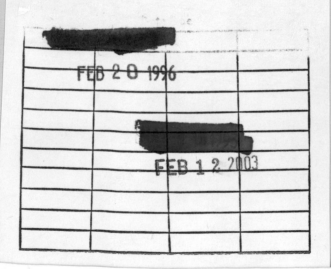

The Old English Riddles
of the *Exeter Book*

The Old English Riddles
of the *Exeter Book*

Edited by *Craig Williamson*

The University of North Carolina Press · Chapel Hill

Manufactured in the United States of America
Library of Congress Catalog Card Number 76-46278
ISBN 0-8078-1272-2

Library of Congress Cataloging in Publication Data

Exeter book.
  The Old English riddles of the Exeter book.

  Bibliography: p.
  Includes index.
  1. Riddles, Anglo-Saxon. I. Williamson, Craig,
1943– II. Title.
PR1760.W5   829'.1   76-46278
ISBN 0-8078-1272-2

This edition is dedicated
To the unnamed riddlers
Who wrought the songs,
To collectors like Leofric
Who saved the *mycel Englisc boc*,
To teachers like Jim Rosier and John Pope
Who inspired me to become a *rynemonn*,
And to the *Rædellewebba* who surely must rejoice
In the riddle of setter and solver
Sharing and celebrating *þas gied*
Across twelve centuries of time.

Contents

Preface

First of all I should thank the Dean and Chapter of Exeter Cathedral for allowing me to use the *Exeter Book* and to take the photographs that are included in the section of "Plates" in this edition. The photographs were taken by W. G. Hoskin and developed by Lance Sims and myself. I should thank the trustees of the British Museum for giving me access to the 1831–32 Robert Chambers transcription (*Brit. Mus. Add. MS. 9067*) of the *Exeter Book* and for providing me with the photograph of marginalia that appears in plate xvi.b in this edition.

I am greatly indebted to previous editors of the *Riddles* and to the lexicographers of Old English who have provided the important and necessary *staþol* for my own work. It would be impossible to thank all of the modern scholars whose works have been of use to me here, but I should thank at least those who have made specific suggestions to me privately about some portion of the text or notes where those suggestions have contributed in a significant way to the readings found in this edition. Those scholars who have so contributed are A. J. Bliss, Alistair Campbell, James A. Hinz, Edward B. Irving, Neil R. Ker, Robert M. Lumiansky, Bruce Mitchell, Martin Ostwald, R. I. Page, John C. Pope, James L. Rosier, J. David Sapir, Eric G. Stanley, Leslie Webster, and Dorothy Whitelock. Two must be singled out for special thanks. Professor Rosier was supervisor of my dissertation edition of these riddles at the University of Pennsylvania, and he continued to offer helpful advice and criticism as I worked on revising that first version and turning it into the final edition. Without Professor Rosier's advice and support I should never have undertaken the venture nor persevered through many long years of work. Professor Pope was a reader of the manuscript edition of the *Riddles* that I submitted for publication. His many pages of detailed comment and criticism were the basis of yet another revision. His willingness to give advice freely on every aspect of this edition was for me something of a *wundor* in itself. I could not, practically speaking, document every instance in which Professors Rosier and Pope offered suggestions that I accepted or that changed in fundamental ways my own readings. Suffice it to say that without the help of those two worthies, this book would be a much poorer offering than it is. Some of my students of Old English at Swarthmore College also offered suggestions about the book—most notably David Sewell and Matthew Abbate. Matthew's help in particular on portions of the glossary was invaluable. If there is a clarity of discussion in the book, it is due in no small way to the provocative questions of my own students. I should say, of course, that many people offered suggestions, and of those suggestions, I accepted some and rejected others. Finally, the responsibility for every reading in the text or notes must rest with me.

A number of institutions offered financial help either in supporting the research that went into the making of the edition or in providing subventions to help offset the cost of publication. I would like to thank especially the Danforth Foundation and the University of Pennsylvania for supporting my graduate school research; Swarthmore College for supporting several summers' research; the National Endowment for the Humanities for a Summer Stipend for Younger Humanists, which I used to study Anglo-Saxon archaeology; and the American Council of Learned Societies for a sabbatical fellowship, which I used to pursue research on anthropological approaches to Old English poetry. I would like to thank The Andrew W. Mellon Foundation for a grant to The University of North Carolina Press that made possible the publication of this book. I am also grateful to the director and staff of the press who labored with such enthusiasm and care over the book.

Finally, I would like to thank my parents for their abiding commitment to my education, my wife, Susan, for her riddlic insights and support, and my daughter, Telory, for enduring what must have seemed a riddle to her—her father's chanting in a strange tongue and his pounding out word-tracks of unknown origin on a loud-clattering word-machine far too late at night.

Acknowledgments

Thanks to the Dean and Chapter, Exeter Cathedral, for permission to print photographs from the *Exeter Book*; to the Trustees of the British Museum for permission to print the photograph from *Add. MS. 9067* (Robert Chambers's 1831–32 copy of the *Exeter Book*); to Brepols for permission to quote from *Aenigmata*, vol. 133 of the *Corpus Christianorum, Series Latina*; to Columbia University Press for permission to quote from *The Anglo-Saxon Poetic Records*; to the Council of the Early English Text Society for permission to quote from Mackie's edition of Part 2 of the *Exeter Book* (o.s. 194); to Féret et Fils and to Jacques Fontaine for permission to quote from *Traité de la Nature* (Fontaine's edition of Isidore's *De Natura Rerum*); to Harvard University Press for permission to quote from the various volumes of the Loeb Library Series; to D. C. Heath and Co. for permission to quote from Klaeber's edition of *Beowulf*; and to Yale University Press for permission to quote from Pitman's edition of *The Riddles of Aldhelm*.

Abbreviations

All abbreviations used throughout this edition are included here with one exception—the special abbreviations for the variant numbers (VN) of riddles in previous *Riddle* editions, which are enclosed in brackets at the beginning of the headnote to each riddle, are explained in the "Note to Variant Numbers" at the beginning of the Notes and Commentary section. Abbreviations used in the Glossary, which are also included here, are explained more fully in the note at the beginning of the Glossary.

a./acc.	accusative
AA	*Acta Archaeologica*
adj.	adjective
adv.	adverb
AEW.	Holthausen's *Altenglisches etymologisches Wörterbuch*, 2d ed.
AN.	anomalous
An.	*Andreas*
Anglia	*Anglia*
Anglia Beibl.	*Beiblatt zur Anglia*
Anm.	Anmerkung
Ap.	*Fates of the Apostles*
Archiv	*Archiv für das Studium der neueren Sprachen und Literaturen*
art.	article
ASPR.	*Anglo-Saxon Poetic Records*, ed. Krapp and Dobbie

Abbreviations

aux.	auxiliary
Az.	*Azarias*
BBzA.	*Bonner Beiträge zur Anglistik*
Beiträge	*Beiträge zur Geschichte der deutschen Sprache und Literatur*
Beo.	*Beowulf*
BJS	*British Journal of Sociology*
Bks.	Ogilvy's *Books Known to the English, 597–1066*
Bo.	*The Meters of Boethius*
Brit. Mus. Add. MS. 9067	*British Museum Additional Manuscript 9067*
Brun.	*The Battle of Brunanburh*
B-T.	Bosworth and Toller's *An Anglo-Saxon Dictionary*
BTS.	Toller's *Supplement* to Bosworth-Toller's *An Anglo-Saxon Dictionary*
BudV.	*Berichte über die Verhandlungen der k. sächsischen Gesellschaft der Wissenschaften zu Leipzig, Phil.-hist. Klasse*
Campbell	Campbell's *Old English Grammar*
cap.	capital (letter)
CCL.	*Corpus Christianorum: Series Latina*
CH.	Clark Hall's *A Concise Anglo-Saxon Dictionary*, 4th ed.
Chr.	*Christ*
cm.	centimeters
Coll.	Aelfric's *Colloquy*
comp.	comparative
conj.	conjunction
CP	*Classical Philology*
cp.	compare
Cr.	Aldhelm's *Creatura* Riddle (no. 100, ed. Pitman, pp. 60 ff.)
Crit.	*Criticism*

CS.	*Christ and Satan*
CT.	contract
d.	dual (in Glossary only)
d./dat.	dative
def.	definite
dem.	demonstrative
DNR.	Bede's *De Natura Rerum*
Dream	*Dream of the Rood*
DRN.	Lucretius's *De Rerum Natura*
EB.	*Encyclopaedia Britannica,* 1969 ed.
ed.	edited by; edition
ed(s).	editor(s)
EETS	Early English Text Society
EGS	*English and Germanic Studies*
EH.	Bede's *Ecclesiastical History* [*Historia Ecclesiastica Gentis Anglorum*]
El.	*Elene*
ELN	*English Language Notes*
Engl.	English (modern)
ES	*English Studies*
ESn.	*Englische Studien*
Etym.	Isidore's *Etymologiae* [*Etymologiarum sive Originum,* ed. Lindsay]
Ex.	*Exodus*
f./fem.	feminine
ff.	following
fig.	figure
Finn.	*The Battle of Finnsburh*
fol.	folio
Fort.	*The Fortunes of Men*
g./gen.	genitive

Abbreviations

Gen.	*Genesis*
ger.	gerund
Germ.	German (modern)
Gifts	*The Gifts of Men*
Guth.	*Guthlac*
Hell	*The Descent into Hell*
Hex.	Ambrose's *Hexaemeron*
Hom. I	*Homiletic Fragment I*
Hom. II	*Homiletic Fragment II*
Hus.	*The Husband's Message*
i./inst.	instrumental
imp.	imperative
impers.	impersonal
ind.	indeclinable
indef.	indefinite
inf.	infinitive
infl.	inflected
interj.	interjection
intr.	intransitive
JD. I	*The Judgment Day I*
JEGP	*Journal of English and Germanic Philology*
Jud.	*Judith*
Jul.	*Juliana*
L.	Latin
Lch.	*Leechdoms,* ed. Cockayne
Leid.	*The Leiden Riddle*
Lewis and Short	Lewis and Short's *A Latin Dictionary*
lit.	literally
m./masc.	masculine

MA	*Medieval Archaeology*
MÆ	*Medium Ævum*
Mald.	*The Battle of Maldon*
Max. I	*Maxims I*
Max. II	*Maxims II*
MED	*Middle English Dictionary*
Men.	*The Menologium*
Met.	Ovid's *Metamorphoses*
M.H.G.	Middle High German
MLN	*Modern Language Notes*
MLQ	*Modern Language Quarterly*
MLR	*Modern Language Review*
MP	*Modern Philology*
MS	*Mediaeval Studies*
MS.	Manuscript
n./nom.	nominative
Napier	Napier's *Old English Glosses*
NEG./neg.	negative
Neoph.	*Neophilologus*
n./neut.	neuter
NH.	Pliny's *Natural History* [*Historia Naturalis*]
NM	*Neuphilologische Mitteilungen*
No./no.	number
NQ	*Notes and Queries*
NR.	Isidore's *De Natura Rerum*
n.s.	new series
NS	*Neuphilologische Studien*
num.	number (in Glossary only)
obj.	object
O.E.	Old English
OED	*Oxford English Dictionary*
O.H.G.	Old High German

Abbreviations

O.I.	Old Icelandic
O.N.	Old Norse
Ord.	*The Order of the World*
o.s.	old series
O.S.	Old Saxon
p./pl.	plural
pers.	person
PG.	*Patrologiae Cursus Completus: Series Graeca,* ed. Migne
Ph.	*The Phoenix*
PL.	*Patrologiae Cursus Completus: Series Latina,* ed. Migne
PMLA	*Publications of the Modern Language Society of America*
poss.	possessive
PP.	preterite-present
pp.	past participle
PPs.	*The Metrical Psalms of the Paris Psalter*
PQ	*Philological Quarterly*
prep.	preposition
pres.	present
PRET./pret.	preterite
pron.	pronoun
prp.	present participle
punc.	punctuation
refl.	reflexive
rel.	relative
Repr.	reprint; reprinted
RES	*Review of English Studies*
rev.	revised
Rid./Rids.	*Riddle; Riddles*
Rim.	*The Riming Poem*

Run.	*The Rune Poem*
s./sing.	singular
SB.	Brunner's *Altenglische Grammatik nach der angelsächsischen Grammatik von Eduard Sievers*, 3d ed.
Seaf.	*The Seafarer*
ser.	series
SN	*Studia Neophilologica*
Sol.	*Solomon and Saturn*
Soul I	*Soul and Body I*
Soul II	*Soul and Body II*
SP	*Studies in Philology*
Sp.	Grein's *Sprachschatz der angelsächsischen Dichter*, in collaboration with F. Holthausen, rev. J. J. Köhler, 1912 ed.
Spec.	*Speculum*
Studies	Sisam's *Studies in the History of Old English Literature*
SUBJ.	subjunctive
subs.	substantive
supl.	superlative
tr.	translator; translated by
trans.	transitive
TSL	*Tennessee Studies in Literature*
v.	verb
Vain.	*Vainglory*
VN	Variant Numbers (*see* "Note to Variant Numbers" at the beginning of Notes and Commentary section)
vol(s).	volume(s)
w.	with
Wand.	*The Wanderer*
Wh.	*The Whale*

Abbreviations

Wid.	*Widsith*
Wife	*The Wife's Lament*
wk.	weak
Wulf	*Wulf and Eadwacer*
WW.	Wright and Wülker's *Anglo-Saxon and Old English Vocabularies*, 2d ed.
ZfdA.	*Zeitschrift für deutsches Altertum*

Introduction

Manuscript, Authorship, Date

The ninety Old English riddles and the single Latin riddle that comprise this edition are edited from a manuscript known as the *Exeter Book* (*Exeter Cath. MS. 3501*), which is kept in the Exeter Cathedral Library in Exeter, England. The riddles occur on folios 101*a*–ll5*a*, 122*b*–123*a*, and 124*b*–130*b* of the *Exeter Book* in the following arrangement:

Folios	Riddles
101*a*–115*a*	1–27, 28a, 29–57
122*b*–123*a*	28b, 58
124*b*–130*b*	59–91

As the numbering indicates, *Rid.* 28 occurs in two versions, printed together in this edition but separated in the manuscript. The Latin riddle is *Rid.* 86. *Riddle* 33 of the *Exeter Book* is also preserved in a Northumbrian version in a manuscript (*Leiden Univ. MS. Voss. Q. 106*) of the University Library at Leiden (see headnote to *Rid.* 33). The total number of riddles in this edition, ninety-one, is somewhat smaller than that of most previous editions, not because any riddles have been omitted, but because several riddles or riddle fragments heretofore printed separately have here been combined. The reasons for adopting these new readings are set forth at length in the headnotes to the individual riddles, numbers 1, 66, 73, and 76.

The *Exeter Book* was donated to Exeter Cathedral by Leofric, first bishop of Exeter, who died in 1072 (for a short biography of the man, see Barlow's introductory essay, "Leofric and His Times," in *Leofric of Exeter* by Barlow et al.). In the list of Leofric's donations to the cathedral (extant in two early versions, one appended to the beginning of the *Exeter Book* and the other in *MS. Auct. D.2.16* of the Bodleian), there is a manuscript described as *.i. mycel Englisc boc be gehwilcum þingum on leoðwisan geworht*, which most authorities take to be the *Exeter Book* itself. Flower (*The Exeter Book of Old English Poetry*, pp.

83 ff.) dates the manuscript between 970 and 990 and believes that several scribes were involved in the copying. But Sisam (*Studies in the History of Old English Literature,* p. 97) doubts that more than a single scribe was employed in the copying and Ker (*Catalogue of Manuscripts Containing Anglo-Saxon* 116, p. 153) notes that "the hand is the same throughout," and I would agree. Of the marginalia, much of it discussed at length in this edition for the first time, little seems to have been penned by the scribe of the main text itself.

The *Exeter Book* in its present state contains 131 parchment leaves "of that comparatively thin kind usually employed by the Anglo-Saxons, so that occasionally the writing shines through from one page to the other" (Förster, *The Exeter Book of Old English Poetry,* p. 55). The first leaf is blank and has not been included in the foliation. The *Exeter Book* proper runs from folios 8–130. The first seven folios and the blank page were added sometime after Leofric's original gift but before the sixteenth century (for a description of the preliminary matter, see Förster, ibid., pp. 44 ff.). The dimensions of the leaves are approximately 31–32 cm. by 22 cm., and the text itself covers an area of about 24 cm. by 16 cm. The number of lines on a page varies from 21 to 23. The manuscript is generally well-preserved, but it has suffered severe damage in several places. Folio 8 is damaged by knife strokes and the spillage of liquid from a cup or mug. The last fourteen leaves suffer mutilation from what appears to be a long diagonal burn. The burn has obliterated portions of *Rids.* 28b, 61, 65, 69–71, 74–75, 77–80, 83–85, and 88–90. In its present state the MS. is rebound with pieces of backing vellum along the mutilated portions so that portions of letters are obscured, but some of these letters may be read in the facsimile photographs for purposes of which the backing strips and glue were removed.

The *Exeter Book* appears to have been an anthology of Old English poems. Sisam notes that "the order of the poems is unpredictable" (*Studies,* p. 291). For example, the riddle collection that begins on folio 101*a* is interrupted at folios 115*a*–122*b* by eight poems: *The Wife's Lament, The Judgment Day I, Resignation, The Descent into Hell, Alms-Giving, Pharaoh, The Lord's Prayer I,* and *Homiletic Fragment II* (here as elsewhere, I use the titles from the *ASPR.*). There follows then on folios 122*b*–123*a* a second version of *Rid.* 28 and another riddle, *Rid.*

58, and then another interruption on folios 123*a*-124*b* by *The Husband's Message* and *The Ruin* before the last section of riddles, *Rids.* 59–91, conclude the *Exeter Book* on folios 124*b*–130*b*. It is not clear from the order whether the original anthology was made over a number of years by one or more authors or whether the book was copied from other anthologies or sources by one or more scribes. It may be that the Anglo-Saxon notion of poetic order remains simply too far removed from our modern sensibilities to be comprehended. Sisam at any rate believes that "the collection was put together by tacking on new groups or items as codices or single pieces came to hand" (*Studies*, p. 97) and also that "it is unlikely that the compilation was first made in the Exeter Book, whose stately, even style indicates that it was transcribed continuously from a collection already made" (ibid.).

It is impossible to say much with any certainty concerning the authorship of the *Riddles*. The *Riddles* were first attributed to Cynewulf beginning in 1857 on the basis of Leo's (*Quae de se ipso Cynewulfus tradiderit*) forcing of runic names out of the text of *Wulf and Eadwacer* in a charade-like fashion unprincipled in method and unsupported by any similar use of mutated runic names anywhere in Old English. Leo's ascription of authorship found some support in Dietrich's reading of the Latin *"lupus"* *Rid.* 86 as a wordplay upon the name of Cynewulf (*ZfdA.* xii, 250) and in Dietrich's solution of *Rid.* 91 as "Wandering Singer" (*ZfdA.* xi, 487 ff.). But in 1888, Bradley (*Academy* xxxiii, 197 ff.) argued convincingly that *Wulf and Eadwacer* was not a riddle at all but the fragment of some dramatic soliloquy similar in tone and matter to *Deor* and *The Wife's Lament*, and in 1891, Sievers (*Anglia* xiii, 15) cast certain doubt upon Leo's reading of runic names and attempted to prove that the *Riddles* predated Cynewulf. Sievers's argument that the *Riddles* dated from the early eighth century was based on the forms in the *Leiden Riddle* (which, as Tupper [p. lvii] points out, is hardly typical of the collection), on the runic "spellings" in *Rids.* 17 and 50 (where, as I explain in the notes, it is often unwise to assume a one-to-one relationship between vocalic runes and certain phonological equivalents represented by letters, and where, as Tupper points out, Sievers reads as "Northumbrian" several forms that also occur in other dialects), and on the spelling of MS. *Agof* at *Rid.* 21.1 (where, as I explain in the notes, Sievers makes several wrong assumptions about the date of the scribal change). Madert (*Die Sprache der altenglischen Rätsel des Exeterbuches und die Cynewulffrage*), however, by comparing the language of the *Riddles* with the known poems of Cynewulf, showed that the *Riddles* had little in common with the Cynewulfian poems. Most editors now take *Wulf and Eadwacer* to be a dramatic lyric, however enigmatic it remains to the modern mind. The solutions to *Rids*. 86 and 91 are still much debated, but I am not without hope that my new solutions to those riddles will help put to rest once and for all the old notion of the author's oblique and cryptic reference to himself in those riddles.

Another possible criterion to be used in the dating of *Riddles* is the existence of what Sievers called hidden disyllabic forms. Sievers (for the various references, see Klaeber's discussion on pp. 274–75 of the third edition of *Beowulf*) noted that in *Beowulf* and other presumably early poems, certain stressed syllables that have undergone contraction through loss of intervocalic *h* or *j* or through coalescence of stem vowels with vowels of inflectional endings produce abnormal metrical patterns unless the contracted syllables are treated as two.[1] Similarly Sievers noted that certain words that were treated as disyllabic in the later stages of the language, and therefore in the relatively late poetry, were sometimes treated as monosyllables by the author of *Beowulf* and other presumably early poets (see Klaeber's discussion of this at the top of p. 276 of his third edition of *Beowulf*), and that often these need to be counted as monosyllables for the proper metrical scansion of the lines.[2] But the use of such metrical tests for the dating of Old English poems has proved inconclusive for several reasons. For one thing, the poets seem to have had a certain freedom of usage and province of traditional language that prose writers did not have. Thus originally disyllabic forms that were contracted to monosyllables in the later stages of the language were still available to some poets as disyllables (see, for example, the use of *heahan* at *Glory I* 27). For

1. Examples of this phenomenon in the *Riddles* (most of which are listed by Sievers in *Beiträge* x, 476–80) occur at *Rids*. 1.3la, 1.54a, 1.80a, 1.87a, 1.94b, 1.96b, 3.3b, 4.5a, 5.4b, 10.8b, 19.5b, 20.7b, 26.13b, 29.24b, 30.14b, 32.4b, 33.14b, 37.1b, 38.24b, 38.27a, 38.52a, 39.7b, 39.9b, 42.1b, 48.5a, 60.5a, 60.6b, 61.2a, 61.5b, 65.16b, 71.8a, and 76.6b.

2. As examples of this phenomenon in the *Riddles*, Sievers (*Beiträge* x, 481) cites forms at *Rids*. 1.88b, 1.92a, 53.5a, and 80.25b (the list should probably include *wæstm* at 87.2b).

another thing, as Klaeber says, "it remains a matter of honest doubt what degree of rigidity should be demanded in the rules of scansion" (p. cix of Klaeber's third edition of *Beowulf*). Thus Sievers would take as disyllabic *sie* or *sy* in the formulaic *hwæt seo wiht sy* that often closes riddles. But the rhetorical pattern could conceivably have generated an exceptional verse type in a formulaic case like this. Similarly Sievers would read disyllabic words at *Rids.* 19.5*b* and 48.5*a* to normalize the pattern |⌣ x x|⌣| (with resolved initial lift in the case of 19.5*b*) into a more regular type A verse, even though such verses read with their monosyllabic forms might well constitute acceptable *exceptional verse types* (cp. *Beo.* 2150*a* and *Guth.* 313*a*, and see Pope's discussion of these on pp. 320–21 of *The Rhythm of Beowulf*). The normalizing of verses on the basis of metrical criteria is especially tricky business in the *Riddles* where in some cases at least the poet or poets seem to have taken a relatively greater freedom from the metrical norms than, for example, the poet of *Beowulf*. Like *Beowulf*, the *Riddles* contain a number of stressed short syllables (for example, *Rids.* 15.11*a*, 18.18*a*, 27.5*a*, 30.11*a*, 36.6*b*, 36.7*b*, 40.2*b*, 44.6*a*, 56.14*b*, 87.1*b*, and 89.12*a*). Unlike *Beowulf*, the *Riddles* contain a relatively large number of metrically deficient and metrically overburdened verses. The reading of such verses depends, of course, to some extent on the editor who may or may not emend. Using a reasonably conservative policy about emending solely on the basis of metrical considerations, I read two apparently authentic trisyllabic verses at 1.33*a* and 19.4*a* and one authentic disyllabic verse at 2.7*b*. One verse, 1.85*a*, has four syllables but is still metrically short. Overburdened verses in the *Riddles* may be grouped according to four categories:

1. B/C: |x x . . . ⌣|x ⌣ x| [See Pope's *Seven Old*
         or (rhythmically)   *English Poems*, p. 128,
         |ᴧx x . . .|⌣ x ⌣ x| for other examples.]

   Rids. 36.5*b* (?)   38.5*b*
      37.10*a*

2. Long C: |x x ⌣|⌣ x x| [Cp. *Seaf.* 85*a*]
         or (rhythmically)
   Rid. 2.5*a* |ᴧx x|⌣ ⌣ x x|

3. A/E or "Truncated A": $|\acute{-} \times \times \ .\ .|\acute{-}|$ [See Pope's *Seven Old English Poems*, pp. 128–29, and *The Rhythm of Beowulf*, pp. xxx and 321, for other examples.]

Rids. 7.10*a*   37.26*a*
　　27.4*a*   87.8*a* (?)

4. Other overburdened verses without precedent, and where one or more factors indicate the possibility of scribal corruption (see notes to individual lines):
Rids. 2.8*a*   36.6*a*
　　23.2*a*   80.35*a*

In each of these cases the metrical abnormality of the verse is discussed fully in the note to the text. In addition to these examples, there are three passages in three separate riddles where the lines in question make sense grammatically and syntactically but where the verses are quite unusual metrically: *Rids.* 2.7*b*–8*b*, 36.5–7, and 63.1–2. In these cases for one reason or another (see the notes to the individual passages), the riddle-poet seems to have taken liberties with the traditional norms of Old English meter. There are seven examples of apparently authentic alliteration on the final stress in the *Riddles*: 1.66, 2.8, 38.5, 53.14, 57.12, 71.2, and 87.6. There are also two apparent cases of *hw* alliterating with *w* at *Rids.* 4.7 and 33.11 (see notes to all of these lines). In a number of the runic passages certain liberties are sometimes taken with the meter, but this is understandable given the nature of the other constraints that are operating (see "A Note on the Runes" at the end of the headnote to *Rid.* 17).

　　Other criteria sometimes used to date Old English poems are Barnouw's (*Textkritische Untersuchungen nach dem Gebrauch des bestimmten Artikels und des schwachen Adjectivs in der altenglischen Poesie*) criteria of frequency of use of the definite article, of the frequency of the definite article plus weak adjective plus noun, and of the occurrence of the weak adjective without the article (for a recent attempt at this sort of dating, see Hacikyan's *A Linguistic and Literary Analysis of Old English Riddles*), but as Klaeber (p. cv in the third edition of *Beowulf*) notes, generalizations based on such fragmentary evidence can hardly be given any decisive weight. This is especially true of the

Riddles where it is hard to generalize from one riddle to the next (different riddles may have been written by different authors at different times) and where with the exception of the one or two extremely long riddles there is hardly enough evidence within the limits of a particular riddle to draw any significant conclusions at all. It is also true in studies of this sort that there is a strong tendency to use a "standard" of dating that is more ambiguous than the authors would like to admit. For more on the problems of using such criteria, the reader should see pp. lx–lxii of Tupper's edition. Ultimately, it seems to me wise to admit a certain amount of humble ignorance in the matter of dating. As Sisam himself says with respect to Cynewulfian poetry:

> Elaborate linguistic and metrical tests have been applied to establish the chronological order of Old English poems. Because these tests leave out of account differences of authorship, of locality, of subject, and of textual tradition, the detailed results, whether of relative order or absolute date, are little better than guess-work hampered by statistics. [*Studies*, p. 6]

Tupper, who also realizes the futility of trying to date the *Riddles* individually or as a group on linguistic or metrical grounds, still surmises with Sievers that "the *Riddles* are the product of the first half of the eighth century, as this was the golden age of English riddle-poetry" (p. lviii), but certainly the greatest known English riddle-writer of Latin riddles was Aldhelm, who lived most of his life in the latter half of the seventh century. It is also true that the discoveries at Sutton Hoo have given archaeologists and students of Old English alike some cause to reexamine their long-established notions about the "golden age of Old English poetry." The problem of identifying the proper "golden age" in the proper kingdom is further complicated by our limited knowledge of early southern texts and by our inability to say exactly what the provenance of the *Riddles* might have been.

The language of the *Riddles* is consistent with the language of the rest of the *Exeter Book* in terms of dialect and form—it is what Förster characterizes as "West-Saxon, but with a strong admixture of such elements as are usually called Anglian" (*The Exeter Book of Old English Poetry*, p. 66). For a discussion of the language of the *Exeter Book*, see Sisam, *Studies*, pp. 97 ff. and for a discussion of dialectical forms in the *Riddles*, see Madert's monograph cited above. A number of the Anglian forms that occur in the *Riddles* appear to be Northumbrian. These may include *bæg* at 2.8*a*, *swe* at 13.3*a* (see also note to 7.6), *wræce* at 18.18*a*, *geonge* at 19.2*b*, *walde* at 27.5*a*, *ehtuwe* at 34.4*a*, *sy* at 38.65*a*, *eðþa* at 41.16*a*, *wær* at 44.1*a* (but see note), *wægas* at 49.6*b*, *wæg* at 51.8*b*, *wido* at 54.2*b* (see note) and *þæh* at 70.9*b*. The reader should see the note to the text in each case as there is sometimes debate about the nature and provenance of the forms. I think it unwise to draw any firm conclusions about the provenance of the *Riddles* as a whole on the basis of what appear to be occasional archaic Anglian or Northumbrian forms. We know in Sisam's words that "the Exeter collection has at some time been copied by one or more scribes who freely substituted forms to which they were accustomed for those in the copy before them" (*Studies*, p. 106), but this does not necessarily mean that the existence of a late West Saxon text with a sprinkling of Anglian forms indicates an early Anglian provenance for the poems. This traditional view of the provenance of *Exeter Book* poems is articulated by Förster who says:

> For the time of the scribe the language must have had a somewhat archaic flavour, both in vocabulary and in phonology. Both peculiarities of the language, the dialectal and the chronological one, may be accounted for by the very probable assumption that the scribe had copied from older originals, wholly or partly written in the Anglian dialect. [*The Exeter Book of Old English Poetry*, p. 66]

But Sisam (*Studies*, pp. 119 ff.) points out that modern notions of early English dialects are often based on texts that are difficult to date and localize with certainty and that the problem is only compounded when we consider the shifting physical and political boundaries of the early English kingdoms. It is also true, as Sisam says elsewhere, that "without early Southern texts, there is no sure distinction between words, forms and constructions unknown to Southern poets in early times, and those, once general, that survived in Anglian only" (*MÆ* xiii, 32). It is also true, as Whitelock has recently noted (*The Audience of Beowulf*, pp. 28 ff.), that Anglian forms may once have attained a literary or social status and that consequently these forms may have been used by non-Anglian poets throughout England. If the archaeological evidence of Sutton Hoo is any guide, we can be sure that early England was a place of commerce and communication both within and without so it does seem likely that a certain admixture of dialect forms should have occurred. In the only case of a riddle extant in two dialect forms, *Rid*. 33 of the *Exeter Book* and the *Leiden Riddle*, most editors agree that while the Leiden text is closer to the original Latin of Aldhelm's "Lorica" Riddle (ed. Pitman, p. 18), it is impossible to tell which of the Old English texts represents the original translation and whether one of the Old English texts was the source of the other (see Dobbie, *ASPR.*, vol. 6, p. cix and Smith, *Three Northumbrian Poems*, pp. 17 ff.). What is clear in this isolated example is that a riddle was communicated from one dialect region to another, and it seems likely in light of Aldhelm's sending his Latin riddles to Northumbria that the communication was a conscious learned and literary exchange. Smith at least (p. 18) does not discount the possibility that Aldhelm was the translator of his own poem, and Sisam reconstructs a scenario for the exchange:

There are no historical reasons why poems composed in the South should not pass to the North and Midlands, assume an Anglian dress or colouring there, and return to the South. The Northumbrian version of the Mailcoat Riddle is found in a ninth-century manuscript at Leyden, together with Latin riddles by Aldhelm, who wrote its Latin original. This would be good evidence that Latin texts composed in the South came into Northumbrian hands in early times, even if Aldhelm's dedicatory letter to the Northumbrian King Aldfrith ('Acircius') were not extant [*Aldhelmi Opera, Mon. Germ. Hist.*, ed. R. Ehwald, 1919, p. 61]. Had Aldhelm himself made the English translation it might travel the same way; and there is nothing in the Northumbrian version to prove that it was not transposed from West Saxon. The Mailcoat Riddle, wherever it was translated, is an example of literary or learned communication. [*Studies*, pp. 122–23]

Blair (*An Introduction to Anglo-Saxon England*, p. 327) notes that Aldfrith was a ruler of some learning who enjoyed a reputation as a poet, and it is not impossible that the bulk of the Old English riddles came to be written as the result of literary communication between the circles of Aldhelm and the king. Some will argue that certain riddles are the product of an oral tradition, and the contention is impossible to prove or disprove. There is no reason to ascribe the so-called obscene riddles to a folk tradition any more than the "straight" riddles. The double entendre riddles are carefully crafted; indeed they must be so to carry out the disguise. We know that there was a learned tradition of Latin riddling in early England, and there is nothing in *Beowulf* or in *The Gifts of Men* or in those portions of the gnomic poems where human crafts and entertainments are described to support directly the notion that the Anglo-Saxons as a people maintained a long tradition of social riddling. Still, lack of positive mention of this sort may mean little, especially as the documents are part of a literary tradition. I do not mean by this discussion to suggest that the Old English riddler or riddlers knew and extensively used the Latin riddle poets; indeed I think that the influence of Latin riddles on the Old English riddles has if anything been overstated in the past.[3] What I do mean to suggest is that whoever wrote the Old English riddles, he or they (I incline to the view that the *Riddles* were written by several men, perhaps of the same school, but this is impossible to prove or disprove) were learned men with access to medieval writings on philosophy and natural history, and they were conscious, careful crafters of verse. They were also, as should be obvious, lovers of nature and of men and careful observers of the world about them.

Manuscript Punctuation

These riddles like the other poems of the *Exeter Book* are not provided with titles in the manuscript. Thus, unlike most Latin riddles of medieval collections, these Old English riddles are not introduced by entitling solutions. The scribe of the *Exeter Book* is fairly consistent in beginning each riddle with a large capital letter or letters and in ending each riddle with an end-punctuation mark or marks such as : 7, :–, or :~. There are unusual marks after *Rids*. 12 and 28a that may or may not be end-punctuation marks (see notes to *Rids*. 12.19 and 28a.9 and plates). There are two places in the MS. where the scribe has apparently combined two riddles into one. The pairs mistakenly combined are *Rids*. 40 and 41 and *Rids*. 45 and 46. Similarly there are four places where the scribe has apparently written one riddle as two: *Rids*. 1, 66, 73, and 76. Most editors print *Rid*. 66 as one riddle on

---

3. In a recent article, Lawrence Shook makes a similar point. He says: "In fact one of the serious obstacles to fully satisfactory scholarship on the Exeter Book riddles over the years has been the determination of scholars to identify the poems of Symphosius, Aldhelm and the other [Latin riddle writers] in their Anglo-Saxon dressing. The results have been disappointing, sometimes even misleading. The Anglo-Saxon riddles, like most Anglo-Saxon poems, display minimal dependence upon Latin models" ("Riddles relating to the Anglo-Saxon Scriptorium," in *Essays in Honour of Anton Charles Pegis*, ed. J. Reginald O'Donnell, p. 219).

structural grounds; a few print *Rid.* 1 as a single riddle. For the first time in this edition, *Rids.* 73 and 76 are each printed as a single riddle where two are indicated in the MS. For the structural arguments involved in each of the four cases, the reader should see the headnotes to the individual riddles. The scribe has in one case (*Rid.* 25.15) placed an end-punctuation mark within the text of a riddle before its proper end, but in this case he simply went on to finish the riddle and to place another end-punctuation mark in the proper place as well. Since one riddle normally ends in the middle of a MS. line and the next begins a new MS. line, there is usually a space, some portion of a line long, separating one riddle from the next. Sometimes when the scribe has finished a MS. line and has only a word or two of the riddle left to write, he will write that word or those words in the next MS. line close to the right-hand margin of script and begin the next riddle in the same MS. line at the left-hand margin and leave a space between the sections of the two riddles. In these cases one MS. line may contain portions of two riddles but it is always clear which portion belongs to each riddle. Often in these cases the short MS. line of the new riddle is followed by a point to separate it from the end of the preceding riddle (the instances are listed in the "Catalogue of Simple Points" in Appendix C), and sometimes a sign such as ⫽ or ⁊ is placed before the tail-end of the preceding riddle as a separation mark as well.

The abbreviations used in the *Riddles* are those commonly employed in the rest of the *Exeter Book.* These include the tilde over a letter, usually a vowel, to indicate the omission of a letter or letters following, frequently over -*ū* for -*um* as in *hwilū* for *hwilum*; also *þ* for *þæt*, *þōn* for *þonne*, and 7 for *ond*. In each case the words sometimes abbreviated also occur unabbreviated in the MS. The abbreviation 7 is in one case used in a compound *7weorc*, apparently an error for *hondweorc* (*Rid.* 3.8). At *Rid.* 38.66 the abbreviation *p´nex* occurs for *pernex*. The standard abbreviations such as the tilde over vowels, 7 for *ond*, and *þōn* for *þonne*, are expanded without comment in the edited text; the unusual abbreviations such as *7weorc* for *ondweorc* or *hondweorc* are noted in the paleographical notes to the text.

Krapp and Dobbie note "there are nearly six hundred acute accent marks in the *Exeter Book*" (*ASPR.*, vol. 3, p. xxiv). There are 48

acute accent marks in the *Riddles*. The significance of the accents follows generally the pattern described by Krapp and Dobbie (ibid.) for the rest of the *Exeter Book*. Of the 48 accents in the *Riddles*, 39 occur over etymologically long vowels. In three cases (*Rids*. 32.6, *áa*; 76.11, *góod*; 77.3, *fóot*), an etymologically long vowel is doubled and the accent is also written above the initial vowel. In three cases there is an accent over the short vowel *o* of *ón* (*Rids*. 4.7; 18.29; 19.6). In two of these cases (*Rids*. 4.7 and 18.29), the accent probably indicates a stress on a postpositive preposition. The third case (*Rid*. 19.6) is more difficult to explain. Three other cases remain. At *Rid*. 23.11 the accent over *wundén locc* is partially erased and is probably an error (perhaps a misplaced accent from the immediately preceding *wif*). At *Rid*. 52.9 the MS. reading *hie ó* is apparently a mistake for *hio* (cp. *Rids*. 33.9, 80.15, and 80.31 where *á* occurs with an accent and is apparently taken by the scribe as an adverb though in all three cases it is actually a verbal prefix). At *Rid*. 83.4 the accent over MS. *gum rínc* is difficult to explain and may also be an error. All of the accents are listed by folio and *Riddle* number in Appendix A at the end of the Introduction.

Krapp and Dobbie note that "nearly eight hundred small capitals occur in the Exeter Book," and of these "somewhat more than half are initial I" (*ASPR*., vol. 3, p. xviii). The small capitals that occur in the *Riddles* are listed in Appendix B at the end of the Introduction. The following summary does not include the questionable cases included and so marked [?] in the Appendix. There are 112 certain occurrences of small capitals in the *Riddles*. Of these, 95 are initial *I*. Of the 95 initial *I* words, 52 are *Ic*. Of the 112 small capitals, 30 are preceded by a point (see the "Catalogue of Simple Points" at Appendix C). Of the 30 occurrences of a small capital in conjunction with a point, 20 mark the juncture between sentences (and in 11 of the 20 cases, the new sentence begins with an adverbial or conjunctive marker); 4 mark the juncture between independent clauses; and 4 mark the juncture between coordinate clauses (in each case a point plus MS. *Ac*). Thus, of the 30 occurrences of a small capital preceded by a point, we may say that 28 of them serve a fairly clear syntactic function.

The occurrences of simple points in the *Riddles* are listed and described in detail in Appendix C. The table includes all points in the text except those used merely to set off runes or numerals and those

elaborate end-punctuation marks described earlier that mark the ends of riddles. Förster argues that in the *Exeter Book* "the dot is almost exclusively used to denote a metrical pause, so that, with Lawrence, we may call it a 'metrical point'" (*The Exeter Book of Old English Poetry*, p. 61). As for those instances of points that occur in the middle of half-lines, Förster notes that "most of these occur at the end of a page, where mechanical circumstances naturally impose upon the scribe a small pause in writing and may well have tempted him to introduce the sign for a pause" (ibid.). Krapp and Dobbie, noting the sporadic nature of pointing in the *Exeter Book*, conclude rather summarily that "for the most part, the pointing of the manuscript cannot be said to be either metrical or structural" (*ASPR.*, vol. 3, p. xxii). Dunning and Bliss, in their recent edition of *The Wanderer*, note that the manuscript point must have served a number of purposes corresponding to the range of modern punctuation signs, and they conclude:

> It cannot be claimed that the punctuation is fully systematic; on the other hand, it is far from being random. With a very limited range of symbols at his command, the scribe has chosen to do three things: to mark out sections in the development of the poem; to call attention to sequences of parallel clauses or phrases; and to indicate places where the reader might misconstrue the syntax. [*The Wanderer*, p. 11]

From the evidence of the Catalogue at Appendix C and from the summary below, it will be clear that the conclusions of Dunning and Bliss with regard to *The Wanderer* are also true with regard to the *Riddles*. Excluding points that mark off runes and numerals in the text, there are 184 simple points in the *Riddles*. Of these 184, a total of 167 occur at the end of either the *a*-line or the *b*-line. While these points may be called metrical, they are not *merely* metrical for they often fall at a point of rhetorical, syntactic, or paleographical significance as will be detailed below. Of the 17 points that do not occur at the end of a half-line, 9 mark the end of a folio page (there are 18 pages so marked but in 9 cases the end of the page corresponds to the end of a half-line); 3 mark the end of a short MS. line where space has been left to separate one riddle from another (in 2 of the 3 cases the tail-end of the preceding riddle is in the same MS. line); 2 mark unusual points of syntactical juncture within the half-line (*Rids.* 41.8 and 57.11); 1 is an error based on a principle of rhetorical pointing (*Rid.* 23.5; this is explained below); and 2 (*Rids.* 20.8 and 52.2) are unexplainable. Of the total 184 points, those that have for certain only metrical significance number 14; those that probably have only metrical significance (marked with a question mark in the table) number 13. There are also 6 points that have no rhetorical or syntactical significance but occur immediately after words marked with an accent (*Rids*. 18.29; 33.9; 38.105; 51.12; 52.9; 79.13) and these points may or may not indicate a vocal or scribal pause; if they do not indicate a pause (if the co-occurrence of the point with the accent in these 6 cases is chance), then these 6 points occurring at the ends of half-lines would also be merely metrical points. There are also 5 cases in the text where because of lacunae it is impossible to tell if points that occur at a metrical juncture have any additional significance. All of this means that of the 167 so-called metrical points, the number of points that have *solely* metrical significance is somewhere between 14 and 38. This leaves a large number of points that have not only a metrical significance but some other significance as well. Of these, a total of 71 points have a rhetorical significance, which means that they occur in conjunction with adverbs or with coordinate or subordinate conjunctions which normally introduce clauses (or occasionally phrases) in the *Riddles*. The point in each case precedes the rhetorical marker. The markers and their number of prepointed occurrences in the *Riddles* follow:

Rhetorical Marker and Prepointed Occurrences

hwilum	20	gif	2
ne	12	eac	1
ac	7	forþon	1
ond	6	hu	1
nu	5	hwonne	1
þonne	4	nymþe	1
swa	3	sona	1
swylce	3	ða	1
oft	2		

For those words occurring only once or twice with a preceding point, the rhetorical significance may be doubtful, but for the rest the significance is clear. One case is especially interesting—that of *Rid*. 23.5 where the sentence begins *Neþeð hwilum* and where the MS. reads *neþeð · hwilum* with a rhetorical point in the middle of a half-line and at the wrong syntactic juncture. Here the scribe's impulse to point rhetorically has overridden his impulses to point metrically or syntactically. This is not always true, for at *Rid.* 71.7 the scribe points after *hwilum* and in the proper metrical and syntactic fashion. In most cases, of course, the point of rhetorical pause or juncture coincides with the point of syntactic juncture and with the point of metrical pause. In terms of a larger rhetorical concern, 3 points occur that separate the main descriptive body of the riddle from the formulaic ending.

The syntactic significance of points depends to some extent on the individual editor's reading of the text. Points occur in the MS. corresponding to points of syntactic significance in this edited text as follows: 47 points occur where I mark the break between sentences (and in 25 of the 47 cases, the new sentence begins with an adverbial or conjunctive marker); 17 occur where I mark the break without a conjunction between independent clauses; 31 occur with one of the rhetorical adverbs or conjunctions listed above where I mark the juncture between coordinate clauses; and 10 occur with the rhetorical markers where I mark the juncture between a subordinate and a main clause. As I have noted in the previous section on small capitals in the text, of 30 occurrences of small capitals in conjunction with a point, 28 have some syntactic significance. The total number of points with some syntactic significance is 105.

I have quoted earlier Förster's statement to the effect that some points are used to mark the end of a folio page. There are 18 of these points in the *Riddles* and they may be classified as having paleographical significance. Other points of paleographical significance include 9 points marking the end of a short MS. line where the line has been shortened—in each case the first MS. line of a riddle—in order to leave a space between the ensuing riddle and the preceding one, or where the tail-end of one riddle occurs at the right-hand margin of one line and where the beginning of the next riddle is in the left-hand portion of the same MS. line, to mark off portions of two different riddles in the same MS. line. There are 5 points that appear to mark the proper metrical stop at the end of a half-line because of possible confusion arising from a nearby point in the MS. There are 4 instances where the scribe appears to have marked a potentially difficult passage, involving two similar or identical words following one upon another, with a point: *Rid.* 1.53, *neah · héa*; 54.7, *oþer · oþer*; 80.32, *sawe · Swa*; and 84.10, *hearde · eard*. There are 5 points noted above in the discussion that occur after words marked with an accent; these may or may not have paleographical significance.

Thus, points are used for a number of things in the *Riddles*; they may carry metrical, rhetorical, syntactic, or paleographical significance. Normally they are significant in at least two categories. The punctuation is certainly not systematic nor is it random. Where a point might be indicated by more than one category of significance, there the scribe has his strongest tendency to point. Sometimes the MS. points, as at *Rid.* 22, are a good guide to a modern editor's punctuation. In other cases, as at *Rid.* 52, the points are not so helpful. Where the points have a rhetorical or syntactic significance, modern punctuation may approximate this, albeit with a wider (and more helpful) variety of signs. Points of paleographical significance are important mainly in the reading and setting up of the text (here the editor acts as a new scribe communicating with the old one). There is no reason to include metrical points in a modern text, even if the points were to be systematic in the manuscript, because the line division and spacing between *a*- and *b*-lines in the text serves the function of a system of metrical points. It is important to understand the medieval scribe's system of pointing in the manuscript insofar as it is possible to do so; it is also important to provide the modern reader with an edited text in which the punctuation facilitates the reading. This I have attempted to do.

In one area, however, it is necessary to retain the MS. system of pointing—this is in connection with the use of runes in the text. Points are used to set off runes in the *Exeter Book* from their immediate context. Förster (*The Exeter Book of Old English Poetry*, p. 62, note 21) first pointed out that where the scribe puts whole groups of runes between points, as in *Rids.* 17 and 73, he means each group of runes to be taken as a word (with the letters indicated by the runes read backwards); and that where the scribe points each rune singly, he means the runes to be taken for their individual letter values, as in *Rids.* 22 and 62, or to be read as the word suggested by the name of the rune, as in *Rid.* 87 and in *The Husband's Message*. Of course it is still difficult in many cases to know for certain what the runes mean. The most unusual use of runes in the *Riddles* is in *Rid.* 62 where each rune singly pointed takes its letter value but where the letters indicated by the runes spell out only the beginnings of the individual words. Krapp and Dobbie (*ASPR.*, vol. 3, p. xxiii) rightly note that the one exception to the rule noted by Förster is at *Rid.* 62.5 where there should evidently be a point after ᛏ.

Modern Scholarship and the Old English *Riddles*

Modern study of the Old English *Riddles* began essentially with Benjamin Thorpe's *editio princeps* of the *Exeter Book* in 1842, entitled *Codex Exoniensis*. Thorpe's text and translation of the *Exeter Book* made the *Riddles* generally available to the scholarly community for the first time. R. W. Chambers notes that Thorpe's chief fault "lay in his careless treatment of the mutilated passages [for] when there was not enough [of the the MS.] preserved to make continuous sense, Thorpe often did not trouble to transcribe such words or portions of words as could be read; and when he indicated a gap by asterisks, he did not give any indication of the size of the gap" (*The Exeter Book of Old English Poetry*, p. 35). Thorpe's own apology for his work on the *Riddles* sounds like a stumped riddle-solver's cry for quarter:

> Of the "Riddles" I regret to say that, from the obscurity naturally to be looked for in such compositions, arising partly from inadequate knowledge of the tongue, and partly from the manifest inaccuracies of the text, my translations, or rather attempts at translation, though the best I can offer, are frequently almost, and sometimes, I fear, quite, as unintelligible as the originals. Though they have baffled me, yet, as they will now be in the hands of the Public, a hope may reasonably be entertained, that one more competent will undertake their interpretation, and with a more favourable result. Of some I have deemed it advisable to give merely the Saxon text, unaccompanied by an effort at translation. [*Codex Exoniensis*, p. x]

Early attempts at solving certain of the *Riddles* had been made by editors who printed anthologies of Old English poetry like Conybeare (*Illustrations of Anglo-Saxon Poetry*) and L. C. Müller (*Collectanea Anglo-Saxonica*), but the first attempt at solving all the riddles came after the published texts of Thorpe and Grein. In 1857–58, Grein published his two-volume *Bibliothek der angelsächsischen Poesie*, but for all he knew about the *Exeter Book* text, Grein relied upon Thorpe. R. W. Chambers points out that Grein "sometimes attempted, by conjecture, to fill the lacunae in the manuscript; but only too frequently fragments of words or letters preserved in the *Exeter Book* (but unrecorded by Thorpe) conclusively refute his [Grein's] conjectures" (*The Exeter Book of Old English Poetry*, p. 36). Grein's greatest contribution to scholarship was his publication of the *Sprachschatz der angelsächsischen Dichter* in 1861 and 1864. Meanwhile Franz Dietrich in two separate articles in 1859 (*ZfdA*. xi, 448 ff.) and 1865 (*ZfdA*. xii, 232 ff.) attempted to solve all of the riddles printed by Grein and Thorpe. Dietrich's effort, especially considering the fragmentary nature of the texts he was using, was incredible. Wyatt aptly says: "By an effort of sympathetic imagination Dietrich enabled himself to see and think with the eyes and mind of an eighth-century Englishman: no other scholar can question his pre-eminence as a solver" (*Old English Riddles*, p. xiv). Many of Dietrich's solutions remain unchallenged after more than a hundred years. In a few isolated instances, Dietrich noted the influence of Latin riddles on the Old English, but Ebert (*BudV*. xxix, 20 ff.) and Prehn (*NS* iii, 145 ff.) tried to show that nearly all of the *Exeter Book* riddles had Latin sources. Prehn's effort especially was misguided and his method unscholarly. His conclusions are refuted by nearly all modern editors (see Tupper, *The Riddles of the Exeter Book*, pp. xxxvii ff.). The clear Latin influence on the Old English *Riddles* amounts to this: (1) two riddles (*Rids*. 33 and 38) are translated from Aldhelm; (2) three riddles (*Rids*. 45, 81, and 82) show the influence of Symphosius. Elsewhere (for example, *Rids*. 14, 20, 35, 36) the Old English *Riddles* sometimes share common motifs with certain Latin riddles, but even when the Latin and the Old English solutions are the same, it is dangerous to generalize about Latin sources since (1) Latin and Old English riddle-writers may have used the same general sources like Isidore's *Etymologiae* or Pliny's *Historia Naturalis* in the composing of their riddles; (2) the riddle-writers may have had independent but similar human perceptions about certain riddle-creatures; and (3) at least in the cases of Anglo-Saxons like Tatwine and Eusebius and perhaps in the case of Aldhelm—except where riddles are directly translated from the Latin, it is impossible to tell if the motif in the Old English riddle came from the Latin or vice versa.

In 1898 the Grein text of the *Riddles* was reedited by Assmann as part of volume 3 of the revised *Bibliothek der angelsächsischen Poesie* by Richard Wülker. The Grein-Wülker text included all of the *Riddles* including fragments and was based upon a new collation of the *Exeter Book*. Moritz Trautmann began publishing articles on the *Riddles* in 1883 and continued for three and a half decades. But Frederick Tupper was the first to publish a complete critical edition of the *Riddles* in 1910, *The Riddles of the Exeter Book*. In his reading of the text, Tupper was the first to take into account the British Museum transcript of the *Exeter Book* (*Brit. Mus. Add. MS. 9067*) made in 1831–32 by Robert Chambers. This transcript proved especially valuable in the reading of certain damaged passages. Wyatt published his edition of *Old English Riddles* in 1912. Trautmann published his edition, *Die altenglischen Rätsel* (*die Rätsel des Exeterbuchs*) in 1915. No critical edition of the *Riddles* has appeared since that time.

In 1933 the *Exeter Book* was photographed and a facsimile published under the title, *The Exeter Book of Old English Poetry*. The facsimile was edited by R. W. Chambers, Max Förster, and Robin Flower. In the case of the damaged folios, those portions of the original vellum glued to backing strips were removed from those strips and the glue was taken off so that more of the text might be accessible to the photographer. Thus in the case of letters located close to the hole in the MS. caused by the burn, more of the text is visible in the facsimile than in the manuscript which has been again rebound (see note to *Rid.* 80.46 ff. and plates comparing similar portions from the MS. and the facsimile). The photographs of the facsimile are excellent though in one case they fail to show runes scratched in the margin in drypoint (see note to *Rid.* 62.right margin and plates showing close-up of the runes), and in another they show a MS. point where none occurs in the MS. (see note to *Rid.* 80.2 and plates). The several essays in the introduction to the facsimile are interesting, especially Förster's noting of the marginalia (p. 64 and note 29), but Förster's reading of a bit of offset blotting as an *ac*-rune (see note to *Rid.* 16.lower margin and plates) is perplexing.

The facsimile was helpful to two later editors of the *Exeter Book*. In 1934 Mackie published part 2 of the EETS edition of *The Exeter Book* (EETS, o.s. 194), and in 1936 Krapp and Dobbie published volume 3 of the *Anglo-Saxon Poetic Records*, which was *The Exeter Book*. Mackie's edition contains text and translation on facing pages but includes only a handful of notes. Krapp and Dobbie's rendering of the text is the best ever accomplished (the one mistake is *Nu* for MS. *ne* at *Rid.* 38.38), though their noting of marginalia is less than adequate. Krapp and Dobbie's textual notes and bibliography are good; their discussion of riddle solutions is brief.

The need for a new and complete critical edition of the *Riddles* at this time should be obvious. The standard edition is still Tupper's though it is completely outdated in many respects. Tupper's use of medieval lore to support his various solutions is admirable; his use of postmedieval folklore is not. As I have indicated elsewhere in the notes and commentary to several riddles, the relevance of late medieval, renaissance, or early modern English folklore to Old English riddles (which are, incidentally, literary creations) is doubtful at best. Tupper's discussion of the marginalia is limited. His reading of the text has been outdated by the work of later editors, especially Krapp and Dobbie. The amount of riddle scholarship that has taken place since 1910 is quite large and the advances in the field of early English archaeology render most of Tupper's discussions in that area obsolete. Krapp and Dobbie in their edition of *The Exeter Book* summarize the riddle scholarship through 1935 but their discussion of solutions is extremely brief because of the nature of their edition. Since the Krapp and Dobbie edition, articles have been published on the *Riddles* affecting solutions and/or disputed passages for over 50 riddles. New solutions have been proposed for over 20 of the *Riddles*. These range in quality from Blakeley's "circling stars" at *Rid.* 20 and Pope's "lyre," and "lighthouse," at *Rids.* 67 and 68—all accepted here for the first time in a critical edition—to Eliason's "elk-hunter" at *Rid.* 73 where that critic confuses the *Ic* of third-person descriptive riddles (*Ic geseah* . . .) with the *Ic* of first-person persona riddles (*Ic eom* . . .) to pronounce the solution, "elk-hunter" instead of "elk." There will no doubt be those who will take equal umbrage at my own solution to that difficult riddle. My own work on riddle solutions in this edition includes some 12 new solutions proposed here for the first time. Some of these— "ship's figurehead" at *Rid.* 72 and "yew-horn" at *Rid.* 26, for example —are based in part on recent archaeological discoveries. In addition, some eight or ten old riddle solutions, such as Brett's "fox" at *Rid*. 13 and Dietrich's "nightingale" at *Rid*. 6, are resurrected and given new supporting evidence. I have tried to solve several of the oldest and most troublesome of the riddlic cruces such as the MS. reading of *hringende an* at *Rid*. 46.1 and the MS. reading of *fremdes ær freondum* at *Rid*. 91.4. In my reading of cruces and in my support of solutions I have tried to use materials most relevant—namely Old English prose and poetry, medieval books like Isidore's *Etymologiae* that might have been used by Anglo-Saxon poets, the evidence of Anglo-Saxon archaeology, and the information in natural histories and encyclopedic works both old and new. Since my own study of linguistic anthropology has led me to the conclusion that literary and speech genres are used in different cultures at different times for quite different purposes, I have kept the use of comparative riddle lore in this edition to a minimum. My discussion of manuscript points is wholly new to *Riddle* editions as is my detailed discussion of manuscript marginalia illustrated by the accompanying plates. The close-up photographs of runes, letters, offset blotting, and other strange marginalia should at least clarify some of the most puzzling problems that have haunted editors of the *Riddles* for years.

The Form and Substance of Old English *Riddles*

There is no reason to believe that the Old English *Riddles* were based on any well-established tradition of social riddling in Anglo-Saxon England. Of course it is impossible to prove or disprove the contention that the *Riddles* in the *Exeter Book* were based on earlier speech genres, but if the tradition of riddling were widespread in England, one might expect some mention of it in the poetry or prose. There is nothing in the court games of *Beowulf* or in the list of social talents in *The Gifts of Men* or elsewhere in the descriptions of crafts and entertainments in the gnomic poems to suggest that the Anglo-Saxons maintained a tradition of social riddling. We do know that there was a Latin literary tradition of riddling and that following the example of Symphosius, many English scholars like Aldhelm, Tatwine, Eusebius, Boniface, and Alcuin composed Latin riddles. Most of these Latin riddles are admittedly a far cry from the Old English. All of the Latin riddles have titles that give their solutions and consequently they are less a literary game than a conscious exercise in the use of metaphor. The riddles of Symphosius (ed. Ohl, *The Enigmas of Symphosius*) are each three lines long; each line is usually a sentence or an independent clause. The construction is regular to the point of boredom. Of the one hundred solutions of Symphosius, some sixteen or seventeen are also solutions of the Old English *Riddles*. Three Old English *Riddles* (45, 81, 82) show the direct influence of Symphosius. Aldhelm's Latin riddles (ed. Pitman, *The Riddles of Aldhelm*) are more varied than those of Symphosius. The riddles range generally from four to ten lines in length though some are longer and one, "Creatura," is 83 lines long. Aldhelm has a few mundane subjects like "earth," "bellows," "nightingale," "swallow," "wine cask," "bookcase," and "pen"; but many of his solutions are exotic like "diamond," "silkworm," "salamander," "minotaur," "lion," "ostrich," "unicorn," "Lucifer," "elephant," and "woman in labor with twins" (*puerpera geminas enixa*). Of Aldhelm's one hundred riddle subjects, some fourteen or fifteen are also subjects of the Old English *Riddles*. Two Old English Riddles (33, 38) are translated from Aldhelm. The later Latin riddles of Tatwine and Eusebius (see *CCL.* cxxxiii, pp. 165–271) show little in common with the Old English *Riddles* except an occasional shared motif. Given then the lack of any documented tradition of social riddling in early England, and given the presence of a Latin literary tradition of riddling, it seems wise to conclude with Ker (*The Dark Ages*, p. 92) that the Old English *Riddles* derived from a Latin literary tradition but that they assumed distinct Old English qualities, namely imaginative portrayal and projection and the power of a dramatic, literary game. It is a mark of Ker's genius to call Old English riddle-writers early metaphysical poets. He says:

> In some of the riddles the miracle takes place which is not unknown in literary history elsewhere: what seems at first the most conventional of devices is found to be a fresh channel of poetry. Many of these quaint poems, taking their start from a simple idea, a single term, expatiate, without naming it, over all the life of their theme, and the riddle, instead of an occasion for intricate paraphrase, becomes a subject of imaginative thought. The poets of the riddles are not content with mere brocading work, though they like that well enough: but, besides, they meditate on their subject, they keep their eye on it. The riddle becomes a shifting vision of all the different aspects in which

the creature may be found—a quick, clear-sighted, interested poem. Though it is only a game, it carries the poetic mind out over the world. [*The Dark Ages*, p. 93]

There are two truths here: (1) that the Anglo-Saxon imagination is extended out into the world, and (2) that the power of the poems, man's record of and identification with that world, is locked into the convention of the riddlic game. It may be true, as Kennedy says, that "the Old English *Riddles* compose a brilliant series of thumbnail sketches of the daily realisms of Old English life" (*The Earliest English Poetry*, p. 134), but the communicative power of the poems is not realistic, at least in a formal sense. Kennedy recognizes this implicitly when he says that the *Riddles* "constitute a mosaic of the actualities of daily experience" (ibid.). The Old English riddlers have meaning to peddle and part of the meaning lies in the game. The riddlers taunt and cajole, they admit and deny, they peddle false hopes and paradoxes, they lead the reader down dark roads with glints of light. And in the end they never confess except to flatter, "Say what I mean." What they mean is the riddle-solver's meaning. What they mean is that reality exists and is at the same time a mosaic of man's perception. What they mean is that man's measure of the world is in words, that perceptual categories are built on verbal foundations, and that by withholding the key to the categorical house (the entitling solution) the riddlers may force the riddle-solver to restructure his own perceptual blocks in order to gain entry to a metaphorical truth. In short the solver must imagine himself a door and open in.

There are two kinds of Old English riddles that are the two poles of the perceptual game. The first kind of riddle is one that begins typically with *Ic eom* or *Ic wæs*. This kind of riddle, like *The Dream of the Rood*, is an imaginative projection, a kind of Anglo-Saxon negative capability. In terms of the game, the riddler pretends to be the creature in question. The voice of the riddle is the voice of the unknown creature cloaked in the disguise of man. The disguise is double. The riddler (man) pretends to be the creature (not man), but the creature describes himself in typically human terms. Thus the wind speaks as a warring servant, the shield as a wounded warrior, the nightingale as an evening poet, mead as a terrible wrestler, gold as an exile, and the book as a mysterious traveler. These projective riddles we may call first-person riddles of personification. The second kind of riddle begins typically with *Ic seah* or *Ic gefrægn* or *Wiht is*. This kind of riddle is a narrative riddle in which man retains his human identity in order to describe the miraculous identity of the riddlic creature. Still the creature that is not human is often described in human terms. Thus the shuttle sings, water watches over its family in the manner of a great mother, stars move as horsemen, soul and body journey through life as master and servant. These narrative riddles we may call third-person riddles of description.

Riddles are a form of literary game; they are also a metaphoric disguise. Typically in the Old English *Riddles* a creature that is not man takes on the cloak of man. There are exceptions of course like the "one-eyed seller of garlic," who is a man disguised as a monster, and the "rake," which is a tool disguised as a domestic beast, and the "Lot and his family" riddle, which is a kinship riddle, but for the most part Old English *Riddles* are anthropomorphic—they describe something not human in human disguise. There are all kinds of riddles (see, for example, Scott's description at pp. 115ff. of his article, "Some Approaches to the Study of the Riddle," in *Studies in Language, Literature, and Culture of the Middle Ages and Later*, ed. Atwood and Hill, pp. 111–27), and the metaphysic of the Old English choice of anthropomorphic riddles is interesting to contemplate. Certainly the first-person riddles like *The Dream of the Rood* may owe something to the classical rhetorical device of *prosopopoeia* (see Margaret Schlauch's "The 'Dream of the Rood' as Prosopopoeia," in *Essays and Studies in Honor of Carleton Brown*, pp. 23–34; and more recently, Marie Nelson's "The Rhetoric of the Exeter Book Riddles," *Spec.* xlix, 421–40, especially pp. 425ff.), but there is nothing in the classical tradition to explain the particular lyric quality—almost a celebration of the nonhuman Other—in the Old English poems. The tradition of speaking things may be related to the early practice of inscribing swords and rings and other jewels with "personalised statements of identity or origin" (Swanton, *The Dream of the Rood*, p. 66), but inscriptions like ÆDRED MEC AH, EANRED MEC AGROF on a Lancashire ring (Okasha, *Hand-list of Anglo-Saxon Non-runic Inscriptions*, p. 89) seem small claims in comparison with the lyric declaration of the *Riddles*. My own view is that the Anglo-Saxon poets, particularly those of the *Riddles* and *The Dream of the Rood*, were imbued with a native strain of negative capability (for the term coined by Keats, see especially his letter to his brothers of 21 December 1817 and his letter to Richard Woodhouse of 27 October 1818 in *The Letters of John Keats*, ed. Forman, pp. 70–72, 227–29), which allowed them to celebrate in human, poetic terms the nonhuman world about them. The celebration is what one African poet calls "dancing the Other." Senghor says of the poet:

> Il vit avec l'Autre en symbiose, *il con-naît à l'Autre*, pour parler comme Paul Claudel. Sujet et objet sont, ici, dialectiquement confrontés dans l'acte même de la connaissance, qui est acte d'amour. "Je pense donc je suis," écrivait Descartes. La remarque en a déjà été faite, on pense toujours *quelque chose*. Le Négro-africain pourrait dire: "Je sens l'Autre, je danse l'Autre, donc je suis." Or danser, c'est créer, surtout lorsque la danse est danse d'amour. C'est, en tout cas, le meilleur mode de connaissance. [*Liberté I*, p. 259]

Formally the Old English celebration of the Other is more sophisticated than the act of symbiosis. In the first-person riddles of persona, the riddler in each case projects himself into the hypothetical consciousness of the bird or shield; then, playing the part of the nonhuman creature, he describes himself in human terms to his human listener (the riddle-solver). It is as if a man wearing the clothes of his fathers took on the disguise of a bird in a riddlic game, and for the purposes of playing that game took on another set of human clothes and began slowly to disrobe until his watcher perceived that he was actually a man playing the part of a bird. In the third-person descriptive riddles the process is simpler as the narrative *Ic* of the riddle remains human and the spinner of the tale and the unraveler attempt to penetrate this mystery of nonhuman things in human disguise. The end result of all of this is, I think, a profound statement about the categories of human perception and the power of human imagination. Real birds do not play men, but men may through the power of poetry play birds. The consciousness of the nightingale in *Rid.* 6 would hardly ring true to the bird itself since the bird sings and does not recreate its singing as a poet. Man may soar past the limits of his own *banhus* but the wings of liberation are the wings of the perceptual mind. When man's perceptual categories become reified the wings no longer function. It is the task of the Old English riddler to challenge his reader in the dark to sprout bright wings. The flight from the *banhus* to the charged world about us is accomplished by the gift of words. As Kenneth Burke says:

In sum, just as the Word is said by theologians to be a mediatory principle between this world and the supernatural, might words be a mediatory principle between ourselves and nature? And just as the theologian might say that we must think of the Word as the bond between man and the supernatural, might words (and the social motives implicit in them) be the bond between man and the natural? Or, otherwise put, might nature be necessarily approached by us through the gift of the spirit of words?

If this were possible, then nature, as perceived by the word-using animal, would be not just the less-than-verbal thing that we usually take it to be. Rather, as so conceived and perceived, it would be infused with the spirit of words. . . . The world that we mistook for a realm of sheerly non-verbal, non-mental, visible, tangible things would thus become a fantastic pageantry, a parade of masques and costumes and guild-like mysteries. [*Anthropological Linguistics*, iv, no. 6, p. 21]

The parade of disguises is a lovely game, all the more so since the riddle-solver must share in the perceiving. The Old English riddlers offer bright jewels and glimmers of song in a surely enlightening literary game.[4]

4. For a recent article on the structure of Old English *Riddles*, see Nigel F. Barley's "Structural Aspects of the Anglo-Saxon Riddle," *Semiotica* x, 143–75, which came to hand after this section of the introduction was completed. For an excellent treatment of the function of riddles in general, see Ian Hamnett's "Ambiguity, Classification and Change: The Function of Riddles," *Man* ii, 379–92.

Appendixes to the Introduction

I n the notes to these appendixes, the reference to Krapp and Dobbie refers to *The Exeter Book*, edited by George Philip Krapp and Elliott Van Kirk Dobbie (Volume 3 of *The Anglo-Saxon Poetic Records*), especially the tables in their introduction, pp. lxviii–lxxxviii. The reference to Mackie is to *The Exeter Book*, Part 2, edited by W. S. Mackie (EETS, o.s. 194). Mackie's reading of the manuscript punctuation is not in tables but in the text itself.

Appendix A

ACCENTS IN THE MANUSCRIPT

MS. Fol.	Rid. No.	Word	MS. Fol.	Rid. No.	Word
101*a*	1.19	fám	106*b*	22.3	gós
101*a*	1.25	sǽ grundas	107*a*[1]	23.11	wundén locc [?]
101*b*	1.31	fréa	107*a*	24.24	ár stafum
101*b*	1.54	héa	109*a*	32.6	áa
102*b*	2.11	mín	109*a*	33.9	á wæfen
103*a*	4.7	ón	109*b*	34.9	fór
103*b*	9.8	wón	110*b*	38.11	mín
103*b*	9.8	wá	111*b*	38.105	swín
105*b*	18.4	wír	112*a*	40.13	rýne menn
105*b*	18.14	gerúm	113*b*	51.12	fǽr
105*b*	18.29	ón	114*a*[2]	52.9	hie ó
106*a*	19.6	ón	114*a*	53.5	úp
106*a*	19.6	mín	114*b*	56.15	rád
106*a*	19.12	án	122*b*	58.1	sǽ wealle
106*a*	20.7	héa	125*b*	67.2	wóh
106*b*	21.13	mán drinc	126*a*	70.5	mín

1. This case is also reported with a question mark by Krapp and Dobbie, p. lxxxviii; it is not reported by Mackie. The left-hand side of the accent is faint and may have been erased. The accent is copied by Robert Chambers in the 1831 British Museum transcript of the *Exeter Book*.

2. In the edited text, MS. *hie ó* is emended to *hio*.

Appendix A—*continued*

MS. Fol.	Rid. No.	Word	MS. Fol.	Rid. No.	Word
126a	70.15	scód	128a	80.31	á loden
126b	72.1	feax hár	128b	80.54	onhlíd
127a	76.11	góod	129a	83.4	gum rínc
127b	77.3	fóot	129b	87.6	mínes
127b	79.4	fáh	130a	89.1	Fréa
127b	79.9	árære	130a	89.8	fród
127b	79.13	dóm	130a	89.13	scóc
128a	80.10	ór	130b³		
128a	80.15	á weorþ[...			

3. Krapp and Dobbie, p. lxxxviii, report an accent over *féond* at their riddle number 93.28 which corresponds to *Rid.* 89.28 in my edition. Mackie does not report this accent. The MS. is smudged over *feond* and is difficult to read, but there is no apparent accent over the word. No accent is reported by Robert Chambers in his 1831 British Museum transcript of the *Exeter Book*.

Appendix B

SMALL CAPITALS IN THE MANUSCRIPT

MS. Fol.	Rid. No.	Word	MS. Fol.	Rid. No.	Word
101*a*	1.8	Ic	108*a*	29.3	Ic
102*a*	1.89	Ic	108*b*	30.11	In
102*b*	3.9	In	109*a*	33.2	Innaþe
102*b*	3.9	Ic	109*b*	35.6	Innað
102*b*	4.6	Ic	109*b*	35.7	In
103*a*	6.6	In	110*a*	37.7	Ne
103*a*	7.3	In	110*a*[2]	37.10	Ne [?]
103*a*	7.3	Innan	110*a*[3]	37.16	Ne [?]
103*b*	10.10	In	110*b*	38.16	Ic
104*b*	13.6	In	110*b*	38.23	Ic
104*b*	14.2	Ic	110*b*	38.28	Ic
104*b*	14.4*a*	Ic	110*b*	38.38	Ic
105*a*	15.2	Innan	111*a*	38.42	Ic
105*a*	15.9	Is	111*a*	38.44	Ic
105*a*	15.9	Innað	111*a*	38.46	Ic
105*b*[1]	18.3	Is	111*a*	38.48	Ic
105*b*	18.17	Ic	111*a*	38.50	Ic
105*b*	18.22	Nymþe	111*a*	38.58	Ic
106*b*	21.2	Ic	111*a*	38.60	Ic
106*b*	21.3	Ic	111*a*	38.62	Ic
106*b*	21.4	Ic	111*a*	38.64	Ic
106*b*	21.7	Ic	111*a*	38.66	Ic
106*b*	21.10	Ne	111*a*[4]	38.72	Ic
107*b*	25.6	In	111*b*[5]	38.78	Ic
107*b*	25.6	Nu	111*b*	38.82	Ic
107*b*	25.9	Sona	111*b*	38.84	Ic
107*b*	25.15	Ic	111*b*	38.88	Ic
107*b*	25.16	Ðe	111*b*	38.92	Mara
107*b*	26.7	In	111*b*	38.92	Ic
107*b*	26.7	Innan	111*b*	38.94	Ic
108*a*	27.7	Ða			

1. Not listed by Krapp and Dobbie.
2. Not listed by Krapp and Dobbie; the *Ne* in question is the first one in the line.
3. Ibid.
4. In the edited text, MS. *Ic* is emended to *is*.
5. Not listed by Krapp and Dobbie.

Appendix B—*continued*

MS. Fol.	Rid. No.	Word	MS. Fol.	Rid. No.	Word
111*b*[6]	38.98	Ic	115*a*	57.17	In
111*b*	38.101	Ac	123*a*	58.13	Ingeþonc
111*b*	38.105	Mara	124*b*[9]	60.1	Ingonges
111*b*[7]	38.105	Ic	125*b*	65.13	Ic
112*a*	39.6	Ne	126*a*	69.2	Iu
112*a*	40.5	Ic	126*a*	70.9	Ic
112*a*	41.1	Ic	126*a*[10]	70.10	Ic [?]
112*a*	41.2	In	127*b*	79.6	Ic
112*b*[8]	44.4	Inne	127*b*	79.12	Ac
112*b*	44.7	Insittendra	128*a*	80.33	Swa
112*b*	45.4	In	128*b*	81.3	Ic
113*a*	46.1	Ic	128*b*[11]	81.5	Ic
113*a*	47.8	Ic	128*b*	81.6*a*	Ic
113*b*	50.1	In	128*b*	81.6*a*	In
113*b*	51.6	In	128*b*	81.6*b*	Ic
113*b*	52.2	In	129*a*	84.9	Ac
114*a*	53.1	In	129*a*	84.15	Nu
114*a*	53.7	Ic	129*a*	84.18	Is
114*a*	53.13	In	129*a*	84.19	Ic
114*a*	54.1	Inne	129*a*	84.21	Ac
114*a*	54.10	Ic	129*b*	84.29	Innan
114*b*	56.9	Isernes	130*a*	89.11	In
114*b*	56.10	Iteþ	130*a*	89.14	Ic
114*b*	56.14	In	130*a*[12]	89.17	Innanweardne
114*b*	57.1	In	130*b*	89.28	Nu
114*b*	57.7	In	130*b*	91.1	Indryhten
114*b*	57.9	In	130*b*	91.8	Ic

6. Ibid.

7. Ibid.

8. Ibid.

9. In the edited text, MS. *Ingonges* is emended to *hingonges*.

10. Not listed by Krapp and Dobbie.

11. Ibid.

12. Not listed by Krapp and Dobbie; the MS. reading here is *In nan weardne* with the manuscript line break after *In*.

Appendix C

CATALOGUE OF SIMPLE POINTS

The following table is a catalogue of simple points used in the manuscript punctuation of the *Riddles*. Included in the table are all points except those used merely to set off runes or numerals within the text and except those elaborate end-points used to mark the close of riddles. For each point the manuscript folio number is listed as well as the *Riddle* and line numbers. Since a number of points occur at the end of the *b* hemistich, the reader should bear in mind that the riddle and line numbers in these cases refer to the word preceding the point and that the word following the point would occur in the next line of the edited text. Under the heading, "Context," the point is listed with the preceding and following word or words. These are in all cases the manuscript readings and not those of the edited text. Under the category, "Meter," an entry is included if the point falls at the end of either hemistich. The entry, "b/a," means that the point falls at the end of the *b*-line; the entry, "a/b," means that the point falls at the end of the *a*-line.

Where the point seems to have some rhetorical and/or syntactic significance, this is listed under the category, "Rhet./Syn." Where the rhetorical and syntactic significance vary slightly, the two are separated by a slash. Thus, for example, under *Rid*. 1.30 the point and context *wrugon · hwilum* is listed under the category, "Rhet./Syn.," as +*hwilum*/Sent. This means that the point has both a rhetorical and syntactic significance—rhetorical because it falls before *hwilum*, which often marks the onset of a new phrase or clause, and syntactic because it occurs at the end of a sentence, as printed in the edited text. The abbreviations used under the category, "Rhet./Syn.," are these:

> CC.: "Coordinate clauses"; the point and a conjunction or conjunctive adverb together mark the separation between two coordinate clauses.
>
> IC.: "Independent clauses"; the point alone marks the juncture between two independent clauses.
>
> Form.: "Formulaic ending"; the point separates the formulaic ending from the rest of the text.
>
> SC.: "Subordinate clause"; the point and a conjunction or conjunctive adverb together mark off a subordinate clause from a main clause.
>
> Sent.: "Sentence"; the point marks the end of a sentence as printed in the edited text.

+ : "In conjunction with"; the word following the sign is usually an adverb or conjunction commonly pointed.

+cap.: "In conjunction with a capital letter"; in which case the point usually falls at the end of a sentence or independent clause, but not always.

// : "Parallel" (subjects, objects, etc., which the point may be used to separate).

? : To indicate editorial doubt as to the significance listed.

Where the point seems to have some paleographical significance, such as falling at the end of a manuscript page or marking off the text of one riddle from another in the same MS. line, this is noted under the category, "Paleography." Most of these explanations are spelled out in full. The notation, "Scribal care," means that the point is used to call attention to a potentially troublesome passage, frequently succeeding words similar or the same.

The presence of dots marked off by a bracket or brackets means, as is the case in the edited text, that the manuscript is damaged with a resulting lacuna.

This catalogue is intended to be the groundwork for further study of the significance of manuscript pointing in the *Riddles*. For my own generalizations from the data, see the section of the Introduction on "Manuscript Punctuation."

Appendix C—*continued*

MS. Fol.	Rid. No.	Context	Meter	Rhet./Syn.	Paleography
101a	1.21	[beatað · stundum][1]	a/b	? // predicates	
101a	1.30	wrugon · hwilum	b/a	+hwilum/Sent.	
101b	1.46	tæcneð · hwilum	b/a	+hwilum/Sent.	
101b	1.53	neah · héa	b/a		Scribal care
101b	1.65	þæt · hwilum	b/a	+hwilum/Sent.	
101b	1.67	wæg fatu · wide	a/b		End fol. 101b
102a	1.70	hludast · þōn	b/a	+þonne/SC.	
102a	1.77	bosme · wætan	b/a	? // objects	
102a	1.82	wæpnum · dol	b/a	Sent.	
102a	1.102	swiþfeorm · saga	a/b	Form./Sent.	End fol. 102a
102b	3.10	læce cynn · onfolc	b/a		
102b	4.4	hrine · þōn	b/a	+þonne/SC.	
102b	4.7	winne · ón	b/a		End fol. 102b
103a	5.8	beom · flode	b/a		See note²
103a	5.9	gæst · :7	b/	End Riddle/Sent.	See note²
103a	7.7	sceate · swa	a/b	+swa/SC.	
103b	8.7	hrægl · sume	b/a	IC.	
103b	8.9	ahof · wind	b/a	? // subjects	
104a	11.11	tredan · :7	b/	End Riddle/Sent.	Part of end-punctuation

1. Mackie marks a point here, but under magnification the "point" appears to be connected with the ligature *s* and somewhat different in shape from other points, so it is difficult to know whether the mark is actually a point or a resting of the pen.

2. These points delimit the last line of *Rid.* 5, thus: · *flode ond foldan ferende gæst* · :7. This may be because of the unusual MS. position of the hemistiches relative to one another. The *a*-line ends one MS. line and the *b*-line is written directly below it in the next MS. line.

Appendix C—*continued*

MS. Fol.	Rid. No.	Context	Meter	Rhet./Syn.	Paleography
104a	12.13	fyrd sceorp · hwilū	a/b	+hwilum/Sent. (?CC.)	
104a	12.15	bosme · hwilū	b/a	+hwilum/CC.	
104a	12.17	wine · hwilū	a/b	+hwilum/CC.	
104b	13.11	witod · forþon	b/a	+forþon/CC.	
105a	15.9	til · wombhord	b/a	? // subjects	
105a	18.2	minū · leof			End fol. 105a
105b	18.21	woc · Nymþe	b/a	+nymþe/SC. (+cap.)	
105b	18.29	ón · bende	b/a		See note[3]
105b	18.31	gestreona · oft	b/a	+oft/Sent.	
106a	19.3	min · woh	b/a		
106a	20.8	streamas · stronge			
106a	20.14	swom · nebe	b/a	+ne/CC.	
106b	21.9	geap · Neto	b/a	+ne/Sent. (+cap.)	
106b	22.1	stefne · hwilum	b/a	+hwilum/CC.	
106b	22.2	hund · hwilū	a/b	+hwilum/CC.	
106b	22.2	gat · hwilum	b/a	+hwilum/CC.	
106b	22.3	gós · hwilū	a/b	+hwilum/CC.	
106b	22.3	hafoc · hwilū	b/a	+hwilum/Sent. (?CC.)	
106b	22.5	hleoþor · hwilum	a/b	+hwilum/CC.	
106b	22.6	gemæne · hwilum	a/b	+hwilum/CC.	

3. Certain otherwise unexplainable points occur immediately after words marked with an accent in the MS. These points may indicate a resting of the pen after the accent is made, or perhaps they are a kind of rhythmic marker indicating a pause or point of vocal emphasis after either a long vowel or a stress on a normally unstressed word.

Appendix C—*continued*

MS. Fol.	Rid. No.	Context	Meter	Rhet./Syn.	Paleography
106b	23.5	neþeð · hwilum	a/b	+hwilum/See note[4]	End fol. 106b
106b	23.6	cyrtenu · ceorles	b/a	+nu/Sent.	
107a	24.14	bifongen · nu	b/a	+gif/Sent. (SC.): See note[5]	
107a	24.17	wite · gif			
107a	24.26	clyppað · frige	a/b	Form./Sent.	
107a	24.27	mære · haeleþum	b/a		End fol. 107a
107b	25.6	bydene · Nu	a/b	+nu/Sent. (+cap.)	
107b	25.8	ceorl · Sona	b/a	+sona/Sent. (+cap.)	
107b	26.3	ge streona · corfen	b/a	? Mark onset of // rhymed participles	
108a	27.6	meahte · Ða	b/a	+ða/Sent. (+cap.)	
108a	29.2	gewlitegad · wrættum	a/b	? // participles	
108a	29.12	bideþ · hwonne	b/a	+hwonne/SC.	
109a	33.4	min · wundene	b/a	IC.	See note above to 18.29
109a	33.9	á wæfan · wyrda	a/b		
109a	33.12	gewæde · saga	b/a	Form./Sent.	
109b	34.3	feowere · fet	a/b		? As a possible analogue to points setting off roman numerals in *Riddles*
109b	35.1	hindan · þriþum	b/a		

4. Here the rhetorical consciousness of the scribe is shown to be greater than his syntactic or metrical awareness. *Hwilum* normally marks the onset of a clause or sentence, but in this case the sentence begins with the verb *neþeð*. The scribe, however, continues his practice of pointing before *hwilum* as in the preceding riddle.

5. Here *gif* begins a new sentence, but the scribe may have marked a point before it thinking to separate the subordinate clause from a preceding main clause.

Appendix C—*continued*

MS. Fol.	Rid. No.	Context	Meter	Rhet./Syn.	Paleography
109*b*	36.1	wæpned cynnes · geoguð myrþe	b/a		Mark end of short MS. line and separate text from text of previous riddle in same MS. line
110*a*	37.6	onweg · Ne	b/a	+ne/Sent. (+cap.)	
110*a*	37.9	biþ · Ne⁶	b/a	+ne/Sent. (?CC.) (?+cap.)	
110*a*	37.15	wære · Ne⁶	b/a	+ne/Sent. (?CC.) (?+cap.)	
110*a*	37.17	dreogan · ne	b/a	+ne/Sent. (?CC.)	
110*a*	37.20	mot · ac	b/a	+ac/CC.	
110*a*	37.24	gesceapu · þæt	a/b	Sent.	
110*a*	37.29	hatte · :7	b/	End Riddle/Sent.	Part of end-punctuation
110*b*	38.9	æfre · *ond*	b/a	+ond/CC.	
110*b*	38.15	ymb clyp þe · Ic	b/a	Sent. (+cap.)	
110*b*	38.19	giefeð · nemæg	b/a	+ne/CC.	
110*b*	38.22	wealdeþ · Ic	b/a	Sent. (+cap.)	
110*b*	38.28	heo · swylce	b/a	+swylce/CC.	
110*b*	38.32	stinceþ · eal	b/a	Sent.	
110*b*	38.39	bihealdan · eac	b/a	+eac/CC.	
111*a*	38.41	gesta · Ic	b/a	Sent. (+cap.)	
111*a*	38.43	geweorþan · *ond*	b/a	+ond/CC.	
111*a*	38.45	hrif · Ic	b/a	Sent. (+cap.)	
111*a*	38.47	utan · Ic	b/a	IC. (+cap.)	

6. In each of these cases, the capital letter is questionable; see Appendix B.

Appendix C—*continued*

MS. Fol.	Rid. No.	Context	Meter	Rhet./Syn.	Paleography
111a	38.51	grena · folm	b/a	IC.	
111a	38.52	bifon · *ond*	a/b	+ond/CC.	
111a	38.59	hunige · swylce	b/a	+swylce/CC.	
111a	38.67	meah te · nis	b/a	+n[e]/CC.	
111a	38.69	æghwær · meis	b/a	IC.	
111a	38.73	wordū · nemnað			End fol. 111a
111b	38.73	nemnað · hefigere	b/a	Sent.	? Indicate proper metrical stop because of possible confusion from preceding point
111b	38.75	clympre · leohtre	b/a	? // comparatives/IC.	
111b	38.77	gæð · fotum	a/b		
111b	38.77	dryge · flinte	b/a	Sent.	
111b	38.79	heardan · hnescre	b/a	? // comparatives/IC.	
111b	38.81	onlyfte · Ic	b/a	Sent. (+cap.)	
111b	38.83	grena · Ic	b/a	IC. (+cap.)	
111b	38.85	gewefen · wundor cræfte	a/b		
111b	38.85	wundor cræfte · nis	b/a	+n[e]/Sent.	
111b	38.87	onworld life · Ic	b/a	IC. (+cap.)	
111b	38.91	sceal · Mara	b/a	Sent. (+cap.)	
111b	38.94	syne · Ic	a/b	IC. (+cap.)	
111b	38.94	he · swylce	b/a	+swylce/CC.	
111b	38.97	delfað · ne[7]	b/a	+ne/Sent.	
111b	38.100	moste · Ac	b/a	+ac/CC. (+cap.)	

7. This word is misread as *nu* by Krapp and Dobbie.

Appendix C—*continued*

MS. Fol.	Rid. No.	Context	Meter	Rhet./Syn.	Paleography
111b	38.104	loccas · Mara	b/a	Sent. (+cap.)	See note above to 18.29
111b	38.105	swín · bearg	b/a	? // subjects	
112a	39.1	edniwu · þæt	b/a	? [MS. fol. missing before *edniwu*]	
112a	39.3	sweartestan · þæs	b/a	Mark // superlatives: See note[8]	
112a	39.4	deorestan · þæs	a/b	Mark // superlatives	
112a	39.5	agen · Ne	b/a	+ne/Sent. (+cap.)	
112a	39.8	geþencanne · þeoda	a/b		
112a	40.17	sindon · Ic	b/a	Sent. (+cap.) See note[9]	
112a	41.2	geardum · þam	a/b		
112a	41.8	care · gif	a/b	+gif/SC.: See note[10]	
112a	41.9	hlaforde · hyreð	a/b		End fol. 112a
112b	41.12	hweorfað · anre	b/a		
112b	42.3	godne · þonne	b/a	+þonne/Sent. (SC.): See note[11]	

8. There are three superlatives at *Rid.* 39.3–4*a*. Two are followed by a MS. point, and the third, *selestan* (39.3*a*), occurs at the end of the MS. line where the space may serve the same separating function as the points in the other two cases.

9. The point marks the formal juncture between two riddles. This is one of two cases where the scribe has mistakenly combined two riddles into one.

10. This is a rare case of a syntactical pause falling within the half-line.

11. Here *þonne* takes a rhetorical point commonly placed before adverbs used as conjunctions. The scribe may have mistakenly assumed that he was marking off the subordinate clause from the main clause as is often the case elsewhere. Here, however, the subordinate clause precedes the main clause.

Appendix C—*continued*

MS. Fol.	Rid. No.	Context	Meter	Rhet./Syn.	Paleography
112b	44.1	wifum · twam			Mark end of short MS. line and separate text of previous riddle in same MS. line
113a	45.6	swealg · Ic	b/a	Sent. (+cap.) See note[12]	
113a	46.1	hringende an · torhtne	b/a		
113a	48.7	ryhte · fedað	b/a	? // predicates	
113a	49.2	swearte · wæran			End fol. 113a
113b	50.1	fergan · under	b/a		Mark end of short MS. line and separate text from text of previous riddle in same MS. line
113b	51.12	fær · genamman	b/a		See note above to 18.29
113b	52.1	gangan · þær	a/b		Mark end of short MS. line and separate text from text of previous riddle in same MS. line
113b	52.2	stondan · In	b/a	(+cap.)	
113b	52.2	to · hror	b/a		
113b	52.4	up · hrand	a/b	? // predicates	
113b	52.7	nyt · tillic	b/a		
113b	52.9	stunda · gehwam	b/a		End fol. 113b
114a	52.9	hie ó · werig	b/a		See note above to 18.29

12. The point marks the formal juncture between two riddles. This is one of two cases where the scribe has mistakenly combined two riddles into one.

Appendix C—*continued*

MS. Fol.	Rid. No.	Context	Meter	Rhet./Syn.	Paleography
114a	53.8	secgan · þær	b/a	IC. ? Mark onset of list of // tree-names	
114a	53.9	acc · *ond*	a/b	? +ond	See note[13]
114a	53.9	iw · *ond*	b/a	? +ond	See note[13]
114a	53.11	anne · wulf heafed treo	b/a	? // objects	
114a	54.2	winnende · wiht			Mark end of short MS. line, the first MS. line of the riddle
114a	54.7	oþer · oþer	a/b		Scribal care
114b	55.4	cirmað · tredað	b/a	IC.	
114b	57.7	gemynd · his	b/a		
114b	57.11	don · swa	b/a	+swa/SC.	
114b	57.16	cwæden · hringes	b/a		End fol. 114b
122b	58.3	wæs · monna	b/a		
122b	58.5	be heolde · ac	b/a	+ac/CC.	
122b	58.8	sið · æfre	a/b		End fol. 122b
123a	58.11	conn · hu	b/a	? +hu/? SC.	
124b	60.1	strong · forð	b/a	? // adjectives	Mark end of short MS. line, the first MS. line of the riddle
125a	61.1	sceal · fægre	b/a		Mark end of short MS. line and separate text from text of previous riddle in same MS. line

13. Conceivably the scribe took *acc* and *iw* as names of runes instead of or in addition to their being names of trees and thus placed points after them.

Appendix C —*continued*

MS. Fol.	Rid. No.	Context	Meter	Rhet./Syn.	Paleography
125a	64.2	hond · wyrm	b/a	+þonne/SC.	End fol. 125a
126a	69.6	wigeð · þōn			
126a	70.3	geaf · [...	a/b	[The lacuna here makes it impossible to guess the function of the point]	
126a	71.2	hruse · *ond*			End fol. 126a
126b	71.7	hwilum · nu	b/a	+nu/SC.: See note[14]	
126b	71.24	hrægn locan · hwilum	a/[***]	[The sense and meter indicate the loss of a half-line before *hwilum*]	
127b	79.8	mot · ac	b/a	+ac/CC.	
127b	79.11	unlytel · Ac	b/a	+ac/CC. (+cap.)	
127b	79.13	dóm · dyran	a/b		See note above to 18.29
127b	80.2	ryne · strongne			End fol. 127b
128a	80.2	[strongne · grimme][15]			
128a	80.5	æfre · neol	b/a	IC.	
128a	80.24	gesweotlad · wlite	b/a	IC.	
128a	80.26	getenge · clæn georn	b/a	? Mark off extended introductory adjectival modifier	

14. Here the scribe has punctuated properly according to syntax and meaning and has rightly ignored the rhetorical rule of pointing before *hwilum*. Cp. the pointing above at 23.5.

15. Mackie marks a point here and there is a point in the facsimile (ed. Chambers, Förster, and Flower, *The Exeter Book of Old English Poetry*), but this is apparently an imperfection in the photographic plate because there is no point in the MS. See note to *Rid.* 80.2 in Notes and Commentary section.

Appendix C—*continued*

MS. Fol.	Rid. No.	Context	Meter	Rhet./Syn.	Paleography
128a	80.32	sawe · Swa	b/a	+swa/Sent. (+cap.)	? Scribal care End fol. 128a
128a	80.35	mode · snottor			
128b	80.43	sceafte · biþ	b/a	Sent.	
128b	81.4	preohtigra · hwilum	b/a	+hwilum/Sent.	
128b	82.3	twa · ond	b/a	+ond/See note[16]	
128b	82.4	heafda · hryc	b/a		? In a line with several points because of numerals, to mark clearly the metrical end of the line
129a	83.1	wombe · hæfde			Mark end of short MS. line and separate text from text of previous riddle in same MS. line
129a	83.1	micle · þryþum	b/a		Mark proper metrical stop because of possible confusion resulting from preceding point. Cp. 38.73 above
129a	83.2	geþrungne · þegn	a/b		Same as preceding example
129a	84.2	sumor · mi[...	? a/b	[The lacuna here makes it impossible to guess the function of the point]	
129a	84.8	...]fgeaf · Ac	b/a	+ac/CC. (+cap.)	
129a	84.10	hearde · eard	b/a	Sent.	Scribal care

16. Here *ond* links parallel objects, but the scribe may have punctuated as if *ond* were a coordinate conjunction.

Appendix C—*continued*

MS. Fol.	Rid. No.	Context	Meter	Rhet./Syn. (+cap.)	Paleography
129a	84.14	meotud · Nu	b/a	+nu/Sent. (+cap.)	
129a	84.17	gum cynnes · anga	b/a		
129a	84.18	bæc · wonn	b/a		
129a	84.20	her · Ac	b/a	+ac/CC. (+cap.)	
129a	84.22	fæste · ne	b/a	+ne/CC.	
129a	84.24	sceata · eardian	a/b		End fol. 129a
129b	85.7	worhte · hwilum	b/a	+hwilum/CC.	
129b	86.1	tenetur · obcu[..]it	b/a	IC.	Latin Riddle
129b	86.2	agnus · et	? a/b	[The meter indicates a possible loss of a word after *agnus*] IC.	
129b	86.3	magnan · dui	b/a		
129b	87.7	middel nihtum · hwilum	b/a	+hwilum/Sent.	
129b	87.8	bregde · nebbe	b/a		End fol. 129b
130a	87.8	nebbe · hyrde	b/a		Mark proper metrical stop because of possible confusion resulting from preceding point. Cp. 38.73 and 83.1 above
130a	88.1	holte · freolic	b/a		Mark end of short MS. line, the first MS. line of the riddle
130a	88.3	sond · gold	b/a	? // objects	
130a	89.8	...]s · hwilū	b/a	+hwilum/CC.	
130a	89.10	eþel · hwilū	a/b	+hwilum/CC.	

Appendix C—*continued*

MS. Fol.	Rid. No.	Context	Meter	Rhet./Syn.	Paleography
130a	89.13	hrimig hearde · hwilum	a/b	+hwilum/CC.	
130b	89.27	fot · Nu	b/a	+nu/Sent. (+cap.)	
130b	89.29	gehleþan · oft	b/a	+oft/IC.	
130b	90.3	sunne · [...	b/a	[The lacuna here makes it impossible to guess the function of the point.]	

Plates

Unless otherwise noted, all photographs are from the *Exeter Book* manuscript. These appear by courtesy of the Dean and Chapter, Exeter Cathedral. The photograph from *Brit. Mus. Add. MS. 9067* (Robert Chambers's 1831–32 copy of the *Exeter Book*) appears by courtesy of the trustees of the British Museum. The photographs of the *Exeter Book* manuscript were taken in early March, 1972, in the Exeter Cathedral Library under the supervision of library officials and the editor of this edition.

The plates are referred to in the paleographical notes to the text and in the notes to the individual lines in the Notes and Commentary.

I. See note to *Rid.* 1.7: (a) superscript *y* above *i* in *hlin* at *Rid.* 1.7 [fol. 101*a*] compared with (b) textual *y* in *hrycge* at *Rid.* 1.12 [fol. 101*a*]. The hand in each case appears to be the same. Scale of both photographs: 2:1.

(a)

(b)

(a)

(b)

II. See note to *Rid*. 1.42: (a) superscript *a* (with subscript caret) inserted between the elements of MS. *up þringe* at *Rid*. 1.42 [fol. 101*b*] compared with (b) textual *a* of *sal*, a portion of MS. *sal wonge* at *Rid*. 1.32 [fol. 101*b*]. The hand is similar but not exactly the same. Scale of both photographs: 2:1.

(a)

(b)

(c)

III. See notes to *Rid*. 3.lower margin and *Rid*. 4.lower margin: (a) marginalic ᚻ (*sigel*) rune between *Rids*. 3 and 4 [fol. 102*b*] and (b) marginalic ᚻ (*sigel*) rune between *Rids*. 4 and 5 [fol. 103*a*] compared with (c) textual ᚻ (*sigel*) rune at *Hus*. 49 [fol. 123*b*]. The first marginalic rune is similar to the textual rune; the second is not. Scale of all photographs: 2:1.

IV. See note to *Rid.* 6.upper margin: (a)
marginalic mark above *Rid.* 6 [fol. 103*a*]
compared with (b) textual *n* in *ne beom* of *Rid.*
5.8 [fol. 103*a*] directly above in the MS.;
compared also with (c) textual ᚢ (*ur*) rune of
Cynewulfian signature at *Chr.* 805 [fol. 19*b*]
and with (d) textual ᚻ (*cen*) rune of
Cynewulfian signature at *Chr.* 797 [fol. 19*b*].
If the mark above *Rid.* 6 is a rune, it more
closely resembles runic ᚢ (*ur*) than ᚻ (*cen*);
but the mark actually resembles no other
mark, rune, or letter in the *Exeter Book*. Scale
of all photographs: 2:1.

(a)

(b)

(c)

(d)

V.

V. See note to *Rid*. 10.15.right margin: marginalic *eoh* rune (Z) with point to the left and pen trailing downward from the last lateral stroke, in the right-hand margin of *Rid*. 10 [fol. 104*a*]. Scale: 2:1.

VI.

VI. See note to *Rid*. 12.right margin: marginalic H (?) to the right of *Rid*. 12 [fol. 104*a*]. Scale: 2:1.

VII.

VII. See note to *Rid*. 12.19: unusual end-punctuation mark following *Rid*. 12 [fol. 104*a*]. Scale: 2:1.

VIII. See note to *Rid*. 15.upper margin: (a) marginalic ᛒ (*beorc*) rune and ᛚ (*lagu*) rune between *Rids*. 14 and 15 and below the textual *fæste* of *Rid*. 14.10 [fol. 105*a*]. The runes are shown in close-up at (b). These marginalic runes should be compared with (c) textual ᛒ (*beorc*) rune at *Rid*. 62.2 [fol. 125*a*] and with (d) textual ᛚ (*lagu*) rune at *Rid*. 73.2 [fol. 127*a*]. The marginalic runes here do not appear to have been made by the same scribe who made the textual runes. Scale of (a): 1:1; scale of (b), (c), and (d): 2:1.

(a)

(b)

(c)

(d)

IX. See note to *Rid*. 15.lower margin: curved mark in margin between *Rids*. 15 and 16 [fol. 105*a*]. Scale: 2:1.

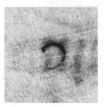

IX.

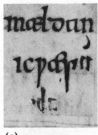

X.

X. See note to *Rid*. 16.right margin: a mark to the right of *Rid*. 16 [fol. 105*a*] appears to be a testing of the pen and nothing more. Scale: 2:1.

(a)

XI. See notes to *Rid*. 16.4 and to *Rid*. 16.lower margin: (a) inclusive photo showing margin-alic offset marks and offset *n* after *wæs* in *Rid*. 16 [fol. 105*a*] and (b) close-up photo of offset marginalic marks falsely identified by Förster as a rune. The marks are offset from the facing folio 104*b*. Scale of (a): 1:1; scale of (b): 2:1.

(b)

XII.

XII. See note to *Rid*. 18.34: *þ* of *firenaþ* altered from *w* [fol. 105*b*]. Scale: 1:1.

XIII. See paleographical note to *Rid*.
19.15: unusual *n* in *min* [fol. 106*a*].
Scale: 1:1.

XIII.

XIV. See note to *Rid*. 28a.right margin: (a)
marginalic *r* with points on either side and (b)
uncertain marginalic mark, both in the
right-hand margin of *Rid*. 28a [fol. 108*a*]; also
for comparison, the interlinear *r* of *bereft* [fol.
10*a*] made by Nowell in the sixteenth
century. The hand of the *r* in the margin of
Rid. 28a is not Nowell's. Scale of all
photographs: 2:1.

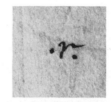

(a)

(b)

(c)

XV. See note to *Rid.* 28a.9: unusual mark following end-punctuation mark at end of *Rid.* 28a [fol. 108*a*]. Scale: 2:1.

XV.

XVI. See note to *Rid.* 38.108: (a) marginalic writing at bottom of folio 111*b* and (b) Robert Chambers's transcription of the marginalia in his 1831 copy of the *Exeter Book* (*Brit. Mus. Add. MS. 9067*). Scale of both photographs: 1:1.

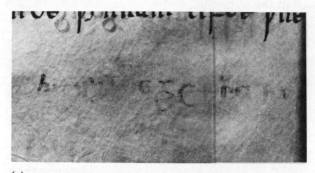

(a)

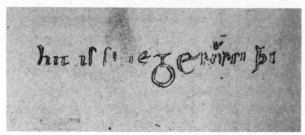

(b)

XVII. See note to *Rid.* 62.right margin: dry-point runes ᛒ ᚾᛏᛦᚠ (standing perhaps for *Beo unreþe!*) scratched in right-hand margin of *Rid.* 62 [fol. 125*a*]. The capital *G* and other penciled marginalia are Hickes's (for an explanation of these, see note to *Rid.* 73.right margin). Scale: 2:1.

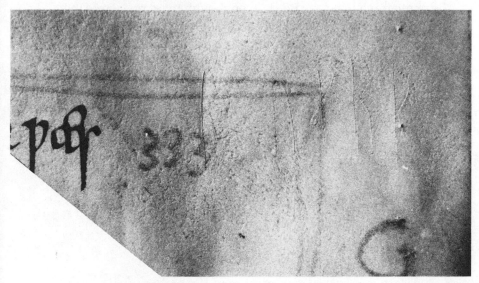

XVII.

XVIII. See headnote to *Rid.* 73 and also note to *Rid.* 73.right margin: right-hand portion of *Rid.* 73 (copied by the scribe as two riddles) and top line of *Rid.* 74 [fol. 127*a*] showing Hickes's penciled markings that include the bracket, the sign 𝟑𝟑 , and the capital *H*. Hickes, who normally bracketed runic riddles with these coded instructions to his copier to copy them, apparently took the top two lines as shown in the photograph to be one riddle even though the scribe wrote them as two. That the lines are one riddle is also my reading. Scale: 1:1.

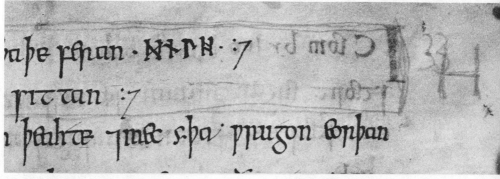

XVIII.

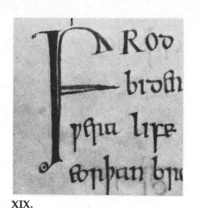

XIX.

XIX. See note to *Rid.* 79.1: the beginning of *Rid.* 79 showing various sizes of capital letters [fol. 127*b*]. Scale: 1:1.

XX. See note to *Rid*. 80.2: (a) manuscript portion of *strongne grimme* at *Rid*. 80.2–3 [fol. 128*a*] showing no evidence of a point between the two words compared with (b) the same portion from the facsimile of 1933 (edited by Chambers, Förster, and Flower) showing a point between the two words. The point in the facsimile is apparently the result of an imperfection or spot of dust on the photographic plate. Scale of both photographs: 2:1.

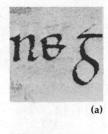

(a)

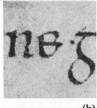

(b)

XXI. See note to *Rid*. 80.46 ff.: (a) portion of MS. folio 128*b* along the edge of the burn compared with (b) same portion of the facsimile where edges have been pulled free of backing vellum for purposes of taking the photograph. Here, typically, more of the script is visible in the facsimile than in the manuscript itself. Scale of both photographs: 1:1.

(a)

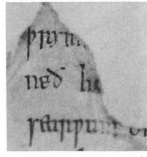

(b)

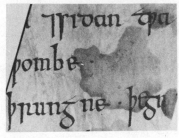

XXII.

XXII. See note to *Rid*. 82.lower margin: blank space and smudge after *Rid*. 82 [fol. 129*a*] showing no trace of ᛒ rune recorded by Wyatt. Scale: 1:1.

XXIII.

XXIII. See note to *Rid*. 86.2: portion of *agnus et capit* from *Rid*. 86 [fol. 129*b*] showing unusual form of *et* and horned *c* form of *a*. Scale: 1:1.

Text

Plan of the Text

The text of the *Riddles* has been transcribed and edited from the *Exeter Book* manuscript in Exeter Cathedral and checked against the manuscript facsimile and where necessary against the British Museum transcript of 1831–32. Common abbreviations in the manuscript, such as 7 for *ond* and þ̄ for *þæt*, are expanded silently (these abbreviations are listed in the section of the Introduction on "Manuscript Punctuation"); uncommon abbreviations, such as *p´nex* for *pernex* (*Rid.* 38.66) and *7weorc* for *ondweorc* or *hondweorc* (*Rid.* 3.8) are noted in the paleographical notes to the text. The word formation of the manuscript has been normalized. Manuscript accents, small capitals, and points are listed in the Appendixes to the Introduction and are discussed in the section of the Introduction on "Manuscript Punctuation." Other departures from the text of the manuscript itself are noted below the edited text in the paleographical notes. In these notes the sign [/] is used to indicate the break coming between the end of one manuscript line and the beginning of the next.

Places in the manuscript that are impossible to read because of some spillage, age, or the mutilation caused by the burn are indicated by bracketed dots in the edited text. Each dot represents a lost letter. Where only a few letters are lost, the count is probably quite accurate. Where many letters are lost, the count is an approximation based on the number of letters in a space of equal size to the lacuna in a nearby manuscript line. Where the lacuna includes the end of a riddle and extends to the right-hand margin of the manuscript, it is difficult to tell the number of lost letters since riddles often end somewhere in the middle of a manuscript line. Where there is no break in the manuscript but where a break is indicated by the sense of the text and often by the meter, these presumed losses are indicated in the edited text by asterisks.

Opposite each of my own riddle numbers in the text, there appears in an open bracket the corresponding riddle number or numbers from the Krapp and Dobbie edition of the *Exeter Book* (*ASPR.*, vol. 3). Variant numbers from other major riddle editions are given in the Notes and Commentary section that follows the entire text of the *Riddles*. In the Notes and Commentary section, riddle solutions are discussed in a headnote, and the textual problems along with variant readings of other editors are discussed in the notes to the individual lines.

1.

Hwylc is hæleþa þæs horsc   ond þæs hygecræftig
þæt þæt mæge asecgan,   hwa mec on sið wræce,
þonne ic astige strong,   stundum reþe,
þrymful þunie,   þragum wræce
5 fere geond foldan,   folcsalo bærne,
ræced reafige?   Recas stigað
haswe ofer hrofum;   hlyn bið on eorþan,
wælcwealm wera.   Þonne ic wudu hrere,
bearwas bledhwate,   beamas fylle;
10 holme gehrefed,   heahum meahtum
wrecen on waþe,   wide sended:
hæbbe me on hrycge   þæt ær hadas wreah
foldbuendra,   flæsc ond gæstas
somod on sunde.   Saga hwa mec þecce,
15 oþþe hu ic hatte   þe þa hlæst bere.
Hwilum ic gewite,   swa ne wenaþ men,
under yþa geþræc   eorþan secan,
garsecges grund.   Gifen biþ gewreged,
fam gewealcen   *   *   *
20 hwælmere hlimmeð,   hlude grimmeð;
streamas staþu beatað,   stundum weorpaþ
on stealc hleoþa   stane ond sonde,
ware ond wæge,   þonne ic winnende,
holmmægne biþeaht,   hrusan styrge,
25 side sægrundas.   Sundhelme ne mæg
losian ær mec læte   se þe min latteow bið
on siþa gehwam.   Saga, þoncol mon,

1.1 ff: For a discussion of whether this first riddle constitutes one, two, or three riddles, see the headnote.

1.7: *hlyn*: MS. *hlin* with a small *y* written above the *i* in a hand similar to that of the scribe (see plate 1.a and note).

1.10: *heahum*: MS. *heanū*.

1.11: *wrecen*: MS. *wrecan*.

1.15b–16a: After *bere* there is an end-punctuation mark; *Hwilum* with a large capital *H* begins a new MS. line. As *bere* is flush with the right-hand margin of script, there is no end-space separating what the scribe appears to have taken to be two separate riddles—the first at lines 1–15, the second at lines 16ff.

      hwa mec bregde   of brimes fæþmum
      þonne streamas eft   stille weorþað,
30   yþa geþwære, þe mec ær wrugon.
      Hwilum mec min frea   fæste genearwað,
      sendeð þonne   under salwonges
      bearm bradan,   ond on bid wriceð,
      þrafað on þystrum   þrymma sumne,
35   hæste on enge,   þær me heord siteð
      hruse on hrycge.   Nah ic hwyrftweges
      of þam aglace,   ac ic eþelstol
      hæleþa hrere: hornsalu wagiað,
      wera wicstede;   weallas beofiað
40   steape ofer stiwitum.   Stille þynceð
      lyft ofer londe   ond lagu swige,
      oþþæt ic of enge   up aþringe,
      efne swa mec wisaþ   se mec wræde on
      æt frumsceafte   furþum legde,
45   bende ond clomme,   þæt ic onbugan ne mot
      of þæs gewealde þe me wegas tæcneð.
      Hwilum ic sceal ufan   yþa wregan,
      streamas styrgan,   ond to staþe þywan
      flintgrægne flod: famig winneð
50   wæg wið wealle.   Wonn ariseð
      dun ofer dype;   hyre deorc on last,
      eare geblonden,   oþer fereð,
      þæt hy gemittað   mearclonde neah
      hea hlincas.   þær bið hlud wudu,
55   brimgiesta breahtm;   bidað stille
      stealc stanhleoþu   streamgewinnes,

    1.32: *salwonges*: MS. *sal wonge*.
    1.35: *hæste*: MS. *hætst*.
    1.37: *aglace*: MS. *aglaca*.
    1.38: *hrere*: MS. *hrera*.
    1.42: *up aþringe*: MS. *up þringe* with a slight space between the words and a small superior *a* in a similar hand (?) inserted between, with an inferior caret marking the addition (see plate II.a).
    1.48: *streamas*: Not in MS.; in the MS. *wregan* ends one MS. line and *styrgan* begins the next.
    1.48: *þywan*: MS. *þyran*.

hopgehnastes,   þonne heah geþring
on cleofu crydeþ.   Þær bið ceole wen
sliþre sæcce   gif hine sæ byreð
60   on þa grimman tid   gæsta fulne
þæt he scyle rice   birofen weorþan,
feore bifohten,   fæmig ridan
yþa hrycgum.   Þær bið egsa sum   —
ældum geywed   þar þar ic yrnan sceal
65   strong on stiðweg.   Hwa gestilleð þæt?
Hwilum ic þurhræse   þæt me on bæce rideð,
won wægfatu,   wide toþringe
lagustreama full,   hwilum læte eft
slupan tosomne.   Se bið swega mæst,
70   breahtma ofer burgum,   ond gebreca hludast,
þonne scearp cymeð   sceo wiþ oþrum,
ecg wið ecge.   Earpan gesceafte
fus ofer folcum   fyre swætað,
blacan lige,   ond gebrecu ferað
75   deorc ofer dreorgum   gedyne micle,
farað feohtende,   feallan lætað
sweart sumsendu   seaw of bosme,
wætan of wombe.   Winnende fareð
atol eoredþreat;   egsa astigeð,
80   micel modþrea   monna cynne,
brogan on burgum,   þonne blace scotiað
scriþende scin   scearpum wæpnum.
Dol him ne ondrædeð   ða deaðsperu;
swylteð hwæþre   gif him soð meotud
85   on geryhtu   þurh regn ufan
of gestune læteð   stræle fleogan,
farende flan.   Fea þæt gedygað
þara þe geræceð   rynegiestes wæpen.
Ic þæs orleges   or anstelle

1.64: *þar þar*: MS. *þara þe*.
1.64: *yrnan*: MS. *hyran*.
1.75: *dreorgum*: MS. *dreontum*.
1.86: *læteð*: With *e* altered from partially erased *a*.

90 þonne gewite   wolcengehnaste
þurh geþræc þringan   þrimme micle
ofer burnan bosm.   Biersteð hlude
heah hloðgecrod;   þonne hnige eft
under lyfte helm   londe near
95 ond me on hrycg hlade   þæt ic habban sceal,
meahtum gemagnad   mines frean.
Swa ic þrymful þeow   þragum winne,
hwilum under eorþan,   hwilum yþa sceal
hean underhnigan,   hwilum holm ufan,
100 streamas styrge,   hwilum stige up,
wolcnfare wrege,   wide fere
swift ond swiþfeorm.   Saga hwæt ic hatte,
oþþe hwa mec ræfe   þonne ic restan ne mot,
oþþe hwa mec stæðþe   þonne ic stille beom.

2.   [K-D.4

Ic sceal þragbysig   þegne minum,
hringan hæfted,   hyran georne,
min bed brecan,   breahtme cyþan
þæt me halswriþan   hlaford sealde.
5 Oft mec slæpwerigne   secg oðþe meowle
gretan eode;   ic him gromheortum
winterceald oncweþe.   Wearm lim
gebundenne bæg   hwilum bersteð,
seþeah biþ on þonce   þegne minum,
10 medwisum men,   me þæt sylfe,
þær wiht wite   ond wordum min
on sped mæge   spel gesecgan.

1.92: *burnan*: MS. *byrnan*.
1.95: *on*: Not in MS.
1.96: *gemagnad*: MS. *ge* [/] *manad*.
1.99: *hean*: MS. *heah*.
2.8: *hwilum*: MS. *hwil um* altered from *hwilcum* by erasure.

3.

Ic eom anhaga, iserne wund,
bille gebennad, beadoweorca sæd,
ecgum werig. Oft ic wig seo,
frecne feohtan— frofre ne wene,
5 þæt me geoc cyme guðgewinnes
ær ic mid ældum eal forwurðe;
ac mec hnossiað homera lafe,
heardecg heoroscearp hondweorc smiþa,
bitað in burgum; ic a bidan sceal
10 laþran gemotes. Næfre læcecynn
on folcstede findan meahte
þara þe mid wyrtum wunde gehælde,
ac me ecga dolg eacen weorðað
þurh deaðslege dagum ond nihtum.

4.

Mec gesette soð sigora waldend,
Crist to compe. Oft ic cwice bærne
unrimu cyn eorþan getenge,
næte mid niþe, swa ic him no hrine,
5 þonne mec min frea feohtan hateþ.
Hwilum ic monigra mod arete;
hwilum ic frefre þa ic ær winne on
feorran swiþe— hi þæs felað þeah
swylce þæs oþres, þonne ic eft hyra
10 ofer deop gedreag drohtað bete.

3.5: *me*: MS. *mec.*
3.6: *forwurðe*: MS. *for wurde.*
3.8: *hondweorc*: MS. *ꝥweorc.*

3.lower margin: At the end of the riddle, in the intervening space between *Rids.* 3 and 4, a rune ᚻ (*sigel*) occurs in a fine hand which appears to be that of the scribe (see plate III.a and note).

4.10: *bete*: MS. *betan.*

4.lower margin: At the end of the riddle, in the intervening space between *Rids.* 4 and 5, a rune ᚻ (*sigel*) occurs in a fine hand which may or may not be that of the scribe (see plate III.b and note).

5.

Hrægl min swigað   þonne ic hrusan trede
oþþe þa wic buge   oþþe wado drefe.
Hwilum mec ahebbað   ofer hæleþa byht
hyrste mine   ond þeos hea lyft,
5   ond mec þonne wide   wolcna strengu
ofer folc byreð.   Frætwe mine
swogað hlude   ond swinsiað,
torhte singað,   þonne ic getenge ne beom
flode ond foldan,   ferende gæst.

6.

Ic þurh muþ sprece   mongum reordum,
wrencum singe,   wrixle geneahhe
heafodwoþe,   hlude cirme,
healde mine wisan,   hleoþre ne miþe.
5   Eald æfensceop,   eorlum bringe
blisse in burgum;   þonne ic bugendre
stefne styrme,   stille on wicum
sittað nigende.   Saga hwæt ic hatte,
þe swa scirenige   sceawendwisan
10   hlude onhyrge,   hæleþum bodige
wilcumena fela   woþe minre.

7.

Mec on þissum dagum   deadne ofgeafun
fæder ond modor;   ne wæs me feorh þa gen,
ealdor in innan.   Þa mec an ongon

6.**upper margin:** In the intervening space between *Rids.* 5 and 6, a mark (see plate
IV.a) occurs which could conceivably be the rune ᚢ (*ur*) or an elongated *n* (see note).
The mark does not appear to have been made by the scribe.
  6.8: *sittað*: MS. *siteð*.
  6.9: *þe*: MS. *þa*.
  6.11: *fela*: With *a* on an erasure.
  7.1: *ofgeafun*: MS. *ofgeafum*.
  7.3: *an*: Not in MS.

welhold mege   wedum þeccan,
5   heold ond freoþode,   hleosceorpe wrah,
swa arlice   swa hire agen bearn,
oþþæt ic under sceate—   swa min gesceapu wæron—
ungesibbum wearð   eacen gæste.
Mec seo friþemæg   fedde siþþan
10   oþþæt ic aweox,   widdor meahte
siþas asettan;   heo hæfde swæsra þy læs
suna ond dohtra,   þy heo swa dyde.

8.   [K-D.10

Neb wæs min on nearwe   ond ic neoþan wætre,
flode underflowen,   firgenstreamum
swiþe besuncen;   ond on sunde awox,
ufan yþum þeaht,   anum getenge
5   liþendum wuda   lice mine.
Hæfde feorh cwico   þa ic of fæðmum cwom
brimes ond beames   on blacum hrægle;
sume wæron hwite   hyrste mine.
Þa mec lifgende   lyft upp ahof,
10   wind of wæge;   siþþan wide bær
ofer seolhbaþo.   Saga hwæt ic hatte.

9.   [K-D.11

Hrægl is min hasofag;   hyrste beorhte
reade ond scire   on reafe hafu.
Ic dysge dwelle   ond dole hwette
unrædsiþas;   oþrum styre
5   nyttre fore.   Ic þæs nowiht wat,
þæt heo swa gemædde,   mode bestolene,
dæde gedwolene,   deoraþ mine

7.4: *þeccan*: MS. *weccan*.
7.6: *swa arlice*: MS. *snearlice*.
8.7: *hrægle*: MS. *hrægl*.
9.2: *hafu*: Not in MS.

won wisan gehwam.   Wa him þæs þeawes
siþþan heah bringað   horda deorast,
10 gif hi unrædes   ær ne geswicaþ.

10.

Fotum ic fere,   foldan slite,
grene wongas,   þenden ic gæst bere.
Gif me feorh losað,   fæste binde
swearte Wealas,   hwilum sellan men.
5 Hwilum ic deorum   drincan selle
beorne of bosme;   hwilum mec bryd triedeð
felawlonc fotum;   hwilum feorran broht
wonfeax Wale   wegeð ond þyð,
dol druncmennen   deorcum nihtum,
10 wæteð in wætre,   wyrmeð hwilum
fægre to fyre;   me on fæðme sticaþ
hygegalan hond,   hwyrfeð geneahhe,
swifeð me geond sweartne.   Saga hwæt ic hatte
þe ic lifgende   lond reafige
15 ond æfter deaþe   dryhtum þeowige.

11.

Ic seah turf tredan—   ten wæron ealra,
six gebroþor   ond hyra sweostor mid—
hæfdon feorg cwico.   Fell hongedon
sweotol ond gesyne   on seles wæge
5 anra gehwylces.   Ne wæs hyra ængum þy wyrs,

9.9: *bringað*: MS. *bringeð*.

10.6: *beorne*: MS. *beorn*.

10.15. right margin: Opposite the last MS. line of *Rid.* 10, in the upper right-hand margin of folio 104*a*, there is a mark (see plate v) resembling the rune Z (*eoh*) with a point to its left and a slight downward trailing of the pen from the end of the last lateral stroke. The strokes of the rune, if indeed it is a rune, are fine and the plane of the letter or rune is at an upward tilt (see note).

11.1: *ten*: MS. *x*.

11.2: *six*: MS. *vi*.

ne side þy sarre,   þeah hy swa sceoldon,
reafe birofene,   rodra weardes
meahtum aweahte,   muþum slitan
haswe blede.   Hrægl bið geniwad
10   þam þe ær forðcymene   frætwe leton
licgan on laste,   gewitan lond tredan.

12.   [K-D.14

Ic wæs wæpen wigan;   nu mec wlonc þeceð
geong hagostealdmon   golde ond sylfre,
woum wirbogum;   hwilum weras cyssað.
Hwilum ic to hilde   hleoþre bonne
5   wilgehleþan;   hwilum wycg byreþ
mec ofer mearce;   hwilum merehengest
fereð ofer flodas   frætwum beorhtne.
Hwilum mægða sum   minne gefylleð
bosm beaghroden;   hwilum ic on bordum sceal,
10   heard, heafodleas,   behlyþed licgan;
hwilum hongige   hyrstum frætwed,
wlitig on wage,   þær weras drincað,
freolic fyrdsceorp.   Hwilum folcwigan
on wicge wegað,   þonne ic winde sceal
15   sincfag swelgan   of sumes bosme;
hwilum ic gereordum   rincas laðige
wlonce to wine;   hwilum wraþum sceal
stefne minre   forstolen hreddan,
flyman feondsceaþan.   Frige hwæt ic hatte.

11.6: *sarre*: MS. *sarra*.

12.right margin: Opposite the first MS. line of the riddle, in the right-hand margin of folio 104*a*, there is a mark (see plate VI) which could be an old Germanic form of the English rune *hægl* or more probably a late capital *H*. The letter does not appear to be written in the hand of the scribe (see note).

12.1: *wigan*: MS. *wiga*.

12.2: *sylfre*: MS. *sylfore*.

12.9: *on*: Not in MS.

12.14: *on*: Not in MS.

12.17: *wraþum*: MS. *wraþþum*.

12.19: Following *hatte* there is an unusual end-punctuation mark (see plate VII and note).

13.

Hals is min hwit   ond heafod fealo,
sidan swa some.   Swift ic eom on feþe,
beadowæpen bere.   Me on bæce standað
her swylce swe on hleorum;   hlifiað tu
5   earan ofer eagum.   Ordum ic steppe
in grene græs.   Me bið gyrn witod
gif mec onhæle   an onfindeð
wælgrim wiga   þær ic wic buge,
bold mid bearnum,   ond ic bide þær
10   mid geoguðcnosle.   Hwonne gæst cume
to durum minum,   him biþ deað witod;
forþon ic sceal of eðle   eaforan mine
forhtmod fergan,   fleame nergan.
Gif he me æfterweard   ealles weorþeð—
15   hine breost berað—   ic his bidan ne dear,
reþes on geruman—   ne ic þæt ræd teale—
ac ic sceal fromlice   feþemundum
þurh steapne beorg   stræte wyrcan.
Eaþe ic mæg freora   feorh genergan
20   gif ic mægburge mot   mine gelædan
on degolne weg   þurh dunþyrel
swæse ond gesibbe;   ic me siþþan ne þearf
wælhwelpes wig   wiht onsittan.
Gif se niðsceaþa   nearwe stige
25   me on swaþe seceþ,   ne tosæleþ him

13.2: *Swift*: With *f* altered from *s*.
13.4: *hleorum*: MS. *leorum*.
13.6: *grene*: MS. *grenne*.
13.9: *bold*: MS. *blod*.
13.14: *æfterweard*: MS. *æfter weard* with *d* altered from *ð* by erasure.
13.15: *breost berað*: MS. *berað* [/] *breost*.
13.15: *bidan*: MS. *biddan*.
13.16: *ne ic*: MS. *nele*.
13.21: *on degolne*: MS. *onde* [/] *golne* with the *e* of *onde* altered from *o*.
13.21: *dunþyrel*: MS. *dum þyrel*.
13.24: *Gif se*: MS. *gifre*.

on þam gegnpaþe guþgemotes,
siþþan ic þurh hylles hrof geræce
ond þurh hest hrino hildepilum
laðgewinnan þam þe ic longe fleah.

14. [K-D.16

Oft ic sceal wiþ wæge winnan ond wiþ winde feohtan,
somod wið þam sæcce fremman, þonne ic secan gewite
eorþan yþum þeaht; me biþ se eþel fremde.
Ic beom strong þæs gewinnes gif ic stille weorþe;
5 gif me þæs tosæleð, hi beoð swiþran þonne ic,
ond mec slitende sona flymað:
willað oþfergan þæt ic friþian sceal.
Ic him þæt forstonde, gif min steort þolað
ond mec stiþne wiþ stanas moton
10 fæste gehabban. Frige hwæt ic hatte.

15. [K-D.17

Ic eom mundbora minre heorde,
eodor wirum fæst, innan gefylled
dryhtgestreona. Dægtidum oft
spæte sperebrogan; sped biþ þy mare
5 fylle minre. Freo þæt bihealdeð,
hu me of hrife fleogað hyldepilas.
Hwilum ic sweartum swelgan onginne
brunum beadowæpnum, bitrum ordum,
eglum attorsperum. Is min innað til,

13.29: *laðgewinnan*: MS. *laðgewin* [/] *num*.
14.2: *fremman*: Not in MS.
14.4: *strong*: With *o* altered from *d* by erasure.
15.upper margin: At the top of folio 105*a*, in the intervening space between *Rids*.
14 and 15 are two figures which resemble the runes � (*lagu*) and ᛒ (*beorc*), the former
immediately above the latter (see plates VIII.a and b). The runes do not appear to have
been made by the main scribe (see note).
15.8: *brunum*: With *n* altered from *m* by an erasure of the initial minim.

10   wombhord wlitig,   wloncum deore;
      men gemunan   þæt me þurh muþ fareð.

16.   [K-D.18

    Ic eom wunderlicu wiht;   ne mæg word sprecan,
    mældan for monnum,   þeah ic muþ hæbbe,
    wide wombe   *   *   *
    Ic wæs on ceole   ond mines cnosles ma.

17.   [K-D.19

    Ic on siþe seah   ·ᚻᚱᚨ
    ᚻ· hygewloncne,   heafodbeorhtne,
    swiftne ofer sælwong   swiþe þrægan.
    Hæfde him on hrycge   hildeþryþe—
5   ·ᛏᚠᛗ·   Nægledne rad
    ·ᚠᚷᛗᛈ·   Widlast ferede
    rynestrong on rade   rofne ·ᚻᚠ
    ᚠᛗᚠᚾ·   For wæs þy beorhtre,
    swylcra siþfæt.   Saga hwæt hit hatte.

18.   [K-D.20

    Ic eom wunderlicu wiht,   on gewin sceapen,
    frean minum leof,   fægre gegyrwed.

    15.lower margin: In the space between *Rids.* 15 and 16 there is a curved mark (see plate ix) which is neither a rune nor a letter; nor is the mark offset blotting from folio 104*b* (see note).

    16.1: *wunderlicu*: With *e* altered from *o*.

    16.4: *wæs*: MS. *wæs* followed by a mirror image *n* with a curved stroke above; these marks are offset blotting from the facing folio 104*b* (see plate xi.a and note).

    16.lower margin: Several marks resembling inverse letters occur in the intervening space between *Rids.* 16 and 17; these marks are offset blotting from the facing folio 104*b* (see plates xi.a and b and note).

    17.right margin: Hickes's penciled markings and his letter *E* appear in the right-hand margin of the runic riddle (for an explanation of Hickes's marks, see note to *Rid.* 73).

    17.1: *on siþe*: Not in MS.

    17.3: *swiftne*: MS. *swist* [/] *ne*.

    17.9: *hit*: MS. *ic*.

Byrne is min bleofag;   swylce beorht seomað
wir ymb þone wælgim   þe me waldend geaf,
5   se me widgalum   wisað hwilum
sylfum to sace.   Þonne ic sinc wege
þurh hlutterne dæg,   hondweorc smiþa,
gold ofer geardas.   Oft ic gæstberend
cwelle compwæpnum.   Cyning mec gyrweð
10   since ond seolfre   ond mec on sele weorþað,
ne wyrneð wordlofes,   wisan mæneð
mine for mengo   þær hy meodu drincað,
healdeð mec on heaþore,   hwilum læteð eft
radwerigne   on gerum sceacan,
15   orlegfromne.   Oft ic oþrum scod
frecne æt his freonde.   Fah eom ic wide,
wæpnum awyrged.   Ic me wenan ne þearf
þæt me bearn wræce   on bonan feore,
gif me gromra hwylc   guþe genægeð;
20   ne weorþeð sio mægburg   gemicledu
eaforan minum   þe ic æfter woc,
nymþe ic hlafordleas   hweorfan mote
from þam healdende   þe me hringas geaf.
Me bið forð witod,   gif ic frean hyre,
25   guþe fremme,   swa ic gien dyde
minum þeodne on þonc,   þæt ic þolian sceal
bearngestreona.   Ic wiþ bryde ne mot
hæmed habban,   ac me þæs hyhtplegan
geno wyrneð   se mec geara on
30   bende legde;   forþon ic brucan sceal
on hagostealde   hæleþa gestreona.
Oft ic wirum dol   wife abelge,
wonie hyre willan;   heo me wom spreceð,
floceð hyre folmum,   firenaþ mec wordum,

18.3: *seomað*: MS. *seo* [/] *mað* with the ð altered from *d*.
18.29: *geara*: MS. *gearo*.
18.34: *firenaþ*: With þ altered from *w* (see plate xii).

35   ungod gæleð.   Ic ne gyme þæs,
     compes   *   *   *

19.   [K-D.21

Neb is min niþerweard;   neol ic fere
ond be grunde græfe,   geonge swa me wisað
har holtes feond;   ond hlaford min
woh færeð,   weard æt steorte,
5   wrigaþ on wonge,   wegeð mec ond þyð,
saweþ on swæð min.   Ic snyþige forð,
brungen of bearwe,   bunden cræfte,
wegen on wægne—   hæbbe wundra fela.
Me biþ gongendre   grene on healfe,
10   ond min swæð sweotol   sweart on oþre.
Me þurh hrycg wrecen,   hongaþ under
an orþoncpil;   oþer on heafde,
fæst ond forðweard.   Fealleþ on sidan
þæt ic toþum tere,   gif me teala þenaþ
15   hindeweardre   þæt biþ hlaford min.

20.   [K-D.22

Ætsomne cwom   sixtig monna
to wægstæþe   wicgum ridan;
hæfdon endleofan   eoredmæcgas
fridhengestas,   feower sceamas.
5   Ne meahton magorincas   ofer mere feolan
swa hi fundedon,   ac wæs flod to deop,
atol yþa geþræc,   ofras hea,

    18.35: MS. folio 105*b* ends with *compes* [without any MS. punctuation following it]; MS. folio 106*a* begins with *Neb*, the first word of *Rid.* 19. The evidence of the gatherings (see note) indicates that a leaf is missing between the folios.

    19.7: *bearwe*: MS. *bearme.*

    19.15: *min*: The MS. *n* has two minims separated by several spaces and connected by a long diagonal so as to resemble a capital *N* (see plate XIII).

    20.1: *sixtig*: MS. *lx.*

    20.3: *endleofan*: MS. *xi.*

    20.4: *feower*: MS. *iiii.*

streamas stronge.　Ongunnon stigan þa
on wægn weras　ond hyra wicg somod
10　hlodan under hrunge;　þa þa hors oðbær
eh ond eorlas,　æscum dealle,
ofer wætres byht　wægn to lande—
swa hine oxa ne teah,　ne esna mægen,
ne fæthengest,　ne on flode swom,
15　ne be grunde wod　gestum under,
ne lagu drefde,　ne of lyfte fleag,
ne under bæc cyrde;　brohte hwæþre
beornas ofer burnan　ond hyra bloncan mid
from stæðe heaum　þæt hy stopan up
20　on oþerne　ellenrofe
weras of wæge　ond hyra wicg gesund.

21.　　　　　　　　　　　　　　　　　　　　　[K-D.23

Agob is min noma　eft onhwyrfed.
Ic eom wrætlic wiht　on gewin sceapen.
Þonne ic onbuge　ond me on bosme fareð
ætren onga,　ic beom eallgearo
5　þæt ic me þæt feorhbealo　feor aswape.
Siþþan me se waldend,　se me þæt wite gescop,
leoþo forlæteð,　ic beo lengre þonne ær,
oþþæt ic spæte,　spilde geblonden,
ealfelo attor　þæt ic æror geap.
10　Ne togongeð þæs　gumena hwylcum
ænigum eaþe　þæt ic þær ymb sprice,
gif hine hrineð　þæt me of hrife fleogeð,
þæt þone mandrinc　mægne geceapaþ,
full ferfæste　feore sine.
15　Nelle ic unbunden　ænigum hyran
nymþe searosæled.　Saga hwæt ic hatte.

20.17: *ne under*: MS. *neon der.*
21.1: *Agob*: MS. *Agof.*
21.1: *onhwyrfed*: With *d* altered from *ð.*
21.3b: *on*: MS. *of.*
21.9: *æror*: MS. *ær.*
21.14: *ferfæste*: MS. *wer fæste.*

22. [K-D.24]

Ic eom wunderlicu wiht— wræsne mine stefne:
hwilum beorce swa hund, hwilum blæte swa gat,
hwilum græde swa gos, hwilum gielle swa hafoc.
Hwilum ic onhyrge þone haswan earn,
5 guðfugles hleoþor; hwilum glidan reorde
muþe gemæne, hwilum mæwes song,
þær ic glado sitte. · X · mec nemnað
swylce · ᚠ · ond · ᚱ · ᛈ · fullesteð
· ᚻ · ond · ᛁ · Nu ic haten eom
10 swa þa siex stafas sweotule becnaþ.

23. [K-D.25]

Ic eom wunderlicu wiht, wifum on hyhte,
neahbuendum nyt. Nængum sceþþe
burgsittendra nymþe bonan anum.
Staþol min is steapheah; stonde ic on bedde,
5 neoþan ruh nathwær. Neþeð hwilum
ful cyrtenu ceorles dohtor,
modwlonc meowle, þæt heo on mec gripeð,
ræseð mec on reodne, reafað min heafod,
fegeð mec on fæsten. Feleþ sona
10 mines gemotes seo þe mec nearwað,
wif wundenlocc— wæt bið þæt eage.

24. [K-D.26]

Mec feonda sum feore besnyþede,
woruldstrenga binom, wætte siþþan,
dyfde on wætre, dyde eft þonan,

22.left margin: Hickes's penciled markings and his letter *F* appear in the left-hand margin of the MS. (for an explanation of Hickes's marks, see note to *Rid.* 73).

22.2: *hwilum*: All instances of *hwilum* in the riddle are preceded by a MS. point (see note).

22.7: · X · : MS. · *x* · , a letter not a rune.

23.10: *seo þe*: MS. *seþe*.

sette on sunnan   þær ic swiþe beleas
5 herum þam þe ic hæfde.   Heard mec siþþan
snað seaxses ecg,   sindrum begrunden;
fingras feoldan,   ond mec fugles wyn
geondsprengde speddropum,   spyrede geneahhe
ofer brunne brerd,   beamtelge swealg,
10 streames dæle,   stop eft on mec,
siþade sweartlast.   Mec siþþan wrah
hæleð hleobordum,   hyde beþenede,
gierede mec mid golde;   forþon me glisedon
wrætlic weorc smiþa,   wire bifongen.
15 Nu þa gereno   ond se reada telg
ond þa wuldorgesteald   wide mære
dryhtfolca helm—   nales dol wite.
Gif min bearn wera   brucan willað,
hy beoð þy gesundran   ond þy sigefæstran,
20 heortum þy hwætran   ond þy hygebliþran,
ferþe þy frodran;   habbaþ freonda þy ma
swæsra ond gesibbra,   soþra ond godra,
tilra ond getreowra,   þa hyra tyr ond ead
estum ycað,   ond hy arstafum,
25 lissum bilecgað,   ond hi lufan fæþmum
fæste clyppað.   Frige hwæt ic hatte
niþum to nytte;   nama min is mære,
hæleþum gifre   ond halig sylf.

25.   [K-D.27

Ic eom weorð werum,   wide funden,
brungen of bearwum   ond of burghleoþum,
of denum ond of dunum.   Dæges mec wægun
feþre on lifte,   feredon mid liste
5 under hrofes hleo.   Hæleð mec siþþan

24.6: *ecg*: MS. *ecge*.
24.8: *geondsprengde speddropum*: MS. *geond sped dropum*.
24.12: *hyde*: MS. *hyþe*.
24.13: *glisedon*: MS. *gliwedon*.

baþedan in bydene.   Nu ic eom bindere
ond swingere;   sona weorpe
esne to eorþan,   hwilum ealdne ceorl.
Sona þæt onfindeð,   se þe mec fehð ongean
10   ond wið mægenþisan   minre genæsteð,
þæt he hrycge sceal   hrusan secan
gif he unrædes   ær ne geswiceð.
Strengo bistolen,   strong on spræce,
mægene binumen—   nah his modes geweald,
15   fota ne folma.   Frige hwæt ic hatte
ðe on eorþan swa   esnas binde
dole æfter dyntum   be dæges leohte.

26.   [K-D.28

Biþ foldan dæl   fægre gegierwed
mid þy heardestan   ond mid þy scearpestan
ond mid þy grymmestan   gumena gestreona—
corfen, sworfen,   cyrred, þyrred,
5   bunden, wunden,   blæced, wæced,
frætwed, geatwed,   feorran læded
to durum dryhta.   Dream bið in innan
cwicra wihta: clengeð, lengeð
þar þar ær lifgende   longe hwile
10   wilna bruceð   ond no wiht spriceð,
ond þonne æfter deaþe   deman onginneð,
meldan mislice.   Micel is to hycganne
wisfæstum menn   hwæt seo wiht sy.

25.7: *weorpe*: MS. *weorpere.*
25.8: *esne*: MS. *efne.*
25.15: MS. *hatte* is followed by a typical end-punctuation mark :– and the next word, MS. *ðe*, begins with a small capital immediately thereafter; another end-punctuation mark also occurs at the proper end of the riddle.
26.9: *þar þar*: MS. *þara þe.*
26.10: *wiht*: MS. *wið.*

27.

Ic wiht geseah   wundorlice
hornum bitweonum   huþe lædan,
lyftfæt leohtlic   listum gegierwed,
huþe to þam ham   of þam heresiþe.
5 Walde hyre on þære byrig   bur atimbran,
searwum asettan,   gif hit swa meahte.
Ða cwom wundorlicu wiht   ofer wealles hrof
seo is eallum cuð   eorðbuendum;
ahredde þa þa huþe,   ond to ham bedraf
10 wreccan ofer willan—   gewat hyre west þonan
fæhþum feran,   forð onette.
Dust stonc to heofonum;   deaw feol on eorþan;
niht forð gewat.   Nænig siþþan
wera gewiste   þære wihte sið.

28a.

Ic eom legbysig,   lace mid winde,
bewunden mid wuldre,   wedre gesomnad,
fus forðweges,   fyre gebysgad,
bearu blowende,   byrnende gled.
5 Ful oft mec gesiþas   sendað æfter hondum
þæt mec weras ond wif   wlonce cyssað.
þonne ic mec onhæbbe,   ond hi onhnigaþ to me,
monige mid miltse,   þær ic monnum sceal
ycan upcyme   eadignesse.

27.2: *hornum bitweonum*: MS. *horna abitweonū*.

27.5: *atimbran*: MS. *atimbram*.

27.9: *bedraf*: MS. *bedræf*.

27.11: *onette*: MS. *o* [/] *netteð*.

28a.right margin: In the right-hand margin of the riddle are two marks: one is a
late *r* with a point on either side; the second consists of two straight lines resembling no
O.E. letter or rune (see plates xiv.a and b and notes).

28a.7: *onhnigaþ*: MS. *on hin gaþ*.

28a.9: At the end of the riddle there is a typical end-punctuation mark and
following that, an atypical one (see plate xv and note).

28b.   [K-D.30b

Ic eom ligbysig,   lace mid winde,
w[.................]dre gesomnad,
fus forðweges,   fyre gemylted,
bear[.] blowende,   byrnende gled.
5 Ful oft mec gesiþas   sendað æfter hondum
þær mec weras ond wif   wlonce gecyssað.
Þonne ic mec onhæbbe,   hi onhnigað to me,
modge miltsum,   swa ic mongum sceal
ycan upcyme   eadignesse.

29.   [K-D.31

Is þes middangeard   missenlicum
wisum gewlitegad,   wrættum gefrætwad.
Ic seah sellic þing   singan on ræcede;
wiht wæs nower   werum on gemonge
5 sio hæfde wæstum   wundorlicran.
Niþerweard onhwyrfed   wæs neb hyre,
fet ond folme   fugele gelice;
no hwæþre fleogan mæg   ne fela gongan.
Hwæþre feþegeorn   fremman onginneð,
10 gecoren cræftum,   cyrreð geneahhe,
oft ond gelome   eorlum on gemonge,
siteð æt symble,   sæles bideþ
hwonne ær heo cræft hyre   cyþan mote
werum on wonge.   Ne heo þær wiht þigeð
15 þæs þe him æt blisse   beornas habbað.
Deor, domes georn,   hio dumb wunað;
hwæþre hyre is on fote   fæger hleoþor,
wynlicu woðgiefu.   Wrætlic me þinceð

28b.2: After *w*, the letter may be *u* or *a*; four spaces after *w* there is a short
descender, probably from *r*.
29.4: *nower werum*: MS. *onwerum*.
29.6: *Niþerweard*: MS. *niþer wearð*.
29.6: *onhwyrfed*: Not in MS.
29.15: *habbað*: MS. *habbad*.

hu seo wiht mæge   wordum lacan
20 þurh fot neoþan.   Frætwed hyrstum,
hafað hyre on halse   þonne hio hord warað,
baru, beagum deall,   broþor sine—
mæg mid mægne.   Micel is to hycgenne
wisum woðboran   hwæt sio wiht sie.

30.   [K-D.32

Is þes middangeard   missenlicum
wisum gewlitegad,   wrættum gefrætwad.
Siþum sellic   ic seah searo hweorfan,
grindan wið greote,   giellende faran.
5 Næfde sellicu wiht   syne ne folme,
exle ne earmas;   sceal on anum fet
searoceap swifan,   swiþe feran,
faran ofer feldas.   Hæfde fela ribba;
muð wæs on middan.   Moncynne nyt,
10 fereð foddurwelan,   folcscipe dreogeð,
wist in wigeð,   ond werum gieldeð
gaful geara gehwam   þæs þe guman brucað,
rice ond heane.   Rece gif þu cunne,
wis worda gleaw,   hwæt sio wiht sie.

31.   [K-D.33

Wiht cwom æfter wege   wrætlicu liþan;
cymlic from ceolan   cleopode to londe,
hlinsade hlude—   hleahtor wæs gryrelic,
egesful on earde.   Ecge wæron scearpe;

29.22: *baru*: MS. *bær.*
29.24: *sio*: Not in MS.
30.2: *wrættum*: MS. *wrætum* with a small *t* added above the line and between the *t* and the *u*. The hand of the small *t* does not appear to be that of the main scribe.
30.8: *fela*: MS. *fella.*
30.10: *fereð*: MS. *fere.*
31.2: *ceolan*: MS. *ceole.*
31.3: *hleahtor*: MS. *leahtor.*

5   wæs hio hetegrim,   hilde to sæne,
     biter beadoweorca.   Bordweallas grof
     heardhiþende.   Heterune bond!
     Sægde searocræftig   ymb hyre sylfre gesceaft:
     "Is min modor   mægða cynnes
10   þæs deorestan   þæt is dohtor min
     eacen uploden;   swa þæt is ældum cuþ,
     firum on folce,   þæt seo on foldan sceal
     on ealra londa gehwam   lissum stondan."

32.   [K-D.34

     Ic wiht geseah   in wera burgum
     seo þæt feoh fedeð.   Hafað fela toþa;
     nebb biþ hyre æt nytte;   niþerweard gongeð,
     hiþeð holdlice   ond to ham tyhð,
5   wæþeð geond weallas,   wyrte seceð.
     Aa heo þa findeð   þa þe fæst ne biþ;
     læteð hio þa wlitigan,   wyrtum fæste,
     stille stondan   on staþolwonge,
     beorhte blican,   blowan ond growan.

33.   [K-D.35

     Mec se wæta wong,   wundrum freorig,
     of his innaþe   ærist cende.
     Ne wat ic mec beworhtne   wulle flysum,
     hærum þurh heahcræft,   hygeþoncum min:
5   wundene me ne beoð wefle,   ne ic wearp hafu,
     ne þurh þreata geþræcu   þræd me ne hlimmeð,
     ne æt me hrutende   hrisil scriþeð,
     ne mec ohwonan   sceal am cnyssan.
     Wyrmas mec ne awæfan   wyrda cræftum,
10   þa þe geolo godwebb   geatwum frætwað.

31.9: *mægða*: MS. *mæg* [/] *da*.
31.11: *uploden*: MS. *upliden*.
33.8: *am*: MS. *amas*.

Wile mec mon hwæþre seþeah   wide ofer eorþan
hatan for hæleþum   hyhtlic gewæde.
Saga soðcwidum   searoþoncum gleaw,
wordum wisfæst,   hwæt þis gewæde sy.

34.   [K-D.36

Ic wiht geseah   on wege feran
seo wæs wrætlice   wundrum gegierwed:
hæfde feowere   fet under wombe
ond ehtuwe
5 monn·h·w·m·wiif·m·x·l·kf wf·hors· qxxs·
                     ufon on hrycge;
hæfde tu fiþru   ond twelf eagan
ond siex heafdu.   Saga hwæt hio wære.
For flodwegas;   ne wæs þæt na fugul ana,
10 ac þær wæs æghwylces   anra gelicnes:
horses ond monnes,   hundes ond fugles,
ond eac wifes wlite.   Þu wast, gif þu const
to gesecganne,   þæt we soð witan—
hu þære wihte   wise gonge.

35.   [K-D.37

Ic þa wihte geseah—   womb wæs on hindan
þriþum aþrunten.   Þegn folgade,
mægenrofa man,   ond micel hæfde gefered
þær þæt hit felde   fleah þurh his eage.
5 Ne swylteð he symle   þonne syllan sceal
innað þam oþrum,   ac him eft cymeð

33.14: *gewæde*: MS. *ge wædu*.

   34.left margin: Hickes's penciled markings and his letters *FF* appear in the
left-hand margin of the riddle (for an explanation of Hickes's marks, see note to *Rid.*
73).

   34.5: This line is probably a scribal interpolation of an earlier marginalic note (see
note).

   35.4: *þæt*: Not in MS.

bot in bosme;   blæd biþ aræred.
He sunu wyrceð;   bið him sylfa fæder.

36.

Ic þa wiht geseah   wæpnedcynnes
geoguðmyrþe grædig: him on gafol forlet
ferðfriþende   feower wellan
scire sceotan,   on gesceap þeotan. ⁓
5 Mon maþelade,   se þe me gesægde:
"Seo wiht, gif hio gedygeð,   duna briceð;
gif he tobirsteð,   bindeð cwice."

37.

Gewritu secgað   þæt seo wiht sy
mid moncynne   miclum tidum
sweotol ond gesyne.   Sundorcræft hafað
maran micle   þonne hit men witen.
5 Heo wile gesecan   sundor æghwylcne
feorhberendra;   gewiteð eft feran on weg.
Ne bið hio næfre   niht þær oþre,
ac hio sceal wideferh   wreccan laste
hamleas hweorfan—   no þy heanre bið.
10 Ne hafað hio fot ne folme,   ne æfre foldan hran,
ne eagena hafað   ægþer twega,
ne muð hafað,   ne wiþ monnum spræc,
ne gewit hafað;   ac gewritu secgað
þæt seo sy earmost   ealra wihta
15 þara þe æfter gecyndum   cenned wære.
Ne hafað hio sawle ne feorh,   ac hio siþas sceal
geond þas wundorworuld   wide dreogan.

36.2: *geoguðmyrþe*: MS. *geoguð myrwe*.
37.2: *tidum*: See note.
37.4: *maran*: MS. *maram*.
37.10: *folme*: MS. *folm*.
37.11: *eagena*: MS. *eage ne*.
37.11: *hafað*: Not in MS.

Ne hafaþ hio blod ne ban;   hwæþre bearnum wearð
geond þisne middangeard   mongum to frofre.
20 Næfre hio heofonum hran,   ne to helle mot,
ac hio sceal wideferh   wuldorcyninges
larum lifgan.   Long is to secganne
hu hyre ealdorgesceaft   æfter gongeð—
woh wyrda gesceapu.   Þæt is wrætlic þing
25 to gesecganne.   Soð is æghwylc
þara þe ymb þas wiht   wordum becneð.
Ne hafað heo ænig lim,   leofaþ efne seþeah.
Gif þu mæge reselan   recene gesecgan
soþum wordum,   saga hwæt hio hatte.

38.   [K-D.40

Ece is se scyppend,   se þas eorþan nu
wreðstuþum wealdeð   ond þas world healdeð.
Rice is se reccend   ond on ryht cyning,
ealra anwalda;   eorþan ond heofones
5 healdeð ond wealdeð—   swa he ymb þas utan hweorfeð.
He mec wrætlice   worhte æt frymþe
þa he þisne ymbhwyrft   ærest sette;
heht mec wæccende   wunian longe
þæt ic ne slepe   siþþan æfre,
10 ond mec semninga   slæp ofergongeþ—
beoð eagan min   ofestum betyned.
Þisne middangeard   meahtig dryhten
mid his onwalde   æghwær styreð;
swa ic mid waldendes   worde ealne
15 þisne ymbhwyrft   utan ymbclyppe.

37.21: *wuldorcyninges*: MS. *wuldor* [/] *cyninge*.

37.24: *is*: Not in MS.

37.27: *hafað heo ænig*: MS. *hafaðhehænig*, with *hafað hænig* written in the normal scribal hand and with *he* inserted into the normal space between these two in a smaller hand.

38.2: *wealdeð*: Not in MS.

38.3: *Rice*: MS. *ric*.

38.11: *betyned*: With *d* altered from *ð*.

Ic eom to þon bleað   þæt mec bealdlice mæg
gearu gongende   grima abregan,
ond eofore eom   æghwær cenra
þonne he gebolgen   bidsteal giefeð;
20 ne mæg mec oferswiþan   segnberendra
ænig ofer eorþan   nymþe se ana God,
se þisne hean heofon   healdeþ ond wealdeþ. —
Ic eom on stence   strengre micle
þonne ricels   oþþe rose sy
25 *   *   *   on eorþan tyrf
wynlic weaxeð;   ic eom wræstre þonne heo.
Þeah þe lilie sy   leof moncynne,
beorht on blostman,   ic eom betre þonne heo;
swylce ic nardes stenc   nyde oferswiþe
30 mid minre swetnesse   symle æghwær,
ond ic fulre eom   þonne þis fen swearte
þæt her yfle   adelan stinceð.
Eal ic under heofones   hwearfte recce,
swa me leof fæder   lærde æt frymþe,
35 þæt ic þa mid ryhte   reccan moste
þicce ond þynne,   þinga gehwylces
onlicnesse   æghwær healde.
Hyrre ic eom heofone;   hateþ mec heahcyning
his deagol þing   dyre bihealdan;
40 eac ic under eorþan   eal sceawige
wom wraðscrafu   wraþra gesta.
Ic eom micle yldra   þonne ymbhwyrft þes
oþþe þes middangeard   meahte geweorþan,
ond ic giestron wæs   geong acenned,
45 mære to monnum,   þurh minre modor hrif.
Ic eom fægerre   frætwum goldes,
þeah hit mon awerge   wirum utan;
ic eom wyrslicre   þonne þes wudu fula
oððe þis waroð   þe her aworpen ligeð.

38.23: *micle*: Not in MS.; in the manuscript *strengre* ends one MS. line, *þōn* begins the next.

38.33: *hwearfte*: With *f* on an erasure.

38.42: *þes*: MS. *þæs*.

50 Ic eorþan eom   æghwær brædre
    ond widgielra   þonne þes wong grena;
    folm mec mæg bifon   ond fingras þry
    utan eaþe   ealle ymbclyppan.
    Heardra ic eom ond caldra   þonne se hearda forst,
55 hrim heorugrimma,   þonne he to hrusan cymeð;
    ic eom Ulcanus   upirnendan
    leohtan leoman,   lege hatra.
    Ic eom on goman   gena swetra
    þonne þu beobread   blende mid hunige;
60 swylce ic eom wraþre   þonne wermod sy
    þe her on hyrstum   heasewe stondeþ.
    Ic mesan mæg   meahtelicor
    ond efnetan   ealdum þyrse;
    ond ic gesælig mæg   symle lifgan,
65 þeah ic ætes ne sy   æfre to feore.
    Ic mæg fromlicor   fleogan þonne pernex
    oþþe earn oþþe hafoc   æfre meahte;
    nis zefferus,   se swifta wind,
    þæt swa fromlice mæg   feran æghwær;
70 me is snægl swiftra,   snelra regnwyrm,
    ond fenyce   fore hreþre;
    is þæs gores sunu   gonge hrædra
    þone we wifel   wordum nemnað.
    Hefigere ic eom micle   þonne se hara stan
75 oþþe unlytel   leades clympre;
    leohtre ic eom micle   þonne þes lytla wyrm
    þe her on flode gæð   fotum dryge.
    Flinte ic eom heardre   þe þis fyr drifeþ

38.56: *ic eom*: Not in MS.
38.61: *þe*: Not in MS.
38.63: *þyrse*: MS. *þyrre*.
38.66: *pernex*: MS. *p´nex*.
38.70: *snelra*: MS. *snel* [/] *ro þōn*.
38.72: *is*: MS. *Ic*.
38.77: *on flode*: MS. *onflonde*.
38.78: *heardre*: With final *e* altered from *a*.
38.78: *fyr*: With possible erasure of a letter after *r*.

of þissum strongan   style heardan;

80   hnescre ic eom micle   halsrefeþre

seo her on winde   wæweð on lyfte.

Ic eorþan eom   æghwær brædre

ond widgelra   þonne þes wong grena;

ic uttor eaþe   eal ymbwinde

85   wrætlice gewefen   wundorcræfte.

Nis under me   ænig oþer

wiht waldendre   on worldlife;

ic eom ufemest   ealra gesceafta

þara þe worhte   waldend user,

90   se mec ana mæg   ecan meahtum

geþeon þrymme   þæt ic onþunian ne sceal.

Mara ic eom ond strengra   þonne se micla hwæl

se þe garsecges   grund bihealdeð,

sweart ansyne— ic eom swiþre þonne he;

95   swylce ic eom on mægene   minum læsse

þonne se hondwyrm   se þe hæleþa bearn,

secgas searoþoncle,   seaxe delfað.

Ne hafu ic in heafde   hwite loccas

wræste gewundne,   ac ic eom wide calu;

100 ne ic breaga ne bruna   brucan moste,

ac mec bescyrede   scyppend eallum;

nu me wrætlice   weaxað on heafde

þæt me on gescyldrum   scinan motan

ful wrætlice,   wundne loccas.

105 Mara ic eom ond fættra   þonne amæsted swin,

bearg bellende,   þe on bocwuda

won wrotende   wynnum lifde

þæt he   *   *   *

38.84: *eaþe*: Not in MS.

38.88: *ufemest*: MS. *ufor*.

38.91: *onþunian*: MS. *onrinnan*.

38.106: *þe*: Not in MS.

38.108: MS. folio 111*b* ends with þ *he*. MS. folio 112*a* begins with *edniwu*. Apparently a MS. folio is missing in between. At the bottom of the MS. folio 111*b* in a faint, nonscribal hand, several letters of varying sizes and shapes occur. These appear to be: *h…s. egC….þ.* where *s* is a high ligature *s* (see plate XVI.a and note).

39.

    *   *   *   edniwu;
þæt is moddor   monigra cynna,
þæs selestan,   þæs sweartestan,
þæs deorestan   þæs þe dryhta bearn
5 ofer toldan sceat   to gefean agen.
Ne magon we her in eorþan   owiht lifgan
nymðe we brucen   þæs þa bearn doð.
Þæt is to geþencanne   þeoda gehwylcum,
wisfæstum werum,   hwæt seo wiht sy.

40.

Ic seah wyhte   wrætlice twa
undearnunga   ute plegan
hæmedlaces;   hwitloc anfeng,
wlanc under wædum,   gif þæs weorces speow,
5 fæmne fyllo.   Ic on flette mæg
þurh runstafas   rincum secgan
þam þe bec witan   bega ætsomne
naman þara wihta.   Þær sceal Nyd wesan
twega oþer   ond se torhta Æsc,
10 an an linan,   Acas twegen,
Hægelas swa some.   Swa ic þæs hordgates
cægan cræfte   þa clamme onleac
þe þa rædellan   wið rynemenn
hygefæste heold,   heortan bewrigene
15 orþoncbendum.   Nu is undyrne
werum æt wine   hu þa wihte mid us
heanmode twa   hatne sindon.

40.4: *speow*: MS. *speop*.
40.11: *Swa ic*: MS. *hwylc*.
40.11: *þæs*: MS. *wæs*.
    40.17: *Rid.* 40 ends with a single point after *sindon* and *Rid.* 41 begins with a small capital immediately thereafter in the same MS. line. Thus, paleographically, *Rids.* 40 and 41 appear to be one riddle.

41.

Ic wat indryhtne   æþelum deorne
giest in geardum   þam se grimma ne mæg
hungor sceððan   ne se hata þurst,
yldo ne adle.   Gif him arlice
5 esne þenað   se þe agan sceal
on þam siðfate,   hy gesunde æt ham
findað witode him   wiste ond blisse;
cnosles unrim   care, gif se esne
his hlaforde   hyreð yfle,
10 frean on fore,   ne wile forht wesan
broþor oþrum.   Him þæt bam sceðeð
þonne hy from bearme   begen hweorfað
anre magan   ellorfuse,
moddor ond sweostor.   Mon se þe wille
15 cyþe cynewordum   hu se cuma hatte,
eðþa se esne   þe ic her ymb sprice.

42.

Wrætlic hongað   bi weres þeo
frean under sceate: foran is þyrel.
Bið stiþ ond heard;   stede hafað godne.
þonne se esne   his agen hrægl
5 ofer cneo hefeð,   wile þæt cuþe hol
mid his hangellan   heafde gretan
þæt he efenlang ær   oft gefylde.

43.

Ic on wincle gefrægn   weaxan nathwæt,
þindan ond þunian,   þecene hebban.
On þæt banlease   bryd grapode,

41.1: See note to *Rid.* 40.17.
42.7: *efenlang*: MS. *efe lang*.
43.1: *weaxan*: MS. *weax*.

hygewlonc hondum;　hrægle þeahte
5　þrindende þing　þeodnes dohtor.

44.　[K-D.46

Wær sæt æt wine　mid his wifum twam
ond his twegen suno　ond his twa dohtor,
swase gesweostor　ond hyra suno twegen,
freolico frumbearn.　Fæder wæs þær inne
5　þara æþelinga　æghwæðres mid,
eam ond nefa.　Ealra wæron fife
eorla ond idesa　insittendra.

45.　[K-D.47

Moððe word fræt—　me þæt þuhte
wrætlicu wyrd　þa ic þæt wundor gefrægn,
þæt se wyrm forswealg　wera gied sumes,
þeof in þystro,　þrymfæstne cwide
5　ond þæs strangan staþol.　Stælgiest ne wæs
wihte þy gleawra　þe he þam wordum swealg.

46.　[K-D.48

Ic gefrægn for hæleþum　hring gyddian,
torhtne butan tungan,　tila þeah he hlude
stefne ne cirmde　strongum wordum.
Sinc for secgum　swigende cwæð:
5　"Gehæle mec,　helpend gæsta."
Ryne ongietan　readan goldes

44.3: *hyra*: MS. *hyre.*

45.6: *Rid.* 45 ends with a single point after *swealg* and *Rid.* 46 begins with a small capital immediately thereafter in the same MS. line. Thus, paleographically, *Rids.* 45 and 46 appear to be one riddle.

46.1: See note to *Rid.* 45.6.

46.1: *for*: MS. *fer.*

46.1: *hring gyddian*: MS. *hringende an.*

guman, galdorcwide,   gleawe beþencan
hyra hælo to Gode,   swa se hring gecwæð.

47.

Ic wat eardfæstne   anne standan
deafne dumban   se oft dæges swilgeð
þurh gopes hond   gifrum lacum.
Hwilum on þam wicum   se wonna þegn,
5   sweart ond saloneb,   sendeð oþre
under goman him   golde dyrran,
þa æþelingas   oft wilniað,
cyningas ond cwene.   Ic þæt cyn nu gen
nemnan ne wille   þe him to nytte swa
10   ond to dugþum doþ   þæt se dumba her,
eorp unwita,   ær forswilgeð.

48.

Wiga is on eorþan   wundrum acenned
dryhtum to nytte,   of dumbum twam
torht atyhted,   þone on teon wigeð
feond his feonde.   Forstrangne oft
5   wif hine wrið.   He him wel hereð,
þeowaþ him geþwære,   gif him þegniað
mægeð ond mæcgas   mid gemete ryhte,
fedað hine fægre;   he him fremum stepeð
life on lissum.   Leanað grimme
10   þam þe hine wloncne   weorþan læteð.

46.7: *beþencan*: MS. *beþuncan*.
47.4: *hwilum on þam*. MS. *hwilū monþā*.
47.11: *forswilgeð*: MS. *fer swilgeð*.
48.4: *Forstrangne*: MS. *fer strangne*.
48.10: *þam*: Not in MS.

49.

[K-D.51

Ic seah wrætlice   wuhte feower
samed siþian;   swearte wæran lastas,
swaþu swiþe blacu.   Swift wæs on fore
fuglum framra;   fleag on lyfte
5   deaf under yþe.   Dreag unstille
winnende wiga,   se him wægas tæcneþ
ofer fæted gold   feower eallum.

50.

[K-D.52

Ic seah ræpingas   in ræced fergan
under hrof sales   hearde twegen
þa wæron genumne   nearwum bendum,
gefeterade   fæste togædre.
5   Þara oþrum wæs   an getenge
wonfah Wale,   seo weold hyra
bega siþe   bendum fæstra.

51.

[K-D.53

Ic seah on bearwe   beam hlifian,
tanum torhtne;   þæt treow wæs on wynne,
wudu weaxende.   Wæter hine ond eorþe
feddan fægre   oþþæt he frod dagum
5   on oþrum wearð   aglachade
deope gedolgod,   dumb in bendum,
wriþen ofer wunda,   wonnum hyrstum
foran gefrætwed.   Nu he fæcnum wæg
þurh his heafdes mægen   hildegieste
10   oþrum rymeð.   Oft hy an yst strudon
hord ætgædre;   hræd wæs ond unlæt

49.4: *framra*: The medial *a* is rubbed slightly at the top so as to resemble *u*.
49.4: *fleag on*: MS. *fleotgan*.
50.3: *genumne:* MS. *genamne*.
51.9: *mægen:* MS. *mæg*.

se æftera,   gif se ærra fær
genamnan in nearowe   neþan moste.

52.   [K-D.54

Hyse cwom gangan   þær he hie wisse
stondan in wincle;   stop feorran to
hror hægstealdmon,   hof his agen
hrægl hondum up,   hrand under gyrdels
5   hyre stondendre   stiþes nathwæt,
worhte his willan: wagedan buta.
þegn onnette;   wæs þragum nyt
tillic esne;   teorode hwæþre
æt stunda gehwam   strong ær þonne hio,
10   werig þæs weorces.   Hyre weaxan ongon
under gyrdelse   þæt oft gode men
ferðþum freogað   ond mid feo bicgað.

53.   [K-D.55

Ic seah in healle,   þær hæleð druncon,
on flet beran   feower cynna:
wrætlic wudutreow,   ond wunden gold,
sinc searobunden,   ond seolfres dæl,
5   ond rode tacn   þæs us to roderum up
hlædre rærde,   ær he helwara
burg abræce.   Ic þæs beames mæg
eaþe for eorlum   æþelu secgan:
þær wæs hlin ond acc   ond se hearda iw,
10   ond se fealwa holen—   frean sindon ealle
nyt ætgædre;   naman habbað anne,
wulfheafedtreo.   þæt oft wæpen abæd
his mondryhtne,   maðm in healle,

52.2: *wincle*: MS. *winc sele*.
52.4: *hrand*: MS. *rand*.
52.9: *þonne hio*: MS. *þon hie ó* followed by a MS. point.
53.1: *healle*: MS. *heall*.

goldhilted sweord.   Nu me þisses gieddes
15 ondsware ywe   se hine on mede
wordum secgan   hu se wudu hatte.

54.   [K-D.56

Ic wæs þær inne   þær ic ane geseah
winnende wiht   wido bennegean,
holt hweorfende;   heaþoglemma feng,
deopra dolga.   Daroþas wæron
5 weo þære wihte,   ond se wudu searwum
fæste gebunden.   Hyre fota wæs
biidfæst oþer;   oþer bisgo dreag,
leolc on lyfte,   hwilum londe neah.
Treow wæs getenge   þam þær torhtan stod
10 leafum bihongen.   Ic lafe geseah
minum hlaforde,   þær hæleð druncon,
þara flana   on flet beran.

55.   [K-D.57

Ðeos lyft byreð   lytle wihte
ofer beorghleoþa   þa sind blace swiþe,
swearte, salopade.   Sanges rope
heapum ferað,   hlude cirmað;
5 tredað bearonæssas,   hwilum burgsalo
niþþa bearna.   Nemnað hy sylfe.

56.   [K-D.58

Ic wat anfete   ellen dreogan
wiht on wonge.   Wide ne fereð,
ne fela rideð,   ne fleogan mæg
þurh scirne dæg,   ne hie scip fereð,

54.7: *biidfæst*: MS. *biid fæft.*
54.12: *flana*: MS. *flan.*

5   naca nægledbord;   nyt bið hwæþre
    hyre mondryhtne   monegum tidum.
    Hafað hefigne steort,   heafod lytel,
    tungan lange,   toð nænigne,
    isernes dæl;   eorðgræf pæþeð.
10 Wætan ne swelgeþ,   ne wiht iteþ,
    foþres ne gitsað;   fereð oft swa þeah
    lagoflod on lyfte.   Life ne gielpeð,
    hlafordes gifum;   hyreð swa þeana
    þeodne sinum.   Þry sind in naman
15 ryhte runstafas,   þara is Rad forma.

57.   [K-D.59

    Ic seah in healle   hring gyldenne
    men sceawian   modum gleawe,
    ferþþum frode.   Friþospede bæd
    God nergende   gæste sinum
5   se þe wende wriþan.   Word æfter cwæð
    hring on hyrede,   hælend nemde
    tillfremmendra.   Him torhte in gemynd
    his dryhtnes naman   dumba brohte
    ond in eagna gesihð,   gif þæs æþelestan
10 goldes tacen   ongietan cuþe
    ond dryhtnes dolg,   don swa þæs beages
    benne cwædon.   Ne mæg, þære bene
    æniges monnes   ungefullodre,
    Godes ealdorburg   gæst gesecan,
15 rodera ceastre.   Ræde se þe wille
    hu ðæs wrætlican   wunda cwæden

56.6: *mondryhtne*: MS. *dryht* [/] *ne*.
56.15: *forma*: MS. *furum*.
57.1: *gyldenne*: MS. *gylddenne*.
57.3: *Friþospede*: MS. *friþo spe* at the end of a MS. line.
57.9: *æþelestan*: MS. *æþelan*.
57.11: *ond*: Not in MS.
57.11: *dryhtnes*: MS. *dryht*.
57.13: *ungefullodre*: MS. *ungaful lodre*.

hringes to hæleþum   þa he in healle wæs
wylted ond wended   wloncra folmum.

58.

Ic wæs be sonde   sæwealle neah
æt merefaroþe;   minum gewunade
frumstaþole fæst.   Fea ænig wæs
monna cynnes   þæt minne þær
5   on anæde   eard beheolde,
ac mec uhtna gehwam   yð sio brune
lagufæðme beleolc.   Lyt ic wende
þæt ic ær oþþe sið   æfre sceolde
ofer meodubence   muðleas sprecan,
10   wordum wrixlan.   þæt is wundres dæl,
on sefan searolic   þam þe swylc ne conn,
hu mec seaxes ord   ond seo swiþre hond,
eorles ingeþonc   ond ord somod,
þingum geþydan,   þæt ic wiþ þe sceolde
15   for unc anum twam   ærendspræce
abeodan bealdlice,   swa hit beorna ma,
uncre wordcwidas,   widdor ne mænden.

59.

Oft mec fæste bileac   freolicu meowle,
ides on earce;   hwilum up ateah
folmum sinum   ond frean sealde,
holdum þeodne,   swa hio haten wæs.
5   Siðþan me on hreþre   heafod sticade,
nioþan upweardne   on nearo fegde.
Gif þæs ondfengan   ellen dohte,

58.1: *be sonde*: MS. *besonde* with *o* on an erasure (the original letter appears to have
been *a* or *u*).

58.9: *meodubence*: MS. *meodu*.

58.12: *seaxes*: MS. *seaxeð*.

58.15: *twam*: MS. *twan*.

mec frætwedne   fyllan sceolde
ruwes nathwæt.   Ræd hwæt ic mæne.

60.   [K-D.62

Ic eom heard ond scearp,   hingonges strong,
forðsiþes from,   frean unforcuð;
wade under wambe   ond me weg sylfa
ryhtne geryme.   Rinc bið on ofeste
5 se mec on þyð   æftanweardne,
hæleð mid hrægle: hwilum ut tyhð
of hole hatne,   hwilum eft fereð
on nearo nathwær;   nydeþ swiþe
suþerne secg.   Saga hwæt ic hatte.

61.   [K-D.63

Oft ic secgan   seledreame sceal
fægre onþeon   þonne ic eom forð boren,
glæd mid golde,   þær guman drincað.
Hwilum mec on cofan   cysseð muþe
5 tillic esne   þær wit tu beoþ,
fæðme on folm[.....]grum þyð,
wyrceð his willa[.......]ð l[......
...........] fulre   þonne ic forð cyme
[...............................]
10 Ne mæg ic þy miþan   [............
...............]an on leohte
[...............................]
swylce eac bið sona   [..................

59.8: *mec*: MS. *þe mec.*
60.1: *hingonges*: MS. *Ingonges.*
60.7: *fereð*: MS. *fareð.*
61.7: *l*[... : After *l*, the upper portion of two minims is visible; the letter after *l* is *u* or *i*.

61.11: Before *an*, two descenders are visible indicating *w* or *þ* for each of the two letters; another two spaces before these two, the tip of a long descender is visible (see note).

..]r[.]te getacnad   hwæt me to[......
15   ....]leas rinc,   þa unc geryde wæs.

62.

Ic seah · ᚹ · ond · ᛁ ·   ofer wong faran,
beran · ᛒ · ᛗ ·   Bæm wæs on siþþe
hæbbendes hyht   · ᚻ · ond · ᚠ ·
swylce þryþa dæl.   · ᚦ · ond · ᛗ ·
5   gefeah, · ᚠ · ond · ᚱ ·   fleah ofer · ᛏ
ᚻ · ond · ᚳ ·   sylfes þæs folces.

63.

Cwico wæs ic—ne cwæð ic wiht;   cwele ic efne seþeah.
Ær ic wæs—eft ic cwom;   æghwa mec reafað,
hafað mec on headre,   on min heafod screp,
biteð mec on bær lic,   briceð mine wisan.
5   Monnan ic ne bite   nymþþe he me bite:
sindan þara monige   þe mec bitað.

64.

Ic eom mare   þonne þes middangeard,
læsse þonne hondwyrm,   leohtre þonne mona,
swiftre þonne sunne.   Sæs me sind ealle
flodas on fæðmum   ond þes foldan bearm,
5   grene wongas.   Grundum ic hrine,
helle underhnige,   heofonas oferstige,

61.14: The letter between *r* and *t* is either *h* or *n*.

61.15: In the MS. *leas* is separated from the preceding element by a space; the last letter of the preceding element is either *e* or *t*. Five or six spaces before *leas* the tip of a short descender (probably *r*) is visible.

62.right margin: Hickes's penciled markings and his letter *G* appear in the right-hand margin of the riddle (for an explanation of Hickes's marks, see note to Rid. 73). Above Hickes's *G*, five runes are scratched in dry-point: ᛒ ᚻᛉᚱᚦ (see plate XVII and note).

64.1: *middangeard*: MS. *mindan geard*.

64.4: *þes*: MS. *þas*.

wuldres eþel,   wide ræce
ofer engla eard;   eorþan gefylle,
ealne middangeard   ond merestreamas
10   side mid me sylfum.   Saga hwæt ic hatte.

65.   [K-D.67

Ic on þinge gefrægn   þeodcyninges
wrætlice wiht,   wordgaldra [.....
............] snytt[......] hio symle deð
fira gehw[..........................
5   ......] wisdome.   Wundor me þæt [......
........................]   nænne muð hafað,
fet ne [.................
............] welan oft sacað,
cwiþeð cy[........................] wearð
10   leoda lareow.   Forþon nu longe m[.]g
[........] ealdre   ece lifgan
missenlice,   þenden menn bugað
eorþan sceatas.   Ic þæt oft geseah
golde gegierwed,   þær guman druncon,
15   since ond seolfre.   Secge se þe cunne,
wisfæstra hwylc,   hwæt seo wiht sy.

66.   [K-D.68–69

Ic þa wiht geseah   on weg feran;
heo wæs wrætlice   wundrum gegierwed.
Wundor wearð on wege: wæter wearð to bane.

64.9: *ealne*: MS. *ealdne*.
64.10: *me*: MS. *mec*.
65.5: The first letter of the word following *þæt* is either *þ* or *w*.
65.7: The letter after *ne* has a long descender.
65.9: Fragmentary short strokes after *cy* may indicate *m* or *ni*.
65.10: The missing letter in the last word is *a* or *æ*.
65.11: Three or four spaces after *m*[.]*g* a long descender is visible.
66.2–3: After *gegierwed* at the end of line 2 there is an end-punctuation mark.
Wundor with a large capital *W* begins a new MS. line. Thus, paleographically, the riddle appears to be two (see headnote).

67.

Wiht is wrætlic þam þe hyre wisan ne conn:
singeð þurh sidan;   is se sweora woh,
orþoncum geworht;   hafaþ eaxle tua,
scearp on gescyldrum.   His gesceapo * * *

68.

    *   *   *
þe swa wrætlice   be wege stonde
heah ond hleortorht   hæleþum to nytte.

69.

Ic eom rices æht,   reade bewæfed.
Stið ond steapwong,   staþol wæs iu þa
wyrta wlitetorhtra;   nu eom wraþra laf,
fyres ond feole,   fæste genearwad,
5 wire geweorþad.   Wepeð hwilum
for minum gripe   se þe gold wigeð,
þonne ic yþan sceal   [.......]fe,
hringum gehyrsted.   Me bi[..........
......]go[..]dryhtne   min[..............
10 ....]wlite bete.

70.

Ic wæs lytel [..........................]
fo[........................

67.1: *hyre*: MS. *hyra*.

67.4: MS. folio 125*b* ends with *gesceapo*; MS. folio 126*a* begins with *þe swa*. These are apparently two riddle fragments with a missing leaf in between (see headnote to *Rid*. 67).

69.7: Two spaces before *fe* the tip of an ascender is visible.

69.8: After *bi*, either *þ* or *l*.

69.10: The last letter of the word preceding *wlite* has a long descender.

70.1: *lytel*: Only the upper portions of *tel* are visible.

........]te geaf   [.................
............]þe   þe unc gemæne [.....
5   ....] sweostor min
fedde mec [.......]   oft ic feower teah
swæse broþor,   þara onsundran gehwylc
dægtidum me   drincan sealde
þurh þyrel þearle.   Ic þæh on lust
10   oþþæt ic wæs yldra   ond þæt anforlet
sweartum hyrde;   siþade widdor,
mearcpaþas træd,   moras pæðde,
bunden under beame,   beag hæfde on healse,
wean on laste   weorc þrowade,
15   earfoða dæl.   Oft mec isern scod
sare on sidan;   ic swigade,
næfre meldade   monna ængum,
gif me ordstæpe   egle wæron.

71.   [K-D.73

Ic on wonge aweox,   wunode þær mec feddon
hruse ond heofonwolcn,   oþþæt me onhwyrfdon,
gearum frodne,   þa me grome wurdon,
of þære gecynde   þe ic ær cwic beheold,
5   onwendan mine wisan,   wegedon mec of earde,
gedydon þæt ic sceolde   wiþ gesceape minum
on bonan willan   bugan hwilum.
Nu eom mines frean   folme bysigo[.
.....]dlan dæl,   gif his ellen deag,
10   oþþe æfter dome   [.]ri[...........
...........]ian   mæ[.]þa fremman,

70.3: Before *te*, traces of three or four minims are visible.
70.5: The word or words before *sweostor* show three long descenders in the following pattern: descender, space or letter, descender, letter, descender, space, *sweostor*.
70.12: *mearcpaþas træd*: MS. *mearc paþas walas træd* (see note).
71.1: *wunode*: MS. *wonode*.
71.2: *heofonwolcn*: MS. *heofon wlonc*.
71.11: The letters before *i* look like *tt* or *gg*.

wyrcan w[........................
......]ec on þeode   utan we[.......
.............................]ipe
15   ond to wrohtstæp[....................
.............] eorp,   eaxle gegyrde
wo[...................................]
ond swiora smæl,   sidan fealwe
[.....................]   þonne mec heaþosigel
20   scir bescineð   ond mec [.........]
fægre feormað   ond on fyrd wigeð
cræfte on hæfte.   Cuð is wide
þæt ic þristra sum   þeofes cræfte
under brægnlocan   *   *   *
25   hwilum eawunga   eþelfæsten
forðweard brece   þæt ær frið hæfde.
Feringe from,   he fus þonan
wendeð of þam wicum.   Wiga se þe mine
wisan cunne   cyðe hwæt ic hatte.

72.   [K-D.74

Ic wæs fæmne geong,   feaxhar cwene,
ond ænlic rinc   on ane tid;
fleah mid fuglum   ond on flode swom,
deaf under yþe   dead mid fiscum,
5   ond on foldan stop—   hæfde ferð cwicu.

71.12: The letter following *w* looks like *o*.

71.13: The *e* of *we* is part of a ligature *ea, eo,* or *ec.*

71.15: The letter following *wrohtstæp* may be *e;* two spaces following this, the tip of a long descender is visible.

71.16: The last letter of the word before *eorp* is *r* or *n.*

71.20: The first letter of the word following *mec* has a long descender.

71.23: *þristra*: MS. *þrista.*

71.24: *brægnlocan*: MS. *hrægn* [/] *locan.*

71.29: *cyðe*: MS. *saga.*

72.5: *ferð*: MS. *forð.*

73. [K-D.75–76

Ic swiftne geseah on swaþe feran
· ᛞ ᚾ ᛚ ᚻ ·
Ic ane geseah idese sittan.

74. [K-D.77

Sæ mec fedde, sundhelm þeahte,
ond mec yþa wrugon eorþan getenge,
feþelease; oft ic flode ongean
muð ontynde. Nu wile monna sum
min flæsc fretan; felles ne recceð
siþþan he me of sidan seaxes orde
hyd arypeð, [...]ec hr[.]þe siþþan
iteð unsodene ea[.......................]d.

75. [K-D.78

Oft ic flodas [.................
................]s cynn[.] minum
ond [...................................
.]yde me to mos[....................
................] swa ic him [...........
........................] ne æt ham gesæt
[......................]flote cwealde
þurh orþonc [..........] yþum bewrigene.

73.right margin: Hickes's penciled markings and his letter *H* appear in the right-hand margin of the riddle (see plate XVIII and note).

73.1–3: The first MS. line of folio 127*a* contains line 1 of the riddle and the runes of line 2 followed by an end-punctuation mark. Line 3 of the riddle begins a new MS. line with a large capital *I*; there is an end-punctuation mark after *sittan*. Thus, paleographically, the riddle appears to be two.

74.1: *Sæ*: MS. *Se*.

74.8: *ea*[... : The letter following *ea* looks like *c* and the letter after that has an ascender; the letter before *d* is probably *o*.

75.5: A letter with a long descender occurs two spaces before *swa*.

75.6: Three minims are partially preserved in the last letter(s) of the word before *ne*; the minims are preceded by the tip of a short descender, probably *r*.

75.8: The tip of a long descender is preserved three or four spaces to the left of *yþum*.

76.

Ic eom æþelinges   æht ond willa;
ic eom æþelinges   eaxlgestealla,
fyrdrinces gefara,   frean minum leof,
cyninges geselda.   Cwen mec hwilum
5   hwitloccedu   hond on legeð,
eorles dohtor,   þeah hio æþelu sy.
Hæbbe me on bosme   þæt on bearwe geweox.
Hwilum ic on wloncum   wicge ride
herges on ende—   heard is min tunge.
10   Oft ic woðboran   wordleana sum
agyfe æfter giedde.   Good is min wise
ond ic sylfa salo.   Saga hwæt ic hatte.

77.

Ic eom bylgedbreost,   belcedsweora;
heafod hæbbe   ond heane steort,
eagan ond earan   ond ænne foot,
hrycg ond heard nebb,   hneccan steapne
5   ond sidan twa,   sagol on middum,
eard ofer ældum.   Aglac dreoge,
þær mec wegeð   se þe wudu hrereð,
ond mec stondende   streamas beatað,
hægl se hearda,   ond hrim þeceð,
10   [.]orst [.....]eoseð,   ond fealleð snaw
on þyrelwombne;   ond ic þæt [.]ol[.........
.............] mæ[.]   wonsceaft mine.

76.1–2: The first line of *Rid.* 76 appears as a single riddle in the MS. There is an
end-punctuation mark after *willa;* the *ic* of line 2 in the riddle has a large capital *I* and
begins a new MS. line. Paleographically, line 1 appears to constitute one riddle; lines
2–12, another (see headnote).

77.1: *bylgedbreost*: MS. *by led breost.*

77.5: *sagol*: MS. *sag.*

77.11: *on*: Not in MS.

77.12: The letter after *mæ* is either *g* or *t.*

78.   [K-D.82

Wiht is [..........................
........]ongende   greate swilgeð
[...............................
......]ell ne flæsc;   fotum gong[..
5   ....]eð,
sceal mæla gehwam   [...............]

79.   [K-D.83

Frod wæs min fromcynn   [..................]
biden in burgum,   siþþan bæles weard
[...........] wera   lige bewunden,
fyre gefælsad.   Nu me fah wara∂
5   eorþan broþor,   se me ærest wearð
gumena to gyrne.   Ic ful gearwe gemon
hwa min fromcynn   fruman agette
eall of earde;   ic him yfle ne mot,
ac ic hæftnyd   hwilum arære
10   wide geond wongas.   Hæbbe ic wunda fela,
middangeardes   mægen unlytel,
ac ic miþan sceal   monna gehwylcum
degolfulne dom   dyran cræftes,
siðfæt minne.   Saga hwæt ic hatte.

78.4: The letter following *gong* looks like *e*.

78.6: After *gehwam* the hole in the MS. extends some 30 spaces to the right-hand margin of the folio. Three or four spaces after *gehwam* a long descender is visible.

79.1: *fromcynn*: MS. *from cym*; the first letter of the next word may be *h* or *n*.

79.3a: The first letter of the word following *weard* (line 79.2*b*) is *d* or *o*; the lower portion of several minims is visible thereafter.

79.3b: *lige*: MS. *life*.

79.4: *warað*: Only the lower portion of *∂* is visible.

79.9: *hæftnyd*: MS. *on hæft nyd*.

80.   [K-D.84

An wiht is on eorþan   wundrum acenned,
hreoh ond reþe;   hafað ryne strongne,
grimme grymetað,   ond be grunde fareð.
Modor is monigra   mærra wihta.
5   Fæger ferende   fundað æfre;
neol is nearograp.   Nænig oþrum mæg
wlite ond wisan   wordum gecyþan,
hu mislic biþ   mægen þara cynna,
fyrn forðgesceaft;   fæder ealle bewat,
10   or ond ende,   swylce an sunu,
mære meotudes bearn   þurh [..........]ed
ond þæt hyhste mæ[.......]es [.]æ[....
...................] dyre cræft[.
....
15   .]onne hy aweorp[...........................]
..]þe ænig þara [........................]
.......]fter ne mæg   [....................
..........] oþer cynn   eorþan [........
..............] þonne ær wæs
20   wlitig ond wynsum   [...........]
Biþ sio moddor   mægene eacen,
wundrum bewreþed,   wistum gehladen,
hordum gehroden,   hæleþum dyre.

80.1: *on eorþan*: Not in MS.

80.1: *acenned*: MS. *acceneð*.

80.2: *strongne*: See note.

80.3: *fareð*: With *e* altered from *a*.

80.8: *mægen*: The beginning of an additional minim protrudes from the upper right-hand corner of the *n* and there is no erasure. Thus the scribe appears to have begun writing *m*, and, realizing his error, to have stopped.

80.12: The letter after *mæ* may be *g* or *t*. One or two spaces before *es* an ascender is visible. The letter preceding the *æ* in the last word may be *g* or *t*.

80.16: The letter before *þe* is *o*, *d*, or *ð*.

80.18: The last letter of the word before *oþer* looks like *a*.

80.19: *þonne*: MS. *þon* with a possible obliteration of the tilde because of the MS. burn.

80.20: In the word before *Biþ*, i.e., in the last word of line 20, the penultimate letter has a short descender and is probably *r*; the letter preceding the letter with the short descender has a long descender.

80.22: *bewreþed*: Only the lower portion of the *b* is visible.

Mægen bi∂ gemiclad,   meaht gesweotlad;
25 wlite biþ geweorþad   wuldornyttingum.
Wynsum wuldorgimm   wloncum getenge,
clængeorn bi∂ ond cystig,   cræfte eacen;
hio biþ eadgum leof,   earmum getæse,
freolic, sellic.   Fromast ond swiþost,
30 gifrost ond grædgost—   grundbedd trideþ—
þæs þe under lyfte   aloden wurde
ond ælda bearn   eagum sawe.
Swa þæt wuldor wife∂   worldbearna mægen,
þeah þe ferþum gleaw   *   *   *
35 mon mode snottor   mengo wundra.
Hrusan bi∂ heardra,   hæleþum frodra,
geofum bi∂ gearora,   gimmum deorra;
worulde wlitiga∂,   wæstmum tydre∂,
firene dwæsce∂;   *   *   *
40 oft utan beweorpe∂   anre þecene,
wundrum gewlitegad   geond werþeode,
þæt wafia∂   weras ofer eorþan,
þæt magon micle   [............]sceafte.
Biþ stanum bestreþed,   stormum [..........
45 ....]len [.........]timbred weall,
þrym[............................]ed
hrusan hrine∂,   h[............]
....................]etenge;
oft searwum biþ [................
50 ....] dea∂e ne fele∂,
þeah þe [.........................
......]du hreren,   hrif wundigen,
[........................]risse.
Hordword onhlid   hæleþum ge[....

80.33: *mægen*: MS. *mæge*.

80.45: Only the upper portion of *len* is visible; conceivably the letters could read *ler*.

80.49: Only the lower half of *biþ* is visible; of the three letters, only the *i* is absolutely certain.

80.53: In the word after *wundigen*, i.e., in the first word of line 53, the first letter has a long descender.

80.54: The two letters after *ge* may be *cy*. Only the lower portion of the letters remains. Five spaces after *ge*, the tip of a long descender is visible.

55 ....]wreoh, wordum geopena,
   hu mislic sy mægen þara cy[...]

81. [K-D.85

Nis min sele swige, ne ic sylfa hlud
ymb * * * ; unc dryhten scop
siþ ætsomne. Ic eom swiftre þonne he,
þragum strengra; he þreohtigra.
5 Hwilum ic me reste; he sceal rinnan forð.
Ic him in wunige a þenden ic lifge;
gif wit unc gedælað, me bið dead witod.

82. [K-D.86

Wiht cwom gongan þær weras sæton
monige on mæðle, mode snottre;
hæfde an eage ond earan twa,
ond twegen fet, twelf hund heafda,
5 hrycg ond wombe ond honda twa,
earmas ond eaxle, anne sweoran
ond sidan twa. Saga hwæt hio hatte.

83. [K-D.87

Ic seah wundorlice wiht; wombe hæfde micle,
þryþum geþrungne. Þegn folgade,
mægenstrong ond mundrof; micel me þuhte
godlic gumrinc; grap on sona,

81.2: *dryhten*: MS. *dryht.*
81.3: *swiftre*: MS. *swistre.*
81.5: *rinnan*: MS. *yrnan.*
82.4: *twegen*: MS. *ii.*
82.4: *twelf*: MS. *xii.*
82.5: *hrycg*: MS. *hryc.*
82.7: *hio*: MS. *ic.*

83.3: *mægenstrong*: MS. *megen* [/] *strong*; the first *e* of the first word has a subscript correction of *e* to *æ*.

5   heofones toþe   *   *   *
      bleowe on eage;   hio borcade,
      wancode willum.   Hio wolde seþeah
      niol [...............]

84.   [K-D.88

      Ic weox þær ic s[........................
      ....] ond sumor   mi[................
      ....]me   wæs min ti[.....
      ....

5   ...]d ic on staðol[....................
      ....]m geong   swa [..........
      ....] seþeana
      oft geond [......................]fgeaf,
      ac ic uplong stod   þær ic [.........]x
10   ond min broþor—   begen wæron hearde.
      Eard wæs þy weorðra   þe wit on stodan,
      hyrstum þy hyrra.   Ful oft unc holt wrugon,
      wudubeama helm   wonnum nihtum,
      scildon wið scurum.   Unc gescop meotud.
15   Nu unc mæran twam   magas uncre
      sculon æfter cuman,   eard oðþringan
      gingran broþor.   Eom ic gumcynnes
      anga ofer eorþan.   Is min innaþ blæc,
      wonn ond wundorlic;   ic on wuda stonde
20   bordes on ende.   Nis min broþor her,

83.6: *borcade*: The *r* could be an *n* (see note).

83.8: Four or five spaces after *niol* the tip of an ascender is visible.

84.1: The *s* is a ligature *s*.

84.3: The letter following *ti* is *r* or *n*.

84.5: The letter before *d* may be *o*.

84.6: The letter before *m* is *u* or *a*.

84.9: Only a small portion of *x* is visible; the *x* appears to be the last letter of the word preceding the abbreviation for *ond*, but a letter may have been lost after the *x*; one or two spaces before the fragmentary *x* a descender is visible.

84.10: *min*: MS. *mine*.

84.18: *innaþ*: Not in MS.

84.18: *blæc*: MS. *bæc*.

ac ic sceal broþorleas   bordes on ende
staþol weardian,   stondan fæste;
ne wat hwær min broþor   on wera æhtum
eorþan sceata   eardian sceal,
25 se me ær be healfe   heah eardade.
Wit wæron gesome   sæcce to fremmanne;
næfre uncer awþer   his ellen cyðde,
swa wit þære beadwe   begen ne onþungan.
Nu mec unsceafta   innan slitað,
30 wyrdaþ mec be wombe;   ic gewendan ne mæg.
Æt þam spore findeð   sped se þe se[....
.............]   sawle rædes.

85.   [K-D.89

[..............................
.......]e wiht   wombe hæfde
[.............................
....]tne leþre   wæs beg[.........
5 ....]on hindan
grette wea[...................
.................]   listum worhte,
hwilum eft [...................
...........]   þygan,   him þoncade,
10 siþþan u[..................
....]   swæsendum   swylce þrage.

86.   [K-D.90

Mirum videtur mihi—   lupus ab agno tenetur;
obcu[..]it agnus *   *   *   et capit viscera lupi.

84.21: *ac*: The *a* takes the form of horned *c* (see note) and is a small capital.
84.22: *stondan*: MS. *stodan*.
84.28: *swa wit*: MS *swawit* with a possible attempted erasure of *a*.
84.29: *Nu*: MS. *hu*.
85.10: The letter after *u* may be *n*, *m*, or *h*.
86.2: *agnus*: With *a* in the form of horned *c* (see note).
86.2: *et*: In an unusual paleographical form (see plate xxiii).
86.2: *capit*: With *a* in the form of horned *c* (see note and plate xxiii).

Dum starem et mirarem,   vidi gloriam magnam:
duo lupi stantes   et tertium tribulantes—
5   quattuor pedes habebant;   cum septem oculis videbant.

87.

[K-D.91

Min heafod is   homere geþuren,
searopila wund,   sworfen feole.
Oft ic begine   þæt me ongean sticað,
þonne ic hnitan sceal   hringum gyrded,
5   hearde wið heardum,   hindan þyrel—
forð ascufan   þæt mines frean
mod · ᚹ · freoþað   middelnihtum.
Hwilum ic under bæc   bregde nebbe
hyrde þæs hordes,   þonne min hlaford wile
10   lafe þicgan   þara þe he of life het
wælcræfte awrecan   willum sinum.

88.

[K-D.92

Ic wæs brunra beot,   beam on holte,
freolic feorhbora   ond foldan wæstm,
weres wynnstaþol   ond wifes sond,
gold on geardum.   Nu eom guðwigan
5   hyhtlic hildewæpen,   hringe be[.......
....]e[...................] byreð
oþrum [...............................]

86.3: *mirarem*: MS. *misarē*.
86.3: *magnam*: MS. *magnan* with the first *a* in the form of horned *c* (see note).
86.4: *duo*: MS. *dui*.
86.4: *tribulantes*: MS. *tribul.*
86.5: *quattuor*: MS. *iiii.*
87.11: *wælcræfte*: See note.
88.3: *weres*: Not in MS.
88.3: *wynnstaþol*: MS. *wym staþol.*
88.5: After *be*, either *g* or *t*.
88.6: After *e* the upper portion of a long ascender is preserved; some eight spaces after the ascender a portion of a ligature *s* or ligature *e* is preserved.

89. [K-D.93]

Frea min [......................
............]de   willum sinum
[...................................]
heah ond hyht[...................
5   ....]earpne,   hwilum [.........
......................]wilum sohte
frea [.....................]s wod
dægrime frod   deo[..........]s;
hwilum stealc hliþo   stigan sceolde
10   up in eþel;   hwilum eft gewat
in deop dalu   duguþe secan
strong on stæpe,   stanwongas grof
hrimighearde;   hwilum hara scoc
forst of feaxe.   Ic on fusum rad
15   oþþæt him þone gleawstol   gingra broþor
min agnade   ond mec of earde adraf.
Siþþan mec isern   innanweardne
brun bennade;   blod ut ne com,
heolfor of hreþre,   þeah mec heard bite
20   stiðecg style.   No ic þa stunde bemearn,
nc for wunde weop,   ne wrecan meahte
on wigan feore   wonnsceaft mine,
ac ic aglæca   ealle þolige
þæt [..]e bord biton.   Nu ic blace swelge
25   wuda ond wætre,   w[..]b[.] befæðme
þæt mec on fealleð   ufan þær ic stonde,

89.1: *min*: Only the initial minim of the *n* remains.

89.4: *hyht*: Only a small upper portion of the *t* remains; after *hyht* a portion of an ascender remains.

89.5: Two or three letters before *earpne* a long descender is visible.

89.7: The letter before *s* may be *a*.

89.9: *hwilum*: MS. *hwilu* with a possible obliteration of the tilde because of the MS. burn.

89.14: *feaxe*: MS. *feax*.

89.14: *on*: MS. *of*.

89.15: *gingra*: MS. *gingran*.

89.24: *þæt [..]e*: MS. *þ [..]e*; the gap is owing to a slight stain in the MS.

[119]

eorpes nathwæt;   hæbbe anne fot.
Nu min hord waraðð   hiþende feond
se þe ær wide bær   wulfes gehleþan;
30 oft me of wombe   bewaden fereð,
steppeð on stið bord   [...............
...] deaþes d[...]   þonne dægcondel,
sunne [......................
..........]eorc   eagum wliteð
35 ond spe[.........................]

90.   [K-D.94

Smeþr[.............................]ad,
hyrre þonne heofon[.................
...............] glædre þonne sunne,
[.............................]style,
5 smeare þonne sealt ry[.....................]
leofre þonne þis leoht eall,   leohtre þonne w[..........]

91.   [K-D.95

Ic eom indryhten   ond eorlum cuð,
ond reste oft   ricum ond heanum,
folcum gefræge.   Fereð wide,
ond me fremde ær   freondum stondeð
5 hiþendra hyht,   gif ic habban sceal
blæd in burgum   oþþe beorhte god.

89.32: See note.

89.34: See note.

90.2: A long descender is preserved in the third space after *heofon*.

90.4: The lower portion of several minims (of *m*, *n*, or *h*) is visible as part of the initial letters of the word after *sunne*.

90.6b: *þonne*: MS. *þon* with the tilde missing, presumably because of the burn.

90.6b: After *w* the lower fragments of several letters remain visible. Five or six spaces after *w* there is a long descender; two or three spaces after the long descender there is a short descender, probably from *r*.

91.4: *fremde*: MS. *fremdes*.

91.6: *beorhte*: MS. *beorhtne*.

Nu snottre men   swiþast lufiaþ
midwist mine: ic monigum sceal
wisdom cyþan;   no þær word sprecan
10 ænig ofer eorðan.   Þeah nu ælda bearn,
londbuendra,   lastas mine
swiþe secað,   ic swaþe hwilum
mine bemiþe   monna gehwylcum.

91.9: *sprecan*: MS. *sprecað*.

Notes and Commentary

Note to Major Editions

The following editions of *Riddles* are referred to in the Notes and Commentary by the editor's name alone:

Thorpe. *Codex Exoniensis*. London, 1842.

Grein. *Bibliothek der angelsächsischen Poesie*. Göttingen, 1857–58.

Assmann. Vol. 3 of Wülker's revised *Bibliothek der angelsächsischen Poesie*. Leipzig, 1898.

Tupper. *The Riddles of the Exeter Book*. Boston, 1910.

Wyatt. *Old English Riddles*. Boston and London, 1912.

Trautmann. *Die altenglischen Rätsel (die Rätsel des Exeterbuchs)*. Heidelberg, 1915.

Mackie. *The Exeter Book*. Part 2. London, 1934.

Krapp and Dobbie. *The Exeter Book* [*ASPR*., vol. 3]. New York and London, 1936.

Baum. *Anglo-Saxon Riddles of the Exeter Book* [translations only]. Durham, N.C., 1963.

Note to Variant Numbers

Enclosed in brackets at the beginning of the headnote to each riddle, there is a list of the variant numbers (*VN*) used by previous editors to refer to that riddle. The bracketed abbreviations are:

VN: Variant Numbers	*Tu*.: Tupper
*Gr*¹.: Grein	*W*.: Wyatt
*Gr*².: Grein-Wülker	*M*.: Mackie
(Assmann)	*K-D*.: Krapp and Dobbie
Tr.: Trautmann	

In the first 64 riddles where the numbers of *Gr*¹. and *Gr*². are the same, the single abbreviation, *Gr*., is used to indicate both. Beginning at *Rid.* 65 (the first riddle omitted by Grein in the 1857–58 edition), the numbers are indicated separately by the superscript. Where a riddle has been omitted by an editor, this is indicated by an "X" where the variant number would normally be (e.g., $Gr^1.X$ or $W.X$).

Note on Quotations of Old English Verse

All quotations from the *Riddles* are from this edition. All quotations from *Beowulf* are from Fr. Klaeber, ed., *Beowulf and The Fight at Finns-burg*, 3d ed., Boston, 1950. All other quotations from Old English verse are from George Philip Krapp and Elliott Van Kirk Dobbie, eds., *The Anglo-Saxon Poetic Records*, New York and London, 1931–53.

1. Wind

[*VN: Gr.2–4; Tr.1; Tu.2–4; W.1–3; M.1–3; K-D.1–3*]

All major editors except Trautmann separate the first riddle as printed here into three riddles with line divisions as follows: (1) lines 1–15; (2) lines 16–30; (3) lines 31–104. Trautmann in 1894 (*Anglia Beibl.* v, 46) and Edmund Erlemann in 1903 (*Archiv* cxi, 49 ff.) first suggested reading the three riddles as one, and the single riddle was so printed by Trautmann in his edition of 1915. Wyatt printed three riddles with the query, "Are the first Three Riddles one riddle?" (p. 66) and the note (p. 68) that the third riddle at least was a continuation of the second. Mackie and Krapp and Dobbie print three separate riddles. Recently Charles Kennedy (*The Earliest English Poetry*, pp. 364 ff.) has argued for the integrity of the second two riddles at least, and Erhardt-Siebold (*PMLA* lxiv, 884 ff.) has argued for the integrity of all three together as one. In my printing of a single riddle, I follow Trautmann, Erlemann, and Erhardt-Siebold. In my offering of the solution, "wind," I have merely extended Kennedy's solution of lines 16–104 to the entire riddle.*

On the basis of paleographical evidence alone, the riddle as printed here would appear to comprise two separate riddles—the first, lines 1–15; and the second, lines 16–104. There is a large capital *H* in *Hwylc* at line 1 and a smaller, quite unadorned capital *H* in *Hwilum* at line 16. There is an end-punctuation mark after *bere* at line 15*b*. Since *bere* extends to the right-hand margin of script on the MS. line, there is no typical end-space to separate the two riddles as written by the scribe. Most editors begin a third riddle at line 31, but there is no evidence to support this reading. MS. folio 101*a* ends with the word *wrugon* (30*b*) followed by a simple point. MS. folio 101*b* begins with the word *hwilum* (31*a*) with no capital. The placing of a simple point after the last word on a MS. page does not indicate the end of a riddle. The manuscript end-page point is a kind of carry-over sign used at the scribe's discretion. It occurs, for example, at the end of folios 101*b*, 102*a*, 102*b*, 105*a*, etc., where there are riddle carry-overs from one MS. page to the next.

*In recent articles Marie Nelson (*Spec.* xlix, 433) and Jackson J. Campbell (*Neoph.* lix, 128 ff.) also argue that the three "storm" riddles should be one. Campbell would solve the riddle as "the power of nature."

The normal division of the text into three riddles is based upon two rhetorical considerations: the commands to the reader initiated by the word *Saga* at lines 14–15 and at 27*b*–30 and the corresponding *Hwilum* beginning at lines 16 and 31. About the use of *hwilum* two things need be said: (1) the marking off of internal divisions of a riddle with *hwilum* at lines 47 and 66 shows that the word itself placed at the beginning of a metric line and at the beginning of a verse paragraph, even at the beginning of a MS. line (as is the case at line 66), does not necessarily indicate the beginning of a new riddle; (2) in fact, we should assume exactly the opposite from the semantic and syntactic function of *hwilum* as it is used in the *Riddles* to delineate general descriptions of character or action, which descriptions in all cases precede it. Two examples may suffice. Since *hwilum* must follow a general description, it never occurs elsewhere in the *Riddles* in the first line of a riddle. The earliest it may occur is in the second line of a riddle, as in the case of *Rid.* 22:

> Ic eom wunderlicu wiht— wræsne mine stefne:
> hwilum beorce swa hund, hwilum blæte swa gat,
> hwilum græde swa gos, hwilum gielle swa hafoc.
>
> [*Rid.* 22.1–3]

Notice that the *hwilum* constructions delineate the general phrase *wræsne mine stefne*. The same thing is true of the summary *hwilum* clauses at the end of *Rid.* 1 as printed here:

> Swa ic þrymful þeow þragum winne,
> hwilum under eorþan, hwilum yþa sceal
> hean underhnigan, hwilum holm ufan,
> streamas styrge, hwilum stige up,
> wolcnfare wrege, wide fere
> swift ond swiþfeorm.
>
> [*Rid.* 1.97–102]

In this case the *hwilum* clauses delineate the general description of action, *þragum winne*, at 97*b*. Kennedy (*The Earliest English Poetry*, p. 365) also points out that this summary *hwilum* description corresponds to the four *hwilum* descriptions of the "wind" beginning at line 16, thus:

Poem	Summary
1. Submarine power of wind	
Lines 16–30	Lines 98*b*–99*a*
2. Subterranean power of wind	
Lines 31–46	Line 98*a*
3. Storm above sea	
Lines 47–65	Lines 99*b*–100*a*
4. Thunderstorm among clouds	
Lines 66–96	Lines 100*b*–102*a*

The initial two sections are transposed in the summary, but both belong to the general category of "earthquake" as explained by Bede (see below) and others. Otherwise the sections fit perfectly. I would agree with Erlemann (*Archiv* cxi, 49 ff.) that the first 15 lines of the riddle introduce the windstorm especially with regard to its power over men, that the four *hwilum* clauses noted above detail the various forms that the wind may take, and that the final lines summarize the body of the poem. Of the six sections of the poem (initial description, four *hwilum* sections, and summary), five end with a reference to the divine Power who rules the might of the wind, and in four of the five cases the reference is put in terms of a rhetorical question to the reader.* Those editors who would argue that the rhetorical questions in themselves mark the ends of riddles must ignore the question at 65*b* where no one marks the end of a riddle and also the correspondence between the *hwilum* clauses in the summary of the riddle (lines 97–102*a*) and the extended *hwilum* descriptions in the main body (lines 16–96).

Most editors who print the riddle as three solve the three riddles as "storm" in its various aspects. Thus Dietrich (*ZfdA*. xi, 461) solves his first riddle (here lines 1–15) as "storm on land and sea"; his second (here lines 16–30) as "sea storm"; his third (here lines 31 ff.) as a three-phase storm, under earth, upon the waves, and overhead. Thus Dietrich has five different storms for three storm riddles; this disjunction is ridiculous. Tupper takes the central riddle (here lines 16–30) to be a "submarine earthquake"; otherwise he accepts Dietrich's parcel of storms. Wyatt prints three separate riddles in his text, solves the first as "storm on land" and the second and third together

*A similar point is made by Kennedy.

as "storm at sea" in his notes, and suggests finally in his table of pre-ferred solutions (p. viii) that all three riddles should be one "storm." Mackie prints three separate riddles and lists Dietrich's five "storm" solutions in his Appendix A along with his own suggestion that the three might together constitute a single "wind" riddle. Trautmann (edition) and Erlemann (*Archiv* cxi, 49ff.) argue for a single "storm" riddle. Krapp and Dobbie print three riddles but note that they could be one. Kennedy (*The Earliest English Poetry*, pp. 364ff.) argues that at least the second two riddles (here lines 16–104) constitute one "wind" riddle. Erhardt-Siebold (*PMLA* lxiv, 884ff.) argues for a single "at-mosphere" riddle, but her solution seems too broad. Shook (*MS* viii, 316ff.) believes the first riddle (here lines 1–15) to be a "fire" riddle, but his explanation of lines 10–14 as the depiction of "a boiling caul-dron containing the flesh of human victims, suspended over a sacrifi-cial fire" (*MS* viii, 318) cannot be taken seriously.

Both Erlemann and Kennedy argue that the details of the riddle derive from medieval and classical notions of meteorology, especially as they are documented by four works: Book II of Pliny's *Historia Naturalis*, Lucretius's *De Rerum Natura*, Isidore's *De Natura Rerum*, and Bede's *De Natura Rerum*. Kennedy argues for the solution "wind." Erlemann solves the riddle as "storm" but recognizes implicitly the "wind" solution when he calls the divine Driver of the creature in the riddle "Gott der Beherrscher und Gebieter des Windes" (*Archiv* cxi, 54). In all four meteorological works noted above, the power of the wind in causing natural storms of all kinds is preeminent. Pliny calls the region below the moon (*infra lunam haec sedes*) the realm of the winds (*ventorum hoc regnum*) and explains that most natural disorders come from this realm:

> Hinc nubila, tonitrua et alia fulmina, hinc grandines, pruinae, imbres, procellae, turbines, hinc plurima mortalium mala et rerum naturae pugna secum. . . . decidunt imbres, nebulae subeunt, siccantur amnes, ruunt gran-dines, torrent radii et terram in medio mundi undique impellunt, iidem in-fracti resiliunt et quae potavere auferunt secum. vapor ex alto cadit rursumque in altum redit. venti ingruunt inanes, iidemque cum rapina remeant. [*NH*. ii.xxxviii.102–3]

Kennedy (*The Earliest English Poetry*, p. 368) points out that Pliny's statement about the plundering winds swooping down upon the land is like the riddler's description beginning at line 66, especially lines

93b–96. The battle of elements in the realm of winds causes mischief to man. Pliny notes that most authorities even attribute the cause of lightning and thunder to the wind:

> Ventorum hoc regnum. itaque praecipua eorum natura ibi et ferme reliquas complexa aeris causas, quoniam et tonitruum et fulminum iactus horum violentiae plerique adsignant, quin et ideo lapidibus pluere interim, quia vento sint rapti; et multa similiter. [NH. ii.xxxviii.102]

Erlemann (Archiv cxi, 54–55) notes that the riddlic conception of God as ruler of winds is an Old Testament notion and cites Bede's description of the wind:

> Ventus est aer commotus et agitatus, sicut flabello brevi potest approbari, nec aliud intelligitur quam fluctus aeris, qui, ut Clemens ait, ex quibusdam montibus excelsis velut compressus et coangustatus ordinatione Dei cogitur et exprimitur in ventos, ad excitandos fluctus, aestusque temperandos. [DNR. xxvi; PL. xc, 246–47]

But the conception of wind in the Old English riddle seems even slightly demonic. Isidore points out that there were two main traditions for viewing the significant power of the wind:

> Venti autem interdum angelorum intelliguntur spiritus, qui a secretis Dei ad salutem humani generis per universum mundum mittuntur. Item nonnumquam venti incentores spiritus poni solent pro eo quod malae suggestionis flatu ad terrena desideria iniquorum corda succendunt, secundum quod scriptum est: tollet eum ventus urens. [NR. xxxvi.iii.19–24]

Clearly the Old English riddler followed the tradition of those who viewed the wind as a scourge.

In lines 16–30 the wind is described as the source of a submarine earthquake and in lines 31–46 as the source of a subterranean quake. The two kinds of quakes are linked by Bede in his chapter, "De Terrae Motu," of De Natura Rerum:

> Terrae motum vento fieri dicunt, ejus visceribus instar spongiae cavernosis incluso, qui hanc horribili tremore percurrens, et evadere nitens, vario murmure concutit et se tremendo vel dehiscendo cogit effundere. Unde cava terrarum his motibus subjacent, utpote venti capacia: arenosa autem et solida carent. Neque enim fiunt, nisi coelo marique tranquillo, et vento in venas terrae condito. Et hoc est in terra tremor, quod in nube tonitruum: hocque hiatus, quod fulmen. Fiunt simul cum terrae motu et inundationes maris, eodem videlicet spiritu infusi vel residentis sinu recepti. [DNR. xlix; PL. xc, 275–76]

The passage derives from Isidore (*NR*. xlvi) and is in turn based on similar descriptions in Pliny and Lucretius. Pliny describes wind-caused earthquakes coming in the midst of a brooding calm in language similar to lines 40*b* ff. of the Old English riddle.* Pliny says:

> Et haec quidem arbitrio cuiusque existimanda relinquantur: ventos in causa esse non dubium reor; neque enim umquam intremiscunt terrae nisi sopito mari caeloque adeo tranquillo ut volatus avium non pendeant subtracto omni spiritu qui vehit, nec umquam nisi post ventos, condito scilicet in venas et cava eius occulta flatu. [*NH*. ii.lxxxi.192]

Pliny also notes that earthquakes may occur at sea where great waves rise up without wind and where the shock waves shake ships (*NH*. ii.lxxxiii), and that these submarine quakes in turn may cause great floodings of the land (*NH*. ii.lxxxvi). Lucretius describes earthquakes in his *De Rerum Natura*, Book VI, lines 536 ff. Kennedy first pointed out the central description at lines 577 ff.:

> Est haec eiusdem quoque magni causa tremoris,
> ventus ubi atque animae subito vis maxima quaedam
> aut extrinsecus aut ipsa tellure coorta
> in loca se cava terrai coniecit ibique
> speluncas inter magnas fremit ante tumultu
> versabundaque portatur, post incita cum vis
> exagitata foras erumpitur et simul altam
> diffindens terram magnum concinnat hiatum.
>
> [*DRN*. vi.577–84]

Elsewhere (*DRN*. vi.561 ff.) Lucretius describes the earthquake's devastation of buildings in terms similar to those of the Old English riddler.

The rainstorms of lightning and thunder described in lines 1–15 and 66–96 also have their basis in the meteorological tracts. I have quoted above the passage from Pliny where that author says that most men attribute the hurling of thunderbolts and lightning to the violence of the winds. Kennedy (*The Earliest English Poetry*, p. 367) points out that the description of thunder at lines 66 ff. of the riddle as being the result of the clashing of wind-driven clouds may derive from Lucretius, who says:

---

*This point was first made by Kennedy, *The Earliest English Poetry*, p. 368.

Principio tonitru quatiuntur caerula caeli
propterea quia concurrunt sublime volantes
aetheriae nubes contra pugnantibu' ventis.

[*DRN*. vi.96–98]

Erlemann (*Archiv* cxi, 52) points to a similar description in Bede's *De Natura Rerum*:

Tonitrua dicunt ex fragore nubium generari, cum spiritus ventorum earum sinu concepti sese ibidem versando pererrantes, et virtutis suae mobilitate in quamlibet partem violenter erumpentes, magno concrepant murmure, instar exilentium de stabulis quadrigarum vel vesicae, quae, licet parva, magnum tamen sonitum displosa emittit. [*DNR*. xxviii; *PL*. xc, 249–50]

Lightning is said to come from the same wind-driven clash. Lucretius describes lightning as the result of winds bursting from black clouds:

Ventus ubi invasit nubem et versatus ibidem
fecit ut ante cavam docui spissescere nubem,
mobilitate sua fervescit; ut omnia motu
percalefacta vides ardescere, plumbea vero
glans etiam longo cursu volvenda liquescit.
ergo fervidus hic nubem cum perscidit atram,
dissipat ardoris quasi per vim expressa repente
semina quae faciunt nictantia fulgura flammae;

[*DRN*. vi.175–82]

When the wind holds this power, there is no need to assign a solution, "fire," to lines 1–15 in the manner of Shook (*MS* viii, 316 ff.).

I have quoted these Latin passages about the wind at length, both because of the importance of Erlemann's and Kennedy's comments, and also because it is important for us as modern readers to understand the broad range of the wind's powers in terms of medieval meterological thought. The central reason for so many editors' printing of three "storm" riddles with five or six different "storm" solutions is the modern scientific inability to see the wind in rainstorms, thunder, lightning, earthquakes, submarine quakes, sea storms, and the like. Certainly the meteorological writers of the time would not have had such an inability. The Old English riddler draws upon a long-established tradition of ascribing to the wind all of the natural disturbances in what Pliny calls "the realm of winds . . . in the region below the moon."

1.1 ff.: The editors close the initial question at various points: Assmann, Mackie, and Krapp and Dobbie after 6*a* as I have it here; Grein, after 7*a*; Wyatt, after 2*b*; Trautmann, after 3*a*; Tupper after 4*a*. The reading with the adverbial time-clause extending from *þonne* at 3*a* through the end of the creature's actions at 6*a* makes the best sense. The important opening lines of the riddle are highlighted in a recent article by Campbell (*Neoph.* lix, 128 ff.) who notes that solver, riddlic creature, and driving Power (the Lord) are all brought into immediate juxtaposition. Campbell's article details the use of rhetorical devices in the poem.

1.2: *wræce*: Most editors gloss the word as preterite subjunctive *wræce*, but Wyatt (p. 67), citing SB. 391 Anm. 1.5 and a similar example at *Jul.* 719, notes that *wræce* may be a present subjunctive Northumbrian form. As *Juliana* is probably Mercian in origin, it is safer to call the form Anglian. The syntax and meter here allow for either a past or a present subjunctive form, but for a clear-cut example of the Anglian form elsewhere in the *Riddles*, see the usage of 18.18.

1.4: *wræce*: The word is here taken as dative or instrumental of *wræc*, "vengeance," for which see B-T., p. 1269. This is apparently the reading of Mackie, who translates *þragum wræce / fere* as "at times travel with havoc" (p. 89). For the form and possible etymology of *wræc*, "vengeance," see *OED* xii, p. 354, under *wreche*, sb. obs. The meter, as Sievers (*Beiträge* x, 510) pointed out, seems to call for a long vowel. Grein (*Sp.*, p. 823) and Bosworth-Toller (p. 1268) take *wræce* as instrumental singular of *wracu*, "hostility," but Tupper notes that this leaves the half-line metrically short, and Krapp and Dobbie doubt the reading. Tupper emends the MS. reading to *wræcca*, "exile, wretch," after a suggestion by Herzfeld (*Die Räthsel des Exeterbuches und ihr Verfasser*, p. 44). Trautmann reads *wræce* as instrumental singular of *wræc*, "Elend, Verderben, Leid" (p. 199), but Tupper and Krapp and Dobbie note that *wræc* with this meaning probably has a short vowel. Thorpe originally read *wræce* as a verb, translating *þragum wræce* as "[I] at times wander," but the present tense of *wrecan* ought to be *wrece*. Wyatt takes *wræce* as a present subjunctive Northumbrian form citing *Jul.* 719 and SB. 391 Anm. 5, but it is not clear why the subjunctive should be used here. Mitchell, *A Guide to Old English* 174.4, p. 92, notes that clauses of time introduced by *þonne* take the indicative.

1.7: *hlyn*: The MS. reading is *hlin* with a small *y* written above the *i*, probably as a correction (cp. the superscript *a* in line 42). Previous editors retain the reading *hlin* and Grein, Tupper, and Krapp and Dobbie note that the superscript *y* is written in a hand different from that of the main scribe. Mackie says that the *y* is "perhaps by another hand." It should be noted that size in itself is not a good criterion for proving a difference of hand. It is difficult to tell with small letters, but the superscript *y* here (see plate 1.a) is quite similar to the textual *y* in shape (see plate 1.b) and appears thus to have been made by the scribe. The *y* is probably a correction since the proper form here is *hlyn*, "noise," not *hlin*, "maple" (cp. *Rid*. 53.9).

1.8b ff.: Cp. *Rid*. 77.7 where the wind is called in riddlic fashion the creature *se þe wudu hrereð*. The motif is a common one. Cp. Aldhelm's Riddle 2, "Ventus," line 1: "Viribus horrisonis valeo confringere quercus" (ed. Pitman, p. 4).

1.10: *holme gehrefed*: "Roofed with water, I am sent. . . . " Cosijn (*Beiträge* xxiii, 128) would emend *holme* to *helme*, but the emendation makes less sense in the context.

1.10: *heahum*: All editors emend MS. *heanū* to *heahum* and for a similar mistake cp. line 99 of this riddle. Erhardt-Siebold (*PMLA* lxiv, 885) retains *heanum meahtum*, "[sent] by lowly agents." Strictly speaking, this is possible in terms of Isidore's statements about the *spiritus incentores* (*NR*. xxxvi.iii.19) noted above in the headnote, but *heahum* seems more appropriate to the immediate context of the line (*ofer hrofum, on eorþan*, etc.). Though the wrath of the divine Power in this riddle seems almost demonic, this probably has more to do with older Anglo-Saxon notions of *wyrd* than with any clear-cut theological conception of "lower agents."

1.11: *wrecen*: The emendation of MS. *wrecan* to *wrecen*, parallel to *sended*, was proposed by Cosijn (*Beiträge* xxiii, 128) and is accepted by Trautmann and Krapp and Dobbie. All other editors and B-T. (p. 1272) take MS. *wrecan* as an infinitive. Mackie translates *wrecan . . . sended*, "sent to wreak destruction," but in all other uses of *wrecan* meaning "to wreak," there is an object, either *torn* or *yrre* (see B-T., *wrecan*, category II). B-T. translates the phrase as "sent driving" with a question mark. Tupper takes *wrecan* as genitive singular of *wrecca* after a suggestion by Grein (*SP.*, p. 824, under *wræcca*).

1.12 ff.: This riddle-within-a-riddle has been the source of some fancy editorial solving. Grein first read *sande*, "sand," for MS. *sunde*, "sea, water," and this was the basis of Dietrich's (*ZfdA*. xi, 460) notion that *þæt ær hadas wreah / foldbuendra* (12*b*–13*a*) referred to the first clothing of men—i.e., leaves. Assmann and Tupper retain Grein's emendation essentially, reading *sonde* for MS. *sunde*. Tupper offers no comment on the reading in his notes. Trautmann took Dietrich to task for his "leaves of Paradise," but Trautmann's own reading of the *sunde* as "das Wasser welches die Menschen beim Baden umfloss, ehe es als Dunst aufstieg und von der Luft getragen ward" (p. 66) is equally unenlightened. Erhardt-Siebold's belief that the covering waters here refer to "the Biblical great flood, in which the clouds outpoured all the water now carried again by the air" (*PMLA* lxiv, 886) is more likely, though technically, of course, the flood waters did not cover all the *foldbuendra* since some were riding in Noah's boat.

1.15–16: For a discussion of whether a new riddle begins at line 16 or not, the reader is referred to the headnote. Other examples of the scribe's possibly mistaking one riddle for two are *Rids.* 67, 73, and 76 as printed in this edition. Another example of the scribe's placing an end-punctuation mark in the text before the proper end of the riddle occurs at *Rid.* 25.15.

1.19: There is no gap in the MS. here but the meter indicates that at least a half-line is missing. Grein and Trautmann read *fam gewealcen* in the *b*-line, supplying *flod afysed* in the *a*-line. Other editors read *fam gewealcen* in either the *a*- or *b*-line with an ellipsis in the other half-line. Cosijn (*Beiträge* xxiii, 128) would read *famge wealcen*, "foamy waves."

1.20: For the use of rhymes elsewhere in *Riddles*, cp. *Rids.* 9.6–7, 13.13, 26.4ff., 32.9, 36.4, 64.6, and 71.22.

1.21b–23a: Normally *weorpan* takes an accusative object, but occasionally it takes the dative (see B-T., p. 1198, under *weorpan*, category I.2).

1.32–33a: Reading *salwonges* for MS. *salwonge*, I translate, " . . . then sends me under the broad bosom of the plain." The reading was first proposed by Wyatt. The half-line at 33*a*, *bearm bradan*, is unusual, but for another apparently authentic trisyllabic verse, cp. *Rid*. 19.4*a*, and see also the discussion of metrically unusual verses in the *Riddles* in the Introduction. Most other editors retain MS. *salwonge* (dat.) and read *bearm* (acc.) as a parallel object, but Krapp and Dobbie note that this involves an unlikely parallelism between dative and accusative. Those taking *bearm* thus as a parallel object are Grein and Assmann (who retain the MS. *bearm bradan* in 33*a*), Holthausen (*Anglia* xiii, 358) and Tupper (who read *bearm* [*þone*] *bradan*), and Herzfeld and Trautmann (who read *bearm* [*on*] *bradan*). Krapp and Dobbie read *salwonges* in 32*b* after Wyatt, but emend 33*a* to *bearm þone bradan* after Holthausen; this insertion of *þone* makes the meter of 33*a* more regular, but it seems idiomatically doubtful in this context. Mackie emends *bearm* to *bearme* after a suggestion by Kock (*Lunds Universitets Årsskrift*, NF., Avd. 1, Bd. 14, Nr. 26, p. 60), but *under* should govern the accusative not the dative when motion is implied.

1.35: *hæste*: Grein, Assmann, and Wyatt retain MS. *hætst* from a verb *hætsan* that Grein defines as "impingere?" (*Sp.*, p. 294) and Wyatt defines as "to drive, throw" (p. 68). The word is not elsewhere recorded and is of doubtful legitimacy. It is not included by Holthausen in the *Wörterbuch*. Even if there were such a verb, we should expect the form *hætseð* here as contracted forms are quite rare in poetry. Cosijn (*Beiträge* xxiii, 128) proposed reading *hæste*, "with violence," and so Tupper, Mackie, Krapp and Dobbie, and myself. Trautmann reads *hæfteð*.

1.35: *heord*: a variant spelling for *heard*, probably an early form: see Campbell 276, p. 117, for an explanation of the form. Most editors retain the MS. reading. Tupper follows Cosijn (*Beiträge* xxiii, 128) in reading *heard*. Wyatt reads *hearde* as an adverb.

1.35: *siteð*: Krapp and Dobbie in a paleographical note say this is "*sited* with *d* altered from *ð*" (p. 181). Other editors read *siteð* without comment. The crossbar on the *ð* is faint and the characteristic pointed tail at the end of the crossbar stroke is lacking, but the body of the letter clearly has the angular ascender of *ð* not *d*. What appears to have happened here is this : the scribe began to make the letter ð, but as he was making the cross bar the point of his pen ran dry and he neglected to return to the word to put the finishing touches on the crossbar tail. Still, there is no doubt that the letter is ð not *d*.

1.36: *hwyrftweges*: Thorpe and Trautmann read *hwyrft weges*, as does B-T., p. 578. All other editors read the compound as I have it—apparently taking the construction as a partitive (Klaeber, *MLN* xxxi, 428, cites a comparable example at *Beo.* 681). Cp. also the partitive construction at *Rid.* 38.65 and see note to that line.

1.38: *hrere*: The MS. *hrera* may be legitimate as a rare Northumbrian form. Campbell 752, p. 324, notes that the variant Northumbrian forms for the first person singular present indicative are -*o* and (less often) -*a*, -*u*, and -*e*. Mackie retains the MS. reading. The rarity of the form and the presence of the regular reading *hrere* at line 7b of this same riddle make the reading *hrera* doubtful here. Krapp and Dobbie normalize the reading as I do. All other editors emend MS. *hrera* to *hreru*, which they take as a variant form of *hrere*. Wyatt notes that *hreru* is a Northumbrian form, but there seems little reason to emend from one rare variant -*a* to another -*u*. Campbell (ibid.) notes that the -*u* ending is a more common variant in the *Vespasian Psalter*, and that would make the reading *hreru* here a Mercian form. Either leaving the MS. *hrera* as a rare Northumbrian form or normalizing to *hrere*, as I have done, seems preferable to reading *hreru*.

1.42: *up aþringe*: Here, as Grein, Tupper, and Krapp and Dobbie note, the small superior *a* inserted between MS. *up* and *þringe* may well be in a different hand (see plate ii.a), though it is difficult to know what constraints the smallness of the letter may have placed upon the scribe. In the direction of its strokes, the superscript *a* appears to be similar to textual *a* (see plate ii.b).

1.43–44: *se mec wræde on . . . legde*: "who first laid bonds upon me." For the construction, cp. *Rid.* 18.29–30 and *Deor* 5. Grein and Assmann read *wræðe* in their text with the same meaning (*Sp.*, p. 825), but the primary spelling in Old English is *wræd* (see B-T., p. 1270; *AEW.*, p. 406).

1.48: The addition of *streamas* to complete the line was suggested by Thorpe (cp. line 100) and is accepted by all editors.

1.54b–55a: "There is the loud ship, the cry of sailors." This is the traditional interpretation. Conceivably the *hlud wudu* could refer to the wind blowing through the shoreline forests and the *brimgiesta breahtm* to the sound of waves, but the use of *gæsta* at 60*b* makes the traditional interpretation more likely.

1.61: *rice*: Klaeber (*MP* ii, 144) would read *rince* in a collective sense and so Trautmann in his text. But the MS. *rice birofen* may be taken as meaning "robbed of [its] power" referring to the ship (see Kock, *Lunds Universitets Årsskrift*, NF., Avd.1, Bd. 14, Nr. 26, p. 60).

1.62: *feore bifohten*: "deprived of life" (B-T., p. 99). Klaeber (*MP* ii, 144) would emend to *fere bifohten*, "attacked by danger," but it is not necessary to emend the MS. when it makes good sense.

1.64: The line as it stands in the MS., *ældum geywed þara þe ic hyran sceal*, is retained by Assmann, Wyatt, and Krapp and Dobbie, though *hyran* does not make much sense in this context and the line lacks alliteration. Tupper reads *hæleðum* for MS. *ældum* after a suggestion by Ettmüller, and this solves the problem of the alliteration but not the problem of meaning. Grein suggested reading *yppan*, "reveal," for MS. *hyran* and so Trautmann. This is a reasonable possibility if the MS. *þara þe* is a partitive genitive referring back to *egsa*. But *þara þe* may be an error for *þar þar* (for my argument that the same error has occurred at *Rid*. 26.9, see note to *Rid*. 26.7*b* ff.), and if we read *yrnan* for MS. *hyran* after a suggestion by Barnouw (*Neoph*. iii, 77), this at least makes excellent sense of the line.

1.66: Because of the alliteration, Grein in a note suggested *rideð on bæce* for MS. *on bæce rideð*, and so Tupper and Wyatt. But for alliteration on the final stress, which appears to be a not uncommon exception to the rule, cp. *Rids*. 2.8, 53.14, 57.12, 71.2, and 87.6.

1.71: *sceo*: Cosijn (*Beiträge* xxiii, 128) would read *sceor* (=*scur*) for this hapax legomenon and so Tupper. Other editors retain MS. *sceo*, "cloud," citing O.N. *ský* and O.S. *skio*. For the possible etymology, see Holthausen, *AEW*., p. 279, under *scio*.

1.72: *Earpan*: Mead (*PMLA* xiv, 189) notes that *eorp* (*earp*), "dark, dusky," occurs elsewhere at *Rid.* 47.11 (where it describes a bookcase or possibly a clay bake-oven) and at *Ex.* 194 (where it refers to a troop of Egyptians).

1.75: *dreorgum*: The emendation of *dreorgum* for MS. *dreontum* was first proposed by Holthausen (*ESn.* xxxvii, 206); it is easily justified on paleographical grounds (MS. *nt* as a misreading of *rg*) and makes for a meaningful variation on the *folcum* of line 73*a*. Thorpe, Tupper, and Mackie read *dreohtum* for MS. *dreontum*, taking *dreohtum* as a form of *dryht*; but as there is no phonological evidence for such a variant, it would be better in terms of the supposed reading here to emend the MS. reading to *dryhtum* as do Wyatt, Trautmann, and Krapp and Dobbie, and to explain the error by assuming that the scribe miscopied *y* as *eo* (possibly under the influence of *deorc*) and *h* as *n*. But all things considered, Holthausen's emendation is easier to justify paleographically and makes better sense of the line.

1.77: *sumsendu*: This hapax legomenon is taken by most editors to mean "humming, buzzing" (B-T., p. 934; *AEW.*, p. 329), related to M.H.G. *summen* and modern German *sumsen, summen*. Bosworth-Toller (p. 934) and Grein (*Sp.*, p. 646) raise the possibility of reading *suinsendu* or *suinsende* as a participle from *swinsian*, "to make music." Normally O.E. *swinsian* is used to refer to pleasing, melodious sounds (B-T., p. 958), but under *swinsung*, B-T. lists two instances of unpleasant sounds (p. 959, category II).

1.85: *on geryhtu*: Holthausen (*Anglia* xxxviii, 77) and Trautmann would supply *forð* after *geryhtu* for the meter (cp. *Jud.* 202), but the line makes sense without the addition and in light of several other deficient verses in the *Riddles* (see Introduction), it seems wiser here not to emend. Krapp and Dobbie note a similarly short verse at *Chr.* 423*a*.

1.87: *farende flan*: Tupper emends *farende* to *fērende* because the verse as it stands seems metrically short. But Sievers (*Beiträge* x, 480) notes that *flān* may originally have been disyllabic *flā-an* and so Trautmann reads *flaan*. It is not necessary to change the spelling here if one bears in mind that there are a number of instances in the *Riddles* where hidden disyllabic pronunciations could regularize the meter. These are listed in the Introduction.

1.92: *burnan*: Grein first suggested reading *burnan* (from *burne*, "stream") for the MS. *byrnan* (from *byrne*, "corselet"). Other editors retain the MS. spelling as a variant form of *byrne*, but this is difficult to justify phonologically. It seems more likely that the scribe has here confused the more common *byrne* with the less common *burne*.

1.95: *on*: Supplied by Grein and accepted by all editors.

1.96: *meahtum gemagnad*: "strengthened by the powers." The emendation of MS. *ge manad* to *gemagnad* was suggested by Trautmann and is accepted by Krapp and Dobbie. For the meaning of *gemagnad*, see the citation from Bede under *gemægened* in B-T., p. 412. Other editors retain the MS. *gemanad* from *gemanian*, "to urge, bear in mind, demand, instruct" (BTS., p. 368), but none of the possible meanings listed by Toller makes much sense here.

1.102: *swiþfeorm*: In Old English the word may mean: (1) abounding in substance, fruitful; (2) violent (see citations at B-T., p. 960). In the glosses, L. *crudescentes* is glossed by O.E. *þæt þa swiðfeormende* (WW. 523.19). Given the range of meanings in both the Old English and the Latin, it seems not unlikely that *swiþfeorm* means here not only "violent" but "swelling." For a similar instance of the Anglo-Saxons' tendency to view anger or violence as a swelling of the spirit, cp. the meanings of *belgan, abelgan, bolgenmod*, etc.

2. Uncertain

[*VN: Gr.5; Tr.2; Tu.5; W.4; M.4; K-D.4*]

This riddle is in many respects the most puzzling riddle in the *Exeter Book*. With its plenitude of rings (some or all of which may be the same), its horde of ambiguous words (*þragbysig, slæpwerigne, lim*), and its occasional anomalies (transitive use of *berstan* at 8*b*, disyllabic verse at 7*b*, anacrusis before type E verse at 8*a*), it has perplexed and will probably continue to perplex the proudest of solvers. The two most likely solutions to the riddle, "bell" and "millstone," were put forth by Dietrich who explained:

Nicht so klar ist nr [2]; der sprechende, der sein bett brechen muss, hat, ringgeheftet, das schicksal seinem diener gehorchen zu müssen, und antwortet, wenn er schlafmüde am morgen durch gruss aufgeregt wird, mit schall und gegenrede. da er dies winterkalt thut, so ist metall oder stein vorausgesetzt als stoff. ich habe früher an die glocke gedacht, welche die form in der sie liegt bricht, und wenn sie gegrüsst, d.h. in bewegung gesetzt wird, dem klöpfel, ihrem diener, gehorchen muss: sie kann springen, so erklärte sich der zusatz 'ein warmes glied (die bewegende menschenhand) berstet zuweilen den gebundenen ring;' bei Symposius sagt das *tintinabulum* [no. 81, Ohl ed.] *patulo componor in orbe.* aber alle aussagen passen auch auf den oberen der beiden *mühlsteine*, zu dem sich der untere als diener verhält, und der sein bett worauf er liegt, das getreide, brechen soll; auch ertönte wohl gerade am frühen morgen am meisten die handmühle, von knecht oder magd in bewegung gesetzt, mit einem zum wohl (*on spêd*) dienenden geräusch. so tritt angemessner das brechen des bettes in die reihe der thätigkeiten des sprechenden und wird das gleich in den anfang gesetzte prädicat *laufgeschäftig* (*þragbysig*) sinnvoller. ähnlich, aber deutlicher, behandelt Aldelmus die beiden mühlsteine [no. 66, ed. Pitman], er nennt sie schwestern die allen die nahrung erarbeiten und gleiche arbeit aber ungleiches loss haben: *altera nam currit, quod numquam alter gessit.* [*ZfdA*. xi, 461]

Most editors accept one of these two solutions. Holthausen (*ESn*. li, 185) first solved the riddle as "lock," but later (*Anglia* xliv, 346) accepted *Handmühle*. Erhardt-Siebold (*PMLA* lxi, 620 ff.) accepts *handmill* and argues that the "ring" is the journal-box or socket in which a pivot (the "warm limb") turns. Tupper accepts the solution, "bell," arguing that the "ring" is the band with which the clapper is tied to the bell and that the "warm limb" is either the bell-ringer's hand or the clapper itself. Trautmann solved the riddle as "flail," though this is less satisfactory in most respects than either "bell" or "millstone." Recently Shook ("Riddles Relating to the Anglo-Saxon Scriptorium," in *Essays in Honour of Anton Charles Pegis*, ed. J. Reginald O'Donnell, pp. 226 ff.) solved the riddle as "feðer" or "penna," taking the "ring" to be the reinforced nib wound about with thread and the breaking of the "ring" to be (somewhat illogically) the breaking of the nib (not the "ring-thread"). Shook's reading of *bed* at 3a as "prayer" is unlikely given the context and his reading of *hringan hæfted* at 2a as "make a noise when taken up" is syntactically impossible. Bradley's notion (*MLR* vi, 433 ff.) that the riddle concerns some necromancer's tale of a dead man called from the grave to wear the oracular collar sounds more like an outwitted riddle-solver's cry in the dark than a plausible solution. Wyatt, Mackie, and Krapp and Dobbie retain the stumped riddle-solver's humility and list the riddle as unsolved and so do I. Neither "bell" nor "millstone" fits, without forcing, all of the descriptive details of the riddle. Indeed the descriptive details themselves are often something of a puzzle (see notes below). Often the ambiguity at the literal level of the riddle (for example, does *slæpwerigne* at 5*a* mean "weary from too much sleep" or "weary from lack of sleep"?) precludes knowing for certain what the creature is metaphorically saying about its underlying actions or nature. Of course this is true to some extent with every riddle, but the number of ambiguities is great here and the number of hard clues small.

2.1: *þragbysig*: B-T. (p. 1065) glosses this as "occupied for a time (?), periodically employed (?)" and this is the reading of most editors (cp. *þragmælum*, "at times, from time to time"). Bright (see Tupper, p. 79, note) suggests the meaning "perpetually" and Clark Hall glosses the term as "long busy (?)." For the latter meaning, cp. *þraglic*, "lasting a long time" (BTS., p. 730). None of the objects that have so far been put forth as possible solutions is "perpetually busy" in the sense that it is in use all of the time. But on the literal level at least it seems likely that the creature which is *þragbysig* and whose perpetual task is to "break its bed" (3*a*) should be as a result *slæpwerigne* or "weary with lack of sleep" (but for another possible meaning of *slæpwerigne*, see below).

2.2: *hringan hæfted*: The MS. reading *hringan* is retained by Thorpe, Wyatt, and Mackie. The *-an* plural ending is probably a late West Saxon form (see Campbell 378, p. 157; and 572, p. 224). Other editors emend MS. *hringan* to *hringum*.

2.3: *min bed brecan*: *break my bed* (since the creature breaks its bed, presumably that is why it is *slæpwerigne*). There is little evidence to support Mackie's translation, "break into my bed," since *brecan* even when it means "to break into, force a way into" (BTS., p. 104, category I.[4]), carries with it the connotations of destruction. The bell may metaphorically "break its bed" of stillness or rest, but this is not very convincing. The millstone more conceivably "breaks its bed" of grain. Neither breaks its bed continuously, if that is the implication of *þragbysig* in 1*a*.

2.3: *breahtme*: probably "with a clamor, noisily," though the spelling *breahtm* is also recorded in several instances for *bearhtm* (BTS., p. 65) so the word could mean "in a flash, instantly."

2.4: *halswriþan*: probably "neck-ring," or "necklace" (cp. *healsbeah* at *Beo.* 2172) though a plural "neck-rings" is also possible. Short of knowing the solution it is impossible to know exactly what the hapax legomenon means.

2.5: *slæpwerigne*: There are two possible meanings for the hapax legomenon, both listed by B-T. (p. 881): (1) "weary for sleep," which would refer to the evening hours; (2) "weary with sleep," which would refer to the early morning hours. B-T. compares *deaþwerig* for the first possibility and *symbelwerig* for the second. If *þragbysig* in 1*a* means "perpetually busy," the creature is presumably "weary for sleep" since it is always working at breaking its bed (3*a*). Holthausen (*Anglia Beibl.* xlvi, 8) would emend *slæpwerigne* to the nominative *slæp-werig* (the adjective thus modifying the *secg oþðe meowle* in 5*b*) because the final drop in 5*a* has one too many syllables for a normal type C verse. But for another verse like the one in question here, cp. *Seaf.* 85*a* and see Pope's discussion of unclassifiable verse types on p. 128 of his *Seven Old English Poems*.

2.7b–8: I retain the MS. reading here with Krapp and Dobbie even though there are a number of unusual metrical and grammatical features in the passage. If we take *bersteð* in a transitive sense as do most editors (elsewhere in O.E. *berstan* is intransitive but Tupper notes that the transitive meaning, common in Middle English, seems required here; and so *Sp.*, p. 50: *"berstan: facere ut quid fragorem edat? frangere?"*), we may translate lines 7*b*–8: "A warm limb sometimes breaks the bound ring." O.E. *lim*, like modern "limb" may refer to "a limb, joint, member of a body, [or] branch of a tree" (B-T., p. 641). Tupper takes the limb here to be the bell-ringer's hand or the clapper of the bell; Erhardt-Siebold takes the limb to be the pivot about which the millstone turns (*PMLA* lxi, 620 ff.). The half-line at 7*b*, *Wearm lim*, is retained by Grein, Assmann, Wyatt, and Krapp and Dobbie, even though it is metrically most unusual. There are a number of possibly trisyllabic verses in *Beowulf* (see Pope, *The Rhythm of Beowulf*, pp. 318–20, 371–72, and the corresponding remarks in his Preface of 1966) and two such verses in the *Riddles* (*Rids*. 1.33*a*, 19.4*a*), and I believe that the disyllabic line here though unusual is probably authentic, especially in light of the poet's "breaking" of metrical rules elsewhere in the poem (5*a*, 8*a*, 8*b*). In two other cases (*Rids*. 36 and 63) the riddler or riddlers have taken similar liberties with the meter in constructing their verses. Mackie indicates a possible ellipsis after *lim*. Tupper reads 7*b* as þæt *wearme lim*; Holthausen as *wearm limwædum* (*Indogermanische Forschungen* iv, 386), *wearmlim guma* (*Anglia* xxxviii, 77), or *wearm limgearwum* (*Anglia Beibl*. xxx, 51). Trautmann reads *wearm lim swenge* with *bundenne bæg* in line 8*a*. The normal reading of *gebundenne* at 8*a* as it is in the MS. makes for a metrically unusual verse (type E with anacrusis or type B with abnormally heavy medial drop), though the verse seems acceptable with its slight irregularity. Line 8*b* has alliteration on the final stress so all editors except Trautmann, Mackie, and Krapp and Dobbie read *bersteð hwilum*. But for similar examples of final alliteration, cp. *Rids*. 53.14, 57.12, 71.2, and 87.6.

2.8: *bæg*: for *beag*. All editors normalize the spelling except Trautmann, Mackie, and Krapp and Dobbie. B-T. (p. 66) lists *bæg*, "collar," as a separate word, but both Grein and Clark Hall take it as a variant spelling of *beag*. For the general process of smoothing from *ēa* to *ǣ*, see Campbell 225, p. 95.

2.9–10: "which (preceding action) is, however, pleasing to my servant, a foolish man, and also to myself," or "which . . . pleases my servant . . . and likewise myself." Tupper notes that the "accusative of specification (þæt *sylfe*) is equivalent to the adverb 'likewise'" (p. 80) and cites similar examples at *Chr*. 937 and *PPs*. 81.3 and 128.1.

2.11: þær: *if*. For the occasional use of þær meaning "if" to introduce a conditional clause, see Mitchell, *A Guide to Old English* 179, p. 96.

3. Shield
[*VN: Gr.6; Tr.3; Tu.6; W.5; M.5; K-D.5*]

L.C. Müller (*Collectanea Anglo-Saxonica*, pp. 63–64) first proposed the solution, "shield," and this has been accepted by all later editors. Dietrich (*ZfdA*. xi, 461) pointed out the possible influence of Aldhelm's Riddle 87, "Clipeus" (ed. Pitman, p. 52), but the resemblance between the Latin and the Old English riddle is slight. The Latin creature describes itself as being made of willow wood and oxhide, as enduring terrible blows to protect its bearer, and as withstanding blows so fierce as to imply its super- (or non-) human nature. The Old English creature is described as a warrior torn by continual strife who must await death without the benefit of a physician's charms.

Metal portions of shields are a fairly common find in Anglo-Saxon graves. The Anglo-Saxon shield ranges in size from 30 cm. to 76 cm. in diameter (Wilson, *The Anglo-Saxons*, p. 115). The shield found at Sutton Hoo was ornate with a number of metal mounts and fittings "mostly in the form of, or decorated with, stylized animals and bird or animal heads" (Bruce-Mitford, *The Sutton Hoo Ship-Burial: A Handbook*, p. 24; see also plates 3, 4, 5, and 12); the shield of the riddle, however, makes no mention of treasure or ornate trappings, so it must have been one of the simpler, more common variety known to the ordinary foot soldier. For more information on Anglo-Saxon shields, see Wilson, *The Anglo-Saxons*, pp. 115 ff., and Keller, *The Anglo-Saxon Weapon Names*, pp. 67 ff. and 224 ff.

3.6: *mid ældum*: probably *among men*, as all editors would have it, though the reading *mid ǣldum, among* (or *by means of*) *flames*, is also possible. For the oblique form of *ǣled*, "fire," cp. genitive singular *ǣldes* at *Chr*. 959.

3.6: *forwurðe*: This is the first person present subjunctive form of *forwurðan* (*forweorðan*). The reading *forwurðe* for MS. *forwurde* was suggested as a possibility by Grein after an earlier suggestion by Ettmüller, but Grein adopted *forwurde* in his text. Holthausen (*Anglia* xliv, 346) and Krapp and Dobbie accept *forwurðe*; all other editors retain MS. *forwurde*, glossing it as a preterite subjunctive form. While it is true that *ǣr* as a conjunction introducing a clause of time normally prefers the subjunctive (Mitchell, *A Guide to Old English* 174, p. 92), the preterite subjunctive usually refers to the past or to the future-in-the-past (Mitchell, ibid. 198, p. 108), neither of which is the case here. When present tense verbs are used in the main clause and when the subjunctive refers to time future, one normally expects the present subjunctive form. For that reason I accept the emendation *forwurðe* as the present subjunctive form.

3.7: *homera lafe*: Cp. *Beo.* 2829 and *Brun.* 6 and the description of the sword at *Rid.* 69.3b–4a as *wraþra laf, | fyres ond feole*.

3.9: *a bidan*: This is the reading of Grein, Assmann, and Wyatt. Other editors read one word, *abidan*. Metrically, the word *a* need not carry the burden of the alliteration (cp. *Beo.* 455b). My own reading here is based on the irony that the word provides in terms of the basic riddlic game of hiding nonhuman creatures in human disguise. To solve the paradoxes of the riddle, one must separate the nonhuman solution from the human metaphor. Thus, while the shield, like man, may sustain wounds in battle, unlike man it may not be healed by the *læcecynn*. Still, despite the shield's particular vulnerability, it is able to sustain over a long period of time many more wounds without dying than man could ever sustain. Though it is wounded time and time again, it must ever await that *laþran gemotes*. Man's hardihood is not so great. Where the shield cannot be easily cured, it cannot also be easily killed. Its strength (wood) is also its weakness. That is the paradox of the riddle.

3.12: *þara þe . . . gehælde*: Mitchell notes that "when the relative pronoun *þara þe* means 'of those who', the verb of the adjective clause can be singular or plural" (*A Guide to Old English* 187.3(d), p. 104). Wyatt, p. 69, makes a similar point.

3.lower margin: At the end of this riddle in the intervening space between *Rids.* 3 and 4, the rune ᛋ (*sigel*) occurs. A comparison of this rune with the textual rune in *The Husband's Message* (line 49) on MS. folio 123b and with similar textual runes in the *Exeter Book* indicates that the marginal rune here was probably made by the main scribe (see plates iii.a and c). The rune is probably meant to indicate the solution of the preceding riddle, L. *scutum* or O.E. *scyld*, though Tupper and Wyatt believe that this rune and a similar S-rune which follows the next riddle both refer to *Rid*. 4. Trautmann believes that the runes refer to the riddles that follow them rather than to the preceding riddles. Krapp and Dobbie note that "it is more natural to suppose that the runes contain clues to the riddles which precede them (since the solution of a riddle is of no interest until the riddle itself has been read)" (p. 325), but of course this ignores the Latin tradition where titles (solutions) are given before the riddles. Since titles are not given to the Old English riddles as we have them, I would agree with Krapp and Dobbie, at least in those instances where, by comparison with the text, the marginal runes appear to have been made by the main scribe. It is difficult to say anything for certain about those rune-like marks (see, for example, the mark that precedes *Rid*. 8), which appear to have been made by a postscribal hand.

4. Sun
[*VN: Gr.7; Tr.4; Tu.7; W.6; M.6; K-D.6*]

The solution, "sun," is accepted by all editors. The sun is mentioned frequently in Old English poetry, but rarely with reference to its dual nature as benefactor and scourge of mankind. The sun is typically portrayed as a benevolent creature (see, for example, *Run*. 45 and *Ord*. 59–67). The tradition for the sun's dual nature as benefactor and scourge may derive from Isidore's *De Natura Rerum*. Isidore maintains that the sun is essentially fire, but that its fierce heat is tempered by the presence of water vapor:

> Nos autem credimus eum sicut habere virtutem inluminandi, ita etiam vaporandi. Igneus est enim sol. Ignis autem et inluminat et exurit. Quidam autem dicunt solis ignem aqua nutriri et ex contrario elemento virtutem luminis et vaporis accipere. Unde frequenter solem videmus madidum atque rorantem: in quo evidens dat indicium quod elementum aquarum ad temperiem sui sumpserit. [*NR*. xv.ii.11–17]

Isidore goes on to compare the role of the sun as benefactor and scourge with that of Christ:

Haec quantum ad naturam eius pertinet. At vero iuxta spiritalem intelle-
gentiam sol Christus est, sicut in Malachia scriptum est: vobis autem qui
creditis orietur sol iustitiae, et sanitas in pinnis eius. Merito autem Christus
sol intellegitur dictus, quia ortus occidit secundum carnem, et secundum
spiritum de occasu rursus exortus est. Item sol inluminat et exurit et opaco
tempore confovet sanos, febricitantes vero flagrantia geminati caloris incen-
dit. Ita et Christus credentes fidei spiritu vegetante inluminat, negantes se
aeterni ignis ardore torrebit. [*NR*. xv.iii.18–26]

This passage is echoed by Aelfric in his *De Temporibus Anni* (i.33,
EETS, o.s. 213, p. 14) and by the Old English poet of *Christ* III. In the
latter poem, the Lord Christ is said to rise on the Day of Doom like
the morning sun:

> Þonne semninga   on Syne beorg
> suþaneastan   sunnan leoma
> cymeð of scyppende   scynan leohtor
> þonne hit men mægen   modum ahycgan,
> beorhte blican,   þonne bearn godes
> þurh heofona gehleodu   hider oðyweð.
> Cymeð wundorlic   Cristes onsyn,
> æþelcyninges wlite,   eastan fram roderum,
> on sefan swete   sinum folce,
> biter bealofullum,   gebleod wundrum,
> eadgum ond earmum   ungelice.

[*Chr*. 899–909]

Hill (*NM* lxx, 672 ff.) suggests that the notion of Christ's dual aspect
on the Day of Judgment has its roots in Gregory's *Moralia in Job*,
XXXII, vii (*PL*. lxxvi, 640–41) where Gregory explains that though the
Lord is immutable, he will appear as calm to the righteous and as
wrathful to the unrighteous: "Unde et in extremo judicio, in semetipso
incommutabilis manens, nulla vicissitudine ac mutabilitate variatur,
sed tamen electis ac reprobis nequaquam sub specie ejusdem incom-
mutabilitatis ostenditur, quia et tranquillus justis, et iratus apparebit
injustis" (*PL*. lxxvi, 640). Clearly the Old English riddler draws here
upon the tradition of the Christ-like sun, but with a new twist: in the
riddle the sun is a personified creature in its own right, a minion
warrior of the lord Christ, burning and nurturing at his overlord's
command. The sun travels *ofer deop gedreag* (line 10) to nourish and
blast like a warrior embued with the fire of judgment.

4.7: *hwilum ic frefre þa ic ær winne on*: Grein emends the *a*-line to *hwi-lum ic [wel] frefre*; Trautmann, to *willum ic frefre*, for reasons of allitera-tion. Tupper, however, points to other instances of *hw* alliterating with *w* at *Wulf* 12, *Rid*. 33.11, and *Chr*. 188 (Tupper's other two exam-ples, *Beo*. 2299 and *Guth*. 352 [K-D numbering], are open to question). The line may be translated, "Sometimes I comfort those whom previ-ously I make war on." Modern English, partly because of Latin influence, would use the perfect, "have made war on," but the pre-sent tense has the advantage of expressing continued action. O.E. *ær* is used with the preterite to translate the pluperfect in Latin (for *ær* as a sign of the pluperfect, see Mitchell, *A Guide to Old English* 168, p. 82), but its use is not rigid. Certainly if *ær* plus preterite corresponds to the Latin pluperfect, then *ær* plus present is the nearest thing to the Latin perfect. Perhaps the best modern English equivalent of the line would be: "Sometimes I comfort those whom I have previously been making war on," since this includes the idea of the continued action.

4.10: *ofer deop gedreag*: literally, *over the deep tumult*. In terms of the bat-tle imagery of the poem (*compe, winne, feohtan*), *gedreag* may refer to the tumult of war. As *deop* often refers adjectivally or substantivally to the sea (see citations in B-T., p. 201), Grein glosses *deop gedreag* as *maris* (*Sp.*, p. 124), and BTS. translates the phrase as *"over the deep tumult of the waves"* (p. 314). BTS. (p. 314) lists *gedræg, gedreag* as a noun meaning "what is drawn together, a concourse, an assembly," related to the verb, *dragan*, "to draw." But as a number of the citations of *gedreag* come from contexts that clearly imply suffering, it is not impossible that some of these occurrences might be related to *dreogan* in the sense of "to suffer" (see BTS., p. 156, *dreogan*, category III), and might mean "suffering." Taking *deop* then in a metaphorical sense (see a number of the examples at B-T., p. 201, and the general cate-gories "literal" and "metaphorical" marked out by BTS., p. 149), and *ofer* with the accusative as "after" (B-T., p. 730, category II.[14][a]), we might translate *ofer deop gedreag* as "after severe suffering." This passage through suffering to a state of comfort may be significant in terms of the medieval tradition of Christ as *sol justitiae* discussed in the headnote to the riddle.

4.lower margin: At the end of this riddle in the intervening space between *Rids.* 4 and 5, the rune ᛋ (*sigel*) occurs. A comparison of this rune with the textual *S* rune in *The Husband's Message* (line 49) on MS. folio 123*b* and with similar textual runes in the *Exeter Book* leaves some doubt as to whether this rune was made by the main scribe or not (see plates III.b and c). It is generally assumed that this rune and the rune between *Rids.* 3 and 4 (see note to *Rid.* 3.lower margin and plate III.a) were both made by the same hand, presumably that of the scribe. But the rune at *Rid.* 3.lower margin shows more similarities in the manner of its strokes to a typical textual *S* rune than does the rune here. I doubt seriously that both marginalic *S* runes were made by the same hand. Whoever made the rune here, it was probably intended by its position to indicate the solution of the preceding riddle, L. *sol* or O.E. *sigel*.

5. Swan
[*VN: Gr.8; Tr.5; Tu.8; W.7; M.7; K-D.7*]

Dietrich's solution, "swan" (*ZfdA.* xi, 462), is accepted by all editors. Dietrich pointed out the only other known references in classical or medieval lore to the song of the swan's feathers in the O.E. *Phoenix* and in the *Epistles* of Gregorius Nazianzenus, a fourth-century Bishop of Constantinople. In the O.E. *Phoenix* the firebird's sweet song is compared to the most delightful melodies known to man—among them the song of the swan's feathers:

> Biþ þæs hleoðres sweg
> eallum songcræftum   swetra ond wlitigra
> ond wynsumra   wrenca gehwylcum.
> Ne magon þam breahtme   byman ne hornas,
> ne hearpan hlyn,   ne hæleþa stefn
> ænges on eorþan,   ne organan,
> sweghleoþres geswin,   ne swanes feðre,
> ne ænig þara dreama   þe dryhten gescop
> gumum to gliwe   in þas geomran woruld.
>
> [*Ph.* 131–39]

The Latin *De Ave Phoenice* upon which the Old English poem is partly based notes only the death-song of the swan, *olor moriens* (line 49), a well-known classical motif, and makes no mention of the singing feathers. In a letter of Gregorius Nazianzenus to Celeusius, a story is told of a debate between swallows and swans over the relative merits of their respective songs. After the swallows chatter with bravado, the swans calmly speak:

'Αλλ' ἡμεῖς μὲν ἕνεκεν ὧν, ὦ αὗται, κἂν εἰς τὴν ἐρημίαν ἀφίκοιτό τις, ὥστε ἀκοῦσαι τῆς μουσικῆς, ὅταν ἀνῶμεν τῷ Ζεφύρῳ τὰς πτέρυγας, ἐμπνεῖν ἡδύ τι καὶ ἐναρμόνιον. [PG. xxxvii, 212]

[Whenever someone comes even into the wilderness for our sake to hear our music, O you (swallows), then, when we raise our wings to Zephyrus, he inhales something sweet and harmonious.]

It is possible that the writer of the Old English riddle knew of Gregory's letter either firsthand or in a Latin translation. The *Catholic Encyclopedia* reports that Gregory's letters were copied and disseminated during his lifetime (vi, p. 793), and Ogilvy notes that Aldhelm and Alcuin knew several of the letters at least from a translation by Rufinus that is now lost (*Bks.*, pp. 153–54). Of the Anglo-Saxons' knowledge of Greek itself, Ogilvy says: "In spite of Bede's testimony to the excellent Greek scholarship of Theodore and Hadrian and their immediate successors, we know almost nothing of the Greek texts available in England before the Conquest" (*Bks.*, p. 146). If the swan's singing feathers were merely a matter of a shared tradition, one would expect the lore to be repeated in Isidore or Ambrose. It is not. Still, the similarity does not in itself prove the use of a Greek source, even in translation. The Whooper or Whistling Swan (*Cygnus Musicus*) does give off a kind of whistling sound in flight. Evans says that "the flight is accompanied by a rushing sound, the note is trumpet-like or whistling" (*Birds*, p. 135). It is possible that Gregory and the Old English riddler were the only meticulous bird-watchers in medieval Christendom.

5.2: *buge*: a form of *buan, to inhabit, dwell*. The verb may be used either transitively or intransitively (B-T., p. 132).

5.2: *wado drefe*: *stir* or *ruffle the seas*. O.E. *drefan* is used with *lagu, wæd*, and *wæter* to indicate movement through the sea (cp. *Rid.* 20.16, *Hus.* 21, *Beo.* 1904).

5.4: *hyrste: trappings.* Tupper (p. 265) defines the word here and at *Rid.* 8.8 as "wings," but *hyrst* is used generally in the *Riddles* to refer to any outer covering (cp. *Rids.* 9.1, 12.11, 29.20, 51.7, and 84.12).

5.7: *swogað:* in this context best translated as "whistle." CH. gives a cacophony of possible sounds: *"to sound, roar, howl, rustle, whistle, rattle"* (p. 333).

5.9: *ferende gæst: a traveling guest* or *stranger* (*gæst, giest*), though in the context of the swan's eerie song, the reading *gæst* (*gāst*), "spirit," cannot be entirely ruled out. In terms of the latter possibility, *ferende gæst* could be a euphemism for the death of the swan. *Feran* is sometimes used to describe the last traveling over the death-road (cp. *Beo.* 27). In the classical tradition, swans were famous for their death-songs (see, for example, Pliny, *NH.* x.xxxii.63; and Cicero, *Tusculanae Disputationes* i.xxx.73). In the O.E. *Phoenix*, the poet's use of *swanes feðre* where the Latin poem has *olor moriens* could conceivably indicate a coalescence of the two traditions.

5.lower margin: For a note on the mark between riddles 5 and 6, mistakenly thought to be a runic C, see under 6.*upper margin* below.

6. Nightingale
[*VN: Gr.9; Tr.6; Tu.9; W.8; M.8; K-D.8*]

The creature of this riddle is clearly a songbird. Dietrich (*ZfdA.* xi, 462) solved the riddle as "pipe" or "nightingale," and later (*ZfdA.* xii, 239) as "wood-pigeon." Trautmann (*Anglia Beibl.* v, 48) solved the riddle as "bell," but accepted Dietrich's "nightingale" in his edition. Holthausen (*Anglia Beibl.* ix, 357) and Swaen (*SN* xiv, 67ff.) favor Trautmann's original "bell." Tupper, Klaeber (*Archiv* clxxxii, 107), and Krapp and Dobbie favor "jay"; Wyatt favors "nightingale"; Mackie (*MLR* xxviii, 76) favors "chough" or "jackdaw"; Young (*RES* xviii, 308ff.) favors "thrush." The bird's modulated song and its power as a poet would seem to indicate "nightingale" or "jay." Tupper notes in his edition:

Of these solutions, 'Nightingale' seems to me distinctly the best, for its varied note is heard in so much poetry of the late Latin period; for instance, in the *Philomela* elegies of the mythical Albus Ovidius Juventinus and Julius Speratus . . . and in the pretty *Luscinia* poem of Alcuin. Yet *Nihtegale* does not fit the rune, and is obviously the reverse of scurrilous; hence this answer, like the others, must be given up. [Tupper, p. 84]

Two things must be said. First, the mark preceding this riddle (see note below and plate IV.a) is certainly not a *C* rune. A comparison of the mark with the runic *C* and runic *U* of the Cynewulfian signature of *Christ* (see plates IV.c and d and note below) will show that the letter is closer to *Ur* than to *Cen*. The mark is, however, unlike any letter or rune in the *Exeter Book* and could hardly have been made by the main scribe. This casts considerable doubt upon those solutions based primarily upon the reading of the so-called *C* rune: wood-pigeon (O.E. *cuscote*), chough (O.E. *ceo*), pipe (L. *camena*), bell (O.E. *clugge*), and to some extent Tupper's "jay" (L. *cicuanus, catanus*). The songbirds must be judged as they fit the descriptive language of the riddle, not as the initial letters of their names correspond to the elusive "rune." Tupper's second reservation about the solution, "nightingale," is the so-called "scurrilous" quality of the bird and its song. This derives from the traditional association of *sceawendwisan* in line 9 (which B-T. defines as "a jesting song, song of a jester," p. 827) with *sceawendspræc*, which occurs once as a gloss to L. *scarilitas* (WW. 533.4). Given the absence, however, of any well-defined dramatic tradition in Anglo-Saxon England, we should be careful of assuming a one-to-one correspondence between the lemma and the gloss. Anderson points out that "Old English Glosses . . . show a general ignorance of the meaning of Latin theatrical terms" (*The Literature of the Anglo-Saxons*, p. 208). At best, *sceawendspræc* probably means literally *showing words* or *words that reveal a story*, and among birds it is the nightingale that is traditionally revered as the story-telling poet (see below).

I agree with Wyatt that the *eald æfensceop* (line 5) could be none other than the sweet-singing nightingale, O.E. *nihtegale*, "singer of the night." The bird is aptly named, for Newton and Gadow point out that the nightingale is "celebrated beyond all other [birds] by European writers for the admirable vocal powers which, during some weeks after its return from its winter-quarters in the south, it exercises at all hours of the day and night" (*A Dictionary of Birds*, pp. 635–

36). Pliny points out that nightingales sing day and night for two weeks in early spring and also notes the modulated sounds of the bird:

Luscinis diebus ac noctibus continuis garrulus sine intermissu cantus densante se frondium germine, non in novissimis digna miratu ave. primum tanta vox tam parvo in corpusculo, tam pertinax spiritus; deinde in una perfecta musicae scientia: modulatus editur sonus, et nunc continuo spiritu trahitur in longum, nunc variatur inflexo, nunc distinuitur conciso, copulatur intorto, promittitur revocato; infuscatur ex inopinato, interdum et secum ipse murmurat, plenus, gravis, acutus, creber, extentus, ubi visum est vibrans—summus, medius, imus; breviterque omnia tam parvulis in faucibus quae tot exquisitis tibiarum tormentis ars hominum excogitavit, ut non sit dubium hanc suavitatem praemonstratam efficaci auspicio cum in ore Stesichori* cecinit infantis. ac ne quis dubitet artis esse, plures singulis sunt cantus, nec iidem omnibus, sed sui cuique. [NH. x.xliii.81–82]

Each nightingale has a repertoire of songs and the singers compete with one another (NH. x.xliii.83). Nightingales are said to practice often and to imitate verses: *meditantur aliae iuveniores versusque quos imitentur accipiunt* (ibid.). Pliny notes elsewhere that magpies or jays often imitate particular words, but that starlings and nightingales have been known after thorough training to speak Greek and Latin sentences like true poets (NH. x.lix.118–20).

Elegies to the nightingale abound in medieval Latin literature. One of the finest is Alcuin's *De Luscinia* (PL. ci, 803). The poem exemplifies the tradition of the nightingale's night-songs, of its modulated tones and varied melodies, of its angelic and devotional praises of the Lord. It is the devotional qualities of the nightingale's song that perhaps prompts the riddler to describe its listeners as *nigende* (var. of *hnigende*) in line 8. Tupper emends the reading to *swigende*, asking, "Why listen with reverence (*hnigan* is always used with that implication) to the scurrilous chatter of a jay?" (p. 85). Why indeed? The chattering of jays would hardly quiet one's soul, while the nightingale's singing could lull one to sleep on the melodious wings of prayer.

6.upper margin: The mark (see plate iv.a) that occurs between *Rids*. 5 and 6 is thought by most editors to be a runic C. This is taken to indi-

---

*Rackham notes that Stesichorus was a "famous Sicilian Greek poet, 632–552 B.C., on whose lips in infancy a nightingale perched and sang" (Loeb edition, p. 344, note).

cate the initial letter of the solution to the foregoing riddle (*cygnus*) or to this riddle (see solutions in headnote). A comparison of the mark with runic *C* and runic *U* of the Cynewulfian signature of *Christ* (see plates IV.c and d) will show that the mark resembles *Ur* more than *Cen*. The mark is unlike any letter or rune, textual or marginalic, in the *Exeter Book* and was certainly not made by the main scribe. If the letter is meant to be a rune, it is probably runic *U* to indicate O.E. *ule* or L. *ulula*, "owl," someone's conjectured solution on the basis of the description of the creature as *eald æfensceop* in line 5. Owls and nightingales are frequently found listed together as nightbirds in the Latin encyclopedic literature. Ambrose, for example, says: "Habet etiam nox carmina sua, quibus vigilias hominum mulcere consuevit; habet et noctua suos cantus. Quid autem de luscinia dicam . . . " (*Hex.* v.xxiv.85; *PL.* xiv, 254). Förster (*The Exeter Book of Old English Poetry*, p. 64, note 29) believes the mark to be "a modern imitation of the old *n* in *ne beom*" directly above in the line of the text (see plate IV.b). The mark may be "modern" but it was made before 1831 since it appears in the manuscript transcription made by Robert Chambers on that date (*Brit. Mus. Add. MS. 9067*). The mark is long and thin and resembles very little the *n* in this or any other medieval text that I have seen. I believe the mark to have been made by a postmedieval peruser of the text who thought himself to be making a "rune-like" letter indicating the solution of the following riddle, "nightingale." The reader was perhaps acquainted with the Latin tradition of entitling riddles with their solutions at their onset.

6.2: *wrencum singe: sing with modulated tones.* For citations of *wrenc* as a modulation of the voice, see B-T., p. 1274, under *wrenc*, heading II. For a vivid description of the nightingale's modulated tones, see the quotation from Pliny in the headnote.

6.3: *heafodwoþe:* The meaning of the hapax legomenon remains a mystery. B-T. and CH. gloss the word as "voice," ignoring the initial element *heafod-*. Grein glosses as *vox capitis* (*Sp.*, p. 308), but it remains unclear whether he intends merely a literal rendering of the terms of the compound or modern English *headvoice*, "the vocal tones of the head register" (*Webster's Third New International Dictionary*, p. 1043). Since the bird is called *eald æfensceop* (line 5), it is tempting to see the creature here as a minstrel poet singing beautiful falsetto songs. The *OED* defines *headvoice* as "one of the higher registers of the voice in singing or speaking, applied both to the second register (that immediately above *chest-voice*), and to the third register or falsetto" (*OED* v, p. 151). Unfortunately the *OED* cites the first documented use of *headvoice* in a book by Dickens in 1849. Still, it is not impossible that another poet in another culture, observing the resonance patterns of falsetto notes, chose to coin the term *heafodwoþ* for *high tones* and to use that word to aptly describe the songs of a nightingale in minstrel disguise.

6.5: *Eald æfensceop*: *old night-singer*. Swaen (*SN* xiv, 63) doubts the appropriateness of calling the nightingale or any other bird *eald* and Klaeber says, "Aber warum 'alt'? Da kann man nur raten" (*Archiv* clxxxii, 108). The etymological significance of *nihtegale* as *æfensceop* should be clear. Pliny points out the bird's predilection for singing both day and night during the early days of spring (*NH.* x.xliii.81), and Ambrose says: "Quid autem de luscinia dicam, quae pervigil custos cum ova quodam sinu corporis et gremio fovet, insomnem longae noctis laborem cantilenae suavitate solatur" (*Hex.* v.xxiv.85; *PL.* xiv, 254). The adjective *eald* does not mean *old in years* so much as *old in time, familiar*. The *OED* lists several such uses of the word in Old English under its heading II: "Belonging to former times or an earlier period as well as to the present; long established" (*OED* vii, p. 97). As the nightingale is famous for its singing in early spring, it may have been like the cuckoo an "old" or traditional harbinger, a bird of welcome (see lines 10*b*–11).

6.8: *sittað*: This is the reading of Grein and all later editors except Trautmann. The understood subject, *they*, refers back to the *eorlum* of line 5. Trautmann reads *sitte*, "I sit," but he also reads *swigende* for MS. *nigende*. It is not clear how the singing bird should sit silently.

6.8: *nigende*: Grein read *hnigende* for MS. *nigende* as "gesenkten Hauptes(?)." This is accepted by Wyatt and Mackie. Ettmüller read *swigende* and Cosijn (*Beiträge* xxiii, 128), *suigende*. *Swigende* is accepted by Tupper and Trautmann. Tupper rightly questions the propriety of men's listening reverently to the song of the *jay*, but Alcuin's comments on the nightingale (see headnote) make it clear that the *æfen-*

sceop was considered an inspirational bird. Krapp and Dobbie retain MS. *nigende* as a variant of *hnigende* and so do I.

6.9: The meaning of this line has been much debated. Taking *scirenige* with Cosijn (see below) as some form of *scericge* (*Sp.*, p. 577: *Spass-macherin; von der Stimme*) and *sceawendwise* as "showing songs" (*Sp.*, p. 573: *cantus scenicus*), I translate lines 9–10*a*, "who like a minstrel (actress?) loudly imitates dramatic (narrative?) songs." For the problem of translating Old English "dramatic" terms, see the headnote. Thorpe and Grein read MS. *sci renige* as *scire nige* with some doubt, associating *nige* with *nigende* in the previous line. While it is clear from Alcuin's *De Luscinia* and other medieval Latin poems on the nightingale why men might "bow" before the melodious and prayerful song of the bird, it is not clear why the bird should also bow. Wyatt reads *scire cige*, "brightly call," after a suggestion by Bosworth-Toller (p. 837 under *scire*). Cosijn (*Beiträge* xxiii, 128) emended *scirenige* to *sciernicge*, citing *scericge*, "actress" at *Shrine* 140.11: *Sea Pilagia wæs æryst mima in Antiochia ðære ceastre, ðæt is scericge on urum geþeode* (cited in B-T., p. 830), and so Trautmann. For -*icge* as a feminine ending, see *Anglia* vi, 178. Sievers (*Anglia* vii, 222) took *scericge* as a form of earlier *sciernicge*. The word, whatever its proper form, is presumably related to O.H.G. and O.S. *scern* (*AEW.*, p. 278). Tupper, Mackie, Krapp and Dobbie, and I retain the MS. spelling but read the word after Cosijn as "actress, female jester." Cassidy and Ringler (Bright's *Old English Grammar and Reader*, 3d ed., p. 464) take *scirenige* for *scīren-īge*, "bright-eyed," without explanation. The spelling *ige* for *eage*, *ege*, "eye," is only recorded once elsewhere in O.E. (WW. 379.22: *Cyclopes: anige þyrsas*), and one might expect the initial element *scir-* instead of *sciren-* (cp. *scirecg*, *scirham*, *scirmæled*). The significance of the hypothetical "bright-eyed" bird is not explained.

6.11: *wilcumena fela*: The reference here may be to the nightingale as a harbinger of spring. Pliny notes that the nightingale sings day and night for two weeks when the leaf-buds are swelling (*NH.* x.xliii.81).

7. Cuckoo
[*VN: Gr.10; Tr.7; Tu.10; W.9; M.9; K-D.9*]

Dietrich's solution, "cuckoo" (*ZfdA*. xi, 463), is accepted by all editors. The parasitic nesting habits of the cuckoo are well known. Evans says that "the eggs are invariably deposited in the nests of other birds, which rear the intruder and feed it until it leaves the country" (*Birds*, p. 353). Pliny reports something of the same chicanery in his *Natural History*: " . . . parit in alienis nidis, maxime palumbium, maiore ex parte singula ova, quod nulla alia avis, raro bina" (*NH*. x.xi.26). The mother cuckoo succeeds in placing her egg in the nest of the foster mother because of the cuckoo's evolved adaptation of egg mimicry (Thomson, *A New Dictionary of Birds*, p. 595). The children of the foster mother suffer as a result of the newcomer to the nest. Pliny notes that the cuckoo, greedy by nature, snatches bits of food from the other chicks and so becomes fat and beautiful—so much so that the mother delights in the cuckoo and neglects the rest of her own children (*NH*. x.xi.27). Modern observation of the cuckoo has shown that the newly hatched bird has even the ability to evict its foster brothers and sisters from the nest (Evans, *Birds*, p. 354). Thus the foster mother has fewer of her own dear ones (lines 10–11) for taking in the cuckoo. The Old English "cuckoo" riddle owes nothing to the "Cuculus" riddle of pseudo-Symphosius, quoted by Wyatt (on the question of the Latin riddle's legitimacy, see Ohl, *The Enigmas of Symphosius*, p. 135).

7.1: *Mec on þissum dagum*: Holthausen (*ESn*. xxxvii, 206) would read *on dagum þissum* or *on þissum dogrum* for reasons of alliteration, but Sievers (*Beiträge* x, 454) considers the MS. reading to be an A-type line and Krapp and Dobbie note the existence of several similar lines in the *Riddles*.

7.3: *an*: The addition of *an* was first proposed by Grein (*Germania* x, 428) and is accepted by all major editors. For the use of *an* as an indefinite article separated from its noun, see Rissanen, *The Uses of "One" in Old and Early Middle English*, pp. 210–11.

7.4: *welhold mege*: Grein and Wyatt read *wel hold me* with *gewedum* in the *b*-line. Wyatt translates the phrase, "very faithful to me," but notes that the half-line is metrically defective. Cosijn (*Beiträge* xxiii, 128) read *mege* for *mage* or *mæg*, "kinswoman," and this reading is accepted by Trautmann, Tupper, Mackie, and Krapp and Dobbie. Early editors read *wel hold* as two words but Holthausen's *welhold* (*Anglia Beibl.* xlvi, 8) is accepted by Trautmann and Krapp and Dobbie. For compounds utilizing initial *wel-*, see B-T., pp. 1185 ff.

7.6: *swa arlice*: Cosijn (*Beiträge* xxiii, 128) first suggested that the MS. *snearlice* was a corruption of *sue arlice* (the scribe having mistaken *u* for *n*), and so Tupper and Mackie read *sue*. Wyatt and Trautmann read *swe*; Grein, Assmann, and Krapp and Dobbie read *swa*. Since MS. *swa* occurs in the next half-line, it seems best for purposes of consistency to read *sue . . . sue* or *swa . . . swa* but not a combination of the two.

7.7 ff.: I translate these lines, "until under an unrelated bosom I grew great with life as was my destiny" (literally, "as were my destinies"). I take *ungesibbum* as dative singular modifying *sceate*, as do most editors. For the meaning of *sceat* as "lap, bosom," see B-T., p. 826, category IV. Wyatt takes *ungesibbum* as a substantive plural and translates as "towards or amongst those who were no kin of mine" (p. 70) and so Mackie. For the meaning of the phrase, *wearð eacen gæste*, cp. a similar phrase at *Gen.* 1000–1001: *siððan Adam wearð / of godes muðe gaste eacen*.

7.9: *friþemæg*: protectress, woman of peace. The form *friþe-* derives from the feminine *friðu*, *freoðo* (see the citations in B-T. under the various spellings). For similar compounds utilizing the initial element, cp. *friðusibb* (*Beo.* 2017), *freoðuwebbe* (*Beo.* 1942, *Wid.* 6, *El.* 88 [*friðowebba*]), *freoðuweard* (*Guth.* 173), and a host of others. Grein first glossed *friþemæg* as "Schützende" (*Sp.*, p. 225, note), and so Assmann, Wyatt, and Mackie. Grein later (*Sp.*, p. 225) accepted Dietrich's reading of *friþe mæg*, "stately, beautiful woman" (*ZfdA.* xii, 251), and so Tupper, Trautmann, and Krapp and Dobbie. Dietrich's reading of a hypothetical O.E. adjective *frið* meaning "beautiful" has little to support it (O.N. *friðr* but no existing forms in O.E.) and the notion of feminine beauty is not particularly appropriate to the context here anyway.

7.10: *aweox*: Holthausen would emend to the subjunctive *aweoxe* (*ESn.* xxxvii, 206) to regularize the meter, and so Tupper and Trautmann.

While *oþþæt* prefers the indicative (see Mitchell, *A Guide to Old English* 174, p. 92, note), it does occur occasionally with the subjunctive when the future is problematical (see, for example, *Genesis* 27:44–45 in Crawford's edition of the Old English *Heptateuch*). Here the growing up of the cuckoo and its leaving the nest might seem problematical, especially to the mother bird bound to feed such a creature, but in the context of so many other indicative verbs and in light of the fact that *oþþæt* takes the indicative elsewhere in the riddles, it seems wiser to keep the MS. reading. The meter though unusual is not unknown. If initial *oþþæt* takes a stress as it sometimes does in the absence of other more frequently stressed words (cp. *Beo.* 9*a* and 219*a*), the verse is one of those like *Beo.* 3027*a* or *Dream* 18*a* or *Rid.* 27.4*a*, which begin like an A3 verse with a light lift and a number of minor syllables leading up to an alliterating lift in the second measure but which end abruptly like type E without a final drop. See my note to *Rid.* 27.4*a* and Pope's discussion of the phenomenon on pp. 128–29 of his *Seven Old English Poems*, and on pp. xxx and 321–22 of *The Rhythm of Beowulf*.

8. Barnacle Goose
[*VN: Gr.11; Tr.8; Tu.11; W.10; M.10; K-D.10*]

Brooke first proposed the solution, "barnacle goose" (*The History of Early English Literature*, p. 179), which is now accepted by all editors. Earlier conjectures included Dietrich's "sea furrow" (*ZfdA.* xi, 463), Trautmann's "bubble" (*Anglia Beibl.* v, 48) and "anchor" (*BBzA.* xvii, 142; *BBzA.* xix, 170 ff.), and Holthausen's "water lily" (*Anglia Beibl.* xvi, 227 ff.). Müller traces the legend of the barnacle goose from the seventeenth century back through the twelfth (*Lectures on the Science of Language*, 2d ser., pp. 533–51). The first literary reference to the strange barnacle bird occurs in the *Topographia Hiberniae* of Giraldus Cambrensis from the twelfth century:

> *De bernacis ex abiete nascentibus; earumque natura.* Sunt et aves hic multae, quae bernacae vocantur; quas mirum in modum, contra naturam, natura producit; aucis quidem palustribus similes, sed minores. Ex lignis namque abieti-

nis, per aequora devolutis, primo quasi gummi nascuntur. Dehinc tanquam ab alga ligno cohaerente, conchilibus testis ad liberiorem formationem inclusae, per rostra dependent; et sic quousque processu temporis, firmam plumarum vestituram indutae, vel in aquas decidunt, vel in aeris libertatem volatu se transferunt. Ex succo ligneo marinoque, occulta nimis admirandaque seminii ratione, alimenta simul incrementaque suscipiunt.

Vidi multoties oculis meis plusquam mille minuta hujusmodi avium corpuscula, in litore maris ab uno ligno dependentia, testis inclusa, et jam formata.

Non ex harum coitu, ut assolet, ova gignuntur; non avis in earum procreatione unquam ovis incubat; in nullis terrarum angulis vel libidini vacare, vel nidificare videntur.

Unde et in quibusdam Hiberniae partibus, avibus istis, tanquam non carneis quia de carne non natis, episcopi et viri religiosi jejuniorum tempore sine delectu vesci solent. [*Topographia Hiberniae* i.xv; ed. Dimock, Rolls Series xxi.5, pp. 47–48]

It was perhaps the early churchmen's fondness for fowl on days of fasting that prompted the strange etymology in the first place. Müller notes certain similarities between barnacles and birds but admits that language itself probably spawned the myth. The etymology of English *barnacle* is still open to question since, as the *OED* notes, "all the evidence shows that the name was originally applied to the *bird* which had the marvellous origin, not to the *shell* which, according to some, produced it" (*OED* i, p. 676, under *barnacle*). No Old English equivalent of the barnacle goose is listed by Whitman (*JEGP* ii, 149 ff.) in his article on Old English bird names. Pliny, in his *Natural History*, comments upon a famous variety of English goose, the *chenerotes*: "Anserini generis sunt chenalopeces et, quibus lautiores epulas non novit Britannia, chenerotes, fere ansere minores" (*NH*. x.xxix.50). Rackham (in the Loeb translation) at least thinks that the *chenerotes* here refers to the English barnacle goose (*branta leucopsis*), though Lewis and Short would define the term here as "a species of small goose or duck; perhaps *anas clipeata*" (p. 326). Swaen (*Neoph*. xxx, 126–27) believes that the riddle actually refers to the Brent Goose (*branta bernicla*) and that the two species may have been confounded in earlier times and the name *barnacle goose* applied to both. But the riddlic description of the creature's coloring (lines 7–8) would apply more closely to the barnacle than to the brent. Clearly the Old English riddler knew the legend of the barnacle goose but whether the folk etymology of *barnacle* existed as early as Anglo-Saxon times or not is likely to remain a moot question sealed in the vaults of history.

8.1–5: I read the lines with *wæs* understood in line 1*b* and with *under-flowen* and *besuncen* as parallel modifiers of the creature, thus: "My beak was in a narrow place and I was below with water, having gone down with the flood, sunk deep in the sea-streams; and I grew up in the sea, covered above by waves (and) close to a floating (piece of) wood (sailing ship?) with my body." Part of the game of the riddle is to pick the right *wudu*. For the use of *an* in 4*b* as an article separated from the following noun by an intervening word, see Rissanen, *The Uses of "One" in Old and Early Middle English*, p. 297, and cp. *Rids.* 13.7 and 73.3.

8.7–8: This is an accurate description of the barnacle goose's colora-tion. Brooke, for example, says:

> The Barnacle is almost altogether in black and white. The bill is black, the head as far as the crown, together with cheeks and throat is white—the rest of the head and neck to the breast and shoulders black. The upper plumage is marbled with blue-gray, black and white. The feathers of back and wings are black edged with white, the underparts are white, the tail black. [*The History of Early English Literature*, p. 179, note]

9. Cup of Wine (or Spirits)
[*VN: Gr.12; Tr.9; Tu.12; W.11; M.11; K-D.11*]

Dietrich (*ZfdA.* xi, 463) first solved the riddle as "night," and so Tup-per. Walz (*Harvard Studies and Notes* v, 261) proposed "gold." Traut-mann (*BBzA.* xix, 173 ff.) solved the riddle as "wine," and so Klaeber (*Anglia Beibl.* xvii, 300 ff.), Wyatt, and Mackie. Mackie prefers the formulation, "beaker of wine," since the *hrægl* in 1*a*, which is typically part of the creature, is clearly the drinking vessel. I follow Trautmann and Mackie: the creature is a cup (probably silver) of intoxicating drink —probably wine or spirits.

Walz argues that *hasofag* (1*a*) is a proper epithet for gold, but Mead in his article on Old English color names notes quite rightly that "*haso* is used with an apparent definiteness of color-feeling, and is applied to the dove, to the eagle, to the curling smoke, to the leaves of plants, and even to the *herestræta*, the highways with their dusty, dirty-white surfaces" (*PMLA* xiv, 192). The word *hasofag* must mean "gray" or even "gray and shining," but not merely *"glänzend"* as even Trautmann *BBzA*. xix, 173) would have it. Tupper accepts the solution, "night," but does not explain how the "bright gems" of night's mantle (the stars) may be *reade*. Tupper admits that the riddle is a companion piece to *Rid*. 25, "mead" (he cites for comparative purposes 9.12*b* and 25.13*a*; 9.7*a* and 25.17*a*; 9.10 and 25.12), but justifies his solution rather weakly with the retort that " 'Night debauch' is quite as well suited to the vinous lines that suggest the later riddle" (p. 90). Lines 3–8*a*, as Tupper himself admits, describe appropriately a strong alcoholic beverage. This creature, like the mead in *Rid*. 25, has the power to overthrow the strong and to mislead the foolish. The creature is falsely praised, and for this *unræd* (9.10*a*; 25.12*a*), man must suffer, though somewhat more severely in this riddle than in the other. The last lines of *Rid*. 9 (see note below) convey the fundamental irony of the poem: if man persists in praising the jeweled cup and its contents as he lifts the drink high, then the Lord will have his just revenge when the dearest of jewels (the soul) is raised high (to heaven on the Judgment Day).

9.1–2: The reading here with the addition of *hafu* in 2*b* to complete the half-line follows that of Wyatt and Mackie. Trautmann first suggested the addition of *hafo* (*BBzA*. xix, 173) or *hafe* (edition). For the Anglian form, first person singular present, *hafu*, *hafo*, cp. *Beo*. 2150, 2523, and 3000, and see Klaeber's note on p. lxxxvii (section 23.5) of his third edition of *Beowulf*. Grein and Krapp and Dobbie supply *minum* at the end of the half-line, but this was rejected by Holthausen (*Anglia Beibl*. ix, 357) as unmetrical. Tupper supplies *sind* at the end of the half-line. The *hrægl* of the liquor, which is certainly the cup, is described as *hasofag* ("gray" or "brilliant gray") in color and studded with ornaments *reade and scire*. This sounds like a silver cup inlaid with garnets or colored glass though technically *reade* could refer to gold (O.E. *read* refers to fire, roses, the Red Sea, blood, swords, and gold: see Mead, *PMLA* xiv, 195ff.). For the general technique of using glass or garnets on silver, see Wilson, *The Anglo-Saxons*, p. 136. For a description of three small silver hanging bowls, which may have been used as drinking cups, see Wilson's account of "The Bowls and Miscellaneous Silver: Form and Function," in *St. Ninian's Isle and Its Treasure* (listed in the Bibliography under "Wilson"), pp. 106ff. See also a description of the silver Northumbrian bowl from Ormside in Kendrick's *Anglo-Saxon Art to A.D. 900*, pp. 150ff. and plate lx. For a number of eighth-to-tenth century silver cups in the Carolingian style (with an apparently southern German bias) found in various parts of Europe, a number of them in sets that appear to indicate that they were used at table, possibly for drinking spirits, see Wilson, "The Fejø Cup," *AA* xxxi, 147–73.

9.3 ff.: The motif of the drink misleading and often overthrowing the man also appears in *Rid.* 25 and in Riddle 80 of Aldhelm, "Calix Vitreus" (ed. Pitman, pp. 46, 48) and in two "De Vino" riddles of the Bern collection, numbers 50 and 63 (*CCL.* cxxxiii A, pp. 596, 610).

9.4: *unrædsiþas*: I accept Klaeber's reading (*Anglia Beibl.* xvii, 300), taking *hwettan* with accusative of person (*dole*) and genitive of thing (*unrædsiþas*). This reading is also accepted by Krapp and Dobbie. Klaeber (*MLN* xxvi, 428) notes that the construction is not recorded elsewhere, but he points out several similar constructions and notes the interchange of genitive constructions with those utilizing *on* and *to*. For the variant genitive singular ending *-as*, see SB. 237 Anm. 1, p. 195, and also Krapp and Dobbie's note to *Wand.* 44. Herzfeld emends to *on unrædsiþas* (*Die Räthsel des Exeterbuches und ihr Verfasser*, p. 68), and this is accepted by Wyatt. Tupper reads *dole* as a modifier of *unrædsiþas*, but *dole* seems to be parallel with *dysge*. Grein apparently reads both *dole* and *unrædsiþas* as objects of *hwette* (*Sp.*, p. 118, 742; and Wyatt, p. 71). Trautmann places *unrædsiþas* in the *styre*-clause, but this makes little sense.

9.6–7: *bestolene . . . gedwolene*: Rhymes are used infrequently in Old English poetry. Cp. the use of rhymes in *Rid.* 26, and see note to *Rid.* 1.20.

9.8: *won wisan*: *evil* or *perverse nature*. The MS. *wón* is marked with an accent to indicate an etymologically long vowel, so the word must be *wōh*, not *wann*.

9.8–10: I follow Krapp and Dobbie in emending MS. *bringeð* to *bringað* in line 9a and I follow Bright (see Tupper, p. 92) in taking *horda deorast* as the "dearest of treasures" or the soul. I translate beginning at 8a: "Woe to them for that custom when they bring high (to Judgment) the dearest of treasures (the soul) if they do not cease from folly before that." The use of language here sets out the central irony of the riddle. The jeweled cup (lines 1–2) is an earthly treasure often raised high in the drinking. The *horda deorast* is a heavenly treasure raised high at the Last Judgment. Judgment shall fall heavily upon man if he worships the lesser treasure at the expense of the greater and heeds not the final raising. The MS. reading as it stands is clearly corrupt, and all editors emend. Cosijn (*Beiträge* xxiii, 128) emends MS. *bringeð* to *þringeð*, taking *horda deorast* as the sun in support of the solution "night." This is also Tupper's reading. Trautmann emends MS. *heah* to *hearm*, taking *horda deorast* as the communion wine. Tupper notes that it is not clear why the wine should bring harm. Kock (*Lunds Universitets Årsskrift*, NF., Avd. 1, Bd. 14, Nr. 26, p. 62) emends MS. *heah bringeð* to *hean hnigeð*; Holthausen (*Anglia* xliv, 347) reads *hean cringeð*. Wyatt reads *heah* with Grein (*Sp.*, p. 309; *deus, Cristus*) as the subject of *bringeð*, but *heah* is not used substantivally elsewhere in Old English to refer to the Deity. In support of Bright's notion of the soul as *horda deorast*, Wyatt cites the description of heaven-bound souls at *Gen.* 1608 as *breosta hord*. Cp. a similar description at *Chr.* 1072.

10. Ox
[*VN: Gr.13; Tr.10; Tu.13; W.12; M.12; K-D.12*]

This is the first of three "ox" riddles in the *Exeter Book*—*Rids.* 10, 36, and 70. *Riddles* 10 and 36 are fashioned about the central paradox: "Living, I break the soil; dead, I bind men." Riddles 83 of Aldhelm, "Iuvencus," and 37 of Eusebius, "De Vitulo," utilize the same motif (see my discussion of the Latin riddles in the headnote to *Rid.* 36). *Riddle* 70 is a narrative portrayal of the ox as a beast of burden. Though all editors agree as to the general solution of *Rid.* 10, there is some disagreement as to the specific term to be used. Dietrich (*ZfdA.* xi, 463) and Trautmann solve it as "das Leder"; Tupper, as "oxhide or leather"; Wyatt, as "skin, hide, leather"; Mackie, as "oxhide." The term, "leather," is too general; the term, "oxhide," is hardly appropriate to the working beast in the beginning of the poem. The *ic* who speaks initially (lines 1–2) is the beast of burden. The conditional beginning with *Gif* in line 3 and extending through all possible futures (*hwilum . . . hwilum*) seems to indicate the live beast musing upon his roles as a servant to men. This is also true in the Latin riddles where the name of the living beast is the entitling solution. It seems, therefore, most appropriate to solve *Rid.* 10 as "ox."

The ox was important to the Anglo-Saxon economy not only because it pulled the plow (*Coll.* 22 ff.) but also because it provided the leather with which the *sceowyrhta* fashioned shoes, slippers, pouches, bags, straps, ropes, and all kinds of clothes (*Coll.* 170–74). The Anglo-Saxon leather-working trade and its terms of speech are discussed by Klump in *Die altenglischen Handwerkernamen*, pp. 20–22, 64–73. For a description of late Anglo-Saxon shoes recently found at Hungate, York, see Page, *Life in Anglo-Saxon England*, p. 84.

10.1–2: Cp. the description of the Anglo-Saxon plow in *Rid.* 19.

10.4: *swearte Wealas*: The word for "Welshman" was used both to mean "foreigner" and "slave" by the Anglo-Saxons (B-T., p. 1173). Tupper notes that *"wealh* was applied, without regard to origin, to bondmen who were, however, largely of Celtic or pre-Celtic blood" (p. 95). For a description of the difficult lot of the Anglo-Saxon slave, see Whitelock, *The Beginnings of English Society*, pp. 108–9.

10.7 ff.: Though the riddle itself is not usually classified as "obscene," the double entendre of these lines should be clear. For a similarly playful description, cp. *Rid.* 43 and the use of *hygewlonc* in that riddle (43.4) with *hygegalan* (10.12) here.

10.9: *druncmennen*: drunken maid (B-T., p. 215; *Sp.*, p. 129). Grein had earlier suggested *duncmennen*, citing O.H.G. *tunc*, but this suggestion was taken up only by Holthausen (*Anglia* xxxv, 168).

10.14: *þe ic*: I who. For the use of the compound relative here, see Mitchell, *A Guide to Old English* 162.2, p. 74, note.

10.15.right margin: The mark in the upper right-hand margin of MS. folio 104a, opposite the last MS. line of *Rid.* 10, resembles the rune Z (*eoh*) with a point to its left and a slight downward trailing of the pen from the end of the last lateral stroke. The trailing may have been carelessly made when the maker of the letter or rune lifted his stylus from the vellum. The *eoh* rune does not appear elsewhere in the *Exeter Book*, but it does occur at *Run.* 35 where the name *eoh* is given by Hickes. Dobbie notes that "the name *eoh*, given . . . by Hickes, appears to be a variant of the word *iw*, 'yew' " (*ASPR.*, vol. 6, p. 155). Elliott notes that the "rune could face either way, Z or Ƨ, and was used to denote either the high front vowel sound *è* as in common Germanic usage and as in the Dover inscription [where Elliott transcribes it *i*] . . . or else the front spirant [ç] as in the word *almeჳttig*, 'almighty', on the Ruthwell Cross" (*Runes*, p. 36) and also that "this twofold function is suggested by the letters *ih* against the rune in the Vienna codex" (ibid.). Page argues that "there is some case for taking Z as a vowel rune in the region of *i*" (*MÆ* xxxvii, 131). If the mark at the end of *Rid.* 10 in the margin of the MS. is this *eoh* or *iw* rune, it may indicate some scribal guess as to the Latin solution of the riddle, "Iuvencus" (see Aldhelm's Riddle 83). This might be by analogy with the ᚻ runes at the end of *Rids.* 3 and 4, which could indicate the Latin solutions, *scutum* and *sol*. In the case of *Rid.* 10, the rune (?) does not appear to have been made by the main scribe, but since no other *eoh* rune appears in the *Exeter Book*, it is difficult to say this with any surety. The fineness and manner of the stroke in some ways resemble the marginalic *r*, also pointed, which occurs to the right of *Rid.* 28a in the margin of folio 108a. For the mark here, see plate v.

11. Ten Chickens
[*VN: Gr.14; Tr.11; Tu.14; W.13; M.13; K-D.13*]

Wright (*Biographia Britannica Literaria*, vol. 1, p. 80) solved the riddle as "the aurelia of the butterfly, and its transformations." Grein (*Germania* x, 308) repeated this as "Raupe aus der Familie der Spanner (Palaenodea oder Geometrae)." The living creatures of the riddle, however, having shed their initial skins, do not fly moth-like to the trees or heavens; rather, they "tread the land" (*turf tredan* in line 1 and *lond tredan* in line 11). Dietrich's solution, "die 22 buchstaben des alphabets" (*ZfdA.* xi, 463–64), is as elusive as the ethereal moth. There are ten, not twenty-two, creatures in the riddle; the parchment "skins" (*fell*) would hardly hang on the wall; and letters would have to be magical indeed to rise up, cast off their clothes, and tread the land. Tupper (*MLN* xviii, 101, and edition, p. 96) solved the riddle as "fingers and gloves," but his explanation of *haswe blede* (line 9) as "the leaves of the manuscript on which the hands are browsing" (p. 98) is not convincing. With reference to Tupper's solution, Krapp and Dobbie point out that "*turf* and *lond tredan* would more readily suggest 'ten toes,' although then the six brothers and four sisters would hardly mean anything" (p. 328). Trautmann's "ten chickens" is accepted by Wyatt, Mackie, and Krapp and Dobbie. Erhardt-Siebold has offered the best explanation to date of the enigmatic "six brothers and four sisters." She says:

> I suggest as the solution to the riddle *Ten Ciccenu* (Ten Chickens). This solution with its ten letters, of which six are consonants (brothers) and four vowels (sisters), would readily explain the number puzzle. The spelling *ciccen* instead of the usual *cīecen* or *cīcen* is characteristic of the Northumbrian dialect; hence, it is another instance corroborating the presumable Northumbrian origin of many of the OE riddles. [*MLN* lxv, 99]

Without pushing the theory of origins too far, this seems a reasonable explanation of the first two lines of the riddle. For the form *ciccenu* see BTS., p. 123, under *cicen*; SB. 119 Anm. 3, p. 98; and Erhardt-Siebold's note 5 on page 100 of the same article. The motif of the young chick shedding its initial "skin" is to be found in Riddle 38 of Eusebius, "De Pullo"; otherwise the two riddles share little in common.

11.3b–5a: Trautmann (*BBzA.* xix, 177 ff.) explains that these lines refer to the inner membranes of the eggshells that are left hanging on the "house" of each chick as the chicks hatch and shed their "skins." Anyone who has seen the newly discarded "house" of a young chick with its "skin" hanging on the wall can attest to the accuracy of the description. Wyatt's thesis that the eggshells are hung on the wall of a man's house as a charm seems to me idle speculation. The fact that eggs were so hung in rare cases in nineteenth-century English houses proves nothing about the Anglo-Saxons' "egg-shell charms." The most natural reading of lines 4b–5a would be, as Erhardt-Siebold (*MLN* lxv, 97 ff.) indicates, "on the wall of each one's house."

11.6: *ne side þy sarre*: The MS. reading is *ne side þy sarra*. This reading is retained by Trautmann in spite of its grammatical difficulties. Krapp and Dobbie read *ne siðe þy sarre* after a suggestion by Cosijn (*Beiträge* xxiii, 128). All other editors read the half-line as printed here. Mackie translates lines 5*a*–6*b*: "None of them was any the worse, / or his side the more painful" (p. 103). In the sense of "side," O.E. *side* normally glosses Latin *latus* (WW. 159.11; 265.18; 307.6; 434.36), and there is no reason to believe that the Old English word (see B-T., pp. 870–71) was any more limited to the meaning "flank" than was the Latin (see Lewis and Short, p. 1042). The paradox at least is clear: the creature sheds skin, yet feels no pain in the process. The paradox is resolved partly in terms of the solution (the "skin" is the shell) and partly in terms of the literal description (*Hrægl bið geniwad*: line 9).

12. Horn
[*VN: Gr.15; Tr.12; Tu.15; W.14; M.14; K-D.14*]

Dietrich's (*ZfdA.* xi, 464) solution, "horn," is accepted by all editors. This is the first of two "great horn" riddles in which the horn is depicted in its uses as war-horn, treasure, and holder of mead. The companion "horn" riddle is *Rid.* 76. These horns are probably great aurochs' horns similar to the drinking horns discovered at Sutton Hoo. Caesar notes in his *De Bello Gallico* that the hunting of the aurochs was an old Germanic custom and that the great horns were collected, adorned, and used as drinking vessels: "Haec studiose conquisita ab labris argento circumcludunt atque in amplissimis epulis pro poculis utuntur" (vi.28). Manuscript illustrations of drinking horns are described by Tupper on p. 99 of his edition; illustrations of playing horns are described by Padelford in his "Old English Musical Terms" (*BBzA.* iv, 55–56). Two other Old English "horn" riddles, *Rids.* 84 and 89, describe inkhorns made not from aurochs' horns but from stags' horns. A possible "horn of yew" riddle occurs at *Rid.* 26.

12.right margin: Opposite the first MS. line of the riddle, in the far right-hand margin of the page, there is a mark (see plate VI). If the mark was intended to be a runic *H* (to indicate the solution, O.E. *horn*), it was fashioned by someone other than the main scribe according to a Germanic rather than an Old English norm. The Germanic runic *H* had a single crossbar while the O.E. *hægl* had a double crossbar (see chart in Elliott's *Runes*, p. 48). The normal Old English runic *H* may be seen in the scribe's hand at folio 127*a* (see plate XVIII for runes of *Rid.* 73). The mark is more probably a postscribal capital *H* meant to indicate the solution "horn." The mark may have been made by the same late reader who made the rune-like *n* at folio 103*a* above *Rid.* 6 to indicate the solution "nightingale."

12.1: *wæpen wigan*: For MS. *wæpen wiga*, all editors except Trautmann read a compound, *wæpenwiga*, "armed warrior." Trautmann and Swaen (*Neoph.* xxvi, 298 ff.) rightly point out that the creature-horn may be literally a *wæpen* on the bull's head or metaphorically a *wiga* as it goes to battle, but that it cannot be a *wæpenwiga* or "armed warrior" since it carries no weapon but is the weapon itself. In this regard, one may compare the beginning of Eusebius's Riddle 30, "De Atramentorio":

> Armorum fueram vice, meque tenebat in armis
> Fortis, et armigeri gestabar vertice tauri.
>
> [*CCL.* cxxxiii, p. 240]

Trautmann and Swaen, following a note by Rieger in his *Alt- und Angelsächsisches Lesebuch*, would read *wæpen wigan*, translating the first half-line thus: "I was the weapon of a warrior (the aurochs)." This makes sense of the contrast between the creature's past (*Ic wæs* . . .) and present (*nu mec* . . .) states as a weapon and a treasure. For the possibility of MS. *wiga* as a legitimate Northumbrian genitive form with loss of -*n*, see Campbell 472, p. 189 and 617, p. 249.

12.2: *sylfre*: Since syncopation seems the rule in all other instances of *seolfor* in the oblique cases (B-T., p. 864; *Sp.*, p. 599), and since the extra syllable in the drop makes for a metrical irregularity, it seems best to normalize the form here with Tupper after a suggestion by Sievers (*Beiträge* x, 459). Other editors retain the MS. reading. For the silver-gilt of the Sutton Hoo drinking horns, see Bruce-Mitford, *The Sutton Hoo Ship-Burial*, p. 33 and plate 19.

12.4–5: For the motif of the horn summoning warriors to battle, cp. the first two lines of Aldhelm's Riddle 68, "Salpix":

> Sum cava, bellantum crepitu quae corda ciebo,
> Vocibus horrendis stimulans in bella cohortes.

[Ed. Pitman, p. 38]

12.9–10: For *behlyðan*, Grein gives the following definition: *"behlyðan (-hleðan?): privare, spoliare* (vgl. *hleða: praedator: Cot.* 170)" (*Sp.*, p. 348), and similarly B-T. (p. 80). Tupper and Mackie supply *on* before *bordum* as I do here (cp. the loss of *on* at line 14). Tupper translates: "Sometimes I shall lie stripped on the tables" (p. 100). Wyatt would retain the MS. reading, taking *bordum* as a form of *borda* instead of *bord* and translating *bordum . . . behlyþed* as "deprived of my ornamented, bejeweled lids or covers" (p. 74) and so Swaen (*Neoph.* xxvi, 299–300). Trautmann emends MS. *behlyþed* to *behlywed*, taking the latter as a word related to *hleow*, "protection," translating the sense as "von Brettern geschützt" (p. 77), and so Krapp and Dobbie. I prefer to read *bordum* as the boards of the table and to supply *on* with Tupper and Mackie. The despoiling of the horn may not refer so much to its ornaments as to its contents. The drinking horn has two treasures—its silver and its mead. The horn in *Rid.* 76 says: *Hæbbe me on bosme þæt on bearwe geweox* (76.7). It is this treasure that is despoiled when the horn lies *on bordum*.

12.10: *heafodleas*: Dietrich (*ZfdA.* xi, 464) took this to mean "los vom haupte" or "separated from the bull's head" and so Trautmann and Swaen (*Neoph.* xxvi, 299). If the element *heafod-* refers to the creature's own head, then the clue here is to the "headless" or open end of the horn through which the treasure (mead) is taken.

12.14: *on wicge wegað*: The addition of *on* to MS. *wicge wegað* was proposed by Holthausen (*Anglia* xxxv, 165) and this reading is accepted by Krapp and Dobbie and myself. Trautmann reads *mec on wicge wegað*, but the pronoun is often ellipted as it is here (see line 3). Other editors retain the MS. reading, placing a semicolon after *drincað* and taking *freolic fyrdsceorp* with *wegað*, but Krapp and Dobbie note that *hwilum* ought to mark the onset of a new clause and that *freolic fyrdsceorp* probably goes with the preceding sentence.

12.14–15: So in Aldhelm's Riddle 68, "Salpix": *Spiritus in toto sed regnant corpore flabra* (ed. Pitman, p. 38).

12.19: The mark (see plate VII) at the end of the riddle is in a place normally reserved for end-punctuation marks. The mark, however, is not a typical punctuation mark. It does not appear to be either a letter or a rune. The mark bears some resemblance to the mark following the end-punctuation sign at the end of *Rid*. 28a.

13. Fox
[*VN: Gr.16; Tr.13; Tu.16; W.15; M.15; K-D.15*]

Dietrich first proposed the solution, "badger" (*ZfdA*. xi, 465). This solution is accepted by Tupper, Trautmann, Wyatt, and Mackie. The solution is based on the creature's digging abilities described in lines 17–22. One source notes that "the badger digs rapidly, easily outdistancing a man with a shovel" (*EB*. ii, p. 1026). The badger is a savage fighter when cornered. He bears sharp teeth and strong claws—these may be the *beadowæpen* of line 3. But the creature of the riddle has a white neck and ruddy or tawny (*fealo*) head and sides. The Old World badger is gray above and black below. It has black stripes, bordered by white, running from its snout through its eyes to its small, inconspicuous ears. It is heavy and squat and walks like all of the heavier mustelids on flat feet with a "slow, rolling, bear-like shuffle" (Walker, *Mammals of the World*, p. 1189). A cornered badger will usually keep to its burrow where even the fiercest of terriers will have trouble rooting him out. The creature of the riddle is *swift* (line 2); it travels over grassy meadows on its toes (*ordum*); it prefers to struggle through *hylles rof* (line 27) to fight in the open.

Walz (*Harvard Studies and Notes* v, 261 ff.) and Holthausen (*ESn*. xxxvii, 206 ff.) argue for "porcupine." Porcupines are dark with white bands on their spines. They walk "ponderously on the sole of the foot with the heel touching the ground [and] run with a shuffling gait or gallop clumsily when pursued" (Walker, *Mammals of the World*, p. 1004). Porcupines are slow; they have tiny ears.

Holthausen's alternative to "porcupine" is "hedgehog" (*ESn.* xxxvii, 206 ff.). Hedgehogs walk "on the sole with the heel touching the ground . . . [in] a waddling walk or trot" (Walker, p. 125). Hedgehogs shelter "in and under logs, among rocks, under the roots of trees and brush piles, in termite mounds, and in burrows" (ibid.). When threatened, the hedgehog rolls itself into a ball and emits a hiss or a loud scream.

Brett (*MLR* xxii, 258 ff.) first argued for the solution "fox," saying:

> The fox's neck is white beneath; his head and sides are *fealo*, if the meaning of that word be yellowish red, like some autumn leaves; he is swift; he has formidable teeth, like the badger, and a conspicuous brush which might be likened to a weapon; his ears tower conspicuously over his eyes; he steps daintily; the habits fit him fairly well, though the badger is a stronger and deeper digger;—here we must remember that the fox will use a badger's old home, and has even been found sharing a hole with him. [*MLR* xxii, 259]

Mead notes that the prevailing meaning of O.E. *fealo* is "pale yellow shading into red or brown" (*PMLA* xiv, 198), and Walker notes that the color of the red fox "ranges from pale yellowish red to deep reddish brown above with white, ashy, or slaty underparts" (*Mammals of the World*, p. 1156). Foxes have bushy cheeks and towering ears. They have knife-like teeth. They move swiftly *in grene græs* (line 6). Like all canines, they walk, trot, or canter fully or partly on their toes (Walker, p. 1148). They live in burrows that they dig for themselves or take over from badgers, often enlarging the holes (Burrows, *Wild Fox*, p. 19). Young says that "the vixen is a 'model mother' . . . noted for gallantry in defence of her young" (*RES* xx, 305). Burrows reports that vixens remove their cubs from disturbed "earths" or burrows (*Wild Fox*, p. 151), as does the creature of this riddle. The natural enemy of the fox is the dog, and was once the wolf (Burrows, p. 160), either of which could be the *wælhwelp* of line 23. The fox does not keep to its burrow for the fight; it needs space to utilize its assets of speed and agility in order to make the kill. It might well struggle *þurh hylles hrof* (line 27) before turning to meet its attacker. Certainly it would secure the safety of its cubs before turning to the death-fight.

Young (*RES* xx, 304 ff.) admits the compelling arguments in favor of "vixen," but offers also the solution, "weasel." Weasels are reddish brown above and white below (*EB.* xxiii, p. 333). They are swift, savage fighters like the fox, with weapon-like teeth. But they have small, flat heads, with short, rounded ears. They are not confined to burrows, but make their nests of dry leaves and herbage in ground holes or hollow trees (*EB.* xxiii, p. 333). They are not particularly known for digging. Young argues that the pursuing *wælhwelp* of the riddle might be a snake after the weasel's offspring (*RES* xx, 306); but a weasel hunts and fights well in a burrow because of its slender body, and Isidore notes that the weasel hunts snakes: "Serpentes etiam et mures persequitur" (*Etym.* xii.iii.3).

13.2: *Swift*: Trautmann emends MS. *swift* to *soft* in support of his solution, "badger."

13.3–5: This passage has been read in a variety of ways. Grein took MS. *sweon* for *sue on*, reading:

> me on bæce standað
> her swylce sue: on hleorum hlifiað
> tu earan ofer eagum;

For the meaning of *sue*, Grein cited O.E. *sugu, suge* ("sow") from the glosses. But no form *sue* exists in O.E. outside of the emended reading here, and Grein later retained MS. *swe* for *swa* (*Sp.*, p. 652) as printed here. Krapp and Dobbie note that "the ears can hardly be both *on hleorum* and *ofer eagum*" (p. 329). They arrange the lines according to MacLean (*An Old and Middle English Reader*, p. 4), as do Tupper, Wyatt, Mackie, and myself. Trautmann reads *swine* for MS. *swe* and *biað* for MS. *hlifiað* in order to support his solution, "badger." Neither Grein's nor Trautmann's "pig" has any place in this poem. For MS. *swe* as a form of *swa*, see Campbell 125, pp. 48–49, and also B-T., p. 940, under *swa*. Mitchell (*A Guide to Old English* 177.2, p. 95) notes that *swylce . . . swa* is usually translated "such . . . as," but here there is no intervening material between the words since *her*, the subject, falls after the verb of the main clause. Literally the phrase reads: "Such hairs stand on my back as [stand] on my cheeks." Mackie's translation, "On my back stand hairs / and likewise on my cheeks" (p. 105), provides a suitable modern equivalent. In lines 4*b*–5*a*, the creature's ears are said to "tower" (*hlifiað*) over its eyes. Of all the animals proposed as solutions to the riddle, only the fox has high, pointed ears.

13.7: *onhæle*: The feminine ending here may be a way of indicating the female fox (cp. *glado* at *Rid.* 22.7). The riddler is not always consistent with respect to the gender of his adjectives (cp. *swift* at 2b, which may, however, be governed by *wiht*), but the occasionally startling feminine form seems significant.

13.9: *ond*: a cumulative conjunction to be read with the implied conditional from line 7 as *ond* [*gif*]. The same construction occurs at *Rid.* 14.8–9. This is as Mackie reads the lines. Trautmann's emendation of MS. *ond* to *gif* is unnecessary.

13.10: *geoguðcnosle*: *children*, literally *youth-kindred*. Wyatt notes this and the following hapax legomena in the poem: *feðemundum* (17), *wælhwelpes* (23), *niðsceaþa* (24), *gegnpaþe* (26), and *laðgewinnum* (29; emended to *laðgewinnan* in my edition; see note to line 29). I also read *dunþyrel* in line 21 as a hapax legomenon.

13.10: *Hwonne*: Previous editors have taken the clause beginning with *hwonne* at 13.10b as part of the preceding sentence. The number of dependent clauses in lines 13.6b–11 according to previous readings prompts Krapp and Dobbie to note that "these lines also offer considerable difficulty" (p.330). The syntax is simplified considerably by taking *Hwonne* as an adverb meaning "when," introducing what Mitchell calls an "adverb clause of time" (see *A Guide to Old English* 159 n. 2, p. 72, and cp. *Max. I*, 104b ff.).

13.11b: "death will be appointed for them (the children)"—i.e., the children are doomed to death if they wait in the dwelling. Cp. the use of *witod* at 6b.

13.14: *Gif*: Previous editors have taken the conditional clause as part of the preceding sentence. But for a similar instance of an introductory *gif* clause, cp. the sentence beginning at line 24.

13.14: *me æfterweard ealles weorþeð*: *chases after me* (*Sp.*, *vestigiis meis instat*; p. 8), literally, *becomes wholly to me a following* (*one*).

13.15a: The meter of the verse as it stands in the MS. is wholly irregular so it seems best to transpose *beráð* and *breost* with Herzfeld, Cosijn (*Beiträge* xxiii, 129), Tupper, and Trautmann. The verse as emended is a not uncommon C2 verse where the second lift is a short stressed syllable.

13.16b: *ne ic þæt ræd teale*: "I do not consider that advisable" (Sedgefield, *MLR* xvi, 61). If the MS. reading, *nele þæt ræd teale*, is retained, then *ræd* must be the subject, *þæt* the object, and *teale* the adverb (*tela*)—which B-T. translates as "good counsel will certainly not require that" (p. 974), and so Wyatt and Mackie. But the syntax seems so convoluted as to put the MS. reading seriously in doubt. Sedgefield's emendation accepted here is easily explained. If the *i* of an original *ic* was a bit above the line (small cap.?), then *ne ic* could easily have been misread as *nele*.

13.17: *feþemundum*: *with forepaws*, literally *with walking-hands*.

13.21: *dunþyrel*: *hill-hole, burrow*. For similar compounds, cp. *dunland*, *dunscræf*, *dunstræt* and words utilizing the final element *-þyrel* (B-T., p. 1085). For MS. *dum þyrel*, Grein and later editors read *dune þyrel*, taking *dune* as genitive singular. Thorpe and Trautmann read *dim* for MS. *dum*. Barnouw (*Neoph.* iii, 77) suggested *duruþyrel*, which was accepted by Trautmann (*Anglia* xlii, 129). Since burrows do not have real "doors," and since *þyrel* already means "opening" (CH., p. 368), the elements seem somewhat redundant. The compound *dunþyrel* seems more likely and requires less drastic emendation of the MS. The reading here is also better than *dune þyrel* because it provides a regular type C verse rather than an irregular A verse with anacrusis.

13.23: *wælhwelpes*: *slaughter-hound*. This probably refers to a dog, but it may refer to a wolf, which was once the single wild predator of the fox (Burrows, *Wild Fox*, p. 160). Cp. the use of *hwelp* at *Wulf* 16, which surely plays upon the connotations of "wolf-cub."

13.26: *gegnpaþe*: *hostile* or *opposing road*. Grein glosses the compound as *via hostilis* (*Sp.*, p. 253); CH., as *opposing path* (p. 150).

13.29: *laðgewinnan*: Wyatt, Mackie, and Krapp and Dobbie retain *laðgewinnum* from MS. *laðgewin* [/] *num*. Wyatt glosses, and Mackie translates the word as dative plural with the proper *-um* ending. But it is not immediately clear why the single *wælhwelp* should turn into a horde of beasts at this point in the poem. Tupper and Grein (*Sp.*, p. 396) gloss the word as dative singular, but neither Campbell (615 ff., pp. 248 ff.) nor Sievers-Brunner (276–77, pp. 221–24) notes this variant dative singular form for weak masculine nouns. Trautmann emends *laðgewinnum* to the normal *laðgewinnan* and this seems the most likely reading.

14. Anchor
[*VN: Gr.17; Tr.14; Tu.17; W.16; M.16; K-D.16*]

Dietrich (*ZfdA*. xi, 452) first solved the riddle as "anchor," and this solution is accepted by all editors. Dietrich cited Symphosius's Riddle 61 as the source of the Old English riddle. The "Ancora" Riddle of Symphosius is :

> Mucro mihi geminus ferro coniungitur uno.
> Cum vento luctor, cum gurgite pugno profundo.
> Scrutor aquas medias, ipsas quoque mordeo terras.

[Ed. Ohl, p. 92]

Line 1 of the Latin has no exact parallel in the Old English. The Old English anchor has a tail (*steort*) instead of twin points (*Mucro . . . geminus*); it is not described as being specifically made of iron, as is the Latin creature. Line 2 of the Latin is analogous to lines 1–2*a* of the Old English. Line 3 of the Latin may find parallels in lines 2*a*–3 of the Old English, though the Old English creature never "bites the land" as does the Latin (*mordeo terras*).

The first four lines of this riddle are, as Sievers (*Beiträge* xii, 457) noted, prevailingly hypermetric. Verses 1*b*, 2*b*, 3*b*, 4*a*, and 4*b* are expanded A lines—to use Pope's terms, hA (*The Rhythm of Beowulf*, p. 110). Line 3*a* can be read as normal (D*4) or hypermetric HB1 (cp. *Dream* 10*a*), but in the context of other hypermetric half-lines the latter reading is more likely. Line 2*a*, if allowed to stand unemended in its MS. reading, *somod wið þam sæcce*, would be a normal half-line (A1), but given the context of hypermetric lines and the oddity of *sæcce* as a verb form, it seems best to emend with Holthausen and Trautmann (see note). The last six lines of the riddle are normal.

14.2a: *somod wið þam sæcce fremman*: The reading here with the addition of *fremman* follows that of Holthausen (*Anglia* xxxv, 169) and Trautmann in order to take *sæcce* as a noun and to restore what is believed to be a hypermetric verse in the context of four full hypermetric lines. Other editors retain the MS. reading without *fremman*. B-T. (p. 808) reads *sæcce* doubtfully as a form of *sæccan*, "to fight, contend," elsewhere unattested. Tupper takes *sæcce* as a northern form of *sacan* and cites Lindisfarne *onsæcco* at Mark 14:31 (B-T., p. 757), but the oddity of the form together with the isolation of the normal half-line in the hypermetric context make it seem likely that something has been lost from the original.

14.3: *fremde*: Cp. the use of *fremde* [MS. *fremdes*] at *Rid.* 91.4.

14.5b: This is an instance where the slightly irregular meter could be resolved if we assume an earlier form *þon* for *þonne*. Cp. *Beo.* 469*b* and see Pope's discussion of the phenomenon at p. 71 of *The Rhythm of Beowulf*.

14.6: *slitende*: Trautmann reads *slitendne* as referring to the anchor, but this is unnecessary. Mackie translates, "and [they], tearing at me, soon put me to flight" (p. 107).

14.9–10a: This is all part of the conditional clause begun at line 8*b*. Mackie translates beginning at 8*b*: "if my tail endures, / and if rocks may hold fast / against my strength" (p. 107).

15. Uncertain
[*VN: Gr.18; Tr.15; Tu.18; W.17; M.17; K-D.17*]

Dietrich first (*ZfdA*. xi, 465) solved the riddle as "ballista," but later (*ZfdA*. xii, 237) offered the solution, "fortress," after a suggestion by Lange. Trautmann (*Anglia Beibl.* v, 48; *BBzA.* xix, 180 ff.) solved the riddle as "oven," but in his edition admitted the dual possibility—"Wurfmange (??) Backofen (?)." Wyatt accepts "fortress"; Tupper, Mackie, and Krapp and Dobbie accept "ballista." Trautmann's "oven" does not at all fit the language of the riddle, and there are problems with both "fortress" and "ballista." The Anglo-Saxons neither built nor occupied Roman-style forts. Their occasional compound walls were wooden and, as the poetry and archaeological evidence tells us, breached normally by fire, not by the hurled stone. The linguistic evidence (see below) indicates some doubt in the Anglo-Saxon mind as to the nature of the Latin ballista. The evidence suggests that neither military commanders nor poets knew much about the fancy catapults of the Romans. The riddler could conceivably have constructed a "ballista" riddle from Latin sources (Vitruvius, *De Architectura* x.i.3; Caesar, *De Bello Civili* vii.25; and Isidore, *Etym.* xviii.x.1–2 all mention Roman catapults of various kinds), but in a riddle collection where most of the subjects would have been recognized by the ordinary Anglo-Saxon, this seems unlikely. Keller (*The Anglo-Saxon Weapon Names*, pp. 62 ff.) believes that the Anglo-Saxons possessed both a simple (*liðere*) and an elaborate (*stæfliðere*) sling, but we have only the conflicting evidence of the glosses for this and in any case neither of the slings could correspond to the elaborately mechnical Roman ballista. Isidore, in his chapter on catapults, mentions the complicated *ballista* and the simpler *funda* and *fundibalum* (*Etym.* xviii.x.1–2). L. *ballista* is glossed by O.E. *stæfliðere, gelocen boge*, and *searu*, and in some cases the Latin includes the amplification *catapulta* or *machina belli* (for the glosses of *ballista*, see WW. 8.15; 143.22; 192.9; 357.21–22). O.E. *liðere* normally glosses L. *funda*, but in two cases it glosses L. *fundibalum* (B-T., p. 644; BTS., p. 619). O.E. *stæfliðere* glosses both L. *fundibalum* and *ballista* (B-T., p. 907). Aldhelm at least knew the L. *fundibalum* as a simple sling made of twisted flax and leather (see his "Fundibalum" riddle 74, ed. Pitman, p. 42). In any case neither the Anglo-Saxon sling nor the Roman ballista would be filled with "noble treasures" (*dryhtgestreona*), nor would they shoot arrows or darts (cp. *hyldepilas, beadowæpnum, ordum, attorsperum* in lines 6–9). Tupper notes that the riddle bears certain resemblances to *Rid.* 21, "bow," but we should bear in mind that the crossbow was unknown in England until the eleventh century (Keller, *The Anglo-Saxon Weapon Names*, p. 54).

Two new solutions to the riddle have recently been proposed. Pinsker (*Anglia* xci, 11 ff.) argues for the solution, "forge" ("Der Schmelzofen"), but this seems to ignore the battle action and imagery of the poem (for example, the use of verbs like *spætan* and *fleogan* to describe the ejection of weapons from the creature's belly and mouth and the use of battle diction such as *sperebrogan, hildepilas*, etc.). Furthermore, there is no mention of heating, hammering, cooling, or quenching —all of which we might expect in a "forge" riddle (for the process of forging, see Davidson, *The Sword in Anglo-Saxon England*, chapter 1). Shook ("Riddles Relating to the Anglo-Saxon Scriptorium," in *Essays in Honour of Anton Charles Pegis*, ed. J. Reginald O'Donnell, pp. 222 ff.) argues rather ingeniously for the solution, "ink-well" (O.E. *blæchorn*, L. *atramentorium*). The solution fits the runes that precede the riddle (see note below) and it makes lovely sense of the concluding line, but there are several major problems with it. The inkwell could conceivably be the *mundbora* of its "flock" of inkdrops, but why should these drops be the *dryhtgestreona*? The inkwell could swallow a spear (the pen), but why plural spears and arrows throughout the poem? And why should the arrows be "bitter" and "venomous"? Shook explains the use of *attorsperum* at 9*a* by saying that "the puzzling hapax legomenon *attorspere* echoes in its first element *attor* the *atra* of Latin *atramentum* and *atramentorium*" (ibid., p. 223), but as O.E. *attor*, "poison, venom," is common both by itself and in compounds and as O.E. *atrum*, "black liquid," appears only rarely in the glosses (see BTS., p. 56; the two words are not etymologically related), there seems little likelihood that an Anglo-Saxon would have recognized such an "echo" (unless of course he were a man of great Latin learning who liked to indulge in bilingual puns!). Shook suggests that *wombhord* (10*a*) naturally suggests *wordhord*, but one could argue by the same reasoning that it suggests *wyrmhord* or some other similar compound. Finally Shook argues that scribal activity was an appropriately "daytime" one (cf. *Dægtidum* at 3*b*), but so one supposes were most other human activities depending upon an abundance of light. What Shook does do rather well is to raise the question of whether the battle descriptions in the riddle are to be taken literally or metaphorically. As no Anglo-Saxon weapons have ever been put forward that would satisfy the requirements of the riddle, potential solvers should perhaps begin to think in figurative terms of those big-bellied creatures that hold great treasures and spit forth spear-like objects.

15.upper margin: In the space between *Rids.* 14 and 15 are two figures that appear to be the runes, ᚱ (*lagu*) and ᛒ (*beorc*) (see plates VIII.a and b) as they are read by Trautmann, Wyatt, Krapp and Dobbie, and myself. A comparison of these marginalic runes with runic *B* at *Rid.* 62.2 and runic *L* at *Rid.* 73.2 (see plates VIII.c and d) will show that the marginalic runes here appear not to have been made by the main scribe. The slant of the runes is different as is the relative proportion of upper-portion to lower-portion *B*. Grein and Mackie read only the runic *B*. Förster believes that "in reality a modern hand has tried to reproduce the peculiar *B*-like e of the old *fæste* [directly above the runes in the MS]; and the hook above it, in the form of an acute, is a mark of reference" (*The Exeter Book of Old English Poetry*, p. 64, note 29). If this is so, the imitation is a poor one indeed (see plate VIII.a). Tupper and Trautmann (edition) believe the runes to stand for L. *ballista* and O.E. *liðere*, and the presence of two runes instead of one at the beginning of the riddle might reflect the same sort of confusion about the exact nature of the war-engine that is evident in the glosses. Wyatt reads runic *B* as standing for O.E. *burg*. Shook (see reference in headnote) takes the two runes ingeniously to stand for O.E. *blæchorn*, but does not explain why two runes should appear here where normally one would suffice.

15.2: *eodor wirum fæst*: There are two problems with the half-line: (1) Is *eodor wirum* to be taken as a compound or as two words? (2) Does *eodor* in either case mean "prince, protector," or "dwelling, enclosure"? My reading of the two words follows that of Trautmann and Tupper. Other editors read *eodorwirum fæst*, which in some ways is metrically more satisfying since *fæst* then takes a primary stress in a type E half-line and the secondary alliteration with *gefylled* is more conspicuous. But the meaning of the elsewhere unattested compound is in doubt. Grein (*Sp.*, p. 163) defines it as "cingulum, sepiens filum metallicum;" B-T., as "a wire enclosure" (p. 252); CH., as "wire fence" (p. 105). O.E. *eodor* may mean "enclosure" (cp. *Beo.* 1037; *Gen.* 2447, 2489), though not necessarily "fence." *Eodor* is used only once elsewhere in a compound with this sense, *eodorbrice* (*Lambd.* 31.31; in B-T., p. 252), which B-T. translates as "fence-breaking" and which CH. (p. 105 under *eodorbrecð*) translates as "breach of enclosure, house-breaking." In fact if *eodor* is taken to mean "prince," the compound might conceivably mean "princely wire" (rings? ornamental wire?). If *eodor* is a single word, which seems more likely, it may, as an appositive with the always animate *mundbora* (1a), mean "protector," or it may, in anticipation of the inanimate thing that is *innan gefylled | dryhtgestreona*, mean "enclosure." This depends on whether one reads the paradox as a linking of the protector with the agent of protection (*mundbora*, "protector" = *eodor*, "enclosure") or as an unusual description of the protector (*eodor*) as *wirum fæst*. Trautmann's resolution of this is to read *eodor* as a pun facilitating the transition between the *mundbora* (1*a*) and the description of the enclosure commencing at 2*b*. Such wordplays are not overly common in Old English poetry, but the use of the pun here would make splendid sense of some very difficult lines.

15.5: *Freo*: Thorpe, Mackie, and Trautmann retain this MS. reading, which is probably archaic for *frea* (Campbell 275, p. 116). Other editors normalize the spelling to *frea*.

15.7: *sweartum*: Pinsker's translation of this as "in schwarzen (Nächten)" (*Anglia* xci, 16) finds no support anywhere in Old English. The same may be said of his considered emendation to *sweorcum*.

15.11: *men gemunan*: Cosijn (*Beiträge* xxiii, 129) would supply *oft* or *þæt* after *men*, and Trautmann in his edition follows Holthausen (*Anglia* xxxv, 165) in reading *men gemunan þæt me* in the *a*-line—all these apparently for metrical reasons. But Herzfeld (*Die Räthsel des Exeterbuches und ihr Verfasser*, p. 49) points to similar half-lines at *Rids.* 44.6*a* and 89.12*a* (my numbering). There is no reason to change the half-line.

15.lower margin: The mark in the end-space of *Rid.* 15 (see plate ix) noted by Wyatt appears to be a stray mark of the pen and nothing more. It does not match up as offset blotting with anything on folio 104*b* (and because of offset blotting after the next riddle it is possible to match up the two folios exactly).

16. Jug (Amphora)
[*VN: Gr.19; Tr.16; Tu.19; W.18; M.18; K-D.18*]

The solution, "der Schlauch," *leather bottle*, was proposed by Dietrich, who reasoned: "Denn er hat ohne sprechen zu können einen mund, er hat einen weiten bauch, und ist mit mehrern seines gleichen auf dem schiffe zu hause" (*ZfdA*. xi, 465). Trautmann rightly questions the relevance of Dietrich's *zu Hause* to the Old English riddle and reports that "Ho[lthausen] fragt auf dem Probebogen: 'Fass?'" (p. 80). Neither solution is supported by the archaeological evidence from Anglo-Saxon England (see below). Shook's more recent offering of O.E. *blæchorn* ("Riddles Relating to the Anglo-Saxon Scriptorium," in *Essays in Honour of Anton Charles Pegis*, ed. J. Reginald O'Donnell, pp. 223–24) assumes a paradox in the opening lines (the dumb creature who nonetheless brings wisdom to mankind), but it ignores the broad hint of the last line that the creature and its contents are typically transported *on ceole* (Anglo-Saxon ink was made locally of tree dye as was continental ink—cp. *Rid.* 24.9 and see Tupper's note to *beamtelge* on p. 129 of his edition). Dietrich and Trautmann were closer to the truth.

Leather bottles were certainly made by the Anglo-Saxon *sceo-wyrhta* or shoewright (see Aelfric's *Colloquy*, lines 170ff.). But these bottles are not likely to have been used in the shipping trade. Leather is subject to mold and rot and would not easily have been stored in a dark, damp shiphold. Furthermore, leather bottles of sufficient size to transport quantities of wine or oil would have been extremely awkward to manage. Wooden barrels like those depicted in the Bayeux tapestry were certainly used in the French wine trade, but none of these barrels exists in the preconquest archaeological materials from England (David Wilson, *The Anglo-Saxons*, pp. 88–90). The only large wine vessels that do exist in the Anglo-Saxon archaeological finds are pottery jugs or *amphorae* that Wilson associates with the German wine trade:

> From the seventh century onwards we have evidence that pottery was imported from the Continent, which must presumably be associated with the German wine trade. The great *relief-band amphorae* . . . some of them three or four feet in height, can have been used for no other purpose than transporting wine." [*The Anglo-Saxons*, p. 89]

These large pottery jugs (see Wilson, fig. 15, p. 88) have a great girth and small mouths. They have handles to facilitate the carrying. They could easily have been stored on shipboard. They were common certainly in Anglo-Saxon England and probably throughout Europe. Isidore says of the *amphora*:

> Amphora vocata quod hinc et inde levetur. Haec Graece a figura sui dicta dicitur, quod eius ansae geminatae videantur aures imitari. Recipit autem vini vel aquae pedem quadratum, frumenti vero modios Italicos tres. Cadus Graeca amphora est continens urnas tres. [*Etym.* xvi.xxvi.13]

The L. *amphora* or *amphoram* is glossed by O.E. *amber* (WW. 354.1; 484.1), which also glosses L. *lagena, urceus, situla,* and *hydria* (B-T., p. 36), so I have listed as the primary solution, the more general equivalent, *jug*.

16. right margin: The mark noted by Wyatt (see his fig. 9) to the right of *mældan* (see plate x) is a testing of the pen and nothing more.

16.3: *wide wombe*: Though single half-lines are known to exist in Old English poetry (see A. J. Bliss, NQ ccxvi, 442–49), the sense of the riddle seems to demand something more here, and I have marked the lacuna after the half-line as do Krapp and Dobbie.

16.4 *wæs*: The mirror *n* (see plate xi.a) following *wæs* in the MS. on folio 105*a* is offset blotting from the *n* of *ne* at *Rid.* 13.22 on MS. folio 104*b*. The curved stroke above the mirror *n* is similarly offset blotting from the lower curved stroke of the *g* in *degolne* (MS. *onde* [/] *golne*) at *Rid.* 13.21 on MS. folio 104*b*. For further offset blotting from the same area, see the following note. It must be borne in mind that the facing pages do not *exactly* match up now, since the book was unbound, photographed, and rebound for the facsimile edition in 1933. Even in the facsimile, however, portions of folio 104*b* that have blotted off onto folio 105*a* appear lighter in color on 104*b* and can easily be recognized on the facing folio by anyone familiar with mirror-image writing.

16. lower margin: The pale letters (see plates xi.a and b), which occur in the intervening space between *Rids.* 16 and 17, were described by Förster as "a peculiar rune-like sign which reminds me of the *ac*-rune in the (unpublished) alphabet in MS. No. 17 of St. John's College, Oxford" (*The Exeter Book of Old English Poetry*, p. 64). The letters are broad, curved, and indistinct. They could hardly be marginalic runes. They are, in fact, offset blotting from the letters *aþa* of *niðsceaþa* (MS. *nið* [/] *sceaþa*) in *Rid*. 13.24 on MS. folio 104*b*. Both this and the above-mentioned instance of offset blotting come from the same area of MS. folio 104*b*, which is close to the left-hand margin about two-thirds of the way down the folio. Neither of these offset blotting marks is reproduced in the extremely careful MS. copy made by Robert Chambers (*Brit. Mus. Add. MS. 9067*) in 1832. Robert Chambers either recognized the marks on folio 105*a* as offset blotting and chose not to copy them, or else the marks did not exist at that time. It seems possible that between the readings of Robert Chambers in 1832 and Förster in 1933, some caustic liquid was spilled on the MS. causing the offset blotting to occur.

17. Ship
[*VN: Gr.20; Tr.17; Tu.20; W.19; M.19; K-D.19*]

The key to this riddle lies in its runic clues. Each group of runes is to be transliterated and read backwards according to a system outlined below. The clues thus furnished are HORS, MON, WEGA, and HAOFOC. Some of the readings are disputed (see below). The horse I take to be the O.E. *merehengest* or *sæmearh*, and likewise the nailed creature to be the *nægledcnearr* or nailed clinker, an ocean-going vessel similar to the one discovered at Sutton Hoo. The hawk, by analogy with *Rid*. 62.3–4, is the sail or *swylce þryþa dæl* (*Rid*. 62.4). The *widlast* of line 6 is the wide road of the sea. This *widlast* is described as *rynestrong* (line 7); similarly the waterway of *Rid*. 80.2 is said to be strong-flowing: *hafað ryne strongne*. My translation of the riddle is as follows:

> I saw a proud and bright-headed horse (HORS) going on the way, a swift creature traveling fiercely over the plain. It carried on its back a battle-power, man (MON). The warrior (WEGA) rode the nailed creature. The wide road carried, swiftly flowing, a bold hawk (HAOFOC). The journey, the expedition of these (of such ones) was all the brighter. Say what it is called.

The riddle ends with a miniature riddle: "What is the swift-flowing road which carries the bold hawk?" That road is the sea; that hawk is the sail; that nailed horse is the ship. On the deck of the ship rides the *hildeþryþe*, MON.

Two main solutions have been proposed for the riddle. One is Hicketier's "falconry" solution (*Anglia* x, 592–96), recently repeated by Erhardt-Siebold (*PMLA* lxvii, 3–6) with no new consideration of the text. Hicketier's solution is based in part upon an emendation of MS. *rad* to *rand* and of MS. runic AGEW to runic WOEÞ (read in reverse as ÞEOW). Hicketier describes his newly discovered *nægled rand* as "der mit buckeln oder wenigstens mit einem buckel in der mitte aus-gestattete schild" (*Anglia* x, 593). The other main solution proposed is Trautmann's "Hors, mon, þew, haofoc" (p. 80), which is little more than a restatement of the literal terms of the riddle. Tupper modified Trautmann's solution slightly by saying that the riddle is "little more than fragments of the world-riddle, 'A man upon horseback with a hawk on his fist'" (p. 108). Tupper supports this "world-riddle" solu-tion by reference to a seventeenth-century riddle culled from the col-lection of one Randle Holme III in *MS. Harl. 1960* (see the collection in *PMLA* xviii, 211 ff.). The Holme riddle bears no structural resemblance to the Old English riddle in question. Indeed, the relevance of any seventeenth-century riddle collection to an Old English tradition is seriously to be doubted. A rapid survey of common riddlic motifs in Archer Taylor's *English Riddles from Oral Tradition* will show that simi-lar riddlic descriptions are used by peoples in different cultures to conceal different solutions. Tupper's statement that "in the pointless Anglo-Saxon logogriphs, the subject is merely stated" (p. 108) is in-genuous. Kock (*Anglia* xliii, 310) points out that the descriptive HORS hidden in simple runic disguise is not likely to be the solution of the riddle, and I agree. Krapp and Dobbie doubt "whether the various in-terpretations of l. 6*a* add anything to the solution, if in fact there is any 'solution' at all" (p. 331). Wyatt notes that the riddle is "not worth the time and ingenuity that have been spent upon it" (p. 78). Recently Eliason has interpreted the riddlic *nægled* (taking final *ne* as adverbial *ne*) as "on or possessing finger nails" (*SP* xlix, 561). The verbal uses of *næglian* in O.E., "to nail or to fasten with nails" (B-T., p. 707), do not support the "fingernail" hypothesis. As for Eliason's "writing" solution, it should be noted that Old English riddles do not conceal solutions that are abstractions of human experience. Even the "writing" creatures of *Rid.* 49 are the discrete *pen and fingers*.

A Note on the Runes: A note here on the general use of runes in the riddle is in order. Förster (*The Exeter Book of Old English Poetry*, p. 62, note 21) first pointed out that where the scribe puts whole groups of runes between points, as in *Rids.* 17 and 73, he meant each group of runes to be taken as a word, with the letters indicated by the runes read backwards (for the MS. pointing of runes, see the Introduction). Presumably the runes here and elsewhere in the *Riddles* are to be read with their Anglo-Saxon runic names (for the names, see the list of runes at the end of the Glossary). In each runic group in this riddle there is one rune whose name properly alliterates with the primary alliteration of the line. Wherever possible, the linear arrangement of runes in the text is according to the alliterative requirements of the lines. Given, however, the double constraint of (1) securing some alliteration and (2) using the runes in terms of their phonological equivalents to spell words backwards in the text, the poet seems not to have been able to have consistently satisfied the requirements of traditional Old English meter as well. Thus the runes, if named, give faulty meter at 1*b* and 5*a* and proper meter at 2*a*. The meter at 7*b* would be proper if *ond* were inserted between the runes. If the alliterating rune in 6*a* were placed in the proper metrical position, the last two runes would be transposed. But if the runic clues are to be properly given and properly solved, clearly the order of presenting runes that represent letters that spell out words in backwards fashion must be consistent at all costs. This enables the reader to discover the key to untangling the runes and to solving the riddle. One could argue, of course, that where the meter is faulty, the text is corrupt, but I believe that the runes as they occur in the MS. make good sense and that therefore in the case of runic passages, the riddler sometimes took metrical liberties that he did not take elsewhere.

17.1: *Ic on siþe seah*: MS. *Ic seah*. Grein completes the *a*-line, *Ic seah* [*somod*] and so does Tupper. Trautmann prints *Ic* [*on siþe*] *seah*, and so do Krapp and Dobbie. Wyatt prefers *Ic seah* [*swoncorne*]; Kock (*Anglia* xliii, 311), *Ic seah* [*sigan*]. Krapp and Dobbie note that Trautmann's reading is supported by the analogy of *on swaþe* at *Rid.* 73.1; it is also supported by the parallel phrasal *on rade* in line 7 of this riddle.

17.1–2: ·ᚻ ᚱ ᚠ / ᚺ· : transliterated SROH, to be read in reverse order as HORS. The ship is a sea horse. Old English kennings for *ship* often utilized one term for *sea* and one for *horse*. Some examples are: *brimhengest* (*Run.* 47; *An.* 513), *sundhengest* (*Chr.* 852, 862), *merehengest* (*Rid.* 12.6; *Bo.* 26.25), *wæghengest* (*Guth.* 1329; *El.* 236), *yðmearh* (*Chr.* 863; *Wh.* 49), *sæmearh* (*An.* 267; *El.* 228, 245; *Wh.* 15), and *lagumearg* (*Guth.* 1332).

17.2: *hygewloncne*: *proud, high-spirited*. The only other occurrence of this compound is at *Rid.* 43.3ff., *bryd grapode, | hygewlonc hondum*, ostensibly to describe the proud woman's kneading of the dough. Both elements are frequently compounded. Cp. *hygerof, hygegrim, felawlanc, modwlanc*.

17.2: *heafodbeorhtne*: *bright-headed*. Brøgger and Shetelig note that Viking figureheads "were decorative . . . and they were carefully embellished to provide a fitting ornament for the ship" (*The Viking Ships*, pp. 139–40). Old English compounds for *ship* that include an element for *prow*—such as *hringedstefna* (*Beo.* 32, 1131, 1897; *El.* 248), *wundenstefna* (*Beo.* 220), *hringnaca* (*Beo.* 1862), and *brondstæfn* (*An.* 504)—like the O.N. *hringhorni* (*Sp.*, p. 361), may indicate that Anglo-Saxon figureheaded prows were also elaborately adorned. See my discussion of ships' figureheads in the headnote to *Rid.* 72.

17.4: *hildeþryþe*: *battle-power* (*Sp.*: *vigor bellicus*), in apposition to the runic MON. The movement from a general to a more specific description of an unknown character is typical in the *Riddles*.

17.5: · ᚴ ᛗ ᛗ · : transliterated NOM, to be read in reverse order as MON. This is the *hildeþryþe* carried *on hrycge* of the ship. Cp. "ship" *Rid.* 34.6 in which creatures are carried *ufon on hrycge*.

17.5: *nægledne*: *the nailed-one*, a substantive adjective. This is a nailed clinker ship similar to the one discovered at Sutton Hoo. The *Exeter Maxims* poet says, "Scip sceal genægled" (*Max. I* 93), and the poet of *Rid.* 56 excludes the possibility of a *ship* solution in the same terms: "ne hie scip fereð, | naca nægledbord" (56.4–5). The family of Noah in *Gen.* 1418 and 1433 ride in a *nægledbord*; and the Norsemen at *Brun.* 53 flee over deep water in their *nægledcnearrum*. Anglo-Saxon ships, like their Viking cousins, were "clench- or clinker-built, i.e., with the lower edge of each plank overlapping slightly the upper edge of the plank below and riveted to it at frequent intervals by clench-nails of iron, clenched on the inside over an iron washer, the rove" (Green, *Sutton Hoo: The Excavation of a Ship-Burial*, p. 49).

17.6: · ᛏ ᚷ ᛗ ᚹ · : transliterated AGEW, to be read in reverse order as WEGA for O.E. *wiga, warrior*. Page (*ES* xliii, 484 ff.) points out the difficulty of transliterating runes into Old English script, especially in the case of vocalic runes where dialects and sound shifts may be involved. Hacikyan (*ELN* iii, 86 ff.) argues that the poet, noticing a vocalic shift from *-i* to *-e* in certain words, may have written runic WEGA for WIGA in order to test or to fool the reader. He mentions the supposedly parallel situation of *Agof* for *Agob* in *Rid*. 21. But *Agof* is non-runic and therefore a different case altogether. It seems more likely, in light of other "variant" vocalic runes (see, for example, runic HAOFOC in lines 7–8), that the problem here is one of transliteration and of equivalence rather than one of deliberate deception on the poet's part. There are several other readings of the four runes, most of them involving an emendation. Krapp and Dobbie point out that "most edd. take *rad*, l. 5*b*, the name of the R-rune, as standing for that rune and to be read with the runes in l. 6*a*" (p. 331). Tupper, for example, reads WEGAR for *wig-gar, lance*, and translates the passage 17.4 ff.: "He (the horse) had on his back strength in war (or 'war-troop'), a man and a nailed spear" (p. 109). There are no nailed spears in either Old English poetry or Anglo-Saxon graves, to my knowledge. Cosijn (*Bëitrage* xxiii, 129), Holthausen (*Anglia Beibl.* ix, 357), Hicketier (*Anglia* x, 593 ff.), and Trautmann (pp. 80–81) all emend the runes drastically to support their cacophony of solutions. Cosijn reads MS. *rad* as runic *R* and transliterates [R]AG WE to read GAR W*ynn*Eh. Holt-hausen reads GAR W*ynn*E. Trautmann adds one rune and emends another to give [R]AG [W]E[þ], reading GA[R] [þ]Eo[W]. Hicketier emends *rad* to *rand* and runic AGEW to WOEþ, reading *rand* þEOW. A conservative editorial policy is nowhere apparent. It does not seem likely that the runes have been here miscopied, since the *Exeter Book* scribe takes special care with passages that are set off by points and that have a high visibility. Most scribal errors in the MS. are committed at points of low visibility such as the MS. *swist ne* for *swiftne* in line 3 of this riddle. Mackie does regard the runic AGEW as valid but reads A GEW, two words, for A WEG, translating "upon the ways" (p. 109). Krapp and Dobbie apparently agree with this reading. But adverbial phrases are not normally hidden in runes. The phrase, *a weg*, has no significance in terms of the solution of the riddle. The runic letters should disguise a noun and they should hide a character of some importance. Given the difficulties of transliterating vocalic runes as noted above, it seems simplest and most straightforward to read MS. runic AGEW for WEGA and to take this for O.E. *wiga, warrior*. Runic WEGA is thus in apposition to runic MON. In *Rid.* 62, two runic clues are similarly repeated with variation: BE[*orn*] and þE[*gn*], and HA[*foc*] and FÆ[*lca*]. Thus there is some precedent for the practice of runic apposition here.

17.6–8: Mackie translates these lines, taking runic MON as the subject:

> Travelling far upon the ways (AGEW)
> swift in his progress, he carried
> a strong hawk (COFOAH).

[Mackie, p. 109]

Krapp and Dobbie apparently accept this reading. Syntactically, one would expect either *widlast* or *rynestrong* to be the subject of *ferede*. The existence of an adjectival *widlast* is a matter of some contention. B-T. (p. 1217) lists the example from this riddle and that of *Gen.* 1021–22: *forþon þu* [Cain] *flema scealt / widlast wrecan, winemagum lað> Grein (*Sp.*, p. 789) lists the latter example as a noun along with the example from *An.* 677. Grein lists the riddlic *widlast* and the *widlastum* from *Wulf* 9 as adjectives. CH. lists the riddlic *widlast* as "*long wandering, long way* or *road*" (p. 407). The only example cited that might be an adjective is the *widlastum wenum* of *Wulf and Eadwacer*. The line in which *widlastum* occurs, however, is complicated by the presence of MS. *dogian*, an unattested verb with no known cognates. Malone ("Two English Frauenlieder," in *Studies in Old English Literature in Honor of Arthur G. Brodeur*, ed. S. B. Greenfield, pp. 106ff.) would emend *dogode* to *hogode* and translate *widlastum* as a noun, thus: "I was mindful of my Wulf in his wanderings, his expectations" (pp. 108–9). This seems to me the most likely reading of this particular *widlast*. In fact, there is no adjectival *last* and I doubt that there is any adjectival *widlast*. O.E. *widlast* means simply *long journey* or *wide road*. The *widlast* in line 6 of this riddle is the wide road of the sea, modified by *rynestrong* (nom. sing. masc.), a hapax legomenon that I take to mean *strong-flowing*.

B-T. notes that *ryne* means, "*A course, run, running*, both in the sense of *motion* and in that of *the path in which motion takes place*" (p. 805). With reference to fluids, it means *a flow* or *flux* (p. 806). Thus, in *Gen.* 159, the waters created by God are described as *heora ryne healdað*, and in *Rid.* 80, the water creature is said to be swift-flowing: *hafað ryne strongne* (80.2). The wide road of the sea is swift-flowing; it carries the bold hawk or bird-like sail.

17.7–8: · ᚻ ᛕ / ᚠ ᛕ ᚠ ᚺ · : transliterated COFOAH, to be read in reverse order as HAOFOC for O.E. *hafoc*. Page (*ES* xliii, 484ff.) points out the difficulty of transliterating runes especially in the case of vocalic runes where exact correspondences may not be well defined and where dialects and sound shifts may complicate the procedure. I take the HAOFOC or *hafoc* to be metaphorically the sail, as the parallel runic HA[*foc*] in *Rid.* 62 is described as *swylce þryþa dæl* (62.4), *a share of the power*. Bruce-Mitford points out that Anglo-Saxon ships, like their Viking contemporaries, were presumably powered by both oars and sails (*The Sutton Hoo Ship-Burial: A Handbook*, pp. 47–50). Bede mentions the ship of Guthfrith, which had both oars and sails (*EH.* v.i, p. 454). Thus oars and bird-like sail would be *þryþa dæl*. The ship-creature of *Rid.* 34 has *tu fiþru* (34.7) but is *na fugol ana* (34.9). Anglo-Saxon or Viking ships might easily have been seen as great birds swimming over the horizon. Thus in *An.* 497, a ship is described as *fugole gelicost*; likewise in *Beo.* 218.

17.8: *beorhtre:* See note to *heafodbeorhtre* above.

17.9: *Saga hwæt hit hatte:* The MS. reading is certainly corrupt, as most editors have surmised, since the human narrator of the third-person descriptive riddle can hardly conclude with "Say what I am called." Presumably the scribe saw the collocation of *saga, hwæt,* and *hatte* and assumed the familiar rhetorical ending of the first-person riddle. For another similar mistake, cp. *Rid.* 82.7. The proper ending for a third-person descriptive riddle may be found at *Rid.* 37.29b: *saga hwæt hio hatte* where *hio* refers to the previous *wiht*. Since no *wiht* appears as the antecedent in this riddle, it is probably wiser to use the neuter *hit*.

18. Sword
[*VN: Gr.21; Tr.18; Tu.21; W.20; M.20; K-D.20*]

Dietrich's solution, "sword" (*ZfdA.* xi, 465) is accepted by all major editors except Trautmann who solves the riddle as "hawk" or "falcon." Swaen (*Neoph.* iv, 258 ff.) properly points out that Trautmann's reading of the text is forced and that Trautmann's knowledge of the medieval art of falconry is slight. Trautmann, for example, emends MS. *wir*, "wire," at line 4*a* to *wirn*, which he reads as *wearn*, "hindrance," then explains that the "bright hindrance" is a hood about the "murderous eye" (*wælgim*) of the bird. Apart from the practice of rewriting the text, Swaen notes that the practice of hooding hawks did not reach Europe until the thirteenth century. Recently Shook ("Old English Riddle No. 20," in *Franciplegius: Medieval and Linguistic Studies in Honor of Francis Peabody Magoun, Jr.*, ed. Jess B. Bessinger, Jr., and Robert P. Creed, pp. 194 ff.) has attempted to shore up Trautmann's case, but Shook's readings though ingenious are often as broadly interpretive as Trautmann's. Shook takes the *wælgim*, for example, to be a "slaughtering-gem" or hawk's talon bound by the *wir* or fist-ring of the handler. He takes the *since ond seolfre* to be the ornate gear of the bird. He believes the solution of the riddle to be a kenning, *heoruswealwe* (*Fort.* 86), "sword-swallow" or "hawk," and thus accounts for the language appropriate to bird and blade. O.E. *heoruswealwe* is both a kenning and a hapax legomenon. Presumably the word was unusual and riddle-like even to an Anglo-Saxon audience. A common accessibility to possible solutions seems a necessary prerequisite to the riddling game. Did the riddle-solvers or readers know the kenning for "hawk"? This seems doubtful since the poet of *The Fortunes of Men* introduced his kenning only after describing the bird clearly as *wildne fugel* and *heafoc* (*Fort.* 85–86). Was the riddle written only for readers of *The Fortunes of Men*? This is not likely. A singular kenning does not seem a plausible solution to a riddle. A kenning is, in fact, a miniature riddle in itself.

Another unlikely solution is Kay's (*TSL* xiii, 133 ff.) double entendre "sword" and "phallus" with an emphasis upon the latter. Certainly there is some sexual joke at the end of the riddle as most editors have realized, but Kay goes too far when he tries to reinterpret the whole of the riddle in terms of the concluding joke. He says, for example:

> In line 4 *wælgim* probably refers to the ultimate victory which results from the sexual slaughter-conquest since the emphasis is on the "glory" (*beorht*, line 3), the "beautiful" (*fægre*, line 2), and indeed on the—*gim*. *Wælgim* suggests a death-orgasm archetype. After being directed sometimes into battle, lines 5–6, we learn that the *wiht* brings home the treasure (conception) as the result of victory. [*TSL* xiii, 137]

There is a double entendre in the riddle (see below), but it is limited to lines 17*b* ff. and it is much more complicated than Kay realizes.

The problem with the riddle is, as Shook rightly notes, that it seems to have two apparently unrelated parts. The first, lines 1–17*a*, describes a weapon, most naturally a sword. The second, lines 17*b*–35, describes the celibacy of the creature. Trautmann and Shook believe that a real, animate, celibate creature is described in the latter half of the poem. Kay believes that a sword is described as a phallus (normally not a very "celibate" creature). Tupper (*MLN* xxi, 97) notes (with tongue in cheek?) that the riddler here may have wandered in "the joy of creation." I believe with Davidson that the description in lines 17*b* ff. may refer on one level to the possible reforging of the sword. Davidson explains the difficulty of the last section of the riddle in terms of the "sword" solution:

> The most puzzling passage is the [creature's] lament that it has no wife and child and can have none unless it leaves its lord's service. The idea of the sword as a bachelor warrior is well enough, but it is worked out in such detail here that one would suspect some special meaning behind it. Two possibilities are that if a sword no longer remained in service it might go back to the armoury with other weapons, and perhaps might go into the smithy and be reforged as a new weapon. Since the sword is a recognized phallic symbol, it is also possible that we have a double entendre here. [*The Sword in Anglo-Saxon England*, pp. 153–54]

The sword is a celibate fighter; it enters the fray without hope of progeny. It brings *real* death to men (not Kay's "death-orgasm"). Women do not love *that* weapon but revile it. The point here is not, as Kay would have it, that the sword is actually a phallus; the point is that the sword is a real and not a metaphoric weapon, that it brings a real and not a metaphoric death. There are certainly two weapons in the last part of the poem, and the hidden "weapon" by implication— the "weapon" that may "battle" and beget children, the "weapon" that the wife loves—is a phallus. The riddlic weapon, the *real* weapon, must battle valiantly without hope of begetting children (it begets only when it fails and is sent to the smithy); it must serve honorably in a real battle and bring death to men, and it reaps for its labors only scorn and insult from a woman. Not so with that other "weapon." One weapon murders men when it faithfully toils, and engenders "children" only when it fails in its duty. The other "weapon" engenders children when it faithfully toils. It can fight and engender, battle and be loved at the same time. The end of the riddle begins to make sense only when we realize that the sword describes itself as *unlike that other "weapon."* Admittedly this is a rather sophisticated use of the double entendre device, but a quick survey of other double entendre riddles in the *Exeter Book* will show that the device is not always used in exactly the same way, and in at least one case (*Rid.* 10.7*b* ff.) the double entendre seems to function for only a part of the riddle as it does here.

The other "sword" riddle in the *Exeter Book* is *Rid.* 69. Neither riddle owes anything to any of the Latin "sword" or "dagger" riddles: Aldhelm's Riddle 61, Tatwine's Riddle 30, and Eusebius's Riddle 36.

18.1: Cp. *Rid.* 21.2.

18.3–4: The *byrne* or "mail coat" of the sword must be the scabbard, though Davidson (*The Sword in Anglo-Saxon England*, p. 153) believes it to be the sword blade. Scabbards were normally made of wood and simply covered with leather or cloth, but sometimes they were adorned with jewels. The Sutton Hoo sword, for example, had scabbard-bosses "with a cross in the centre of a unique petal-like design, set up in wedge-shaped covered cells between them" (Bruce-Mitford, *The Sutton Hoo Ship-Burial: A Handbook*, p. 76). The *wælgim* is probably a scabbard jewel associated with the death-dealing destruction of the sword.

18.6b ff.: The poet of the *Exeter Maxims* writes that *Gold geriseþ on guman sweorde, | sellic sigesceorp* (*Max. I* 125–26), and Davidson notes that this description "is well borne out by surviving hilts and scabbards with rich ornamentation, as well as allusions to swords decorated with gold in Anglo-Saxon wills of the tenth and eleventh centuries"

(*The Sword in Anglo-Saxon England*, p. 151). For the use of gold and other treasures in the decoration of the hilt, see Davidson, ibid., pp. 64 ff.

18.11: *wordlofes*: Editors before Krapp and Dobbie read *word lofes* as two words, but Pontán (*MLR* xii, 71) pointed out that the verb *wyrnan* always governs the genitive of thing so the reading here must be a compound; so also B-T., p. 1266, who cite O.N. *orðlof*.

18.16b–17a: It is important to note the sequence leading up to this reference to the occasional injury of friends. The sword's actions have been described in the hall *for mengo þær hy meodu drincað* (line 12) where it is appropriately sheathed (*healdeð mec on heaþore*, line 13a). Inappropriately, by implication, it is drawn and used against friends —and the earlier reference to mead drinking is hardly happenstance. Too much drinking often leads to a table catastrophe. So the poet of *The Fortunes of Men* says:

> Sumum meces ecg   on meodubence
> yrrum ealowosan   ealdor oþþringeð,
> were winsadum;   bið ær his worda to hræd.

> [*Fort.* 48–50]

And many of the Anglo-Saxon *Laws* warn against the drawing of swords at table—so the *Laws* of Hlothære and Eadric indicate:

> Gif man wæpn abregde þær mæn drincen *and* ðær man nan yfel ne deþ, scilling þan þe þæt flet age, *and* cyninge XII scll'.
> Gif þæt flet geblodgad wyrþe, forgylde þem mæn his mundbyrd *and* cyninge L scill'. [Liebermann, ed. *Die Gesetze der Angelsachsen*, vol. 1, p. 11]

18.17a: *wæpnum awyrged*: *hated (cursed) among weapons*. Tupper cites a similar description of a sword at PPs. 143.11: *of þam awyrgedan wraðan sweorde*. For this sense of *awiergan*, see CH., p. 30, category I, and also cp. *awyrgedlic*, "detestable, abominable" (B-T., p. 84; CH., p. 31) and *awyrgednes*, "wickedness, cursedness" (B-T., p. 84). Trautmann proposed to read *wæpnum awyrded* (*Anglia* xlii, 130) after a suggestion by Grein, or *wordum awyrged* (edition, p. 82, note).

18.17b ff.: For a discussion of the implied comparison in the last half of the riddle, see the headnote.

18.18: *wræce*: Most editors gloss the form here as preterite subjunctive *wrǣce*, but the syntax would appear to demand the present subjunctive. For the form, present subjunctive *wræce*, which appears to be Anglian, see the note to *Rid.* 1.2. For the meter, see Pope's category C23 on p. 296 of *The Meter of Beowulf*.

18.20 ff.: I translate beginning at line 20: "nor will the family from which I sprang be increased by children of mine unless I must depart lordless from my possessor who gave me rings." The sword while it serves honorably in battle remains celibate, but by implication when it falters (and does not *frean hyre, I guþe fremme*: 24b–25a), it leaves its lord and returns to the smithy to beget "children." The instrumental plural *-an* ending of *eaforan* is probably a late West Saxon form (cp. *hringan* at *Rid.* 2.2 and *secgan* at *Rid.* 61.1 and see notes). Davidson (*The Sword in Anglo-Saxon England*, p. 29) notes at least one example of a sword that appears to have been made from strips of pattern-welding from older worn swords, and also gives the accounts from several sagas of swords remade from blades broken in battle (pp. 162 ff.). The relative clause at line 21b is usually taken as referring to the *mægburg* as I have translated it (see B-T., p. 1147 under *wacan*, also Holthausen, *ESn.* li, 185, and Wyatt, p. 79). Schücking (see note in Krapp and Dobbie, p. 332) takes the relative clause as referring to *eaforan* and translates, "durch Kinder von mir, die ich in die Welt setzte," and similarly, Shook ("Old English Riddle No. 20," in *Franciplegius*, p. 201); but the verb *wacan* means "to be born, to come into being" (B-T., p. 1147), not "to bear" in a transitive sense. In the cases cited by B-T., it is the children who are the subject of the verb *wacan*, while references to the parents are in the oblique case. Cp., for example, *Gen.* 1646–47: *of þam eorle woc I unrim þeoda*; likewise *Gen.* 2764–65: *Abrahame woc I bearn of bryde*.

18.23: *þe me hringas geaf*: A number of Anglo-Saxon swords unearthed by the archaeologists have had rings of one sort or another attached to the hilt. Some, mainly those found in Kentish cemeteries, have a fixed ring attached to the pommel and a loose ring linked to this. Others have not rings, but a metal fitting shaped to represent one ring held inside another. The significance of the ring or ring-knob (as the metal fittings in the shape of rings are now called) in each case has been the subject of some debate (see Davidson, *The Sword in Anglo-Saxon England*, pp. 71 ff., for a list of ring-swords and for a summary of opinions as to the significance of the rings). At first it was thought that the rings might have been used for the attachment of a useful cord or thong or for the attachment of an amulet, but most of these theories now seem doubtful. The ring-knobs of course would not be useful for attaching anything. It is now thought that the rings may have been used in all cases as a symbol of a liege-lord relationship, especially as we know that "the gift of a sword from the king or leader to a warrior entering his service was considered to form a bond of mutual obligation and loyalty between them" (Davidson, ibid., pp. 75–76). For a recent discussion of ring-swords and their significance, see Evison, "The Dover Ring-sword and Other Sword-rings and Beads," *Archaeologia* ci, 63 ff.

18.29: *geara*: The MS. *gearo* is retained by Grein, Assmann, and Mackie, but both the meter and the sense would seem to demand *gēara* as Herzfeld (*Die Räthsel des Exeterbuches und ihr Verfasser*, p. 44) proposed —and so Tupper, Wyatt, Trautmann, and Krapp and Dobbie.

18.32 ff.: Tupper notes that this is "the only picture of the shrew or scold in Old English poetry" (p. 113), but the purpose here is not so much to paint the picture of a scold as it is to indicate the difference between the woman's response to the real weapon which kills and her response to the other implied "weapon" which engenders (see headnote).

18.34: *firenaþ*: with *þ* altered from *w* (see plate xii). This has not been previously noted by the editors.

18.36: Förster (*The Exeter Book of Old English Poetry*, p. 59) points out that folio 105*b* ends a full eight-leaf quire, but that the next quire lacks a whole sheet, one leaf at the beginning (here) and one at the end (see gap between *Rids.* 38 and 39). Though *Rid.* 19 begins properly on folio 106*a*, there is no end-punctuation after *compes* (the last word on folio 105*b*), and if *compes* begins a new verse as seems likely from a metrical standpoint, there is certainly something lost between the folios. All editors except Wyatt and Mackie indicate a lacuna in the manuscript. Most editors read *compes* at the end of 35*a*, but Holthausen (*Anglia*

Beibl. ix, 357) and Trautmann put *compes* at the beginning of a new verse for metrical reasons. *Ic ne gyme þæs compes* is barely conceivable as an Old English half-line. It might be an example of what Pope calls minor deviations from, or combinations of, types B and C (see p. 128 of his *Seven Old English Poems*), but the examples that Pope lists all have only a single-syllable drop between the lifts and this verse has a two-syllable drop. All things considered, it seems wiser and safer to begin a new line with *compes* as do Holthausen and Trautmann. Of course, given the lacuna, it is impossible to know for certain whether *þæs* was an article or an emphatic demonstrative, but in the absence of other information it seems best to steer clear of metrically irregular lines.

19. Plow
[*VN: Gr.22; Tr.19; Tu.22; W.21; M.21; K-D.21*]

Dietrich's solution, "plow" (*ZfdA*. xi, 465 ff.), is accepted by all editors. B. Colgrave believes that the plow in this riddle may be similar to that depicted in *MS. Cott. Tib. B. V.* (*MLR* xxxii, 19 ff.), but David Wilson notes that in the reconstruction of Anglo-Saxon tools, manuscript iconography must be used with extreme caution for "an artist illuminating a manuscript would not necessarily go out in the fields and look at a plough before he drew it: he would be much more likely to copy a drawing from another manuscript, which may itself have been painted in Padua or Paris" (*The Anglo-Saxons*, pp. 73–76). No Anglo-Saxon plows and only a few plowshares have survived. Wilson's own hypothetically constructed plow has a heavy wheel but no moldboard. Its furrow was "cut and turned by a coulter which was shifted at the end of each furrow, so that the next furrow would lie in the same direction" (ibid., p. 76). For a description of the life of the "lord" who paradoxically serves the plow, see Aelfric's *Colloquy*, lines 22–33.

19.1: *neol*: a form of *neowol*, for which B-T. lists two basic meanings: I. *prone, prostrate*; II. *deep down, low, profound* (pp. 715–16). The occurrence in this riddle is listed under the first meaning, but either is appropriate to the context. Cp. *El.* 831, where Judas digs a hole *under neolum niðer næsse*.

19.2: *geonge*: a Northumbrian form of *gangan* (Campbell 173, p. 66).

19.2–3: I take the *har holtes feond* to be the gray ox, as first suggested by Dietrich (*ZfdA.* xi, 466). The structure of the clauses here quite simply indicates the fore and aft of plowing: *me wisað . . . feond*, and *hlaford . . . æt steorte . . . wrigaþ on wonge*. With the exception of Krapp and Dobbie, other editors emend 4a to regularize the meter—but for another apparently authentic trisyllabic half-line, cp. *Rid.* 1.33a. Sievers (*Beiträge* x, 519) suggested reading *on* before *woh*, and so Wyatt; but Tupper notes that *on woh* normally means "wrongly, wrongfully" not "bent." Tupper adds *se* before *woh*, and so Mackie; Trautmann adds *se þe*. Cosijn (*Beiträge* xxiii, 129) fancifully takes the *har holtes feond* to be the iron of the share related by implication to an unmentioned axe.

19.8: *wægne*: Clearly this indicates a wheeled plow, but several varieties are possible (see Wilson, *The Anglo-Saxons*, fig. 10a, for a picture from the Bayeux tapestry and Page, *Life in Anglo-Saxon England*, p. 78, for a picture from *Brit. Mus. MS. Cotton Julius A VI*). Colgrave (*MLR* xxxii, 282) interprets the *wægne* here as "the fore-carriage which Virgil calls the *currus*," but the words glossed by O.E. *wægn* or *wæn*, L. *plaustrum* and *carrum*, are as general as modern English *wagon* or *cart*.

19.10: *sweotol*: Trautmann emends to *sweotole*, presumably reading *sweotole sweart* as *manifestly dark*. But a dark track may also be *sweotol*. Cp. *Blickl. Homl.* 203.36 (in B-T., p. 951): *Ða fotlastas wæron swutole and gesyne*.

19.12: *orþoncpil*: Trautmann, Wyatt, and Mackie read two words, *orþonc pil*, but for a similar compound utilizing initial *orþonc-*, see *orþoncbendum* at *Rid.* 40.15. One *orþoncpil* is the colter, the other is the share.

19.13–14: *Fealleþ on sidan | þæt ic toþum tere*: What I tear with my teeth falls to the side. Krapp and Dobbie point out that "the coulter . . . can hardly be said to 'fall to the side'" (p. 333). Mackie reads the clause beginning with *þæt* in line 14a as a clause of result and translates,

"Another in my head . . . leans to the side, / so that I tear with my teeth . . . " (p. 113). This is a misreading of *teran* as an intransitive verb. The only possible object for *tere* is the noun clause beginning with *þæt* in line 14*b*.

20. Wagon of Stars
[*VN*: *Gr.23*; *Tr.20*; *Tu.23*; *W.22*; *M.22*; *K-D.22*]

Dietrich (*ZfdA*. xi, 466) solved the riddle as "month," the sixty riders representing the sixty half-days of the month, the eleven horses, the four Sundays plus seven feast days. Thus, says Dietrich, the month is December and the far shore, the new year. This solution has been more or less accepted by all editors except Trautmann, though Krapp and Dobbie do admit that the explanation is far-fetched for "if we count the days of the month by half-days, we would expect the other numbers to be doubled also" (p. 333). Trautmann, disregarding the numbers, solves the riddle as "bridge." Recently, Blakeley (*RES* n.s. ix, 241–47) has interpreted the *wægn* of line 9 as Charles's Wain (Ursa Major) and has proposed the solution, "circling stars." Blakeley explains:

> The dangerous sea that must be crossed is the vast expanse of the sky. Once in every twenty-four hours the Wain leaves the horizon—which in the latitudes of the British Isles it seems almost to touch—and travels round the Pole Star till it comes down again toward the land. . . . The horsemen and horses are the stars near to the Wain, which travel with it. We are told that the eleven horses are loaded under the pole of the Wain. If the horses are stars, this gives perfect sense. The pole of the Wain was a familiar object in the heavens centuries before this riddle was invented; so Ovid (*Met*. x.447), "Flexerat obliquo plaustrum temone Bootes." . . . Under the pole of the Wain is the constellation now called "Canes Venatici." This constellation in fact does consist of eleven stars visible to the naked eye. [*RES* n.s. ix, 243]

Blakeley points out that the *wægn* of the heavens is mentioned in Alfred's *Boethius*—*An þara tungla / woruldmen hata ð wænes þisla* (*Bo.* 28.9–10)—and in Aelfric's *De Temporibus Anni*:

> Arcton hatte an tungel on norðdæle se hæfð seofon steorran *and* is forði oðrum naman gehaten Septembrio þone hata ð læwede men Carles wæn se

ne gæð næfre adune under ðissere eorðan swa swa oðre tunglan doð. Ac he went abutan hwilon up, hwilon adune, ofer dæg *and* ofer niht. [ix.6; ed. Henel, EETS, o.s.213, p. 68]

The Aelfric passage is derived from Isidore who says:

> *De Arcturo*: Arcturus ille est quem Latini Septentrionem dicunt, qui septem stellarum radiis fulgens in se ipso revolutus rotatur, qui ideo plaustrum vocatur quia in modum vehiculi voluitur et modo tres ad summa elevat, modo quattuor inclinat. Hic autem in caeli axe constitutus semper versatur et numquam mergitur, sed dum in se ipso voluitur, et nox finitur. [*NR.* xxvi.iii.18–23]

Blakeley notes that the Old English riddle may owe something to Riddle 53 of Aldhelm, "Arcturus," the first four lines of which describe the movement of the mysterious wagon of stars:

> Sidereis stipor turmis in vertice mundi:
> Esseda famoso gesto cognomina vulgo;
> In giro volvens iugiter non vergo deorsum,
> Cetera ceu properant caelorum lumina ponto.
>
> [Ed. Pitman, p. 28]

As the L. *arcturus* revolves without rushing downward, so too the O.E. *wægn* carries men and horses from one shore to another without falling from the air—*ne of lyfte fleag* (line 16). Here the common emendation of MS. *of* to *on* has completely obscured the proper solution to the riddle.

20.1: *sixtig*: The number here may refer simply to a multitude of stars. Blakeley (*RES* n.s. ix, 244) refers to an article by Tucker on "Sixty As an Indefinite Number in Middle English" (*RES* xxv, 152–53) and notes that similar examples may be found in Laȝamon's *Brut* and *Piers Plowman*. The convention is not common in Old English, but Blakeley notes that it may have been suggested to the Anglo-Saxons by the common Latin use of *sescenti* to signify "multitude" and by the less common use of *sexaginta* (cp. Martial, *Epigrams*, xii.26, cited by Blakeley, p. 244). Blakeley notes the significant use of "sixty" for "multitude" by Alcuin in a riddle-like poem about an ivory comb:

Mirum animal duo habens capita et dentes lx
non elefantinae magnitudinis sed
eburneae pulchritudinis.

[Wattenbach and Duemmler,
Monumenta Alcuiniana, p. 153;
cited by Blakeley, p. 244]

20.3: *endleofan*: These are the eleven stars of the constellation, Canes Venatici, which are visible to the naked eye (Blakeley, *RES* n.s. ix, 243).

20.4: *fridhengestas*: Thorpe in a note suggested *fyrdhengestas* and this was accepted at one time by Bosworth-Toller who translated the word as "war-horses" (p. 254, under *eoredmæcg*). Elsewhere (p. 337, under *fridhengest*), Bosworth-Toller translates the word as "stately horses" following a suggestion by Dietrich (*ZfdA.* xii, 251). But the evidence for an O.E. form, *frid-* or *frið-*, cognate with O.N. *friðr*, and meaning "beautiful," is slight (see note to *Rid.* 7.9). Tupper and Mackie emend the MS. reading to *friðhengestas* and translate "horses of peace." Trautmann reads *fridhengestas*, which he glosses in the singular as "gefleckter Hengst" with a question mark. I am inclined here to accept Grein's early notion in a note to his text that O.E. *frid-* here is related to O.H.G. *parafrit*, "horse." Kock (*Lunds Universitets Årsskrift*, NF., Avd. 1, Bd. 14, Nr. 26, p. 63) queries: "Is not *frid-* the Latin-Romanic *vered-*, *fred-* in *veredus*, *fredus*, 'courier's horse,' *paraveredus*, *palafredus*, Low Germ. *perd-*, Germ. *Pferd*, Engl. *palfrey*?" Kock's reading is apparently accepted by Krapp and Dobbie.

20.4: *feower sceamas*: The word *sceam* does not occur elsewhere in Old English. Holthausen notes: *scéam* m. 'Schimmel' (Pferd), zu *scéawian*, *scíene*, vgl. nis. *skjōmi* 'Licht, Strahl', ais. ~ 'Schwert', *skjōni* 'Apfel-schimmel'" (*AEW.*, p. 273). Bosworth-Toller (p. 822) and Grein (p. 572) define *sceam* as "white horse" with a question mark; Clark Hall, as a "pale grey or white horse?" (p. 292). But this may be a case where the literal context has deceived the lexicographers. Blakeley points out that there are four stars in the constellation Canes Venatici that are brighter than the other seven and notes that the riddler may have been thinking of these stars as the "white horses" (*RES* n.s. ix, 243–44). If this is true, the word *sceam* may be more closely related to O.E.

scima, "light, brightness, splendor" as its spelling would seem to indicate. For *scima* Holthausen notes: "*scīma* m. 'Strahl, Licht, Glanz', as. ahd. *scīmo*, nis. *skīma*, got. *skeima* 'Leuchte', zu ai. *chāyā́* 'Glanz, Schimmer', vgl. *scéam, scima, scīnan, scīr*" (*AEW.*, p. 279). If O.E. *sceamas* is related to *scima*, it might be translated as "bright ones" or "shiners." These are the four brightest of the eleven visible stars of Canes Venatici that are found *under hrunge* (line 10), "under the pole" of the heavenly wain.

20.16: *ne of lyfte fleag*: All editors except Mackie emend MS. *of* to *on* in order to duplicate the pattern of line 14*b* and to make sense of the solution, "month." Blakeley (*RES* n.s. ix, 246) points out that the phrase makes perfect sense in terms of the actual movement of the wain in the skies. Unlike many stars that rise and set in the course of an evening, the stars of Charles's Wain or Ursa Major revolve about the pole and are always visible at night (Olcott's *Field Book of the Skies*, rev. ed., p. 62). The same point is made by Aldhelm in his Riddle 53, "Arcturus," lines 2–4 (see headnote). It is interesting to note that the word for the constellation Arcturus in "common speech" in Aldhelm's riddle is *essedum*, "chariot," a Celtic word (Lewis and Short, p. 660).

21. Bow
[*VN: Gr.24; Tr.21; Tu.24; W.23; M.23; K-D.23*]

Dietrich (*ZfdA.* xi, 466) solved the riddle as "bow," and this solution is accepted by nearly all editors. Trautmann suggests that the bow here is actually a crossbow (*die Armbrust*), but crossbows were unknown in England until they were brought over by the French in the eleventh century (Keller, *The Anglo-Saxon Weapon Names*, p. 54). For a summary of the archaeological evidence for the reconstruction of the Anglo-Saxon bow, see Wilson, *The Anglo-Saxons*, pp. 123–24. For a list of references to bows and arrows in Old English literature, see Keller, *The Anglo-Saxon Weapon Names*, pp. 197 ff.

21.1: *Agob*: All previous editors retain the MS. form, *Agof*, though most accept Sievers's explanation of the form:

Im urtext stand also *agob*, und ein abschreiber hat hier wie sonst das aus-
lautende *b* nach der gewohnheit seiner zeit in *f* umgesetzt. Silbenauslau-
tendes *b* für germ. ƀ (vgl. *Beiträge* xi, 542 ff.) geht aber auch im allgemeinen
nicht über die mitte des 8. jahrhunderts hinaus während es sich im inlaut
etwas länger zu halten scheint. [*Anglia* xiii, 15]

Certainly the original reading must have been *Agob* and some scribe
after the eighth century must have "corrected" the *b* to *f*, but the
original as well as the "correction" could have occurred any time be-
tween the eighth and the tenth centuries (any scribe used to making
the alteration of the early form might have done so mechanically
here). Still it does seem likely that the mistake arose because some
scribe at some point was copying an exemplar containing riddles or
poems in which the spelling *b* for voiced *f* was common and had to be
changed to accord with the scribe's own usage. Wyatt's notion that
Agof is a bit of *philological* chicanery on the part of a poet who "had
seen the change of final *b* to *f* and . . . utilised it here to befog his
auditors" (p. 81) seems less likely. Nowhere else in the *Riddles* are
runes or secret letters used in such a deliberate, phonologically gaming
fashion. In fact, a general use of this sort would make code words all
but impossible to decode, since one could never be sure which par-
ticular phonological change was to be reversed. Schlutter (*ESn.* xli,
453–54) would reverse only the consonants in *Agof* to read *Afog*,
which he associates with the Old Northumbrian base of *afu(h)lic*,
"perverse" (BTS., p. 27), but he does not attempt to explain the rela-
tionship between *afuh* and *afog*, and his translation of lines 1–2a ("Ver-
dreht is mein name, wieder verdreht / bin ich, ein kunstreich ding")
is most unlikely.

21.2: Cp. *Rid*. 18.1.

21.3: The editors retain the MS. *of bosme* in 3*b*, but as the bow is being
bent (*þonne ic onbuge*) in readiness for the shot, it makes more sense to
read *on bosme*. In terms of the real action (the bending of the bow), line
3*a* means "when I bend"; but in terms of the metaphoric game (the
bow masquerading as a warrior) it may mean "when I yield." This
creates a typical riddle-like paradox: when this creature bends and
takes an arrow in the breast, it does not die; instead, it sends forth the
arrow to kill another.

21.4a: Cp. *Rid.* 15.9, *Chr.* 768, *Jul.* 471, *An.* 1331, and *Mald.* 47, 146. Such weapons are "deadly," not necessarily poisonous.

21.8: *oþþæt*: Trautmann reads *oþþe* but this makes less sense of the passage. The bow here spits out its venom as a result of being released. This is one of those cases noted by Mitchell where "clauses of time with *oþ(þæt)* often shade into result" (*A Guide to Old English* 180, p. 98).

21.8: *spilde geblonden*: Mackie translates this as "fraught with destruction" (p. 115), but the "mixing" here (the primary sense of *geblandan*) seems more ominous. For the possible meaning of *geblandan*, "to infect, corrupt," which denotes possession of evil moral qualities, see BTS., p. 296, under category V. This meaning surely derives from the extended meaning, "to mix, prepare with (harmful) ingredients" (BTS., category III). A good translation might be "infected with destruction." Cp. the uses of *geblandan* at *An.* 33 and *Guth.* 668.

21.9b: The unemended verse, *þæt ic ær geap* (as printed by Grein, Assmann, Wyatt, and Krapp and Dobbie) needs a drop after *ær* to be acceptable metrically (B1). Sievers (*Beiträge* x, 519) first suggested reading *æror* for *ær*, and so Tupper, Mackie and myself. Trautmann proposes to emend *geap* to *geseap* (edition), or *geþeah* (*Anglia* xlii, 131 ff.); Holthausen would emend to *gegrap* (*Anglia Beibl.* xxx, 51). But the form *geap* from O.E. *geopan*, "to take to oneself, to receive" (B-T., p. 427; *Sp.*, p. 258) is probably legitimate.

21.10 ff.: The clause at 11*b* is the subject of *togongeð*; thus Mackie translates, "What I am speaking about does not easily pass away from any man, if what flies from my belly reaches him . . . " (p. 115). Erhardt-Siebold (*MLN* lxv, 93 ff.) would emend *sprice* in line 11*b* to *spirce* in order to translate 11*b* as "what I spirt about," but O.E. *spircan* means "to sparkle" (BTS., p. 708) and is used with reference to fire or to objects that are on fire.

21.13 ff.: I translate beginning at 13*a*: *so that he buys* (or *pays for*) *the evil drink with his strength, the perilous* (literally, *danger-* or *calamity-fast*) *cup with his life.* For the MS. *full wer fæste* I read *full ferfæste* with *fer-* for *fær-*, "danger, sudden attack." The weak adjective *ferfæste* (acc. sing. neuter) modifies *full*, "cup," and the phrase *full ferfæste* is a variation of *þone mandrinc* in the preceding line. The early editors (Grein, Assmann, Wyatt) keep the MS. reading, *full wer fæste*, taking *wer* as the subject of *geceapaþ* in the previous half-line and *full* as an object appositive to *mandrinc* with *fæste* as an adverb. Tupper, following a suggestion by Bright, takes *fullwer* as a compound meaning " 'complete wer' or 'wergild,' 'complete recompense for a life' " (p. 121), and so Mackie. Trautmann reads *full befæste* (edition) or *full forfæste* (*Anglia* xliii, 247). Krapp and Dobbie read *fullwered*, "mead-cup," after a suggestion by Holthausen (*Anglia* xliv, 348). Erhardt-Siebold (*MLN* lxv, 93 ff.) reads *full wege*, "full cup," as appositive to *mandrinc*. But if the compound word or set of two words is to refer to the cup, one would expect, I think, some strongly negative qualification such as *man-* in the word *mandrinc* in line 13*a*, or such as *biter* in the phrases *bitran drync* (*Guth.* 868) and *bittor bædeweg* (*Guth.* 985) in the other famous *poculum mortis* passages. For a discussion of the "cup of death" motif in Old English poetry, see Carleton Brown's article, "*Poculum Mortis* in Old English," *Spec.* xv, 389 ff.

22. Jay
[*VN: Gr.25; Tr.22; Tu.25; W.24; M.24; K-D.24*]

The solution, as Dietrich (*ZfdA.* xi, 466) first surmised, is indicated by the runes, to be grouped together and transliterated GÆROHI, rearranged as HIGORÆ, and read, as Trautmann and Krapp and Dobbie rightly pointed out, for O.E. *higoræ*, the feminine form of *higora*, "magpie, jay." The use of the feminine adjective *glado* in line 7*a* (cp. the use of *onhæle* at *Rid.* 13.7*a*) would appear to substantiate the notion that the female jay is here intended. It is not clear whether the Anglo-Saxons actually considered the female jay more loquacious than the male or whether this is an early instance of antifeminism projected upon the bird.

There is also some confusion as to the modern meaning of O.E. *higora*. B-T. gives the definition, "*a magpie* or *a woodpecker*" (p. 535); CH. gives "*jay, magpie, jackdaw, woodpecker*" (p. 182). Jays, jackdaws, and magpies belong to the subfamily *garrulinae* of the family *corvidae*, several members of which are known mimics. Woodpeckers, on the other hand, belong to the family *picidae*, whose cries are "somewhat harsh, consisting of more or less continuous notes according to the species" (Evans, *Birds*, p. 458). The distinction between the jay (L. *pica*) and the woodpecker (L. *picus*) is clear in the Latin encyclopedic literature. Pliny notes that woodpeckers were used for taking auguries (*NH*. x.xx.40), while jays or magpies were often trained to mimic words (*NH*. x.lix.118 ff.). Isidore also calls the *picus* a bird of augury (*Etym*. xii.vii.47) while he describes the *pica* as a well-known mimic:

> Picae quasi poeticae, quod verba in discrimine vocis exprimat, ut homo. Per ramos enim arborum pendulae inportuna garrulitate sonantes, et si linguas in sermone nequeunt explicare, sonum tamen humanae vocis imitantur. De qua congrue quidam ait (Mart. 14,76):
>
> > Pica loquax certa dominum te voce saluto:
> > si me non videas, esse negabis avem.
>
> [Etym. xii.vii.46]

Dietrich (*ZfdA*. xi, 466–67) points to the possible confusion in early English glosses between L. *picus* and L. *pica*. The common jay or *pica* is glossed only once in O.E. as *agu* (WW. 132.12), a word that does not appear elsewhere. The less common bird, *picus*, is glossed frequently as *higre, fina* (WW. 39.36), *fina* (WW. 132.14), *higere* (WW. 260.14), *higere uel gagia* (WW. 286.9). In a fifteenth-century vocabulary, both *picus* and *pica* are bracketed and glossed by one word, *pye* (WW. 702.4–5). O.E. *higere* also glosses L. *gaia, uel catanus* (WW. 132.5) and L. *cicuanus* (WW. 364.10; 13.18 [*higrae*]). As *agu* does not appear outside the glosses, and as the jay was certainly a common bird, it seems likely, as Dietrich contends, that L. *pica* and L. *picus* were confused by the Old English glossators. Whitman (*JEGP* ii, 162) doubts that the *higora* of *Rid*. 22 can be a woodpecker. Certainly the mimicking bird must be the *pica glandaris* described by Pliny and the *pica* of Isidore noted above.

Whether this classical and medieval *pica* is a *magpie* or a *jay* may be a moot point. The birds are closely related and both are known mimics. Since A. H. Evans says of English magpies that they chatter, while jays "vary their harsh, grating utterances by mimicking other species" (*Birds*, p. 555), I have chosen to call the L. *pica* a jay.

22.2: *hwilum*: All seven instances of *hwilum* in this riddle are preceded by a MS. point. The riddle thus exhibits a consistent scheme of rhetorical pointing (see section on "Manuscript Punctuation" in the Introduction).

22.2: *hwilum beorce swa hund, hwilum blæte swa gat*: Holthausen (*ESn.* xxxvii, 207) suggests several emendations to improve the alliteration, but for *b* alliterating with *bl*, see *Rid.* 38.16, 35.7, 89.24, etc.

22.5: *guðfugol*: war-bird, eagle. Cp. *guðhafoc* (*Brun.* 64), and *herefugol* (*Ex.* 162).

22.7: *glado*: Cp. the use of *onhæle* at *Rid.* 13.7a and see note. The riddler is not always consistent in his use of gender with reference to the unknown creature, but the occasionally startling use of the feminine form seems significant.

22.7: The MS. letter, *x*, is presumably a scribal error for runic *G*, since the poet refers in line 10 to *þa siex stafas*. Manuscript runic traditions are often influenced by similar-looking letters, but this small *x* in no way compares with the runic *G* at *Rid.* 17.6.

22.9a: For metrical reasons Tupper supplies *ond* and Trautmann *swylce* at the beginning of the half-line; Holthausen (*Anglia Beibl.* ix, 357) supplies *samod* at the end. But for a similar metrical irregularity in runic passages, cp. *Rid.* 62.3b and 4b and see "A Note on the Runes" in the headnote to *Rid.* 17.

23. Onion
[*VN: Gr.26; Tr.23; Tu.26; W.25; M.25; K-D.25*]

Dietrich first solved the riddle as "onion or leek" (*ZfdA.* xi, 467), and later (*ZfdA.* xii, 240) with Lange, as "hemp" after a suggestion by Bouterwek (*Cædmon's des Angelsachsen biblische Dichtungen*, vol. 1, p. 310). Trautmann first solved the riddle as "rose hip" or "den rosenbutz, frucht der wilden rose" (*Anglia Beibl.* v, 49, and *BBzA.* xix, 184ff.), but later accepted "onion" in his edition. Walz (*Harvard Studies and Notes* v, 263) solved as "mustard." Tupper (*MLN* xviii, 103) first accepted Dietrich's "hemp," and afterwards (*MLN* xxi, 101, and edition, p. 123) "onion." Wyatt, Mackie, and Krapp and Dobbie accept the original "onion." Tupper classifies the riddle as "obscene," but surely some will find more pleasure in it than lack of propriety. The theme of the slain slayer in the riddle is echoed at "onion" *Rid.* 63.5–6. The motif derives from Riddle 44 of Symphosius (see headnote to *Rid.* 63 for the Latin).

23.1: *wifum on hyhte: for the purpose of (bringing about) joy to women.* Mackie (p. 115) translates more freely, "bringing joy to women." For a similar use of *on* marking end or purpose in conjunction with *hyht*, cp. *Run.* 45: ᚻ (*sigel*) *semannum symble biþ on hihte.*

23.2: *neahbuendum nyt*: Normally *neahbuendum* might constitute a half-line in and of itself (cp. similar examples at *Beo.* 95*b*, 309*b*, 1006*a*, and 1355*a*); thus Sievers (*Beiträge* x, 480) would emend *neahbuendum* to *neahbundum* to produce a more regular type E verse, and so Swaen (*Neoph.* xxxi, 147), Tupper, and Trautmann. Other editors choose to keep the normal form of *-buend* at the cost of accepting the metrical irregularity.

23.4: *Staþol*: For the MS. *staþol*, Trautmann reads *stapol* for the shaft of the onion. Most onions do not have shafts that could be called *steapheah*. A scallion has a long stalk, but the onion as described at line 8 seems to be of the red, bulbous variety. Swaen (*Neoph.* xxxi, 147) would read *staþol* for "bulb," but it is also difficult to see how the bulb could be *steapheah*. I read *staþol* for *foundation* or *ground* (see B-T. under *staþol*, p. 912, category III) and translate lines 4–5*a*: "My ground is high; I stand in a bed, shaggy somewhere below." In a charm for bewitched lands, the writer of the *Leechdoms* uses *staþol* in a similar fashion: "Nim þonne ele *and* hunig *and* beorman . . . *and* do þonne halig wæter ðæron *and* drype þonne þriwa on þone staðol þara turfa *and* cweþe . . . " (*Lch.* i.398.5–11). Cp. *Dan.* 580 ff.: *se wyrtruma / stille wæs on staðole*; and *Rid.* 69.2 ff.: *staþol wæs iu þa / wyrta wlitetorhtra*. The *staþol* in *Rid.* 23 is *steapheah* for two different reasons on two different levels of meaning. Onions are normally planted in loose ground raised high into mounds or rows. The onion's hidden double has a high "foundation" in the act of love.

23.4: *steapheah*: Grein and Wyatt read *heah* at the beginning of the second half-line, but the *b*-verse so constituted is metrically unacceptable. Holthausen (*Anglia Beibl.* ix, 357) first proposed reading *steapheah* as it is here (citing *heahsteap* at *Gen.* 2840), and so all other editors.

23.7: *modwlonc*: *proud, haughty,* or possibly, with sexual connotations, *licentious*; for a similar use of *-wlonc*, cp. *felawlonc* at *Rid.* 10.7 and *hygewlonc* at *Rid.* 43.4.

23.8: *ræseð mec on reodne*: *rushes on me (who am) red* (Wyatt). For the word order, Tupper cites *Rid.* 10.13 (my numbering): *swifeð me geond sweartne*. Cp. also the description of Guthlac pursued by death at *Guth.* 995–96: *ac hine ræseð on / gifrum grapum*. Grein, in a note, first suggested *ræreð* for MS. *ræseð* and *on reoðne* ("zur Rüttelung?") for MS. *on reodne*. Later (*Sp.*, pp. 544, 550), he accepted the MS. reading. Trautmann's reading of *ræreð mec on reodne*, " 'erhebt mich an einen roten' (d.i. *mūð*, den Mund)" (p. 87), is something of an assault in itself. Bright suggests *hreode*, "reed, stalk" (see note in Tupper) for MS. *reodne*, but O.E. *hreod* normally means "reed," a plant in its own right, and not the "stalk" of any plant (see B-T., p. 557, and BTS., p. 564).

24. Bible
[*VN: Gr.27; Tr.24; Tu.27; W.26; M.26; K-D.26*]

The solution, "book," was first proposed by L. D. Müller (*Collectanea Anglo-Saxonica*, p. 63). Dietrich elaborated: "Das *buch* und zwar als fell am thier, und als zubereitete membrane, als eingebundne und verzierte handschrift, welche viel nützliches gewährt und selbst den namen eines heiligen buchs haben kann" (*ZfdA.* xi, 467). Tupper notes that the book need not necessarily be a Bible: "The friendly aid and lofty guidance brought by the Book to men are the themes of many riddles" (p. 130). But the book is more than helpful for the creature says: *nama min is mære, / hæleþum gifre, ond halig sylf* (lines 27–28). If this is to be a recognizable clue, surely the Bible is intended. Wyatt gives the solution, "Bible or book"; Trautmann, "Haut—Buch—Bibel." Mackie lists "Bible Codex."

The use of parchment prepared from animal skins as a material for writing upon may be traced back to Eumenes, king of Pergamum in the second century B.C., whose supply of papyrus from Egypt was withheld because of a feud. Pliny says: "Mox, aemulatione circa bibliothecas regum Ptolemaei et Eumenis, supprimente chartas Ptolemaeo, idem Varro membranas Pergami tradit repertas; postea promiscue patuit usus rei qua constat immortalitas hominum" (*NH.* xiii.xxi.70). The preparation of parchment in the Middle Ages is described in a ninth-century manuscript (noted by Tupper, p. 126, as *Bibl. Cap. Canonicorum Lucensium*, I, Cod. 4; Tupper gives only a translation from another source) printed by Ludovico Muratori in his *Antiquitates Italicae*:

> *De Pargamina*: Pargamina quomodo fieri debet. Mitte illam in calcem, *et* jaceat ibi per dies tres. Et tende illam in cantiro. Et rade illam cum nobacula de ambas partes; *et* laxas desicarre. Deinde quodquod volueris scapilatura facere, fac, *et* post tingue cum coloribus. [*Antiquitates Italicae*, 1774 ed., vol. 4, p. 683]

The same manuscript also describes the gilding of the parchment skin:

> *Inauratio pellis*: Tollas pellem rubeam, *et* pumicas eam diligenter, *et* temperas aquam tepidam, *et* labas ea diligenter, quoadusque limpidam aqua egrediatur. Deinde tendis in cantario, *et* lamnizas usque tres vices. Post hec tendis in axe mundam. Sic facies desuper, *et* cum ligno mundo cuoequas diligenter. Postquam autem exsiccata fuerit, tollis albumen obi, *et* sungia* munda, *et* intinguis in ipsum lacrimem: *et* inducis semel per ordinem. Si autem non sufficit, inducis iterum. Et cum siccatum fuerit, ponis petalum. Deinde intinguis spungiam in aquam, *et* premis, *et* cum siccatum fuit, polis. Deinde super cum pelle munda fricas. Iterum polis similiter, *et* dracanto inauratur, ita tamen, ut mittas in aquas sub nocte, quoadusque sobatur. [*Antiquitates Italicae*, 1774 ed., vol. 4, pp. 693–94]

The scriptorium of an ordinary Benedictine monastery is described by Falconer Madan in *Books in Manuscript* in his chapter 4. Wattenbach

---

*The Latin *sungia* here is apparently an error for *spungia*.

(*Das Schriftwesen im Mittelalter,* p. 208) notes the following early tenth-century description of parchment preparation from "Ein Mönch von St. Gallen . . . an Bischof Salomon":

> Cultro membranas ad libros presulis aptans,
> Pumice corrodo pellique superflua tollo,
> Et pressando premens ferrumque per aequora ducens,
> Linea signatur cum regula recta tenetur.
> Tunc quoque litterulis operam dans saepe legendis,
> Quod minus aut majus scriptor depinxit anhelus,
> Rado vel adjungo, placeant ut grammata domno.
>
> > [E. Dümmler, *St. Gall. Denkm. in den*
> > *Mittheilungen d. Züricher Antiq. Ges.* xii, 247:
> > quoted in Wattenbach, p. 208]

For other Old English riddles on writing or writing materials, see *Rids.* 49, 58, 65, 84, 89, and 91. For a recent article on "Riddles Relating to the Anglo-Saxon Scriptorium," by Lawrence Shook, see *Essays in Honour of Anton Charles Pegis,* ed. J. Reginald O'Donnell, pp. 215–36.

24.1 ff.: Cp. the initial lines of Tatwine's Riddle 5, "De Membrano": "Efferus exuviis populator me spoliavit, / Vitalis pariter flatus spiramina dempsit" (*CCL.* cxxxiii, p. 172).

24.3: *dyde eft þonan: took me out again.* For the meaning of *don* as "to put, bring, take," see BTS., p. 155, category IV.

24.6: *seaxses:* For the variant form, cp. *Lch.* ii.56.7.

24.6: *sindrum begrunden: with all impurities ground off* (B-T., p. 876), apparently with reference to the sharpness of the *seaxses ecg* in the preceding half-line. Holthausen (*AEW.,* p. 294) defines *sinder* as "Sinter, Schlacke, Abfall von Metall, Hammerschlag," noting a number of cognate forms. O.E. *sinder* glosses L. *scoria* (WW. 45.28); O.E. *sindor* glosses L. *caries, putredo lignorum, uel ferri . . . uel uestutas* (WW. 200.23–24).

24.7: *fugles wyn:* the quill.

24.8a: *geondsprengde speddropum:* The emendation here was first proposed by Grein and so Assmann, Tupper, Mackie, and myself. Wyatt and Krapp and Dobbie retain the MS. *geond speddropum* with *geond* governing the preceding *mec*, and Krapp and Dobbie translate 7*b*–8*a*, "And the bird's delight went over me with useful drops." But if *geond* is to take a primary stress it ought to alliterate and it does not, so it seems likely that something has been lost here. Grein's emendation improves the sense because it separates the action of the quill in sprinkling the parchment with ink-letters from its returning to the inkwell for more ink. Trautmann would emend to *geondspedde dropum* and Holthausen (*Indogermanische Forschungen* iv, 386) to *geondspaw speddropum*.

24.8 ff.: For the theme of the black tracks, cp. the *lastas, / swaþu swiþe blacu* of *Rid.* 49.2–3. The same motif occurs in Aldhelm's Riddle 59, "Penna," and in Riddles 32, "De Membrano," and 35, "De Penna," of Eusebius.

24.9: *brerd*: the *rim* of the inkhorn.

24.11 ff.: Of the binding and decorating of medieval manuscripts, Madan notes:

> The common binding in the Middle Ages for books of some size and interest was leather, plain or ornamented, white or brown, fastened over solid wooden boards, with raised bands, four or five or more in number, across the back. The sewing of the sheets and passing of the thread over these bands usually results in a firmness and permanence which no ordinary modern book possesses. . . . the oak sides are as permanent as the back, and the solid pegging, by which the parchment strings issuing from the thread-sewn back are wedged into the small square holes and grooves cut in the inner oak sides, is a sight worth seeing for workmanship and indestructibility. . . . the finest books received an ivory, silver, or even gold binding, and the sides were carved or worked into embossed figures and set with jewels. [*Books in Manuscript*, pp. 48–49]

24.12: *hyde*: The emendation was suggested by Grein and is accepted by all major editors.

24.13b–14a: "Consequently the bright works of smiths glistened on me." The reading of *glisedon* for MS. *gliwedon* was proposed by Trautmann. All other editors keep *gliwedon* and assume a meaning, "to adorn," elsewhere unattested. Normally *gleowian* (*gliowian, gliwian*) means "to sing, play (music), make merry, jest." Toller (BTS., p. 476, under *gliwian*) reads line 13a as *gierede mec mid golde forþ* and 13b as *on me gliwedon* translating 13a as "[he] went on to adorn me with gold" and 13*b*–14*a* as "on me played the fair work of smiths," and explaining that *gliwedon* here refers to "the sound made by the metal ornaments and clasps when the book was moved about or opened." Toller's reading seems a bit forced and the meter of his verse 13*a* is highly questionable (Toller cites a D*4 verse at *An.* 1108*a* as a possible parallel, but that verse has after its initial resolved lift a drop of two not three syllables as is the case with his reading of the on-verse here).

24.16: *mære*: Third person plural subjunctive of *mæran*. For the form of Old English plural subjunctives ending in -e, see Bloomfield, *JEGP* xxix, 100–113. Wyatt's and Trautmann's emendation to *mæren* is unnecessary.

24.17: *nales dol wite*: Mackie (*MLR* xxi, 300) reads *wite* rightly as third person present subjunctive of *witan* and translates, "Let not the foolish man impute blame," or in his edition, "Let no fool find fault." He explains that this may refer either to the fool finding fault with the lavish ornamentation of the Bible Codex or to the greater fool's finding fault with the extolling of God. The fool here might also be the man bound to the oral tradition who refused to accept the viability of the written word (some such skepticism is evident in *Rid.* 45). Other readings of the half-line are less satisfactory. Grein and most other editors read *dolwite* as one word and translate variously as *poena temeritatis* (*Sp.*, p. 118), *the pain of a wound* (BTS., p. 154), and *the pains of hell* (Tupper). Trautmann emends *dol wite* to *dolwice*, "Tun eines Toren," and begins a new sentence at 17*b*. For the other readings, all of them unlikely, see Krapp and Dobbie, p. 336.

24.18 ff.: Aldhelm similarly describes the power of the word over men's lives in the closing lines of his Riddle 59, "Penna."

25. Mead
[*VN: Gr.28; Tr.25; Tu.28; W.27; M.27; K-D.27*]

Dietrich (*ZfdA*. xi, 467 ff.) first solved the riddle as "whip", but later (*ZfdA*. xii, 239) offered Lange's solution, "mead," which has been accepted by all editors. Storms (*Anglo-Saxon Magic*, p. 134) notes that the keeping of bees is an old Germanic custom for which "the oldest historical evidence dates from the fourth century B.C., when Pythias of Massilia, a Greek merchant, mentions the culture of bees by Germanic tribes." The rights and duties of the Anglo-Saxon beekeeper or *beoceorl* are detailed in the *Rectitudines Singularum Personarum*, chapter 5 (Liebermann, ed., *Die Gesetze der Angelsachsen*, vol. 1, p. 448). The value of honey-producing bees is not to be doubted—in the *Laws* of Alfred, the bee thief is punished as severely as the horse thief and the stealer of gold (Liebermann, ed., vol. 1, p. 54).

25.2: *burghleoþum: mountain slopes*. B-T. (p. 135) defined the word that occurs here and at *Ex*. 70 as "a fortress-height, the hill on which a city is built," and most editors choose one of these meanings. Mackie translates the compound as "fortress-like hill"; Tupper as "city-heights" after a suggestion by Brooke; Trautmann as "Abhang bei Stadt oder Dorf." But BTS. takes *burghleoþ* as a form of *beorghliõ* as does Grein (*Sp.*, p. 46). This is also the reading of Kock (*Anglia* xlv, 124) and of Krapp and Dobbie and is the reading adopted here.

25.7–8: The reading of *weorpe* for MS. *weorpere* and of *esne* for MS. *efne* was proposed by Holthausen (*ESn*. xxxvii, 207) and is accepted by Tupper, Trautmann, and Krapp and Dobbie. Other editors take MS. *weorpere*, "thrower," as parallel with *bindere* and *swingere* and MS. *efne* as a form of the verb *efnan*, "to throw down, lay low" (see B-T., p. 242). But the normal meaning of *efnan* is "to achieve, perform," and the position of *hwilum* according to the unemended reading is, as Krapp and Dobbie point out, unusual. Rather the *esne* (cp. line 16) is parallel to, and forms a contrast with the *ealdne ceorl*. The old man is wiser in his drinking habits and is therefore thrown less readily than the headstrong young warrior.

25.9 ff.: Cp. the remarks of Tacitus on the power of beer to subdue the Germanic tribes: "Sine apparatu, sine blandimentis expellunt famem.

adversus sitim non eadem temperantia. si indulseris ebrietati sugge-
rendo quantum concupiscunt, haud minus facile bitiis quam armis
vincentur" (*Germania* xxiii; ed. Hutton, p. 296).

25.10: *mægenþisan*: "mighty rush." B-T. defined *mægenþyse* as "vio-
lence, force" citing for *-þyse* Icelandic *þysja*, "to rush" (p. 656). Holt-
hausen (*ESn.* xxxvii, 207) also took *-þisan* as a form of *-þyssa*, "Toser"
(for the cognate forms see *AEW.*, p. 375, under *ðyssa*), then retracted
this in favor of the emendation *mægenwisan* after a suggestion by
Grein (*Anglia* xxxv, 169), and finally reverted to his original opinion in
the *Wörterbuch* (see *ðysse*, p. 375). Trautmann reads *mægenwisan*; other
editors keep the MS. reading after Holthausen.

25.12: Cp. *Rid.* 9.10.

25.13 ff.: In placing a full stop after *geswiceð* in line 12, I follow
Wyatt and Mackie. Other editors read the phrases beginning at 13a as
a continuation of the previous sentence. Trautmann supplies *ond* at
the beginnings of lines 13 and 14 and *bistroden spræce* at 13b for MS.
strong on spræce. Grein (*Germania* x, 428) suggested *strongan spræce* at
line 13b as parallel with *strengo*, both governed by *bistolen*, and so
Assmann and Kock (*Anglia* xliv, 256 ff.). But the point here is, as other
editors point out, that drunken men cannot hold their tongues. That
is the meaning of the riddler's statement at 14b: *nah his modes geweald*.
The dangers of drunken speech at the mead-table are well documented
in Old English poetry. The poet of *The Fortunes of Men*, for example,
explains how the heavy drinker who cannot hold his tongue becomes
a *selfcwalu* or suicide:

> Sumum meces ecg   on meodubence
> yrrum ealowosan   ealdor oþþringeð,
> were winsadum;   bið ær his worda to hræd.
> Sum sceal on beore   þurh byreles hond
> meodugal mæcga;   þonne he gemet ne con
> gemearcian his muþe   mode sine,
> ac sceal ful earmlice   ealdre linnan,
> dreogan dryhtenbealo   dreamum biscyred,
> ond hine to sylfcwale   secgas nemnað,
> mænað mid muþe   meodugales gedrinc.

[*Fort.* 48–57]

The motif of the drink overthrowing the man that appears in this riddle also appears in Riddle 80 of Aldhelm, "Calix Vitreus" (ed. Pitman, pp. 46, 48) and in two "De Vino" Riddles of the Bern collection, numbers 50 and 63 (*CCL.* cxxxiii A, pp. 596, 610). The physical effects of strong liquor are set forth by Theodore in his *Liber Poenitentialis*: "Hoc est ebriositas, quando statum mentis mutant, et linguae balbutiunt, et oculi turbantur, et vertigo erit capitis, et ventris distensio, ac dolor sequitur" (chap. xxvi; ed. Thorpe, *Ancient Laws and Institutes of England*, vol. 2, p. 32).

25.15: The end-punctuation mark after *hatte* probably indicates that a scribe was misled by the formulaic half-line at 15*b* into thinking the riddle had ended. The fact that Đe (16*a*) does not begin a new MS. line shows that the scribe immediately perceived his error.

26. Yew-Horn?
[*VN: Gr.29; Tr.26; Tu.29; W.28; M.28; K-D.28*]

Thomas Wright (*Biographia Britannica Literaria*, vol. 1, p. 79) first proposed the solution, "John Barleycorn," and this was accepted by Brooke, Wyatt, Mackie, and in the form, "beer or ale," by Tupper. Dietrich (*ZfdA.* xi, 468) proposed "wine cask," citing Aldhelm's Riddle 78, *Cupa Vinaria*, and rightly noting that the riddlic creature must be made of wood. Trautmann solved as "harp," and Kock (*Lunds Universitets Årsskrift*, NF., Avd.1, Bd. 14, Nr. 26, pp. 63–64) agreed at least that a stringed instrument was indicated by the language of the riddle. Shook (*MS* xx, 93 ff.) argued for the solution, *Testudo*, "tortoise-lyre," citing Riddle 20 of Symphosius. My own solution, proposed here for the first time, is "yew-horn," a horn made of yew wood, similar to the Celtic horn dredged up recently from the River Erne in Northern Ireland (see the *Ulster Journal of Archaeology*, ser. 3, xxxii, 101–4 and plate iv).

Wright's solution, "John Barleycorn," was most forcefully argued by Brooke (*The History of Early English Literature*, pp. 152–53) and Tupper. Both quote the poem, "John Barleycorn," by Robert Burns.

Burns carefully describes the barley being planted and harvested and finally being turned into brew:

> They filled up a darksome pit
> With water to the brim,
> They heaved in John Barleycorn,
> There let him sink or swim.

> They laid him out upon the floor,
> To work him farther woe,
> And still, as signs of life appear'd,
> They toss'd him to and fro.

> They wasted, o'er a scorching flame,
> The marrow of his bones;
> But a miller us'd him worst of all,
> For he crush'd him between two stones.

[Quoted in Brooke, p. 152]

The riddlic creature undergoes a dire fate described in lines 4–6 of the riddle, but it should be noted that it is not washed, crushed, burned, or boiled. One source notes that "the three main stages of the brewing process are: mashing, boiling and fermentation" (*EB.* iv, 165). Beer cannot be made without a bit of boiling. It should also be noted that while barley is *scearp*, it is certainly not *heard*. Dietrich (*ZfdA.* xi, 468) rightly notes that the creature described in lines 1–3 must be a hardwood tree. Dietrich's "wine cask" is somewhat better suited to the beginning of the riddle than "John Barleycorn," but it is equally ill-suited to the end. The *Dream* of line 7 that is *in innan / cwicra wihta* and that sounds onomatopoeically—*clengeð, lengeð* (line 8)—must be music. While alive the creature has no power to speak nor does it desire to do so; dead, it begins to talk after a fashion (*meldan mislice*).

Trautmann's solution, "harp," has never been given the close consideration that it deserves. Certainly, as Kock (see reference above) and Krapp and Dobbie note, the riddlic creature appears to be a musical instrument made of wood. Trautmann quotes Riddle 20 of Symphosius and two *lyre* riddles from Reusner's *Aenigmatographia sive Sylloge Aenigmatum et Griphorum Convivalium* (Frankfort, 1602) to illustrate the central motif of *harp* or *lyre* riddles: "The living are silent; the dead sing." The motif is appropriate to any musical instrument carved out of wood. Small wooden objects are rare finds in Anglo-Saxon archaeological sites because wood rots under normal conditions of the soil. Two Anglo-Saxon lyres remain partially preserved, one from Sutton Hoo and another from a seventh-century barrow at Taplow, Buckinghamshire—both are made of maple wood (See Rupert and Myrtle Bruce-Mitford's article in *Antiquity* xliv, 7–12). Maple is a hard wood though not the *heardestan* of Anglo-Saxon woods. Maple trees are not *scearp*, nor are they *grimm*. Shook (*MS* xx, 93 ff.) would read the superlatives of the first three lines of the riddle as descriptive of a tortoise shell out of which is formed a tortoise-lyre or *testudo*. Several objections may be raised to this solution. No portion of the earth (*foldan dæl*) is fairly adorned (*fægre gegierwed*) with tortoise shells. Tortoise shells are not *scearp*, nor are tortoises *grimm*. Shook notes that "OE *grimm* 'fierce' echoes . . . the *saevo* of Symphosius' *saevo prodita fato*" (*MS* xx, 96), but it is the turtle's fate that is "cruel" in the Latin, not the turtle itself. Furthermore, there is neither linguistic nor archaeological evidence to support the presence of tortoise lyres in medieval Britain. Shook's solution does not fit the language of the riddle as well as Trautmann's.

Still the problem of the maple wood remains. The wood described in the first three lines of the riddle would appear to be the yew. The yew is a hard wood, harder than maple, probably the hardest of Anglo-Saxon woods. In *Rid*. 53, when four woods are mentioned, the yew is called *se hearda iw* (53.9). In *The Rune Poem* the yew is described:

> Z (eoh) byþ utan   unsmeþe treow,
> heard, hrusan fæst,   hyrde fyres,
> wyrtrumun underwreþyd,   wyn on eþle.

> [*Run*. 35–37]

The yew is not only the *heardestan* of trees, it is also the *scearpestan* in the sense of "most bitter," and the *grymmestan* or fiercest of killers. The flat, needle-like leaves of the yew contain a poisonous alkaloid mentioned by classical writers as fatal to horses and cattle and some- times to men. Ovid (*Met*. iv.432) and Lucan (*De Bello Civili* vi.645) refer to the deadly yew trees shading the road to the underworld. Isidore says: "Taxus venenata arbor, unde et toxica venena exprimun- tur" (*Etym*. xvii.vii.40). Pliny details the grim appearance of the tree and the poisonous quality of its fruit:

Similis his etiamnunc aspectu est, ne quid praetereatur, taxus minime virens gracilisque et tristis ac dira, nullo suco, ex omnibus sola bacifera. mas noxio fructu, letale quippe bacis in Hispania praecipue venenum inest: vasa etiam viatoria ex ea vinis in Gallia facta mortifera fuisse conpertum est. hanc Sextius milacem a Graecis vocari dicit, et esse in Arcadia tam praesentis veneni ut qui obdormiant sub ea cibumve capiant moriantur. sunt qui et taxica hinc appellata dicant venena quae nunc toxica dicimus, quibus sagittae tinguantur. [NH. xvi.xx.50–52]

These associations are repeated by Aldhelm, who says in the final lines of his *Taxus* Riddle 69:

Sed me pestiferam fecerunt fata reorum,
Cumque venenatus glescit de corpore stipes,
Lurcones rabidi quem carpunt rictibus oris,
Occido mandentum mox plura cadavera leto.

[Ed. Pitman, p. 40]

Elliott notes similar associations of the yew with poison, death, and the underworld in several European traditions, among them Germanic and Celtic (*Spec.* xxxii, 250 ff.). Thus the yew is the hardest and grimmest of trees and its leaves and berries are the *scearpestan* in the sense of "most bitter" (for this meaning of O.E. *scearp*, see B-T., p. 825 under IIa. *acrid*; also CH., p. 292: "*biting, bitter, acid*").

Lines 4–6 of the riddle describe the cutting of the yew, the preparation of its wood, and the fashioning of some object or instrument that is carried into the homes of men. One source notes that "yew lumber has been used for cabinetwork, implements requiring strength and durability, and particularly for making bows" (*EB.* xxiii, p. 892). The wooden objects that the Anglo-Saxons may have fashioned from the yew remain obscured by the twin graves of rot and time, but there is at least the recent evidence from Taplow that one iron- and another bronze-bound bucket were made of yew (information courtesy of the British Museum). The object described in this riddle appears to be an instrument of sorts. There is *Dream* (line 7) in the wood; it is the sound of *cwicra wihta* (line 8), presumably of men, since the "speaking" creature in terms of the central paradox of the riddle (lines 9–12) is not "living" but dead. The living yew is a fierce and grim creature, yet it speaks not; the dead wood begins to speak and sing. The living yew is a killer; the dead yew brings *dream* to the halls of men. I believe the creature of this riddle to be a horn made of yew, similar to the one dredged up recently from the River Erne in Northern Ireland and dated roughly from the eighth to the tenth century (D. M. Waterman, "An Early Medieval Horn from the River Erne," *Ulster Journal of Archaeology*, ser. 3, xxxii, 101–4, and plate IV). This horn appears to have been fashioned very nearly in the manner described in lines 4–6 of the riddle. Waterman describes its present appearance:

> The horn consists of a wooden tube, shaped from a solid piece of yew, to which a mouthpiece and mounts of bronze are attached by rivets. It is 58 cm. long, slightly curved in the length, with a diameter at the mouthpiece of 2.5 cm. and at the opposite end, allowing for distortion due to the damage here, of about 8 cm. The bronze mouthpiece has a moulded orifice and is accommodated in a rebate so that it lies flush with the surface of the wood tube, the enclosed end of which is carefully funnel-shaped. Originally twelve bronze mounts were set out along the length of the tube, of which three are missing, although their positions are established by areas of smoother, less eroded wood and by the remains of rivets or of the holes which they had occupied. The surviving mounts are made from lengths of thin bronze sheeting, 1.2–5.0 cm. in width, the ends of which are overlapped. [*Ulster Journal of Archaeology*, ser. 3, xxxii, 101]

A similar horn, said to be of willow, was found at Becan in 1791 and is now preserved in the National Museum of Ireland, Dublin (see Waterman, pp. 101 ff.). Both horns exhibit long irregular cracks running down the length of the wood and Waterman notes that "it would seem . . . that the River Erne horn, like that from Becan, was produced by cleaving longitudinally a solid block of wood and assembling the two halves after hollowing and shaping to match" (*Ulster Journal of Archaeology*, ser. 3, xxxii, 103). Wilde describes the fashioning of the Becan horn as follows:

> It seems to have been originally a solid piece, which in that state was split from end to end; each of the pieces into which it was thus divided was then hollowed or grooved on the inside, and tapering in such a manner that, when joined again, these grooves, applying to each other, formed a circular and conical perforation through the whole length, resembling that of a trumpet or horn. To secure the pieces in this position they were bound together on the outside by a long fillet of thin brass, about an inch and a quarter broad, wrapped around them in a spiral from one end to the other, with upwards of an inch of interval between the rolls, and fastened to the wood with small brass nails. The ends were secured by circular plates, probably of the same metal, as appears from marks still remaining on the surface of the wood, these pieces having been lost. [*Catalogue of the Museum of Antiquities of the Royal Irish Academy*, p. 244; cited by Waterman]

Thus the wood of both horns was cut and prepared, bound and adorned, and presumably carried to the halls of men where it resounded with the voice of living creatures. The combination of bronze and yew was a common Celtic style of the early Christian period. Waterman notes:

> At this time [eighth- to tenth-century] indeed it was yew wood, the same material from which the horn is fashioned, that was most widely employed as backing for bronze-work, as on the shrines and crosier shafts of the period; and from yew also, were turned or carved so many of the vessels and implements found on habitation sites, in particular at the crannogs of Lagore and Ballinderry. [*Ulster Journal of Archaeology*, ser. 3, xxxii, 103]

To my knowledge no yew-horns have been discovered in Anglo-Saxon graves, but wooden objects are rare archaeological finds, and wooden instruments are often reconstructed after the excavation with a great deal of hindsight. The Anglo-Saxon "harp" from Sutton Hoo, now thought to be a lyre (*Antiquity* xliv, 7–12) is a good case in point. Padelford (*BBzA.* iv, 54) notes that the etymology of O.E. *stocc* would seem to indicate a straight wooden trumpet; the same might be said of *bieme*, which is related to *beam* (Holthausen, *AEW*, pp. 17, 23). The yew-horn mentioned above is, of course, Celtic, but the Celts exerted some influence on the brass-work style of the Anglo-Saxons—at least in the case of hanging bowls. It is not impossible that the Anglo-Saxons, under Celtic influence, also made wooden horns from the yew and adorned them in Celtic fashion. Admittedly, the language of the riddle does not strictly define *horn* or any other instrument, but clearly an artifact of yew seems intended. If lines 9–12 of the riddle refer to the creature itself, as I think they do, then the central paradox noted by Trautmann in several riddlic analogues is established—the living creature is silent while the dead creature speaks. This makes some sense in terms of the natural history of the creature described in lines 1–8: the creature lives and adorns a portion of the earth; it is cut and killed, shaped and fashioned, bound and adorned, and carried to the halls of men where *Dream bið in innan* (line 8). The creature could not be a lyre for two reasons: (1) it would be most difficult to fashion a lyre out of a wood so hard as yew; and (2) the two extant lyres known to have come from Anglo-Saxon England are made of maple wood. The riddle must remain unsolved in many respects until more wooden objects have been unearthed and reconstructed from the Anglo-Saxon period. Still, the solution, "horn of yew," deserves some careful study by riddlists and archaeologists alike.

26.2: To secure the alliteration of this line, Ettmüller would emend MS. *scearpestan* to *hwæssestan* and Grein would read *heoruscearpestan*. Holthausen (*Anglia* xxxv, 169) would emend MS. *heardestan* to *sceardestan*, and so Trautmann. But Tupper cites an article by Kluge (*Beiträge* ix, 446) in which the rhyming of suffixes is shown to be an acceptable alternative to normal alliterative patterns.

26.4 ff.: Most of the descriptive terms here fit the hypothetical fashioning of the wooden horn based on the archaeological evidence at hand. The most difficult verse is 5b: *blæced, wæced*. The wood may have been bleached by the sun in the process of drying or it may have been bleached by an agent as a part of, or preliminary to, some schematic decorating of the horn. The wood may have been "weakened" by the process of cutting, grooving, twisting, and nailing. There is also the remote possibility that the wooden horn, like a number of cow horns, may have been weakened systematically in some way in order to twist it into a certain shape. For the use of rhymes in *Riddles*, see note to *Rid.* 1.20.

26.7b ff.: These lines as they are in the MS. have been the cause of some difficulty. I read *þar þar* for MS. *þara þe* at 9b and *wiht* for MS. *wið* at 10b (the latter emendation after a suggestion by Trautmann) and translate the passage: "The joy (or music) of living beings (men) is in the inside: it clings, lingers (there) where before, alive, for a long time it (the creature) delights and does not speak at all, and then, after death, it begins to proclaim, speak variously." Thus the essential paradox of the wooden horn is articulated: living, the yew says nothing; dead, it begins to speak as the music of men rises up inside of it. For other examples of the *þar þar* (*þær þær*) construction, see B-T., p. 1031 under *þær*, category I.(c)(2). For the meaning of *clengan*, see BTS., p. 128, and *OED* (ii, p. 490) under *clenge*, v.2, "to cling, adhere, remain," and also *MED* (ii, p. 304) under *clengen*, v.(2), "to cling, adhere, remain." For *lengan*, see B-T., p. 629, one definition being "to delay, tarry." For the meaning of *deman*, "to proclaim, celebrate," see BTS., p. 148 under category IV. Most previous editors take MS. *þara þe* as parallel with *cwicra wihta*, but the translation even in terms of the solution, "barleycorn," has never been very clear. My reading makes sense of the lines and also explains the use of the singular verbs at 10*a* ff. The meaning of O.E. *clengan* is debated, but Toller's reading remains the best. He translates beginning at line 7*b*: "Joy is within, remains, is prolongued" (p. 128), and this reading is accepted by Tupper, Mackie, Krapp and Dobbie, and myself. Grein (*Sp.*, p. 89) reads *clengan* as a possible form of *glengan* and defines the word as *ornare* with the note, "oder ist dies subst. acc.(?)." Kock (*Lunds Universitets Årsskrift*, NF., Avd. 1, Bd. 14, Nr. 26, p. 64), following Grein's note, reads both *clengeð* and *lengeð* as nouns with an -*eþ* or -*oþ* ending (cp. *langoð*, var. *langeð*- from O.E. *langian*), but his O.E. *clengian* is unattested and O.E. *lengian* occurs only once (B-T., p. 629). Trautmann translates *clengan* as "heften, haften machen," and begins a new sentence at 8*b*. The MS. reading at 10*b*, *ond no wið spriceð*, is somewhat awkward. One must assume an understood object (and a somewhat far-removed subject) and translate with Mackie: "and [men] say nothing against them" (p. 119). Baum's "and naught gainsays" (p. 48) is less happy. Tupper and Wyatt read *no* as a simple adverb. Trautmann's emendation of *wiht* for MS. *wið* makes reasonable sense of the line and is easy to justify paleographically.

26.11–12: Bright translates these lines with reference to the barley beer drinkers: "And then after death (i.e., drunken sleep), they indulge in large discourse and talk incoherently" (see Tupper, p. 138, note). This is a rather tame reading of O.E. *deaþe*, which I think must refer to the creature's being cut and killed in line 4 of the riddle. One might suppose old beer drinkers to argue before rather than after their drunken sleep.

26.12b: *to hycganne*: This is the first of five occurrences of the inflected infinitive after *to* that Sievers (*Beiträge* x, 482) would emend to the uninflected form on metrical grounds. The five occurrences are:

1.	Micel is tō hycganne	*Rid.* 26.12*b*
2.	Micel is tō hycgenne	*Rid.* 29.23*b*
3.	Long is tō secganne	*Rid.* 37.22*b*
4.	Þæt is tō geþencanne	*Rid.* 39.8*a*
5.	sæcce tō fremmanne	*Rid.* 84.26*b*

There are two occurrences of the inflected infinitive after *to* in the *Rid-*

dles that Sievers finds metrically acceptable, both *tō gesecganne* (C1) at *Rids*. 34.13*a* and 37.25*a*. In the five cases cited above, all of which would be D*1 verses if allowed to stand (see Pope, *The Rhythm of Beowulf*, pp. 308–10 and 365, especially those examples with a drop of several syllables after the first lift [which may in some cases like *Micel* above be a resolved lift] and those examples of similarly inflected infinitives in D*1 verses in *Beowulf*: 473*a*, 1724*b*, 1941*a*, 2093*a*, and 2562*a*), Sievers believed that the inflections resulted in unmetrical or metrically rare verses and that they were probably the result of an overzealous scribal practice of normalizing infinitives to what had become the regular inflected form. The problem is a difficult one. Klaeber, after agreeing with Sievers in his early editions (see section 12, p. 277 of the third edition of *Beowulf*), decided to restore the manuscript forms in his third edition and argued somewhat obscurely in the "Second Supplement" (p. 466, note to line 473) that there was a subtle syntactic distinction between the inflected and uninflected forms as they stand in the MS. In general, past editors of the *Riddles* have allowed the MS. readings to stand without much comment on the problem. Trautmann reads *fremman* at *Rid*. 84.26*b* (where he is able to take *-ne* as adverbial *ne* at the beginning of the next half-line) and marks the final *-ne* in the other four cases with dots below the letters to indicate that the endings might be late scribal additions. Other editors allow the MS. readings to stand. Since in all five cases that Sievers would emend there is a similarity of construction and of meter, and since D*1 verses of a similar if not exactly parallel nature can be found elsewhere in Old English poetry, it seems to me best to let the MS. readings stand.

27. Moon and Sun
[*VN: Gr.30; Tr.27; Tu.30; W.29; M.29; K-D.29*]

Dietrich (*ZfdA*. xi, 468–69) solved the riddle as "moon and sun," citing *Bo*. 4.10–11: *hwilum eac þa sunnan sines bereafað I beorhtan leohtes*. Dietrich's solution is accepted by all editors except Trautmann. Trautmann first argued for "swallow and sparrow" (*Anglia Beibl*. v,

49), and later for "bird and wind" (*BBzA*. xix, 189 ff.; edition, pp. 90–91). I agree with Tupper (pp. 139–40) that Trautmann's reading of lines 1–3 of the riddle is far-fetched. Trautmann says of the *hornum* and the *lyftfæt*:

> Dieses wesen (ein vogel) führt zwischen seinen hörnern (dem ober- und unterkiefer seines schnabels) beute. Die beute ist ein leichtes und kunstvoll bereitetes luftgefäss (ein gras- oder strohhalm oder eine feder). [*BBzA*. xix, 191]

Tupper points out that the *lyftfæt leohtlic* (line 3), like the *leohtfatu* at *PPs*. 135.7, is likely to be a bright heavenly body. Tupper also notes that there is no particular reason for the "wind" to drive the "bird" *west þonan* (line 10). The same objections apply to Walz's solution, "cloud and wind" (*Harvard Studies and Notes* v, 264).

According to Isidore, there were two conflicting opinions in the Middle Ages with regard to the source and the nature of moonlight (*NR*. xviii.i–iii). Both derive from Augustine's commentaries upon the Psalms (see Augustine's discussion, "In Psalmum X: Enarratio," *PL*. xxxvi, 131–33). Isidore explains in his chapter "De Lumine Lunae," in *De Natura Rerum* that according to one tradition the moon is thought to generate its own natural light, while according to the other it is thought to receive light from the sun (*alii dicunt lunam non suo fulgere lumine, sed a sole accipere lumen*). Among those who accept the second tradition are clearly the Old English riddler and also Aelfric who describes the nature of moonlight in his *De Temporibus Anni*, i.31–32:

> Soðlice se mona *and* ealle steorran underfoð leoht of ðære micclan sunnan, *and* heora nan næfð nænne leoman buton of ðære sunnan leoman;
> *And* ðeah ðe seo sunne under eorðan on nihtlicere tide scine, þeah astihð hire leoht on sumere sidan þære eorðan þe ða steorran bufon us onliht; *and* ðonne heo upagæð, heo oferswið ealra ðæra steorrena *and* eac þæs monan leoht mid hire ormætan leohte. [Ed. Henel, EETS, o.s. 213, pp. 12, 14]

The Old English riddle is informed by this tradition of the moon as a "taker of light"—but there is something else at work here—for although Tupper would take the *huþe* of 2b to be merely moonlight, Wyatt is surely right when he explains that the *huþe*, which is carried *hornum bitweonum* (2a), must be the earthlit dark portion of the moon cradled by the crescent light (cp. *Sir Patrick Spens*, "I saw the new moon late yestreen / Wi' the auld moon in her arm"). When the moon is only a thin crescent, old or new, we can often make out the rest of the disc faintly illuminated by sunlight reflected from earth to moon. Since earth phases are exactly the opposite of moon phases, the nearly "full earth" reflects a maximum amount of light on the nearly "new moon" (for a good description of this, see Rudeaux and Vaucouleurs, *Larousse Encyclopedia of Astronomy*, pp. 116 ff.). The notion of "earthlight" does not enter into medieval discussions of the moon, but the Old English riddler in true scientific fashion told what he saw. Cassidy and Ringler give a good explanation of the details of the poem:

> A few days before new moon the moon rises shortly before dawn. A thin sunlit crescent half encircles the rest of its surface, which is earth-lit and clearly if dimly visible (2–3). Before the moon can rise to the zenith (5–6), dawn appears on the horizon (7–8) and the earthlit portion of the moon fades to invisibility (9a). She pursues her westward course (9b–11). A wind comes up (12a) and dew falls (12b) as night yields to morning (13a). During the next few days (new moon) the moon will be entirely invisible (13b–14). [*Bright's Old English Grammar and Reader*, 3d ed., pp. 341–42, note].

Whitman (*SN* xli, 93 ff.) views the moon in this riddle according to a tradition that he traces to Cyril of Alexandria as "a symbol of the forces of evil . . . a bastard light, inconstant, and an inhabitant of the darkness" (*SN* xli, 97), but the treatment in the riddle seems more heroic than Christian. The moon is a plundering warrior and not a Satanic prince.

27.4a: *ham:* Tupper and Trautmann emend to *hame* to produce an orthodox type A verse, but the irregular verse as it stands, something approximating type E with light secondary stress or a truncated type A without a final drop, is not wholly without parallels (cp. for example *Beo.* 2150a and 3027a and the examples listed by Pope in his *Seven Old English Poems*, pp. 128–29). See Pope's discussion of the phenomenon on pp. xxx and 321–22 of *The Rhythm of Beowulf*.

27.5a: For metrical reasons, Herzfeld (*Die Räthsel des Exeterbuches und ihr Verfasser*, p. 50) would emend *byrig* to *burge*, and Holthausen (*ESn.* xxxvii, 208) would read *on byrg þære* or would place *walde* after *byrg*. But A3 verses with a short penult sometimes occur in the poetry (cp. *Wand.* 46a, *Beo.* 1514a, and see Pope's discussion of short A3 verses at pp. 273–74 of *The Rhythm of Beowulf*); and even if one were to resolve the final lift ˊx, the verse would have a parallel in the immediately preceding on-verse. For *walde* as a variant of *wolde*, see SB. 428 Anm. 4, p. 357, and Campbell 156, p. 60.

27.6b: The verb *beon* is ellipted.

27.7: *ofer wealles hrof*: B-T. translates this as "over the mountain top" (p. 1174). Marckwardt and Rosier note that the phrase "may be taken to mean something like *over the horizon*, but within the (figurative) terms of the poem the roof's wall refers back to the *byrig* in line 5" (*Old English Language and Literature*, p. 198, note 9).

27.9: *to ham*: Marckwardt and Rosier note that this phrase is "apparently in some contrastive sense to *to þam ham* (= *hame*) in line 4; perhaps read *at (her) home, from home*" (*Old English Language and Literature*, p. 199, note 10). More recently Joyce has pointed out that there is in the apparent opposition between the two uses of *ham* "an ironic reversal; for the moon intending to keep light in the night-time darkness overhead (4–6) is forced to retreat to the darkness beyond the horizon after the recapture of light by the sun" (*Annuale Mediaevale* xiv, 7).

27.11: *fæhþum*: This is the only recorded dative or instrumental plural form of the word and it may indicate means ("by means of feuds") or manner ("with hostilities," "hostilely"). Grein (*Sp.*, p. 172) believes this to refer to the sun, but clearly it is the moon that goes west against her will (line 10) with a score to settle.

27.13–14: Cassidy and Ringler believe these lines to refer to the disappearance of the moon during the new moon phase on subsequent evenings (see headnote), but the lines may more simply indicate the disappearance of the moon over the western horizon.

28. Tree (Wood)
[VN: Gr.31; Tr.28; Tu.31; W.30; M.30; K-D.30]

This is the only riddle in the *Exeter Book* for which there are two texts. Both texts are included in this edition under the numbers 28a and

28b. *Rid.* 28a occurs in proper sequence on folio 108*a*; *Rid.* 28b occurs on folio 122*b* between *Homiletic Fragment II* and *Rid.* 58. The two versions are essentially the same, though *Rid.* 28b is defective at lines 2 and 4 because of the manuscript burn. Grein, Assmann, Tupper, and Wyatt print a single composite reading of the two riddles. Trautmann, Mackie, and Krapp and Dobbie print both. I follow Trautmann's practice of including both versions under the same headnote. In the notes to individual lines below, where a note applies to one version only, it is so marked.

Dietrich (*ZfdA.* xi, 469) first solved the riddle as "rainwater," though he was hard-pressed to explain lines 4–9 in terms of the solution. Of line 4 he says nothing. Of lines 5–6 he says, "Es geht oft von männern gesendet und geküsst von hand zu hand, offenbar beim waschen vor und nach dem mahle." The water in lines 7–9 he believes to be the holy *Taufwasser.* Tupper rightly points out that line 4 of the riddle, which describes the creature as *bearu blowende, byrnende gled*, presents a serious obstacle to the "rainwater" solution. Recently Pinsker (*Anglia* xci, 15 ff.) has revived some of Dietrich's ideas in support of a similar solution, "snowflake." Pinsker explains the troublesome line 4 as follows:

> Der Vergleich mit einem "blühenden Hain" (v. 4a) liegt nahe durch die weisse Farbe, ob man nun an tatsächlich mit Schnee bedeckte Baumäste denkt oder an das Wirbeln weisser Punkte im Schneeschauer. . . . Die einzige Schwierigkeit bietet die "brennende Glut" in Vers 4b. Schnee ist zwar nicht heiss, aber die im Schneesturm erfrorenen Hände brennen zunächst wie Feuer. [*Anglia* xci, 16]

This theory of the frost-bitten hand Pinsker uses to explain the hand-passing and kissing of lines 5–6 of the riddle that supposedly refer to "das Anhauchen oder Absaugen der vom Frost schmerzenden Hände" (ibid.). Since, as Pinsker says, "Schnee ist zwar nicht heiss," he emends MS. *legbysig* (28a.1) or *ligbysig* (28b.1) to *lyftbysig.* Likewise in the last lines of the riddle he emends MS. *ycan upcyme* to *ywan upcymes* in order to sustain his notion that the melted snow, having moistened the fields, rises and points out to the farmer bowed over his crops "den Reichtum der aufspriessenden Saat." This manipulation of text and meaning is hardly legitimate.

Most editors accept the solution put forward by Blackburn (*JEGP* iii, 4 ff.) who solves the riddle as "*an beam* in the various senses that the word carries in Old English, *tree*, *log*, *ship*, and *cross* (probably also *harp* and *bowl*)" (*JEGP* iii, 4, and note 1). In his translation, Blackburn indicates the line references as follows:

Lines 1–2: tree	5: harp
3*a*: ship	6: cup?
3*b*–4*a*: tree	7–9: cross
4*b*: log	

Tupper, Mackie, and Krapp and Dobbie accept Blackburn's solution. Wyatt lists the riddle as unsolved. Trautmann, who earlier had proposed the solution, "Ährenfeld" (*Anglia Beibl.* v, 49), accepts Blackburn's *beam* with certain reservations. Trautmann rightly notes that in terms of the wordplay O.E. *beam* may mean "tree," "log," or "cross," but not "ship," "harp" (except in certain compounds like *gleobeam*), or "cup." He takes Blackburn's *beam* to mean "tree" in lines 1–4 and "cross" in lines 5–9. If the riddle is facilitated mainly by a wordplay, then Trautmann's reading is certainly correct. But I believe that the riddle treats the various aspects and uses of a tree—first (lines 1–4), in the forest, troubled by lightning, tossed by wind, surrounded by the glory of its foliage, made one with weather, quick to go forth (as wood for carving? as a log for burning? or perhaps in the b-text [*fyre gemylted*] as fruit for the melting pot?): a blooming grove, a burning ember. From line 5 on, the tree is presented as wood fashioned by art: first a cup (lines 5–6), then a cross (lines 7–9). There is a certain irony in the poem that links lines 1–4 with lines 5–9: the creature, having been forced onto the death-road by man, is, as an art object crafted by man, loved (5–6) and worshiped (7–9) by all men.

28a.right margin: In the right-hand margin of *Rid.* 28a (folio 108*a*) there are two marks (see plates xiv.a and b). The upper one is a very late *r* with a point on either side. It is hard to tell who made the letter or what its significance might be (a hazarded solution, *rood*?). The letter was not made by Nowell in the sixteenth century as a comparison between it and an interlinear *r* on folio 10*a* (see plate xiv.c) will readily show. The second mark resembles no Old English letter or Anglo-Saxon rune and is probably just a testing of the stylus. Conceivably the lower mark could be a *C* rune made in the style of the Old Norse *kaun* (see Elliott, *Runes*, p. 48), but there is no reason why an Old Norse rune should appear here. The mark does in some respects resemble a similar mark on the pommel of the Gilton sword, but the meaning of the mark on the sword is still much in doubt. For the mark on the sword, see Bately, "Interpretation of the Runes on the Gilton Pommel," *Archaeologia* ci, 99 ff.

28a.1: *legbysig*: 28b.1 *ligbysig*: Thorpe and Grein misread the text at 28b.1 as *lic bysig*, and so Blackburn (*JEGP* iii, 7). Assmann reported the MS. reading correctly but printed *lic bysig* as an emendation in the text. Later editors report the b-text correctly. Tupper, in his composite text, reads *legbysig*; Wyatt, *lig bysig*.

28b.2: In the b-text, the traces of letters still showing after *w* are consistent with *uldr*. The restoration *w[uldre bewunden, we]dre gesomnad* seems likely. The restoration was first proposed by Trautmann, who however misread the initial letter as *u* in *u[uldre*.

28.3: *fus forðweges*: O.E. *fus* often means "ready to depart after death" (see BTS., p. 275, category III) and *forðweg* also means sometimes "the way forth from life" (cp. *Beo.* 2625). The words are used again in conjunction at *Men.* 217–18: *he gast ageaf on godes wære, | fus on forðweg*.

28.5–6: Blackburn (*JEGP* iii, 4) first noted that line 6 might refer to the cup, and Holthausen (*Anglia Beibl.* xxx, 51) argued that lines 5–6 refer to a wooden cup. Creatures traditionally kissed in riddles are drinking cups. The word *cyssan* occurs in two other riddles in the *Exeter Book*. The "beaker" at *Rid.* 61, which is carried *þær guman drincað* (61.3), proclaims: *Hwilum mec on cofan cysseð muþe* (61.4). And the drinking horn of *Rid.* 12 says *hwilum [mec] weras cyssað* (12.3). The theme of kissing the cup also appears in Aldhelm's Riddle 80, "Calix Vitreus" (see quotation in headnote to *Rid.* 61), in Bern Riddle 6, "De Calice" (*CCL.* cxxxiii A, p. 552), and in Lorsch Riddle 5, "De Cupa Vinaria" (*CCL.* cxxxiii, p. 351).

28a.9: At the end of the a-text riddle on folio 108*a*, after MS. *eadig nesse* there follows a typical end-punctuation mark and after that an unusual one (see plate xv), which resembles somewhat the unusual end-punctuation mark at the close of *Rid.* 12 (see note and plate for that riddle). The reason for the unusual mark remains unclear in both cases.

29. Bagpipe
[*VN: Gr.32; Tr.29; Tu.32; W.31; M.31; K-D.31*]

Dietrich's solution, "bagpipe" (*ZfdA*. xi, 469), is accepted by all editors except Trautmann and Holthausen. Trautmann first solved the riddle as "fiddle" (*Anglia Beibl*. v, 49), which hardly fits the gangly, bird-like creature, and later retreated to the solution, "ein Musikgerät," with the qualification, "Nicht gemeint ist der Dudelsack" (edition, p. 92). Trautmann's singular antipathy to *der Dudelsack* remains something of a mystery. Holthausen (*Anglia Beibl*. xxx, 51) solves the riddle as "organistrum" ("drehleier, leierkasten"), but the notion of an Anglo-Saxon hurdy-gurdy is fanciful indeed. Dietrich believes the bagpipe to be the O.E. *swegelhorn*, which glosses the L. *sambucus* (WW. 44.37) and *symphonia* (Hpt. Gl. 445.19, cited in B-T., p. 947; cp. WW. 483.17). Dietrich says:

> Das seltsame singende ding nr [29], mit dem schall im fusse und den zwei brüdern am halse, ist die *sackpfeife* ags. *svegelhorn* (sambuca, symphonia gl. Ald.) mit den zwei flöten am obern ende des dumpf tönenden schlauches. noch jetzt sieht man zuweilen auf den strassen Londons schottische knaben mit dem alten, bei allen deutschen stämmen so beliebten dudelsack; wenn dann das hörnerne mundstück den kopf und leib des vom arme des knaben geschlagenen schlauches anschwellt, während die finger auf den flöten ruhen die in den hals des schlauches münden, dann ist allerdings die vollste ähnlichkeit des dinges mit einem vogel da, der mit seinem schnabel den mund des bläsers berührt . . . [*ZfdA*. xi, 469]

Padelford, in his article, "Old English Musical Terms" (*BBzA*. iv, 49 ff.), agrees with the "bagpipe" solution to the riddle, but argues for the Latin names, *musa*, *chorus*, and *camena* as the proper terms of reference. L. *musa* is glossed by O.E. *pipe oððe hwistle* (WW. 311.22); *camena* by *sangpipe* (*Prudentius Glosses* 389.26, cited by B-T., p. 816). Padelford says of the *chorus*:

> Chorus is the usual name for the bagpipe among the church writers. It will be remembered that Giraldus called the *chorus* an instrument of Wales

and Scotland. In the Boulogne and Tiberius manuscripts . . . are drawings of the chorus, which, from the fragments of Latin accompanying them, are suggested by the following from Pseudo-Jerome: 'Synagogae antiquis temporibus fuit chorus quoque simplex pellis cum duabus cicutis aereis: et per primam inspiratur, per secundam vocem emittit' (*PL*. xxx, 125). These instruments are conventional, having a round body, and two pipes opposite each other. In the Tiberius manuscript is a second chorus, which has a square body, and two pipes for blowing, instead of one. [*BBzA*. iv, 51]

Bright agrees with the "bagpipe" solution and makes the following observations:

The bagpipe looks like a bird carried on the shoulders with the feet projecting upward (= the drones, two in number). The poet speaks of these legs in the air as *fēt ond folme fugele gelīce* (l. 7); the *neb* (l. 6) is the chanter and is at the foot of the instrument (ll. 17, 20). The gender of the parts is important. The chanter (the sister) is the female voice, it carries the high notes and the tune; the deep-voiced brothers are the drones (ll.21–23). [Quoted in Tupper, p. 144]

29.4: For the *b*-line, *werum on gemonge*, cp. line 11*b*, *eorlum on gemonge*. The MS. *a*-line is clearly deficient. Holthausen (*Anglia Beibl.* xxx, 51) reads *wiht wæs on wonge*; Mackie (*MLR* xxviii, 76) reads *wiht wæs on wynne*. Krapp and Dobbie point out that "neither of these readings provides a suitable syntax for the comparative *wundorlicran* in the next line" (p. 338). Cosijn (*Beiträge* xxiii, 129) reads *wiht wæs no hwæðre*, citing line 8, and so does Tupper. Kock (*Anglia* xliv, 112) reconstructs the half-line to read *wiht ne wæs þæs onwene*, and translates lines 4–5: "however strange a thing on earth might be, / this creature had a shape more wondrous still" (*Anglia* xliv, 113). Herzfeld (*Die Räthsel des Exeterbuches und ihr Verfasser*, p. 68) reads *wiht wæs nower*, and so do Trautmann, Wyatt, and Krapp and Dobbie. The loss of *-wer* before *werum* and the transposition of *no* to *on* is easy to justify paleographically. The construction is strange, but taking *sio* as a relative in line 5, we may translate lines 4–5: "There was no creature anywhere (literally, "There was nowhere a creature") among men which had a more wonderful shape."

29.6: The line as it stands in the MS. is obviously corrupt. All editors read *Niþerweard* for MS. *niþer wearð*. Grein, Assmann, Wyatt, and Krapp and Dobbie keep the reading, *Niþerweard wæs neb hyre*, but the on-verse so constituted is metrically short (cp. *Rid*. 19.1*a*, *Neb is min niþerweard*, and *Rid*. 32.3*b*, *niþerweard gongeð*). The addition of *onhwyrfed* as I have it was first suggested by Herzfeld (*Die Räthsel des Exeterbuches und ihr Verfasser*, p. 68). Herzfeld also suggested the possibility of adding *gongende* after *Niþerweard*. Holthausen in the same place would supply *geneahhe* or *genyded* (*Indogermanische Forschungen* iv, 387), *beged* (*Anglia* xxxviii, 77) or *hnæged* (*Anglia Beibl.* xlvi, 9). Tupper supplies *æt nytte* after *Niþerweard*, citing *Rid.* 32.3*a*. Trautmann reads *Niþerweard wæs neb* as the *a*-line and *hyre* [*no wæron*] as the *b*-line in order to justify his solution, "fiddle." Likewise Holthausen (*Anglia Beibl.* xxxii, 136 ff.) in another of his reconstructions, closed the *a*-line with *neb* and read *hyre neoðan wæron* in the *b*-line. Kock (*Anglia* xliv, 112 ff.) takes *Niþerweard wæs neb hyre* as the complete *a*-line, supplying *neol wæs hnecca* for the *b*-line, but the on-verse so constituted is metrically overcrowded.

29.20b ff.: These are difficult lines. I agree with Tupper who translates the passage as follows: "She (the instrument), when she holds the treasure (i.e., is inflated), without clothes (so BTS., p. 61) (yet) proud of her rings, has on her neck her brothers [bass-pipes or drones]—she, a kinswoman with might" (p. 145). All editors except Thorpe read MS. *bær* as nominative singular feminine, but the proper form, as Holthausen (*Anglia Beibl.* xlvi, 9) pointed out, must be *baru* (see Campbell 643.1, p. 264), and so I have emended the form in the text. Thorpe reads *bærbeagum* as a compound, "with bearing-rings." Bright (see Tupper, p. 145, note) first suggested that the *hord* of 21*b* was the treasure of the bag—i.e., the air. Bright and Wyatt take the *hio* of 21*b* to be the chanter and not the whole instrument. Wyatt emends line 23*a* to read *mæg mid mægum* to refer to chanter and drones. Trautmann takes *hord* to be the music of the fiddle, *broþor* to be the strings, and *bær* as *bær* for "Trage, Bahre."

29.23: *hycgenne*: Sievers (*Beiträge* x, 482) would emend the inflected form here to the uninflected *hycgan* for metrical reasons (see note to *Rid.* 26.12*b*).

30. Ship
[*VN: Gr.33; Tr.30; Tu.33; W.32; M.32; K-D.32*]

Conybeare (*Illustrations of Anglo-Saxon Poetry*, pp. 210ff.) solved the riddle as "wagon," and Bouterwek (see *Sp.*, p. 276, under *grindan*) solved as "millstone," but Dietrich's (*ZfdA*. xi, 469ff.) solution, "ship," is accepted by all other editors. Ships played a large part in the communication network of Anglo-Saxon England. Page notes that "rivers were extensively used, so that many inland towns were ports reached by rivers no longer commercially navigable" (*Life in Anglo-Saxon England*, p. 15), and Wilson says that "whenever possible . . . merchandise was transported by water" (*The Anglo-Saxons*, p. 91). For information on Anglo-Saxon ships, see the headnotes to "ship" *Rids*. 17, 34, and 62. For an account of the mercantile system of Anglo-Saxon England, see Wilson, ibid., pp. 80ff.

30.1–2: Cp. the opening lines of *Rid*. 29.

30.4: *grindan wið greote*: *grind against the shore*. Tupper cites a parallel passage at *Guth*. 1333ff.: *se hærnflota . . . grond wið greote*.

30.7: *searoceap*: *skillfully made merchandise*. Grein glosses the word as *merx vel res artificiosa* (*Sp.*, p. 587); B-T., as *an ingenious piece of goods, a curious implement* (p. 852); CH., as *artistic object* (p. 300). *Ceap* originally meant *cattle*, and then by extension, *a sellable object* or *a commodity* (B-T., p. 148). Cp. *searofær* (*Rim*. 65), *searopil* (*Rid*. 87.2), *searowundor* (*Beo*. 920), and *orlegceap* (*Gen*. 1994). Trautmann emends MS. *searoceap* to *searocest*, "sinnreicher kasten," citing *mereciest* at *Gen*. 1317.

30.9: *muð*: Dietrich (*ZfdA*. xi, 470) cites *Gen*. 1364: *merehuses muð*. Wyatt calls this *muð* the hatchway. Bruce-Mitford notes that the Sutton Hoo ship was a "great open rowing boat" (*The Sutton Hoo Ship-Burial: A Handbook*, p. 47). Boats do appear with great, high holds and hatchway doors in *Oxford Bodleian MS. Junius 11* (see Page, *Life in Anglo-Saxon England*, illustrations on pp. 20, 85), but this may derive from a strictly literary or artistic tradition. The exact nature of holds and hatches on Anglo-Saxon ships must await the discovery of further archaeological materials.

30.10: *fereð*: The MS. reading, *fere*, is not easily explained. Grein gives the following definition: "*fere* = *fære acc. zu* faru *f. das Tragen*,

Bringen; (scip) fere foddorwelan (*gen.*) folcscipe (*dat.*) dreogeð, wist inwigeð (fere dreogeð = fereð)" (*Sp.*, p. 192). The idiom *fare dreogan* is found nowhere else in Old English. Krapp and Dobbie note that the accusative singular of *faru* should be *fare*, citing *Gen.* 1746 and *Ex.* 555. B-T. (p. 296 under *foddorwela*), Tupper, and Mackie follow Grein. Wyatt emends MS. *fere* to *fær*, accusative singular neuter for "journey," but otherwise follows Grein. Trautmann and Krapp and Dobbie emend MS. *fere* to *fereð* (from *ferian*, "to carry") and this reading gives the best possible sense to the passage.

30.10: *folcscipe dreogeð*: works for the people (*nation?*). *Dreogan* occurs as an intransitive verb at *Gen.* 2284, *Az.* 3, and *Sol.* 60 in the B text (B-T., p. 212). I read *folcscipe* as dative singular with Grein and Bosworth-Toller, though my reading of the passage is different from theirs (see previous note). For the meaning of *folcscipe dreogeð*, Krapp and Dobbie quote Sedgefield's gloss, "performs a social service" (*An Anglo-Saxon Verse Book*, p. 190), but the glossing of *folcscipe* as "social service" is dubious indeed. Grein, Bosworth-Toller, and Clark Hall all gloss the compound as *nation* or *people*. Trautmann in his edition cites the supposedly analogous passage at *Beo.* 1470, *drihtscype dreogan*, which he defines as "Herrentaten verrichten." But he glosses *folcscipe* as *Volk* (acc. sing.), and the meaning of the implied *Volk verrichten* remains obscure.

30.11a: For the meter (short A2a in which the second lift consists of a single short syllable), cp. *Rid.* 89.12*a*.

31. Iceberg
[*VN: Gr.34; Tr.31; Tu.34; W.33; M.33; K-D.33*]

Dietrich's solution, "eisscholle" (*ZfdA.* xi, 470) is accepted by all editors though there is some disagreement as to whether the creature is an ice floe (river ice or sea ice) or an actual iceberg (broken off from a glacier). The opening lines seem to indicate "sea ice" or "iceberg," but Trautmann says: "Unmöglich: das Meer um ganz England und Schottland herum gefriert nicht" (p. 94). A number of sources (King,

An Introduction to Oceanography, pp. 110 ff. and Jenkins, *A Textbook of Oceanography*, pp. 85 ff.) make it clear that while sea ice or pack ice (ice formed directly by the freezing of seawater) is not found in British waters, icebergs from east Greenland occasionally are. King says for example that "the southerly extent of the ice-bergs varies greatly from year to year. . . . In years rich in ice-bergs they penetrate at times as far as 30°N, when they drift east towards the Azores or even the British coasts" (p. 111). Jenkins (p. 89) charts North Atlantic icebergs with phenomenal drift between 1900 and 1916, and several of these would have been within range of an Anglo-Saxon sailor such as King Alfred's Ohthere. Finally, Edward Smith, who went on an iceberg-charting expedition in 1928, says of erratic icebergs:

> There are records of occasional bergs, "erratics" that wander from the better recognized paths of travel to be carried hither and thither in irregular tracks. Being relatively large and massive the processes of melting and erosion often fail to affect their destruction until they have completed long journeys. . . . Probably several of the reports of ice sighted in the vicinity of the British Isles, or the Faroe Islands, rare phenomena but nevertheless authentic, refer to bergs that have drifted from northeast Greenland via the East Iceland current." [*The Marine Expedition to Davis Strait and Baffin Bay Under Direction of the United States Coast Guard, 1928, Part 3, Arctic Ice, with Especial Reference to Its Distribution to the North Atlantic Ocean*, 1931, p. 75]

Dietrich and Tupper cite several late Latin analogues utilizing the genealogical motif of *mater et filia*. The tradition, as noted by Ohlert (*Rätsel und Rätselspiele der alten Griechen*, p. 54), is as old as Pompeius's *Commentum Artis Donati*, a book well known to English grammarians (Ogilvy, *Bks.* p. 224). Pompeius says:

> Aenigma est, quo ludunt etiam parvuli inter se, quando sibi proponunt quaestiunculas, quas nullus intellegit. dic mihi, quid est hoc, est quaedam filia matris et mater filia est filiae suae? hoc qui potest intellegere,
>
> mater me genuit, eadem mox gignitur ex me?
>
> aenigma est; hoc autem significat, aquam soluta glacie posse procreari, iterum ipsam aquam coactam glaciem posse facere. ergo et de aqua fit glacies, et de ipsa glacie fit aqua. aenigma est hoc. [Keil, ed. *Grammatici Latini*, vol. 5: *Artium Scriptores Minores*, p. 311]

Tupper points out that the tradition is noted by Aldhelm in his *Epistola ad Acircium* (see Giles, ed. *Sancti Aldhelmi . . . Opera*, p. 230). The motif is also used in *The Meters of Boethius* 28.59 ff.:

Hwa wundrað þæs
oððe oþres eft,   hwi þæt is mæge
weorðan of wætere;   wlitetorht scineð
sunna swegle hat;   sona gecerreð
ismere ænlic   on his agen gecynd,
weorðeð to wætre.

[*Bo.* 28.59–64]

The creature of the riddle is called *wrætlicu* and *cymlic*. The jeweled creature ice is also described by the poet of *The Rune Poem*:

ᛁ (is) byþ oferceald,   ungemetum slidor,
glisnaþ glæshluttur,   gimmum gelicust,
flor forste geworuht,   fæger ansyne.

[*Run.* 29–31]

Ice is also described by the poet of the *Exeter Maxims*: *Forst sceal freosan . . . is brycgian, | wæter helm wegan* (*Max.* I 71–73). For a different treatment of the iceberg theme, cp. *Rid.* 66.

31.2: *cymlic from ceolan cleopode to londe*: *The beauty cried out from her throat* (*gorge*) *to the land.* I have emended MS. *ceole* to *ceolan.* Mackie and Baum both translate *from ceole* as "from its keel," and both Wyatt and Tupper gloss *cēol* as "keel, ship," though they do not specify its meaning in this particular case. O.E. *cēol* cannot mean "keel" (see CH., p. 67; BTS., p. 121; *OED* v, p. 657ff. and *AEW.*, p. 46). The first documented use of "keel" (*cule*) to mean *keel of a boat* listed by the *OED* is from Trevisa in the fourteenth century. The word for *keel* in Latin is *carina*, which may also mean *ship*. L. *carina* occurs with the following glosses in Old English: *bythne* (WW. 11.18), *scipes botm* (WW. 166.5), *scipesbotm* (L. *Cimba, uel carina*: WW. 181.37), *bythme* (WW. 288.3), and *bytne* (WW. 362.31). L. *carinae* is glossed by *scipes* (WW. 376.33). *Carina* is never glossed by the O.E. *cēol.* O.E. *cēol* is the gloss for the following Latin terms: *celox* (WW. 12.29; 276.5; 363.37), *celox, uel cilion, i. species nauis* (WW. 203.31), and *ciula* (WW. 205.6). The problem is dealt with in a number of ways. Dietrich (*ZfdA.* xi, 470) reads *from ceole* as modifying *cwom . . . liþan* and translates somewhat freely as "vom kiele, d.h. auf dem meere, gefahren." Trautmann questions this and says: "Unmöglich: das Meer um ganz England und Schottland herum gefriert nicht." Trautmann suggests in his edition *from cĕosle*, "vom Sande," with reference to the iceberg's breaking off from the glacier. Barnouw (*Neoph.* iii, 78) reads *from cele* or *from ciolde*, "out of the cold," and Trautmann (*Anglia* xlii, 134 ff.) suggests the use of *cealde*, *cole*, or *ceolde* as more regular forms. Krapp and Dobbie note that "the MS. *ceole* seems to refer to the iceberg itself, the sound being represented as coming *from ceole* to the shore" (p. 340). This begs the question. Does the creature cry out *from the ship*? Metaphorically, the iceberg as a wave-traveler is equated with a ship; it does not ride one. It seems to me to make clearest sense to read *cymlic* as a substantival adjective, "the beautiful one," and to emend MS. *ceole* to *ceolan*, a form of *ceole*, "throat, gorge." The creature cries out from its throat to the land. Something of the same wording is used in the *Paris Psalter* at *Psalm* 113.16: *Ne cleopigaở hi care, þeah þe hi ceolan habban.*

31.5: *wæs hio hetegrim, hilde to sæne*: she was fiercely cruel [yet] slow to battle. This is the reading of Mackie, who takes *to*, as I do, as a preposition following *hilde* and governing it, marking purpose or sphere of action. Brooke notes that the MS. reading might aptly describe the iceberg as "slow in beginning the war, but when engaged, bitter in battle-work" (*The History of Early English Literature*, p. 181, note). Tupper and Wyatt read *to* as an adverb modifying *sæne*, but this reading overemphasizes the slowness of the creature and deemphasizes its grim sense of purpose. Klaeber (*MP* ii, 144–45) would read *on wene*; Herzfeld (*Die Rätsel des Exeterbuches und ihr Verfasser*, p. 68) would read *to sæge*, "zugeneigt," which Tupper notes does not appear elsewhere in Old English. Holthausen would read *to cene* (*ESn.* xxxvii, 208) or *næs to sæne* (*Anglia Beibl.* xxx, 52). Trautmann reads *hilde unsæne*. Krapp and Dobbie doubt the MS. reading but note that none of the emendations are very convincing. It is possible the MS. *sæne* represents the corruption of an infinitive after *to* (one possibility might be *hilde to secan*). For other uses of *hetegrim*, cp. *An.* 1395 and 1562.

31.6: *Bordweallas*: probably *ship-walls*, though in terms of the battle imagery a pun on *shield-walls* (cp. *Beo.* 2980, *Brun.* 5, and *Mald.* 277) cannot be ruled out. Wyatt believes that *bordweallas* here refers literally to the "sides of ships hung round with shields" (p. 92). There are illustrations of Norman and English ships in the Bayeux tapestry (see Stenton, ed., plates 6, 7, 30, 43, and 44), which have "shield-walls," but Charles Gibbs-Smith in a note to the illustrations says:

> When armed troops are on board, their shields are seen arranged over-lapping inside the gunwales . . . but this is probably a technical error on the part of the designer, based on insufficient knowledge of the sea. It is well known and documented that in the Viking ships—and the same rule would apply here—shields were only allowed to be displayed along the gunwales when in port. Before the ship was got under way, they were stowed else-where on board for the good reason that their position would interfere with the seamen who had to man the oars—as they would have to be prepared to do at any minute with the limited navigational facilities of the single square sail. [In Stenton, *The Bayeux Tapestry*, p. 182, notes to plates 42–44]

31.7: *heardhiþende*: *the hard-plundering one.* Krapp and Dobbie note that "the editors read *heard ond hiþende*, except Wyatt, Trautmann, and Mackie, who read *heard, hiþende* as an asyndeton, but the compound seems more probable here" (p. 340). For a similar compound, cp. *heardhicgende* at *Beo.* 394 and 799.

31.7: *Heterune bond!*: B-T. (p. 535) defines *heterun* as "*a charm causing hate or evil*," and Mackie translates the half-line as "it wrought a baleful spell" (p. 125). But *run* can also mean *mystery* or *secret* (see B-T., p. 804, categories II and III), and it seems likely here that the *hateful mystery* that the iceberg "binds" or "locks in" is the deadly portion of ice below the water. Cosijn (*Beiträge* xxiii, 129) would read *onband* for *band* here, citing *Beo.* 501: [*Unferð*] *onband beadurune*. But the curse of the iceberg is not loosed like the smoothly articulate tongue—it is rather locked like the rage of a warrior whose passion is steeled for the coming battle.

31.9–11b: I translate: "My mother, of the most precious (or excellent) of the race of females, is what my daughter is." This is the reading of all editors except Mackie who takes *min* (9a) not as a possessive adjective but as the genitive of *ic* and *deorestan* (10a) not from *deore*, "precious," but from *deor*, "bold," and translates: "The mother of myself, who am the boldest of the female sex, is what is my daughter, when grown up in strength" (p. 125). But if *þæs deorestan* agrees with *min* (which refers to the *mægð*), would we not expect the feminine gender? Also Mackie's reading renders the syntax unnecessarily difficult.

31.11: *uploden*: For the MS. *upliden*, Grein reads *up liden* under both *li-ðan*, "to travel, sail" (*Sp.*, p. 423) and *leodan* (*liodan*), "to spring up, grow" (*Sp.*, p. 413). Bosworth-Toller (p. 643), Tupper, and Wyatt gloss the phrase as "grown up" under *liðan* with some question. Clearly the phrase, *eacen upliden*, as it is in the MS., is related to the verb, *leodan*, "to spring, grow" (B-T., p. 630) and to *aleodan*, "to grow up," which is used to describe water again at *Rid.* 80.31. The context at *Rid.* 80 is similar to this one:

> Fromast ond swiþost,
> gifrost ond grædgost— grundbedd trideþ—
> þæs þe under lyfte aloden wurde
> ond ælda bearn eagum sawe.

[Rid. 80.29–32]

Aleodan also occurs at *PPs.* 106.36. For the occurrences of *leodan* and *geleodan*, see Grein, *Sp.*, p. 413. The past participle always occurs in the form, *-loden*, so I have emended the text to exemplify that spelling here. O.E. *up-* is a common verbal prefix. I would read the form *uploden* here to mean "grown up" from the infinitive *upleodan*, which is unattested but which would function in a capacity similar to that of *aleodan*. The iceberg's mother, water, is also its daughter *eacen uploden*, "grown up pregnant." The water is eternally conceiving, as is the ice. For the reading of *eacen* as "pregnant," cp. the description of Beado-hild at *Deor* 11: *þæt heo eacen wæs*.

32. Rake
[*VN: Gr.35; Tr.32; Tu.35; W.34; M.34; K-D.34*]

Dietrich (*ZfdA.* xi, 470) first solved the riddle as "rake," and so all later editors. Trautmann (*Anglia Beibl.* v, 49) first proposed "bee," but later withdrew this in favor of Dietrich's "rake" (edition). Trautmann cites Riddle 60 of Symphosius, "Serra," but the only thing that the Latin riddle shares with the Old English one is that both the rake and the saw have teeth.

32.2: So Isidore says: "Rastra quoque aut a radendo terram aut a raritate dentium dicta" (*Etym*. xx.xiv.6).

32.5: *geond weallas*: *about walls* (Mackie, p. 125)? *among the hills* (B-T., p. 1174)? Since *weall* normally means (1) wall, or (2) cliff, Mackie's reading seems the more likely. Wyatt and Trautmann would also read "hills." The reference may be to domestic gardening. Otherwise an emendation to *wealdas* might be in order.

33. Mail Coat
[*VN: Gr.36; Tr.33; Tu.36; W.35; M.35; K-D.35*]

Dietrich (*De Kynewulfi Poetae Aetate*, pp. 16 ff.; *ZfdA*. xi, 470) solved the riddle as "mail coat" and pointed out that both this and the *Leiden Riddle*, a Northumbrian version of the same riddle, were translations of Aldhelm's Riddle 33, "Lorica." The *Leiden Riddle* is preserved in the *Leiden University MS. Voss. Q. 106* on the lower half of folio 25*b* (see Smith, *Three Northumbrian Poems*, pp. 7 ff. and Dobbie, *ASPR.*, vol. 6, pp. cviii ff. for a discussion of the MS.). The Leiden MS. contains primarily, besides the riddle, a Greek litany, the Latin Riddles of Symphosius, a list of the Latin Riddles of Aldhelm along with the riddles themselves, and a short epilogue (Smith, pp. 7–8). The *Leiden Riddle* appears to have been added in the space remaining at the end of the MS. I reprint Dobbie's edition of the riddle, which is based in large part upon Smith's earlier reading:

> Mec se ueta uong, uundrum freorig,
> ob his innaðae aerest cæn[.]æ.
> Ni uaat ic mec biuorthæ uullan fliusum,
> herum ðerh hehcraeft, hygiðonc[.....].
> 5 Uundnae me ni biað ueflæ, ni ic uarp hafæ,
> ni ðerih ðreatun giðraec ðret me hlimmith,
> ne me hrutendu hrisil scelfath,
> ni mec ouana aam sceal cnyssa.
> Uyrmas mec ni auefun uyrdi craeftum,

10 ða ði geolu godueb geatum fraetuath.
Uil mec huethrae suae ðeh uidæ ofaer eorðu
hatan mith hęliðum hyhtlic giuæde;
ni anoegun ic me aerigfaerae egsan brogum,
ðeh ði n[...]n siæ niudlicae ob cocrum.

[*ASPR.*, vol. 6, p. 109]

The Latin riddle upon which both the Exeter and the Leiden riddles
are based is Aldhelm's Riddle 33, "Lorica." Since there are a number
of difficult weaving terms in the text and since there are a number of
bad translations of the Latin, I include Wyatt's translation, which is a
good one:

	O.E.
Roscida me genuit gelido de viscere tellus;	[1–2]
Non sum setigero lanarum vellere facta,	[3–4]
Licia nulla trahunt nec garrula fila resultant	[5–6]
Nec crocea Seres* texunt lanugine vermes	[9–10]
Nec radiis carpor duro nec pectine pulsor;	[7–8]
Et tamen en vestis vulgi sermone vocabor.	[11–12]
Spicula non vereor longis exempta faretris	

[Ed. Pitman, p. 18]

The dewy earth brought me forth from her cold womb. I am not made of a
hairy fleece of wool; no leashes draw me tight, nor do threads vibrate with
vocal sound, no Chinese worms weave me from downy floss of saffron hue; I
am not plucked at by the shuttle, nor struck by the ruthless sley; and yet, lo! I
shall be called a garment in common parlance. I fear not darts drawn from
long quivers. [Wyatt, p. 93]

In general the Old English riddler uses two lines to translate one line
of the Latin, though the order of the lines is rearranged and in some
places there is a departure from the sense of the Latin text (see notes
below). The last line of the Latin corresponds to the last two lines of
the *Leiden Riddle*; these lines are missing in the Exeter version and a
two-line rhetorical ending is substituted in their place. There are two
other riddles having to do with weaving in the *Exeter Book*, *Rids.* 54
and 86, and the reader should see the headnotes to those riddles. In
Rid. 33 the weaving terms are part of the negative qualification of the

---

*"Seres: Σῆρες, a people of Eastern Asia (the modern Chinese), celebrated for their
silken fabrics" (Lewis and Short, p. 1678); see, for example, Pliny, *NH.* vi.xx.54–55.

riddlic definition: this shirt is not woven by normal means—it is a shirt of mail.

Although the mail shirt is mentioned fairly frequently in Old English poetry, particularly in *Beowulf*, not many byrnies have been found in the graves. Green (*Sutton Hoo: The Excavation of a Royal Ship-burial*, p. 77) describes mail shirts found at Thorsbjerg in Schleswig, at Vimose in the Danish island of Fyen, at Vendel in Uppland, Sweden, and at Benty Grange, near Monyash in Derbyshire, but Wilson (*The Anglo-Saxons*, p. 125) argues that "nothing survives of the Benty Grange mail and it is possible that it was merely the neck guard of the helmet (a helmet with a mail neck guard occurred in the more or less contemporary grave 6 at Valsgärde in Sweden)." On the other hand, there is solid evidence for the chain mail found at Sutton Hoo. Bruce-Mitford reports:

> Lying in folds at the bottom of this deposit [i.e., under the Great Silver Dish] was a mass of rusted iron mail, the remains of a mail coat. Radiography of the rusted mass shows that the rows of rings were alternately riveted and welded. In the riveted rows the ends of each ring were hammered into a spatulate shape, made to overlap, and fastened with a minute bronze rivet. As the folds had rusted into a solid lump it is not possible to reconstruct the shape or size of the original garment or to say, for example, whether it had sleeves. No buckles or other metal fittings that might possibly have been associated with a coat of mail were revealed in the radiographic survey. [*The Sutton Hoo Ship-Burial: A Handbook*, p. 37]

Keller (*The Anglo-Saxon Weapon Names*) treats the various known kinds of mail (pp. 93ff.) and the various Old English words for body armor or chain mail (pp. 255ff.). The numerous references to chain mail in *Beowulf* indicate the importance of the armor in epic terms. For example, the coming of Beowulf's band is described:

> Guðbyrne scan
> heard hondlocen,   hringiren scir
> song in searwum,   þa hie to sele furðum
> in hyra gryregeatwum   gangan cwomon.
>
> [*Beo.* 321–24]

And Beowulf, when he comes into the Danish hall, speaks to Hrothgar with an appropriately bright introduction by the poet: "Beowulf maðelode—on him byrne scan, / searonet seowed smiþes orþancum" (*Beo.* 405–6).

33.3: Literally, "I do not know myself made from fleeces of wool," but more freely, "I know I am not made from wool fleece."

33.4: *hygeþoncum min*: *in* (*by*) *the thoughts of me*, or more freely, *in my thoughts*. The reading of the personal pronoun was suggested by Wyatt. Kock (*Lunds Universitets Årsskrift*, NF., Avd. 1, Bd. 14, Nr. 26, p. 20) takes *min* as an uninflected adjective after the noun. There is no corresponding passage in the Latin, and the Leiden MS. is damaged here.

33.5 ff.: For the use of rhetorical devices (*anaphora* and *polysyndeton*) patterned on the Latin, see J. J. Campbell, *MP* lxiii, 195. Another list of weaving terms may be found in the *Gerefa* (*Anglia* ix, 263, section 15; also in Liebermann, *Die Gesetze der Angelsachsen*, vol. 1, p. 455, section 15, with notes at vol. 3, p. 254).

33.5: *wefle*: O.E. *wefl* normally means *weft* or *woof* (the thread that crosses horizontally back and forth through the vertical warp), or the weft thread on the shuttle (see B-T., pp. 1182–83). Here, clearly in contrast with *wearp*, the word means "weft." Aldhelm's "Licia" (line 3) normally meant "leashes, leash-rods," but it also had a secondary sense of "weft" (see Zandvoort, *EGS* iii, 47 for a discussion of this point).

33.6: *ne þurh þreata geþræcu þræd me ne hlimmeð*: This corresponds to the Latin *nec garrula fila resultant*, and the meaning of *þurh þreata geþræcu*, which must be the equivalent of or an expansion of L. *garrula*, has been the subject of some contention. Dietrich and Grein originally thought the *þreat* to have been some part of the loom (for a summary of early ideas about the passage, see Zandvoort, *EGS* iii, 47–48) and the idea was recently resurrected by Ekwall, who said in a review of Smith's edition of the *Leiden Riddle*: "A ðreat must have been some part of the loom. I suggest that it was the name of one of the weights that kept the warp taut. ðerih ðreata giðraec [sic] would then mean 'owing to the pressure of the weights'" (*MLR* xxix, 80). Zandvoort (*EGS* iii, 48) notes that this is plausible but that it has nothing to do with *garrula* in the Latin riddle. Also, the term *þreat* does not occur in the *Gerefa* list of weaving implements (*Anglia* ix, 263, section 15) where one might expect it. Toller (BTS., p. 434, under *geþræc*) translates *þurh* *þreata geþræcu* as "through thick-coming torments," suggesting that this might refer to "the process to which the thread is subjected in weaving." Tupper translates *þreata geþræcu* as "'the pressing of multitudes'—that is, 'the force of many strokes'" (p. 152). Gerritsen (*ES* xxxv, 262) suggests that "'the crowded many' instrumental in making thread resound is *the system of leashes*." It seems to me that Toller is on the right track. L. *garrula* refers to the sound of the vibrating threads in the loom and O.E. *þurh þreata geþræcu*, "through the rush of many," seems to be an explanation of the source of the sound (*þræd . . . hlimmeð*) in terms of battle imagery. Battle language is also used in "web and loom" *Rid.* 54, and the hostility between warp and woof is part of the game in the Latin *Rid.* 86 of the Exeter collection. Both warp and woof move in the process of weaving. In *Rid.* 54 the weft or woof moves as the shuttle darts back and forth, and the two sides of the warp move up and down like great feet (54.6–8), presumably with the movement of the leash-rod. The song of the shuttle is traditional in poetic descriptions of weaving, but both warp and weft threads make a kind of music, and I think the Old English riddler meant to refer to the entire symphony of threads when he wrote this line.

33.7: *hrisil: shuttle.* The word glosses L. *radius* (B-T., p. 562; BTS., p. 567).

33.8: *am:* This word corresponds to the L. *pectin* of Aldhelm and must refer to the weaver's reed or sley that is used to compact the fabric by beating up the weft. Both Holthausen (*AEW.*, p. 3) and Erhardt-Siebold ("The Old English Loom Riddles," in *Philologica: The Malone Anniversary Studies*, ed. Thomas A. Kirby and Henry Bosley Woolf, p. 14) connect the Old English word (which occurs as *aam* in the *Leiden Riddle*) with L. *hamus.* The word also occurs as *amb* in the *Gerefa* (*Anglia* ix, 263, section 15, line 13). The word should not be confused with O.E. *hām*, which glosses L. *cauterium* (see Schlutter, *Anglia* xxx, 258 ff.) and which Holthausen defines as "Brenneisen" (see *AEW.* under *ām*, category [2]). Toller (BTS., p. 35) cites the glosses for the "branding iron" along with the occurrence of the "reed" in the *Gerefa*; Campbell (*Addenda* to BTS., p. 4) notes that the "sense in citations in Suppl. is *branding-iron*," but this applies only to the glosses and not to the citation from the *Gerefa*. The MS. reading in *Rid*. 33 is *amas*, but this is not possible with the singular verb. Thorpe suggested *uma*, "weaver's beam," a word that occurs only as a gloss for *scafus* (BTS., p. 1088), and Dietrich (*De Kynewulfi Poetae Aetate*, p. 19) suggested *ama* as the nominative singular noun. Trautmann accepts Dietrich's emendation to *ama*. But the forms in the *Leiden Riddle* (*aam*) and in the *Gerefa* (*amb*) indicate the likelihood of the proper reading *am* here and this is accepted by all other editors.

33.9: The translation of *wyrd* is always a difficult matter (for the range of possible meanings, see Stanley, *NQ* ccx, 285ff.). Mackie translates *wyrda cræftum* as "by the skill that the fates have given" (p. 127); Baum, as "with fatal wiles" (p. 41). Both place too much emphasis upon the older meanings of *wyrd*, though Mackie's reading is certainly preferable to Baum's. I prefer Erhardt-Siebold's translation of *wyrda cræftum* as "with inborn skill" (in her article noted above in *Philologica: The Malone Anniversary Studies*, p. 13). Note that the Leiden version has singular *wyrdi* for plural *wyrda* here.

33.11: Holthausen (*Anglia* xxxv, 168) would read *hwile* for *wide* for the alliteration, but the alliteration of *w* and *hw* is not unknown. Cp. *Rid*. 4.7.

34. Ship
[*VN: Gr.37; Tr.34; Tu.37; W.36; M.36; K-D.36*]

This riddle is complicated by the presence of the cryptic writing in line 5. Dietrich (*ZfdA*. xi, 470ff.) recognized the code in which consonants *b, f, k, p,* and *x* are substituted for their respective preceding vowels—*a, e, i, o,* and *u*. The medieval tradition for the code is outlined in some detail by Tupper (pp. 154–55). By a fantastic process of letter shifts and emendations, Dietrich derived the solution, *"sugu mid V. ferhum,"* or "sow with a litter of five pigs." Dietrich's explanation of the last half of the riddle in light of his solution is a sublime and surreal vision:

Nun ist aber der vogel im zweiten theile des räthsels noch übrig zu lösen; er ist nur fortsetzung des scherzes von den flügelohren, und ist eben noch die sau, denn die ähnlichkeiten mit ross und weib, die der vogel haben soll, sind schon prädicate des gegenstandes im ersten theile; wie die sau wegen der mähne ein pferd ist, so ist sie wegen ihres mutterleibs und ihrer zitzen ein weib und wegen ihrer schnauze und ihres gebisses dem hunde ähnlich. [*ZfdA.* xi, 471]

Grein's emendation *foldwegas* is rejected for the MS. *flodwegas*, great wallowing pools for pigs! This reading was rightly doubted by Trautmann (*Anglia Beibl.* v, 49) and Holthausen (*ESn.* xxxvii, 208) who read the script in line 5 as coded Latin words for the preceding Old English forms: *homo* for *monn*, *mulier* for *wiif*, and *equus* for *hors*. According to Wyatt and later editors, the *h·w·m* must be read as *h·[p]·m·[p]·*; the *·m·x·l·kf w* as *·m·x·l·k·f·[r]·*; the *f·hors ·qxxs·* as *hors ·fqxxs··*. Krapp and Dobbie note that the line is probably a scribal interpolation, saying:

Lines 4 and 6 belong together on the evidence of the alliteration, and it is very probable that l. 5 was not originally a part of the text. Line 5 is best explained as a marginal note, intended as an aid to the identification of the eight feet, which was copied into the text through carelessness or misunderstanding. For a similar instance of the copying of a marginal note into the text, see *Gen.* 1543–1549, note, in Records I, 179. [P. 341]

I agree with Krapp and Dobbie. The cryptic line has only made solving the riddle more difficult. Trautmann's explanation of the first half of the riddle in support of his solution, "Mann, Weib, Ross," may be taken as a typical example:

Meine genauere Deutung ist: Ein Mann und eine Frau sitzen auf einem Pferde; der Mann trägt einen Vogel auf der Hand und die Frau einen Hund im Arm und ein Kind im Leibe (oder der Mann trägt den Hund, die Frau den Vogel). Die 4 Füsse unter dem Bauche sind die des Rosses, die 8 auf dem Rükken die des Kindes, des Vogels und des Hundes. Die Füsse des Mannes und der Frau zählen nicht; denn sie sind weder unter dem Bauch noch auf dem Rücken des Pferdes. [P. 98]

Trautmann proposes to emend MS. *flodwegas* to *foldwegas* or to read lines 9–14 as a separate "ship" riddle. Tupper plausibly extends Trautmann's "ship" to the entire riddle. He says:

The ship has "four feet under its belly," the four oars . . . and "eight above on its back," those of the man, woman, and horse on its deck. . . . The horse, man, dog, bird, and woman, of which it bears the likeness (i.e., which it carries), supply, if we add the ship's figure-head, the two wings, twelve eyes, and six heads. The phrase *tu fiþru* may refer also to the ship's sails, and thus stress the likeness to a bird. [P. 156]

Wyatt, Mackie, and Krapp and Dobbie accept this reading, though Wyatt notes that "apparently the feet of the dog and the bird don't count" (p. 95). Erhardt-Siebold (*PMLA* lxiii, 3–6) suggests that the "eight feet above" belong to the four oarsmen and that the horse is a *yðmearh* or *sundhengest* (see notes to *Rid.* 17.1 and 62.1). She solves the riddle, however, not as "ship," but as "water-fowl hunt," with a fantasy certainly equal to Dietrich's:

> The company must be a party of hunters on their way home with their dogs and killed game, that is, the birds, safely in the punt. The birds, numerous, let us hope, are in the womb of the larger bird, the punt or duckingsink, and, for this reason, our poet discovers in the boat a feature also of a woman.
> How many dogs are there on board? Evidently, two. They supply the two heads and four eyes that we had been looking for in the first part of the riddle, when the puntsmen, not yet homeward-bound, were still engaged in shooting birds with bow and arrow. During this earlier period the dogs had of course left the punt so that their legs could not be counted among those on deck. But their heads and eyes certainly did count in the hunt . . . [*PMLA* lxiii, 5]

Apparently the birds' heads, eyes, and feet do not count. The dogs' heads and eyes count, but their feet do not. No wonder Wyatt wishes the riddle "at the bottom of the Bay of Portugal" (p. 93). Eliason (*SP* xlix, 562ff.) accepts Trautmann's notion of the two riddles, solving the second as "boat" and the first as "a pregnant horse with two pregnant women on its back" (*SP* xlix, 564). This is a burden too heavy to bear.

I accept Tupper's "ship" solution. The reader should see my headnotes to *Rids.* 17 and 62 where ships are described in similar terms. I believe the ship to be a four-oared boat with sail similar to the Viking boat, Skuldelev 3, excavated in 1962. Olsen and Crumlin-Pedersen note that "the ship is a lightly built cargo vessel, of modest draught but well-suited for sailing, and could be pulled ashore fairly easily and even hauled overland for short distances" (*AA* xxxviii, 132). They point out that the boat was powered by both oars and a sail and that "when the ship was rowed it was largely the oars at [strakes] 3 ½A and 2 ½F that were used; a maximum of four oars, each manned by an oarsman although the two pairs of oars did not necessarily always have to be worked at the same time" (*AA* xxvii,

128). Though this boat is a tenth-century Viking boat, it is probable that the Anglo-Saxons had some such boat for sailing their inland waterways. Greenhill (*Antiquity* xlv, 41) notes that older types of Viking and Anglo-Saxon ships may have continued to be built for a long period. Wilson notes that early Anglo-Saxon ships cannot have differed greatly from their Viking contemporaries (*The Anglo-Saxons*, pp. 91–92). The ninth-century Graveney boat whose length and breadth is similar to that of Skuldelev 3 is now thought to have been a barge converted from an earlier sailing boat (*Antiquity* xlv, 89 ff.). Bede notes in his description of Guthfrith's journey to Farne Island to visit Aethelwald that the boat was powered by oars and a sail. When a storm arises, he says: "Positis nobis in medio mari, interrupta est serenitas qua vehebamur, et tanta ingruit tamque fera tempestatis hiems, ut neque velo neque remigio quicquam proficere, neque aliud quam mortem sperare valeremus" (*EH*. v.i, p. 454). When the storm is over, the boat is landed and hauled onto the shore (*ab undis exportaremus*), so the ship was presumably a light sailing vessel equipped also with oars.

In this riddle, the "four feet below" are the oars in the water; the "eight feet above" are the feet of the four oarsmen who are also the travelers. The *monn*, *wiif*, and *hors* are to be discounted as a scribal interpolation of an originally marginalic note. The *tu fiþru* refers to the bird-like sail. The *widlast* carries in *Rid*. 17 the runic HAOFOC. The runic HAfoc in *Rid*. 62 is described as *þryþa dæl*, "a share of the power." The ships in *An*. 497 and *Beo*. 218 are called *fug(o)le gelicost*. The ship has *tu fiþru* (line 7) but is certainly *na fugul ana* (line 9). The man, horse, and bird of line 11, I take to be the runic MON, HORS, and HAOFOC of *Rid*. 17 and the runic BEorn, WICg, and FÆlca of *Rid*. 62. The man is a sailor; the horse is a ship (*yðmearh, sundhengest*); the bird is a sail. The "likeness . . . of a hound" and the "shape of a woman" I take to be figureheads of the ship, fore and aft. The English ship depicted in the Bayeux tapestry has a dog-like head fore and a human head aft (Stenton, *The Bayeux Tapestry*, plate 7). Some of the ships' figureheads noted recently by Bruce-Mitford (*AA* xxxvii, 199 ff.) resemble dogs as much as anything else. The reader should see my discussion of ships' figureheads at *Rid*. 72. Thus there are in the riddle four sailors (manning four oars or "lower feet") and two ships' figureheads accounting for the eight feet, six heads, and twelve eyes. There is no need to postulate the presence of real dogs, birds, or women. The unwitting scribe who copied line 5 into the text has only added a bad guess to the riddle to make the solution if anything more difficult than it already was.

34.4: *ehtuwe*: a Northern form of *eahta*, *eight* (SB. 325 Anm. 8, p. 254). Sievers also cites the Northumbrian form *æhtowe* in *Rushworth Gospel* glosses.

34.5: The cryptic line (see discussion in headnote above) is printed here as it occurs in the MS. and as it is printed by Krapp and Dobbie who read the line as a scribal interpolation of an earlier marginalic note. The marginalic note was presumably an unenlightened guess as to the nature of the "four feet below and eight feet above."

34.9: *flodwegas*: Grein, Cosijn (*Beiträge* xxiii, 129), and Trautmann emend the MS. reading to *foldwegas*, presumably to justify their solutions.

34.12–14: I read *to gesecganne* as a gerund, the object of *const* from O.E. *cunnan* in the sense of *to know* or *understand*. I translate the lines: "You know, if you understand speaking, what we know to be the truth—what the nature of this creature is" (literally, "how the nature of this creature goes"). Most editors take *const* here to mean "be able"; thus Mackie translates, "If you can, you will know how to explain" (p. 127), and Wyatt, "Thou knowest how to say, if thou canst" (p. 95). But *cunnan*, *to be able*, normally takes the infinitive, and *witan* takes an object, a noun or a noun clause (see B-T., pp. 174, 1243–44). Forms of the verbs *cunnan* and *witan* meaning "to know and understand" are often used in juxtaposition in Old English. Compare for example, *Ex.* 28–29 and *Beo.* 180*b*–81.

35. Bellows
[VN: Gr.38; Tr.35; Tu.38; W.37; M.37; K-D.37]

This is one of two "bellows" riddles in the *Exeter Book*. The other, a fragmentary riddle, occurs at *Rid.* 83. Dietrich first solved *Rid.* 35 as "wagon" (*ZfdA*. xi, 472), later (*ZfdA*. xii, 238) as "bellows." All editors accept Dietrich's second solution. The riddle has nothing in common with Aldhelm's Riddle 11, "Poalum," but lines 5–7 of the Old English riddle share something in common with Riddle 73 of Symphosius, "Uter" (or "Follis"):

> Non ego continuo morior, dum spiritus exit;
> Nam redit adsidue, quamvis et saepe recedit:
> Et mihi nunc magna est animae, nunc nulla facultas.
>
> [Ed. Ohl, p. 104]

The similarity was first cited by Dietrich (*ZfdA*. xii, 238, note 6).

Tupper (p. 157) cites a number of manuscript illustrations of the smith at work. The poet of *The Gifts of Men* describes the craft of the smith:

> Sum mæg wæpenþræce,   wige to nytte,
> modcræftig smið   monige gefremman,
> þonne he gewyrceð   to wera hilde
> helm oþþe huþseax   oððe heaþubyrnan,
> scirne mece   oððe scyldes rond,
> fæste gefeged   wið flyge gares.
>
> [*Gifts* 61–66]

In Aelfric's *Colloquy* (lines 220 ff.) the smith claims to be the most important of the workers because he makes the tools for everyone else. For more on the smith's craft, see Klump, *Die altenglischen Handwerkernamen*, pp. 32 ff. and 97 ff.

35.2: *aþrunten*: See note to *Rid.* 43.5.

35.2: *Þegn folgade*: *A servant attended it* (*served it*). The object of *folgian* is understood to be the *wihte* of line 1*a*. For the sense of *folgian* as "to follow as a servant" or "to be attendant upon," see B-T., p. 300 under general category II of *folgian* and also BTS., p. 230 under section (2).

35.2b–4: I translate the lines as follows: "A servant attended it, a mighty man, and (one) who had accomplished much when [*þær*] what filled [*felde* = *fylde*] it flew through its eye." This is essentially the reading of Wyatt who, however, places *gefered* at the beginning of line 4*a* as do all other editors. The line arrangement with *gefered* at the end of 3*b* makes for a more natural syntactic and metrical pattern. Verse 3*b* is thus an orthodox A verse with anacrusis *ond* (for A1 off-verses with anacrusis, see p. 329 of Pope's *The Rhythm of Beowulf*) and verse 4*a* is an orthodox A3 verse (see Pope's category A66, p. 264 of *The Rhythm of Beowulf*). For the occasional translation of *þær* as "when," see Mitchell, *A Guide to Old English* 168, p. 85. The omission of *þæt* in the MS. may have been due to the similarity of *þær* and *þæt*. Thorpe in a note first proposed *fyligde* for MS. *felde*. Dietrich (*ZfdA*. xi, 472) first suggested *his filled* for MS. *hit felde*, taking *filled* as "Fülling" and reading *þær his filled fleah þurh his eage* as a single phrase that Grein (see Tupper, p. 158, note) translated as: "wo seine Füllung (?) flog durch sein Auge." Later (*ZfdA*. xii, 238, note 6) Dietrich returned to the MS. reading, explaining: "er floh da man es (v.4, das ding) fällte d.h. niederdrückte." Tupper prefers Dietrich's original reading, though he emends MS. *hit felde* to *his fyllo*—which is certainly better than Dietrich's *filled*. Tupper refers in his note to "the 'much accomplishment' (*micel . . . gefered*) of the *þegn*" (p. 158) without explanation and without citing similar uses of the past participle. Mackie reads *þær his fyllo* with Tupper but translates *þær* as "when" and *fyllo* as "what filled it" so that his translation approximates Wyatt's and my own. Trautmann retains the MS. reading with a colon after *felde* and translates: "der Schmid hatte viel hingeschafft wo es füllte (viel Luft in den Blasebalg)" (p. 99). Barnouw (*Neoph.* iii, 78) questions this intransitive use of *fyllan* and suggests reading *þæt* for MS. *þær* translating: "and what filled it had travelled much." This is the reading accepted by Krapp and Dobbie.

35.7: *blæd*: Cp. the gloss *blædbylig* for L. *follis* at WW. 241.33.

35.8: Cp. the same motif at *Rid.* 31.9 ff. The bellows creates wind; wind in turn "recreates" (sustains, lends form and substance to) the bellows.

36. Bull Calf (Young Ox)
[*VN: Gr.39; Tr.36; Tu.39; W.38; M.38; K-D.38*]

This is the second of three "ox" riddles in the *Exeter Book* (see also *Rids*. 10 and 70). Dietrich's solution, "der junge stier" (*ZfdA*. xi, 472) is accepted by all editors. The riddle shares several common motifs with Riddles 83 of Aldhelm, "Iuvencus," and 37 of Eusebius, "De Vitulo." The Latin riddles are:

> Iuvencus
> Arida spumosis dissolvens faucibus ora
> Bis binis bibulus potum de fontibus hausi.
> Vivens nam terrae glebas cum stirpibus imis
> Nisu virtutis validae disrumpo feraces;
> At vero linquit dum spiritus algida membra,
> Nexibus horrendis homines constringere possum.
>
> [Ed. Pitman, p. 50]

> De Vitulo
> Post genitrix me quam peperit mea, sepe solesco
> Inter ab uno fonte rivos bis bibere binos
> Progredientes; et si vixero, rumpere colles
> Incipiam; vivos moriens aut alligo multos.
>
> [CCL. cxxxiii, p. 247]

The Latin riddles share the common motif of the four fountains and the central paradox of the living leather: "Living, I break the soil; dead, I bind men." The fountain motif may be found in lines 2*a*–4 of the Old English riddle; the paradox of the living leather concludes the Old English poem. The Old English riddle is a third-person descriptive riddle rather than a first-person personificative riddle as are both of the Latin riddles. Lines 1, 2, and 5 of the Old English have no counterpart in the Latin. Ebert (*BudV*. xxix, 50, note) believes that the *Mon* of line 5 in the Old English refers either to Aldhelm or to Eusebius, but this is to confuse the conventional narrator of descriptive riddles with the author himself. Line 5 serves rather to set up a dramatic situation, a speech act within the riddle, in order to lend emphasis to the concluding paradox, much as the riddler in *Rid*. 37 concludes with a miniature riddle.

36.2: *geoguðmyrþe*: *the pleasure of youth* (i.e., drinking milk). This reading for the MS. *geoguð myrwe* was proposed by Holthausen (*ESn.* xxxvii, 208) and is accepted by Tupper, Trautmann, Mackie, and Krapp and Dobbie. Trautmann would transpose the words in the *a*-line to read *grædig geoguðmyrþe* for metrical reasons (producing an A2a verse with double resolution instead of the rare A* verse), but the meter as it stands is legitimate if rare (cp. *Beo.* 438*a* and 1649*a* and see Pope's list of A* on-verses, especially his category A61, on p. 263 of *The Rhythm of Beowulf*). Wyatt retains *geoguðmyrwe* as a form of *geoguð-myru*, "gladness of youth," and BTS. lists the compound *geoguþ-myru* as "the tenderness of youth," citing O.H.G. *marawi, muruwi* (p. 384). Krapp and Dobbie note that "such a word in Anglo-Saxon is doubtful, and it seems better to emend with Holthausen" (p. 342), but the adjective *mearu* (*mæru, meru, myru*), "tender" does exist (see B-T., p. 675) and the form *myrwan* occurs at least once in an oblique case (WW. 465.13: *Per tenera: ðurh ða myrwan*). In *Rid.* 36, however, the compound appears to be a noun, and the only attested Old English noun form of *mearu* is *mearuness* (B-T., p. 675; BTS., p. 634). Until there is more proof for a noun form, *myru*, in Old English, it seems best to accept Holthausen's reading.

36.2b–4: I translate the lines: "As a gift to him (the young ox), the life-saving one (the mother ox) let four fountains shoot forth brightly, let them murmur to his (the young ox's) delight." For a discussion of particular words and phrases, see the following notes.

36.3a: *ferðfriþende*: Grein originally translated this as "Der Befrieder der Geister" or "Gott" (see Tupper, p. 159, note, and Trautmann, p. 100, note) but later took the word as an accusative plural modifier of *weallan* meaning "vitam servans" (*Sp.*, p. 193). So Tupper, Trautmann, and Mackie take the subject of *forlet . . . sceotan* to be the young ox and translate line 3 as "four life-saving fountains." But the one who lets the four fountains shoot forth is the mother, not the child. So Kock (*Lunds Universitets Årsskrift*, N.F., Avd. 1, Bd. 14, Nr. 26, p. 64) and Krapp and Dobbie take *ferðfriþende* as a substantive, the "life-sustaining one," i.e., the mother cow. This makes much better sense of the lines.

36.3b: For the motif of the four fountains, see lines 1–2 of Aldhelm's Riddle 83 and lines 1–2 of Eusebius's Riddle 37 quoted above.

36.4b: *on gesceap þeotan*: For the meaning of this B-T. says: "The passage describes a calf sucking from its mother; if *þeōtan* is an infinitive, it must refer to the sound made by the milk coming from the teat, but perhaps *gesceap-þeōte* may be a compound noun meaning the teat" (p. 1053). Wyatt notes that the only known compound utilizing initial *gesceap-* is *gescæphwile* at *Beo.* 26. Mackie renders *on gesceapþeotan* as "in their appointed channels" (p. 129), a rather grandiose circumlocution for cows' teats. Wyatt's reading of *on gesceap* as "into the creature, the calf" (p. 97) is even more fanciful. Grein takes *þeotan* as a verb (*strepere, prorumpere cum strepitu: Sp.,* p. 713) and translates the phrase as "nach Geschick tosen" (see Wyatt, p. 97, note), and so Trautmann. The O.E. *þeotan* is surely meant here to describe the sound of the milk flowing (see *þeotan* as a gloss for *murmurans, bombosa, bombose,* cited in B-T., p. 1053, under *þeotan,* section II). For the meaning of *him . . . on gesceap,* Kock (*Lunds Universitets Årsskrift,* NF., Avd.1, Bd. 14, Nr. 26, p. 64) cites the Old Icelandic *hánum í skap,* "to his nature, to his mind, to his pleasure," and translates the Old English as "to his delight." For a similar usage, cp. *Rid.* 71.6: *wiþ gesceape minum.* Kock's reading is accepted by Krapp and Dobbie and myself.

36.5–7: The lines may well be corrupt here since there are a number of metrical irregularities. Barnouw (*Textkritische Untersuchungen,* p. 214) would take *seo wiht* in 6a to be a scribal addition. Holthausen (*ESn.* xxxvii, 208) first read the lines as prose and later (*Anglia* xxxv, 166) as corrupt lines, reconstructing *wealduna* for MS. *duna* and *cwicne* for MS. *cwice* or (*Anglia Beibl.* xlvi, 9) *wealldura* for MS. *duna* and *gebindeð cwice* for MS. *bindeð cwice.* Trautmann supplies *hio* before *duna* and *he* before *bindeð.* Though verses 6b and 7b would be more normal if read according to Holthausen's or Trautmann's emendations, they are not as they stand in the MS. unparalleled in Old English poetry. For short A1 lines of this sort in the off-verse, see p. 333 of Pope's *The Rhythm of Beowulf,* especially his category A98. Line 7a is also acceptable as type A3 with anacrusis (see Pope's category A68 on p. 265 and cp. *Beo.* 1477a). Line 5b is barely acceptable with a stress on *me* (sometimes in exceptionally weak verses the pronoun will take a stress) as what Pope calls a minor deviation from or combination of types B and C (see p. 128 of his *Seven Old English Poems*). These deviant forms seem to have an initial drop of two or more syllables and a drop after the first lift of only one syllable, so line 6a here cannot qualify technically even under this rubric. Barnouw would emend 6a but given the high degree of metrical irregularity in the surrounding lines, it seems unwise to emend 6a (for another example of a passage showing a kind of metrical eccentricity, cp. *Rid*. 63.1–2). Most editors keep the lines as they are in the MS., and Mackie translates: "That creature, if it continues to live, will break up the downs; if it is rent to pieces, it will bind living men" (p. 129). For the motif, cp. *Rid*. 10.14–15 and lines 3–6 of Aldhelm's Riddle 83 and lines 3–4 of Eusebius's Riddle 37 (quoted in the headnote).

37. Speech (O.E. Word, To Gesecganne)
[*VN: Gr.40; Tr.37; Tu.40; W.39; M.39; K-D.39*]

This is one of the most difficult riddles in the *Exeter Book* to solve. Dietrich (*ZfdA*. xi, 472) offered the solution, "day," citing *The Rune Poem* 74 ff.:

> ᚻ (dæg) byþ drihtnes sond,   deore mannum,
> mære metodes leoht,   myrgþ and tohiht
> eadgum and earmum,   eallum brice.
>
> [*Run*. 74–76]

Though Wyatt accepts the solution, "day," he finds "no allusion to the poverty of the day in any dictionary or collection of proverbs ancient or modern" (p. 97). Moreover, the solution, "day," does not fit much of the language of the riddle. Day does not seek out each man individually (*sundor*), nor does it necessarily wander (it is the heavenly bodies that wander). There seems to be no reason to speculate on the final fate of day (lines 22–25). There is no reason why any statement about day (lines 25–27) should be true. Several of the same objections may be raised with regard to Tupper's solution, "moon," which is accepted by Mackie. The moon is visible (line 3a), but it is visible at once to all men in the same location at any one time—it does not visit each man separately. The moon is certainly *niht þær oþre* (7b); the creature of the riddle is not. The moon is not proverbially poor; in fact, in terms of Tupper's own solution of the final riddle, the moon carries a treasure of light (cp. *Rid.* 27.1–4). All statements about the moon are not true. Trautmann solves the riddle as "time," but this solution fits the language of the riddle even less than "day" or "moon." Recently, Erhardt-Siebold has argued for the solution, "creature death" (*PMLA* lxi, 910ff.), noting that "the question of the admissibleness of hypostatizing deprivative notions such as darkness, nothing, death or negative conceptions like ugliness, evil, sin had been occupying speculative minds since the time when Plato in his *Parmenides* first raised the problem . . . " (*PMLA* lxi, 911). But death and darkness do not stalk as creatures in and out of Old English poetry. There are no Old English riddles for "good," "evil," "sin," "death," or any other abstraction of human experience. If death were a creature to the Anglo-Saxons, it would certainly not be *sweotol ond gesyne* (3a), for the poet of the *Exeter Maxims* says: "Deop deada wæg dyrne bið lengest" (*Max. I* 78).*

I believe that the key to this riddle lies in the deliberate ambiguity of lines 24b–25a—*þæt is wrætlic þing / to gesecganne*—which may be translated either as "That is a marvelous thing to be told" or as "Speaking is a marvelous thing." The solution to the riddle is *word* in the sense of O.E. *cwide* or *spræc*, modern English "spoken words" or "speech."† Everything that signifies the creature by words is true

---

*In an article in the April 1976 issue of *Speculum*, "The Solution to Old English Riddle 39," Paul Meyvaert argues that the solution to this riddle is "cloud" and that the riddle has its parallels in Aldhelm's "Nubes" Riddle 4 (ed. Pitman, p. 6); but of the three motifs in the Latin riddle (the cloud's changing color, the cloud's exile in the skies, and its greening of the world by means of its rain), only the theme of exile appears in the Old English (and is not unique to this riddle). Meyvaert's "cloud," like Tupper's "moon," fits certain details of the riddle (the creature's wandering and its lack of limbs, for example), but it does not adequately explain why the creature should "visit each man separately," nor does it explain why every solution to the riddle should paradoxically be the right one. For another recent argument for the "cloud" solution (briefer than Meyvaert's and without reference to Aldhelm) see Christopher Kennedy's "Old English Riddle No. 39," *ELN*, xiii, 81–85.

†As Fred Robinson ("Artful Ambiguities in the Old English 'Book-Moth' Riddle," in *Anglo-Saxon Poetry: Essays in Appreciation: For John C. McGalliard*, ed. Lewis E. Nicholson and Dolores Warwick Frese, pp. 355–62; see footnote to headnote of *Rid.* 45) has

(25*b*–26). Paradoxically, every hazarded solution to the riddle is true because it indicates the creature itself. The solver has only to tell a solution (*reselan recene gesecgan*) with "true words" (but all spoken solutions are true!) in order to indicate the answer, "word" or "speech." Language is certainly "mid moncynne miclum tidum / sweotol ond gesyne" (2–3*a*); even to many modern-day anthropologists, language is the essentializing feature of mankind. Words come to each man separately (*sundor æghwylcne*) as each separately hears and perceives, and the words themselves travel in a mysterious way. The Old English riddler says: "Sundorcræft hafað / maran micle þonne hit men witen"—here again the deliberate ambiguity conceals the solution, "language." The sentence may be translated either as "It has a special power much greater than men know of it" or "It has a special power much greater *when men know it.*" Speech has none of the physical attributes of living creatures (*Ne hafað hio fot ne folme*, etc.) and yet it lives (*leofaþ efne seþeah*) in some substantial way. Speech is a "continuous miracle" as Cassirer has said: "Speech is meaning—an incorporeal thing—expressed in sounds, which are material things" (*Word* i, 114). Language is neither living nor dead; it somehow transcends the categories (indeed it defines and expresses them). The paradox is expressed by the Old English riddler in his summary riddle-within-a-riddle: *Ne hafað heo ænig lim, leofaþ efne seþeah* (line 27). This is essentially the point made some twelve centuries later by Cassirer when he said:

---

just recently argued that the *wyrd* of *Rid.* 45.2 may besides its usual meaning of "event, fate," be a pun on *gewyrd*, "speech, conversation, collection of words, sentence" (see B-T. under *gewyrde*, BTS. under *gewyrd*), so too we may postulate a pun on *wyrda* at line 24*a* here. Thus it is not only the twisted or obscure destiny of events (or the fates) that is so hard to predict at 24*a* but the unusual or obscure fate of the words themselves (as Isidore indicates at *Etym.* ix.i.13 quoted below). The riddler is careful to wrap the pun on *wyrda* in the context of *to secganne* at 22*b* and *to gesecganne* at 25*a*, thus calling our attention to the underlying meaning of the two passages. It should also be noted that one of the reasons why it is so difficult (why it would take so long) to predict the final outcome of speech is that every summary statement adds a new dimension to the creature's life. The only possible moment of surely saying what the fate of speech is is the moment when all speech is finished—the moment when alas there is no speech left for the summary. This magnificent paradox is surely what the riddler means when he says "that fate (of the creature, of the words) is a wonderful thing to be told" and at the same time, "Speaking is a marvelous thing."

To speak of language as a thing that comes into being and withers, that has its youth, its prime of life, its senility, and its death is to speak in a mere metaphor. Such a metaphor is admissible if we understand it in the right way and use it with all the necessary critical reservations and limitations. Biologists and linguists are often engaged in the same battle against a common adversary, a battle that may be described by the slogan: structuralism versus mechanism; morphologism against materialism. In this combat they may allege similar arguments; they may make use of the same logical weapons. But that does not prove that there is any identity in their subject-matter, that, in an ontological sense, we can put human language on the same level as plants or animals. Language is neither a mechanism nor an organism, neither a dead nor a living thing. It is no thing at all, if by this term we understand a physical object. It is—language, a very specific human activity, not describable in terms of physics, chemistry, or biology. [*Word* i, 110]

Language resists the categorical distinction between the living and the dead, between the animate and the inanimate, between the spirit and the flesh. Language cannot exist without men; yet it lives after men. No man may predict what the final forms of language may be— *hu hyre ealdorgesceaft æfter gongeð* (line 23). Isidore says in this regard: "Item quaeritur qua lingua in futurum homines loquantur: nusquam reperitur" (*Etym.* ix.i.13). The life of the *word* is elusive indeed: it has no substance, yet it lives. The miniature riddle at the end of the riddle states the fundamental paradox of language: *Ne hafað heo ænig lim, leofaþ efne seþeah* (line 27). The reader is told to guess the solution to the riddle with *soþum wordum* (line 29) but *soð* is, as we know from lines 25–26, *æghwylc / þara þe ymb þas wiht wordum becneð* (see note below). Every guess signifies the riddle by words, so all solutions are true. As Cassirer says, language cannot be explained except by metaphor. It lives and lives not. *Þæt is wrætlic þing / to gesecganne*.

37.2: *tidum*: With the exception of Krapp and Dobbie, all editors report the MS. reading, *ticlum*. Krapp and Dobbie note that the reading is *tidum* with a continental *d*. Though the form is unusual, it is not unknown in the *Riddles*. Cp. for example the *d* of *videtur* at *Rid.* 86.1. Erhardt-Siebold translates the phrase, *miclum tidum*, as "in great times," corresponding to the L. *magna* or *maxima tempora* (*PMLA* lxi, 912), but it is not clear in terms of her own solution why death should only be present at "great times." I prefer to translate the phrase as "for much (of the) time," or "at many times" (see the possibilities suggested by Marckwardt and Rosier, *Old English Language and Litera-*

ture, p. 199, note 2). Speech, though a distinguishing characteristic of mankind, is not always present.

37.3: *sweotol ond gesyne: evident (plain) and perceivable.* Both words may mean *visible* with reference to an object, but B-T. (p. 951, category III) notes that *sweotol* can mean "clear to the understanding, free from obscurity, plain," and BTS. (p. 412, *gesine*, category III) notes that *gesyne* can mean "to be perceived by the mind, evident, manifest." Thus the half-line does not rule out the solution, "language." It may in fact be a ruse to mislead the riddle-solver into thinking that a material object is meant. This sets up the essential paradox in the rest of the poem, which is summarized in line 27: "It has no limb; yet it lives."

37.3b–4: Either "It has a special power much greater than men know it (to have)" or more probably, "It has a special power much greater when men know it." In a multilingual England, the Anglo-Saxons must have been acutely aware of the power that knowledge of a language or of several languages conferred upon a man.

37.5–6: The description is technically true of speech. Men may share a common language, but each man has his own idiolect. Acoustically, no two utterances are ever exactly the same. This may seem overly subtle but it is no more subtle than the Anglo-Saxons' notion of the moon stealing light from the sun (*Rid.* 27).

37.6a: *feorhberendra:* For other examples of this rare verse type (D3), see Pope's categories D14 and D15 on pp. 305 and 361–62 of *The Rhythm of Beowulf*.

37.10a: *Ne hafað hio fot ne folme:* Most editors retain MS. *folm,* but Krapp and Dobbie rightly note that the proper grammatical form is *folme.* The meter of the verse thus constituted is unusual but not unknown—a sort of combination of types B and C (see Pope's discussion of this on p. 128 of his *Seven Old English Poems*). Holthausen (*Anglia* xxxviii, 78) would read *Ne hafað hio folme ne fot* or *nafað fot ne folme* to regularize the meter or would read the verse (*Anglia* xliv, 349) as I have it as hypermetric. But an isolated hypermetric half-line is not likely and it seems best here to read the verse as a minor deviation from, or combination of, types B and C as indicated above.

37.11a: Grein and most editors supply *hafað* after emended *eagena* (MS. *eage ne*) to complete the verbal parallelism and to satisfy the metrical requirements of the half-line. Thorpe, Mackie, and Krapp and Dobbie read line 11*a* as *ne eagena*, but the frequent appearance of *eagena* as *eagna* in the poetry makes it unlikely that the word can carry a double stress.

37.14: *earmost*: Trautmann would read *earuwost*, "swiftest," but it seems unwise to emend a perfectly acceptable MS. reading in light of a conjectured solution. I cannot find any proverbially poor creature in either Anglo-Saxon or Latin writings that would fit exactly the description in the riddle. This could be, however, a reference to the traditionally gossamer nature of words in contrast to their very substantial power mentioned in line 19. See, for example, Whiting and Whiting's *Proverbs, Sentences, and Proverbial Phrases from English Writings Mainly before 1500* under category W643, "Words are (Word is) but wind (varied)", which quotes, among other examples, Aelfric's *Eower word syndon winde gelice* (*Lives*, vol. 1, p. 196, l. 19) and category W632, which quotes the late fourteenth century *Camb. Univ. Lib. MS. II 6.26*: "For it is a comoun sawe, and soth it is, Worde and wynde and mannes mynde is ful schort, but letter writen dwellith" (quoted in Whiting and Whiting, p. 668).

37.18: *bearnum*: Wyatt (p. 97) and Trautmann (*Anglia* xlii, 135) suggest *beornum*, but Mackie (*MLR* xxviii, 77) notes that *bearn* is used at *JD. I* 40 in the sense of "men" or "children of men." Clark Hall defines *bearn* as "child, son, descendant, off-spring, issue . . . children of men" (p. 35). The word choice here, with its emphasis upon succeeding generations, is appropriate to the riddle subject, language.

37.22bff.: For the difficulty of predicting what the final fate of words may be, see the quotation from Isidore cited in the headnote. As I have explained in the lengthy footnote to the headnote, the phrase *woh wyrda gesceapu* may contain the pun: (1) *wyrd* = "event, fate"; (2) *gewyrd* = "speech, conversation, words." This ambiguity sets up the ambiguity of the following sentence so that we may translate on two levels: (1) "It takes a long time to say how its state goes afterwards—the twisted (or obscure) destinies of events. That (fate) is a wonderful thing to speak of"; (2) "It takes a long time to say how its state goes afterwards—the obscure destinies of words. Speaking is a marvelous thing."

37.22b: *secganne*: Sievers (*Beiträge* x, 482) would emend the inflected infinitive here to the uninflected form for metrical reasons (see note to *Rid.* 26.12*b*).

37.24–25: *þæt is wrætlic þing | to gesecganne*: Either "That is a marvelous thing to be told," or "Speaking is a marvelous thing." For the use of the gerund in the latter sense, see Mitchell, *A Guide to Old English* 205*e*, p. 112.

37.25b–26: "Each of the things signified by words about this creature is true." This is essentially the reading of Mackie. By and large the editors do not comment upon the meaning of these lines though the lines are difficult to translate. Normally O.E. *becnan* meaning "to signify" takes an object (see the citations under the various spellings in B-T. and BTS.—*becnan, bicnan, bicnian, bycnian*). Since *þas wiht* is already the object of *ymb*, the object of *becnan* must be *æghwylc | þara þe* ("each of those things," "everything") unless the object is understood. Mackie translates *becneð* in the passive as I do, "Each part of what has been indicated in words with regard to this creature is true" (p. 131), apparently taking the subject of *becneð* to be an understood *mon* (thus rendering the passive voice). For a similar instance of the indefinite pronoun left unexpressed, cp. *Beo.* 1365 and see Klaeber's discussion in section 4 of "Language. Manuscript," on pp. xcii–xciii of his third edition of *Beowulf*. If we take *æghwylc | þara þe* to mean not "each of those things" but "each of those persons," then we must postulate an understood object and a rather free translation of *is* in 25*b*, thus translating, "Each of those people who signifies (something) about this creature with words 'speaks the truth'" (literally, "Each is true who speaks . . . "). The only other alternative is to transpose *ymb þas wiht* into *wiht ymb þas* with Herzfeld (*Die Räthsel des Exeterbuches und ihr Verfasser*, p. 51), taking *wiht* as the pronoun, "something," and the phrase *ymb þas* as "about this (one)." In line 26*a* Holthausen (*ESn.* xxxvii, 208) would supply *æfre* after *wiht* or would read *þas wiht ymbe* for metrical reasons, and Tupper would read *wihte* for *wiht*, but for similar lines approximating truncated type A without final drop, cp. *Beo.* 3027*a* and *Rid.* 27.4*a* and see my note to the latter.

37.28–29: Though this sounds like a standard closing formula, it is not. This is the only instance of *reselan* in Old English. Furthermore, the meaning of *soþum wordum* in this instance must be influenced by the use of both words in lines 25–26 above. If I am correct in my interpretation, the reader is asked to tell the solution of the riddle with "true words," but since all words signify the creature, any answer given will be "true." The importance of *recene* becomes clear: the quicker the answer, the quicker the signification. Only those who fail to speak any solution will fail to signify the creature with "true words."

38. Creation
[*VN: Gr.41; Tr.38; Tu.41; W.40; M.40; K-D.40*]

Dietrich (*ZfdA.* xi, 455) first pointed out that the riddle is a fairly close rendering of Aldhelm's Riddle 100, "Creatura" (ed. Pitman, pp. 60–66). The solution, "creation," is accepted by all editors, though Mackie prefers the form, "nature." Pitman translates Aldhelm's "Creatura" as "nature," but I have retained the form, "creation," since L. *creatura* is glossed by *gesceaft* in O.E. (WW., 317.41; Napier 1.692; 40.35). There are several opinions as to the slavishness of the translation. Herzfeld says of this riddle and of *Rid.* 33, another translation from Aldhelm:

> Was diese zwei Räthsel von den übrigen scheidet, ist der Umstand, dass die metrische Gliederung mit der syntactischen ganz zusammenfällt, während sonst die Regel besteht, dass beide sich kreuzen. . . . Damit hängt zusammen die Seltenheit der Variation, die sonst so oft zur Ausfüllung von Versen dient und zu neuen Gedanken überleitet. [*Die Räthsel des Exeterbuches und ihr Verfasser*, p. 28]

There are, however, a small number of rather remarkable departures from the Aldhelm text. Some variations seem intended; others do not. In my own reprinting of Aldhelm's text from Pitman's edition, I have marked the corresponding lines in the Old English version to the right of the text. Where some question arises as to the use of Aldhelm's lines by the Old English riddler, I have indicated this with a question mark. In the case of Aldhelm's line 43, the situation is somewhat complicated. The Old English riddler appears to have used *Durior aut ferro*, translating *ferro* as *style* (line 79); he has also used the construction *sed mollior* (*hnescre ic eom micle*: line 80), but has substituted his description of the *halsrefeþre* (line 80*b*–81) for the L. *tostis . . . extis*. This is a delicate bit of creativity that should give some pause to those who think of the Anglo-Saxons as "primitive." The full text of the Aldhelm "Creatura" is included, even those lines that are not used by the Old English riddler:

Creatura

	Conditor, aeternis fulcit qui saecla columnis,	
	Rector regnorum, frenans et fulmina lege,	1–5
	Pendula dum patuli vertuntur culmina caeli,	
	Me varium fecit, primo dum conderet orbem.	6–7
5	Pervigil excubiis: numquam dormire iuvabit,	8–9
	Sed tamen extemplo clauduntur lumina somno;	10–11
	Nam Deus ut propria mundum dicione gubernat,	12–13
	Sic ego complector sub caeli cardine cuncta.	14–15
	Segnior est nullus, quoniam me larbula terret,	16–17
10	Setigero rursus constans audacior apro;	18–19
	Nullus me superat cupiens vexilla triumphi	20–21
	Ni Deus, aethrali summus qui regnat in arce.	21–22
	Prorsus odorato ture flagrantior halans	
	Olfactum ambrosiae, necnon crescentia glebae	
15	Lilia purpureis possum conexa rosetis	23–32
	Vincere spirantis nardi dulcedine plena;	
	Nunc olida caeni squalentis sorde putresco.	
	Omnia, quaeque polo sunt subter et axe reguntur,	
	Dum pater arcitenens concessit, jure guberno;	33–37
20	Grossas et graciles rerum comprenso figuras.	
	Altior, en, caelo rimor secreta Tonantis	38–39
	Et tamen inferior terris tetra Tartara cerno;	40–41
	Nam senior mundo praecessi tempora prisca,	42–43
	Ecce, tamen matris horno generabar ab alvo	44–45
25	Pulchrior auratis, dum fulget fibula, bullis,	46–47
	Horridior ramnis et spretis vilior algis.	48–49
	Latior, en, patulis terrarum finibus exto	50–51
	Et tamen in media concludor parte pugilli,	52–53

	Frigidior brumis necnon candente pruina,	54–55
30	Cum sim Vulcani flammis torrentibus ardens,	56–57
	Dulcior in palato quam lenti nectaris haustus	58–59
	Dirior et rursus quam glauca absinthia campi.	60–61
	Mando dapes mordax lurconum more Ciclopum,	62–63
	Cum possim iugiter sine victu vivere felix.	64–65
35	Plus pernix aquilis, Zephiri velocior alis,	
	Necnon accipitre properantior, et tamen horrens	66–69
	Lumbricus et limax et tarda testudo palustris	
	Atque, fimi soboles sordentis, cantarus ater	70–73
	Me dicto citius vincunt certamine cursus.	
40	Sum gravior plumbo: scopulorum pondera vergo;	74–75
	Sum levior pluma, cedit cui tippula limphae;	76–77
	Nam silici, densas quae fudit viscere flammas,	78–79
	Durior aut ferro, tostis sed mollior extis.	79–80?
	Cincinnos capitis nam gesto cacumine nullos,	
45	Ornent qui frontem pompis et tempora setis,	98–99
	Cum mihi caesaries volitent de vertice crispae,	102–3
	Plus calamistratis se comunt quae calamistro.	[None]
	Pinguior, en, multo scrofarum axungia glesco,	
	Glandiferis iterum referunt dum corpora fagis	105–7
50	Atque saginata laetantur carne subulci;	108 ff.?
	Sed me dira famis macie torquebit egenam,	
	Pallida dum iugiter dapibus spoliabor opimis.	
	Limpida sum, fateor, Titanis clarior orbe,	
	Candidior nivibus, dum ningit vellera nimbus,	
55	Carceris et multo tenebris obscurior atris	[None]
	Atque latebrosis, ambit quas Tartarus, umbris.	
	Ut globus astrorum plasmor teres atque rotunda	
	Sperula seu pilae necnon et forma cristalli;	
	Et versa vice protendor ceu Serica pensa	
60	In gracilem porrecta panum seu stamina pepli.	84–85
	Senis, ecce, plagis, latus qua panditur orbis,	82–83
	Ulterior multo tendor, mirabile fatu;	
	Infra me suprave nihil per saecula constat	86–88
	Ni rerum genitor mundum sermone coercens.	89–91
65	Grandior in glaucis ballena fluctibus atra	92–94

Et minor exiguo, sulcat qui corpora, verme   95–97
Aut modico, Phoebi radiis qui vibrat, atomo;
Centenis pedibus gradior per gramina ruris
Et penitus numquam per terram pergo pedester.
70 Sic mea prudentes superat sapientia sofos,
Nec tamen in biblis docuit me littera dives
Aut umquam quivi, quid constet sillaba, nosse.
Siccior aestivo torrentis caumate solis,
Rore madens iterum plus uda flumine fontis;
75 Salsior et multo tumidi quam marmora ponti   [*None*]
Et gelidis terrae limphis insulsior erro,
Multiplici specie cunctorum compta colorum,
Ex quibus ornatur praesentis machina mundi,
Lurida cum toto nunc sim fraudata colore.
80 Auscultate mei credentes famina verbi,
Pandere quae poterit gnarus vix ore magister
Et tamen infitians non retur frivola lector!
Sciscitor inflatos, fungar quo nomine, sofos.

[Ed. Pitman, pp. 60–66]

Broadly speaking, the lines of the Old English and the Latin riddles correspond in the following fashion:

	Old English	*Latin*
Lines	1–81	1–43
	82–97	59–66
	98–108	44–50

It should be noted that two lines of the Old English are repeated exactly: lines 50–51 and 82–83. Dietrich (*Commentatio de Kynewulfi Poetae Aetate*, p. 25; see Tupper, p. 163, note) suggested, as a way of explaining the Old English departure from the Latin sequence, that perhaps an earlier version of the Aldhelm "Creatura" was used by the Old English riddler. Tupper rightly points out that this does not readily explain "the appreciable weakening of technique in the later part of the English riddle" (p. 163). Tupper believes that the first eighty-one lines of the Old English riddle were completed by one careful translator and that the last 27 lines were added by another careless translator who drew heavily upon the work of the first. This might help to explain the repetition of the Old English lines at 82–83. Rather than translate lines 61–62 of the Latin afresh, the new translator merely chose to repeat the old translation corresponding to somewhat similar Latin lines. Tupper also believes that the translator of the first eighty-one lines is the same translator of Aldhelm in *Rid.* 33, and that the writer of *Rid.* 64 drew upon lines 82–97 of this riddle. I would agree with the first contention; the second is somewhat more difficult to sustain. For other Old English "creation" riddles, the reader should see *Rid.* 64 and also *Rid.* 90.

38.2: *wreðstuþum wealdeð*: The MS. reading for the *a*-line is *wreðstuþum*, which is retained by Grein and Wyatt. But both the sense and the meter require something after *wreðstuþum*. Holthausen (*Indogermanische Forschungen* iv, 387) supplied *weardað*; Trautmann, *fæstnað* (text) or *trymmeð* (p. 102, note). Tupper supplied *wealdeþ* citing the *fulsit . . . columnis* of Aldhelm's Latin and the phrase *healdeð ond wealdeð* at lines 5 and 22 of this riddle. Tupper's reading is accepted by Mackie and Krapp and Dobbie.

38.5b: The verse as it stands in the MS. is accepted by most major editors even though it is most unusual. For alliteration on the final stress, cp. similar examples at *Rids.* 1.66, 2.8, 53.14, 57.12, 71.2, and 87.6. For the metrical pattern, what Pope calls a minor deviation from or combination of types B and C, cp. *Seaf.* 46*a*, *Mald.* 220*a*, and the *Riddle* examples listed in the Introduction, and see Pope's discussion of the pattern on p. 128 of his *Seven Old English Poems*. Grein (in a note), Sievers (*Beiträge* x, 520), Tupper, and Wyatt all suggest changing the word order to secure at least normal alliteration. Trautmann and Holthausen make more drastic changes in the text by transferring *healdeð ond wealdeð* from the *a*-line to the *b*-line. In the *a*-line, Trautmann reads *hea hrofas*; Holthausen (*Anglia Beibl.* xlvi, 9) reads *halig dryhten*. Holthausen also reads *heofonas* for *heofones* in line 4*b*.

38.16: *to þon bleað*: Herzfeld (*Die Räthsel des Exeterbuches und ihr Verfasser*, p. 51) transposes to *bleað to þon* for metrical reasons, and so Tupper and Trautmann.

38.23–25: The MS. reading of these lines indicates a double lacuna as printed by Mackie:

> ic eom on stence   strengre . . .
> þonne ricels   oþþe rose sy
> on eorþan tyrf . . .

Other editors print the lines as follows:

> Ic eom on stence   strengre [micle]
> þonne ricels   oþþe rose sy,
> [þe swa ænlice]   on eorþan tyrf
>
> > [Grein, Wyatt, Tupper in his text]
>
> Ic eom on stence   strengre þonne ricels
> oþþe rose sy   [seo *or* þe] on eorþan tyrf
>
> > [Tupper, p. 166, note]
>
> Ic eom on stence   strengre þon ricels
> oþþe rose sy,   [þe] on eorþan tyrf
>
> > [Trautmann]

My own reading in the text follows that of Krapp and Dobbie. It seems fruitless to speculate over the reading of the lacuna at line 25*a*. The two-line readings of Tupper and Trautmann are unsuitable because the second line lacks proper alliteration.

38.41: *wom*: Wyatt reads *wonn* after an earlier suggestion by Grein (*Germania* x, 429), calling this "an unexampled form for accusative plural" (p. 31). Wyatt also suggests the possibility of *wōn* as a weak plural of *wōh*. But Grein (*Sp.*, p. 758) lists *wam, wom* as an adjective in its own right with occurrences here (defined as *malus*) and at *PPs.* 102.10 (defined as *flagitiosus, scelestus*). The passage from the *Paris Psalter* is:

> Na þu be gewyrhtum,   wealdend, urum
> wommum wyrhtum   woldest us don,
> ne æfter urum unryhte   ahwær gyldan.
>
> > [*PPs.* 102.10]

The corresponding passage from the Vulgate reads: "Non secundum peccata nostra fecit nobis: neque secundum iniquitates nostras retribuit nobis" (Psalms 102.10). Grein's reading of the adjective *wom* as *malus* is accepted by Tupper, Trautmann, and Krapp and Dobbie. In *Rid.* 38, the O.E. *wom wraðscrafu wraþra gæste* corresponds to the Latin *tetra Tartara* of Aldhelm. Tupper cites a similar use of *wom-* at *Chr.*

1533–34: *fæge gæstas / on wraþra wic, womfulra scolu.* . . . . Trautmann reads *wræcscrafu* for MS. *wraðscrafu* after an early suggestion by Grein.

38.42: *þes*: Mackie retains the MS. *þæs* as a variant of *þes*. Wyatt reads *þæs* as genitive singular, referring back to *heofon* in line 38 or forward to *middangeard* in line 43, or as "a vague reference to what precedes ('I am much older than the circuit thereof')" (p. 102). This contorted translation is not convincing.

38.46: Tupper notes that *frætwum goldes* renders Aldhelm's *fibula* at line 25 of the Latin. Of the *fibula* Isidore says: "Fibulae sunt quibus pectus feminarum ornatur, vel pallium tenetur a viris in humeris, seu cingulum in lumbis" (*Etym.* xix.xxxi.17).

38.49: *wāroð*: seaweed. In one extant version of Aldhelm's *Creatura* (*MS. Cambridge University Libr. Gg. V, 35*), the word *algis* is glossed by O.E. *warum* (Napier, 23.13). O.E. *war* or *waar* also glosses L. *alga* in other instances (WW. 5.1, 268.27, 349.7).

38.50–51: These lines are repeated at lines 82–83 below. See headnote above for comments.

38.56: *ic eom*: Supplied by Grein and later editors except Trautmann who reads *ond com*.

38.61: *on hyrstum*: in the woods. The phrase corresponds to *campi* in Aldhelm's Latin. Grein (*Sp.*, p. 383) translated the phrase as *im Blatt-schmuck(?)*, but Tupper and Wyatt are undoubtedly right in reading *on hyrstum* as "in the hursts" after a suggestion by Thorpe. Tupper notes that "in this sense the word appears nowhere else in the poetry, but is found often in the *Charters* (B-T., p. 584) both as simplex (with place-names) and compound" (p. 167).

38.65: *ætes*: This is evidently a partitive genitive with the negative verb: "though I should never see any (of) food." For a similar example, cp. Aelfric's Homily 20, line 408, in Pope's edition (vol. 2, p. 659, and p. 666, note) where the reading should probably be *ne his a seon*. Cp. also the partitive use of *hwyrftweges* with the negative form *nah* at *Rid.* 1.36 and see note to that line.

38.65: *sy*: optative first person singular of *seon*, "to see." For a catalogue of similar forms (*si, sii* in Northumbrian texts), see SB. 374 Anm. 4–6, pp. 288–89. See also Holthausen, *ESn*. li, 186. Holthausen later (*Anglia Beibl*. xlvi, 9) takes *sy* as "be," reading *me* for MS. *ic*, but there is no reason to so alter the MS.

38.66: *pernex*: Dietrich (*ZfdA*. xi, 455) points out that this mythical bird arises from the translator's misunderstanding of Aldhelm's *plus pernix aquilis* (L. *pernix* can be easily confused with *perdix*, "partridge"). Tupper and Wyatt point out that Chaucer made a similar mistake in his *House of Fame* 1392 by translating the phrase, *pernicibus alis*, of Virgil (*Aeneid* iv.180) as "partriches winges."

38.70–71: *snægl . . . regnwyrm . . . fenyce*: This corresponds to Aldhelm's "Lumbricus et limax et tarda testudo palustris" (*Creatura* 37), though the slow-moving turtle has been replaced by the marsh frog. In the Cambridge MS. of Aldhelm (noted above) the glosses are: for *Lumbricus, angeltwicce*, for *limax, rensnægl*, for *testudo, byrdlingc* (Napier, 23.20–22). Whitman (*Anglia* xxx, 383) points out that normally *snægl* is the gloss to *limax* (WW. 121.31, 231.29, 433.1); *yce* to *botrax* (WW. 161.9, 195.23, 361.32) or *rana* (477.4); *regnwyrm* to *lumbricus* (WW. 31.9, 477.2, 122.22 [*renwyrm uel angeltwicce*]).

38.73: *þone we wifel wordum nemnað*: Here the riddler forgets momentarily who is speaking (the personified "Creation"). Trautmann supplies *se* before *þone* in his edition and later (*Anglia* xliii, 249) reads *þone w*[*is*]*e wifel wordum nemnað*. Holthausen would read either *þone þe wifel wordum* [*wise*] *nemnað* (*Anglia Beibl*. xxx, 52) or *þone we* [*won*] *wifel wordum nemnað* (*Anglia Beibl*. xlvi, 9). Aldhelm's *cantarus* (*Creatura* 38) is glossed by *scarabeus, scernwibba* in the Cambridge MS. (noted above), but *cantarus* is the lemma elsewhere for *wibil* (WW. 11.28) and *wifil* (WW. 198.19, 363.4).

38.79–80: The relationship of these lines to Aldhelm's line 43 is discussed in the headnote.

38.82–83: The riddler, perhaps now a new translator, repeats lines 50–51 above.

38.84: Mackie gives the MS. reading: *ic uttor . . . eal ymbwinde*. Grein and Wyatt read *ic uttor eal ymbwinde* with a short half-line, depending upon the placement of the caesura. Holthausen would supply *ana* (*Anglia Beibl.* ix, 358) or *eaþe* (*ESn.* xxxvii, 208) after *uttor*; Trautmann supplies *fela*; Tupper, *eaþe*. Krapp and Dobbie note that Tupper's reading is supported by line 53*a* above.

38.88: The MS. reading, *ic eom ufor ealra gesceafta*, is retained by all editors except Trautmann who reads *ic eom ufor ealra [eorþan] gesceafta* for metrical reasons. But the problem is not so much with the meter (the MS. reading of the on-verse would qualify as short C2, Pope's category C21) as it is with the grammar. O.E. *ufor* is not recorded elsewhere with the genitive as it is here. Normally we might expect *ufor þonne* (Tupper glosses *ufor* here as "higher than") followed by a nominative noun (cp. similar uses of the comparative in this riddle) or *ufemest* with the genitive (see examples at B-T., p. 1087). I have emended MS. *ufor* to *ufemest* as this seems the best and simplest way of making sense of the line. Other editors retain the MS. reading without comment.

38.91: *onþunian*: The MS. reads *onrinnan*, which does not alliterate. Grein first read *onþinnan* in his edition and later (*Germania* x, 429) *onþunian*, translated as *"intumescere, se jactare"* (*Sp.*, p. 729). Grein's *onþunian* is accepted by all later editors except Trautmann, who retains *onrinnan* in his text, suggesting *on-* or *oþþringan* ("entweichen") in his notes (p. 104).

38.94: *sweart ansyne*: *dark in aspect*, referring to the whale. For a similar construction, cp. *Run.* 31, *fæger ansyne*, which B-T. (p.45) translates as "fair in aspect." The reading was first proposed by Herzfeld (*Die Räthsel des Exeterbuches und ihr Verfasser*, p. 69) and is accepted by Trautmann and myself. Other editors read *sweartan syne*, "with dark eye," or "with dark vision," but Herzfeld's reading is closer to the Latin of Cr. 65. Another possibility would be to read *sweartan ansyne*, "with dark appearance," but it is better to avoid the emendation. Krapp and Dobbie raise the possibility of reading *syne* for *sinu, seonu*, "sinew" (p. 345, note), but the whale's sinew here is of less·importance than its outer (visible) aspect.

38.94: *swiþre*: Grein and Tupper read *swiþra*, but Wyatt (p. xxxvi, and p. 103, note) and Krapp and Dobbie note that the Old English riddler is inconsistent in this and other riddles with respect to the gender of the disguised object.

38.94: *þonne*: Here as elsewhere occasionally in the poem (cp. 26*b* and 28*b*) the meter would be more regular if we assumed an originally monosyllabic *þon* for the MS. *þonne* (see note to *Rid.* 14.5*b*).

38.96: *hondwyrm*: In the Aldhelm manuscripts, *handwyrme* glosses *uerme* (Napier 23.50) in one case; *i. briensis, hondweorm* glosses *uerme* in another (Napier 25.1). Elsewhere *handwyrm* or a close equivalent *hondwyrm, honduyrm*) glosses *surio, uel briensis, uel sirineus* (WW. 122.18), *uricus* (WW. 275.15), *briensis* (WW. 9.31, 358.32), and *ladascapiae, briensis* (WW. 29.34). In a long passage in the *Leechdoms* that concerns internal and external "worms" that plague man (*Lch.* ii.120.18 ff.), the writer makes it clear that "handworms" exist close to the surface of the skin. The cure for "handworms" is not a potion but a salve:

> Wiþ hond wyrmum *and* deaw wyrmum genim doccan oððe clatan þa þe swimman wolde þa wyrttruman meng wið fletan *and* wið sealt læt standan þreo niht *and* þy feorþan dæge smire mid þa saran stowa. [*Lch.* ii.122.21–24]

The subsequent paragraph in the *Leechdoms* describes handworms as "worms that eat the hands" and dew worms as worms that attack the feet. Salves are recommended for the former, hot coals for the latter. Since the salves are made with red nettle and salt, among other things, it seems likely that these handworms are some sort of parasite living close to the surface of the skin, which might be driven out by these preparations. These worms do not seem to be the *exiguo, sulcat qui corpora, verme* of Aldhelm's *Creatura* 66. Corpse worms are described in another section of the *Leechdoms* (*Lch.* ii.126.4 ff.) and are to be treated with an entirely different "cure."

38.98: *Ne*: Krapp and Dobbie misread *Nu* for MS. *ne*.

38.106: *þe*: Suggested by Bright (Tupper, p. 34, note) and so all later editors except Wyatt.

38.108: MS. folio 111*b* ends with *þ̄ he*. A folio leaf appears to be missing between folios 111*b* and 112*a*. At the bottom of MS. folio

111*b* several letters and trial strokes appear in a faint medieval hand that does not appear to be that of the main scribe (see plate xvi.a). As far as I can ascertain, the letters read: *h....s. egC....þ.* (see plates) with *s* the initial part of a ligature. The passage is copied in somewhat the same form by Robert Chambers in his transcript of the *Exeter Book* for the British Museum (*Brit. Mus. Add. MS. 9067*) made in 1831 (see plate xvi.b). The passage is noted by Assmann who says: "Unten steht von andrer hand und mit andrer tinte, jetzt fast ganz verwischt: *hit is,* dann noch ungefähr 12 mir nicht mehr im zusammenhange lesbare buchstaben" (p. 211, note). Tupper reports the letters as *sio creatura pr* (p. 34, note). Since these letters were not visible in their entirety to Chambers in 1831 and are not so visible now, Tupper's reading seems highly doubtful. Several of the "letters" appear to be trial strokes and nothing more. The letters are not at all visible in the photographic facsimile of Chambers, Förster, and Flower of 1933 (*The Exeter Book of Old English Poetry*). Recently Konick (*MLN* liv, 262) has interpreted the passage as a bridge between the unfinished *Rid.* 38 and the fragment, *Rid.* 39. Konick believes the two riddles to be one. But the letters are clearly marginalic comment, not part of the text. Textual and marginalic spaces are clearly defined in the *Exeter Book.* It should also be noted that *Rid.* 38 is a first-person riddle in which the disguised creature speaks (*Ic eom . . .*). *Rid.* 39 is a third-person riddle in which a narrator (*Ne magon we . . .*) speaks of the creature (*hwæt seo wiht sy*). The two riddles could not possibly be one.

39. Water
[*VN: Gr.42; Tr.39; Tu.42; W.41; M.41; K-D.41*]

The beginning of this riddle is missing, apparently because of the loss of a MS. folio (see note to *Rid.* 38.108 above). The word, *edniwu,* followed by a MS. point begins folio 112*a*. Dietrich (*ZfdA.* xi, 473) solved the riddle fragment as "earth"; Trautmann (*Anglia Beibl.* v, 49), as "fire." Tupper (*MLN* xviii, 104) first solved the riddle as "wisdom"; later (edition, p. 171), as "water." Recently, Konick (*MLN* liv, 259 ff.) has argued that this riddle fragment is a continuation of the previous "creation" riddle, but he misreads the trial strokes in the lower margin of folio 111*b* as part of the text and ignores the distinction between the riddlic subject of *Rid*. 38 (where *Ic* is the "creation") and the riddlic observers or narrators of *Rid*. 39 (where *we* refers to human beings). For the reading of the marginalic strokes at the bottom of folio 111*b*, see my note to *Rid*. 38.108.

I accept Tupper's second solution, "water." Tupper (p. 171) points out that the "ice" of *Rid*. 31 [this edition] says: *Is min modor mægða cynnes / þæs deorestan* (31.9–10). Likewise the riddler says of "water" at *Rid*. 80.4: *Modor is monigra mærra wihta*. The same motif may be found in Aldhelm's Riddle 29, "Aqua," where the creature says, "Nam volucres caeli nantesque per aequora pisces / Olim sumpserunt ex me primordia vitae" (ed. Pitman, p. 16) and in Aldhelm's Riddle 73, "Fons," where the creature says, "Quis numerus capiat vel quis laterculus aequet, / Vita viventum generem quot milia partu?" (ed. Pitman, p. 42).

39.8: *geþencanne*: Sievers (*Beiträge* x, 482) would emend to *geþencan* (see note to *Rid*. 26.12*b*).

40. Cock and Hen
[*VN: Gr.43; Tr.40; Tu.43; W.42; M.42; K-D.42*]

In the manuscript this riddle and the following riddle appear as one. Each riddle disguises a pair of creatures, but the pairs are certainly unlike. The scribe has made a similar mistake in combining *Rids*. 45 and 46.

Dietrich's solution, "cock and hen" (*ZfdA*. xi, 473), is accepted by all editors. The solution is based upon the runes whose names are given in lines 8–11 of the riddle. There must be in the solution two of *Nyd* (runic N), one of *Æsc* (runic Æ), two of *Ac* (runic A), and two of *Hægl* (runic H). Combined and rearranged, the runes spell two words, O.E. *hana* (cock) and *hæn* (hen). Tupper classifies the riddle as an "obscene riddle," presumably because of the *hæmedlac* or *love-game* played by the birds.

40.2: *plegan*: Sievers (*Beiträge* x, 520) would read *plegian* for metrical reasons, and so also Trautmann, but as A1 lines with a short stressed syllable do occur in the off-verse occasionally in Old English poetry (see Pope's category A98, p. 333, in *The Rhythm of Beowulf*, and cp. *Rid.* 36.6*b* and 36.7*b*), it seems better to retain the MS. reading.

40.3: *hæmedlaces*: *coition*, literally *wedding* or *love game*. Cp. *hæmedceorl* and *hæmedwif*, *hæmedscipe* and *hæmedðing* (CH., p. 165).

40.3: *hwitloc*: *fair-haired*. Cp. *hwitloccedu* at *Rid.* 76.5.

40.10: *an an linan*: *ān an līnan*: *a single one on the line*. Rissanen notes that "the appositive position of *one* is no doubt due to the demands of poetic diction" (*The Uses of One in Old and Early Middle English*, p. 41).

40.11: *Swa ic*: The MS. *hwylc* has never been very plausibly explained either as a relative or as an interrogative (for the various readings, see Krapp and Dobbie, pp. 345–46). The emendation is simply explained. A Northumbrian or Mercian *sue ic* if run together with a somewhat high *i* (or small capital *i*) could easily have been misread by a scribe as *suelc*; this then would have become West Saxon *swylc*, then *hwylc* by attraction to the *h* alliteration of the line. This is the only reading that makes sense of the preterite tense *onleac* at 12*b*. Thus the riddler explains to those who *bec witan* how he has by means of rune-learning solved the puzzle. I translate beginning at 11*b*: "Thus I have unlocked with the power of a key the fastenings of the treasure-door which held the riddle (guarded its solution?) mind-fast against riddle-solvers, concealed in its heart by cunning bonds."

41. Soul and Body
[*VN: Gr.44; Tr.41; Tu.44; W.43; M.43; K-D.43*]

Dietrich first proposed the solution, *der Geist und der Leib*, in 1859:

> Der edle gast . . . mit seinem diener, der zugleich sein bruder ist, ist der *geist* und der *leib*, ihre verwandte, die zugleich mutter und schwester ist, und von der sie scheiden müssen, ist die *erde*. ihre mutterschaft ist bekannt genug; als schwester, weil von demselben vater geschaffen . . . [*ZfdA.* xi, 473]

This solution is accepted by all editors. Wyatt prints the form, "body and soul (mind)," in his edition (p. 103), but neither the intellectual qualities of *mens* nor the deliberative qualities of *animus* seems relevant to the Old English riddle. Rather, the distinction is drawn between the inner and the outer realities of man. Isidore says: "Duplex est autem homo: interior et exterior. Interior homo anima, [et] exterior homo corpus" (*Etym.* xi.i.6). The possible confusion between *anima* and *animus* is usually carefully delineated in medieval Latin writings.

The only resemblances between this riddle and Riddle 25 of Eusebius, "De Animo," are those which would derive from a common theological tradition. The motif of the soul and body as fellow travelers through life is a common one in Old English poetry. Cp., for example, the final plea of the poet of *Juliana*:

> Is me þearf micel
> þæt seo halge me   helpe gefremme,
> þonne me gedælað   deorast ealra,
> sibbe toslitað   sinhiwan tu,
> micle modlufan.   Min sceal of lice
> sawul on siðfæt,   nat ic sylfa hwider,
> eardes uncyðgu;   of sceal ic þissum,
> secan oþerne   ærgewyrhtum
> gongan iudædum.

[Jul. 695–703]

41.1a: *indryhtne*: Trautmann reads *indryhten*, "Inherr, Hausherr," but the adjective, like *deorne*, is a modifer of *giest* in line 2*a*.

41.1b: *æþelum deorne*: *excellent in (noble) lineage*; so Grein (*Sp.*, p. 5), Tupper, and Trautmann take *æþelum* from *æþelu* and *deorne* from *deore*. The formula, *æþelum deore*, glossed in *Sp.*, p. 5, as "origine praenobilis," occurs at *Ex.* 186, *Beo.* 1949, and with a variation (*cyning æþelum god*) at *Beo.* 1870. Wyatt takes *æþelum* to be a form of the adj. *æðele*, "noble," apparently translating the entire phrase as "dear to noble (ones)," and Mackie takes *æþelum* as an adverb and *deorne* as a form of *deor*, "brave," translating the phrase as "(a) nobly brave (guest)," but in light of the formulaic use of *æþelum deore* noted above, these latter two readings are less likely. According to the reading as I have it, the soul has an excellent lineage since (as we know from the *Soul and Body* poems) it comes from God (see, for example, *Soul II* 22 ff.).

41.2: *giest in geardum*: Cp. *Chr.* 819–20: *somod siþian sawel in lice, | in þam gæsthofe.*

41.4: *adle*: A similar form occurs at *Guth.* 1022. Grein lists two separate words, *adl* and *adle*, both defined as *morbus* (*Sp.*, p. 2), but Krapp and Dobbie's contention that *adle* is a variant spelling for the nominative singular seems more likely.

41.5: *esne*: *servant* (but for its variety of meanings in other contexts, see B-T., p. 258). R. I. Page says of the lower classes of Anglo-Saxon society that "beneath the freemen were the slaves, different grades of them, and the laws mention other groups of underprivileged people whose exact positions are obscure; for example . . . the *esne* who is sometimes equated with the slave and sometimes not" (*Life in Anglo-Saxon England*, p. 258). This ambiguity of meaning may be appropriate to the riddle, since the body is called a *broþor* in line 11.

41.5: *agan*: Wyatt and Mackie read *a gan*, "always go," but this makes for an awkward rhythm and a rather prosaic meaning. Other editors read *agan*, "own, possess," without comment, though the sense in which the *esne* might "own" the *giest* is not perfectly clear. Normally one would assume, as do most editors, that the relative *se þe* refers back to the subject, *esne*, of the main clause; but as the relative takes its case from the adjective clause, *se þe* here could refer either to the *esne* (body) or to the *him* (soul) (see Mitchell's discussion of adjective clauses in *A Guide to Old English* 162, pp. 73 ff.). If we take the relative to refer to *him* or the soul, and *agan* to mean "to rule" (cp. *Beo.* 31 and the various *-agend* compounds in *Beowulf*), then we may translate beginning at line 4*b*: "If the servant serves honorably the one who rules . . . " This makes much better sense of the lines and sets up the parallelism that follows.

41.8: All previous editors take *cnosles unrim* as a phrase parallel with the objects *wiste* and *blisse* in the preceding half-line and *care* as the accusative singular object in the following clause. But it is not clear why the good soul and body should have *cnosles unrim*, literally *a* *countless number of children* or *kin*. This does not seem to bother the editors though Mackie tries to get around the problem by translating the phrase as "abundant plenty." The problem is solved if we take *care* as genitive singular (cp. *PPs.* 140.1: *ceare full*) and translate *cnosles unrim care* as "a countless number of offspring of sorrow" or more freely, "a countless progeny of sorrow," and punctuate the lines so that the new clause begins at 7*a* instead of 7*b*. The slight midverse break after *care* is unusual but not unknown (for different sorts of examples, cp. *Gen.* 17*a*, and *Rids.* 46.7*a*, 57.12*b*, 62.5*a*, 63.1*a*, and 63.2*a*).

41.8b–11: The clause beginning with *gif* in 8*b* is continued with *ne* at 10*b*; I translate the lines: "if the servant obeys his lord and master badly on the way and will not as a brother be afraid of (*or* for) the other." My punctuation follows that of Grein and Assmann; all other editors begin a new clause or sentence at 10*b*. My translation of lines 10*b*–11*a* follows that of Klaeber (*MP* ii, 145–46, note 1). Grein (*Sp.*, p. 215) glosses *forht* as *terribilis, formidolosus*, and so Tupper, and Mackie (who translates, "The one brother must not be a cause of fear to the other."). Trautmann emends *forht* to *forþ* explaining that "nicht will der eine Bruder dem anderen immerdar gehören." But Klaeber's reading, accepted by Krapp and Dobbie, makes good sense especially with the clause at 10*b*–11*a* taken as an extension of the preceding clause as it is here.

41.14: *moddor ond sweostor*: Since body, soul, and earth were all created by God, they are siblings; thus, earth is a sister to her brothers, body and soul. Since the whole man, both body and soul, was created from the earth, earth is mother to both body and soul. Isidore makes it clear that both body and soul are created from the clay:

> Homo dictus, quia ex humo est factus, sicut [et] in Genesi dicitur (2,7): 'Et creavit Deus hominem de humo terrae.' Abusive autem pronuntiatur ex utraque substantia totus homo, id est ex societate animae et corporis. Nam proprie homo ab humo. [*Etym.* xi.i.4]

41.16: *eðþa*: a Northumbrian form of *oððe* (SB. 317, p. 249). Cp. *aeththa* of *Bede's Death Song: Northumbrian Version*, line 4.

42. Key
[VN: Gr.45; Tr.42; Tu.45; W.44; M.44; K-D.44]

Dietrich (*ZfdA*. xi, 473–74) solved the riddle as "key" or "dagger-sheath." Krapp and Dobbie note that "either solution is possible" (p. 346). Grein (*Sp.*, p. 301) translates *hangellan* in line 6 as "*pendulum (mentula)*." Tupper prefers "key" to "dagger-sheath" but notes that "it is unwise to dogmatize over the answers to Anglo-Saxon riddles of this class [for] it is probable that the collector himself knew and cared little about the original solutions, since any decorous reply would adorn his unseemly tale" (p. 176). The riddle is less an "unseemly tale" than a skillfully wrought double entendre riddle-game with "key" and its shadow-solution competing for the reader's attention. Tupper, Wyatt, Trautmann, and Mackie accept the solution, "key." For a "key" riddle without the double entendre, compare *Rid*. 87.

42.2: *foran is þyrel*: Some Anglo-Saxon keys have been discovered with holes in the flat part of their tongues (see Wilson, *Anglo-Saxon Ornamental Metalwork 700–1100 in the British Museum*, items 40 and 140 and plates). The holes were presumably functional in certain kinds of locks.

42.7: *efenlang*: Wyatt and Mackie follow Grein in retaining the MS. form *efelang* [MS. *efe lang*]; Tupper and Krapp and Dobbie and I follow Trautmann in emending to *efenlang* after the analogy of *efeneald* and *efenswið*. All editors gloss the word as "equally long" or "just as long." Tupper and Trautmann give the case here as accusative singular neuter (other editors do not give the case) so that the word modifies the neuter *hol* in line 5 and the relative *þæt* in line 7. Thus the hanging thing is said to seek out the equally long hole that it has often filled before. But Tupper at least in his note (p. 177) implies that *efenlang ær* may be a phrasal, and if we take the adjective here to be nominative singular masculine modifying *he*, we might translate beginning at 5*b*: "He wants to greet with the head of his hanging thing that known (intimate?) hole that he has often filled (when he was) just as long as before." The question here is whether the creatures are said to be of matched length (as fits the literal solution) or whether one of the creatures periodically attains the requisite length for matching (as in the case of the double entendre). Presumably the ambiguity is intended.

43. Dough
[*VN: Gr.46; Tr.43; Tu.46; W.45; M.45; K-D.45*]

Dietrich (*ZfdA*. xi, 474) doubtfully proposed the solution, "bee," but Trautmann (edition, p. 107, note) and Herzfeld (*Die Räthsel des Exeterbuches und ihr Verfasser*, p. 69) independently arrived at the solution, "dough." This answer has been accepted by all subsequent editors. Tupper traces the history of "dough" riddles and describes the various kinds of Anglo-Saxon bread (p. 177), but the Old English riddle is no mere testament to the good wife's baking skills. It is rather an elaborate conceit based upon the role of the Anglo-Saxon wife as *hlæf-dige*, "lady, mistress of the house" (B-T., p. 539), literally "kneader of the dough." The lady in the riddle is making more than cakes. The hidden comparison of those *banleas* wonders is certainly the main point of the double entendre riddle.

43.1: *on wincle*: *in a corner*. Swaen (*Neoph*. xxxi, 148) notes that this is "the only instance of *wincel* corner, which occurs in a few place-names, such as A.S. *Wincel-cumb* [see B-T., p. 1231], modern Aldwinkle . . . cognate languages have Dutch *winkel* and German *Winkel*." Cp. *in wincle* (MS. *Inwinc sele*) at *Rid*. 52.2 and see note to that line.

43.1: *weaxan*: For the MS. *weax*, Dietrich (*ZfdA*. xi, 474) suggested the possibility of *weax=wēacs=wāces*, genitive singular of *wāc*, "weak, soft," and so Grein (*Sp.*, p. 766) with a question. Sievers (*Beiträge* x, 520), Wyatt, and Swaen (*Neoph*. xxxi, 148) would emend MS. *weax* to *waces*. Herzfeld (*Die Räthsel des Exeterbuches und ihr Verfasser*, p. 69) proposed *weascan*; Holthausen (*Indogermanische Forschungen* iv, 387) proposed *weaxan*, and so Tupper, Trautmann, Mackie, and Krapp and Dobbie. While it is true as Swaen points out that O.E. *nathwæt* occurs three other times with the genitive (*Rids*. 52.5, 59.9, and 89.27), this does not necessarily constitute a rule of usage. Like Tupper, I prefer the reading, *weaxan*, because it provides a parallel infinitive with *þindan*, *þunian* and *hebban*, and because it is most appropriate to the context of the double entendre.

43.1: *nathwæt*: Cp. the similarly delightful ambiguity of *nathwæt* at *Rids.* 52.5 and 59.9 and of *nathwær* at *Rids.* 23.5 and 60.8.

43.4: *hygewlonc*: See note to *Rid.* 23.7.

43.5: *þrindende*: Thorpe reads *þindende*, and so does Wyatt. Mackie reads *þrintende*. Grein retains MS. *þrindende* (*Sp.*, p. 724), citing M.H.G. *drinden*. All other editors read *þrindende*. The form *þrinteð* occurs at *Vain.* 24, and the form *aþrunten* at *Rid.* 35.2. Grein notes these as separate forms (*Sp.*, pp. 724, 725). Sievers-Brunner notes:

> Neben Formen von ð*rintan* steht das Part. Präs. ð*rindende* Rätsel; neben dem Part. Prät. ãð*runten* auch ein Part. ãð*rūten*, das, wenn es kein Schreibfehler (Ausslassen des Abkürzungsstriches für *n*) ist, wohl zu einem reduplizierenden Verbum . . . * ð*rūtan* gehört, vgl. das schw. Verbum II ð*rūtian* und altn. *þrútinn* Adj. geschwollen und Verbum *þrútna* anschwellen. [SB. 386 Anm. 5, p. 297]

Swaen (*Neoph.* xxxi, 148) notes the occurrence of *aþruten* at *Lch.* ii.44.14 and ii.218.19.

44. Lot and His Family
[*VN: Gr.* 47; *Tr.*44; *Tu.*47; *W.*46; *M.*46; *K-D.*46]

The solution, "Lot with his two daughters and their sons," was proposed by Wright (*Biographia Britannica Literaria*, vol. 1, p. 81). Tupper quotes several analogues but notes that the riddle "seems to have had no vogue in the Middle Ages" (p. 178). The story of Lot's incest was certainly known from Genesis 19. Augustine refers to it in *De Civitate Dei* (*PL.* xli, 509), and so does Isidore in his *Etymologiae* (vii.vi.26). The narrative sequence leading to Lot's seduction is somewhat complex. God sends two angels to destroy the wicked city of Sodom and the angels are befriended by Lot. The angels warn Lot to flee from the city with his family and not to look back on the devastation. Lot's wife disobeys the angels and looking back in flight is turned into a pillar of salt. Lot wanders off with his daughters to live in a cave in the hills. The daughters despair of ever finding husbands and conspire to seduce Lot. They ply him with wine and visit his bed. The *Old English Heptateuch* relates the act: "Eft hi fordrencton ðone unwaran Loð . . . *and* se fæder nyste hu he befeng on hi, ne hwænne heo aras, for hys druncennysse. Hi wæron ða eacnigende" (ed. Crawford, EETS, o.s. 160, p. 134). The Old English riddle is based on the resulting confusion of kinship terms. Lot's daughters are also his wives. His sons are also his grandsons. The daughters are sisters and co-wives. The sons are grandsons, uncles, and nephews (see note to line 6).

44.1: *Wær:* Campbell (288, p. 122) notes that in the *Kentish Glosses to Proverbs*, *wær* is an inverted spelling for *wer*, indicating an earlier orthography. Wyatt takes *wær* as a Northumbrian form. Cp. the use of *wær* for *wer* in *L. Edm. B.* and in the *Rushworth Matthew*, cited in B-T., p. 1205 under *wer*, section IV.

44.3: *swase gesweostor ond hyra suno twegan | freolico frumbearn:* dear *sisters and their two sons, (both) noble first-born children.*

44.6: *eam ond nefa: uncle and nephew*, though *nefa* sometimes means *grandson* (see Lorraine Lancaster, "Kinship in Anglo-Saxon Society," *BJS* ix, 230 ff.). Lot is grandfather and father to both boys but uncle to none (since he has no sister). It seems that *eam ond nefa* must refer to *þara æþelinga æghwæðres* (line 5), as one might expect from the syntax. Each son is, in fact, *eam* and *nefa* to the other. Since both daughters and sons are derived from Lot, they are all by one definition siblings. Taking one son as Ego 1, his mother's brother (*eam*) is the other son or Ego 2. If each son is *eam* to the other, then each must also be *nefa*, as that is the reciprocal relation (son of ego's sister).

45. Bookworm
[VN: Gr.48; Tr.45; Tu.48; W.47; M.47; K-D.47]

Grein's solution, "die Büchermotte," is accepted by most editors, though strictly speaking it is *der Bücherwurm* that feasts upon the vellum. In this respect it is interesting to note that the initial half-line contains a double disguise: *moððe* for *wyrm* and *word* for *bec*. Moths cannot live winging about in books, and worms do not eat spoken words (see below). Dietrich (*ZfdA*. xi, 451) first pointed out the resemblances between the Old English riddle and Riddle 16, "Tinea," of Symphosius. The Latin riddle is:

> Littera me pavit, nec quid sit littera novi.
> In libris vixi, nec sum studiosior inde.
> Exedi Musas, nec adhuc tamen ipsa profeci.
>
> [Ed. Ohl, p. 48]

The differences between the Latin and the Old English riddles are clear. The Latin riddle begins with its title and proceeds line by line, rephrasing the central paradox of the poem. It refers to neither moths nor songs. It is a first-person riddle narrated by the scarcely disguised worm. The Old English riddle begins with a shocking statement and moves on to an elaborate commentary with an implied lament for things past. The Old English riddler is less concerned with the cuteness of the paradox of the illiterate worm than he is with the mutability of songs as they pass from the traditional *wordhord* of the *scop* into the newer and strangely susceptible form of literate *memoria*.*

45.1: *word: speech* (*words*). The usage here is probably plural (cp. *wordum* at 6*b*) and is to be taken in the sense of "spoken words" or "speech" (see B-T., pp. 1264–65); this meaning is reinforced by the

---

*In an article that just appeared ("Artful Ambiguities in the Old English 'Book-Moth' Riddle," in *Anglo-Saxon Poetry: Essays in Appreciation: For John C. McGalliard*, ed. Lewis E. Nicholson and Dolores Warwick Frese, pp. 355–62), Fred Robinson details the use of puns in the riddle. He notes that *wyrd* (2*a*), "event, fate," may be a pun on *gewyrd*, "speech, conversation, collection of words, sentence" (see B-T., under *gewyrde*, BTS. under *gewyrd*); that *þystro* (4*a*), "darkness" may carry connotations of "ignorance"; that *cwide* (4*b*), "speech, sentence, statement," may be a pun on a form of *cwidu*, "what is chewed"; that *staþol* (5*a*) may mean both "foundation," and "intellectual foundation, content of a thought or argument"; and that *swealg* (6*b*) may mean both "swallow" and "take into the mind, imbibe (wisdom)" (see B-T., p. 947). These points have been incorporated into the glossary.

later uses of *gied* and *cwide* in the poem. The *OED* lists this occurrence of "word" as the first-known instance meaning "a written (engraved, printed, etc.) character or set of characters representing this" (*OED* xii, p. 281, under category 12c). As "word" does not occur with the same meaning elsewhere until 1521, its meaning here in the Old English is somewhat dubious. The lexicographer appears to have taken the uncloaked meaning for the literal disguise. Neither moths nor worms can eat spoken words—that is the paradox of the riddle. The *wera gied sumes* are susceptible to the *stælgiest* because they have passed from the *wordhord* to the delicious *memoria* of the vellum sheet.

45.4b–5a: *þrymfæstne cwide / ond þæs strangan staþol*: B-T. translates this as "a glorious saying and the strong man's firm support" (p. 912), taking *strangan* as genitive singular and the half-lines as parallel variations; but since *ond* rarely occurs in preference to asyndetic parataxis where parallel variations of the same referent are introduced, Mackie's reading of *strangan* as accusative singular modifying *staþol* in his translation, "his excellent language and its firm support," is to be preferred. Thus the poet refers in a wittily ironic way to the parchment itself as the worm's food. Trautmann equates genitive singular *þæs strangan* with *bocstæfes* and then explains, "der Buchstabe ist stark durch den Gedanken, den er darstellt und dadurch, dass er in die Ferne und in die Zukunft wirkt" (p. 108), but a more likely reading along similar lines is that of Cassidy and Ringler who translate line 5a as "'And (the very) foundation of that mighty (utterance)'—i.e., the vellum upon which it was written" (*Bright's Old English Grammar and Reader*, p. 342, note). I prefer Mackie's reading.

45.5: *stælgiest*: The oxymoron is difficult to translate into modern terms. One should keep in mind the Anglo-Saxon standards of hospitality and remember that those who broke the neighborly code by stealing from their friends were often put to death.

46. Paten or Chalice
[*VN: Gr.49; Tr.46; Tu.49; W.48; M.48; K-D.48*]

Dietrich (*ZfdA*. xi, 474–75; *ZfdA*. xii, 235) solves the riddle as "chrismal," or "pyx," the vessel that holds the chrism. Tupper prefers the solution, *huseldisc*, or paten, to Dietrich's *huselbox*. Wyatt solves the riddle as "chalice"; Mackie, as "paten or chalice." Trautmann says, "Dass es sich um ein kirchliches Gerät handelt, kann nicht bezweifelt werden" (p. 108), but notes that the round *hring* (line 1) can hardly refer to a box.

The language of the riddle defines an object used in a religious context, presumably the mass. The phrase, *readan goldes*, in line 6 would seem to indicate "chalice" rather than "paten." The English ecclesiastical laws mention in a number of contexts that chalices should be made of gold or at least of molten material; patens are never similarly described (see Thorpe's edition of *Ancient Laws and Institutes of England*, vol. 2, p. 253, line 21; p. 292, line 20; p. 350, line 22; p. 384, lines 6–8). Aelfric says, for example, in his "Pastoral Epistle": "And witað þæt beo ælc calic geworht of myldendum antimbre, gilden oððe seolfren, glæren oððe tinen; ne beo he na hyrnen ne huru treowen" (ed. Thorpe, *Ancient Laws*, vol. 2, p. 385). Aldhelm, in his *Carmina Ecclesiastica*, describes an altar with a gold chalice and a silver paten:

Plurima basilicae sunt ornamenta recentis:
Aurea contortis flavescunt pallia filis,
Quae sunt altaris sacri velamina pulchra,
Aureus atque calix gemmis fulgescit opertus,
Ut caelum rutilat stellis ardentibus aptum,
Ac lata argento constat fabricata patena:
Quae divina gerunt nostrae medicamina vitae.

[*Carmina Ecclesiastica* 3.69–75;
ed. Ehwald, *Aldhelmi Opera*, p. 18]

The primary concern of the churchmen appears always to be with the chalice and not with the paten—at least in terms of its composition.

In terms of the ritual of the mass, however, the outcry of the riddlic creature may be more suited to the paten than it is to the chalice. The creature paradoxically speaks while keeping silent (*swigende cwæð*) at line 5: *Gehæle mec helþend gæsta*. The silent statement is probably a religious inscription on the object (cp. *Rid*. 57, lines 11–12 and 15 ff. where the "wounds" of the chalice "speak"). If the Old English plea in line 5 corresponds to some portion of the mass, that portion is probably the last petition of the Pater Noster before the fraction or breaking of the bread: *libera nos a malo* (see Jungmann, *The Mass of the Roman Rite*, pp. 469 ff.). Jungmann notes that in the medieval mass the Pater Noster was sometimes accompanied by certain external rites, namely, the raising of the paten and chalice, or of the paten alone (Jungmann, *Mass*, pp. 469 ff.). Hardison, who draws heavily upon the work of Amalarius, Bishop of Metz in the ninth century and a prominent figure at the court of Charlemagne, describes the ritual action at the end of the Pater Noster in these terms:

> The subdeacons . . . bow again during the Pater Noster. Then, at the *libera nos a malo*, deacons and subdeacons raise their heads. The transition from the *tristia* of the Passion to the *gaudium* of the Resurrection is, for Amalarius, the turning point of the Mass. It is hinted at in the presentation of the paten, and the hint becomes more overt at the general raising of heads. [Hardison, *Christian Rite and Christian Drama in the Middle Ages*, p. 71]

Thus the presentation of the paten may mark the passage from the supplication to the celebration of the mass. If the cry of the creature at line 5 of the Old English riddle corresponds to the Latin plea, *libera nos a malo*, then the creature of the riddle may be the paten and not the chalice. Still the problem of the *readan goldes* (line 6) in terms of Aldhelm's description of paten and chalice would remain.

46.1: *hring gyddian*: For the MS. *hringende an*, all editors except Trautmann and Krapp and Dobbie read *hring ærendean*, but Krapp and Dobbie note that such a half-line is suspicious metrically. The spelling of *ærendean* is also suspicious. Klaeber (*MP* ii, 145) would read *hring ændean* or *hring endean*, explaining *ændean* as a form of *ærndean* or *ærendian* with the suppression of the *r*. Trautmann reads *endean* for *endian* and says: "Unser 'begann' kann bedeuten 'sprach' (aus 'begann zu sprechen'): könnte nicht *endian* das oft heisst 'aufhören zu reden', aus dieser Bedeutung die einfache 'reden' gezogen haben?" (p. 108). This flight of fantasy defies comment. O.E. *endian* means "to make an end of, to complete, finish" (BTS., p. 190), not "aufhören zu reden." Krapp and Dobbie rightly doubt all of these readings and retain MS.

hringende an as *hring endean*, saying: "However we explain the MS. form *endean*, a word meaning 'speak' is indicated by *cwæð*, l. 4, and *gecwæð*, l. 8, and by the expected antithesis with *butan tungan*, etc., in ll. 2–3" (p. 347). With this I would agree. I suggest, however, that the original reading may have been *hring gyddian*, which would make good sense of the half-line and which would be acceptable metrically (cp. *Beo.* 3133*a*: *flod fæðmian*). In the original text, if the verb had taken the Anglian form *geddian* and if one of the g's had been dropped by haplography, then a scribe might have tidied up *hringeddian* into *hringende an*.

46.2b: Grein originally supplied *reordian* after *tila* and read in line 3: *þeah he hlude stefne ne cirmde, strongum wordum*. The reading here was proposed by Klaeber (*MP* ii, 145) and followed by all modern editors.

46.6–7: Holthausen (*Anglia* xxxv, 171; xxxviii, 78; *Anglia Beibl.* xxx, 53; xlvi, 9) proposes a number of unlikely emendations in these lines in order to read the verbs as either preterite plural indicative or as infinitives. Other major editors read *ongietan* and *beþencan* (MS. *beþuncan*) as optatives. Grein and Wyatt retain the form *beþuncan* in the MS., but this form does not occur elsewhere and seems highly suspicious here. The slight midverse break after *guman* in 7*b* is unusual but not unknown (for other examples, see the note to *Rid.* 41.8).

47. Uncertain
[*VN: Gr.50; Tr.47; Tu.50; W.49; M.49; K-D.49*]

Dietrich (*ZfdA*. xi, 475) solved the riddle first as "falcon-cage," later (*ZfdA*. xii, 236) as "bookcase." Tupper, Mackie, and Swaen (*Neoph.* xxxi, 145–46) accept "bookcase." Trautmann (*BBzA*. xix, 183 ff., and edition) solved the riddle as "oven." Shook recently ("Riddles Relating to the Anglo-Saxon Scriptorium," in *Essays in Honour of Anton Charles Pegis*, ed. J. Reginald O'Donnell, pp. 224–25) solved the riddle as "pen and ink." The word *eardfæstne* in line 1*a* if taken literally would certainly indicate something in close proximity with the ground like a clay bake-oven. Thus the *wonna þegn* (4*b*) who sends treasures *golde dyrran* (cp. the myth of Midas) into the mouth of the creature might be the cook. On the other hand, the use of the weak adjective *dumban* in 2a if it is meant to be a substantive ("a dumb one") along with *unwita* at 11a certainly seems to indicate in ironic fashion something like a bookcase that contains knowledge but comprehends nothing (cp. the use of *dumba* at *Rid.* 57.8 where the chalice though "dumb" speaks through its "wounds" or carved inscriptions and also Riddle 89 of Aldhelm, "Arca Libraria"). Books may also be *golde dyrran* (cp. *Rid.* 24.18 ff.) and of use to men. But the difficulty with "bookcase" is that the *wonna þegn* in the *Riddles* is typically a low-class servant (cp. *Rids.* 10.4, 10.8, 50.6, and 70.11), and Dietrich's explanation of the thane who is *sweart ond saloneb* as "der schrein aus eichenholz mit eisernem schloss und schlüssel versehen" (*ZfdA.* xii, 237) is not very convincing. Shook's reading of the "dark-nosed thane" as the pen itself is more plausible, and his reading of *lacum* (3b) as a form of *lacu*, "stream, pool," is ingenious; but the pen at work as it swallows ink (2b) can hardly be *eardfæstne*. Shook tries to get around this objection by arguing that the pen is originally in its pen rack or in its original abode as a reed, but the creature of the riddle swallows its "gifts" or "streams" (depending upon the reading of *lacum*) right from the beginning. Perhaps the book itself might be said to stand *eardfæstne* and to swallow streams of ink that the dark thane (the pen) provides, but I am not sure a book could reasonably be called *eorp* (11a). Furthermore, the collocation of *eardfæstne* and *lacum* (with Shook's reading *lacu*=pool) certainly hints that the creature may be something out of doors (though such hints are often misleading in riddles). It would help to know for certain the meaning of *gopes* in 3a, but this has so far eluded all editors. Given the uncertainties, it seems wisest to list the solution as "uncertain," though of all the solutions, I think "book" has the greatest possibilities.

47.1–2a: Rissanen (*The Uses of "One" in Old and Early Middle English*, pp. 70–71) notes that the use of *an* here (*eardfæstne anne*) is the only Old English case of a prop word *an* occurring after an adjective and surmises that the adjective here is probably used as a noun. Thus Mackie translates, "I know of one that stands fixed to the ground, deaf and dumb." But the weak adjective *dumban* may be construed as a noun (cp. *se dumba* at line 10b) in which case we could translate, "I know of a certain dumb thing that is fixed to the ground and deaf." I have punctuated the lines according to this latter reading.

47.3: *þurh gopes hond*: The meaning and derivation of O.E. *gop* continues to elude the scholars (myself included). Tupper reports Grein's original hypotheses about the word: "Grein, *Spr.* I, 520, accepts the reading of the MS. and defines doubtfully either as 'servus' (pointing to O.N. *hergopa*, 'serva bello capta'; cf. *gēopan*, 'capere') or as 'listig,' with reference to *gēap*, 'callidus'" (p. 181). Tupper rightly notes that "against the first etymology, speaks the length of the vowel in the present word; against the second, the difficulty of associating phonetically *gōp* and *gēap*" (ibid). Holthausen (*ESn.* lxxiv, 325) also notes that the meter favors *gōpes* not *gŏpes* and suggests emending *hond* to *honda* if *gŏpes* is required. If the word has a short vowel then it might be related, as Grein points out, to O.E. *gēopan* (pp. *gopen*?), and B-T. cites the following cognate forms for that verb: "*Scot.* gowpen *to lift* or *lade out with the hands*: *Icel.* gaupn: *O.H.Ger.* coufan *both hands held together in the form of a bowl*" (p. 427). On the possible meaning of O.E. *gōp*, Holthausen says: "*Gōp* muss wohl zu *gapian* 'gaffen' gehören, also 'Gaffer' bedeuten, vgl. ais. *glópr* 'Tölpel, plumper Mensch' neben *glap* 'Ungebühr,' schwed. ~ 'Ritz, Spalt, Öffnung,' *glapa* 'offenstehen'" (*ESn.* lxxiv, 325). For the possible existence of O.E. *gapian*, see under *gape* in the *OED* and also cp. O.E. *ofergapian* (B-T., p. 733). Whatever the meaning, Holthausen is certainly right when he says, "Gemeint ist gewiss der *wonna þegn* in V.4" (*ESn.* lxxiv, 325).

47.3: *gifrum lacum*: *useful gifts* or *useful streams*. Most editors take *lacum* from *lāc*, "gift," but Shook (see reference in headnote) suggests that it comes from *lacu*, "pool, stream." Either reading is possible metrically though the first would be more regular. Barnouw (*Neoph.* iii, 78) suggests *ceacum* for *lacum*, translating the phrase as "with greedy jaws," but this is certainly unnecessary. Trautmann questions Grein's reading of *gifrum* as "heilsam, nützlich," and says: "Kann *gifre* 'lecker' bedeuten? oder is *gifnum* 'gegebenen' das Echte?" (p. 109). O.E. *swelgan* may take either an accusative or an instrumental (dative) object (B-T., p. 947).

48. Fire
[*VN: Gr.51; Tr.48; Tu.51; W.50; M.50; K-D.50*]

Dietrich (*ZfdA.* xi, 475) solved the riddle as "dog," but a dog is not *torht* (line 3), nor is it *wundrum acenned* (line 1), at least no more so than man. Herzfeld (*Die Räthsel des Exeterbuches und ihr Verfasser*, p. 69) and Trautmann (*Anglia Beibl.* v, 50) solved the riddle as "fire," and this solution is accepted by all later editors.

48.2: *dumbum twam*: the flint and steel used to engender the fire. Cp. the first two lines of the Bern Riddle 23, "De Ignis Scintilla":

> Durus mihi pater, dura me generat mater,
> Verbere nam multo huius de viscere fundor.
>
> [*CCL.* cxxxiii A, p. 569]

Cp. also the first line of Aldhelm's Riddle 44, "Ignis": *Me pater et mater gelido genuere rigore* (ed. Pitman, p. 24). Tupper (p. 182) notes the glosses *ferrum* and *silex* to *pater* and *mater* respectively in the *Royal MS. 12, C. XXIII* manuscript of the Aldhelm riddle.

48.4: *Forstrangne oft*: Trautmann reads *forestrangne*, but Krapp and Dobbie rightly note that the intensifying prefix *for-* is well attested. Trautmann also reads the half-line here as part of the previous sentence. He begins a new sentence at line 5*a*.

48.5: *wrið*: B-T. (p. 1275) and all major editors except Krapp and Dobbie read *wrið* as a syncopated third person singular present form of *wriðan*, "to bind," but the meter of the half-line thus construed is suspicious (type E with light secondary accent or truncated type A: see Pope's category F3 on p. 320 of *The Rhythm of Beowulf*). Trautmann, recognizing this problem, would emend to the unsyncopated form *wriðeð*. But Sievers (*Beiträge* x, 476) and Holthausen (*Anglia Beibl.* xxx, 53) note that the form *wrið* here could originally have been disyllabic *wriheð* or *wrieð* from O.E. *wrion, wreon* (early *wrihan*), "to cover," and so Krapp and Dobbie, who note that "the reference is apparently to the covering of the fire with ashes" (p. 348). For other "hidden" disyllabic forms in the *Riddles*, see the Introduction.

48.10: *þam*: Supplied by Holthausen (*Anglia Beibl.* xlvi, 9) and accepted by Trautmann and Krapp and Dobbie. The sense of *him* in lines 5*b* and 8*b* may be carried over into the final sentence, especially if one were to place a semicolon after *lissum* (line 9*a*) instead of a period (none of the other editors who retain the MS. reading do this), but Holthausen's reading gives the passage needed clarity. The passage itself is broken in the MS. as the scribe wrote *grimme þe hi* at the end of one MS. line, *ne wloncne* at the beginning of the next.

49. Pen and Fingers
[*VN: Gr.52; Tr.49; Tu.52; W.51; M.51; K-D.51*]

Dietrich (*ZfdA.* xi, 475) solved the riddle as "dragon." Trautmann (*Anglia Beibl.* v, 50) first proposed "horse and wagon" and later (*BBzA.* xix, 195–98) "pen (and three fingers)" or simply "quill" (*die Feder*). The solution, "pen and fingers" is accepted by all modern editors. The pen would not necessarily have to be a quill, since reed pens were also known to have been used in the Middle Ages—but the riddlic motif of the birds suggests a quill pen.

The Old English riddle shares little with Aldhelm's Riddle 59, "Penna," except the motif of the black tracks (see note below). Tupper rightly points out, however, that the motif of the three fingers appears in both Riddle 30 of Aldhelm, "Elementum," and in Riddle 6 of Tatwine, "De Penna." Aldhelm describes the letters of the alphabet as born from a bird:

> . . . et volucris penna volitantis ad aethram;
> Terni nos fratres incerta matre crearunt.
>
> [Ed. Pitman, p. 16]

The three brothers are the fingers; the mother is the quill pen. Tatwine describes his pen as *vincta tribus* (*CCL.* cxxxiii, p. 173). Most of the Latin "pen" riddles are built upon the paradox of the bird-like creature that is caught and forced to travel the flat land. The Old English paradox is that the bird-like creature also dives and travels the land all in the same essential (writing) action. For other Old English riddles having wholly or partly to do with writing, see *Rids.* 24, 58, 65, 84, 89, and 91.

49.2: *swearte wæran lastas*: Cp. *sweartlast* at *Rid*. 24.11. The motif of the dark tracks also occurs in Riddle 59 of Aldhelm and in Riddle 35 of Eusebius.

49.4: *framra*: Early editors read MS. *frumra*, though Tupper (p. 38, note) remarks that "the *u* of MS. *frumra* may be an *a* with its top faintly marked." Mackie and Krapp and Dobbie rightly read MS. *framra*. It appears that the scribe may have begun to change *a* to *u*, then thinking better of his plan, to have left the *a* in the MS. with only a faint upper stroke. As for the meaning of *fuglum framra*, Trautmann says: "Stärker als der Vogel ist die Feder; denn sie trägt ihn" (p. 110). But the comparison is a more general one, and *fuglum* is in the plural. Mackie translates the phrase, "more rapid than birds" (p. 145), but I would prefer "bolder than birds." This creature flies like a bird, but it also dives and struggles on the road. Once part of a bird, it is now greater than all birds. Tupper would read *fultum* for MS. *fuglum*, taking *fultum fromra* as the subject of the sentence beginning at line 2*b* and translating the phrase as "the support of swift ones" (p. 184), which he takes to be a bird's wings. But the *fore* here is not the journey of some bird before the plucking of quills; it is the journey of the quill creature and its supporting friends. One feather could hardly support a whole bird, to say nothing of "birds."

49.4: *fleag on lyfte*: Early editors and Wyatt retain the MS. *fleotgan lyfte* assuming an adjective *fleotig*, "floating," which is unattested. Trautmann, who earlier read *fleag geond lyfte*, proposed *fleotga an lyfte* in his edition, glossing unattested *fleotig* as "fliessend, schwimmend." Cosijn (*Beiträge* xxiii, 130), Tupper, and Kock (*Anglia* xliv, 258) all read *fleag on lyfte*, which is accepted by Krapp and Dobbie and is also the reading here.

49.6: *winnende wiga*: the hand or arm of the scribe.

49.6: *wægas*: Northumbrian for *wegas*. This MS. reading is retained by Trautmann and Mackie; other editors normalize the form. For the Northumbrian form, see Campbell 328, p. 135.

49.7: *ofer fæted gold*: See the description of the gilding of vellum in the headnote to *Rid*. 24. The "Bible" creature of that riddle is *gierede* . . .

mid golde (24.13). Cp. the *hiþendra hyht* of *Rid.* 91.5, which I take to be a kenning for gold.

50. Flail?

[*VN: Gr.53; Tr.50; Tu.53; W.52; M.52; K-D.52*]

Dietrich (*ZfdA*. xi, 476) first solved the riddle as "two buckets," but Grein (*Germania* x, 308), rightly noting that the *wonfah Wale* (6a) is close to only one of the two creatures (5a; see note below), altered Dietrich's solution to "well-buckets," and so Wyatt. But there is nothing in the riddle to define the context of a well (as there is, for example, in "well sweep" *Rid.* 56), and as the creatures are brought *under hrof sales* initially, Trautmann's "flail" seems the best solution yet offered. Trautmann explains:

> Die beiden gefangenen sind der stiel und der knüppel. Sie heissen treffend gefangene, weil sie aneinander gefesselt sind. Die fesseln sind der riemen, der zwei-, drei- oder vierfach durch die öse des stieles und durch die öse des knüppels geht und so beide teile des dreschflegels mit einander verbindet. Dass beide hart sind wird niemand bestreiten. Die dunkelfarbige Welsche, die mit dem einen der gefangenen enge verbunden ist und beider weg lenkt, ist eine welsche magd oder sklavin, die den stiel des flegels in der hand hält und drischt. [*Anglia* xvii, 397]

Thus Trautmann accepts "flail" and gives up his earlier "broom" (*Anglia Beibl.* v, 50) solution. Tupper, Mackie, and Krapp and Dobbie accept "flail." The OED (iv, p. 277, s.v. *flail*) notes that the O.E. *fligel*, which occurs in the "Gerefa" (*Anglia* ix, 264, line 8) like its modern counterpart in many countries, was "an instrument for threshing corn by hand, consisting of a wooden staff or handle, at the end of which a stouter and shorter pole or club, called a swingle or swipple [was] so hung as to swing freely." Manuscript illustrations of the Anglo-Saxon flail may be found in the threshing scenes for December in "The Labors of the Months" illustrations of *MS. Cott. Jul. A. VI*, and *MS. Cott. Tib. B. V.* (see Webster, *The Labors of the Months*, plates 33b and 34b), and a representation in stone on the baptismal font in the Burnham Deepdale Church (ibid., plate 91, figure 9). It must be admitted that there is little in the riddle to define the actual process of the threshing, but the same lack of detail provides problems for almost any solution.

50.1: *ræpingas*: a variant of *ræpling*, meaning *captive* (B-T., p. 784; CH., p. 277). This is the only such spelling, but *ræpling* occurs several times in the prose. Cp. the verb, *ræpan*, *to bind* or *fetter*, and also the compound, *ræplingweard*, "warden" (B-T., p. 784).

50.3: *þa wæron genumne nearwum bendum*: *which were seized (held) by tight bonds*. The relative *þa* refers back to the *ræpingas* of line 1. The emendation of MS. *genamne* to *genumne*, past participle of *geniman*, was first suggested by Thorpe, and is accepted by B-T. (p. 420), Trautmann, Wyatt, and Mackie. The form *genumne* is a contraction of *genumene*, nominative plural masculine to agree with *þa*, the subject of the relative clause. Holthausen (*ESn.* xxxvii, 209) proposed the emendation of MS. *genamne* to *genamnan*, plural of a noun *genamna*, "namensvetter, gleichnamiger, genosse," citing O.H.G. *ginamno*. Grein (*Sp.*, p. 492) and BTS. (p. 377) accept this reading, as do Tupper and Krapp and Dobbie. Clark Hall (p. 246) lists the form *genamn* with a question as to its authenticity. The evidence for the existence of a noun, *genamn*, from the verb, *genemnan*, in Old English is slight. The two possible occurrences are here and at *Rid.* 51.13 where the MS. reading is *genamnan*. The latter case seems more likely to be a noun. The relative clause in *Rid.* 50.3 seems clearer with the reading of the past participle, *genumne*.

50.5: *Þara oðrum wæs an getenge / wonfah Wale*: *A [O.E. an] dark Welshwoman (servant) was close to one (of two)*. For uses of *an* as an article separated from the following noun by an intervening word, see Rissanen, *The Uses of "One" in Old and Early Middle English*, p. 297. For the use of *oðer* to mean "one of two" in a context where two definite objects are referred to, see B-T., p. 769 under category I. For the use of *Wale* as *slave*, see note to *Rid.* 10.4.

50.6: *seo*: Cp. the parallel use of the demonstrative as a relative pronoun in line 3 of the riddle. The relative *seo* is preceded by a comma because the clause is nonrestrictive. It explains the carrying action of the clearly defined *wonfah Wale*, who is mentioned several times in the

Riddles (10.4; 10.8; 70.12). The relative *þa* in line 3 is not preceded by a comma because the clause in that instance is restrictive. It defines the peculiarly bound nature of the mysterious *ræpingas*.

51. Ram
[VN: Gr.54; Tr.51; Tu.54; W.53; M.53; K-D.53]

Dietrich (*ZfdA*. xi, 476) solved the riddle as "battering ram" and so all later editors. Trautmann (*Anglia Beibl*. v, 50) first proposed the solution, "spear," but later in his edition accepted Dietrich's "ram." O.E. *ram* (*ramm*) occurs occasionally in the glosses either as the animal or the war tool (L. *aries* may be either), and it occurs as a war tool in Alfred's translation of Gregory's *Pastoral Care* (ed. Sweet, p. 161, line 5; p. 163, lines 10, 14–18). *Ram* does not occur in any original Old English context and there is no archaeological evidence for the existence of an Anglo-Saxon battering ram. Since, as Hollister points out, there were no Anglo-Saxon castles, and since "the very concept of a system of fortifications throughout England was a novelty which had not existed in late-Saxon times" (*Anglo-Saxon Military Institutions*, p. 141), there would have been no need for the deployment of an Anglo-Saxon ram. Presumably, knowledge of the Roman ram was passed down to the Anglo-Saxons through literary (see, for example, Vitruvius, *De Architectura* x.xiii.1) and iconographic sources. For the various kinds of Roman rams, see Keller, *The Anglo-Saxon Weapon Names*, p. 66. The ram in the riddle corresponds to the simple Roman ram "carried by the men who worked it, often consisting of a mere wooden beam with a bronze or iron ram's head at one end for battering down the walls of the besieged town" (ibid.). Aldhelm's Riddle 86, "Aries," describes in two of its lines (see below) a battering ram, but Aldhelm's riddle plays mainly upon the various meanings of L. *aries* and so bears little resemblance to the Old English riddle.

51.2: *þæt*: Omitted by Holthausen (*Anglia Beibl*. ix, 358) and Trautmann for metrical reasons. Anacrusis is very rare before type A in the off-verse but not unknown (see Pope's categories A18, A19, and A20 on p. 329 of *The Rhythm of Beowulf*).

51.8: *wæg*: Northumbrian for *weg* (Campbell 328, p. 135); the reading is retained by Trautmann and Mackie while other editors normalize the form.

51.10: *Oft hy an yst strudon*: *Often they have plundered in a storm (of battle)* or *Often they have violently plundered*. The reading was first suggested by Tupper (who emended *an yst* to *on yste*), and so Wyatt and Krapp and Dobbie (who read *an yste*) and also Mackie (who retains the MS. reading as I do). Storm imagery is often used metaphorically in battle descriptions in Old English poetry. Since *yst* is a feminine *i*-stem noun, *an yst* may be taken as preposition (*on*) plus accusative, marking manner (B-T., *on*, category B.II.(9), p. 746; *Sp.*, p. 531, second column at the top, *on neod, on ellen, on lust*). For the MS. *an yst* Grein and Assmann would read *earyst* for *earust*, "alacerrime," and Klaeber (*MP* ii, 145) would read *anys* for *anes*. Trautmann would read *anwist* in apposition to *hord*, but O.E. *anwist* means literally "being in a place" or "living in a place" and by extension "habitation," but not in a limited sense "house," or "fortress" (see the citation from *Ex.* 18 in B-T., *onwist*, p. 762).

51.11b ff.: I translate the lines as follows: "The second [man] was active and quick if the first [ram] had to risk danger (or attack) for his comrade in a tight place." The reading follows that of Holthausen (*ESn.* xxxvii, 208 ff.) who first suggested taking *genamnan* as "namensvetter, gleichnamiger, genosse" (citing O.H.G. *ginamno*) and Krapp and Dobbie. Tupper would emend *genamnan* to *genamna* and would translate, "if the first, a comrade in a tight place, had to venture into danger," and so Mackie. Earlier editors—Grein, Assmann, and Wyatt—followed Thorpe's original reading of *gif se ærra fær genam* in 12*b* (which is metrically impossible) and *nan in nearowe* in 13*a*. Trautmann would emend *genamnan* to *genumnan*, which he takes to be the genitive singular feminine form of the past participle of *geniman* and as referring to the captured fortification. Trautmann takes MS. *fǽr* for *fær*, "journey" and explains: "die Mannschaft hinten war in grosser Bewegung, wenn vorne der Kopf des M[auerbrechers] Einbruch in die Feste wagen durfte" (p. 112). The combination *fær . . . neþan* certainly seems as likely (cp. *Bo.* 13.58–59: *weg . . . geneðeð*) as *fær . . . neþan*, but the scribe has marked the long vowel with an accent in the

MS. and he is usually careful to do this when a confusion in meaning would occur without it (cp. the use of the accent in *wón* at *Rid*. 9.8).

52. Churn
[*VN: Gr.55; Tr.52; Tu.55; W.54; M.54; K-D.54*]

This delightful double entendre riddle, in which the love play is more overt than hidden, was solved by Dietrich (*ZfdA*. xi, 476) as "baker's boy and oven." Trautmann (*Anglia Beibl*. v, 50) solved the riddle as "churn," and this answer is accepted by all later editors. Wyatt points out that one is more apt to become tired (line 8*b* ff.) of churning than of baking, and Tupper notes that *"wagedan buta* seems . . . more fittingly said of churning than of the oven-feeding of the baker's boy" (p. 188). In most of the double entendre riddles the anatomical solution is more covert; the game seems to be a shared mutual understanding of the hidden meaning. Here the love play seems center stage, and one might speculate that the original game consisted of inducing the riddle-solver to guess the "wrong" solution, that is the anatomical one, in order to offer him the "plain" solution and proof of his salacious imagination.

The O.E. *cyrn*, "churn," and *cysfæt*, "cheese vat," are mentioned in the *Gerefa* (*Anglia* ix, 264, section 17, lines 8–9). The shepherd of Aelfric's *Colloquy* describes his milking and making of cheese and butter: "Ic agenlæde hig [sceap] on heora loca, *and* melke hig tweowa on dæg . . . *and* cyse *and* buteran ic do" (*Coll*. 39–41). In the Laws entitled *Rectitudines Singularum Personarum* printed by Liebermann, the following description of the cheesemaker's task is given: "Be cyswyrhte: Cyswyrhtan gebyreð hundred cyse, *and* þæt heo of wringhwæge buteran macige to hlafordes beode; *and* hæbbe hire ða syringe ealle butan ðæs hyrdes dæle" (ed. Liebermann, *Die Gesetze der Angelsachsen*, vol. 1, p. 451, section 16). The creature described in the last lines of the riddle is the O.E. *butere*, the child of the churn.

52.2: *in wincle*: The MS. reading is *Inwinc sele* (with small capital *I*), but this makes no sense. For *wincsele*, Thorpe, Assmann, and Wyatt read *winsele*, but Krapp and Dobbie note that neither a churn nor an oven would stand in the main hall, but rather in an outbuilding. Grein, Tupper, Trautmann, and Mackie read *wincle*, "corner," which is supported by a similar reading at *Rid.* 43.1 (see note to that riddle). This is the reading adopted here. Holthausen (*ESn.* xxxvii, 209) would read *staþole* for *wincsele*, but there is no need for such a radical change. Krapp and Dobbie retain the MS. *wincsele*, apparently for want of a satisfactory emendation.

52.5: *nathwæt*: See note to *Rid.* 60.8.

52.9b: Where the MS. has *þon hie ó*, Grein, Assmann, Tupper, and Mackie emend to *þonne hio*; I follow them. Wyatt reads *þonne hie o*, taking *o* as *ā*, "ever." Trautmann reads *þon hio o*. Krapp and Dobbie read *þon hio*, taking *þon* as a variant for *þonne*. The passage is clearly corrupt. Originally a tilde may have been misplaced from its position over *þon* since *þōn* is a common abbreviation for *þonne* in the *Exeter Book*. A second scribe may have changed the misplaced tilde to an accent mark. The adjective *strong* at the beginning of the half-line refers to the *þegn* or *hyse* who does the churning; the word *hio* refers to the churn, or in terms of the double entendre, to the woman in the corner. Mackie translates lines 7–10*a* as follows:

> The thane hurried; his good servant
> was sometimes useful; nevertheless, though strong,
> he always became tired, and weary of the work,
> sooner than she.

[Mackie, p. 147]

For the meaning of *ær þonne* as "sooner than" or "before," see BTS., p. 17, under *ær*, category II.(1), and cp. *Beo.* 1182*b* ff.

53. Uncertain
[*Gr.*56; *Tr.*53; *Tu.*56; *W.*55; *M.*55; *K-D.*55]

This is a difficult riddle to solve because lines 1–7*a* and 12*b*–16 seem to define some kind of weapon holder and lines 7*b*–12*a* seem to define a rood or possibly the traditional gallows with posts and a cross-bar. The relationship between the weapon holder and the gallows has never been very successfully explained. Dietrich (*ZfdA*. xi, 476) first solved the riddle as "shield," and later (*ZfdA*. xii, 237) as "scabbard." Krapp and Dobbie note that "neither of these solutions seems particularly appropriate" (p. 349). This is particularly true with respect to the composition of the creature; it is made of four woods—maple, oak, yew, and holly—and adorned with gold and silver. We know from the archaeological evidence that Anglo-Saxon shields were made of linden wood and that scabbards were lined with leather or fleece and sometimes covered with cloth (see Keller, *The Anglo-Saxon Weapon Names*, pp. 46, 67 ff.; Davidson, *The Sword in Anglo-Saxon England*, pp. 88 ff.; Bruce-Mitford, *The Sutton Hoo Ship-Burial: A Handbook*, p. 76). Wyatt believes the scabbard to have been "divided into quarters by a cross; probably each quarter was made of a different wood" (p. 106), but the structural weakness of such a hybrid should be obvious. A more typical description of a scabbard is contained in Tatwine's Riddle 30, "De Ense et Vagina":

> Armigeri dura cordis compagine fingor,
> Cuius et hirsuti extat circumstantia pepli;
> Pangitur et secto cunctum de robore culmen
> Pellibus exterius strictim, quae tegmina tute
> Offensam diris defendunt imbribus aulam.

> [*CCL*. cxxxiii, p. 197]

Trautmann's solution, "harp," is even more unlikely. The *hearpe* of *Beowulf* is now thought to have been a round lyre similar to the Sutton Hoo lyre and to that found in the seventh-century barrow at Taplow, Buckinghamshire, both of which are made of maple wood (see the Bruce-Mitfords' article in *Antiquity* xliv, 7 ff.). The pegs of the Sutton Hoo lyre were made of poplar or willow, but the instrument can hardly have been made of four woods. Two other solutions, "sword rack" and "cross," have been proposed. Liebermann (*Archiv* cxiv, 163 ff.) proposed the solution, "gallows or sword rack," based upon a hypothetical acrostic in lines 9–10. Liebermann took the initial letters of the four trees—*hlin*, *acc*, *iw*, and *holen*—and arranged them to read *ialh* (taking the *l* from (*h*)*lin* and the *h* from *holen*), which he equated with *gealg*, the compound element from *gealga* in *gealgtreow*, "gallows tree, cross." There are several problems with this reading. First, though runes are sometimes used in this game-like fashion in the *Riddles*, acrostic letters are not. Second, when the game is played it is usually announced (cp. *Rid.* 40.5ff.). Third, one must translate the *i* from the *iw* in this riddle into the *ge* from *gealg* (Liebermann cites the examples of *hiniongae* from *Bede's Death Song*) and ignore the *h* of *hlin*. Fourth, one must read *gealg* for *gealga*. Also there is no evidence in Old English literature or in Anglo-Saxon archaeology for the existence of an early English sword rack. There is no Old English word for sword rack and there are no manuscript illustrations of sword racks in any early English manuscripts that I have seen. The poetic descriptions of swords in Old English literature and the relatively small number of swords that have been found in Anglo-Saxon graves would seem to indicate that the Anglo-Saxon sword was an heirloom, at once a weapon and a jewel, a prized possession of a wealthy and powerful man, and a thing to be guarded and treasured. It is unlikely that such an heirloom would have been left in a sword rack either at home or in a neighbor's house. One might suppose that swords would be set aside in the pleasure of good company, but a number of the Anglo-Saxon laws make it clear that men wore their swords even while drinking at table. The *Laws* of Hlothære and Eadric, for example, state:

> Gif man wæpn abregde þær mæn drincen *and* ðær man nan yfel ne deþ, scilling þan þe þæt flet age, *and* cyninge XII scll'.
> Gif þæt flet geblodgad wyrþe, forgylde þem mæn his mundbyrd *and* cyninge L scill'. [Liebermann, ed. *Die Gesetze der Angelsachsen* vol. 1, p. 11]

Swords must have been kept somewhere at some times when they were not in use—probably in some kind of strong (perhaps ornamental) box or chest that could be easily and securely locked. In *Waldere*, at least, the speaker at the beginning of Fragment II speaks of a sword *ðe ic eac hafa / on stanfate stille gehided* (lines 2–3), and while this *stanfæt* could be a jeweled scabbard, it sounds more like an ornamental box (one's reading of *stanfæt* depends in part on who one takes to be the speaker of these lines; for this problem, see the notes on the lines in question in the editions of Norman and Dobbie). Still, the connection between such an ornamented swordchest and the rood or gallows of lines 7*b*–12*a* is obscure at best.

Tupper, in an attempt to explain lines 7b–12a satisfactorily, solves the riddle as "cross." For the description of the wood in lines 9–10, Tupper notes the report in Stevens's *The Cross in the Life and Literature of the Anglo-Saxons* that "Chrysostom, for example, had applied the words of Isaiah: 'The glory of Lebanon shall come unto thee, the fir tree, the pine tree and the box together, to beautify the place of my sanctuary; and I will make the place of my feet glorious' [Isaiah 60:13], to the different parts of the cross" (Stevens, p. 10). In somewhat similar fashion in the Pseudo-Bede *Flores* the cross is described:

> Crux Domini de quatuor lignis facta est, quae vocantur cypressus, cedrus, pinus, et buxus. Sed buxus non fuit in cruce, nisi tabula de illo ligno supra frontem Christi fuit, in qua conscripserunt Judaei titulum: Hic est Rex Judaeorum. Cypressus fuit in terra usque ad tabulam, cedrus in transversum, pinus sursum. [*PL*. xciv, 555]

Stevens notes that the enumeration of woods was sometimes eclectic, but it seems a far cry from these patrological descriptions to that of the Old English riddle. A more serious problem with Tupper's interpretation is that he must read *abæd* in line 12 as a strong form of a weak verb *ābǣdan*, which he defines as "ward off, restrain" (p. 241) instead of "to force, compel, demand" (BTS., p. 1). On the face of it, *abæd* would appear to come from *abiddan* and to mean "to receive" (see note to the line below). Tupper would like his cross to "ward off" weapons but that is certainly stretching both the meaning of *abæd* and the natural syntax of the line.

In short, there is no completely satisfactory solution to the riddle. My guess is that the creature is an ornamented sword box and that somehow (either by an unknown wordplay or because of some unknown similarity of function or design) the box is being compared to a gallows or rood in the riddle.

53.5: *þæs:* for *þæs þe* (with the relative particle lost by attraction?). Lines 5–6a may be translated as "and the sign of the cross of Him who raised that ladder for us to the heavens" or as "and the sign of the cross of Him who raised us to the heavens by that ladder."

53.12: *wulfheafedtreo:* *wolfshead-tree, the gallows* or *cross.* Cp. O.E. *weargrod* and *weargtreow.* Tupper (p. 191) notes that *wulfesheafod* was "the legal expression for an outlaw, who may be killed like a wolf, without fear of penalty," and quotes the laws of Edward the Confessor (chap. 6.2): *Lupinum enim caput geret a die utlagationis suae, quod ab Anglis wluesheved nominatur.*

53.12 ff.: I translate beginning at line 12*b*: "That (creature) often received a weapon for its lord, a treasure in the hall, a gold-hilted sword." This follows the reading of Toller at BTS., p. 2, under *abiddan*, category IV.(3). Grein (*Sp.*, p. 32) took *abǣd* as the equivalent of *abǣdeð* meaning "adigere, exigere," and so B-T., p. 2, and Tupper, p. 192. But none of the occurrences of *abǣdan* in BTS. (p. 1) fit the meaning, "to repel or restrain," and these citations also indicate that the proper third-person form of the verb ought to be *abǣdeð* (present) or *abǣd(d)e* (past). Neither Grein nor Tupper gives an explanation of the form for the weak verb. Herzfeld (*Die Räthsel des Exeterbuches und ihr Verfasser*, p. 60) and Madert (*Die Sprache der altenglischen Rätsel des Exeterbuches und die Cynewulffrage*, p. 44) take *abǣd* as a dialectical form of *abēad* without explanation. But if the form *abēad* is required, it would be better to emend the text and to assume that the scribe confused the form of *abēodan* with the form of *abiddan*.

53.14: *þisses gieddes*: For metrical reasons, Tupper and Wyatt read *gieddes þisses* after a suggestion by Herzfeld—but for other examples of alliteration on the final stress, cp. *Rids.* 1.66, 2.8, 38.5, 57.12, 71.2, and 87.6. Holthausen would supply *mon* or *secg* after *gieddes* (*ESn.* xxxvii, 209; *Anglia Beibl.* xlvi, 9).

53.15: *on mede*: B-T., following a suggestion by Thorpe, read this as one word, *onmede*, from a hypothetical verb, *onmedan*, defined as "to take upon one's self, to presume" (p. 756), apparently related to O.E. *onmedla*, "pride, glory." This reading is accepted by Tupper, Wyatt, Mackie, and Cosijn (*Beiträge* xxiii, 130). But other editors have noted that *on* must take a primary stress of its own because of the metrical and alliterative demands of the line. Grein (*Sp.*, p. 458) takes *medan* as "impers. *muten, in mentem venire.*" Trautmann (p. 176) glosses *medan* as "gelusten(?)." Toller (BTS., p. 634) takes *hine* as the object of *on* and translates the phrase *hine on mede* as "gives courage to himself" (literally, "puts courage into himself"). Similarly Krapp and Dobbie take *medan* as a verb related somehow to *mōd* and take *on* as a prepositional adverb bearing stress and alliteration, citing similar examples at *Guth.*

373, *Jul.* 277, and *Beo.* 41. Sedgefield (*MLR* xvi, 61) would emend the phrase to *him ne ormede*, "despairs not," but since the verb *ormedan* does not occur elsewhere, this hardly solves the problem of the line.

54. Web and Loom
[*VN: Gr.57; Tr.54; Tu.57; W.56; M.56; K-D.56*]

Dietrich (*ZfdA.* xi, 476) solved the riddle as "web and weaver's loom," and this is accepted by Tupper, Mackie, and Krapp and Dobbie. Lange solved the riddle as "turning lathe" (see *ZfdA.* xii, 238, note); Trautmann, as "flail." Wyatt accepts Trautmann's "flail." There is little in the riddle to suggest the threshing of grain. Of the *Daroþas* in line 4, Trautmann says: "*Daroþas* . . . sind leichtere *gāras*, somit ein treffender bildlicher Ausdruck für Halme" (pp. 115–16). Wyatt explains this further by translating, "The spears of straw were a misery to the flail" (p. 107), but one might expect the threshing flail to torment the grain. Dietrich's explanation of the loom in terms of the language of the riddle is somewhat more cogent. Drawing upon the account of the old weaver's vertical loom in Olaus Olavius's *Oeconomische Reise durch Island*, Dietrich illuminates the riddlic description:

Die *winnende wiht* ist das gewebe, und zwar der senkrecht vom baume, dem alten jugum, herabhängende und durch steingewichte unten angespannte aufzug, dessen oberes ende um den baum gewickelt und daher *bîfäst* ist (v.7), dessen unteres ende aber, welches desto mehr hinaufrückt, je mehr fertig gewoben und oben aufgewickelt wird, sich bei der arbeit bewegt (*bisgo dreág*), denn es schwebt in der luft (*leólc on lyfte* v.8) und ist nur im anfang dem boden nah. dieser aufzug nun erleidet dreifache kampfesnoth. erstlich durch das hin- und hergehende krumme holz (*holt hwearfende*), welches den eintragsfaden durchführt, aber noch kein schiff, sondern ein einfaches holz (*wido*) ist, und zwar ein *wudu searwum fäste gebunden* . . . weil der faden künstlich darum gebunden ist, altn. heisst es *vinda*. zweitens empfängt der eintrag wundenschläge (v.3) durch das schlagbret, altn. *skeið*, ein schwertähnliches bret, welches der weber in freier hand schwingt, um den eingetragnen faden fest zu schlagen. drittens sind auch speere (*daroðas*) weh dem wesen, denn mitten durch den leib des aufzugs stecken fünf queer durchgehende stäbe, woven die drei obersten die schäfte heissen, denen noch der scheideschaft und das scheidebret folgt. der mit hellem laub (v.9) behangene baum ist der obere balken, worauf die wulste des noch ungewobenen aufzugsgarnes hängen. das überbleibsel des kampfes ist das gewebe, welches, etwa als *gafolhwîtel*, in die herrenhalle gebracht wird. [*ZfdA*. xii, 238–39, note 7]

In the main, I agree with Dietrich's description of the working loom, though I take the *wido* (line 2) or *holt hweorfende* to be a shuttle skillfully bound (*searwum . . . gebunden*) by the woof to the web, and no piece of "simple wood." I also agree with Erhardt-Siebold that "the two feet [lines 6–7] can only be the weighted ends of the two rows of warp-threads" ("The Old English Loom Riddles," in *Philologica: The Malone Anniversary Studies*, ed. Thomas A. Kirby and Henry Bosley Woolf, p. 15).

Dietrich (*ZfdA*. xi, 476) also points out the similarity between the riddlic description of weaving and the spinning song of the Valkyria in chapter 157 of *Njal's Saga* (ed. *Jónsson*, pp. 413–14). Another warlike description of weaving is to be found in Book 6 of Ovid's *Metamorphoses* where a weaving contest between the Maeonian Arachne and Pallas occurs:

> Haud mora, constituunt diversis partibus ambae
> et gracili geminas intendunt stamine telas:
> tela iugo vincta est, stamen secernit harundo,
> inseritur medium radiis subtemen acutis,
> quod digiti expediunt, atque inter stamina ductum
> percusso feriunt insecti pectine dentes.
> utraque festinant cinctaeque ad pectora vestes
> bracchia docta movent, studio fallente laborem.
>
> [*Met*. vi.53–60]

54.2: *wido*: a variant accusative singular of *wudu*, "wood." Tupper notes that the regular Northern form would be *wiodu*. Campbell (218, p. 92) notes the form *uuidu-* in the *Epinal Glossary* and Bosworth-Toller lists the form *uuido* at *Cod. Dip. B.i.*344,11 (B-T., p. 1277). The form *widu* occurs at *Bo*. 13.55.

54.3–4: Normally *fon* takes an accusative object, but for another instance of *fon* with the genitive, cp. *Sol.* 434.

54.5: *weo*: Dietrich (*ZfdA*. xii, 238, note) explained *weo* as a variant of *wēa*, and so Mackie and Krapp and Dobbie. I accept this reading. Wyatt reads *wēa* in the text. Grein (*Sp.*, p. 816) took *weo* as a form of *wōh* translated as *"iniqui, nachteilig."* Tupper apparently accepts this reading. Lange emends *weo* to *wið* (see *ZfdA.* xii, 238, note). Trautmann queries: "Doch ist nicht *weo* verderbt aus *wic* (*wic>wio>weo*)?" (p. 116).

54.6–8: Dietrich saw the two feet described here as the upper and lower ends of the web in the loom. Trautmann rightly doubted this interpretation. The feet, as Erhardt-Siebold makes clear, are the weighted ends of the warp threads, a row on each side of the lower separating rod of the loom. Erhardt-Siebold explains that "one of these ends or feet 'stands still,' whereas, in successive shedding operations, the other foot 'moves up and down near the ground'. . . . Consequently, what our poet in line 1 says he saw, must have been a web in a loom with a parting-plank and a single leash-rod" ("The Old English Loom Riddles," in *Philologica: The Malone Anniversary Studies*, ed. Thomas A. Kirby and Henry Bosley Woolf, p. 15).

54.12: *þara flana*: The reading here follows that of Tupper and Mackie. The genitive is governed by *lafe* in line 10*b*. For the MS. *þara flan*, Grein and Wyatt read *þara flangeweorca* and Holthausen (*Anglia Beibl.* xxxvi, 219) reads *þara flanþraca*, but one might expect the singular rather than the plural form of a compound utilizing -*geweorc*. Krapp and Dobbie read *þara flana geweorc*, taking *geweorc* as a parallel accusative noun with *lafe* in line 10. But *laf* is used more often in the *Riddles* with a genitive. The creature in *Rid.* 69, for example, is called *wraþa laf*, *| fyres ond feole* (69.3–4), and the creature "shield" in *Rid.* 3 is said to feel the bite of those *homera lafe* (3.7)—swords. For the meter of the half-line as here emended (A3), see Pope's category 64 on p. 264 of *The Rhythm of Beowulf*.

55. Swallows
[*VN: Gr.58; Tr.55; Tu.58; W.57; M.57; K-D.57*]

Many solutions have been proposed for the dark-coated creatures of this riddle. Dietrich first proposed "swallows" or "gnats" (*ZfdA.* xi, 477), and later "starlings" (*ZfdA.* xii, 239). Trautmann first proposed "hailstones" (*Anglia Beibl.* v, 50), then "raindrops" (*Anglia* xvii, 397 ff.), then "storm clouds" (*BBzA.* xix, 200), and finally in his edition, "swifts." Brett (*MLR* xxii, 257 ff.) and more recently Erhardt-Siebold (*PMLA* xlii, 1–8) proposed "jackdaws," and Garvin proposed "bees" (*Classica et Mediaevalia* xxvii, 294–95). Tupper prefers the solution, "swallows," while Wyatt likes Dietrich's "gnats or midges." Shook most recently ("Riddles Relating to the Anglo-Saxon Scriptorium," in *Essays in Honour of Anton Charles Pegis*, pp. 225 ff.) proposed "musical notes" (penned on a page), which seems a trifle far-fetched. Krapp and Dobbie believe that "only those [solutions] which involve birds are at all worthy of consideration" (p. 351), and I agree.

Several of the descriptive words or phrases of the riddle are used typically to describe birds: *lyft byreð*, *cirmað*, and *salopade*. The *lyft* bears the swan in *Rid.* 5.4, and also the barnacle goose in *Rid.* 8.9. The nightingale sings, *hlude cirme*, in *Rid.* 6.3. Wyatt argues that O.E. *cirmað* might well describe the wing vibration of gnats, while Garvin (*Classica et Mediaevalia* xxvii, 294 ff.) holds out for the humming of bees. The citations for *cirman* in B-T. (p. 156) do not support either contention. Enemies, armies, birds, and beasts cry out with O.E. *cirman*. The initial element, *salo-*, of *salopade* is used typically in compounds to describe birds (see note to *Rid.* 55.3 below). It should be noted that bees are ringed with color, that gnats have no bountiful song and that musical notes though black do not inhabit wooded headlands or chirp about the hills.

The birds indicated by the riddle are *lytle wihte* (line 1). This phrase could not apply to Erhardt-Siebold's "jackdaws," which are by her own reckoning, "13 to 14 inches long and have a wingspread of 8.6 to 9.5 inches" (*PMLA* xlii, 5). The birds in the riddle are small and dark-coated; they travel in swarms. They nest on hillsides or in the houses of men. These gregarious birds could only be swallows whose fondness for man-made structures is well known. A. L. Thomson describes the swallows in terms appropriate to the riddle:

> Swallows are rather small birds, ranging from 3¾ to 9 inches (a good deal depending on the proportion of the tail). . . . The plumage, especially on the upper parts, tends to be dark—black, brown, green, or blue, often with a metallic luster. . . . They are gregarious birds, sometimes very markedly so, and the flocks roosting together before autumn migration may be of immense size. . . . Another point of evolutionary interest is the extent to which some

species have become dependent on man-made structures for their nesting sites. Although some species use either the natural or the artificial site, according to circumstances, others practically never use anything except a building. [*A New Dictionary of Birds*, p. 791]

The common distinction in classical literature between *hirundo agrestis* and *hirundo domestica* is noted by Jacques André in *Les Noms d'Oiseaux en Latin* (pp. 92–93). When Pliny speaks of field swallows, he makes the following distinction: "Alterum est hirundinum genus rusticarum et agrestium quae raro in domibus diversos figura sed eadem materia confingunt nidos" (*NH.* x.xlix.93).

It is perhaps the domesticity of those swallows that "*tredað . . . hwilum burgsalo | niþþa bearna*" (lines 5–6) or at least man's accessibility to their haunts that accounts for their place in the Anglo-Saxon *Leechdoms*. Swallows' nests, their ashen bodies, and at one point small stones from the maws of fledglings are described as important ingredients for herbal or ritual cures (*Lch.* ii.100, 156, 306; iii.44). Certainly the swallows' melodious songs were known to the inhabitants of Anglo-Saxon halls. This is perhaps the tradition upon which the writer of the *Life of St. Guthlac* draws in describing: "Hu ða swalawan on him sæton and sungon. . . . Twa swalewan heora sang up ahofon and hi setton on ða sculdra ðæs halgan weres Guðlaces" (quoted in B-T., p. 944, and in Whitman, *JEGP* ii, 161).

55.1: *Ðeos lyft byreð:* Cp. *Rid.* 5.4 where the swan is lifted by its *hyrste . . . ond þeos hea lyft;* and *Rid.* 8.9 where the barnacle goose is raised: *mec . . . lyft upp ahof.* Shook takes *Ðeos lyft* not as "wind, air, or sky," but as "'this thing which lifts' and which is not in this case the air but the musical scale, the ledges or other devices by means of which a scribe records the rise and fall of musical notes" ("Riddles Relating to the Anglo-Saxon Scriptorium," in *Essays in Honour of Anton Charles Pegis*, pp. 225–26), but the reading is highly doubtful in light of the fact that *lyft* everywhere else in Old English refers to the actual air or atmosphere in one of its guises (see the citations in B-T. and the categories of meaning outlined in BTS.).

55.2: *beorghleoþa: hillsides* or *cliff faces.* In compounds, initial *beorg-* can mean either *hill* (cp. *beorgstede*) or *mountain* (cp. *beorgseðel*). Either habitat is a possible nesting place for swallows. Mackie translates *beorghleoþa* as "steep hills" (p. 149); Baum, as "headlands" (p. 21); Crossley-Holland (*Storm*, p. 26), as "hill-slopes."

55.2: *blace: black.* Baum (p. 21) takes *blace* for *blāc*, "bright," instead of for *blæc*, but the meter will not sustain Baum's reading.

55.3: *salopade: dark-coated.* The word is a hapax legomenon, but cp. *saloneb* (*Rid.* 47.5), *sealobrun* (*Finn.* 35), and *sal(o)wigpad* (*Fort.* 37; *Jud.* 211; *Brun.* 61). All of the compounds but *saloneb* refer in all cases to birds.

55.3: *Sanges rope: bursting with song* (literally, *bountiful of song*). Krapp and Dobbie note that "for the MS. *rope*, Thorpe suggested *rowe*, 'gentle'. . . . Grein in a note proposed *rofe*. . . . Neither *rofe* nor *rowe* is very appropriate here" (p. 351). Bosworth-Toller mention the gloss, *roopnis*, for L. *liberalitas* (WW. 30.27) and define *rop* as *liberal, bountiful* (p. 802). Another gloss, *ropnes* for L. *liberalitas*, occurs at WW. 433.7.

55.5–6: Swallows were well known in classical times for their habitation in the halls of men. Cp. Virgil's description in an epic simile:

> Nigra velut magnas domini cum divitis aedes
> pervolat et pinnis alta atria lustrat hirundo,
> pabula parva legens nidisque loquacibus escas,
> et nunc porticibus vacuis, nunc umida circum
> stagna sonat.
>
> [*Aeneid*, xii.473–77]

55.6: *Nemnað hy sylfe:* Mackie translates, "Name them," and Tupper reads with Thorpe, "Name them yourselves." Krapp and Dobbie read with Brett (*MLR* xxii, 257 ff.), "They name themselves." Thus they take the bird's name to be an onomatopoeic representation of its song. Erhardt-Siebold (*PMLA* xlii, 1–8) and Garvin (*Classica et Mediaevalia* xxvii, 294–95) argue for the onomatopoeic names of **ca* (unattested for *jackdaw*) and *beon* (*bees*) respectively. Since the riddle-solver is normally addressed in the singular, the use of the plural verb here would tend to support the reading, "They name themselves." Admittedly O.E. *swealwe* does not imitate the swallows' chirping, but we know so little about alternative bird names that the Anglo-Saxons may have used that it seems unwise to base a solution primarily upon an onomatopoeic name. Shook (see reference above) maintains that musical notes (do, re, mi, etc.) "name themselves," but this is not strictly true either in the penned form (where the notes are voiceless symbols of man-made or instrumental tones) or in the sung form (where the tones are uttered but do no uttering).

56. Well Sweep
[*VN: Gr.59; Tr.56; Tu.59; W.58; M.58; K-D.58*]

Dietrich (*ZfdA.* xi, 477) solved the riddle as "der ziehbrunnen" or "draw-well," and this answer is accepted by most editors. Tupper gives the solution, "well with well-sweep"; Wyatt and Mackie, "riding-well." Holthausen (*Indogermanische Forschungen* iv, 387) was the first to note that the riddle describes not so much the well as the "well sweep" and this solution is accepted by Krapp and Dobbie and more recently by Blakeley (*RES* n.s. ix, 247 ff.). Blakeley notes that the well sweep, which is still common in many European countries, "consists of a long beam pivoting on an upright support, which is nearer one end than the other; to the end of the longer, but lighter, part of the beam is attached a pole or a rope which carries the bucket up and down in the well, and the other end of the beam is weighted to help in raising the bucket" (ibid., p. 248). There is still editorial disagreement as to the name of the creature indicated in lines 14b–15 of the riddle (see note below). The riddle has nothing in common with Riddle 71, "Puteus," of Symphosius.

56.5: *naca nægledbord*: For a discussion of Anglo-Saxon nailed clinker ships, see the headnote to *Rid.* 17.

56.14b: For metrical reasons Holthausen (*Anglia* xxxv, 166) would add *me* or *min* after *naman* or he would read *naman in* instead of *in naman*, and Trautmann would read *þry in naman sind*; but for other (admittedly rare) A1 verses with short stressed penult, see Pope's *Rhythm of Beowulf*, p. 272, nos. 100, 101, and p. 333, nos. 98 and 99.

56.15: *forma*: Trautmann retains the MS. *furum* but notes "*furum* ist sinnlos"; other editors emend. Grein (in a note) first suggested *fruma* or *forma* and later (*Germania* x, 308ff.), *fultum*. Mackie accepts *fruma*; Wyatt and I, *forma*; Tupper, *fultum*. Dietrich (*ZfdA*. xi, 477) suggested *furðum*; Holthausen (*Indogermanische Forschungen* iv, 387), *furma*. Krapp and Dobbie read *foran*. The emendation is determined in large part by one's reading of the last two lines. Some think that *Rad* is meant to indicate the rune ᚱ, and that the name of the creature has three letters beginning with R. Holthausen's *rōd*, "rod," is the most likely candidate. Normally O.E. *rōd* does not mean "rod" as in modern English, but the word does occur once in the Homilies—*Ðone Iacobum Iudæa leorneras ofslogan mid webwyrhtan rode* (cited in BTS., p. 689)—and in the compound *seglrod* at *Ex.* 83. Another word *rodd*, presumably the precursor of modern English "rod," occurs in a twelfth-century homily (cited by Campbell in his *Addenda* to BTS., p. 53, and by the *OED* under *rod*, category I.2), but this word has one letter too many for the name in question here. Other editors take the word *rad* to be the initial element of a compound in which the last element would have three letters. Thus Grein (*Germania* x, 308) argues for the solution *radpyt*, "riding-well," but *radrod*, "riding-rod, sweep?" might be more appropriate since it is the pole and not the pit that is the subject. Blakeley (*RES* n.s. ix, 247ff.) argues for the solution, *radlim*, "moving beam," which he takes to be the well sweep. Blakeley derives the word *lim* from the riddle itself in the following curious fashion: he believes that the runes ᛚ, ᛁ, and ᛗ are indicated from the names *lagu*, *is*, and *mon*, which occur as elements in the words *lagoflod* (line 12), *isernes* (line 9), and *mondryhtne* (line 6). To this one may object that *mon* in line 6 is an editorial interpolation, that runes are not used elsewhere in the *Exeter Book* as hidden components of other words, and that the obvious possibilities of *dæg* in line 4 must be ignored. Dietrich's earlier reading (*ZfdA*. xi, 477) of *þry . . . ryhte runstafas* as the three consonants in the word, *burna*, is also not very likely—especially since O.E. *burn* (*burna*) refers generally to moving water and not to a well or well sweep (B-T., p. 136).

57. Chalice
[VN: Gr.60; Tr.57; Tu.60; W.59; M.59; K-D.59]

Dietrich's solution, "chalice" (*ZfdA*. xii, 235, especially note 2), is accepted by all editors except Trautmann who doubts the solution but offers nothing better in its place. For a discussion of the *huselfatu* of the mass, the reader is referred to the headnote to *Rid*. 46. I take the *wunda* of line 16 to be carvings on the creature—letters or icons that inspire faith and that enable the dumb creature to "speak" of Christ before the congregation:

> Word æfter cwæð
> hring on hyrede, hælend nemde
> tillfremmendra.

[*Rid*. 57.5–7]

Presumably the letters or icons, the metaphoric wounds of the creature, must have been visible to the worshipers in order to have inspired faith. The creature could only be a large gold chalice, similar perhaps to the Tassilo chalice, an eighth-century gilt-bronze vessel of English or Anglo-Carolingian style (see David Wilson, *The Anglo-Saxons*, p. 141, and plate 61). The Tassilo chalice is elaborately carved with letters, designs, and icons. Its "wounds" are an ornate articulation of the Christian message.

57.4: *nergende*: For the use of the uninflected form of the participle where *nergendne* might be expected, see SB. 305 Anm. 1, p. 245.

57.9: *æþelestan*: The emendation follows Holthausen (*Anglia Beibl*. ix, 358) and Tupper for metrical reasons. Trautmann supplies *he* after *æþelan*. Other editors leave the half-line short as it is in the MS. For the meter of the line as emended here, see Pope's category C11, pp. 350–51 of *The Rhythm of Beowulf* and cp. *El*. 1106*b*, *þær þa æðelestan*, and *El*. 1024*a*, *mid þam æðelestum*.

57.11 ff.: Grein read lines 11–12 as follows:

> dryht dolgdon...........
> swa þæs beages benne cwædon.
> Ne mæg þære bene [to þæs beages dolgum]

Wyatt and Mackie read *dryhten dolgen* in line 11*a* and indicate a second ellipsis where Grein supplied the bracketed reading. Trautmann reads:

> dryht[maðmes] dolg.   Don swa þæs beages
> benne cwædon: ne mæg þære bene

taking *Don* as an optative, "Let us do." Tupper reads:

> ond Dryhtnes dolg,   don swa þæs beages
> benne cwædon.   Ne þære bene mæg

and translates lines 7–12*a* as follows: "Brightly into his [the worshiper's] mind the dumb thing (the Chalice) brought the name of the Lord, and into his eyesight, if he [the worshiper] was able to perceive the token of the very noble gold and the wounds of the Lord, (and) do just as the wounds of the ring proclaimed" (p. 198). Presumably the reference here is to letters or icons on the chalice that may direct the worshiper to the proper prayerful frame of mind. Krapp and Dobbie accept Tupper's reading though they retain the MS. reading in line 12*b* (as I do) with the unusual alliterative pattern. Holthausen (*Anglia* xxxviii, 78), like Tupper, would emend for purposes of proper alliteration, but he reads *þære bene ne mæg*. There is no reason to assume that the alliterative rules were not occasionally broken. Cp. the final alliterative stress at *Rids.* 1.66, 2.8, 53.14, 71.2, and 87.6. The midverse break after *mæg* in 12*b* is unusual but not unknown (for other examples, see the note to *Rid.* 41.8). Tupper translates lines 12*b* ff. as follows: "The prayer of any man being unfulfilled, his spirit can not attain to (seek) God's city. . . . " (p. 198). For the reading of *ungefullodre* in 13*b* as "unfulfilled," see *Sp.*, p. 739, and B-T., p. 1107. This reading is accepted by all major editors. Cosijn (*Beiträge* xxiii, 130) would read *ungefullodra* for MS. *ungafol lodre*, translating as "of the unbaptized."

58. Reed Pen? Rune Staff?

[*VN: Gr.61; Tr.58; Tu.61; W.60; M.60; K-D.60*]

This riddle occurs on folios 122*b* and 123*a* of the *Exeter Book* and directly precedes the poem now called *The Husband's Message*. The scribe has punctuated the riddle and the three main sections of *The Husband's Message* (lines 1–12, 13–25, and 26–53 in the Krapp and Dobbie edition) alike (with a large beginning capital and elaborate end-punctuation), so it is difficult to know whether he at least took the four verse sections to be four different poems, parts of the same poem, or parts of different poems. As there is some similarity between the beginning lines of the riddle as printed here (and as printed by all major editors) and *The Husband's Message*, and as there are resemblances between the speakers of the two poems (whether the speaker of *The Husband's Message* is a personified *beam* or a human agent is still a matter of some debate), some critics have argued that the two poems (or four MS. poems) are actually one. The most notable proponents of this theory are Blackburn (*JEGP* iii, 1–13) and Elliott (*JEGP* liv, 1–8) who argue that the poems comprise a love letter or perhaps a rune staff sent by a husband or estranged lover to the unidentified woman of the poem, and Kaske (*Traditio* xxiii, 41–71) who sees the poem as a speech of the cross with the following three (allegorical, moral, and anagogical) senses: "as an address by the Cross to the Church following the Atonement, as a special and strongly hortatory vision of the Cross granted to an individual, and as an appearance of the Cross in the role of celestial convoy" (*Traditio* xxiii, 70). Kaske's argument, a symphony of patrological learning, simply stretches the details of the combined texts so far as to be beyond belief; a good example of his fancy footwork is his explanation of the references to water in lines 1–2 and 6–7 of the riddle as the stream running by either the Tree of Knowledge of Good and Evil or the Tree of Life in the Garden of Eden (for the employment of what Greenfield calls the "fallacy of similarity" in Kaske's argument, see *The Interpretation of Old English Poems*, chapters 1 and 6). Whether the speaker of the riddle is a reed pen or a rune staff is a debatable point, but the speaker of *The Husband's Message* seems clearly human. Leslie lists the following reasons against taking the speaker of *The Husband's Message* as a personified *beam* and in favor of taking him as a human messenger:

First, he has been in the habit of making frequent voyages (*Hus.* 6), behaviour not reconcilable with a particular rune-stave, whose significance is for the one voyage from the husband to his wife. Secondly, the speaker's reference to the man *se þisne beam agrof* (*Hus.* 13) suggests that the speaker and the rune-stave are not one and the same person, especially since the speaker has already referred to himself directly as *mec* in line 3. Thirdly, the terms he uses of his master, *mondryhten min* (*Hus.* 7), *mines frean* (*Hus.* 10) and *min wine* (*Hus.* 39), indicate a lord and retainer relationship with which the limited and temporary nature of a rune-stave appears incompatible. Finally, in lines 30 ff. the speaker is recounting what the husband told him—*þæs þe he me sægde* (*Hus.* 31); the verb *sægde* is much more appropriate to a human messenger than to a rune-stave whose function is essentially the conveyance of a written message. [*Three Old English Elegies*, pp. 13–14]

Greenfield (*The Interpretation of Old English Poems*, pp. 145 ff.) essentially agrees with Leslie's reading.* The relationship between the personified speaker of the riddle and the intended reader is an impersonal and general one—the references to *unc* and *þe* facilitate the riddlic

*In an article that appeared too late to be included in the discussion here, Margaret Goldsmith ("The Enigma of *The Husband's Message*," in *Anglo-Saxon Poetry: Essays in Appreciation*, ed. Lewis E. Nicholson and Dolores Warwick Frese, pp. 242–63) argues that the speaker of both riddle and lyric (which she reads as one poem) is "the Reed, symbolizing primarily Holy Writ, the word of God" and that "the Reed's own life, dramatically severed from its place of origin and given a more than human power in the new life, is a similitude of the central theme of the poem that man, born in 'the world,' must be re-born in the life of the spirit and then follow Christ to His Kingdom" (p. 261). The argument is too long and complicated to be rehearsed in the space of a note; it suffers some of the same deficiencies as Kaske's but is in the main much more convincing.

Since Leslie, Kaske, Greenfield, Goldsmith, and others who deal with the two poems argue about the meaning of the runes in *The Husband's Message*, I should briefly set forth my own reading of the runes in that poem. The runes are pointed so as to indicate compound words in the first two instances and a single word in the third. I take ᚻ and ᚱ to indicate *sigelrad*, "sun-road," and ᛦ and ᛈ to indicate *earwynn*, "sea-joy" (for the possibilities of *ear* as a runic name meaning either "sea" or "soil," see Elliott, *JEGP* liv, 4), and ᛗ to indicate *mon*, "man." The passage is deliberately enigmatic (though within the context of a personal lyric poem), and I solve the puzzle within the poem as "ship." The mini-riddle of the runes may be stated thus: "What flies through the heavens, takes joy in riding the sea, and bears man?" The structural similarities between this runic puzzle and the runic "ship" *Rids.* 17 and 62 should be clear. The man and the sea are common elements; the hawk of the runic riddles here has a "sun-road" through which to fly; the runic horse is missing here but the necessary notion of traveling the sea and sky is carried by the runic *-rad*. The question of why the poet in *The Husband's Message* chooses to end his poem in such a runic and riddlic fashion remains to be answered. Though I do not entirely agree with the apocalyptic reading put forward by either Kaske or Goldsmith, I do sense that the lord of this poem has passed beyond the mere confines of middle-earth so that perhaps the riddlic ship is no mere ship of reunification but a ship of the dead, either mythic or real. Could one not imagine the magic runes of the poem carved into a staff and placed on board a ship like the one at Sutton Hoo?

game. The *ic* and *þe* of *The Husband's Message* both have past histories, present personalities, and contemplated future actions (all bound up with the lord)—they seem to have a psychological reality that the personae of the riddle do not. In the one poem we are interested in what the characters represent (so that we may solve the riddle); in the other we are interested to know who the characters are and what the human relationship between them has been and will be.

All major editors print the riddle separately as I have printed it in this edition. Dietrich (*ZfdA.* xi, 477) solved the riddle as "die rohr-flöte" or "reed flute," citing the influence of Symphosius's Riddle 2, "Arundo":

> Dulcis amica dei, ripae vicina profundae,
> Suave canens Musis; nigro perfusa colore,
> Nuntia sum linguae digitis signata magistris.
>
> [Ed. Ohl, p. 36]

Leslie (*JEGP* lxvii, 453) notes that "the first six and a half lines of the Old English poem are much more vivid and detailed than their brief counterpart in Symphosius (l. 1b), whose influence upon our poet has been considerably exaggerated." The Symphosius riddle describes a reed that is used both as a pen and as a flute. Tupper, following a suggestion by Edward Müller (*Die Rätsel des Exeterbuches*, p. 18), believed the same to be true of the Old English riddle, primarily on the basis of lines 7–10. But Leslie comments:

> In the first place, a reed pipe can hardly be described as mouthless; in the second place, *wordum wrixlan* is a highly stereotyped phrase, which refers either to conversation, as in *Beowulf*, 366, or to the composing of verse, as in *Beowulf*, 874. In all probability we have here the paradox of a pen communicating without a mouth, and of both presenting a communication, and being communicated to, by the writer. [*JEGP* lxvii, 454]

For the motif of the mouthless communicator that appears in a number of Latin and Old English riddles having to do with writing, see the note below. With the possible exception of the partly interpolated *meodu*[*bence*] in Tupper's reading, there is nothing in the riddle that would indicate that the creature is a musical instrument.

Most editors then solve the riddle, partly after Dietrich, as "reed" or "reed pen" (so Tupper, Trautmann in his edition, Wyatt with some reservations, Mackie and more recently Leslie, *JEGP* lxvii, 451 ff., and

Whitman, *PQ* l, 180 ff.). Trautmann had first (*Anglia Beibl.* v, 50) solved the riddle as "rune staff" following the suggestion of Strobl (*ZfdA.* xxxi, 55 ff.) and anticipating the reading of later editors who saw the poem as part of *The Husband's Message*. The collocation in line 13 of *eorles ingeþonc ond ord somod* and the immediately resulting message (14 ff.) would tend to support "rune staff" since the activity that requires the thinking (and thus presumably the making of the message) is the cutting itself. But the cutting could conceivably refer to the fashioning of the reed pen, and the habitat of the creature (in or near the water) certainly favors "reed." The fact that the creature itself speaks in the hearer's presence might tend to favor "rune staff," though certainly by extension the pen as well as the author might be said to "speak" through the medium of the written word. The fact that the message seems to be an extended one of personal nature might tend to indicate the written word, but much can be made of a few runes (as readers of the literature on *The Husband's Message* well know).

Several of the solutions put forward in the past may, I think, be discounted. Morley's (*English Writers*, vol. 2, p. 38) "letter-beam cut from the stump of an old jetty" is little more than a restatement (however surreal) of the terms of the riddle. Colgrave and Griffiths (*MLR* xxxi, 545 ff.) believe that the riddlic creature is not a rune staff or a piece of wood but a piece of the kelp-weed, *Laminaria digitata*, an alga with a thick stem, a suitable substance, they note, for the cutting of runes. Apparently the weed may be incised when wet; when the weed is dry the incisions disappear and then reappear when the material is wetted again. Though Colgrave and Griffiths tried the process of kelp-carving and found it to be suitable for the sending of runic messages, they cite no medieval evidence for the weed's having been used in such a fashion. Furthermore, there is in the language of the riddle no indication of ghost-like disappearing and reappearing runes nor is there any indication of the cyclic wetting and drying process. The rune-weed is a product of the moderns' boundless imagination.

58.1–2b: Colgrave and Griffiths (*MLR* xxxi, 545 ff.) argue that these lines define a creature of the sea, but Leslie (*JEGP* lxvii, 452–53) notes that "*Sæwealle* (l. 1) is as likely to mean 'shore' as 'cliff' [he cites *Beo.* 1924 as an example]; many of the contexts of *faroð* refer rather to shore than to sea [BTS., p. 206]; and *mere* may be a lake as well as the sea, as in the references to Grendel's mere in *Beowulf*." Leslie notes that the habitat described here may be "the brackish water of a coastal marsh, beside the sand and near the seashore," which is the ideal habitat of the reed *Phragmites communis* (*JEGP* lxvii, 453). Blackburn, who takes the riddle to be part of *The Husband's Message* (see headnote) says of the initial description here: "The location of the tree from which the wood for the letter was taken suggests a particular kind of wood suitable for the purpose, perhaps willow or swamp cedar" (*JEGP* iii, 7, note).

58.9: *ofer meodubence*: The MS. has *ofer meodu*, but the sense and meter demand something more. Grein first proposed in his edition to read *ofer meodubence*, and so Tupper, Mackie, Krapp and Dobbie, and myself. This reading is sometimes used in support of the "reed flute," but for another kind of "message" used in a similar context, cp. *Rid.* 65.13–15 where the riddler describes a book:

> Ic þæt oft geseah
> golde gegierwed,   þær guman druncon,
> since ond seolfre.

Grein later (*Germania* x, 429) proposed the reading *ofer meodudrincende*, and so Assmann and Blackburn (*JEGP* iii, 6). Wyatt proposed reading *ofer meodusetla* (acc. pl.); Trautmann, *ofer meoduwongas*; and Wrenn (see Kaske's note 70 at *Traditio* xxiii, 67), *ofer meodubyrig*; but there is no certainty that *ofer* would take the accusative here, since the idea of motion across is not very strong.

58.9b–10a: The motif of the "mouthless speaker" is a common one in riddles of writing subjects. References abound in both Old English and Latin. The book in *Rid.* 65 *nænne muð hafað* (65.6) and yet it "speaks." The book in *Rid.* 91 travels far and makes wisdom known to men; yet it *sceal . . . no þær word sprecan / ænig ofer eorðan* (91.9–10). The "letters" of Riddle 7 of Eusebius sing: *Et licet alta loquamur, non sonus auribus instat* (*CCL.* cxxxiii, p. 217). The "parchment-sheets" in Riddle 32 of Eusebius say: *Antea per nos vox resonabat verba nequaquam, / Distincta sine nunc voce edere verba solemus* (*CCL.* cxxxiii, p. 242).

58.14 ff.: The interpretation of these lines varies greatly according to the solution proposed and according to whether or not one reads the riddle as part of *The Husband's Message*. If the solution to the riddle is "rune staff" (whether or not it is part of the other poem), the *þe* is presumably the wife or lover who is the recipient of the message. If the solution is "reed pen," then the pen must metaphorically "speak" to the lady through the written word. With either solution the *þe* could conceivably refer to the reader and the *unc* to the reader and riddlic creature together. In these terms it requires the words of two (personified message and reader together) who *wordcwidas . . . mænden*. Leslie (*JEGP* lxvii, 456–57) rightly notes that there are similar dramatic games played in other riddle conclusions (cp. *Rids.* 34 and 37), but he interprets the passage somewhat differently. He takes the speaker (*ic*) to be the reed pen who is addressing its writer (*þe*), the two together constituting the *unc* of line 15.

59. Helmet? Shirt?
[*VN: Gr.62; Tr.59; Tu.62; W.61; M.61; K-D.61*]

Riddle 59 begins the second major section of riddles in the *Exeter Book*. These include *Rids.* 59–91, which occur consecutively on folios 124*b*–130*b* of the manuscript. Between *Rid.* 58, which ends on folio 123*b*, and this riddle, which begins on folio 124*b*, are the poems, *The Husband's Message* and *The Ruin*.

Dietrich (*ZfdA.* xi, 477) solved the riddle as "shirt"; Trautmann, as "shirt of mail" (*Die Brünne, Das Panzerhemd*). Tupper believes a "shirt or kirtle" was intended and notes the lusty double entendre. Wyatt solves the riddle as "helmet" on the basis of lines 5–6 and 9*a*, but as one may stick a head into a shirt as well as a helmet, it seems best to list both solutions as equally possible. The thing that is *ruwes nathwæt* in line 9*a* may be either a chest or a head; in fact, in terms of the double entendre game being played it makes little difference which "acceptable" solution is given. The point is to recognize the game or perhaps in the riddler's terms to catch the solver out.

59.5: Wyatt notes rightly that O.E *stician* as a transitive verb normally means "to stab, pierce," and as an intransitive verb means "to stick, remain fast" (p. 111). So Grein (*Sp.*, pp. 307, 636) and Wyatt take *heafod* to be the subject of intransitive *sticade* here ("his head stuck fast into my 'breast'"), but the verbs *sticade* (5b) and *fegde* (6b) seem to be parallel and surely the subject of both is the *frea* (3b) who dons the riddlic creature. Thus Tupper, Trautmann, and Mackie take *heafod* to be the object of transitive *sticade* ("he stuck his head into my 'breast' and fixed me on tightly . . . ").

59.7 ff.: I translate as follows: "If the zeal of the receiver endured, something hairy had to fill me thus adorned." For the MS. *þe mec frætwedne*, Grein, Assmann, and Wyatt retain *þe* and emend *frætwedne* to *frætwede*, reading *þe mec frætwede* as "who adorned me." Tupper, Mackie, Krapp and Dobbie, and I retain MS. *frætwedne* and drop the *þe*. This seems to make better sense of the passage. Trautmann reads *þe mec frætwede*, but takes *frætwede* as an accusative singular feminine participle because his solution, "mail coat," O.E. *byrne*, is feminine. But Wyatt (pp. xxxv ff.) points out the many inconsistencies in the *Riddles* with regard to gender, so an emendation of this sort is unnecessary.

60. Borer
[*VN: Gr.63; Tr.60; Tu.63; W.62; M.62; K-D.62*]

The literal solution to this delightful double entendre riddle appears to be a boring tool of some sort. Dietrich (*ZfdA*. xi, 478) first solved the riddle as "der bohrer des zimmermanns," and Wyatt believes that "some boring tool is intended" (p. 110). Trautmann solved the riddle as "der Brandpfeil," by which he meant a burning arrow shot from an *arcubalista* or crossbow, but Swaen (*Neoph.* xxvii, 220) notes that "first of all 'Brandpfeile' were not shot from arbalests (crossbows), and secondly this weapon makes its first appearance in England in 1079." For a discussion of Anglo-Saxon slings and their shot, see the headnote to *Rid.* 15. Tupper mistakenly took Trautmann's "Brandpfeil" to mean "poker or fire-rod" (p. 202) and accepted this as the solution to the riddle. Mackie and Krapp and Dobbie also accept "poker," as does Swaen (*Neoph.* xxvii, 220). There are several problems with the solution, "poker." A poker might be *heard* but not necessarily *scearp*. There is no reason that a poker should be described as clearing for itself a path (*me weg sylfa / ryhtne geryme*) through a narrow place (*on nearo nathwær*). These descriptions are more suitable to a boring tool of some kind. Tupper takes the *hrægle* of line 6 to be a man's garment that he wraps around the poker on account of the heat, but it could just as easily refer to a piece of cloth used to handle the hot bit or end of the boring tool. In either case the use of the word *hrægl* is appropriate largely in terms of the double entendre solution to the riddle.

The Old English words for "borer" are *bor*, *nafubor*, *nafugar*, and perhaps *timbor* or *lynibor* (for the last two see Quinn, *PQ* xlv, 435; Toller, BTS. p. 726, thinks that *timbor*, a gloss for *rotum uel taratrum* [WW. 273.8], may be an error for *tyrnbor*, and I would agree; the legitimacy of *lynibor*, a misplaced lemma in *MS. Cotton Cleopatra A III* remains in doubt despite Quinn's arguments). The word *næfebor* occurs in the *Gerefa* list (*Anglia* ix, 263.3); the others occur in the glosses (see WW. 1.7; 44.11; 45.26; 50.25; 106.16; 220.3; 227.25; 241.6; 273.8; 273.9; 273.12–13 [?]; 333.36; 386.26; 408.39; 550.24; and *Leo.* 121 and *Cot.* 63, cited in B-T., p. 116). For information on boring-bits and other Anglo-Saxon woodworking tools, see David Wilson's "Anglo-Saxon Carpenters' Tools" listed in the Bibliography.

60.1: *hingonges: going forth.* The word sometimes means metaphorically "death," but here it is to be taken rather more literally as it is appositive to *forðsiþes* in line 2. The MS. reading of *Ingonges* (with a small capital *I*) makes perfect sense as it stands but it leaves the line without alliteration. The emendation here is made by all editors.

60.7: *fereð*: This verb is parallel with *tyhð* in 6*b*; the subject of both is the *hæleð* of 6*a*, and the object is the *mec* of 5*a*, the creature. For the MS. *fareð*, which makes little sense, Grein suggested *fegeð*. Wyatt reads *fare ic*; Mackie, *fereð*. Other editors retain the MS. reading.

60.8: *nathwær*: The reference is typically obscure in order to facilitate the double entendre. Cp. a similar use at *Rid.* 23.5 and also the use of *nathwæt* at *Rids.* 43.1, 52.5, and 59.9.

60.9: *superne*: Trautmann takes this as "die Südländerin, d.i. die aus dem Süden stammende *arcubalista*" (p. 121), thus taking the adjective as a substantive noun and the object of *nydeþ*. Other editors take the implied object of the sentence to be the creature of the riddle and read *superne secg* as "the southern man." It is not clear why the wielder of the boring tool (or in terms of Tupper's solution, of the poker) should be a "southern man," but Tupper guesses that "as the actor in one of the obscene riddles, 'the southern man' is obviously in the same class as 'the dark-haired Welsh,' the churls and esnes, often people of un-English origin, who figure in these folk-products" (p. 203). There is, of course, no reason to assume that all double entendre riddles derive from folklore. Conceivably, the *superne secg* here could be related in meaning to the *superne gar* at *Mald*. 134, but the meaning of *superne* in that context is also much in doubt. There is one other admittedly remote possibility here, namely that the word *superne* (modifying either the *secg* or the implied *mec* of the riddle) is meant to indicate somewhat obliquely the direction of the thrust. Such uses are not uncommon in double entendre jokes.

61. Beaker
[*VN: Gr.64; Tr.61; Tu.64; W.63; M.63; K-D.63*]

Dietrich (*ZfdA*. xi, 478) solved the riddle as "beaker," citing the influence of Aldhelm's Riddle 80, "Calix Vitreus." The initial lines of the Aldhelm riddle trace the geological history of the glass and have nothing in common with the Old English riddle. The theme of the beautiful creature held and kissed by man is, however, common to both riddles. Aldhelm says in lines 5–9 of his riddle:

> Nempe volunt plures collum constringere dextra
> Et pulchre digitis lubricum comprendere corpus;
> Sed mentes muto, dum labris oscula trado
> Dulcia compressis impendens basia buccis,
> Atque pedum gressus titubantes sterno ruina.

[Ed. Pitman, p. 48]

The motif occurs in a similar context at *Rids*. 28a and 28b with reference to a wooden cup.

Dietrich's solution is accepted by all editors except Trautmann who initially offered the solution, "flute" (*Anglia Beibl.* v, 50), and later changed to "flask or can" (edition, p. 121). The last lines of the riddle, however fragmentary, appear to indicate that the drinking vessel was made of glass. The creature at line 10*a* cannot conceal something, presumably its contents; at line 11*b* the likely restoration would give us [*siþþ*]*an on leohte*, "when in the light." The liquid of the beaker may also be *getacnad* or even [*to*]*r*[*h*]*te getacnad* at line 14*a*.

Glass beakers are a common find in Anglo-Saxon graves. Wilson notes:

> Glass of Anglo-Saxon type, made both in Britain and on the Continent, is found in some profusion [in Anglo-Saxon graves]. The commonest forms are the squat jars and the palm cups; less common are the bag beakers, and only two examples are known from this country of glass drinking-horns (both from Rainham, Essex). These rarer types, as well as the slightly more common, but hideous, claw-beakers, were almost certainly manufactured on the Continent and imported into this country by the wealthy. It is a noticeable feature that many of the glass vessels found in graves of the pagan period will not stand upright—a feature which can be observed in the later manuscripts, and in the Bayeux tapestry, where glasses are seen to lie and not stand on the table. [*The Anglo-Saxons*, p. 105]

The drinking virtues of a glass that will not stand upright on the table should be obvious. For illustrations of Anglo-Saxon glassware, the reader should see Wilson, ibid., p. 103; Page, *Life in Anglo-Saxon England*, p. 153; and De Baye, *The Industrial Arts of the Anglo-Saxons*, plates xiv–xv.

61.1–2: Taking *secgan* as a late West Saxon dative plural (see Campbell 378, p. 157, and 592 note 4, p. 224, for the ending), I translate: "Often I must fittingly be of service to men in (their) hall-joy." All other editors except Trautmann emend MS. *secgan* to *secga* apparently translating as does Mackie: "Often I must be of good service to men's joy in the hall." Trautmann emends to *secga an* and reads:

> Oft ic secga   an seledreame
> sceal fægre onþeon. ...

61.11: On paleographical evidence alone, the word before *on leohte* was probably *siþþan* or something very close to that.

61.14–15: The line arrangment here follows that of Trautmann, Mackie, and Krapp and Dobbie. Other editors read ...]*te getacnad* at the end of line 14 and begin a new line with *hwæt*, reading a longer lacuna than is indicated in the manuscript. The missing passage at the end of line 13 (as printed in this edition) is not longer than 20 spaces; the passage at the end of line 14 and beginning of line 15, not longer than 10. Grein, Wyatt, and Tupper read each lacuna as covering the space of two half-lines, but since a normal half-line is 15 to 18 spaces, this reading is hardly supported by the manuscript spacing.

62. Ship
[*VN: Gr.65; Tr.62; Tu.65; W.64; M.64; K-D.64*]

This riddle is a companion piece to *Rid*. 17, another "ship" riddle. Both riddles bear runic reference to a strange horse carrying a man and a bird on a journey. The runes of this riddle are to be read, according to the system first outlined by Hicketier (*Anglia* x, 597ff.), as the initial letters of the words indicating the disguised characters. I take the runes to indicate the words: wic*g*, be*orn*, ha*foc*, þe*gn*, fæ*lca*, and eas*por*. The runic wic*g*, like the runic hors of *Rid*. 17, is a *sundhengest* or *ȳðmearh*, an Anglo-Saxon sailing vessel similar to the one discovered at Sutton Hoo. Old English kennings for *ship* commonly utilize an element for *horse* (cp. *brimhengest, merehengest, wæghengest, sæmearh, lagumearg*). The runic be*orn* or þe*gn* of this riddle, like the runic mon or wega (wiga) of *Rid*. 17, is the seaman or warrior who rides on the ship. The runic ha*foc* or fæ*lca* (*falca*), like the runic haofoc of *Rid*. 17, is the bird-like sail. A ship is elsewhere described as "*fug(o)le gelicost*" (*An*. 497; *Beo*. 218). The ship of *Rid*. 34 has "*tu fiþru*" (34.7) but is "*na fugul ana*" (34.9). The metaphoric ha*foc* is described in this riddle as *þryþa dæl* (line 4), *a share of the power*. Bruce-Mitford points out that Anglo-Saxon ships, like their Viking contemporaries, were presumably driven by both oars and sails (*The Sutton Hoo Ship-Burial: A Handbook*, pp. 47–50). Bede mentions the ship of Guthfrith, which had both oars and a sail (*EH*. v.i, p. 454). Thus the sail or metaphoric ha*foc* would only be *þryþa dæl*. The sail is also described here as *hæbbendes hyht* (line 3), *the lifter's joy*, a kenning for *sail* with reference to the hoisting mast. The form *hæbbendes* is usually taken as a present participle from *habban*, but it may come from *hebban* as well (see spellings under both headings in B-T., and also CH. under *hæbb-*). Grein lists the phrase *daraõ hæbbende* from *Jul.* 68 (K-D. print this as *daraõhæbbende*) as a present participial use of *hebban* (*Sp.*, p. 322). Grein also lists the compound element *-hæbbende* in several instances for the same compound under both *habban* and *hebban*. The word *hyht* plus a genitive is also used for a kenning at *Rid.* 91.5. The two creatures, mast and sail, are often found together in Old English poetry. Thus, the *Maxim* poet says, "Mæst sceal on ceole, / segelgyrd seomian" (*Max.II* 24–25), and the boat of Beowulf is defined in typically recognizable terms: "Þa wæs be mæste merehrægla sum / segl sale fæst" (*Beo.* 1905–6). The runic EASP should indicate, by analogy with the other runic groups of the riddle, one word and not two, as most editors would have it (see note below for the various readings). I take runic EASP for EASP*or*, the water-track or sea-trail of the ship's wake. O.E. *easpor* is unattested, but the elements are common and *ea* is commonly compounded. The runic EASP*or* has no runic counterpart in *Rid.* 17, but it does correspond referentially at least to the *widlast . . . rynestrong* of *Rid.* 17. Both riddles end with a riddlic reference to the sea. The single track of the ship's wake is implied in the description of the "ship" at *Rid.* 30.6–8 which must *on anum fet* travel far—*swiþe feran, / faran ofer feldas*. My translation of *Rid.* 62 is as follows:

> I saw a horse (WIcg) going over the plain, carrying a man (BEorn). A hawk (HAfoc) was for both on that journey the lifter's joy and also a share of the power. The warrior (þEgn) rejoiced; the hawk (Fælca) flew over the water-track (EASPor) of the whole company.

Several other solutions to the riddle have been proposed, none of them wholly appropriate to the text. Grein (*Germania* x, 309) read all of the runes together (with an emendation of runic D for þ) as *aspide-uf* and *beah*, a snake-eating bird and serpent. Dietrich (*ZfdA.* xi, 479 ff.) read with the same emendation *pea beah-swifeda*, "der ringgeschweifte pfau." Trautmann's solution, "Wicg, bern, haofoc, þew" (p. 122) is a restatement of the literal terms of the riddle. Tupper's solution, "a man upon horseback with a hawk on his fist" (p. 108) is based on a seventeenth-century analogue that bears no structural re-semblance to the Old English riddle in question. Erhardt-Siebold's "falconry" solution (*PMLA* lxiii, 6) is a summary term for Trautmann's literal restatement. Erhardt-Siebold takes runic þEow, however, "to be a dog and not a man servant" (*PMLA* lxiii, 6). Eliason (*SP* xlix, 553ff.) solves the riddle as "writing," taking EASPoru as "ink-tracks." Eliason interprets "the horse bearing a man and hawk as the three fingers and pen tip, upon which rests the hand and over which is the pen plume" (*SP* xlix, 560). Wyatt notes that "the riddle is still unsolved, though it offers no guerdon of immortality" (p. 112). Krapp and Dobbie remark that "regardless how we interpret the runes in detail, it is clear that this riddle is a companion to Riddle [17], with the same characters, the man, the horse, and the hawk" (p. 368). According to the solution outlined above, the man is a sailor, the horse is a ship, and the hawk is a sail. Together they travel leaving one sea track for the whole com-pany.

62.right margin: In the right-hand margin near Hickes's penciled markings, five runes are scratched in dry-point: ᛒ ᚢᚾᚱᚦ (see plate XVII). These runes were noted by Förster (*The Exeter Book of Old En-glish Poetry*, p. 64) and by no other editors. The runes have never been photographed until now. The runes were transliterated by Förster as B UGRÞ but the shortness of the slanted stroke in the third rune makes the reading B UNRÞ more likely. There are no Old English words like either collocation of letters, but R. I. Page suggested mischievously in a private communication that the runes might stand for *Beo unreþe*, which I take as a frustrated scribe's (and jokester's) comment upon the absurd difficulty of the runic riddle: "Don't be cruel!" There is no indication of the runes in the MS. copy made by Robert Chambers in 1832 (*Brit. Mus. Add. MS. 9067*), but there is little doubt that the runes are genuine, so Chambers must have overlooked them with most other readers of the MS.

62.1: · ᚹ· *ond* · ᛁ· : transliterated *W ond I*, to be read according to the system proposed by Hicketier (*Anglia* x, 597ff.) as the initial letters of the hidden word, WIcg. This reading is generally accepted by all editors.

62.2: · ᛒ· ᛗ· : transliterated *BE*, to be read as the initial letters of ʙᴇ*orn*. This reading is generally accepted. Trautmann (*Anglia* xxxviii, 369) reads ʙᴇ*rn* as a Northumbrian form.

62.3: *hæbbendes hyht*: *the lifter's joy*, a kenning for *sail* with reference to the *hæbbende* or *mast* (see discussion in headnote above). Initial *hæbb-* may be a form of either *habb-* or *hebb-*. Thus two translations are possible: "the owner's joy" (Mackie, p. 205; Baum, p. 55), or "the lifter's joy." The reading, "owner's joy," does not seem to me to be particularly defining in terms of any of the proposed solutions. The "lifter's joy" certainly helps to define the runic ʜᴀ*foc* as a sail.

62.3: · ᚻ· *ond* · ᚠ· : The MS. pointing of runes in this riddle (see Introduction on "Manuscript Punctuation") indicates that the runes are to be taken singly for their individual letter values, and according to a system first outlined by Hicketier (see headnote) as the initial letters of words indicating the disguised characters. The runes here are transliterated *H ond A*, to be read as the initial letters of ʜᴀ*foc*. A similar runic ʜᴀᴏꜰᴏᴄ occurs at *Rid.* 17.7–8 as part of another ship-creature. For the ʜᴀ*foc* as metaphoric sail, see the headnote to this riddle and also the headnote to *Rid.* 17. The runes here as elsewhere are presumably to be read with their Old English runic names (for the names, see Elliott, *Runes*, pp. 48–49). Thus read, the runes facilitate the alliteration of the lines; but here as elsewhere in the *Riddles* (cp. *Rid.* 17) where runic passages occur, there are a number of metrically irregular lines (for a discussion of this problem, see "A Note on the Runes" in the headnote to *Rid.* 17).

62.4: *swylce þryþa dæl*: *and also a share of the power*. Anglo-Saxon ships, like their Viking contemporaries, were presumably powered by both oars and sails (see headnote). English boats depicted in the Bayeux tapestry show the use of poles, oars, and a sail as powering devices (Stenton, *The Bayeux Tapestry*, plate 5). Bede mentions the ship of Guthfrith that had both oars and a sail (*EH.* v.i, p. 454). Thus the sail might aptly be described as *þryþa dæl*. Cp. the *tu fiþru* (sail) and *feowere fet* (oars) of *Rid.* 34.

62.4: · ᚦ· *ond* · ᛗ· : transliterated *Þ ond E*, to be read as the initial letters of ᚦ*ᴇgn*. This ᚦ*ᴇgn* is merely a repetition of the runic ʙᴇ*orn*, as runic ᴡᴇɢᴀ (ᴡɪɢᴀ) is a repetition of runic ᴍᴏɴ in *Rid.* 17. Trautmann (*Anglia* xxxviii, 369) reads þɛw as a Northumbrian form. Holthausen (*ESn.* li, 187) reads þɛow as does Mackie. Other editors generally accept Hicketier's þɛgn.

62.5: · ᚠ· *ond* · ᚫ · transliterated F *ond* Æ, to be read as the initial letters of Fᴁlca or perhaps FAlca. For the difficulty of transliterating vocalic runes, see Page, *ES*, xliii, 484ff., and also the "variant" readings of runic HAOFOC and runic WEGA in *Rid.* 17. The runic Fᴁlca is a repetition of runic HAfoc above, as runic þɛgn is a repetition of runic BEorn. Hicketier (*Anglia* x, 598ff.) supports his reading FAlca by analogy with O.H.G. *falko* and by reference to the name *Westerfalca* in an Anglo-Saxon genealogy. The genealogy reads: "Wilgils Westerfalcing, Westerfalca Sæfugling, Sæfugel Sæbalding" (ed. Thorpe, *The Anglo-Saxon Chronicle*, vol. 1, p. 30, *Cott. Tib. A VI*). Holthausen (*ESn.* li, 187) reads FUgol with emendation of runic Æ to U, or Fᴁhðe (*Anglia* xliv, 349) with *ond* inserted before MS. *fleah*, or Fᴁle (*Anglia* xlvi, 55), an unattested bird whose mythical existence is supported only by a misreading of *Christ* 645: *se fæla fugel*. See also next note. The midverse break after *gefeah* in 5a is unusual but not unknown (for other examples, see the note to *Rid.* 41.8).

62.5–6: · ᛠ / ᛋ· *ond* · ᛈ· : transliterated EA S *ond* P, to be read as the initial letters of a single word which I take to be EASPor or water-track, the wake of the ship. Normally there should be a point between the first two runes and Krapp and Dobbie rightly note (p. xxiii) that the lack of a point here marks the single exception to an otherwise consistent scheme of MS. pointing for runes in the *Exeter Book*. Usually runes that occur in groups marked off by points at either end are to be read as words with the letters in reverse (cp. *Rid.* 17), but the reading SEA does not give much meaning here and the leaving of a single rune ᛈ to indicate another word is not in keeping with the practice established by the other runic references in this riddle. Some editors take the runes to indicate two words, one beginning with EA and the other with SP, but there is no paleographical justification for this either in this riddle or elsewhere. It seems best to follow the usage set in previous instances in this riddle and to read the runes here as the initial letters of the word indicated. The word *easpor* is unattested in Old English, but the elements are common and *ea* is commonly compounded (cp. *eafisc, eagang, eahstream, earisc*). O.E. *spor* appears in the compound *fotspor* (*Lch*. iii.286.3) and with a genitive of reference either to the creature making the track (*wulfes spor*) or to the substance in which the track is made (*spor landes*; see the examples cited in B-T., p. 903). Other editors read the runes as indicating different words. Hicketier (*Anglia* x, 599 ff.) reads EA and sPEArhafuc. Trautmann reads EArh and sPere. Tupper follows Trautmann; Wyatt follows Hicketier. Holthausen reads EArd and sPed (*ESn*. li, 187), or EArd and sPor (*Anglia* xliv, 349), or EArdas and sPed (*Anglia* xlvi, 55). Later (*ESn*. lxxiv, 327), Holthausen reads EArdas and sPere adding *swa* at the beginning of line 6a; reading FÆre as genitive singular feminine of *faru* in 5a, he translates the last two lines as: "Er (der Habicht) freute sich der Fahrt flog wie ein Speer über die Wohnstätten des Volkes selbst." But neither the use of runes to indicate a word in an oblique case nor the separation of the last runic group into two seems likely. Eliason (*SP* xlix, 559–60) reads EA and sPoru as appositives: "*ea* (line 5) is the ink, i.e., the writing, also called the *sporu* (line 6) of the group, *sylfes þæs folces*." Runes, however, are not arranged elsewhere in the *Exeter Book* in this fashion to indicate a pair of appositive words.

63. Onion
[*VN: Gr.66; Tr.63; Tu.66; W.65; M.65; K-D.65*]

Dietrich first solved the riddle as "onion" (*ZfdA*. xi, 480), citing Symphosius's Riddle 44, "Cepa," as a possible source. The solution is accepted by all editors though Trautmann maintains, "Der Zug *ær ic wæs, eft ic com* [sic] lässt sich besser auf den Lauch, und zwar den Schnittlauch, als auf die Zwiebel anwenden" (p. 123). Tupper notes that only the final motif of the Old English riddle, that of "the biter bitten," is found in the Symphosius riddle. The Latin of Symphosius is:

> Mordeo mordentes, ultro non mordeo quemquam;
> Sed sunt mordentem multi mordere parati.
> Nemo timet morsum, dentes quia non habet ullos.

[Ed. Ohl, p. 76]

Lines 1–2 of the Latin correspond to lines 6–7 of the Old English. Line 3 of the Latin riddle has no parallel in the Old English; lines 1–5 of the Old English riddle have no parallel in the Latin. Dietrich explains the significance of the initial motif of the Old English riddle:

> Die zwiebeln werden in dem jahre wo sie gesät sind der hauptmasse nach nicht brauchbar, sie müssen in einem zweiten jahre wieder in die erde gelegt werden, um die gehörige grösse zu erlangen; daher hier vom sterben die rede ist und vom wiederkommen aus einem früheren vorhandensein. [*ZfdA*. xi, 480]

The onion at *Rid*. 23 is also described as a slain slayer, though in a somewhat different vein.

63.1–2: These lines are highly, perhaps deliberately, eccentric. The riddler seems to have been ruled by rhetorical conventions of antithesis and paradox to the point of ignoring traditional Old English metrical norms. Herzfeld (*Die Räthsel des Exeterbuches und ihr Verfasser*, p. 55) would read verses 1*a* and 2*a* as hypermetric—1*a* as hypermetric B and 2*a* as "vielleicht zum Typus D," but Whitman (*NQ* ccxiii, 203) notes that the inclusion of two parallel antithetical clauses separated by a caesura within the limits of a single half-line is most unusual. Midverse breaks, though rare, do occur elsewhere in Old English poetry (some are listed in the note to *Rid*. 41.8). Of verse 1*b* Herzfeld says, "Mit dem Halbvers . . . weiss ich nichts anzufangen" (p. 55). Whitman believes that the traditional line division here is incorrect or that the lines represent somehow "a clumsy expansion of some Latin line, probably hexameter" (*NQ* ccxiii, 203). But there is nothing in either *Rid*. 33 or *Rid*. 38, both translations from the Latin of Aldhelm, which would provide an analogue to such a clumsy handling of a Latin line. One might conceivably arrange the first two lines as three in the following manner:

> Cwico wæs ic— ne cwæð ic wiht;
> cwele ic efne seþeah. Ær ic wæs;
> eft ic cwom. Æghwa mec reafað,

This arrangement too has its drawbacks since it introduces two trisyllabic half-lines and a number of other metrical irregularities. It places the main stress in *cwele ic efne seþeah* on *efne* instead of *cwele*, which runs counter to normal metrical expectation and also to the rhetorical expectation set up by the pattern of the preceding phrases (*Cwico . . . ne cwæð . . . cwele*). The only other possible reading of the lines would be one postulating 1*b* and 2*b* as single half-lines somewhat similar to the O.N. *ljóðaháttr* described by Bliss (*NQ* ccxvi, 442 ff.). The lines might read:

> Cwico wæs ic— ne cwæð ic wiht;
> Cwele ic efne seþeah.
> Ær ic wæs; eft ic cwom.
> Æghwa mec reafað,

The general pattern of this rearrangement of the lines is exactly that of the *ljóðaháttr* stanza, but in Old Norse continued alliteration is rare while double alliteration in the single half-line is common (Bliss, *NQ* ccxvi, 443). There is in *Widsith* 59 ff. something like the tripartite pattern postulated above if we would rearrange the *Widsith* lines as follows:

> Mid Wenlum ic wæs   ond mid Wærnum
> Ond mid wicingum.
> Mid Gefþum ic wæs   ond mid Winedum
> Ond mid Gefflegum.
> Mid Englum ic wæs   ond mid Swæfum
> Ond mid Ænenum.

[Wid. 59–61]

This arrangement does not always give alliteration in all three half-lines, or even in two, but alliteration would be a special problem with any list of names. One distinguishing feature of the *Widsith* passage is that the single half-line always functions as a variation of the preceding two half-lines. This is not the case in the riddle where rhetorically *æghwa mec reafað* belongs not with what precedes it but with what follows. In short, there is no absolutely satisfactory way of arranging the lines and no easy way of explaining the metrical oddities except to chalk them up to a poet with some notion of rhetorical conventions and some radical ideas about breaking the rules of Old English meter.

63.3: *headre*: a variant of *heaðre*, from *heaðor*, "confinement" (see BTS., p. 526, and *Sp*., p. 306). Krapp and Dobbie note a similar variant, *hador*, at *Beo*. 414. Cp. *heaþore* at *Rid*. 18.13.

63.5: *nymppe*: All editors except Trautmann and Krapp and Dobbie normalize the form to *nympe*. Krapp and Dobbie cite a note to a similar form, *yrmpðu*, at *Chr.* 614, which they say "should stand as an interesting phonetic variant with intrusive *p*, as in Mod. Eng. *warmth*" (p. 252). Cp. the form *nybðe* in the *Vespasian Psalter* cited by Sievers (SB. 187 Anm., p. 151).

64. Creation
[*VN: Gr.67; Tr.64; Tu.67; W.66; M.66; K-D.66*]

Conybeare (*Illustrations of Anglo-Saxon Poetry*, p. 213) first solved the riddle as "the omnipresent power of the Deity, comprehending at once the most minute and most vast portions of his creation," but Dietrich's simpler "creation" (*ZfdA*. xi, 480) has been accepted by all modern editors. Dietrich noted similarities between this riddle and *Rid.* 38 and thought that the shorter version was based upon lines 61 ff. of Aldhelm's "Creatura" (*ZfdA*. xi, 480; *ZfdA*. xii, 235; the Aldhelm riddle is printed in the headnote to *Rid.* 38). Herzfeld (*Die Räthsel des Exeterbuches und ihr Verfasser*, pp. 6–7) regarded *Rid.* 64 as a condensed form of the entire *Rid.* 38. Tupper (p. 164) believes that this riddle displays no knowledge or use of Aldhelm's Latin, nor of the first section (lines 1–81) of *Rid.* 38, but that it is a "very free reshaping of some of the material" furnished by the hand in *Rid.* 38.82–97. The *hondwyrm* appears in both poems (and may have been inspired in each case by the Latin *exiguo, sulcat qui corpora, verme* in line 66 of Aldhelm), but apart from that it is difficult to say whether the grander sentiments of *Rid.* 64 were inspired by *Rid.* 38, Aldhelm's "Creatura," or both. At any rate this "creation" riddle is shorter than its predecessor and less bound to the recurrent notion of paradoxical pairs. To be sure the creature is *mare* (1a) and *læsse* (2a), but it is also *leohtre* (2b) and *swiftre* (3a) without being either "darker" or "slower."

64.2: *hondwyrm*: See note to *Rid.* 38.96.

64.8: *ofer engla eard*: Cp. the flight of the divine and inscrutable Christ-bird at *Chr.* 645 ff.:

> Swa se fæla fugel   flyges cunnode;
> hwilum engla eard   up gesohte,
> modig meahtum strang,   þone maran ham,
> hwilum he to eorþan   eft gestylde,
> þurh gæstes giefe   grundsceat sohte,
> wende to worulde.

> [*Chr.* 645–50]

65. Bible
[*VN: Gr¹.X; Gr².68; Tr.65; Tu.68; W.67; M.67; K-D.67*]

This riddle fragment was not edited by Thorpe or Grein, and Dietrich made no comment upon it. Trautmann's solution, "Bible," is accepted by Tupper. Mackie lists the possibilities, "Bible," and "cross." Wyatt says: "The readable passages of this mutilated riddle give no reasonable clue to the solution" (p. 113). But the great teacher, *leoda lareow* (line 10), which speaks to men without a mouth (line 6) and which is richly adorned with gold and silver (lines 14–15), can only be a religious book, presumably the Bible. The riddle shares a number of common themes with "Bible" *Rid.* 24. The making of medieval manuscripts is discussed in the headnote to that riddle. For other riddles wholly or in part about writing materials, the reader should see *Rids.* 24, 49, 58, 84, 89, and 91.

65.2 ff.: For the various reconstructions of the lacunae, the reader should see Krapp and Dobbie, pp. 368–69. As all of the readings are editorial speculation, I have not produced them here.

65.6: For the motif of the mouthless creature who speaks wisdom, cp. Eusebius's two riddles, "De Littera" (Riddle 7) and "De Membrano" (Riddle 33), which are quoted in the headnote to *Rid.* 91.

65.14: *golde gegierwed*: Cp. the "Bible" creature of *Rid.* 24, which is *gierede . . . mid golde* (24.13), and the "pen" of *Rid.* 49, which travels *ofer fæted gold* (49.7). See also the description of the gilding of vellum in the headnote to *Rid*. 24.

66. Iceberg

[*VN: Gr¹.68; Gr².69; Tr.66,67; Tu.69; W.68; M.68; K-D.68,69*]

In the MS., lines 1–2 appear to be one riddle; line 3 appears to be another. Two riddles are printed by Thorpe, Trautmann, and Krapp and Dobbie on paleographical evidence alone. All other editors print the three lines as one riddle on the basis of formal evidence within the text. Tupper and Wyatt point out that by analogy with *Rid*. 34.1–2, the opening two lines appear to be a formulaic introduction and nothing more. I concur with this. Short riddles must have well-wrought tricks; otherwise they fail. The trick in this riddle is the variation from the general *on weg* (line 1), "on the way," to the specific *on wege* (*on wǣge*), "in the water" (line 3), which along with the paradox in line 3*b* is meant to elicit the solution *iceberg*. Tupper notes that "the double meaning of *wĕg* thus serves the riddler's turn" (p. 208). It matters little that the iceberg is treated in somewhat different fashion elsewhere (*Rid*. 31). Certainly the same creature may have a variety of treatments (see, for example, the various ship riddles and the onion riddles with or without double entendre). For other instances of one riddle appearing paleographically as two, cp. *Rids*. 1, 73, and 76 as printed in this edition. In two places the scribe has copied two riddles together as one (*Rids*. 40 and 41 and *Rids*. 45 and 46). All editors who print this riddle as two riddles readily admit that the first, lines 1–2, hardly constitutes a riddle at all. The riddle-master deserves the benefit of the doubt. Of those editors who print the lines as one riddle, Grein solves as "winter" (see Tupper, p. 208); Dietrich, as "ice" (*ZfdA*. xi, 480); Wyatt apparently as "petrified wood" (p. 113); and recently, Eliason, as "Christ walking on the sea" ("Riddle 68 of the *Exeter Book*," in *Philologica: The Malone Anniversary Studies*, ed. Thomas A. Kirby and Henry Bosley Woolf, pp. 18–19). Of the four, only "ice" solves the paradox in line 3*b*: *wæter wearð to bane*. Eliason reads *Wundor* in line 3*a* as "miracle," but Christ can hardly be described as "water changed to bone." The "wonder," which travels *on wege*, is certainly the iceberg. This is the only solution to the riddle that makes any sense of the paradox.

66.3: *wæter wearð to bane*: Unusual metaphors for ice were not unknown in classical times. Compare, for example, Seneca's description in his *Naturalium Quaestionum* iii.25:

> Aqua enim caelestis minimum in se terreni habens cum induruit, longioris frigoris pertinacia spissatur magis ac magis, donec omni aëre excluso in se tota compressa est et umor, qui fuerat, lapis effectus est. [Ed. Gercke, p. 122]

The Old English riddler's metaphoric substitution of bone for ice is in keeping with the anthropomorphic spirit of the *Riddles*.

67. Lyre
[*VN: Gr¹.69.1–4; Gr². 70.1–4; Tr.68.1–4; Tu.70.1–4; W.69.1–4; M.69.1–4; K-D.70.1–4*]

All previous editors take *Rids*. 67 and 68 as printed in this edition to be one riddle. The reading here follows that of Pope (*Spec.* xlix, 615 ff.) who argues persuasively that a folio is missing between folios 125 and 126 in the MS. Pope says:

> Folio 125 is the last leaf of quire XVI [for the quires, see Förster, *The Exeter Book of Old English Poetry*, pp. 56 ff.] as now constituted, and this quire has only 7 leaves instead of the usual 8. Further, the first two leaves of the quire, folios 119 and 120, are detached half-sheets with folds (mere stubs) on their right (verso) sides. If folio 119, the first leaf of the quire, had lost its other half, this other half would have followed folio 125 and completed a quire of eight. The second leaf, folio 120, would have been a half-sheet from the beginning, being matched asymmetrically by another half-sheet in sixth position, folio 124. A precisely similar arrangement of half-sheets in a quire of eight leaves was originally to be found in the second quire of the Exeter Book, where the half-sheet in second position between folios 15 and 16 has been lost, thus producing a gap in the text of Cynewulf's *Ascension*. [*Spec.* xlix, 616–17]

Pope's reading is supported by the gap in sense and meter between folios 125b and 126a—particularly by the shift from third person verbs in *Rid*. 67 to the first person *stonde* in *Rid*. 68. Past editors who read the two riddle fragments as one supplied a verb after *gesceapo* at 67.4, and a number emended MS. *stonde* to *stondeð*, but the relationship between the creature that *singeð þurh sidan* (67.2) and the creature that *be weg stonde*[ð] (68.2) has never been very clearly explained.

Dietrich (*ZfdA.* xi, 480) first solved the combined riddle fragments as "shawm, shepherd's pipe," explaining, "Ein ding mit gebogenem halse . . . und mit zwei achseln singt durch die seite, ist also wahrscheinlich ein flötenartiges instrument, ich denke die *schalmei* der hirten, hier mit zwei seitenklappen, dem hautboi ähnlich, versehen, und mit einem gebogenen mundstück besetzt, welches ich selbst an hirtenflöten gesehen habe" (*ZfdA.* xi, 480). Dietrich's "shawm" is accepted by Tupper, Wyatt, and Mackie, though Tupper notes somewhat skeptically that "the name [*shawm* from O.F. *chalemie*] does not appear in English until long after the Conquest; and Padelford [*BBzA.* iv, 1 ff.] finds no trace of the instrument in the Anglo-Saxon manuscripts cited by Strutt and Westwood" (p. 209). In short, there is no medieval crooked flute with a double set of shoulders; what flutes there are certainly do not stand *heah ond hleortorht* (68.3) by the road or way.

Trautmann (*Anglia Beibl.* v, 51) first solved the combined riddle fragments as "Roggenhalm," a flute made from a stalk of rye, and later (edition, p. 125), as "Harfe" or "harp." Trautmann's "harp" (O.E. *hearpe*, now thought to be actually a round lyre) is accepted by Pope for the first riddle fragment (see below). Holthausen (*Anglia Beibl.* xxx, 51) solved the combined riddles as "organistrum," but the Anglo-Saxon hurdy-gurdy is certainly a chimera of the modern mind.

Erhardt-Siebold ("The Old English Loom Riddles," in *Philologica: The Malone Anniversary Studies*, ed. Thomas A. Kirby and Henry Bosley Woolf, pp. 9–17) solved the combined riddle fragments as "shuttle" in a most ingenious fashion. She took *singeð þurh sidan* to refer to the shuttle's singing through the lateral warp threads of the loom. She took the shuttle itself to be *scearp* ("sharp") and to have two sets of shoulders (translating 3*b*–4*a* as "the pointed thing has two shoulders on its shoulders"). She took the creature that is *heah ond hleortorht* (68.3) to be the loom itself, which ruled the fate of the shuttle (supplying *lædeð* after *gesceapo* at 67.4*b*). But the description of the sharp and doubly shouldered shuttle is not very convincing, nor is the reading of 67.2*a*, which surely must mean that the creature sings through its own sides. The connection between the fragments rests upon an addition to the MS. reading at 67.4*b* and an emendation of MS. *stonde* to *stondeð* and even with these changes the syntax is most unusual, particularly in the use of *þe swa*. Finally the loom, though conceivably *hleortorht*, is certainly not *heah* and certainly does not stand *be wege*.

Pope's argument in favor of a missing folio between the riddle fragments is convincing on paleographical and textual grounds. It very nicely eliminates the need to connect the creature that "sings through its sides" with that other towering and "bright-cheeked" creature that stands *be wege*. Pope tentatively solves the first riddle fragment as printed in this edition as "lyre," and I accept that solution. The lyre sings through its sides; it has a crooked or curved neck that is skillfully wrought; it has apparel (see note to *scearp* below) on its shoulders. For a description of the Sutton Hoo lyre and a similar round lyre found in a seventh century barrow at Taplow, Buckinghamshire, see R. L. S. and Myrtle Bruce-Mitford, "The Sutton Hoo Lyre, *Beowulf*, and the Origins of the Frame Harp," *Antiquity* xliv, 7–12, with illustrations. For Pope's reading of the second riddle fragment, see headnote to *Rid.* 68.

67.4: *scearp*: Most editors read *scearp* as a modifier of *eaxle* in line 3. Mackie translates, "upon its shoulder-blades / it has two sharp shoulders" (p. 209), apparently with reference to the contorted flute. But if *scearp* is the adjective meaning "sharp," it cannot in its uninflected state modify the feminine plural accusative *eaxle*. Erhardt-Siebold takes *scearp* as a substantival adjective referring back to *wiht* and translates, "The pointed thing / has two shoulders on its shoulders" (see reference in headnote) with reference to a highly contorted shuttle. Pope (*Spec.* xlix, 620–21) suggests emending *scearp on gescyldrum* to *scearpan gescyldru*, or in terms of the "lyre" solution reading *scearp* as "a variant dialectal spelling or a miswriting of the neuter noun *sceorp* 'apparel'" (*Spec.* xlix, 620). For the dialectal *ea* for *eo* Pope cites Campbell 278 (b) and (c). For *sceorp*, "apparel, dress, ornament," Pope cites for comparative purposes *sigesceorp* (*Max. I*, 126), *fyrdsceorp* (*Rid.* 12.13 by my numbering), *guðsceorp* (*Jud.* 328), *heorusceorp* (*Hell* 73), *hildesceorp* (*Beo.* 2155), and *hleosceorp* (*Rid.* 7.5).

67.4b: Grein and most later editors supply *dreogeð* after *gesceapo* in their reading of the two riddle fragments as one. Trautmann supplies *bideð*; Erhardt-Siebold (see headnote) supplies *lædeð*.

68. Lighthouse?
[*VN: Gr*¹.*69.5–6; Gr*².*70.5–6; Tr.68.5–6; Tu.70.5–6; W.69.5–6; M.69.5–6; K-D.70.5–6*]

All previous editors read this riddle as a continuation of *Rid.* 67 (see discussion in headnote to *Rid.* 67), but Pope (*Spec.* xlix, 615 ff.) argues persuasively that a folio is missing between the two riddle fragments. Pope notes that the form *stonde* in 2*b* marks this riddle as a first-person persona riddle in contrast to the previous third-person narrative riddle. He also notes that the concluding riddle fragment as it now stands resembles the conclusions to *Rids.* 6 and 25 and that the fragment was probably preceded immediately by the half-line *Saga* (or *Frige*) *hwæt ic hatte*. Pope notes that the creature that stands *be wege* "tall and cheek-bright, for service to men" is probably a lighthouse, and I would agree. Pope cites the analogous Riddle 92 of Aldhelm, "Faros Editissima," which he notes may have been inspired by Isidore's famous description of the lighthouse that stood on Pharos at the entrance to Alexandria (*Etym.* xv.ii.37). Aldhelm's Latin riddle is as follows:

> Rupibus in celsis, qua tundunt caerula cautes
> Et salis undantes turgescunt aequore fluctus,
> Machina me summis construxit molibus amplam,
> Navigeros calles ut pandam classibus index.
> Non maris aequoreos lustrabam remige campos
> Nec ratibus pontum sulcabam tramite flexo
> Et tamen immensis errantes fluctibus actos
> Arcibus ex celsis signans ad litora duco
> Flammiger imponens torres in turribus altis,
> Ignea brumales dum condunt sidera nimbi.
>
> [Ed. Pitman, p. 54]

Pope notes that Aldhelm had probably seen lighthouses on either side of the channel, citing Bede's mention of *farus* (*EH*. i.xi) and also an archaeological investigation by R. E. M. Wheeler, "The Roman Lighthouses at Dover" (*Archaeological Journal* lxxxvi, 29–46).

68.2b: *be wege*: either "by the way" (*wĕg*) or "by the water" (*wēg, wǣg*). Pope (*Spec.* xlix, 618) in the text of his article inclines toward the latter reading even though he admits that the meter strongly supports the former, but in a supplementary note at the end of the article he questions his own reading, noting that N. H. Pearson suggested that "lighthouses mark seaways," and that consequently it might be better to take *be wege* as "by the way." This is the reading I accept.

69. Sword
[*VN: Gr¹.70; Gr².71; Tr.69; Tu.71; W.70; M.70; K-D.71*]

Dietrich (*ZfdA.* xi, 480) solved the riddle as "cupping-glass." Trautmann proposed "iron helmet" (*Anglia Beibl.* v, 51), "iron shield" (*Anglia Beibl.* xxv, 278), and "bronze shield" (edition). Tupper solved the riddle as "sword or dagger," after a suggestion proposed and rejected by Dietrich. Tupper's solution is accepted by Holthausen (*Anglia Beibl.* xxx, 53) and Mackie. Wyatt solved the riddle as "iron, first in the ore, then made into a weapon." The riddle as it remains indicates that the creature is a weapon made of metal and adorned with gold. It is *wire geweorþad* (line 5a) and *hringum gehyrsted* (line 8a) and in these respects much like the "sword" of *Riddle* 18, which speaks of its *beorht . . . wir* (18.3b–4a) and lord-given *hringas* (18.23). In fact the reference in this riddle to adorning rings makes the solution, "sword," most likely. Anglo-Saxon sword hilts were sometimes adorned with rings or ring-knobs to symbolize the liege-lord relationship (see note to *Rid.* 18.23). Davidson (*The Sword in Anglo-Saxon England*, p. 154) also believes this to be another sword riddle. For more on Anglo-Saxon swords, see the headnote to *Rid.* 18.

69.1: *reade bewæfed*: Davidson notes that "the red worn by the sword can be explained by red gold, or jewels like the popular garnet set in the hilt, while no doubt the secondary meaning of red blood is also hinted at here" (*The Sword in Anglo-Saxon England*, p. 155). I think that *reade* probably refers to the use of garnets with gold—see, for example, the pommel and scabbard bosses from the Sutton Hoo sword in Plate D of Bruce-Mitford's *The Sutton Hoo Ship-Burial: A Handbook*, opposite p. 33.

69.2: *stið ond steapwong:* "hard and steep-cheeked." The reading of *steapwong* was first proposed by Holthausen (*Anglia Beibl.* ix, 358) and is accepted by Trautmann, Krapp and Dobbie, and myself. For a similar compound utilizing *-wang, -wenge,* cp. *harwenge,* "grey-bearded," cited by BTS. (p. 509). For other *bahuvrihi* compounds in Old English (cp. *blachleor, bolgenmod, bliðheort*), see Girvan, *Beowulf and the Seventh Century,* p. 6. For characteristic examples of adjective plus adjective with comparable stress and rhythm, see a number of the examples in Pope's categories A36, 38, 45, 46, and 47 in *The Rhythm of Beowulf,* pp. 258–60. Other editors take *steap wong* as separate words, but stylistically such a half-line (two adjectives linked by *ond* and modifying a noun in the same half-line) is most unusual. Grein and Assmann take *wong* as appositive with *æht* in line 1*a*; Tupper and Wyatt (and Mackie in his translation) begin a new sentence with line 2*a*, taking *wong* as appositive with *staþol*.

69.2b–3a: *staþol . . . wyrta wlitetorhtra*: Davidson interprets this as an unusually poetic description of the forging process:

> The explanation given for the first part of this riddle has been to take the 'hard high field' to refer to iron in the earth. But a different solution is suggested by the word *wlitetorht* which does not merely mean 'beautiful' but has the idea of brightness and radiance, and this gives a more effective and telling meaning to the passage. If the iron is the piece from which the blade is forged, a hard, flat piece raised high upon the anvil and beaten by the hammer so that brilliant sparks, like flowers, are seen to spring from it, we have a fine imaginative picture. Moreover, it leads on naturally to the use of the fire and the file, referring to the working and filing down of the sword-blade. [*The Sword in Anglo-Saxon England*, p. 155]

Davidson's metaphoric interpretation is based in part on an unlikely reading of line 2*a* (see preceding note). As for *wlitetorht*, it occurs once elsewhere where it describes the shining sun (*Bo.* 28.61). But a similar word, *wlitebeorht*, is used on a number of occasions (see citations in B-T., p. 1260) to describe the land. Two examples are especially instructive: *Beo*. 92–93: *se Ælmihtiga eorðan worh(te)*, / *wlitebeorhtne wang*; and *Gen*. 1804: *þær him wlitebeorhte wongas geþuhton*. Davidson's reading is ingenious, but I think it is wrong. The "place of bright plants" here must be the same "bright plains" referred to so often in the poetry—the land in bloom.

69.3b–4a: Cp. the use of the kenning, *homera laf*, for sword at *Rid*. 3.7, *Beo*. 2829, and *Brun*. 6.

69.7: *yþan*: Trautmann emends the MS. *yþan* to *ywan* to suit his solution, "shield." The doctoring of legitimate Old English passages to bolster one's solution is not a sound editorial practice.

69.8: *hringum gehyrsted*: For a discussion of Anglo-Saxon sword-rings, see the note to *Rid*. 18.23.

69.8b–10: My reading of the half-line arrangement with the lacuna follows that of Mackie. There are other possibilities. The reading of Krapp and Dobbie is:

Me [.]i[........
..........]go[.]   dryhtne min[..
......................]wlite bete.

According to my reading, the first three half-lines contain 16, 17, and 17 spaces, and the last line contains 30 (approximately two half-lines of 15). According to the reading of Krapp and Dobbie, the first three half-lines contain 10, 13, and 13 spaces, and the last line contains 35. Since the average half-line is 15 or 16 spaces, my own reading seems preferable to the imbalanced reading of Krapp and Dobbie.

70. Ox
[*VN: Gr¹.71; Gr².72; Tr.70; Tu.72; W.71; M.71; K-D.72*]

This is the third of three "ox" riddles in the *Exeter Book* (see also *Rids*. 10 and 36). The riddle was first solved as "axle and wheels" by Dietrich (*ZfdA*. xi, 480) and Prehn (*NS* iii, 243), but Grein (*Sp*., p. 671, under *teon*) read *feower . . . swæse broþor* as *mamillas vaccae* and the riddle was solved as "ox" by Brooke (*The History of Early English Litera-ture*, p. 136) and Trautmann (*Anglia Beibl.* v, 50). The solution, "ox," is accepted by all recent editors. Trautmann's solution takes the form, "der Zugochse."

The importance of the ox to Anglo-Saxon agriculture is discussed in the headnote to *Rid.* 10. The farmer in Aelfric's *Colloquy* begins and ends his day tending the oxen. Isidore notes: "Iuvencus dictus, quod iuvare incipiat hominum usus in colenda terra" (*Etym.* xii.i.28). The motif of the young ox suckling at the four fountains may be found in *Rid.* 36.3–4, and in Riddle 83 of Aldhelm, "Iuvencus," and in Riddle 37 of Eusebius, "De Vitulo." The Latin riddles are quoted and dis-cussed in the headnote to *Rid.* 36. The motif of the four fountains ap-pears here as the *feower . . . swæse broþor* (6b–7a). The breaking of the young ox to the plow is described by Pliny in his *Natural History*: "Domitura boum in trimatu, postea sera, ante praematura; optume cum domito iuvencus inbuitur" (*NH.* viii.lxx.180).

70.4b: Holthausen (*ESn.* li, 188) would restore the half-line to read *þe unc gemæne* [*wæs*].

70.5: The restoration of [*wæs*] before *sweostor*, suggested by Chambers and Flower (*The Exeter Book of Old English Poetry*, p. 78), would fit the pattern of the still visible descenders (see my paleographical note to the line). Krapp and Dobbie's suggestion, [*þ wæs*] *sweostor min* (p. 370, note) is somewhat more tentative.

70.9: *þæh*: Holthausen (*Anglia Beibl.* ix, 358) would emend the MS. reading to *þāh*, and so Wyatt; but Tupper and Madert (*Die Sprache der altenglischen Rätsel des Exeterbuches und die Cynewulffrage*, p. 53) read *þæh* as a northern form of West Saxon *þeah* (cp. *bæg* at *Rid.* 2.8a and see Campbell 225, p. 95, and SB. 119 Anm. 2 and 5, pp. 97 ff. for the forms).

70.10b–11a: "And I gave that (i.e., taking milk from the cow) up to a dark herdsman." For a similar translation, see Tupper, p. 210, and Mackie, p. 211. For the form *anforlætan*, see BTS., p. 41. Grein, Assmann, and Krapp and Dobbie read *an forlet*; other editors read the compound.

70.12: *mearcpaþas træd*: The MS. reading, *mearcpaþas walas træd*, though clearly overburdened (cp. *ofer mearcpaðu* at *An.* 788*a* and *El.* 233*a* and *be mearcpaðe* at *An.* 1061*b*), is retained by Grein, Assmann, Tupper, and Mackie. Tupper (p. 285) reads *Walas* as an unattested adjectival form of *Wealh*, and Mackie translates the half-line as "trod the paths on the Welsh march" (p. 211). Grein, in a note, suggested *Wala* for *Walas*, and so Trautmann and Wyatt (likewise B-T., p. 1173). Krapp and Dobbie print the half-line as it is in the MS. but conjecture: "it may be that *paþas* and *walas* represented two attempts by the scribe to reproduce a partly illegible word" (p. 370). The presence of *pæðde* in the next half-line may mean that the scribe wrote *paþas* because he was anticipating *træd* and put in a natural object for it, but even if the original reading had been something like *mearc Wala træd*, it is not clear why the ox should have been characteristically defined as walking the boundary or country of the Welsh. My own guess, following up on the suggestion of Krapp and Dobbie, is that the original *mearcpaþas* was corrupted into something like *mearcwawas*, and that two scribal conjectures written in above the *-wawas* in the form of *paþas* and *walas* were then both incorporated into the text by a later scribe.

70.13: Pliny describes the yoking of oxen: "Araturos boves quam artissime iungi oportet, ut capitibus sublatis arent—sic minime colla contundunt" (*NH.* xviii.xlix.177).

70.15: *isern scod*: Cp. the remarks of the farmer in Aelfric's *Colloquy* when asked if he has any help: "Ic hæbbe sumne cnapan þywende oxan mid gadisene, þe eac swilce nu has ys for cylde *and* hreame" (*Coll.* 29–30). A farmer in one of the scenes in the Bayeux tapestry is aided by a man using a long stick as a goad (see Stenton, *The Bayeux Tapestry*, detail from plate 12).

71. Spear
[*VN: Gr¹.72; Gr².73; Tr.71; Tu.73; W.72; M.72; K-D.73*]

Dietrich (*ZfdA*. xi, 481) solved the riddle as "die lanze," "lance, spear," and this solution is accepted by all editors except Trautmann, who prefers "der Mauerbrecher," "battering ram." The creature that has a small neck (*swiora smæl*, line 18*a*) and that is carried in its master's hand (line 8) cannot be a heavy battering ram (for the "ram," see *Rid.* 51). Trautmann notes that lines 22*b* ff. better describe a ram than a spear, and Krapp and Dobbie agree; but the *eþelfæsten* of line 25 may not be a real fortress so much as a body stronghold, a house of flesh like the *brægnloca* of line 24, burst by the spear. When the body of the enemy warrior is pierced, the *eþelfæsten* . . . *þæt ær frið hæfde* (lines 25–26) bursts, and life or the soul *feringe from* . . . *fus þonan | wendeð of þam wicum* (lines 27–28). The *wic* is the body (for the plural used in the singular sense, see note below), that old *banhus*, here the *eþelfæsten* and *brægnloca* left by the life spirit as carrion on the field of battle.

The spear was probably the commonest offensive weapon used by the Anglo-Saxons. Spearheads are a common find in Anglo-Saxon graves, both of commoner and king. Wilson (*The Anglo-Saxons*, p. 120) notes that no complete Anglo-Saxon spear has survived but that an entire spear was found relatively intact in a grave at Oberflacht in Germany. For more on Anglo-Saxon spears, see Wilson (ibid.), pp. 118–20; Keller, *The Anglo-Saxon Weapon Names*, pp. 18 ff. and 128 ff.; Bruce-Mitford, *The Sutton Hoo Ship-Burial*, p. 29.

The motif of the flourishing tree, uprooted and carried off to another fate, is common to *Rids*. 71 and 51 and also to *The Dream of the Rood* (lines 28 ff.), and perhaps to the lost beginning of *The Husband's Message*. The poet of *The Rune Poem* plays upon the common meanings of *æsc*, "ash tree," and "ash spear," when he says:

> ᚫ (æsc) biþ oferheah,   eldum dyre,
> stiþ on staþule,   stede rihte hylt,
> ðeah him feohtan on   firas monige.

[*Run. 81–83*]

71.2: For metrical reasons, Tupper and Wyatt read *onhwyrfdon me* for MS. *me onhwyrfdon* after a suggestion by Herzfeld—but there is no reason to assume that the alliterative rules were not occasionally broken. Cp. the final alliterative stress at *Rids.* 1.66, 2.8, 53.14, 57.12, and 87.6.

71.6: *wiþ gesceape minum*: "against (contrary to) my nature." Cp. *him . . . on gesceap* at *Rid.* 36.2*b* ff.

71.8: *mines frean*: For metrical reasons, Tupper reads *frean mines*; Holthausen (*Anglia* xxxv, 172) and Trautmann (edition) read *mines fregan*. Other editors retain the MS. reading of the half-line: *Nu eom mines frean*. With a monosyllabic pronunciation of *frean* and a stress on adverbial *Nu* in the initial position, the verse would be irregular but not without parallels (cp. *Beo.* 2150*a*, *Seaf.* 9*a*, *Rid.* 27.4*a* and note). With disyllabic pronunciation of *frean* (see my discussion of the phenomenon in the Introduction), the verse would be a regular A3 verse (see Pope's category A70 on p. 266 of *The Rhythm of Beowulf*).

71.10: Tupper reads *dome ri...* but there is at least one letter missing before *ri* in the manuscript.

71.16: Assmann, Tupper, Trautmann, and Wyatt read *...n eorp*, but Mackie rightly notes (p. 213) that the last letter of the word before *eorp* may be *r* or *n*. Krapp and Dobbie print *...]eorp*, but there is a clear space in the MS. separating *eorp* from the preceding word. *Eorp* would thus properly alliterate with *eaxle*. O.E. *eorp*, "dark, dusky" also occurs at *Rids.* 1.72, 47.11, and 89.27.

71.19a: I allow for 21 spaces here, the length of the longest half-line (line 1*b*) in the riddle. The lacuna in the MS. extends to the right-hand margin so it is impossible to say where the MS. line may have ended, but a count of spaces on an average-line basis to an average end-point at the right margin would seem to indicate 23 to 24 spaces. The line must have been overly long or it must have ended several spaces short of the normal margin of writing.

71.20: The alliteration would indicate that the letter whose long descender remains visible in the MS. is *s*.

71.24: The sense and meter indicate the loss of at least a half-line after *brægnlocan*, and so all editors. The reading *brægnlocan* for MS. *hrægnlocan* was proposed by Grein (*Germania* x, 429) and is accepted by Wyatt, Tupper, and Mackie. Thorpe in a note proposed *hrægllocan* and so Trautmann. Assmann and Krapp and Dobbie retain the MS. reading for want of a satisfactory solution. Another possibility might be *hringlocan* for "mail coat." Mackie translates lines 23–24: "that among bold comrades I, with the cunning of a thief / within my head." I believe that *under brægnlocan* refers not to the locus of the spear's cunning but to the locus of its attack—in terms of the metaphor used here, the place of its plunder. The *brægnloca* refers to the head just as *banloca* (*Beo.* 742, 818; *Chr.* 769; *Jul.* 476) in Old English poetry refers to the body. The example from *Christ* may give some indication of the missing passage in the riddle:

> Forþon we fæste sculon   wið þam færscyte
> symle wærlice   wearde healdan,
> þy læs se attres ord   in gebuge,
> biter bordgelac,   under banlocan,
> feonda færsearo.

[*Chr.* 766–70]

Presumably a verb like *gebugan* that would alliterate with *brægnlocan* was lost in the lacuna at line 24*b*. I believe the *brægnloca* to be the same riddlic reference to the body as the *eþelfæsten* at line 25*b* and the *wic* at line 28*a*.

71.25: *eþelfæsten*: This stronghold or house is the *banhus* or body. The reference to breaking and entering here carries on the essential metaphor of the *þeofes cræfte* at line 23*b*.

71.26: *þæt ær frið hæfde*: "that before had security"—the body, once secure and whole, has been pierced and the warrior who is *feringe from* (27*a*) is now dying.

71.27: *Feringe from*: "Bold (eager) for the journey." Cp. *forðsiþes from* at *Rid.* 60.2. *Feringe* is genitive singular.

71.27: *fus*: "eager for the journey from this world." For this particular meaning of *fus*, see BTS., p. 275 under category III. The poet of the *Exeter Maxims* says, for example:

> Fus sceal feran,   fæge sweltan
> ond dogra gehwam   ymb gedal sacan
> middangeardes.

[*Max.* I 27–29]

Guthlac likewise says in his death speech: *Nu of lice is, / goddreama
georn, gæst swiðe fus* (*Guth.* 1298–99). The departure of the ghost from
the body (*Guth.* 1305 ff.) follows directly in *Guthlac* as it does in this
riddle.

71.28: *wendeð of þam wicum*: "travels from the building." Bosworth-
Toller (p. 1212) and also Klaeber (in his glossary to *Beowulf*) note that
wic often occurs in the plural form with a singular meaning. The
building here is the *eþelfæsten* of line 25 and the *brægnlocan* of line
24—this is the old *banhus* or body from which the spirit turns at death.
The body is broken (lines 22b–26) and the spirit is eager to travel
(lines 27–29a).

71.28b–29: I read *cyðe* for MS. *saga* at 29b in order to secure the
alliteration and to make better sense of the lines. The conclusion of
the riddle is a challenge to the hypothetical warrior to draw upon his
experience and knowledge to solve the riddle: "Let the warrior who
knows (= who might know) my nature declare what I am called."
With my emendation, the concluding challenge issued in the third
person subjunctive to the hypothetical solver is exactly like that found
at *Rid.* 41.14–15. Without the emendation, there is no alliteration in
the last line. Reading MS. *saga* (where I have *cyðe*) in 29b, the other
editors take the lines in various ways. Grein and Assmann place a
colon after *wicum* and regard *wiga* as vocative with second person
singular subjunctive *cunne* and second person imperative *saga*. This is
also the reading of Tupper and Krapp and Dobbie who begin a new
sentence with *Wiga*. Krapp and Dobbie accept the lack of alliteration
in the last line; Tupper places *wisan* at the end of line 28b and supplies
soþe at the beginning of line 29a. Wyatt, Trautmann, and Mackie take
the clause beginning with *wiga* at 28b as referring back to *he* in 27b.
Mackie translates beginning at 27a:

> The warrior who knows my nature
> goes in haste, speedy of movement,
> away from that city. Say what I am called.

> [Mackie, pp. 213, 215]

But the use of the subjunctive *cunne* does not make much sense with
this reading since the killed warrior who is *Feringe from . . . fus* (line
27; see previous notes) certainly knows very well the nature of the

spear. Wyatt and Mackie accept the lack of alliteration in the last line; Trautmann emends MS. *wisan* (29*a*) to *siþas* after a suggestion by Holthausen (*Anglia* xxxv, 172 ff.).

72. Ship's Figurehead
[*VN: Gr¹.73; Gr².74; Tr.72; Tu.74; W.73; M.73; K-D.74*]

This riddle has been the editors' delight and the mea culpa of modern scholarship. Dietrich (*ZfdA*. xi, 482) proposed the solution, "cuttle-fish," citing Aldhelm's "Luligo" (ed. Pitman, no. 17, p. 10) only to abandon the solution later for lack of evidence (*ZfdA*. xii, 248). Walz (*Harvard Studies and Notes* v, 266) picked up the banner for "cuttle-fish." Holthausen (*Anglia Beibl*. xxxvi, 220) proposed the solution, "swan." Trautmann (*BBzA*. xix, 202) solved as "water" in its various forms—spring (*fæmne geong*), ice floe (*feaxhar cwene*), and snow (*ænlic rinc*)—and so Wyatt. Tupper argued in several places (p. 214; *MLN* xvii, 100; *MLN* xxi, 103 ff.) for the classical "siren," and Krapp and Dobbie find his evidence at least "impressive." Erhardt-Siebold first argued that the poem was no riddle at all but a philosophical conundrum based upon a fifth-century fragment of Empedokles (*MÆ* xv, 48 ff.), then later solved the "riddle" as "soul" (*MÆ* xxi, 36). Whitman (*ELN* vi, 1–5) offered the summary solution, "writing," taking both *fæmne* and *cwene* as "the white feathery sections of the quill" of some seabird.

Tupper notes that the riddle must satisfy many conditions:

> The monster must be at once a woman, both old and young, and a handsome man. It must fly with the birds and swim in the flood. It must dive into the water, dead with the fishes, and yet when it steps on the land it must have a living soul. [P. 214]

Tupper points to various sirens—one a bird-woman, one a mermaid, one a she-falcon with a fishy tail—but none of them all things at once, *on ane tid* (line 2). Tupper's dead divers (*deaf under ȳðe dead mid fiscum*) are Homeric sirens transformed into rocks. The resurrected siren is nowhere apparent in Old English poetry. O.E. *meremen* does occur as a gloss several times (see B-T., p. 680), and the old *merewif* (*Beo*. 1519) is certainly known to readers of *Beowulf*. Still, Grendel's mother, though a valiant warrior, is no haunting beauty and no flying bird, and she certainly lies in unresurrected sleep after her underwater bout with Beowulf.

Trautmann's "water" has more potential as a solution, but its resemblances to the known "water" *Riddle* 80 are slight indeed. The creature of our riddle swims *on flode*. It may be objected that water is the *flode*. Also if water is *dead* under the waves, there is no reason why it should be *cwicu* anywhere else.

The creature of this riddle is likely to be a carved figurehead of wood mounted on a ship's prow in Viking fashion, similar perhaps to those figureheads depicted on the ships of the English fleet in the Bayeux tapestry (see Stenton, *The Bayeux Tapestry*, plates 6 and 7). One of the heads in the tapestry resembles an anthropomorphic beast, the other a beastly man. Scandinavian ships are known to have carried detachable bird-like or dragon-like heads on their prows as early as the Migration period. One such head, the famous Appels Head now in the British Museum, is described by De Laet:

> Head and neck of a monster (dragon?) . . . carved in oak (total height: 1490 mm.). . . . The object consists of three parts: head, neck and a perforated tenon by means of which it could be fastened to some or other larger ensemble. The head is almost spherical and was carved with a sharp knife. The head itself is prolonged by a wide open beak. The pupils of the eyes are in high relief, around which runs a circle in lower relief. From the point of the beak and over the top of the head runs a kind of crest which continues over the neck. On both sides of the beak, enclosing the open mouth, one sees another rim in relief, probably representing the lips. Inside the open beak, four sharp teeth are carved on both sides of the upper jaw. The oval neck is very long. [*AA* xxvii, 129]

Other heads may have resembled horses, dragons, or even men (see the various illustrations in Brøgger and Shetelig's *The Viking Ships*). Brøgger and Shetelig note that the English ships depicted in the Bayeux tapestry are of typical Viking style (*The Viking Ships*, p. 185), and Wilson believes that Scandinavian ships cannot have differed much in appearance from their Anglo-Saxon contemporaries (*The Anglo-Saxons*, pp. 91–92). Vierck too surmises that "figure-heads were to be found on Anglo-Saxon ships," noting that "this is born out from a 3.9 cms long bronze model of a ship which was found in a Kentish cemetery at Sibertswold (grave 177). . . . The ship-model served as the sword-pommel of a seax from around 700 A.D." (*Helinium* x, 139). Most editors agree that some figurehead is to be counted among the heads of *Rid.* 34, whose solution is *ship*. Baum notes that the *wifes wlite* of that riddle or "form of a woman is probably an ornamental design or figurehead" (p. 56), and I agree. Similarly, I take the creature of *Rid.* 72 to be a figurehead in the shape of a woman, *fæmne geong*, which is *feaxhar*, literally *gray-haired* because of the weathering of the wood. The figurehead would appear, perhaps in siren-like form, as a gray-colored girl, charging the waves like a beautiful warrior, flying through the air above the waves with seabirds and diving at times through the waves or salt spray with the fishes. The figurehead would be literally *dead mid fiscum*, being carved of wood; but, moving over the wave in the shape of a feminine creature, it would certainly have a living spirit (*ferð cwicu*). It would stand on the land (*on foldan stop*) either as part of a light boat drawn up on the shore (see, for example, the smaller of the figureheads from the River Scheldt now in the British Museum, which must have come from such a boat) or more probably as the figurehead of a heavy vessel, detached from the prow when the vessel came to port. De Laet points out that "it is known that the animal prow figures could and in certain circumstances had to be removed" (*AA* xxvii, 136). Brøgger and Shetelig note "an old heathen law mentioned in *Landnama*, stating that the dragon-heads should be detached before land was sighted so as not to frighten the protecting spirits ashore" (*The Viking Ships*, p. 140). In proper sequence the Bayeux tapestry shows an English ship in the harbor with no figurehead (Stenton, *The Bayeux Tapestry*, plate 5) and a fully laden ship at sea (Stenton, plates 6 and 7) with both an animal and a human figurehead. In an analogous situation the tapestry shows the Norman fleet approaching the English coast and three of the four ships have figureheads (Stenton, plate 44); then in the subsequent landing scene, none of the ships drawn up on the beach has a figurehead (Stenton, plate 45). In his commentary upon the landing scene, Gibbs-Smith says that "emptied vessels are seen drawn up on the beach: the designer evidently did not feel it worth while to embellish the latter with carved stem or sternposts" (Stenton, *The Bayeux Tapestry*, p. 171). What seems more likely is that the designer employed here a Nordic tradition with respect to figureheads. Ships' figureheads are admittedly rare in archaeological finds, either because they were detached from the prows before the ships were buried, or because they were buried and later detached by thieves, or else because they were simply worn away by time and weather like most of the ships' prows located near the topsoil. Perhaps the figurehead of the riddle is intended to be a Viking figurehead. Certainly the Viking ships were well known to Anglo-Saxons. But it may, as well, be an Anglo-Saxon figurehead. The Anglo-Saxon ships described in *Beowulf* had great ring-necked prows and it is not unlikely that the prows were mounted with figureheads like those of their Viking counterparts or like those depicted in the Bayeux tapestry. (For a recent discussion of ships' figureheads, see R. L. S. Bruce-Mitford's "Ships' Figure-Heads of the Migration Period" in his *Aspects of Anglo-Saxon Archaeology*, pp. 175–87.)

72.1: *feaxhar*: gray-haired, a hapax legomenon (*Sp.*: *comam canam habens*, p. 182). For uses of *har* as an Old English color word, see Mead's "Color in Old English Poetry," *PMLA* xiv, 190 ff. Mead notes that "in *feaxhar cwene* the color element appears to predominate" (p. 190).

72.5: *ferð*: so all editors except Grein who retains the MS. *forð*, defining *cwicu* as *vivacitatem* (Grein-Wülker, p. 226, note).

73. Piss
[VN: *Gr¹.74,75; Gr².75,76; Tr.73,74; Tu.75,76; W.74,75; M.74,75; K-D.75,76*]

In the manuscript lines 1 and 2 appear to constitute one riddle; line 3 appears to constitute another. The riddle is thus printed as two by all other editors. Hickes, however, in copying out the runes of the *Exeter Book* for illustrations in his *Grammaticae Islandicae Rudimenta*, appears to have read all three lines as one riddle. His penciled lines bracket the riddlic texts as one riddle (see plate xvⅢ) and the lines appear with the runes as figure H on page 4 of his *Grammaticae*. In explanation of the lines, Hickes says: "Tab. H personam celeri gressu festinare visam, foeminamque solitarie sedentem describit" (*Grammaticae Islandicae Rudimenta*, p. 5 of pt. 3 of his *Linguarum Veterum*

Septentrionalium Thesaurus). There is some structural basis for this reading of the lines. *Ic ane geseah* (line 3*a*) echoes *Ic swiftne geseah* (line 1*a*). The creature in line 1 is seen to travel; the woman in line 3 is seen to sit. The contrast seems intentional. Maranda ("The Logic of Riddles," in *Structural Analysis of Oral Tradition*, ed. Pierre and Elli Köngäs Maranda, pp. 209 ff.) notes the same contrast in a set of Finnish riddles with various solutions. Paleographically the riddle appears to be two, but the scribe has mistakenly copied one riddle as two at *Rids*. 1, 66, and 76 as printed in this edition. Grein implicitly recognizes the structural similarity between lines 1 and 3 when he says of his Riddle 75 (here, line 3): "War hier auch der rätselgegenstand . . . in runen angegeben?" (see Grein-Wülker, p. 226 note). Most editors who print line 3 as a separate riddle agree that one or both of their riddles are fragments. Grein, Tupper, and Trautmann, following a suggestion by Thrope, emend the rune ᚱ to the rune ᚾ, thus reading runic DNUH for MS. runic DNLH, and solve the riddle as *hund*, "hound," by reading the runes in reverse order. All consider line 3, their second riddle, to be an unsolved fragment. But the runes in the *Exeter Book* appear to have been copied here and elsewhere with particular care. The runes are marked off by points and have a high visibility, and the scribe tends to make errors at points of low rather than of high visibility. Mackie (*MLR* xxviii, 77) accepts the MS. reading of runic DNLH as an anagram of the consonants of Hæl*e*ND and notes that the lines (here, lines 1–2) refer to "Christ as a hunter in pursuit of sin." The pursuit of sin has no place in this riddle. Mackie (edition, p. 242) reads line 3 as a riddle for "hen" after a suggestion by Wyatt. Line 3 by itself hardly delimits any solution. Eliason (*SP* xlix, 554 ff.) reads the three lines as one riddle, taking runic *D* and *N* in line 2 to indicate vowels following *D* and *N* in the alphabet, namely *E* and *O*, and thus reading the runic clue as EOLH, "elk." Normally, however, codes of this kind involve substituting consonants for *preceding* rather than following vowels (cp. the presumably interpolated line at *Rid*. 34.5 and Isidore's description of the standard code at *Etym*. i.xxv.1 ff.). If Eliason's *eolh* has merit, it is certainly lost in his reading of *idese* as "doe" and in his solving the entire riddle as "elk-hunter," the *Ic* of lines 1 and 3 who shoots the elk and leaves Mrs. Elk at home alone to mourn. Here Eliason ignores the basic structure of third-person descriptive riddles. When a riddle begins with *Ic . . . geseah*, the narrator is not the disguised creature (*Ic eom . . .*) but the riddler himself. By Eliason's logic, the solution to *Rid.* 45 for example would be "librarian" (*Me þæt þuhte . . .*) instead of "bookworm."

Since the standard code described by Isidore and used elsewhere (*Rid.* 34.5) in the *Exeter Book* reveals nothing like a solution from runic DNLH, one is left with Mackie's idea that the vowels have merely been omitted. I read the runes in reverse order not as HæLeND, but as HLαND, "piss." Elliott (*Runes*, p. 16) notes that runic *H* may be used in Old English as an aspirate. O.E. *hland* or *hlond* glosses L. *lotium* (WW. 30.34, 439.22, 476.30; *Bibliothèque Nationale MS. Lat. 7586*, fol. 139r, cited by Meritt, *JEGP* lx, 448) and *lotio* (WW. 501.15, 525.9). O.E. *hlom*, uel *micga* glosses *lotium* (WW. 117.25). The lemma *lotii* occurs with glosses *i. urine, hlondes, micgan* (Napier 1.3264) and *hlondes, miggan* (Napier 1.3274). The word *hland* occurs three times in the *Leechdoms* as *biccean hlonde* (i.362.18), *gæten hland* (ii.40.20), and *hlond* (ii.156.14). The *OED* lists O.E. *hland* under *lant*, "Urine, *esp.* stale urine used for various industrial purposes, chamber-lye" (*OED* vi, p. 62), but the specialized meaning, "stale piss," only arises in the seventeenth century. There is nothing in the Old English *Leechdoms* or in the glosses to define an "industrial" context. Latin *lotium* certainly means "piss" (see *Etym.* xi.i.138; and also Aldhelm, *De Virginitate*, line 2532, which reads: "Ut nullum paries mingentem lotia nosset": ed. Ehwald). The word *hland* is not listed in any of its possible forms in the *MED*. In its cognate forms in Old Icelandic and Old Norse, *hland* also means "piss." Cleasby and Vigfusson note five occurrences of *hland* (Nj. 199, Fs. 147, N.G.L. i.29, Grág. ii.132, and Skm. 35: see their abbreviations and editions used), and the compounds *hland-ausa, -skjóla*, and *-trog*, all meaning "urine trough"; *hland-for* and *-gröf* meaning "sewer"; and *hland-blaðra* meaning "bladder" (*An Icelandic-English Dictionary*, 2d ed., p. 269). *Hland* is an appropriate word for human "piss." It is normally listed as a neuter noun, but in its unmodified occurrences it could be confused with the masculine. The riddler uses the adjective *swiftne* to modify the runic creature of the riddle, but Wyatt (pp. xxv–xxvi) notes that the gender of the riddlic creature does not in several cases agree with the gender of the modifiers and pronouns in the riddlic descriptions.

I translate the riddle as follows:

I saw a swift one travel on the track:
HL*a*ND (piss).
I saw a woman sitting alone.

The distinction between the sounds of men and women pissing is noted by Hymes in a rather different cultural context (see his "The 'Wife' Who 'Goes Out' Like a Man: Reinterpretation of a Clackamas Chinook Myth," *Social Science Information*, vii, 173–99, esp. p. 178, note 3, and his discussion of onomatopoetic Chinook terms for pissing). In the Old English riddle, the distinction is one of sight (*Ic . . . geseah*). The swift piss of man is seen to travel on the road or track. The piss of woman by implication is hidden. The riddler does not see the *hland* of woman; he merely sees the woman "sitting alone" (*ane. . . idese sittan*). In some cultures where people still piss without benefit of commode, the woman squats modestly with her skirt lifted a few inches above the ground and pisses unobtrusively in the grass, while the man stands to piss a clearly visible stream. The distinction between modes of pissing is often the source of jokes and stories as in the case detailed by Hymes (see reference above). This is the musing distinction made, I think, by the Old English riddler—men piss on the path while women may only be seen squatting alone. The solution should not offend. It has several virtues: (1) it requires no emendation of the runes; (2) it leaves no remaining unsolved riddle fragments in the text; (3) it makes dramatic sense of the seeming obscurity of the lines; (4) it has a certain riddlic humor not to be overlooked.

73.right margin: Hickes's penciled markings and his letter *H*, which appear in the right-hand margin of the runic riddle (see plate XVIII), are explained by Förster:

> The runic passages of the *Exeter Book* early attracted the interest of antiquaries. Hickes had drawings made of all of them (except the *wynn* and the *monn* passages) and had them reproduced on Plates IV, V, and VI of his *Grammaticae Islandicae Rudimenta*, which forms Part III of his famous *Linguarum Veterum Septentrionalium Thesaurus* (Oxford, 1703). The passages to be reproduced from the riddles were indicated by pencil marks in the manuscript . . . and Roman letters were added in the margin, corresponding to the same letters in Hickes's tables. [*The Exeter Book of Old English Poetry*, p. 63, note 25]

In each case where runes occur in the *Riddles* and in the case of *Rid*. 34 where the cryptic letters occur, Hickes has marked the entire riddle with a bracket, a code sign to the copier ꝫꝫ, and a capital letter corresponding to the same letter in his table of reproductions. Hickes's marks occur at the following places in the *Riddles*:

MS. Folio	Rid. No.	Hickes's Letter
105*a*	*Rid*. 17	E
106*b*	*Rid*. 22	F
109*b*	*Rid*. 34	FF
125*a*	*Rid*. 62	G
127*a*	*Rid*. 73	H

74. Oyster
[*VN: Gr*¹*.76; Gr*².*77; Tr.75; Tu.77; W.76; M.76; K-D.77*]

Dietrich's solution, "oyster" (*ZfdA*. xi, 483), is accepted by all editors. The creature of the riddle is footless and unable to move. It is covered by water close to the shore. It opens its "mouth" often to the sea, presumably to catch food; it in turn is caught and eaten by man. Bede mentions that mollusks occur off the coast of England (*EH*. i.i, p. 15), and the Anglo-Saxon fisherman in Aelfric's *Colloquy* numbers *ostran* among his catch (*Coll*. 106–8). The oysters of the riddle are stripped of their "skins" and eaten raw. Isidore notes that "ostrea dicta est a testa, quibus mollities interior carnis munitur" (*Etym*. xii.vi.52). Apparently the tender meat devoured *unsodene* (line 8) was not always so healthful. The practitioner of the *Leechdoms* treats of fevers that "cumað þa oftost of mettum *and* of cealdum drincan swa swa sindon cealde ostran" (*Lch*. ii.244.1–2).

74.1: *sundhelm*: *sea-guard*. B-T. defines *sundhelm* as "*a water-covering, the sea which covers*" (p. 935) and similarly Clark Hall; but as the compound is rare, I prefer the more literal reading that approximates Grein's "*maris galea i.e. mare tegens*" (*Sp*., p. 646). Cp. the only other use of *sundhelm* at *Rid*. 1.25.

74.5: *recceð*: Grein and Trautmann emend to *receð*, but Campbell notes that "W-S has always *ċċ* in the verb except once in Aelfric's *Colloquy*" (287, p. 122, note 1). See the citations in B-T. under *recan*, p. 788.

74.6: *seaxes orde*: O.E. *seax* may refer to any single-edged long knife used for cutting enemies or food (Wilson, *The Anglo-Saxons*, p. 113). B-T. notes two distinct categories—cutting knives and daggers (p. 853), but the ambiguity noted by Wilson is appropriate to the riddlic context where a personified creature (food) sings of his death (dinner).

74.7: Holthausen's reconstruction of the *b*-line, [*ond m*]*ec hr*[*a*]*þe siþ-þan* (*ESn.* xxxvii, 209 ff.), fits the spaces of the MS. if *ond* is contracted in the usual fashion.

74.8: The final *d* of the line is accepted on the authority of Chambers and Flower. It is not legible in the facsimile, but it occurs on the edge of the burn where photographic reproduction is most difficult.

75. Lamprey?
[*VN: Gr¹.X; Gr².78; Tr.76; Tu.78; W.77; M.77; K-D.78*]

Because of the damaged state of the MS., the riddle is rarely "solved" by editors. Holthausen (*Anglia* xxiv, 265) conjectured "ein im wasser lebendes tier (auster? fisch? krebs?)." Trautmann queried, "Liegt ein zweites Austerrätsel vor?" (p. 129). Tupper notes the parallel occurrences of *flode* and *yþa* in *Rid.* 74 and concludes with Trautmann that this is another oyster riddle. But the creature of this riddle is migratory: *ne æt ham gesæt* (line 6). The oyster, which lies on the bottom of the sea or which sits anchored to rocks or submerged objects (*EB.* xvi, pp. 1193 ff.), hardly fits the way-faring description. Furthermore, the oyster exhibits no special power of killing (*cwealde / þurh orþonc*). It sits and sifts particles of food from the seawater. It is hardly a traveling or a feasting fish.

Five major clues to the sea creature's identity emerge from the remaining fragments of the riddle:

1. The creature is found with, or associated with its kin (*cynn[.] minum*) at some stage in its growth, perhaps at an early stage corresponding to the early lines of the riddle

2. The creature has a strange and presumably strictly defining food ([*d*]*yde me to mos*[*e*] . . .)

3. The creature is migratory (*ne æt ham gesæt*)

4. The creature has a skillful method of killing (*cwealde / þurh orþonc*)

5. It kills its victims covered by waves (*yþum bewrigene*)—probably in the sea.

These clues imply that the creature is a migratory fish with a special adaptation (*orþonc*) for killing. The fish might well be the sea lamprey, or O.E. *lampredon*, well known to the Anglo-Saxon fisherman (*Coll.* 101). The lamprey is a migratory fish: it travels from stream to sea and back to its stream again to spawn a new generation. Bridge notes that "in the spring the Sea-Lamprey ascends the rivers to spawn, and, after depositing its eggs in furrows which it excavates in the river-bottom, it returns to the sea" ("Fishes," chap. 16 of the *Cambridge Natural History*, vol. 7, p. 427). The infant lampreys remain with their siblings for several years in the river bottom "as toothless, nearly blind, worm-like larvae known as ammocoetes" (*EB.* xii, p. 631). When the young lampreys acquire their adult characteristics, they leave their freshwater homes for the sea.

Bridge also notes that the full-grown lampreys are carnivorous and that they have a peculiar adaptation for killing their prey: "They feed by attaching themselves to the bodies of Fishes by their suctoral buccal funnels, and then rasping off the flesh with their lingual teeth; while thus engaged they are carried about by their victims" ("Fishes," see reference above, p. 426). The sea lamprey, like the creature of the riddle, kills its wave-covered victims (*yþum bewrigene*) with a special power or adaptation (*cwealde / þurh orþonc*).

Tupper argues that line 4a of the riddle, referring to the creature's food, should be read: [*d*]*yde me to mos*[*e*], by analogy with *An.* 27. The poet of *Andreas* describes the Mermedons' special culinary habits, not unlike those of the lamprey:

Swelc wæs þeaw hira
þæt hie æghwylcne   ellðeodigra
dydan him to mose   meteþearfendum,
þara þe þæt ealand   utan sohte

[*An.* 25–28]

By itself the analogue proves nothing about the riddle, but the language is strikingly similar, and the phrase is used nowhere else to describe normal eating patterns of either man or beast. Certainly the riddlic creature is likely to eat what it kills, and the sea lamprey is one of the few creatures who could be so clearly defined in terms of its killing and feasting. The sight of the sea lamprey attached to fish drawn from the deep must have been as grotesquely inspiring to the Anglo-Saxon imagination as it is today.

75.2: *cynn*[.]: The letters *cynn* occur close to the end of a MS. line with the hole in the parchment directly after them. It is impossible to say whether a letter or letters followed *cynn*. Krapp and Dobbie note that "the meter favors *cynn*[e] *minum*" (p. 372).

75.4: .]*yde me to mos*[.: Tupper restores to [*d*]*yde me to mos*[*e*], citing *An.* 27 (quoted in headnote above).

75.7: ...]*flote cwealde*: Holthausen (*Anglia* xxiv, 265) restores to [*on*] *flote cwealde*, which seems a likely reading. Krapp and Dobbie print *flote cwealde* as a single half-line, but there is no way of knowing whether a word is left out before the half-line or not. Thus, I have punctuated with the lacuna extending directly to *flote* as do Trautmann, Wyatt, and Mackie.

76. Horn
[*VN: Gr¹.77,78; Gr².79,80; Tr.77,78; Tu.79,80; W.78,79; M.78,79; K-D.79,80*]

As I have indicated in the paleographical notes, line 1 of this riddle appears paleographically to constitute one riddle; lines 2–12, to constitute another. All previous editors print the riddle as two. The problem with this arrangement is that line 1 does not structurally constitute a riddle. It is only a general opening statement that might apply to any number of solutions. Dietrich (*ZfdA*. xi, 483) took line 1 to be a variant of line 2 (as printed here), and so also did Wyatt. Trautmann says of the single-line riddle (line 1): "Wieder ein blosser Anfang eines Rätsels" (p. 129). No solution has ever been put forward for the single-line riddle. I agree with Dietrich and Wyatt that line 1 here is a variant of line 2. The structural similarities should be obvious. I believe that the riddle moves from the general to the particular in its opening lines and that the two riddles as they are in the manuscript should constitute one riddle as I have printed it here. (Alternatively, the scribe could have been copying a defective exemplar, in which a missing leaf or some other defect caused all but the first line of a riddle to be lost.) The scribe has on other occasions mistakenly written two riddles as one (*Rids*. 40 and 41; *Rids*. 45 and 46). I have argued elsewhere (*Rids*. 1, 66, and 73) that he has also on occasion separated one riddle into two. The reading adopted here makes for an excellent riddle beginning. The creature of the riddle is both the prince's "property and joy" and his "comrade" or "shoulder-companion." Literally the horn may be *eaxlgestealla* if it is carried on a strap that is slung over the shoulder.

Several answers have been proposed for the riddle as it is traditionally printed (lines 2–12 here). Dietrich (*ZfdA*. xi, 483) proposed "falcon" or "hawk," and this was accepted by Prehn (*NS* iii, 283) and Brooke (*The History of Early English Literature*, p. 147). Trautmann (*Anglia Beibl*. v, 51) and Walz (*Harvard Studies and Notes* v, 267 ff.) argued for the solution "spear" or "sword." Müller (*Die Rätsel des Exeterbuches*, p. 18) and Trautmann (*BBzA*. xix, 203 ff.) argued for "horn" and so Herzfeld, Tupper, and Mackie. The opening lines of the riddle could apply to any of the solutions, though lines 7 and 10–11*b* could only apply to the horn filled with mead. Line 7 is a riddle within a riddle: "I hold in my belly what grew in the wood." This is the mead that is described in *Rid*. 25 as *brungen of bearwum* (25.2). The horn is both war-horn and mead-horn, a summoner to battle and a reward for song. The riddle is a companion to "horn" *Rid*. 12. The reader should see the headnote to that riddle.

76.1–2: See discussion in headnote.

76.4 ff.: Cp. the office of Wealhtheow during the several feasts in the Danish hall in *Beowulf*.

76.8–9a: Cp. *Rid*. 12.5*b*–6*a*.

76.9b: *heard is min tunge*: Swaen (*Neoph*. xxvi, 300) would take *tunge* in the sense of "language" (see B-T., p. 1019 under II[2]), translating, "my voice is loud." But Trautmann's reading seems more likely: "Könnte nicht *tunge* = 'Mundstück' sein?" (p. 129). This is also the reading of B-T. (pp. 1019–20).

77. Weathercock
[*VN: Gr¹.79; Gr².81; Tr.79; Tu.81; W.80; M.80; K-D.81*]

Dietrich (*ZfdA*. xi, 483) first solved the riddle as "ship," and later (*ZfdA*. xii, 234–35) as "visored helmet" (*Maskenhelm*) after a suggestion of Lange's. Trautmann solved the riddle as "weathercock" (*Anglia Beibl*. v, 51), and this solution is accepted by all later editors.

Needham (*English Weathervanes*, chap. 1) traces the history of weathervanes. The first Western reference to a weathervane mounted atop a building occurs in Vitruvius's *De Architectura*:

> . . . Andronicus Cyrrestes, qui etiam exemplum conlocavit Athenis turrem marmoream octagonon et in singulis lateribus octagoni singulorum ventorum imagines excalptas contra suos cuiusque flatus designavit, supraque eam turrim metam marmoream perfecit et insuper Tritonem aereum conlocavit dextra manu virgam porrigentem, et ita est machinatus, uti vento circumageretur et semper contra flatum consisteret supraque imaginem flantis venti indicem virgam teneret. [*De Architectura* i.vi.4]

Needham notes that "there is little indication of other very early weathervanes except, it is reported, that Rome had a somewhat similar building to the 'Tower of Winds,' and that in the 4th century a female figure turned in the wind over a building in Constantinople" (*English Weathervanes*, p. 11).

There are no known Latin words for "weathervane" (Vitruvius uses *venti index*) before the thirteenth century (*ventilogium, ceruca*). The earliest example of a Germanic word for "weathervane" or "weathercock" is O. H. G. *wetirhano*, a twelfth-century gloss for L. *cheruca* (see

Grimm, *Deutsches Wörterbuch*, under *wetterhahn*). The first English occurrence of "weathercock" is a thirteenth-century gloss *veder-coc* for L. *ventilogium* in Alexander Neckam's *De Utensilibus* (Wright, *A Volume of Vocabularies*, p. 115).

The medieval weathercock seems to have grown out of a tradition whereby "tower-cocks" (French *coq du clocher*, German *Turm-Hahn*) were placed on cathedral towers as a sign of watchfulness and warning (see the articles by Bouet, Gerlach, Leclerq, and Perret de la Menue listed in the Bibliography; for the significance of the cock, see Ambrose, *Hex.* v.88). Needham (*English Weathervanes*, p. 12) notes that "a contemporary drawing in the 10th-century *Benedictional of St. Ethelwold* shows the weathercock on the tower of Winchester Cathedral," and Bouet (*Bulletin Monumental* xv, 532–33) notes the poetic description of the same Winchester Cathedral tower by Wolstan in his *Life of St. Ethelwold*:

> Additur ad specimen stat ei quod vertice gallus
> Aureis ornatu grandis et intuitu
>
> .   .   .   .
>
> Impiger imbriferos qui suscipit undique ventos
> Seque rotando suam praebet eis faciem.
>
> [Cited by Bouet, ibid., p. 533]

Needham also notes that "a part of the Bayeux Tapestry, which is over 800 years old, shows a man, with a weathercock in his hand, about to mount the roof of Westminster Abbey (dedicated to St. Peter), built during the time of Edward the Confessor, and consecrated in 1065" (*English Weathervanes*, p. 12; for the tapestry see Stenton, ed. *The Bayeux Tapestry*, plate 32). In the picture of the Bayeux tapestry at least, it is not clear whether the cock being placed on the tower is actually a weathervane or merely a decorative "Turmhahn."

77.1: *bylgedbreost: puff-breasted*. This is the reading of Tupper and Mackie. Other editors retain *byledbreost* (MS. *by led breost*), which they define in various ways. Grein (*Sp.*, p. 80) gives the definition, "*rostrato pectore praeditus(?)*." Holthausen (*Anglia* xxxv, 173) and Trautmann would take *byled-* as a derivative of *bȳl*, but it is hard to imagine a carbuncled bird. Wyatt glosses *byledbreost* as "with breast like a beak, puff-breasted" (p. 136), but if the latter meaning is intended, then the initial element in the compound is more likely to come from the verb *belgan*, "to puff up" than from *byl*, "blotch, sore," or from *gebilod*, "having a beak" (for the last, see B-T., p. 373; the word occurs once in the Old English version of the *Hexameron of St. Basil*).

77.1: *belcedsweora*: "swollen-necked" according to the lexicographers. Grein and Clark Hall relate initial *belced-* to *bælc* and Grein defines *bælc* as "inflatus et tumens animus, superbia, arrogantia" (*Sp.*, p. 80), related to O.N. *bälkr*. *Bælc* occurs with this meaning at *Jud.* 267 and *Gen.* 54.

77.5: *sagol on middum*: "a pole in the middle" or "a pole between (the sides)." The emendation of MS. *sag*, a hapax legomenon of uncertain meaning, to *sagol* was proposed by Tupper and is accepted by Mackie. O.E. *sagol* normally means "pole, staff, club" as it glosses L. *fustis* (see B-T., p. 813), but Tupper notes that it translates L. *vectis* in a passage describing the poles or rods used to carry the ark of the covenant in the Old English version of the *Pastoral Care* (ed. Sweet, EETS, o.s. 45, pp. 170–71). It is also used to translate L. *sudis* in an Old English translation of Gregory's *Dialogues* (see citation in BTS., p. 693). Holthausen (*Anglia Beibl.* xxx, 4) argues that *middum* in this phrase is a late (inverted) spelling variant of *middan*. All other editors retain the MS. *sag* though there is much disagreement as to the meaning of the word. Thorpe thought it might be an error for *sac*. Ettmüller rendered *sag* as L. *onus*, "burden," and so Grein in one of his early readings (as cited in Tupper, p. 219) and Wyatt. Once Grein had read *sag* as "eine senkung" and this reading is taken up by Trautmann, BTS., and Krapp and Dobbie. BTS. (p. 693) connects the word with O.E. *sigan* as does Trautmann in his glossary (p. 182); in his notes (p. 130) Trautmann connects the word with O.E. *sægan*. In somewhat similar fashion Dietrich had explained the word in terms of his first "ship" solution: "eine öffnung auf dem verdeck zum hinabsenkung (*sægan*) der waaren" (*ZfdA.* xi, 483). Kock (*Lunds Universitets Årsskrift*, NF., Avd. 1, Bd. 14, Nr. 26, pp. 65–66) connects *sag* with *sigan*, but he translates the word as "perch" and reads *sag on middum* as "a perch in the middle (of the people)" parallel to *eard ofer ældum* at line 6b. The problem with connecting *sag* with *sigan* is that no other form *sag* occurs and the form *sige*, "setting, sinking," does occur at *Bo.* 13.56.

A hypothetical O.E. *sāg* meaning "groove" or "channel" might be related to Middle English *sough* or *sow*, "ditch or drain" see (*OED* x, p. 460, under *sough*, sb. 2, and *OED* x, p. 490, under *sow*, sb. 2), but the Middle English word (whose origin the *OED* lists as unknown) normally means "a channel to carry water," and so does not seem appropriate here. Given the ambiguities of O.E. *sag*, it seems best to emend with Tupper.

77.7: *þær*: Mitchell (*A Guide to Old English* 179, p. 96) notes that *þær* can sometimes introduce a conditional clause and can be translated as "when" (section 168, p. 85). This appears to be the case here. The sense of the conditional continues through line 11*a*. For a good translation, see Mackie, p. 219.

77.7: *þær mec wegeð*: If the verb *wegeð* here comes from *wecgan*, "to shake," as most editors would have it, the half-line is a rare short A3 verse (see Pope's categories 104–6 on pp. 273–74 of *The Rhythm of Beowulf*) with extremely light stress in the first measure. Thus Holthausen (*Anglia* xxxv, 173) would supply *wind* after *mec* (cp. *Bo*. 7.35a: *þeah hit wecge wind*), and Trautmann would emend *wegeð* to *wrēgeð*, "bewegt, erregt." Sievers (*Beiträge* x, 520) would emend *wegeð* to *wǣgeð*, but Krapp and Dobbie rightly note that it is possible to retain MS. *wegeð* as a variant spelling of *wǣgeð*. I translate beginning at 6*b*: "I suffer torment when what shakes the forest torments me."

77.8: *stondende*: Trautmann emends to *stondendne* but this is unnecessary as participles may be found in inflected or uninflected form (see Krapp and Dobbie, p. 373, note, and Klaeber, *MLN* xxxi, 429).

77.11: *on þyrelwombne*: "on the stomach-pierced one" (see the note on *sagol* above). The addition of *on* was first suggested by Holthausen (*Anglia Beibl*. ix, 358).

77.12: *mæ[.]*: The reading here follows that of Krapp and Dobbie and of Chambers and Flower. Trautmann and Mackie read *mæg*; Tupper and Wyatt, *mæt*; but as the lower portion of the last letter is obliterated, it is impossible to tell whether *g* or *t* was intended.

78. Harrow?
[VN: Gr¹.X; Gr².82; Tr.80; Tu.82; W.81; M.81; K-D.82]

This riddle is not edited by Thorpe or Grein, and Dietrich does not comment upon it. The only solution offered is Holthausen's "crab" (*Anglia Beibl.* xxx, 53). In the remaining fragments of the riddle, the creature is described as having *ne flæsc* or, if we accept Holthausen's reconstruction of line 4a, *fell ne flæsc* (*Anglia* xxiv, 265), presumably "no skin or flesh." The crab does not have skin in the ordinary sense of that word, but it does have flesh as anyone who has eaten boiled crabmeat must know. This certainly was an Anglo-Saxon delicacy as the fisherman in Aelfric's *Colloquy* mentions among his sea catch *ostran and crabban* (*Coll.* 106). There is nothing in the riddle as it stands to indicate that the creature comes from the sea.

Reading a reconstructed [g]*ongende* in 2a with most editors, I translate line 2 as follows: "Traveling, [the creature] swallows ground." Grein (*Sp.*, p. 654) notes that *swelgan* may be used with the accusative or the instrumental. Examples of *swelgan* taking the dative/instrumental case in the *Riddles* are: 12.15, 15.7, 24.9, 45.6, 47.2, 56.10, 89.24. Tupper (p. 220) reads MS. *greate* as a form of *greot*, "sand, earth, dirt," citing *Gen.* 909: *þu scealt greot etan*. This seems the likeliest reading. The word could be an adjective ("great"), modifying a lost word in the next line, but it could not very well be an adverb meaning "hugely" as Mackie would have it (p. 219). The creature's ability to swallow dirt as it moves is its distinguishing characteristic. Also, it has neither skin nor flesh, and this would seem to indicate an implement made of metal or wood. The creature travels on its "feet," which are unfortunately left undescribed because of the lacuna in line 5. On the basis of this admittedly sketchy description, I believe the creature to be a harrow similar to the one depicted in the Bayeux tapestry (see Stenton, *The Bayeux Tapestry*, plate 12 and detail of the plate). The harrow is a sharp-toothed instrument dragged across the ground after the initial plowing in order to break up clods of soil. Wilson (*The Anglo-Saxons*, p. 76) notes that the Anglo-Saxons probably used harrows similar to the one shown in the Bayeux tapestry. As the harrow moves, it picks up clods of dirt and oftentimes draws them through its teeth to lay them back upon the ground in the form of fine soil. No other tool could "swallow dirt" except perhaps a spade, but a spade would have a single foot and not the plural *fotum* (line 4).

78.4: *fotum gong*[..: Holthausen (*Anglia* xxiv, 265) reconstructs the line to read *fotum gong*[*eð*], which is probably right. Cp. *Rid.* 10.1: *Fotum ic fere*.

79. Gold
[*VN: Gr¹.80; Gr².83; Tr.81; Tu.83; W.82; M.82; K-D.83*]

Dietrich (*ZfdA.* xi, 484) solved the riddle as "ore"; Trautmann solved the riddle as "money." Tupper and Krapp and Dobbie accept "ore." Wyatt lists the solution, "ore, metal, money." Mackie prefers "metal" or "gold." The last five lines of the riddle clearly point to a coinage of some sort so I prefer the solution "gold." O.E. *gold* can mean either the substance gold or gold artifacts or money (BTS., p. 482). The Old English riddle has several themes in common with Riddle 91 of Symphosius, "Pecunia":

> Terra fui primo, latebris abscondita terrae;
> Nunc aliud pretium flammae nomenque dederunt,
> Nec iam terra vocor, licet ex me terra paretur.
>
> [Ed. Ohl, p. 124]

The common motifs are: (1) the creature's home in the earth; (2) the journey from earth to another place; (3) metamorphosis by fire; (4) the acquisition of worldly power. Of course, the emphasis in the Old English riddle is upon the forced nature of the journey—the creature is stolen from its home and separated from its kin. It can do nothing directly to harm its captor; yet ironically it takes unto itself power to bind others in the world. The curse of gold is legendary. Man steals gold from the ground, and the gold in turn steals man's peace and security. This is nowhere more evident than in *Beowulf*. The gold-adorned heirlooms of the poem are symbols of the feud—past, present, and future. The gleaming sword is more often than not a rich token of the *guðdeað* or *bealocwealm* of its previous owner. The treasure is never taken and worn freely as the poet says:

Sinc eaðe mæg,
gold on grund(e)   gumcynnes gehwone
oferhigian,   hyde se ðe wylle!

[*Beo.* 2764*b*–66]

79.1: *Frod*: This word (see plate xix) provides an interesting example of the varying sizes of capital letters that occur at the beginnings of riddles. The initial *F* is a large capital; the next *R* is a small capital, which is larger than most small capitals found within the text (in non-beginning words); the *O* is slightly smaller than the *R*—it is the size of a regular small capital; the final *d* is smaller still, but slightly larger than a regular *d*.

79.2: *bæles weard*: Trautmann emends to *bæles wearð*. Kock (*Lunds Universitets Årsskrift*, NF., Avd. 1, Bd. 14, Nr. 26, p. 66) emends to *bæle wearð* with *bæle* in the instrumental parallel with *lige* and *fyre*.

79.3: *lige*: The emendation of *lige* for MS. *life* was proposed by Holthausen (*Anglia* xxiv, 265) and is accepted by Tupper, Trautmann, Mackie, and myself. Other editors retain MS. *life*. The reading cannot be certain because of the lacuna, but the passage as it stands makes more sense with *lige bewunden* parallel to *fyre gefælsad* (4*a*).

79.4–6: Dietrich (*ZfdA.* xi, 484) and Tupper take the *eorþan broþor* at 5*a* to be Tubal-Cain, the legendary first smith (see *Gen.* 1082ff.), but it does not seem likely that the smith who presently (*Nu me . . . warað*) guards and heats (lines 1–4*a*) the creature is the same man of the past —presumably a miner and not a smith—who stole the creature from its home in the ground. Wyatt believes the *eorþan broþor* to be "fire, through whose agency the ore was brought into the service of men" (p. 118), but *guma* (here *gumena*, line 6*a*) is not elsewhere used in the *Riddles* to refer to creatures. *Guma* always refers to men. Trautmann says "Der Bruder der Erde heisst der Mensch hier wie [*Rid.*] 41.14" (p. 131). In *Rid.* 41 (in Trautmann's numbering and my own), the earth is called mother and sister to body and soul, because man and earth were both formed by God, but man was formed from the earth. Kock (see reference above) takes *eorþan broþor* as an accusative appositive of *me*. Essentially I agree with Trautmann that the enemy here is man in all his guises—miner, smelter, forger, and artisan.

79.6–8: I translate: *I remember well who first wasted* (or *mined?*) *the whole race from which I sprang out of its native soil*. Most editors take MS. *agette* as *āgētte* from the weak verb *āgētan*, "to waste, destroy" (BTS., p. 29), though Krapp and Dobbie note that "it is hard to see how such a meaning can be fitted into this passage," and suggest that "the word *agette* undoubtedly refers to a mining operation, but in exactly what way, is not apparent" (p. 374). Kock (see reference above) and Mackie translate *agette* as "took away," or "drew out," apparently taking the verb as a preterite form of the strong verb *āgitan*, which Toller (BTS., p. 29) notes may mean "to find, get to know," or "to get, take away." Under the second meaning, Toller lists one example, that of *āgēton* at *An.* 32, but his parenthetical query, "(-gētton?)," presumably indicates that he believes the verb to be really the preterite of weak *āgētan*. Indeed an examination of the *Andreas* passage and the four passages cited under *āgētan* (*Rid.* 79.7, *An.* 1143, *Fort.* 16, and *Brun.* 18) shows that all deal with the death-dealing power of spears as instruments of destruction so that Toller's proposed emendation of the *Andreas* passage seems well justified. In this riddle passage, in order to accept Kock's and Mackie's meanings, one would have to emend the MS. reading to the proper preterite form *āgeat* (which would give trouble metrically) or to a subjunctive form *āgēate* or *āgēte*. The passage as it stands would not support a subjunctive reading, but if we were to emend 6*b* to *Ic ne ful gearwe gemon* or *Ne ic ful gearwe gemon* (postulating that the *ne* disappeared because of its proximity with the *-ne* of the preceding *gyrne*), then the subjunctive might be justified. This would however necessitate a double emendation so I prefer to let the passage stand as it is and to postulate with Krapp and Dobbie a lost meaning for weak *āgētan* referring to some mining operation. The weak *āgētan* derives from strong *gēotan*, which may mean *to pour* (*off* or *away*), *cause to flow, found, cast, make with molten metal* (BTS., p. 389). Trautmann (*Anglia* xliii, 252) first thought of reading *fruman* as a verb or of emending *fruman* to *fremman* and taking *agette* as the preterite optative of *āgitan*, "erkennen, verstehen, wissen," but in his edition he gave these up and suggested the possibility of emending *agette* to *apohte*. Holthausen (*Anglia Beibl.* xxx, 53) suggested reading *forma* for *fruman* or (*Anglia* xliv, 350 ff.) adding *æt* or *on* before *fruman*.

79.8b: "I may not treat him evilly." The sense of the main verb must be supplied after the auxiliary.

79.9a: All editors omit MS. *on*. Trautmann and Holthausen (*Anglia* xliv, 351) would read *ic [him] hæftnyd*, but this is unnecessary.

79.10: *wunda fela*: Grein and all later editors except Mackie emend *wunda* to *wundra*, but the "wounds" here may well be stamped impressions, letters or figures on the coins. Cp. the *wunda* at *Rid*. 57.16 that speak to men. Wilson (*The Anglo-Saxons*, p. 86) notes that the first Anglo-Saxon coins were struck in the late seventh century. Before that Roman and Merovingian coins were sometimes used. Wilson notes that the first Anglo-Saxon coinage was gold, but that by the late eighth century the Anglo-Saxons had turned to making silver coins. For a discussion of the early seventh-century Merovingian gold coins found at Sutton Hoo, see Bruce-Mitford, *The Sutton Hoo Ship-Burial: A Handbook*, pp. 54 ff.

79.13: *dyran*: Trautmann in his notes suggests reading *dyrnan*, but the power of the gold has already been called *degolfulne*, and its *cræft* may be precious as well as secret.

80. Water
[*VN: Gr¹.81; Gr².84; Tr.82; Tu.84; W.83; M.83; K-D.84*]

Dietrich's solution, "water" (*ZfdA*. xi, 484) is accepted by all editors. The creature is described here as *Modor . . . monigra mærra wihta* (line 4), and in *Rid*. 39 the water is called *moddor monigra cynna* (39.2). For examples of the same motif in Aldhelm's "Fons" and "Aqua" riddles, see the headnote to *Rid*. 39. Tupper follows Prehn in noting similarities between the opening of the Old English riddle and Riddle 23 of Eusebius, "De Aequore," which begins: *Motor, curro, fero velox, nec desero sedem* (*CCL*. cxxxiii, p. 233). But the paradox of movement and stasis in the Latin line is nowhere evident in the Old English riddle. The water of the Old English riddle *hafað ryne strongne* (line 2; cp. *Rid*. 17.6–7) and *be grunde fareð* (line 3).

The water of this riddle is the mother of many creatures; so Ambrose says of water in the *Hexaemeron*: *eadem sit omnium nutrix* (*Hex.* iii.xv.62; *PL.* xiv, 196). The creature has as many guises as water has forms; again, Ambrose says: *Una nempe atque eadem est aqua, et in diversas plerumque sese mutat species* (*Hex.* iii.xv.62; *PL.* xiv, 195). Pliny details the power and diversity of water in his *Natural History* in the introduction to the books on medicines obtained from aquatic animals. Pliny says:

> Aquatilium secuntur in medicina beneficia, opifice natura ne in illis quidem cessante et per undas fluctusque ac reciprocos aestus amniumque rapidos cursus inprobas exercente vires, nusquam potentia maiore, si verum fateri volumus, quippe hoc elementum ceteris omnibus imperat. terras devorant aquae, flammas necant, scandunt in sublime et caelum quoque sibi vindicant ac nubium obtentu vitalem spiritum strangulant, quae causa fulmina elidit, ipso secum discordante mundo. quid esse mirabilius potest aquis in caelo stantibus? at illae, ceu parum sit in tantam pervenire altitudinem, rapiunt eo secum piscium examina, saepe etiam lapides subeuntque portantes aliena pondera. eaedem cadentes omnium terra enascentium causa fiunt prorsus mirabili natura, si quis velit reputare, ut fruges gignantur, arbores fruticesque vivant, in caelum migrare aquas animamque etiam herbis vitalem inde deferre, victa confessione omnes terrae quoque vires aquarum esse beneficii. quapropter ante omnia ipsarum potentiae exempla ponemus. cunctas enim enumerare quis mortalium queat? [*NH.* xxxi.i.1–3]

The forms of water are many; the power of water is untold. In the same spirit, the Old English riddler says: *Nænig oþrum mæg . . . wordum gecyþan / hu mislic biþ mægen þara cynna* (lines 6–8). The power of the riddler is to describe the miraculous and to enclose the limitless by signifying words.

80.1: *on eorþan*: The phrase was first supplied by Bülbring (*Literaturblatt* xii, 158) to complete the half-line and is accepted by Tupper and Krapp and Dobbie. Herzfeld (*Die Räthsel des Exeterbuches und ihr Verfasser*, p. 70) would read *An wrætlicu wiht* or *Is an wiht* as the initial half-line. Trautmann reads *An worold wiht is* for the half-line. Other editors retain the deficient MS. reading, *An wiht is*. For a similar opening half-line, cp. *Rid.* 48.1.

80.2: *hafað ryne strongne*: For similar uses of *ryne*, cp. *Gen.* 159 and *Rid.* 17.6–7. In the manuscript facsimile of Chambers, Förster, and Flower (*The Exeter Book of Old English Poetry*, folio 128a, at the top of the page) a faint dot occurs between *strongne* and *grimme* that might be mistaken for a MS. point (see plate xx.b). Mackie (p. 220) marks a point after *strongne*, but there is no point in the manuscript itself (see plate xx.a) and no sign of any erasure. The dot in the facsimile is apparently from an imperfection in the photographic plate.

80.6: *neol is nearograp*: *deep down is its clutch*. The word *nearograp* is a hapax legomenon and is usually translated as "close grasp" (B-T., p. 712; CH., p. 247; *Sp.* [*prensionis artae?*], p. 496), though Mackie reads the slightly variant "throttling grip." The power of the current or the tide runs deep. The "tight grasp" of the water is its ability to touch at all points any object submerged in it. The ominous overtones of such a *grap* should not be discounted (cp. the various uses of *grap* in *Beowulf*). Trautmann reads *nearograp* as an adjective, "zugreifend," and places a comma after *is*.

80.11 ff.: My policy with regard to partially obscured or obliterated letters has been a conservative one. I print only those letters that can be read with certainty in either the manuscript or in the facsimile (next to the burn, letters are often more readily visible in the facsimile now than they are in the manuscript itself: see note to line 46 and corresponding plates). Those readers interested in editorial reconstructions of totally obliterated half-lines or full lines should consult the notes in Krapp and Dobbie. The practice of reconstructing the lacunae in Old English poetry seems to me highly questionable, given the often idiosyncratic nature of the lines.

80.12: *mæ*[.......]*es*: Only this much of the word(s) can be read with certainty from the manuscript and facsimile. Robert Chambers (*Brit. Mus. Add. MS. 9067*) could not read the letters after *mæ* with any certainty and neither can I. Other editors have been less cautious. Assmann reads *mæ*.....*þes*; Tupper, *mæst* . . *þes*; Mackie, *mæ*[*g*]*e*[*n halg*]*es*; Krapp and Dobbie, *mæge*[.....]*es*. Wyatt follows Tupper (with a five-space lacuna). Trautmann reconstructs *mægen halges*. Chambers and Flower (*The Exeter Book of Old English Poetry*, p. 79) read *mæge.. ...es*, but Mackie rightly notes that the horizontal stroke visible after *mæ* may be that of a *g* or a *t*.

80.12: Before the final æ all editors except Tupper print *g*; Tupper prints *t*. There is no way of telling whether the upper portion of the letter that is still visible in the MS. is that of a *g* or a *t*.

80.17: I follow Trautmann and Krapp and Dobbie in my reading of the partially visible letters of this line. Wyatt, Mackie, Chambers and Flower, and Tupper read *far* or *f. r* instead of *fter*.

80.19b: Holthausen (*Anglia* xxxviii, 80) restores the half-line to [*for*]*þon ær wæs*, then emends *ær* to *æror* for metrical reasons. Holthausen's assessment of a metrical norm in the midst of a lacuna is ridiculous.

80.22–23: Holthausen (*ESn.* xxxvii, 210; *Anglia* xxxv, 167) rearranges the lines to suit his metrical taste. Tupper (p. 224) points out that the lines are metrically fine as they stand in the MS. and that "the metrical a-priorism of Holthausen is dangerous."

80.29b–32: I translate the lines as follows: "It treads the ground, boldest and strongest, greediest and most eager of whatever has grown up under the sky and (of whatever) the children of men may have seen." Mackie takes *ælda bearn* as the object of *sawe*, but it is not clear how the water might watch men. Krapp and Dobbie read *sawe* as a variant of *sawen*, preterite plural subjunctive, and note similar instances of *-e* plural subjunctive endings at *Rid.* 24.16 (my numbering), *Ord.* 7, *Hell* 83, and refer to a discussion by Bloomfield (*JEGP.* xxix, 100 ff.). This reading makes the most sense. For a similar use of the subjunctive with superlatives, cp. *Rid.* 39.2–5. My translation follows that of Baum.

80.33: All editors except Tupper accept Grein's emendation of MS. *mæge* to *mægen*, though there is little agreement on the meaning of the line. Wyatt would begin a new sentence with *Swa* (as I have done), translating the line, "So that glory weaves the might of the children of the world," or he would place a comma after *sawe* at the end of line 32, translating line 33, "as the might of the children of the world weaves that glory" (p. 119); he does not profess to know what the line means in either case. I prefer Wyatt's first reading, which agrees with Mackie's translation of the line: "So the glorious creature weaves the might of the children of the world" (p. 225). This is, I think, a reference to the power of water to weave the destiny of all the creatures of the world. This is not unusual in light of the riddler's statement at line 4. Tupper's reading is less likely. He retains MS. *mæge* and emends MS. *wifeð* to *wifa*, taking line 33 as a parenthetical statement, translating: "So (lives) the glorious woman, kinswoman of world bairns" (p. 224), citing *Beo.* 1391, *Grendles magan*, for the meaning of *mæge*. Tupper glosses *wuldor* as a noun, but translates it here as an adjective. The only possibility for Tupper's reading would be to postulate a compound, *wuldorwifa* (cp. *Wuldorfæder, wuldorgast, wuldormaga*, etc.), but I prefer Mackie's reading.

80.34: There is no gap in the MS. here but the lack of continuity in the sense of the passage indicates that at least a half-line has been lost. I have followed the traditional practice of reading *mon mode snottor* in a single half-line at 35a, though the verse so constituted is metrically overburdened as Sievers (*Beiträge* x, 508) noted unless *snottor* was originally the variant *snotor* to the poet. Since *mode snottor* is a metrically acceptable half-line in itself (cp. *Rid.* 82.2b, and *Precepts* 87b), it seems just as likely that *mon* was part of some preceding half-line now lost. Grein, who read 35a as I have it here, supplied *gefrigen hæbbe* at 34b and so Assmann, Tupper, and Trautmann.

80.39: There is no gap in the MS. here, but the meter would seem to indicate the loss of a half-line. Krapp and Dobbie point out that the *worulde* of line 38a may be carried over as the object here in order to give the line sense as it stands, but this makes for an awkward syntax since there are intervening verbs and one intervening object. It seems more likely that the object of line 40 was contained in the presumably lost half-line. It should be noted that line 40a, though metrically acceptable as it is (and as it is printed by most editors), could stand with only *utan beweorpeð* leaving *oft* somewhere in the preceding half-line. So Trautmann reads the hypothetically restored lines 39b–40a as [*Hio foldan*] *oft* / *utan beweorpeð*.

80.46 ff.: It should be noted that in many passages around the burn in the manuscript, the words are more clearly visible now in the facsimile of Chambers, Förster, and Flower (*The Exeter Book of Old English Poetry*) than they are in the manuscript itself. The reason for this is not hard to find. Chambers and Flower note:

The reader who turns to this facsimile, and then to most of the editions, will be surprised to find that he is able to read letters which have often been recorded by the editors as missing. The reason of this is that such letters, though always there, were long obscured by the strips of vellum which were used to bind the broken sheets of parchment together.

Before this facsimile was made, these strips were removed, and the facsimile therefore shows in these places almost all that can now be read in the original manuscript, and more than could be read till quite recently. [*The Exeter Book of Old English Poetry*, p. 68]

After the photographs were made for the facsimile, the damaged portions along the burn were again remounted so that small portions of the text were obscured. A small portion of the text for the lines here along the burn is reproduced in the section of plates in both the manuscript and facsimile versions (see plates xxi.a and b).

81. Fish and River
[*VN: Gr¹.82; Gr².85; Tr.83; Tu.85; W.84; M.84; K-D.85*]

Dietrich (*ZfdA.* xi, 485) first solved the riddle as "fish and river," citing the influence of Symphosius's Riddle 12:

> Flumen et Piscis
> Est domus in terris clara quae voce resultat.
> Ipsa domus resonat, tacitus sed non sonat hospes.
> Ambo tamen currunt hospes simul et domus una.
>
> [Ed. Ohl, p. 44]

Tupper (*MLN* xvii, 3; and edition, p. 225) traces the history of the Symphosius riddle in medieval writings. The influence of Symphosius on the first two and one-half lines of the Old English riddle seems clear. The common motifs include: house and houseguest, speaker and silent companion, two comrades bound on a journey. Lines 3*b*–7 of the Old English riddle are altogether new. Here the contrast is drawn between two creatures—one swift and strong and the other slow and enduring. The paradox is pointed: while the swift one rests, the slow one runs on. The resolution of the paradox points to the solution: one creature dwells in the other and will die if separated from its companion. The two belong together. The poet of *Maxims II* says: *Fisc sceal on wætere / cynren cennan* (*Max. II* 27–28).

81.2: Krapp and Dobbie note that "the scribe of the MS. left the space (about seven letters) between *ymb unc* and the end of the MS. line vacant, and began the next line with *dryht*, apparently recognizing that something has dropped out of the text at this point" (p. 376). Tupper (p. 59, note) chastises Grein and Wyatt for failing to note the paleographical "gap" in the text. But the space after *ymb unc* is a traditionally defining one. Since *Rid.* 80 appears to end exactly (a few letters are missing because of the burn) at the right-hand margin of the MS., there is no defining end-space to separate *Rid.* 80 from *Rid.* 81. The scribe has thus begun *Rid.* 81 with a short MS. line leaving a characteristic end-space at the beginning of this riddle in order to compensate for the lack of space at the end of the preceding one. The same practice may be observed in the MS. between the following riddles: 2 and 3 (fol. 102*b*), 21 and 22 (fol. 106*b*), 44 and 45 (fol. 112*b*), 53 and 54 (fol. 114*a*), 56 and 57 (fol. 114*b*), 28b and 58* (fol. 122*b*), 59 and 60 (fol. 124*b*), 62 and 63 (fol. 125*a*), and 86 and 87 (fol. 129*b*). This list does not include examples of short first lines where the final portion of the preceding riddle (one or two words) has been written toward the right-hand margin of the same MS. line (portions of two riddles thus occurring in the same MS. line). What does seem likely is that the scribe, in his concern for marking this end-space, has left out a portion of the text. Tupper restores the line: *ymb unc [domas dyde, unc] Driht[en] scop*. The repetition of *unc* might thus account for the scribe's mistake. Tupper, however, places a semicolon after *hlud* at the end of line 1 and begins a new phrase with *ymb* in line 2. This is a most unusual construction. Nowhere else in the *Riddles* does *ymb* begin a phrase in this manner. It seems to me more likely that the *unc-*, which might have occurred in line 2a, was an adjectival form of *uncer* and that the half-line served as a phrasal modifying *ne [eom] ic . . . hlud* telling where the creature is silent ("about the house"? "about the hall"?). At the end of the MS. line the scribe might easily have passed from this *uncer* (*uncere, uncerne?*) to

---

Rid. 28b is grouped with *Rid.* 28a in this edition; in the MS. it precedes *Rid.* 58 (see headnote to *Rid.* 28).

the following *unc* leaving the resulting lacuna. I have punctuated the line according to this reading with a semicolon after the lacuna. This is also the punctuation of Wyatt and Grein. A number of arbitrary reconstructions have been proposed for the line, but I prefer to leave the lacuna as it stands in the MS.

81.3: *swiftre*: Thorpe and Trautmann emend to masculine *swiftra*, but Tupper (p. 226, note) and Wyatt (p. xxxvi) note similar inconsistencies with regard to gender in other riddles.

81.5: *rinnan*: Tupper's emendation of *rinnan* for MS. *yrnan* to secure the alliteration of the line is accepted by Trautmann, Mackie, and myself. Other editors retain the MS. reading. For "The Chronology of *R*-Metathesis in Old English," and an explanation of the sound changes involved in the shift from *rinnan* to *irnan*, see Stanley's article in *EGS* v, 103–15.

82. One-eyed Seller of Garlic
[*VN: Gr¹.83; Gr².86; Tr.84; Tu.86; W.85; M.85; K-D.86*]

Dietrich (*ZfdA*. ix, 485) first proposed the solution, "organ," but later (*ZfdA*. xii, 248) withdrew this in favor of "one-eyed seller of garlic," citing Symphosius's Riddle 94 as a possible source. All subsequent editors have accepted this solution. The riddle of Symphosius is just as obscure as the Old English riddle, except for the gift of its title:

> Luscus Alium Vendens
> Cernere iam fas est quod vix tibi credere fas est:
> Unus inest oculus, capitum sed milia multa.
> Qui quod habet vendit, quod non habet unde parabit?
>
> [Ed. Ohl, p. 128]

Ohl points out, "Were it not for the title, this enigma would probably defy solution!" (*The Enigmas of Symphosius*, p. 128). Were it not for the Latin (available at least to modern scholars), the Old English riddle would certainly defy solution. The sight of old garlic- or onion-sellers lurching many-headed across the Anglo-Saxon marketplace may have been more common to Old English riddle-solvers than it is to us, but presumably not all of those grisly garlic-sellers were one-eyed.

The Latin riddle, of course, offers its grotesque title and solution immediately: *Luscus Alium Vendens*. The Old English riddle offers no such crutch. Formally, the Latin riddle is divided into three distinct parts, corresponding to the lines: an opening challenge of credibility offered to the reader, a short riddlic description of the creature, and a concluding reference to the riddlic seller. The Old English riddle begins with the slightly ominous, *"Wiht cwom gongan"* (cp. *Beo.* 710 ff.) to the meeting of men, then proceeds to the extended description of the monstrous *wiht*, and concludes with the formulaic posture of riddling. There is no mention of a seller in the Old English riddle.

The Latin riddle is an entitling metaphoric game, however grotesque. If no title had been given, the generous hint of *Qui quod habet vendit* would remain. There is no hint of any solution in the Old English riddle. Rather it seems intended to defy solution. In this sense, it is what Archer Taylor calls a *neck riddle*:

> Another very curious variety of enigma consists in a description of a scene that can be interpreted only by the one who sets the puzzle. The terms used are not confusing, but the situation itself seems inexplicable. In many northern European versions of such puzzles the speaker saves his neck by the riddle, for the judge or executioner has promised release in exchange for a riddle that cannot be guessed. ["The Varieties of Riddles," in *Philologica: The Malone Anniversary Studies*, p. 6]

While not all neck riddles are designed to escape the hangman, certainly all are designed to confuse the solver. This is an old and deliberate disguise. Samson's perfect riddle, "Out of the eater came something to eat, / Out of the strong came something sweet" (Judges 14:14) was solved by his antagonists only after Delilah had pried the answer (*bees in the carcass of a lion*) from him after seven days' weeping. Whether the Old English *Riddle* 82 was meant to stand in this tradition of deliberately obscure riddles, or whether the reader was meant to know the riddle of Symphosius, we cannot know. We can surmise that without the entitled efforts of Symphosius, a good deal of critical weeping would surely have been spent on this riddle.

82.2: *monige on mæðle: many at a meeting.* Cp. *An.* 1626: *manige on meðle*. Padelford (*BBzA.* iv, 46), who likes Dietrich's original "organ" solution, maintains that the line is suggestive of an ecclesiastical setting. The citations of *mæðl* in Grein (*Sp.*, pp. 438ff.) do not sustain this view.

82.4: *twelf hund heafda*: *twelve-hundred heads*. The exact number of heads (cp. Symphosius's *capitum sed milia multa*) is probably dictated by the alliterative requirements of the line.

82.7: *Saga hwæt hio hatte*: Here, as in *Rid*. 17.9, the MS. reading is certainly corrupt since the human narrator of a third-person descriptive riddle cannot conclude with "Say what I am called." The emended form *hio* here refers to the *wiht* in line 1. A similar case occurs at the end of *Rid*. 37.

82.lower margin: Wyatt notes at the end of this riddle "an unrecorded sign (B-rune?)" (Wyatt, fig. 18 and note). No sign is visible in the MS. (see plate xxii), even under ultraviolet light, and no sign was recorded by Robert Chambers in his transcript of 1832 (*Brit. Mus. Add. MS. 9067*). Wyatt's "rune" remains unrecorded for good reason.

83. Bellows
[*VN: Gr¹.84; Gr².87; Tr.85; Tu.87; W.86; M.86; K-D.87*]

Dietrich (*ZfdA*. xi, 485) first solved the riddle as "cask and cooper," explaining, "indem er es mit dem *himmelszahne*, oder ohne mythologischen schmuck mit dem donnernden *keile*, angreift und sein auge, das *spundloch*, zuschlägt." Müller (*Die Rätsel des Exeterbuches*, p. 19), Trautmann (*Anglia Beibl.* v, 50) and Tupper solved the riddle as "bellows" on the basis of similarities between this and *Rid*. 35, and so Mackie and Krapp and Dobbie. The first three lines of *Rids*. 83 and 35 are so similar as to indicate that one riddlic beginning was probably used as a source for the other.

83.2: *folgade*: For the meaning, "to attend," see note to *Rid*. 35.2.

83.4b: The object (the creature) is ellipted. Translate: "He grabbed onto (it)." For a similar construction, cp. *Rid*. 23.7*b*.

83.5: *heofones toþe*: *heaven's tooth*—i.e., *the wind* (Tupper, p. 227). Tupper cites a similar description in Riddle 41 of the Bern collection, "De Vento":

> Os est mihi nullum, dente nec vulnero quemquam,
> Mordeo sed cunctos silvis campisque morantes.
>
> [*CCL.* cxxxiii A, p. 587]

83.5b: There is no indication of any loss in the MS., but the alliterative pattern would indicate a loss of at least a half-line.

83.6: *bleowe on eage*: Cp. *Rid.* 35.4b: *fleah þurh his eage*. The verb is from *blawan*, often used to describe the passage of wind or breath (BTS., p. 96). Cp. the translation of *flantium follium* in Aelfric's *Colloquy* as *blawendra byliga* (WW. 100.2). Grein, in a note, first suggested reading *bleow* or *bleaw* for MS. *bleowe*, so Tupper and Wyatt read *bleow* in their editions. The spelling *bleowan* occurs several times in the homilies (see BTS., p. 96); the form *bleowe* is probably subjunctive. It may be argued that the verb *fleah* in the analogous half-line in *Rid.* 35.4 occurs in the indicative, but the preceding half-line (at least) has been lost here so we do not know whether the verb occurs in a clause normally taking the subjunctive or not. In light of the uncertainty it seems best to leave the form as it is in the MS.

83.6: *borcade*: The hole in the MS. has obliterated the lower portion of the *r* so that the letter resembles an *n*. It is impossible to tell whether the original reading was *borcade* or *boncade*, but since there is no known word in Old English remotely resembling *boncade*, I think we are justified in reading *borcade*. Thorpe and Trautmann report MS. *borcade*; all other editors report MS. *boncade*. Krapp and Dobbie state explicitly that "the lower tip of *n* is quite visible in the MS." (p. 376), but only the right lower tip is visible and this is the same paleographically in both *r* and *n*. All editors read *borcade* in the edited texts, assuming a verb *borcian*, "to bark," perhaps related to *beorcan*. This is also Holthausen's conjecture (*AEW.*, p. 30). The reading is certainly tenuous, but it makes more sense than *boncade*.

83.7: *wancode*: Thorpe, Grein, and Wyatt emended the MS. reading here to *þancode*, which in its meaning, "rejoiced," makes good sense but does away with the double alliteration in the initial half-line.

Trautmann retains MS. *wancode* as a form of *wancian*, "wanken," else-where unattested and so do Mackie, Krapp and Dobbie, and Camp-bell (the latter in his *Revised and Enlarged Addenda* to BTS., p. 64). Krapp and Dobbie note that "an A.S. *wancian* would correspond phonologically to O.H.G. *wankōn*, 'waver, vacillate'" (p. 377). Traut-mann in his notes also suggests the possibility of *wacnode*, "ward (da-durch dass die Luft ausfloss) schwach" (p. 134). Tupper reads *wanode* from *wanian* (*wonian*), "to wane, decrease." A similar possibility might be to read *wacode* from *wacian*, "to languish, grow weak." But it is dif-ficult to know what the intended meaning is because the crux of *bor-cade* or *boncade* in the previous half-line remains unsolved. Under these circumstances it seems best to retain the MS. reading.

84. Inkhorn
[*VN: Gr¹.85; Gr².88; Tr.86; Tu.88; W.87; M.87; K-D.88*]

This riddle is one of two "inkhorn" riddles; the other is *Rid*. 89. Other "horn" riddles occur at *Rids*. 12 and 76 where the motif is much different from the one used here. Dietrich (*ZfdA*. xi, 485–86) first solved the riddle as "staghorn" or "antler" and this form is retained by Wyatt and Mackie. Tupper and Trautmann prefer the more specific "inkhorn" and so do I. This is partly a matter of preference, but as the past tense is used in the early descriptive passages of the poem (when the horn was on the stag's head) and the present tense is used beginning at line 17 (where the horn is described as an inkhorn), the present identity of the riddlic creature would seem to be "inkhorn."

The only other inkhorn riddle from early England is Eusebius's Riddle 30, "De Atramentorio." The Latin riddle has little in common with the Old English "inkhorn" riddles, but it is interesting to com-pare the constructions. Eusebius writes:

> Armorum fueram vice, meque tenebat in armis
> Fortis, et armigeri gestabar vertice tauri.
> Vas tamen intus habens sum nunc intestina amara
> Viscera, sed ructans bonus ibit nitor odoris.

> [*CCL*. cxxxiii, p. 240]

The same contrast between present and past life exists in both riddles. The descriptions of the ink are different. The Latin creature describes itself as a weapon whereas the English creature does not (cp., however, a similar description at *Rid.* 12.1). The Latin horn is made from the head of a bull (*vertice tauri*) whereas the Old English horn comes from a wild forest creature (lines 12 ff.), certainly a stag. Erhardt-Siebold (*Die lateinischen Rätsel der Angelsachsen*, p. 69) notes another medieval Latin reference to the inkhorn in the *Vita Columbae*: *hodie mei corniculum atramenti inclinans effundet* (chap. 25; quoted in Erhardt-Siebold).

84.9b: The letter *x* is mistakenly reported by Chambers and Flower (*The Exeter Book of Old English Poetry*, p. 80, note) and by Mackie (p. 229, note) as a *y*. Trautmann and Krapp and Dobbie rightly report the letter as *x*. Only the lower fragment of the left-slanting diagonal is visible in the manuscript, but this is enough to determine the letter. The slight tail on the stroke where the pen has been picked up moves up and to the left as in the case of *x* and not to the right as in the case of *y*.

84.10: *ond min broþor*: For MS. *ond mine broþor* [with *ond* abbreviated], Trautmann would emend to *wiþ minne broþor*. Tupper would read *ond broþor min*. All other editors follow the more conservative emendation of Grein as it is here.

84.15: *Nu*: Trautmann reads *þæt* in place of MS. *Nu* [small cap. *N*] and reads the half-line as a continuation of the sentence begun at line 14*b*. There is no reason to alter the text in such a drastic fashion.

84.17b–18a: *gumcynnes / anga ofer eorþan*: literally, "the single one of humankind on earth," but this is both hyperbolic and metaphoric— the horn is a suffering and separated warrior. The underlying meaning is something like "an isolated one of my kind on earth."

84.18b: The MS. reading, *is min bæc*, which is retained by Grein and Wyatt, is attacked by Sievers (*Beiträge* x, 520) as being unmetrical. Holthausen (*Indogermanische Forschungen* iv, 388) suggested *is min [agen] bæc* and so Tupper, Mackie, and Krapp and Dobbie, but it is not clear why the horn's back should be any darker than its front. Trautmann's emendation, *is min [innaþ] b[l]æc*, which I have accepted, at least makes good sense of the lines. The repetition of minims in *min innaþ* could easily have caused the initial scribal error.

84.21: *ac*: For the horned *c* form of *a*, here a small capital, see the note to *Rid.* 86.2.

84.21 ff.: This passage was misunderstood by Dietrich who said:

> Wenn nun das horn sagt, jetzt stehe es auf holz (*Beo.* 1317: *healwudu*), am ende des bretes, und müsse da bruderlos feststehen, so ergiebt sich, es ist das dem giebel des ehedem meist hölzernen hauses zum schmuck dienende *firsthorn* [Dietrich cites *Ruin* 22: *heah horngestreon*; *Rid.* 1.38: *hornsalu*; *Beo.* 704: *hornreced*]. um da aufgesteckt werden zu können muste der untere theil des hornes innerlich ausgebohrt werden, daher die klage über das aufreissen (ll. 32 ff.), wodurch der suchende, d.h. der pflock der es tragen soll, gelingen findet. [*ZfdA.* xi, 486]

The misreading is repeated by later editors and translators like Wyatt and Brooke. Tupper notes the similarity in progression between this riddle and "inkhorn" *Rid.* 89 and wisely surmises that the *wuda* of line 19 and the *bordes on ende* of line 20 refer to the wooden table or desk upon which the inkhorn stands. Tupper (p. 228) also notes several manuscript illustrations depicting the inkhorn on the desk or table.

84.26: *fremmanne*: Sievers (*Beiträge* x, 482) would emend to *freman* for metrical reasons (see note to *Rid.* 26.12*b*). Trautmann and Wyatt read *fremman* in line 26*b* and *ne næfre* in line 27*a*. Tupper, Mackie, and Krapp and Dobbie read the lines as they are here.

84.29: *unsceafta*: monsters. Grein (*Sp.*, p. 743) gives the definition, *Ungeheuer*; CH. (p. 384), "monster(?)." B-T. and BTS. do not list the word. Literally *unsceaft* must mean "uncreation." For at least the general meaning, cp. the use of *untydras* at *Beo.* 111 ff. where the offspring of Cain are described:

> þanon untydras   ealle onwocon,
> eotenas ond ylfe   ond orcneas,
> swylce gigantas,   þa wið Gode wunnon
> lange þrage;

[*Beo.* 111–14]

Tupper notes that "the 'monsters' are, of course, the iron and steel weapons that scrape and hollow out the Inkhorn" (p. 229), but they are more likely plundering quills that seize ink from the belly of the inkhorn. Cp. the same motif at *Rid.* 89.28ff.

85. Uncertain
[*VN: Gr¹.X; Gr².89; Tr.87; Tu.89; W.88; M.88; K-D.89*]

This riddle fragment was not edited by Thorpe or Grein, and Dietrich did not comment upon it. Tupper notes that the *wombe* of line 2 and the *leþre* of line 4 may indicate either "leather bottle" or "bellows," but many riddlic creatures have a *wombe* or "belly" and the word *leþre* may be a form of *lyþre*, "evil, wicked" (cp. the form in *Psalm 50* [*ASPR.*, vol. 6, p. 90], line 41: *ðurh lichaman leðre geðohtas*).

My line arrangement for the first five lines follows that of Trautmann. Krapp and Dobbie read *se wiht* at the end of the first line (though the *s* is not visible in the MS. or in the facsimile or in the 1831 transcript made by Robert Chambers for the British Museum), but this leaves by my count a line of 41 spaces for line 1, which is unusually large. Trautmann's arrangement, which adds an extra line, gives a more normal reading. In the latter half of my text, I follow the Krapp and Dobbie reading.

85.4: *beg*[...]: The MS. reads *be g* before the lacuna.

85.5: *on*: The *o* is on the authority of the 1831 transcript by Robert Chambers (*Brit. Mus. Add. MS. 9067*).

85.8: *eft*: The *t* is on the authority of Chambers and Flower (*The Exeter Book of Old English Poetry*, p. 81). Only a small portion of the letter is visible in the MS. and in the facsimile.

85.9: *þygan*: Apparently a form of *þicgan*, "to take, receive, eat," though Trautmann would read *þȳ gān*. Holthausen (*Anglia* xxxviii, 81) suggests *þȳgan* = *þȳwan*, "drücken."

86. Web (O.E. Wulflys) and Loom?
[*VN: Gr¹.86; Gr².90; Tr.88; Tu.90; W.X; M.89; K-D.90*]

This is the only Latin riddle to be found among the Old English riddles of the *Exeter Book*. The text itself has been the cause of much editorial concern. The metrical form of the riddle is in doubt. Dietrich (*ZfdA*. xi, 486) thought the lines to be "rhythmical hexameters," but Krapp and Dobbie rightly note that if this is true the form is much distorted. Holthausen (*ESn*. xxxvii, 210) believed the lines each to contain six stresses with caesura and medial rhyme, but his reading depends on emendations in the case of four out of five lines. In my version of the riddle I have returned essentially to the more conservative reading of Grein, though I allow for a possible lacuna in line 2. My translation, which follows that of Mackie, is as follows:

> It seems to me marvelous—   a wolf is held by a lamb;
> the lamb has lain down (?) * * *   and seizes the belly
> of the wolf.
>
> While I stood and wondered,   I saw a great glory:
> two wolves standing   and troubling a third—
> they had four feet;   they saw with seven eyes.

This riddle is not glossed in the Old English glossary at the end of this edition.

The solution to the riddle has given the editors much trouble, though most agree that some wordplay on either L. *lupus* or O.E. *wulf* or both is intended. Dietrich (*ZfdA*. xi, 486) first took the various meanings of L. *lupus* ("pike" in line 2 and "hops" in line 4) to be the subject of the riddle. Later (*ZfdA*. xii, 250) he argued that the *lupus* of line 1 was a perch and that the riddle was somehow a wordplay on the disguised author's name, "Cynewulf." Edmund Erlemann (*Archiv* cxi, 59 ff.) and Fritz Erlemann (*Archiv* cxv, 391) elaborate upon the "Cynewulf" charade, but their arguments are unconvincing. The linking of *ewu* (L. *agnus*) and *wulf* (L. *lupus*) makes some sense (cp. the runic signature at *Jul.* 704–8), but there is nothing in the Latin riddle to explain the remaining *Cyn* of "Cynewulf," and there is nothing in the "Cynewulf" charade that corresponds to the last three lines of the riddle. Edmund Erlemann circumvents the latter problem by proclaiming blithely that the *duo lupi* of line 4 in this riddle are the equivalent of the runic *LF* in the Cynewulfian signature at *Jul.* 708. This kind of scholarship knows no bounds.

Henry Morley (*English Writers*, vol. 2, pp. 224 ff.) replaced one unlikely solution with another. He disputed the "Cynewulf" solution and proposed the "Lamb of God." He says:

> The marvel of the Lamb that overcame the wolf and tore its bowels out is of the Lamb of God who overcame the devil and destroyed his power. . . . The great glory then seen was of "the lamb that had been slain," the Divine appointment of the agony of one of the three Persons of the Trinity. The four feet were the four Gospels; and the seven eyes refer to the Book of Revelation, where the seven eyes of the Lamb are the seven Spirits of God sent forth into all the earth. The last line but one may here be misinterpreted, but the sense of the whole can be no other than this. [*English Writers*, vol. 2, p. 225]

For those who doubt that the three wolves of line 4 represent Christ and the crucified thieves, Morley offers the possibility that the two wolves troubling a third might be the Old and New Testaments troubling the devil since "in either sense the wolf is used as a rending and destroying power; in one sense a destroyer of evil, and in the other a destroyer of good" (*English Writers*, vol. 2, p. 225, note). One hopes at least that the Anglo-Saxons were clearer in their use of religious symbols. Mackie and Tupper appear to accept Morley's solution, though Tupper admits that it seems overwrought. Trautmann and Krapp and Dobbie are dubious about all previous solutions, but they offer nothing new in their place.

I believe that the riddle involves a wordplay on O.E. *wulflys*, "fleece of wool" (CH., p. 425), which occurs as a gloss for *Cana uellus* (WW. 198.26) where *cana* is apparently a mistake for *lana* (Wülker, note). O.E. *wulflys* is obviously a combination of *wul* and *flys*, but the riddler makes a game of construing the word as *wulf* plus *flys* where the lamb (*agnus*) holds the wolf (*lupus*) and indeed seizes (*capit*) the belly or entrails (*viscera*) of the wolf and thus metaphorically commandeers its last letter. Thus the *flys* seizes *f* from the *wulf*. The charade can only be solved in terms of Old English—that presumably is why it is included in the collection even though it is a Latin riddle. If the *wulflys* were on the loom, the rest of the riddle might be explained as follows: The two wolves of line 4, which torment a third wolf, might be the odd and even ends of the warp threads hanging on either side of the frame of the old vertical loom—these two "wolves" tormenting the third or weft thread as it was passed back and forth in the loom (weaving from top to bottom). For a description of the vertical loom, see Erhardt-Siebold, "The Old English Loom Riddles" in *Philologica: The Malone Anniversary Studies*, pp. 9–17. The two "warp-wolves" would have one foot apiece. This is clear from the description of the "web" in *Rid.* 54:

> Hyre fota wæs
> biidfæst oþer; oþer bisgo dreag,
> leolc on lyfte, hwilum londe neah.

[*Rid.* 54.6–8]

Erhardt-Siebold notes here that in successive shedding operations, one foot moves up and down (as the weaver pushes the weft threads up with the batten or reed) while the other stands still (p. 15). Thus the "warp-wolves" would each have a foot, accounting for two of the four feet in line 5 of the riddle; the weft-wolf moving horizontally in the terms of *Rid.* 54 would have none. The other two feet might be the feet of the loom itself, which stands on two feet and leans against a wall (see the picture of the Norwegian loom, fig. 1, in the article by Erhardt-Siebold). Thus the web or *wulflys* in the loom has two wolves (warp threads) tormenting the third (weft thread). The whole contraption of "web in loom" has four feet—two from the warp threads and two from the loom. This may seem fanciful but certainly no more fanciful than "Lamb of God." The solution proposed here satisfies at least most of the descriptive criteria of the riddle.

The last half-line of the riddle has been a constant puzzle to the editors no matter what the solution proposed. Tupper, in accepting Morley's solution, is content to say that "the phrase 'cum septem oculis' certainly smacks of the Apocalypse" (p. 231). In terms of my own solution, the "seven eyes" might refer to the round baked rings that served the Anglo-Saxons as loom weights to weigh down the warp threads on both sides of the loom. Even on a small loom, however, one would expect an even number of loom weights as the rings would hang normally in pairs on either side of the frame. It is possible here that the riddler meant to refer to seven *pairs* of eyes, fourteen rings together, seven on each side in a row. This is not an unlikely configuration for a small Anglo-Saxon loom. One archaeological find at Sutton Courtenay produced fourteen loom weights in a position that indicated that all or some may have fallen directly from the loom (E. T. Leeds, *Early Anglo-Saxon Art and Archaeology*, p. 26). In another case, Marta Hoffmann, in *The Warp-weighted Loom*, notes the find of an early La Tène loom in Germany "where two clearly separate rows of pyramidal loom weights, fourteen in all, lay near a wall" (p. 312). Though the evidence is admittedly slight, it does indicate the possibility of a small, vertical, warp-weighted loom with seven pairs of "eyes" or rings that might have been used by the Anglo-Saxons.

86.1: Following the practice adopted for the use of Latin quotations in these notes, I have normalized initial *u* to *v* in the following words: *videtur* (line 1), *viscera* (line 2), *vidi* (line 3), and *videbant* (line 5).

86.1: *videtur mihi*: Tupper and Mackie follow Holthausen's (*ESn.* xxxvii, 211) reading of *mihi videtur* for the purpose of establishing medial rhyme. Other editors retain the MS. reading as I have done. The continental *d* in *videtur* occurs also in *tidum* at *Rid.* 37.2 (see note).

86.2: *obcu*[..]*it*: My reading here follows that of Trautmann and of Chambers and Flower. The two lost letters cannot be made out either in the manuscript or in the facsimile. Grein's reading of the word was *obcurrit*; this reading was accepted by Tupper. Mackie (*MLR* xxviii, 77) noted: "Now that the binding round the hole in the parchment has been removed it is clear that the last two letters of the first line are not *rr* but *bu*, so that the verb is not *obcurrit* but *obcubuit*." Chambers and Flower (*The Exeter Book of Old English Poetry*, p. 81) agree that the letters could not be *rr*, but they prefer to leave a lacuna in the text rather than accept Mackie's reading. Krapp and Dobbie accept Mackie's reading of *obcubuit*. It should be noted in this case as in many others that where letter fragments occur in the manuscript close to the edge of the burn, it is often impossible to distinguish between possible ink marks and scorched vellum or vellum darkened over a period of years by the presence of glue.

86.2: *agnus* * * * : Grein and Trautmann read *agnus et* as it is in the manuscript without admitting the possibility of a lacuna here, but the line does seem to be short. Tupper, Mackie, and Krapp and Dobbie follow Holthausen (*ESn.* xxxvii, 211) in supplying *rupi* after *agnus*. Tupper notes: "Now if *agnus* be 'Christ,' and *lupi* 'the Devil,' there seems to be little doubt that *rupi* refers to the rock (Peter) upon which the Church is built (Matthew 16:18); Christ, through his Church, destroys the Devil" (p. 231). I have chosen to retain the MS. reading but to allow for the possibility of a lacuna after *agnus* without offering a guess as to the word or words lost and without basing my solution on any restoration of the passage. This seems to me to be the wisest course. For the double-c form of *a* in *agnus*, see the following note.

86.2: The *a* of *agnus* and the *a* of *capit* both take the "horned or double-c" form described by Ker on p. xxviii of his *Catalogue of Manuscripts Containing Anglo-Saxon*. Ker notes that the scribes who used the form seem to have used it more for Latin than for Old English. For the *a* in *capit*, see plate XXIII.

86.3: *mirarem*: Trautmann and Krapp and Dobbie retain the MS. *misarem*; all other editors emend to *mirarem*. This reading seems more likely in terms of the *gloriam magnam* of the *b*-line.

86.3: *magnam*: For MS. *magnan*, most editors would read *magnam*. Mackie and Tupper follow Holthausen in reading *parem* in order to establish a rhyme with *mirarem* (MS. *misarem*). For the horned *c* form of *a*, see note to line 2 above.

86.4: *duo*: Trautmann and Krapp and Dobbie retain MS. *dui*; other editors emend to the proper form *duo*.

86.5: *quattuor*: As I have followed the practice of spelling out numerical abbreviations in Old English, I do the same for Latin. This is also Tupper's practice.

87. Key

[*VN: Gr¹.87; Gr².91; Tr.89; Tu.91; W.89; M.90; K-D.91*]

Dietrich (*ZfdA.* xi, 486) solved the riddle as "key," citing the resemblance between this riddle and Riddle 4 of Symphosius, "Clavis" (ed. Ohl, p. 38). Trautmann (*Anglia Beibl.* v, 51) first solved the riddle as "sickle," but accepted "key" in his edition. All other editors accept

"key." The resemblances between the Latin riddle of Symphosius and the Old English riddle are slight. In the Latin riddle, the key guards and is guarded in return (*Servo domum domino, sed rursus servor ab ipso*); in the Old English riddle, it is the implied lock that guards and the key that opens. A double entendre "key" riddle may be found at *Rid*. 42.*

Whitelock (*The Beginnings of English Society*, p. 152) points out that in the upper classes at least, Anglo-Saxon women often had control of household furnishings, treasure repositories, and keys. *The Laws of King Cnut* state that if a man brought home stolen goods, his wife was to be held accountable as an accomplice in the crime only if the goods were found in the repositories to which she held the keys (ed. Thorpe, *Ancient Laws and Institutes of England*, vol. 1, p. 418). Thorpe notes similar provisions in several old Scottish laws (ibid., note b). For Anglo-Saxon keys from the archaeological digs, see Wilson, *Anglo-Saxon Ornamental Metalwork 700–1100 in the British Museum*, items 38, 40, 46, 132, 140, and plates.

87.1: *geþuren*: Grein (*Sp.*, p. 726), Sievers (*Beiträge* x, 458), Tupper, and Trautmann read *geþrüen* for metrical reasons to supply a regular A1 verse. Sievers-Brunner note that the form here and at *Beo*. 1285 (MS. *geþuren*: Klaeber reads *geþruen*; Dobbie, *geþuren*) and at *Bo*. 20.134 (MS. *geþruen* corrected by a dot and superscript *u* to *geþuren*) may be derived from an otherwise lost verb *geþrüan* (Class 7) and not, as has been supposed (as in B-T., p. 458), from *geþwĕran*. O.E. *geþweran* normally means "to stir, beat, churn," and B-T. would take the occurrences in question here as poetical extensions meaning "to beat, forge." Sievers thinks the otherwise unattested *geþruan* would mean "to forge." Since the poetical occurrences of the form would all be metrically more regular if the original form were *geþruen*, it is tempting to emend; but since the MS. spelling in each case (if we count the MS. correction at *Bo*. 20.134) is *geþuren*, I hesitate to do this. For similar examples of short A1 verses in the *b*-line involving a stress on a short syllable, see Pope's *The Rhythm of Beowulf*, p. 333.

---

*For a recent interpretation of *Rid*. 87 as a double entendre "keyhole" riddle, see Edith Williams's "What's So New about the Sexual Revolution?" *Texas Quarterly* xviii, 46–55.

87.2: *searopila wund*: Normally *wund* takes the instrumental (cp. *Rid.* 3.1); Tupper (p. 234) notes this as the single instance in which it takes the instrumental genitive.

87.3: *begine*: from *beginan*, "to swallow" (*BTS.*, p. 72). This is also the reading of Swaen (*ESn.* xl, 323). *BTS.* notes a similar use of *beginan* in the *Dialogues of Gregory* 324.26: "Se draca hæfþ beginen in his muðe min heafod and forswolgen," for the Latin: *draco caput meum in suo ore absorbuit* (*BTS.*, p. 72). Trautmann would take MS. *begine* for *begnide*, translating, "ich bereibe" (p. 137), or for *begime*, translating "ich besorge, verwalte" (*Anglia* xliii, 253).

87.5: *þyrel*: All previous editors take this to be an adjective and translate *hindan þyrel* as "pierced from behind." But O.E. *þyrel* may be either an adjective or a noun (see B-T., p. 1085; this instance of the word is not glossed in either B-T. or BTS.), and if we take *þyrel* as a noun here, we may translate beginning at line 4a: "when, girt with rings, I must strike hard (adv.) against hard, the hole from behind, shove forward what protects my lord's joy," etc.

87.6: Tupper and Wyatt read *frean mines* for metrical reasons, but for the word order cp. *Rid.* 71.8 and for the meter (B1) with light first-measure stress on the pronoun, cp. *Beo.* 558b.

87.7: *mod · ᛝ ·*: Dietrich (*ZfdA.* xi, 486) first read the contraction as *modwen* or *modwylm*, but Sievers (*Anglia* xiii, 4ff.) rightly read *modwyn*, "treasure." Krapp and Dobbie note two instances of *wyn(n)* represented by Roman *w* (*El.* 788, 1089) and four instances of its representation by runic ᛝ (*Ap.* 100; *El.* 1263; *Chr.* 804; *Run.* 22).

87.8: All editors, including Sievers (*Anglia* xiii, 4), allow the line to stand as it is, though in normal circumstances the first three words of the on-verse would all be unstressed. Tupper takes the verse to be a B-verse with stress on *under* (p. 234), but it seems more likely that *Hwilum* should take a stress here as it does sometimes in *Beowulf* (cp. *Beo.* 175a, 1728a, 1828b, etc.) and that the verse is one of those unusual ones that Pope says "resemble type A3 in that a number of minor syllables lead up to an alliterating lift, but [in which] there is no final drop, the ending being abrupt like that of type E" (*Seven Old English Poems*, p. 128). Pope cites, for example, two verses similar to

the one in question here: *Dream* 18a: *Hwæðre ic þurh þæt gold*; and *Mald.* 22a: *Þa he hæfde þæt folc*. See also Pope's discussion of *Beo.* 3027a on pp. xxx and 321 of *The Rhythm of Beowulf.*

87.11: *wælcræfte*: Mackie notes that "the *fte* of *wælcræfte* is almost illegible owing to a stain in the parchment" (p. 232). The letter *f* is still visible under a microscope; the letters *te* are not. R. W. Chambers noted in 1933 that "the final *e* comes out clearly under the ultra-violet rays" (*The Exeter Book of Old English Poetry*, p. 81). Robert Chambers in 1832 was able to read the entire word, *wælcræfte*, for his transcription (*Brit. Mus. Add. MS. 9067*). The letters *te* are thus printed on the authority of Chambers and Chambers.

88. Beech / Book (O.E. Bōc)

[VN: Gr¹.X; Gr².92; Tr.90; Tu.92; W.90; M.91; K-D.92]

This riddle was not printed by Thorpe or Grein and Dietrich did not comment upon it. Trautmann first solved the riddle as "beech" (*Anglia Beibl.* v, 51), then later suggested "beech-wood shield" (edition, p. 137) or "beech battering-ram" (*Anglia* xliii, 246). Trautmann's "beech" is accepted by Tupper. Holthausen (*ESn.* xxxvii, 211) first solved the riddle as "ash," but later (*Anglia Beibl.* xxx, 54) accepted Trautmann's "beech." Wyatt solved the riddle as O.E. *bōc*, "*beech*, with its several uses, and *book*" (p. 122), and so Mackie listed the solution, "beech, book" (p. 242). I accept Wyatt's formulation of the solution: the riddle turns on the homonymic uses of O.E. *bōc* (see note to line 3 below).

The beech tree was well known to the Anglo-Saxons. Hoops says: "Und da die Buche in der angelsächsischen Periode wiederholt in Urkunden auftritt und, wenigstens in Südengland, durchaus den Eindruck eines alteinheimischen Baumes macht, ist sie sicher auch zur Römerzeit vorhanden gewesen und nur Caesars Beobachtung entgangen" (*Waldbäume und Kulturpflanzen im germanischen Altertum*, p. 259). Another source notes that beech mast has traditionally been a food for pigs (*EB.* iii, 370). Pliny says in his *Natural History*: "Glans fagea suem hilarem facit, carnem cocibilem ac levem et utilem sto-macho, iligna suem angustam, non nitidam, stringosam" (*NH*. xvi. vii.25). Tupper argues with some reason that the *brunra beot* of line 1 is the beech-mast fodder for pigs.

88.1: *brunra beot*: *the boast of brown creatures*, fodder for pigs (see Pliny's comment above). In *Rid*. 38, the riddler describes an unlimited "creation" as being fatter than pigs in a beech forest:

> Mara ic eom ond fættra   þonne amæsted swin,
> bearg bellende,   þe on bocwuda
> won wrotende   wynnum lifde
>
> [*Rid*. 38.105–7]

Mead (*PMLA* xiv, 193) notes that *brun* has a large range of meanings in Old English, from dusky to red. Holthausen (*ESn*. xxxvii, 211) emends *brunra* to *brunna* and translates the phrase as "der stolz der bäche," or "the pride of streams."

88.3: *weres wynnstaþol*: For the MS. *wym staþol*, all editors read *wynn-staþol*, "the foundation of joy." Assmann and Wyatt keep the tri-syllabic half-line of the MS. reading. Mackie and Tupper read *ond wynnstaþol*. Holthausen reads *wynnstaþol weres* (*Anglia Beibl*. ix, 348), *wynn on staþole* (*ESn*. xxxvii, 211) or *wera wynnstaþol* (*Anglia Beibl*. xxx, 54). Trautmann reads *wlitigra wynnstaþol*, "'die Wonnestätte Schöner,' nämlich *fugla*" (p. 138). Krapp and Dobbie read *weres wynn-staþol* to agree with the *b*-line, *wifes sond*, and note the message sent by a man to his wife in *The Husband's Message*. For the significance of *wynnstaþol* here, Tupper cites *þæs strangan staþol* of *Rid*. 45.5 and the description of books at *Sol*. 240: *gestaðeliað staðolfæstne geðoht*. As for the connection of the "books" to the "beech" riddle, Tupper says, "Though Sievers, like many earlier scholars (B-T., p. 113), calls into question the traditional etymology, every Anglo-Saxon found the origin of 'book' (*bōc*) in the 'beech-tree' (*bōc-trēow*), for, as our riddle shows us, beech-bark was used by him for writing" (p. 236). The etymological connection between "book" and "beech" is still very much in doubt (see *OED* i, p. 988, under *book*), especially since the earliest known form is the word for "writing-tablet" and not for "beech." But since O.E. *boc* and *boctreow* are recorded in the glosses for L. *fagus* or *aesculus*, the tree and the book, whatever their etymological connections, were homonyms in Old English, at least for some speakers; and this wordplay lies at the heart of the riddle.

88.4: *gold*: For the MS. *gold*, Holthausen proposed *gōd* (*Anglia Beibl.* ix, 358) or *golf*, "fussboden" (*Anglia Beibl.* xxx, 54), but Krapp and Dobbie note that *"golf* is recorded only in Old Norse, and does not give a particularly appropriate meaning here" (p. 380). Trautmann (*Anglia* xliii, 254) reads *gold* for "treasure" with reference to the tree itself. But Tupper rightly notes that *"gold* may well refer to the adornments of the Book" (p. 236). In *Rid.* 24.13 the book is *gierede . . . mid golde* and the book in *Rid.* 65.14 is *golde gegierwed*. The companion of the book in *Rid.* 91 is *hiþendra hyht* (91.5), which I take to be a kenning for gold.

88.5: *hildewæpen*: Tupper (p. 236) cites the bequest of a beech shield in the *Wills* (ed. Thorpe, *Diplomatarium Anglicum* 561.5; A.D. 938): "Ic ge-ann Siferþe mines bocscyldes."

88.7: The end of the riddle is obliterated by the MS. burn and it is impossible to tell how many letters may have been lost. The count indicated by the ellipsis is to the right-hand margin of the MS.

89. Inkhorn
[*VN: Gr¹.88; Gr².93; Tr.91; Tu.93; W.91; M.92; K-D.93*]

This riddle is a companion piece to "inkhorn" *Riddle* 84. The riddle was first solved by Dietrich as "das tintenfass aus hirschhorn" (*ZfdA.* xi, 486), and the solution is accepted by all editors. Mackie prefers the more general solution, "antler, horn," and Wyatt, the solution, "horn (antler, inkhorn)." But the creature's present identity in the poem is clearly an inkhorn (see lines 24 ff. where the present tense is used to describe the present condition of the creature). For a comparison of the Old English "inkhorn" riddles with Riddle 30 of Eusebius, "De Atramentorio," the reader is referred to the headnote to *Rid.* 84.

89.5: . . .]*earpne*: Only the lower portion of *ea* is visible in the MS., but there is enough to ascertain the letters.

89.8: *deo*[.........]*s*: Most editors postulate the reading *deope streamas*. Grein, Tupper, and Wyatt believe that final *amas* is certain from the lower fragments showing in the MS. Trautmann is certain of final *eamas*. But Chambers and Flower (*The Exeter Book of Old English Poetry*, p. 82) note that the reading of *streamas* is highly doubtful on MS. evidence alone and so report only final *s* with certainty as I have done here. This is also the reading of Mackie and Krapp and Dobbie.

89.11: *duguþe secan*: The editors gloss this as "to seek gain, benefit," or "to seek safety," but the *duguþe* here could be the stag's comitatus —i.e., the herd. For other examples of plural *duguþe* in the accusative meaning *homines*, see *Sp.*, p. 132, column 1.

89.13b–14a: "Sometimes the gray frost shook out of his hair." This is the reading of all editors except Mackie who translates, "Sometimes the gray one shook the frost from his hair." But as deer are not normally gray and as the weak adjective here probably is used to indicate a quality characteristic of the thing modified, it is better to take the *hara . . . forst* as the subject of an intransitive *scoc* (O.E. *sceacan* may be either transitive or intransitive). For another instance of the "gray frost," cp. *Andreas* 1256*b*–59*a*:

> Weder coledon
> heardum hægelscurum, swylce hrim ond forst,
> hare hildstapan, hæleða eðel
> lucon, leoda gesetu.
>
> [*An.* 1256–59]

89.14: *on*: Grein, Assmann, and Wyatt would retain MS. *of*, but the reading makes no sense in conjunction with *oþþæt* in line 15. The horn must ride *on* the stag until his "younger brother" (the new horn) takes his place. Tupper and later editors read *on* for MS. *of*. Cp. the use of *on* at *Rid.* 84.11 where the motif is the same.

89.15: *gleawstol*: All editors except Mackie read this as "joy seat," and Grein, Assmann, Wyatt, and Tupper emend *gleaw-* to *gleow-*, but Mackie's reading of *gleawstol* as "seat of wisdom"—i.e., the stag's head—makes much more sense.

89.23: Trautmann would read here: *ac ic aglæc a eall* [*a*]*þolige*, but there is no reason to change the MS. reading in this fashion. The reading here depends upon whether one takes *aglæca* for *aglæc*, "trouble, misery," or for *aglæca*, "wretch." Wyatt and Krapp and Dobbie agree upon the former (though Wyatt glosses the occurrence here as accusative plural, and Krapp and Dobbie take *aglæca . . . ealle* as a partitive); Tupper and Mackie agree upon the latter. Wyatt believes that the "torments" of the horn are wounds inflicted by nails that fasten the horn to a wooden inkstand. Mackie and Tupper, who read *þætte* for MS. *þ* [..]*e* in 24*a*, take the adjective *ealle* with the relative clause to refer to cutting tools.

89.24: *þæt* [..]*e*: The MS. reading is *þ* [..]*e*, the gap owing to a slight stain. It is impossible to tell whether one or two letters have been lost. The British Museum transcript has *m* in the blank space, but Chambers and Flower note only that "two minims are clear under the ultra-violet rays" and leave the reading with a lacuna as it is here (*The Exeter Book of Old English Poetry*, p. 82). This is also the reading of Krapp and Dobbie. Grein read *þæt* and so Trautmann. Assmann, Mackie, and Tupper read *þætte* with various degrees of MS. vision and interpolation. Wyatt reads *þ[a þ]e*. Trautmann emends MS. *bord* to *brord*, translating "Spitzen," but Krapp and Dobbie note that *brord* is more probably masculine (p. 380). At any rate, there seems to be enough confusion in the MS. without Trautmann's emending of the text.

89.24: *blace swelge*: Cp. *beamtelge swealg* at *Rid.* 24.9 and the same motif in the last two lines of Riddle 30 of Eusebius, "De Atramentorio" *Vas tamen intus habens sum nunc intestina amara / Viscera, sed ructans bonus ibit nitor odoris* (CCL. cxxxiii, p. 240).

89.28: *hiþende feond*: Tupper identified this plunderer as the pen or quill. Cp. the role of the *unsceafta* in *Rid.* 84: *Nu mec unsceafta innan slitað, / wyrdaþ mec be wombe* (*Rid.* 84.29–30).

89.30: *bewaden*: The meaning of this hapax legomenon is debated by the lexicographers, though the editors make little mention of it. Dietrich took the word in the sense of "ausgehöhlt," and so Grein (*Sp.*, p. 749) and B-T. (p. 96) give the tentative definition: "a quo aliquid abiit(?)." BTS. (p. 88), citing parallel examples of *befaran*, *beferan*, and *beridan*, defines the verb as "to reach, come upon, surprise?" and reads the participle in this case as "surprised." Wyatt, taking the prefix in a privative sense, translates *bewaden* as "deprived." Mackie and Tupper translate *bewaden* as "having emerged." Swaen (*Neoph.* xxvi, 302) follows Trautmann in translating *bewaden* as "begangen, mit Tinte belaufen gefüllt." By analogy with *be-faran*, *be-feran*, *be-ridan*, *be-gan* (*be-gangan*), *be-wadan* ought to mean literally "to ride about" and perhaps "to surround." Thus the quill pen might be "surrounded" or "covered" with ink.

89.32: *deaþes d*[...]: The letters here are all on the authority of Chambers and Flower, though Mackie also claims to have been able to read them. They are no longer visible in either the manuscript or the facsimile and they were not recorded by Robert Chambers in his 1831 transcription (*Brit. Mus. Add. MS. 9067*). More of the letters may have been visible to Chambers and Flower (*The Exeter Book of Old English Poetry*, p. 82) since they uncovered portions of the MS. that were glued to the vellum backing alongside the hole.

89.34: ...]*eorc*: The *e* and *o* are on the authority of Chambers and Flower.

90. Creation?
[*VN: Gr¹.X; Gr².94; Tr.92; Tu.94; W.92; M.93; K-D.94*]

This riddle was omitted by Thorpe and Grein, so Dietrich did not comment on it. Tupper was the first to note that "the few surviving phrases of this badly damaged fragment exhibit a striking likeness to the comparatives of the 'Creation' riddles" (p. 238), *Rids.* 38 and 64 in this edition. Trautmann accepted "creation" with a question (p. 139), and Mackie (*MLR* xxviii, 78) read "creation or nature."

90.1: *Smeþr*[...: Assmann, Trautmann, Tupper, and Wyatt all read *Smiþ* for the obscured MS. *Smeþr*. Chambers and Flower (*The Exeter Book of Old English Poetry*, p. 82) and Mackie (*MLR* xxviii, 78) were the first to read *Smeþr*.

90.2: *hyrre þonne heofon*: Cp. a similar description of "creation" at *Rid*. 38.38: *Hyrre ic eom heofone*.

90.3: Trautmann notes that *glæd* is used with reference to the sun at *Ph*. 92 and 289.

90.4: Holthausen (*Anglia* xxxviii, 82) would restore [*heardre þonne*] *style*. Cp. *Rid*. 38.79: *style heardan*.

90.5: *sealt ry*[...: In the MS. the word division comes between *sealt* and the following word, which begins with *ry*, as is printed here and in Grein-Wülker, Wyatt, and Mackie. Holthausen (*Anglia* xxiv, 266) and Tupper emend MS. *sealt ry*[... to *sealt sy*. Trautmann and Krapp and Dobbie retain the MS. reading without the MS. word division and read *sealtry*[... There is no known word in Old English that begins in this fashion. Krapp and Dobbie do not comment upon the reading. Trautmann connects *ry* with *ryhae* (*ryhe*, "rug"), which he notes as a gloss for *uilla* and *uillosa* in the *Epinal Glossary* (see the listings under *ryhe* in B-T., p. 805). Trautmann defines *sealtry* as follows: "*'Sēaltrӯ'* = 'Salzumschlag' (d.i. ein in Salzlake getauchtes Tuch)?" (p. 139). What Trautmann's briny cloth has to do with "creation" is anyone's guess. The comparative *smeare* comes from *smeah*, which means "crafty, subtle, penetrating" (B-T., p. 887). This does not seem immediately appropriate to the old "salt rug."

91. Book
[*VN: Gr¹.89; Gr².95; Tr.93; Tu.95; W.93; M.94; K-D.95*]

Dietrich (*ZfdA*. xi, 487 ff.) solved the riddle as "wandering singer," and this solution was accepted by Prehn (*NS* iii, 262), Brooke (*The History of Early English Literature*, p. 8), Nuck (*Anglia* x, 393 ff.), and Hicketier (*Anglia* x, 584 ff.). Tupper solved the riddle as "moon," citing parallels between this and *Rid*. 27 (my numbering), "moon and sun." Trautmann first (*Anglia* vi, Anz., p. 168) solved the riddle as "riddle," later as "soul" or "spirit" (edition: *der Geist*), and similarly Holthausen (*Anglia Beibl*. xxxvi, 220) as "der Gedanke." Mackie prefers "moon";

Wyatt, "wandering singer" or "riddle." Krapp and Dobbie note: "All
these solutions, except perhaps 'riddle,' can be defended, but none
seems especially appropriate" (p. 381). Recently, Erhardt-Siebold,
taking the *hiþendra hyht* of line 5 to be ink, solved the riddle as "quill"
(*MLN* lxii, 558–59). I take *hiþendra hyht* to be a kenning for gold, and
solve the riddle as "book." Any editor's solution depends in large
part upon his reading of lines 3*b*–6, which I translate as follows: "The
plunderers' joy (gold) travels far, and, once estranged from friends,
stands on me (shines from me?), if I should have glory in the cities or
bright wealth." Medieval manuscripts were often gilded and book
covers were inlaid with gold (see descriptions in the headnote to
Rid. 24). The presence of gold is noted in several of the Old English
"writing" riddles. The "Bible" at *Rid.* 24 is *gierede . . . mid golde* (24.13)
and similarly the "Bible" at *Rid.* 65.16. The "pen" of *Rid.* 49 travels
ofer fæted gold (49.7). Gold is the *hiþendra hyht* of this riddle. This is
the only reading that makes sense of the conditional at lines 5*b*–6.
That gold is often transported from afar and estranged from its friends
in the earth is clear from *Rid.* 79 where the creature "gold" remembers
hwa min fromcynn fruman agette / eall of earde (79.7–8). The Bibles of
Rids. 24 and 65 are both teachers of men. This riddlic creature notes:
Nu snottre men swiþast lufiaþ / midwist mine (lines 7–8*a*). The Bible of
Rid. 65 "speaks" though it has no tongue; the book of this riddle
makes wisdom known to many though it speaks no words (lines
8*b*–9). The motif is similar to that used by Eusebius in two riddles,
"De Littera" (Riddle 7) and "De Membrano" (Riddle 33):

> De Littera
> Innumerae sumus, et simul omnes quaeque sonamus,
> Una loqui nequit; nos tetrae ludimus albis.
> Et licet alta loquamur, non sonus auribus instat;
> Praeteritum loquimur, praesens et multa futura.
>
> [*CCL*. cxxxiii, p. 217]

> De Membrano
> Antea per nos vox resonabat verba nequaquam,
> Distincta sine nunc voce edere verba solemus;
> Candida sed cum arua lustramur milibus atris;
> Viva nihil loquimur, responsum mortua famur.
>
> [*CCL*. cxxxiii, p. 242]

The power of the written word is strong: it utters wisdom without voices. This accounts for the importance of the *midwist* of the book. The manuscript word is strong, but it is also, as we know from *Rid.* 45, strangely susceptible. In the former riddle the word was prey to the worm; in this riddle the words (or "tracks" of the book) are sometimes lost not in the sacred obscurity of allegorical meaning as Erhardt-Siebold implies, but in the paleographical obscurity of the new "tracks" and in the old obscurity of the riddlic word. Here, in one sense, Trautmann is right about the "riddle," for the Old English riddler has concluded his game not only with a challenge to his future riddle-solvers but with a challenge to his editor (the new scribe) as well. The game is just; the rewards are great—greater than the *hiþendra hyht* long since lost from the pages of the book.*

91.3: *Fereð wide*: Thorpe, Tupper, Wyatt, Trautmann, and Krapp and Dobbie emend MS. *fereð* to *fere* and read the half-line with the preceding sentence. Grein, Assmann, and Mackie retain MS. *fereð* as the subject of the kenning *hiþendra hyht*, as I have it here. In terms of the "book" solution, the gold travels far, then "stands on (or shines from) the book" when the book is gilded or bound with gold.

91.4: *fremde ær freondum*: Since there is no genitive noun in the sentence, the MS. *fremdes* cannot be legitimate unless it is an elsewhere unattested genitival adverb, which is not likely. Brooke (*The History of Early English Literature*, p. 8) proposed *fremdum* for MS. *fremdes* and this emendation is accepted by Tupper, Wyatt, and Mackie. Tupper translates the passage beginning at line 4: "And to me, (who was) formerly remote from friends (so the Moon refers to his periods of lonely darkness), remains booty" (p. 239). After a number of proposed emendations (*Anglia* vi, Anz., p. 168; *Anglia* vii, Anz., p. 210;

---

*Recently, K. S. Kiernan in "*Cwene*: The Old Profession of Exeter Riddle 95" (*MP* lxxii, 384–89), has argued for the solution, "prostitute." His argument is at times ingenious, rarely judicious. I cite as examples his contention that "*blæd* and *god* [91.6] are both variations on *hyht* [91.5], and refer to the sex act," and his reading of lines 10b ff. as referring to the woman's menstrual period as he translates: "Though now the sons of men, of land-dwellers, very much seek out my observances (*lāstas*), I will conceal mine with a bandage (*swaþe*) for a while from each man" (ibid., pp. 386–87). It should be noted that persons and professions are not normally Old English riddle subjects—the exceptions being "Lot and his family" (*Rid.* 44), which is a unique kinship riddle based on a biblical tradition, and the "one-eyed seller of garlic" (*Rid.* 82), which is a translation of a Latin riddle.

BBzA. xix, 206), Trautmann finally settled upon the reading, *fremdes fær freondum*, taking *freondum* for *freogendum*, a dative singular participle, and translating: "und mir, dem Liebenden, droht Überfall eines Fremdlings (des Todes)" (p. 140) in terms of his solution, "der Geist." Krapp and Dobbie follow Grein in retaining the MS. reading for want of a satisfactory solution to the crux. For MS. *fremdes*, I read *fremde*, a nominative singular adjective modifying *hiþendra hyht*, and I translate the phrase, *fremde ær freondum* as "once estranged from friends" with reference to the separation of the gold from its homeland (cp. *Rid.* 79.7–8) in the ground. The gold is taken from its kin and carried off to adorn the book. Cp. the use of *fremde* at *Rid.* 14.3.

91.4: *stondeð*: Tupper translates this as "remains (to me)"; Mackie, as "falls to my lot." But the phrase *me . . . stondeð* may literally mean "stands on me." Cp., for example, *Beo.* 1037–38: *þara anum stod | sadol searwum fah.* Another possibility, though less likely, is that the phrase here means "shines out from me." The use of *standan* to mean "stand out from, shine" may be found six times in *Beowulf*, for example at lines 726–27: *him of eagum stod | ligge gelicost leoht unfæger.* The dative of reference, *him*, agrees with the dative *me* in the riddle, but we might expect some qualifying phrase analogous to *of eagum*, which is not to be found in the riddle. Since the *hiþendra hyht* may refer to the gilding of manuscript pages (see a description of the process in the headnote to *Rid.* 24), it is worthwhile noting the several examples of *standan* listed by BTS. (p. 710) with reference to "matter contained in a book." One example from the preface to the Old English Genesis is: "Stynt on þære bec on þam forman ferse" (see BTS., p. 710).

91.5: *hiþendra hyht*: Tupper sees the plunderers' joy as a booty of light stolen by the moon from the sun and he cites the *huþe* of *Rid.* 27.4 (my numbering) as a parallel case in point. But the context here does not define two warriors fighting over booty. Nor does Tupper mention that another of his "moon" creatures in *Rid.* 37 (my numbering) is called *earmost ealra wihta* (37.14). It should also be noted that *hiþendra* is in the plural and cannot refer to the moon. Tupper does not explain who his thieves of light are. Erhardt-Siebold (*MLN* lxii, 558–59) would read *hiþendra hyht* as a kenning for ink, citing the *hiðende feond* or quill that plunders the inkhorn in *Rid.* 89. But there is no mention of birds or bird feathers in this riddle, and it seems unlikely that we are to extrapolate from one hidden meaning to another—especially in the case of kennings where the solutions are usually self-contained (as in *hranrad* = sea). The *hiþendra hyht* ought simply to be a treasure of some sort, and I believe it to be the gold used to gild the leaves and to ornament the bindings of medieval books. For a use of *hyht* in a similar context, cp. *Andreas* 1113–14: *næs him to maðme wynn,* / *hyht to hordgestreonum.*

91.6: *beorhte god:* The reading here depends upon whether one takes MS. *god* as *gōd,* "good, wealth," or as *god,* "God." Grein, Dietrich (*ZfdA.* xi, 488), Trautmann (*Anglia* vi, Anz., p. 166), Wyatt, and Mackie read *gōd* and therefore emend MS. *beorhtne* to *beorhte* as I have done here. If *gōd* is singular, the adjective is weak. For a similar use of a weak adjective where a strong one might be expected, cp. *Beo.* 873*b* and 1733*a*. The weak adjective would provide the proper meter. If *gōd* is plural, then the adjective is a variant neuter accusative plural form (possibly early or late West Saxon; see Campbell 641, p. 263). Tupper and Trautmann assume *god,* "God," and so do not emend. Krapp and Dobbie keep this MS. reading for want of a good solution that would justify one reading or the other. Trautmann elsewhere (*BBzA.* xix, 207) proposed reading *beorhtan gong,* and Tupper likes this with respect to his moon, though he is willing to give some old Teutonic god a home in the heavenly body. Bright (see Tupper, p. 67, note) suggests *beorhte* or *beorhtan gold.* This would agree in some respects with my reading of *hiþendra hyht,* though it would be too clear an indication of the solution to the riddle, so I prefer to retain MS. *god,* "wealth."

91.7 ff.: The book is a creature that makes wisdom known to many without speaking any words. For the same motif in other "book" riddles, see the headnote to the riddle.

91.9: *no þær word sprecan:* The auxiliary *sceal* is understood from line 8*b*. All other editors except Trautmann retain the MS. reading *sprecað* in the line; the subject is understood in this case to be either *snottre men* from line 7 or simply "they" with reference to the *monigum* of line 8. Tupper translates: "I shall to many reveal wisdom; nor do they speak any word on earth (the Moon's teachings, unlike those of an earthly master, are conveyed and received in silence)" (p. 239). Tupper does not explain why medieval scientists studying the moon should themselves keep silent nor does he explain how the negative conjunction operates to negate anything in the preceding clause. Syntactically, since there is no subject in the negative syndetic clause, one would expect the subject to be that of the preceding positive clause and that the structure of the sentence would take the approximate form: "I did this . . . yet I did not do that." The form is typical for riddles and it often expresses a paradox of sorts as it does here: "I shall make wisdom known to many; yet I shall not speak any word over earth." Trautmann recognizes essentially this form by reading *sprece* for MS. *sprecað*, but the form *sprecan* is more suitable since it is parallel to *cyþan* and makes use of the understood auxiliary *sceal*.

Glossary

Arrangement and Contents

The order of head-words in the Glossary is alphabetical. The ligature æ is treated as *ae*, falling between *ad* and *af*. The letters þ and ð are treated as variants of the same letter following *t* in the Old English alphabet. Words beginning with the prefix *ge-* are listed according to their stems (for example, *ge-hwylc* follows *hwylc*, and *ge-sceaft* falls between *sceacan* and *scēam*). When variant forms of a word occur, the one most frequently used in the text is generally chosen as the head-word, and the variant form is often cross-referenced (for example, "nīol, *see* nēol"). Hard-to-recognize verb forms, and nouns and adjectives with unusual forms in the oblique cases are also cross-referenced (for example, "fēhð, *see* fōn," and "wōn, *see* wōh"). After the head-word comes the notation of the grammatical category to which the word belongs (see below) and then the definition(s) of the word. When all listed definitions of a head-word are questionable, each is followed by a question mark (*shiner? bright creature? white horse?*); when one or more of the definitions seem more possible than another, the questionable definition is listed last and is preceded by a question mark (*proud, haughty, ?licentious*). When words have separate and distinct categories of meaning, these are given in separate sections marked off by boldface numbers or letters, and citations are entered under the proper section.

The order and manner of syntactic description is given below. In the listing of entries, when a variant form occurs, it is duly noted in the citations with one exception—the interchangeability of þ and ð are assumed; thus the spelling *oðþe* for the more common *oþþe* would not be noted while the Northumbrian variant *eðþa* would. Variant forms are noted under the appropriate syntactical description after the normal forms have been listed (for example, the accusative plural forms of *eaxle* appear as follows: "ap. eaxle 67.3, 82.6, exle 30.6"). When no form of a word is given after a syntactic description (for example, "ns. 38.31"), the head-word is to be supplied. The sign ~ signifies the same word as cited immediately before; thus in the entry, "PRET. 3s. drefde 20.16 (lagu ~, *swam*)," the notation, "lagu ~," stands for "lagu drefde." Idiomatic usages, ambiguities, and queries are generally indicated parenthetically after the citation number in question. When a question mark precedes an entry (?cræft[. 80.13) or citation number (?80.12) or follows a grammatical notation (asf?), this is generally because there is some ambiguity due to the mutilation of the text; the word itself may be fragmentary (and this will be indicated in the Glossary) or the surrounding context may be lost. When a manuscript reading varies from the textual reading, the manuscript reading is normally given in brackets after the citation (forwurðe 3.5 [MS. for wurde]); when an entire word has been supplied, the citation number itself may occur in brackets (hafu [9.2]). A list of runes appearing in the *Riddles* may be found at the end of the Glossary.

The following paragraphs describe the style and sequence of syntactic description in the Glossary. The common abbreviations used in the Glossary are indicated in parentheses.

1. *Nouns.* Nouns are indicated by the gender marking—masculine (m.), neuter (n.), or feminine (f.)—immediately following the head-word. Occasionally the marking may indicate a double gender (m.n.) or a plural noun (m.p.). The singular (s.) forms are given first and then the plural (p.). The order of cases is nominative (n), accusative (a), dative (d), instrumental (i), genitive (g). Thus the case listings run in order from nominative singular (ns.) to genitive plural (gp.).

2. *Adjectives.* Adjectives are indicated by the common abbreviation (adj.) following the head-word. As with nouns, all singular (s) forms are given and then all plural (p) forms; the order of the cases follows that of the nouns. Within each number/case category (e.g., ns), the order of gender and strong/weak classification is as follows: masculine (m.), masculine weak (m.wk.), neuter (n.), neuter weak (n.wk.), feminine (f.), feminine weak (f.wk.). Thus the listings for adjectives run in order from nominative singular masculine (nsm.) to genitive plural feminine weak (gpf.wk.). Comparative (comp.) and superlative (supl.) forms follow the regular forms and their number, case, and gender are similarly marked (the reader should remember that all comparatives are weak; as is the common practice, this is not marked).

3. *Pronouns.* Pronouns are indicated by the common abbreviation (pron.) following the head-word. For pronouns, the order and manner of syntactical description follows that of the regular adjectives except that in certain cases (e.g., *ic, hwā*), pronouns have limited possibilities with respect to gender. Also with pronouns, the number is occasionally dual (d.).

4. *Verbs.* Verbs are indicated by the common abbreviation (v.) after the head-word along with a notation indicating the traditional grammatical class to which they belong: strong verbs are indicated by arabic numbers 1 through 7; weak verbs by roman numbers I through III; preterite-present verbs by PP.; anomalous verbs by AN.; contract verbs by CT. Occasionally a nonstandard verb may be marked by two classes. As part of the definition of the verb, there is sometimes a parenthetic notation that the verb is reflexive (refl.), indefinite (indef.), transitive (trans.) or intransitive (intr.), or a notation that the verb occurs with (w.) an object of a particular case (e.g., w. dat., w. acc., w. dat. of person and acc. of thing). In the citations, the indicative mood for verb forms should be understood unless otherwise indicated; likewise the

present tense. Otherwise each designation of mood and tense applies to all citations that follow until another designation is used. The order of forms for verbs is as follows: *A*. infinitive (inf.); *B*. present indicative forms (mood and tense unmarked), first to third singular (1s., 2s., 3s.) followed by first to third plural (1p., 2p., 3p.); *C*. preterite indicative forms (PRET.), first to third singular followed by first to third plural; *D*. subjunctive present (SUBJ. pres.) and subjunctive preterite (SUBJ. pret.) forms; *E*. imperative (imp.), present participle (prp.), past participle (pp.), and gerund (ger.) forms; *F*. negative (NEG.) forms listed in the same order as *A–E* above. Uninflected participles precede inflected forms; the latter are marked with the usual adjectival notation. I have followed the traditional practice of disregarding possible case, number, and gender for the uninflected past participles, but the reader should note that it is often impossible to distinguish between the zero-inflection (nsm., for example) and the uninflected form. Indeed, the past participles in the *Riddles* which have no inflectional endings may nearly all be classified as nsm., nsn., nsf., or asn., so that they appear to be treated as strong, long-stemmed monosyllabic adjectives. Where the participles are used substantively as nouns to refer to possible riddle-solvers, companion creatures, or the creature itself (which sometimes exhibits a changing gender in the course of a *Riddle*), it is often difficult to identify the gender with any certainty.

5. *Adverbs*. Adverbs are indicated by the common abbreviation (adv.) following the head-word. Comparative (comp.) and superlative (supl.) forms follow the regular forms.

6. Other forms include prepositions (prep.), conjunctions (conj.), numbers (num.), and interjections (interj.). Citations for prepositions are normally ordered according to the case of the object (e.g., all occurrences of *on* with the dative followed by all occurrences of *on* with the accusative). Numbers may be indeclinable (ind.) or occasionally inflected (infl.).

Nearly all of the abbreviations used in the Glossary are explained in the preceding paragraphs. Others rarely used are for the most part common and should cause the reader no difficulty. Abbreviations used in the Glossary are included in the general set of abbreviations listed at the beginning of this edition.

A

ā, adv. *always, ever*: 3.9, 81.6, aa 32.6.

ābelgan, v.3. *irritate, anger* (w. dat.): 1s. ābelge 18.32.

ābēodan, v.2. *announce*: inf. 58.16.

ābiddan, v.5. *get by asking, receive*: PRET. 3s. ābæd 53.12.

ābrecan, v.5. *storm, conquer*: SUBJ. pret. 3s. ābrǣce 53.7.

ābrēgan, v.I. *terrify*: inf. 38.17.

ac, conj. *but*: 1.37, 3.7,13, 13.17, 18.28, 20.6, 34.10, 35.6, 37.8,13,16,21, 38.99,101, 58.6, 79.9,12, 84.9,21, 89.23.

āc, m. **1.** *oak*: ns. ācc 53.9. —**2.** *name of runic A*: np. Ācas 40.10.

ācennan, v.I. *bring forth, bear (child)*: pp. ācenned 38.44, 48.1, 80.1 [MS. acceneð].

adela, m. *mud, filth*: is. adelan 38.32.

ādle, f. *disease*: ns. 41.4.

ādrīfan, v.1. *drive away*: PRET. 3s. ādrāf 89.16.

æfensceop, m. *evening singer*: ns. 6.5.

æfre, adv. *ever, always*: 37.10, 38.9,65,67, 58.8, 80.5. NEG. **nǣfre**, *never*: 3.10, 37.7,20, 70.17, 84.27.

æftanweard, adj. *behind, in the rear*: asm. æftanweardne 60.5.

æfter, **A. prep.** w. dat. **1.** *after*: 10.15, 18.21 (*following? in consequence of?* or adv?), 25.17, 26.11, 76.11 (or as meaning #3?), 84.16. —**2.** *along*: 28a.5, 28b.5 (~ hondum, *from hand to hand*), 31.1. —**3.** *according to*: 37.15. —**4.** *after, in pursuit of*: 71.10. —**B. adv.** *afterwards, then*: 37.23, 57.5.

æftera, comp. adj. *latter, second*: nsm. 51.12.

æfterweard, adj. *following*: nsm. 13.14.

ǣghwā, pron. *each, every(one)*: ns. 63.2.

ǣghwǣr, adv. **1.** *everywhere*: 38.13,18,30,37,50,82. —**2.** *anywhere*: 38.69.

ǣghwæðer, pron. *each*: gsm. ǣghwæðres 44.5.

ǣghwylc, pron. *each (one), every(one)*: nsn. 37.25; asm. ǣghwylcne 37.5; gsm. ǣghwylces 34.10.

ǣgþer, pron. *each, either*: as. 37.11. See **āwþer**.

ǣht, f. *property, possession*: ns. 69.1, 76.1; dp. ǣhtum 84.23.

ælde, m.p. *men*: dp. ældum 1.64, 3.6 (or a form of *ǣled*?), 31.11, 77.6; gp. ælda 80.32, 91.10.

ǣled, m. *fire, flame*: dp. ældum 3.6 (or a form of *ælde*?).

ǣnig, adj. or (as subs.) pron. *any(one)*: nsm. 38.21, 58.3, ?80.16; nsf. 38.86; asn. 37.27 [MS. hænig], 91.10; dsm. ǣnigum 21.11,15, ǣngum 70.17; dsn. ǣngum 11.5; gsm. ǣniges 57.13. NEG. **nǣnig**, *not any, none*: nsm. 27.13, 80.6; asm. nǣnigne 56.8; dsm. nǣngum 23.2.

ǣnlīc, adj. *unique, solitary, glorious*: nsm. 72.2.

ǣr, **A. adv.** *before, before that, earlier, formerly, once*: 1.12,30, 4.7, 9.10, 11.10, 21.7, 25.12, 26.9, 29.13 (*early, soon* in conj. hwonne ǣr), 42.7, 47.11, 52.9 (~ þonne, *before, sooner than*), 58.8, 63.2, 71.4,26, ?80.19, 84.25, 89.29, 91.4. —**B. conj.** *before*: 1.26, 3.6, 53.6.

ǣrendsprǣc, f. *message*: as. ǣrendsprǣce 58.15.

ǣrest, **A. adv.** *first*. 38.7, ærist 33.2. —**B. supl. adj.** *first*: nsm. 79.5. (*the first*).

ǣror, adv. *before, formerly*: 21.9 [MS. ær].

ǣrra, comp. adj. *former, first*: nsm. 51.12.

æsc, m. **1.** *ash-spear*: dp. æscum 20.11. —**2.** *name of runic Æ*: ns. 40.9.

æt, prep. w. dat. **1.** *at, in, by* (time, place, circumstance): 1.44, 19.4, 29.12,15, 32.3, 33.7, 38.6,34, 40.16, 41.6, 44.1, 52.9, 58.2, 75.6, 84.31. —**2.** *from* (*at the hands of*): 18.16.

ǣt, m. *food*: gs. ǣtes 38.65 (partitive).

ætgædre, adv. *together*: 51.11, 53.11. *See* **tōgædre.**

ǣtren, adj. *deadly, venomous*: nsm. 21.4.

ætsomne, adv. *together*: 20.1, 40.7, 81.3. *See* **tōsomne.**

æþele, adj. *noble*: nsf. æþelu 76.6; supl. gsn.wk. æþelestan 57.9 [MS. æþelan].

æþeling, m. *nobleman, prince*: gs. æþelinges 76.1,2; np. æþelingas 47.7; gp. æþelinga 44.5.

æþelu, f.p. *nobility, lineage*: ap. æþelu 53.8; dp. æþelum 41.1.

āgan, v.PP. **1.** *have, possess*: SUBJ. pres. 3p. āgen 39.5. —**2.** *have control, rule*: inf. 41.5. NEG. **nāgan,** *have not*: 1s. nāh 1.36; 3s. nāh 25.14.

āgen, adj. *own*: asn. 7.6, 42.4, 52.3.

āgētan, v.I. *waste, destroy, ?mine*: PRET. 3s. āgētte 79.7.

āgifan, v.5. *give*: 1s. āgyfe 76.11.

āglāc, n. *torment, misery*: as. 77.6; ds. āglāce [MS. aglaca] 1.37; gp. āglǣca 89.23 (or ns. of *āglǣca*?).

āglāchād, m. *state of misery? state of awesomeness* (cp. the uses of *āglǣca* in *Beowulf* which refer both to monsters and hero)? ds. āglāchāde 51.5.

āglǣca, m. *wretch*: ns. 89.23 (or gp. of *āglāc*?).

āgnian, v.II. *claim, appropriate*: PRET. 3s. āgnade 89.16.

agob, *see* **boga.**

āhebban, v.6. *raise, lift up*: 3p. āhebbaδ 5.3; PRET. 3s. āhōf 8.9.

āhreddan, v.I. *recapture*: PRET. 3s. āhredde 27.9.

āleodan, v.2. *grow (up)*: pp. āloden 80.31.

ām, m. *weaver's reed, slay*: ns. 33.8 [MS. amas].

āmǣstan, v.I. *fatten*: pp. āmǣsted 38.105.

an, *see* **on.**

ān, adj. or (as subs.) pron. *one, a certain one*: nsm. 13.7, 40.10, 80.10 (*only*); nsm.wk. āna 38.21; nsn. ān 19.12; nsf. ān [7.3], 50.5, 80.1; asm. ānne 47.1, 53.11, 82.6, 89.27, ǣnne 77.3; asn. ān 82.3; asf. āne 54.1, 72.2, 73.3 (adv? *alone*); dsm. ānum 8.4, 23.3 (*alone*), 30.6; isf. ānre 80.40; gsf. ānre 41.13; dpm. ānum 58.15 (*alone*); gp. ānra 11.5, 34.10. NEG. **nān,** *not one, none*: asm. nǣnne 65.6.

āna, adv. *alone*: 34.9, 38.90. *See* **ān.**

ānǣd, n. *solitude*: ds. ānǣde 58.5.

ānfēte, adj. *one-footed*: asf. 56.11.

anfōn, v.7CT. *receive*: PRET. 3s. anfēng 40.3.

ānforlǣtan, v.7. *relinquish*: PRET. 3s. ānforlēt 70.10.

ānga, adj. *lone*: nsm. 84.18 (*solitary?*).

ānhaga, m. *lone-dweller, recluse*: ns. 3.1.

anstellan, v.I. *bring about*: 1s. anstelle 1.89.

ansȳn, f. *view, aspect, form*: ds. ansȳne 38.94.

anwalda, m. *ruler (Lord)*: ns. 38.4.

ārǣran, v.I. *raise up, establish*: 1s.
ārǣre 79.9; pp. ārǣred 35.7.
ārētan, v.I. *gladden*: 1s. ārēte 4.6.
ārīsan, v.1. *arise*: 3s. ārīseð 1.50.
ārlīce, adv. *honorably, kindly*: 7.6
[MS. snearlice], 41.4.
ārstæf, m. *kindness, benefit*: ip. ār-
stafum 24.24.
ārȳpan, v.I. *tear off*: 3s. ārȳpeð 74.7.
āscūfan, v.2. *shove forward*: inf. 87.6.
āsecgan, v.III. *declare*: inf. 1.2.
āsettan, v.I. *set up, build*: inf. 7.11
(sīþas ~, *to make journeys*), 27.6.
āstīgan, v.1. *arise*: 1s. āstīge 1.3; 3s.
āstīgeð 1.79.
āswāpan, v.7. *sweep away*: 1s. āswāpe
21.5.
ātēon, v.2CT. *take out, draw out*:
PRET. 3s. ātēah 59.2.
ātimbran, v.I. *build*: inf. 27.5 [MS.
atimbram].
atol, adj. *awful, terrible*: nsm. 1.79;
nsn. 20.7.
āttor, n. *venom*: as. 21.9.
āttorspere, n. *deadly spear*: dp. āttor-
sperum 15.9.
ātyhtan, v.I. *produce*: pp. ātyhted
48.3.
āþringan, v.3. *press out, burst forth*:
1s. āþringe 1.42.
āþrintan, v.3. *swell*: pp. āþrunten
35.2.
āweaxan, v.6,7. *grow up*: PRET. 1s.
āwōx 8.3, āwēox 7.10, 71.1.
āweccan, v.I. *awake, rouse*: pp. npn.
āweahte 11.8.
āwefan, v.5. *weave*: PRET. 3p.
āwǣfan 33.9.
āweorpan, v.3. *cast away*: pp. āwor-
pen 38.49; ?āweorp[.. 80.15.
āwergan, v.I. *cover, bind*: SUBJ. pres.
3s. āwerge 38.47.
āwōx, *see* āweaxan.

āwrecan, v.5. *drive away*: inf. 87.11.
āwþer, pron. *either (of two)*: ns. 84.27.
See ǣgþer.
āwyrgan, v.I. *curse*: pp. āwyrged
18.17.

B

bæc, n. 1. *back*: ds. bæce 1.66, 13.3.
—2. under bæc, *backwards*: 20.17,
87.8.
bæg, *see* bēag.
bǣl, n. *fire*: gs. bǣles 79.2.
bær, adj. *bare*: nsf. baru 29.22 [MS.
bær]; asn. bær 63.4.
bærnan, v.I. *burn*: 1s. bærne 1.5, 4.2.
See byrnan.
bām, *see* bēgen.
bān, n. *bone*: as. 37.18; ds. bāne 66.3.
bānlēas, adj. *boneless*: asn.wk. bān-
lēase 43.3.
baþian, v.II. *bathe*: PRET. 3p. baþe-
dan 25.6.
be, prep. w. dat. 1. *by, beside, along*
(local): 19.2, 20.15, 58.1, 68.1, 80.3,
84.25,30, bi 42.1. —2. *by, during*
(temporal): 25.17.
beadu, f. *battle*: ds. beadwe 84.28.
beaduwǣpen, n. *battle-weapon*: ap.
beadowǣpen 13.3; dp.
beadowǣpnum 15.8.
beaduweorc, n. *battle-work*: gp.
beadoweorca 3.2, 31.6.
bēag, m. *ring, collar*: as. 70.13, bǣg
2.8; gs. bēages 57.11; dp. bēagum
29.22.
bēaghroden, adj. *ring-adorned*: nsf.
12.9.
bealdlīce, adv. *boldly*: 38.16, 58.16.
bēam, m. 1. *tree*: ns. 88.1; as. 51.1;
gs. bēames 53.7; ap. bēamas 1.9.
—2. *beam (yoke?)*: ds. bēame 70.13.

—3. *timber, wood*: gs. bēames 8.7. *See* **wudubēam**.

bēamtelg, m. *tree-dye, ink*: ds. bēamtelge 24.9.

bearg, m. *barrow-pig, castrated boar*: ns. 38.106.

bearm, m. *bosom, lap*: ns. 64.4; as. 1.33; ds. bearme 41.12.

bearn, n. *child*: ns. 18.18, 80.11; as. 7.6; np. 24.18, 38.96, 39.4,7, 80.32, 91.10; dp. bearnum 13.9, 37.18; gp. bearna 55.6. *See* **frum-, worldbearn**.

bearngestrēon, n. *procreation*: gp. bearngestrēona 18.27.

bearonæs, m. *woody headland*: ap. bearonæssas 55.5.

bearu, m. *grove, wood*: ns. 28a.4, ?bear[.] 28b.4; ds. bearwe 19.7 [MS. bearme], 51.1, 76.7; ap. bearwas 1.9; dp. bearwum 25.2.

bēatan, v.7. *beat*: 3p. bēatað 1.21, 77.8.

bēcnan, v.I. *signify*: 3s. bēcneð 37.26; 3p. bēcnaþ 22.10.

bed, n. *bed*: as. 2.3; ds. bedde 23.4. *See* **grundbedd**.

bedrīfan, v.1. *drive*: PRET. 3s. bedrāf 27.9 [MS. bedræf].

befæðman, v.I. *enclose, contain*: 1s. befæðme 89.25.

bēgen, num. *both*: nm. 41.12, 84.10,28; nn. būta 52.6; dm. bām 41.11, bǣm 62.2; gm. bēga 50.7; gf. bēga 40.7.

begīnan, v.1. *swallow*: 1s. begīne 87.3.

begrindan, v.3. *grind off*: pp. begrunden 24.6.

behealdan, v.7. **1.** *hold, possess*: PRET. 1s. behēold 71.4. —**2.** *behold, see*: SUBJ. pret. 3s. behēolde 58.5. *See* **bihealdan**.

behlȳþan, v.I. *despoil, strip*: pp. behlȳþed 12.10.

belācan, v.7. *play about*: PRET. 3s. beleolc 58.7.

belcedswēora, adj. *swollen-necked*: nsm. 77.1.

belēosan, v.2. *lose* (w. dat.): PRET. 1s. belēas 24.4.

ge-**belgan,** v.3. *become enraged*: pp. gebolgen 38.19. *See* **ābelgan**.

bellan, v.3. *grunt*: prp. nsm. bellende 38.106.

bemīþan, v.1. *conceal*: 1s. bemīþe 91.13.

bemurnan, v.3. *lament*: PRET. 1s. bemearn 89.20.

bēn, f. *prayer*: ds. bēne 57.12.

bend, m.f.n. *bond*: ap. bende 1.45, 18.30; dp. bendum 51.6; ip. bendum 50.3,7. *See* **orþoncbend**.

benn, f. *wound*: np. benne 57.12.

bennian, v.II. *wound*: inf. bennegean 54.2; PRET. 3s. bennade 89.18.

ge-**bennian,** v.II. *wound*: pp. gebennad 3.2.

bēobrēad, n. *honey in the comb*: as. 38.59.

beofian, v.II. *tremble*: 3p. beofiað 1.39.

bēon/wesan, v.AN. *be*: **1.** ordinary present indicative forms: inf. wesan 40.8, 41.10; 1s. eom 3.1, 13.2, 15.1, 16.1, 18.1,16, 21.2, 22.1,9, 23.1, etc. (52 times); 3s. is 1.1, 9.1, 13.1, 15.9, 18.3, 19.1, 21.1, 23.4, 24.27, 26.12, etc. (43 times); 3p. sindon 40.17, 53.10, sindan 63.6, sind 55.2, 56.14, 64.3. —**2.** present indicative forms of bēon: 1s. bēom 1.104, 5.8, 14.4, 21.4, bēo 21.7; 3s. bið 1.7,18,26,54, 58,63,69, 2.9, 11.9, 13.6, etc. (40 times); 1p. bēoþ 61.5; 3p. bēoð

14.5, 24.19, 33.5, 38.11. —**3.** PRET.
forms: 1s. wæs 12.1, 16.4, 38.44,
54.1, 58.1, 63.1,2, 69.2, 70.1,10,
72.1, 88.1; 3s. wæs 7.2, 8.1, 11.5,
17.8, 20.6, 29.4,6, 30.9, 31.3,5, etc.
(35 times); 1p. wǣron 84.10,26;
3p. wǣron 7.7, 8.8, 11.1, 31.4,
44.6, 50.3, 54.4, 70.18, wǣran 49.2.
—**4.** SUBJ. forms: pres. 3s. sȳ
26.13, 33.14, 37.1,14, 38.24,27,60,
39.9, 65.16, 76.6, 80.56; sīe 29.24,
30.14; pret. 3s. wǣre 34.8, 37.15.
—**5.** NEG. forms: pres. 3s. nis
38.68,86, 81.1, 84.20.
beorcan, v.3. *bark*: 1s. beorce 22.2.
beorg, m. *hill*: as. 13.18.
beorghliþ, n. *hillside? cliff-face?* ap.
beorghleoþa 55.2. *See* **burghliþ.**
beorht, adj. *bright*: nsm. 18.3; nsf.
38.28; asm. beorhtne 12.7; asn.wk.
(or ap. strong?) beorhte 91.6 [MS.
beorhtne]; apf. beorhte 9.1; comp.
nsf. beorhtre 17.8. *See* **heafod-
beorht.**
beorhte, adv. *brightly*: 32.9.
beorn, m. *man, warrior, hero*: ds.
beorne 10.6 [MS. beorn]; np. beor-
nas 29.15; ap. beornas 20.18; gp.
beorna 58.16.
bēot, n. *boast*: ns. 88.1.
beran, v.4. *bear, carry*: inf. 53.2,
54.12, 62.2; 1s. bere 1.15, 10.2,
13.3; 3s. byreð 1.59, 5.6, 12.5,
55.1, 88.6; 3p. berað 13.15; PRET.
3s. bær 8.10, 89.29; pp. boren 61.2.
See **oðberan.**
berend, *see* **feorh-, gǣst-, segn-
berend.**
berstan, v.3. **1.** *burst, crash* (intr.): 3s.
biersteð 1.92. —**2.** *burst, break*
(trans?): 3s. bersteð 2.8. *See* **tō-
berstan.**
bescīnan, v.1. *shine upon*: 3s. be-
scīneð 71.20.

bescyrian, v.I. *deprive* (w. dat.):
PRET. 3s. bescyrede 38.101.
besincan, v.3. *sink*: pp. besuncen 8.3.
besnyþþan, v.I. *deprive* (w. dat.):
PRET. 3s. besnyþede 24.1.
bestelan, v.4. *deprive* (w. dat.): pp.
npm. bestolene 9.6. *See* **bistelan.**
bestreþan, v.I. *bestrew? heap up?* pp.
bestreþed 80.44.
bētan, v.I. *improve, amend*: 1s. bēte
4.10 [MS. betan], ?69.10.
betra, *see* **gōd.**
betȳnan, v.I. *close*: pp. betȳned
38.11.
beþencan, v.I. *entrust*: SUBJ. pres.
3p. beþencan 46.7 [MS. beþun-
can].
beþennan, v.I. *stretch over, cover*:
PRET. 3s. beþenede 24.12.
bewadan, v.6. *surround, ?cover*: pp.
bewaden 89.30.
bewǣfan, v.I. *wrap, clothe*: pp.
bewǣfed 69.1.
beweorpan, v.3. *surround*: 3s. be-
weorpeð 80.40.
bewindan, v.3. *wind round*: pp. be-
wunden 28a.2, 79.3.
bewitan, v.PP. *watch over*: 3s. bewāt
80.9.
bewrēon, v.1,2CT. *cover, conceal*: pp.
asf. bewrigene 40.14, apm? be-
wrigene 75.8.
bewreþian, v.I. *sustain, support*: pp.
bewreþed 80.22.
bewyrcan, v.I. *make, construct*: pp.
asm. beworhtne 33.3.
bi, *see* **be.**
bicgan, v.I. *buy, acquire, procure*: 3p.
bicgað 52.12.
bid, n. *lingering, halt*: as. 1.33.
bīdan, v.1. **1.** *await, expect* (w. gen.):
inf. 3.9, 13.15 [MS. biddan]; 3s.
bīdeþ 29.12; 3p. bīdað 1.55. —**2.**
remain: 1s. bīde 13.9; pp. biden
79.2.

biddan, v.5. *entreat, ask someone* (acc.) *for something* (gen.): PRET. 3s. bæd 57.3.

bīdfæst, adj. *fixed*: nsm. biidfæst 54.7 [MS. biid fæft].

bidsteal, n. *halt*: as. 38.19 (~ giefeð, *stands at bay*).

bifeohtan, v.3. *deprive by fighting* (w. dat. of thing): pp. bifohten 1.62.

bifōn, v.7CT. *surround, encircle*: inf. 38.52; pp. bifongen 24.14.

bihealdan, v.7. *see, behold*: inf. 38.39; 3s. bihealdeð 15.5, 38.93. *See* **behealdan**.

bihōn, v.7CT. *hang round*: pp. bihongen 54.10.

bilecgan, v.I. *cover, envelop*: 3p. bilecgað 24.25.

bill, n. *sword*: is. bille 3.2.

bilūcan, v.2. *lock up, enclose*: PRET. 3s. bilēac 59.1.

bindan, v.3. *bind*: 1s. binde 10.3, 25.16; 3s. bindeð 36.7; PRET. 3s. bond 31.7; pp. bunden 19.7, 26.5, 70.13. *See* **unbindan**.

ge-**bindan,** v.3. *bind*: pp. gebunden 54.6, asm. gebundenne 2.8.

bindere, m. *binder*: ns. 25.6.

biniman, v.4. *deprive*: PRET. 3s. binōm 24.2 (w. gen.); pp. binumen 25.14 (w. dat.).

birēofan, v.2. *deprive* (w. dat. of thing): pp. birofen 1.61, npn. birofene 11.7.

bisgo, f. *labor*: as. 54.7.

bistelan, v.4. *deprive* (w. dat.): pp. bistolen 25.13. *See* **bestelan**.

bītan, v.1. *bite*: 1s. bīte 63.5; 3s. bīteð 63.4; 3p. bītað 3.9, 63.6; PRET. 3p. biton 89.24; SUBJ. pres. 3s. bīte 63.5; SUBJ. pret. 3s. bite 89.19.

biter, adj. *bitter, fierce*: nsf. 31.6; dpn. bitrum 15.8.

bitwēonum, prep. w. dat. *between*: 27.2 [MS. abitweonū].

biþeccan, v.I. *cover*: pp. biþeaht 1.24.

blac/blæc, adj. *black*: nsm. blæc 84.18 [MS. bæc]; dsn. blacum 8.7; ism. blace 89.24; npn. blace 1.81, blacu 49.3; npf. blace 55.2.

blāc, adj. *bright*: dsm.wk. blācan 1.74.

blǣcan, v.I. *bleach*: pp. blǣced 26.5.

blǣd, m. **1.** *wealth, glory*: as. 91.6. —**2.** *breath*: ns. 35.7 (w. pun on meaning #1).

blǣtan, v.I. *bleat*: 1s. blǣte 22.2.

blandan, v.7. *mix*: SUBJ. pret. 2s. blēnde 38.59.

ge-**blandan,** v.7. **1.** *trouble, agitate*: pp. geblonden 1.52. —**2.** *infect, taint, corrupt*: pp. geblonden 21.8.

blāwan, v.7. *blow*: SUBJ. pret. 3s. blēowe 83.6.

blēað, adj. *timid*: nsm. 38.16.

blēd, f. *shoot, flower, fruit, crop*: ap. blēde 11.9.

blēdhwæt, adj. *fruitful*: apm. blēdhwate 1.9.

blēnde, *see* **blandan**.

blēofāg, adj. *variegated*: nsf. 18.3.

blīcan, v.1. *shine*: inf. 32.9.

bliss, f. *bliss*: as. blisse 6.6, 41.7; ds. blisse 29.15.

blōd, n. *blood*: ns. 89.18; as. 37.18.

blonca, m. *white horse*: ap. bloncan 20.18.

blōstma, m. *blossom*: ds. blōstman 38.28.

blōwan, v.7. *bloom*: inf. 32.9; prp. nsm. blōwende 28a.4, 28b.4.

bōc, f. *book*: ap. bēc 40.7.

bōcwudu, m. *beech-wood*: ds. bōcwuda 38.106.

bodian, v.II. *announce*: 1s. bodige 6.10.

boga, m. *bow*: ns. agob [MS.
Agof] = boga 21.1. *See* **wīrboga.**
bold, n. *building*: as. 13.9 [MS. blod].
bona, m. *slayer*: ds. bonan 23.3; gs.
bonan 18.18, 71.7.
bonnan, v.7. *summon*: 1s. bonne 12.4.
bora, *see* **feorh-, mund-, wōð-bora.**
borcian, v.II. *bark?* PRET. 3s. borcade
83.6.
bord, n. *board, table*: as. 89.24
(*shield?*),31; gs. bordes 84.20,21;
dp. bordum 12.9. *See* **hlēo-,
nægled-bord.**
bordweall, m. *ship-wall* (w. pun on
shield-wall?): ap. bordweallas 31.6.
bōsm, m. *bosom*: as. 1.92, 12.9; ds.
bōsme 1.77, 10.6, 12.15, 21.3, 35.7,
76.7.
bōt, f. *recompense, renewing*: ns. 35.7.
brād, adj. *broad*: asm.wk. brādan
1.33; comp. nsf. brǣdre 38.50,82.
brægnloca, m. *brain-house, head*: as.
(or ds?) brægnlocan 71.24 [MS.
hrægn locan].
brēag, m. *eyelid*: gp. brēaga 38.100.
breahtm, m. *noise, tumult*: ns. 1.55;
is. breahtme 2.3 (adv?); gp.
breahtma 1.70.
ge-**brec,** n. *crash, noise*: np. gebrecu
1.74; gp. gebreca 1.70.
brecan, v.4. *break, break into*: inf. 2.3;
1s. brece 71.26; 3s. briceð 36.6,
63.4. *See* **ābrecan.**
bregdan, v.3. *draw*: 1s. bregde 87.8;
SUBJ. pres. 3s. bregde 1.28.
brēost, n. *breast* (often in plural with
singular meaning): np. 13.15. *See*
bylgedbrēost.
brerd, m. *rim*: as. 24.9.
brim, n. *sea*: gs. brimes 1.28, 8.7.
brimgiest, m. *sea-guest*: gp. brim-
giesta 1.55 (*sailors? waves?*).
bringan, v.I,3. *bring*: 1s. bringe 6.5;

3p. bringað 9.9 [MS. bringeð];
PRET. 3s. brōhte 20.17, 57.8; pp.
brōht 10.7, brungen 19.7, 25.2.
brōga, m. *terror*: np. brōgan 1.81. *See*
sperebrōga.
brōþor, m. *brother*: ns. 41.11, 79.5,
84.10,20,23, 89.15; np. 84.17; ap.
29.22, 70.7.
ge-**brōþor,** m.p. *brothers*: np. 11.2.
brōþorlēas, adj. *brotherless*: nsm.
84.21.
brū, f. *eye-brow*: gp. brūna 38.100.
brūcan, v.2. *use, enjoy* (w. gen.): inf.
18.30, 24.18, 38.100; 3s. brūceð
26.10; 3p. brūcað 30.12; SUBJ.
pres. 1p. brūcen 39.7.
brūn, adj. *brown, gleaming*: nsn.
89.18; nsf.wk. brūne 58.6; asm.
brūnne 24.9; dpn. brūnum 15.8;
gpm. brūnra 88.1.
brȳd, f. *bride, consort*: ns. 10.6, 43.3;
ds. brȳde 18.27.
būend, *see* **eorð-, fold-, lond-,
nēah-būend.**
būgan, v.2. *bow, bend, turn*: inf. 71.7;
prp. isf. būgendre 6.6 (~ stefne,
with modulated voice). *See* **onbūgan.**
būgan, v.I. *inhabit*: 1s. būge 5.2, 13.8;
3p. būgað 65.12.
bunden, *see* **searo-, un-bunden.**
būr, n. *bower, chamber*: as. 27.5.
burg, f. *dwelling, city*: as. 53.7; ds.
byrig 27.5; dp. burgum 1.70,81,
3.9, 6.6, 32.1, 79.2, 91.6. *See*
ealdor-, mǣg-burg.
burghliþ, n. *mountain-slope*: dp. burg-
hleoþum 25.2. *See* **beorghliþ.**
burgsæl, n. *city-house*: ap. burgsalo
55.5.
burgsittende, m.p. *citizens*: gp.
burgsittendra 23.3.
burna, m./**burne,** f. *stream*: as.
burnan 20.18; gs. burnan 1.92
[MS. byrnan].

būta, *see* bēgen.

būtan, prep. w. dat. *without*: 46.2.

byden, f. *tub*: ds. bydene 25.6.

byht, m. *bight, bay*: as. 20.12.

byht, n. *dwelling*: ap. 5.3.

bylgedbrēost, adj. *puff-breasted*: nsm. 77.1 [MS. by led breost].

byrnan, v.I. *burn*: prp. nsf. byrnende 28a.4, 28b.4. *See* bærnan.

byrne, f. *mail-coat*: ns. 18.3.

bysig, *see* līg- (lēg-), þrāg-bysig.

bysigian, v.II. *occupy*: pp? bysigo[. (or ns. bysigu, *trouble, affliction?*) 71.8.

ge-bysgian, v.II. *busy, agitate*: pp. gebysgad 28a.3.

C

cǣge, f. *key*: gs. cǣgan 40.12.

cald, adj. *cold*: comp. nsm. caldra 38.54. *See* winterceald.

calu, adj. *bald*: nsm. 38.99.

caru, f. *sorrow*: gs. care 41.8.

ge-cēapian, v.II. *buy*: 3s. gecēapaþ 21.13.

ceaster, f. *city*: as. ceastre 57.15.

cēne, adj. *bold*: comp. nsm. cēnra 38.18.

cennan, v.I. *conceive, bring forth*: PRET. 3s. cende 33.2; pp. cenned 37.15. *See* ācennan.

cēol, f. *ship*: ds. cēole 1.58, 16.4.

ceole, f. *throat*: ds. ceolan 31.2 [MS. ceole].

ceorfan, v.3. *cut*: pp. corfen 26.4.

ceorl, m. *churl, countryman*: as. 25.8; gs. ceorles 23.6.

ge-cēosan, v.2. *choose*: pp. gecoren 29.10.

cirman, v.I. *cry*: 1s. cirme 6.3; 3p. cirmað 55.4; PRET. 3s. cirmde 46.3.

clǣngeorn, adj. *yearning after purity*: nsf. 80.27.

clamm, f. *bond, fastening, chain*: ap. clamme 40.12, clomme 1.45.

clengan, v.I. *cling, remain (prolonged)*: 3s. clengeð 26.8.

cleopian, v.II. *call, cry out*: PRET. 3s. cleopode 31.2.

clif, n. *cliff*: ap. cleofu 1.58.

clympre, m? *lump*: ns. 38.75.

clyppan, v.I. *embrace*: 3p. clyppað 24.26. *See* ymbclyppan.

cnēo, n. *knee*: ap. 42.5.

cnōsl, n. *kindred, family, offspring*: gs. cnōsles 16.4, 41.8. *See* geoguð-cnōsl.

cnyssan, v.I. *strike*: inf. 33.8.

cofa, m. *chamber*: ds. cofan 61.4.

comp, m. *fight, battle*: ds. compe 4.2; gs. compes 18.36.

compwǣpen, n. *war-weapon*: ip. compwǣpnum 18.9.

cræft, m. *craft, power, skill, cunning*: as. 29.13; is. cræfte 19.7, 40.12, 71.22 (adv?),23, 80.27; gs. cræftes 79.13; ip. cræftum 29.10 (adv?), 33.9; ?cræft[. 80.13. *See* hēah-, sundor-, wæl-, wundor-cræft.

cræftig, *see* hyge-, searo-cræftig.

Crist, m. *Christ*: ns. 4.2.

crūdan, v.2. *crowd, press*: 3s. crȳdeþ 1.58.

cuma, m. *guest, stranger*: ns. 41.15. *See* wilcuma.

cuman, v.4. *come*: inf. 84.16; 3s. cymeð 1.71, 35.6, 38.55; PRET. 1s. cwōm 8.6, 63.2; 3s. cwōm 20.1, 27.7, 31.1, 52.1, 82.1, cōm 89.18; SUBJ. pres. 1s. cyme 61.8; 3s. cyme 3.5, cume 13.10. *See* forðcuman.

cunnan, v.PP. *know, know how, be able* (w. obj. or inf.): 2s. const 34.12; 3s. conn 58.11, 67.1; PRET. 3s. cūþe

57.10; SUBJ. pres. 2s. cunne 30.13;
3s. cunne 65.15, 71.29.

cūþ, adj. *known*: nsm. 91.1; nsn.
31.11, 71.22; nsf. 27.8; asn.wk.
cūþe 42.5 (*familiar? intimate?*). See
unforcūð.

cwelan, v.4. *die*: 1s. cwele 63.1.

cwellan, v.I. *kill*: 1s. cwelle 18.9;
PRET. 1s? cwealde 75.7.

cwēn, f. *woman, queen*: ns. 76.4; np.
cwēne 47.8.

cwene, f. *woman*: ns. 72.1.

cweðan, v.5. *say*: 3s. cwiþeð 65.9;
PRET. 1s. cwæð 63.1; 3s. cwæð
46.4, 57.5; 3p. cwædon 57.12;
SUBJ. pret. 3p. cwæden 57.16. See
oncwe þan.

ge-cweðan, v.5. *say*: PRET. 3s.
gecwæð 46.8.

cwic/cwicu, adj. *living*: nsm. cwic
71.4, cwico 63.1; asn. cwico 8.6,
cwicu 72.5; apm. cwice 36.7; apn.
cwice 4.2, cwico 11.3; gpf. cwicra
26.8.

cwide, m. *speech, saying*: as. 45.4 (w.
pun on *cwidu*, n., *what is chewed?*).
See **galdor-, sōð-, word-cwide.**

cyme, see **seld-, up-cyme.**

cȳmlīc, adj. *beautiful*: nsf. 31.2.

ge-cynd, f. *kind, nature, condition*: ds.
gecynde 71.4; dp. gecyndum
37.15.

cyneword, n. *fitting word*: ip.
cynewordum 41.15.

cyning, m. *king*: ns. 18.9, 38.3; gs.
cyninges 76.4; np. cyningas 47.8.
See **hēah-, þēod-, wuldor-cyning.**

cynn, n. *family, race, kind*: ns? 80.18;
as. cyn 47.8; ds. cynne 1.80,
?cynn[.] 75.2; gs. cynnes 31.9,
58.4; ap. cyn 4.3; gp. cynna 39.2,
53.2, 80.8, ?cy[...] 80.56. See
**from-, gum-, læce-, mon-,
wæpned-cynn.**

cyrran, v.I. *turn*: 3s. cyrreð 29.10;
PRET. 3s. cyrde 20.17; pp. cyrred
26.4.

cyrten, adj. *beautiful*: nsf. cyrtenu
23.6.

cyssan, v.I. *kiss*: 3s. cysseð 61.4; 3p.
cyssað 12.3, 28a.6.

ge-cyssan, v.I. *kiss*: 3p. gecyssað
28b.6.

cystig, adj. *bountiful*: nsf. 80.27.

cȳþan, v.I. *announce, make known*: inf.
2.3, 29.13, 91.9; PRET. 3s. cȳðde
84.27; SUBJ. pres. 3s. cȳþe 41.15,
71.29 [MS. saga].

ge-cȳðan, v.I. *announce, make known*:
inf. 80.7.

D

dǣd, f. *deed*: is. dǣde 9.7.

dæg, m. *day*: as. 18.7, 56.4; gs. dæges
25.3 (adv.),17, 47.2 (adv.); dp.
dagum 3.14, 7.1, 51.4.

dægcondel, f. *day-candle, sun*: ns.
89.32.

dægrīm, n. *number of days*: ds.
dægrīme 89.8.

dægtīd, f. *day-time*: dp. adv.
dægtīdum, *by day, in the day-time*:
15.3, 70.8.

dæl, n. *valley*: ap. dalu 89.11.

dǣl, m. *part, share*: ns. 26.1, 58.10,
62.4, ?71.9; as. 53.4, 56.9, 70.15; ds.
dǣle 24.10.

ge-dǣlan, v.I. *separate*: 1p. gedǣlað
81.7.

daroþ, m. *dart, spear*: np. daroþas
54.4.

dēad, adj. *dead*: nsm. 72.4; asm.
dēadne 7.1.

dēaf, adj. *deaf*: asm. dēafne 47.2.

dēagol, adj. *secret*: asm. dēgolne

13.21; apn. dēagol 38.39. *See* **dē-golful**.

deall, adj. *proud* (w.dat.): nsf. 29.22; apm. dealle 20.11.

dēað, m. *death*: ns. 13.11, 81.7; ds. dēaþe 10.15, 26.11, ?80.50; gs. dēaþes 89.32.

dēaðslege, m. *death-blow*: ap. 3.14.

dēaðspere, n. *death-spear*: ap. dēaðsperu 1.83.

dēaw, m.n. *dew*: ns. 27.12.

dēgol, *see* **dēagol**.

dēgolful, adj. *secret*: asm. dēgolfulne 79.13.

delfan, v.3. *dig (out)*: 3p. delfað 38.97.

dēman, v.I. *declaim, proclaim*: inf. 26.11.

denu, f. *valley*: dp. denum 25.3.

dēop, adj. *deep*: nsm. 20.6; asn. 4.10; apn. 89.11; gpn. dēopra 54.4.

dēope, adv. *deeply*: 51.6.

dēor, adj. *brave, bold*: nsf. 29.16; dsm. dēorum 10.5.

dēoran, v.I. *praise, glorify*: 3p. dēoraþ 9.7.

deorc, adj. *dark*: nsf. 1.51; npn. 1.75; dpf. deorcum 10.9.

dēore, adj. *dear, precious, excellent*: nsm. 15.10; asm. dēorne 41.1; comp. nsm. dēorra 80.37; supl. asn. dēorast 9.9, gsn.wk. dēorestan 31.10, 39.4. *See* **dȳre**.

dohtor, f. *daughter*: ns. 23.6, 31.10, 43.5, 76.6; np. 44.2; gp. dohtra 7.12.

dol, adj. *foolish, stupid*: nsm. 1.83, 18.32, 24.17; nsn. 10.9; apm. dole 9.3, 25.17.

dolg, n. *wound*: np. 3.13; ap. 57.11; gp. dolga 54.4.

ge-**dolgian**, v.II. *wound*: pp. gedolgod 51.6.

dōm, m. 1. *(great) judgment, glory*: ds. dōme 71.10; gs. dōmes 29.16.
—2. *authority, power*: as. 79.13. *See* **wīsdōm**.

dōn, v.AN. 1. *make, perform, do*: inf. 57.11; 3s. dēð 65.3; 3p. dōð 39.7, 47.10 *(prepare)*; PRET. 1s. dyde 18.25; 3s. dyde 7.12. —2. *put, bring, take*: PRET. 3s. dyde 24.3, ?.]yde 75.4.

ge-**dōn**, v.AN. *cause*: PRET. 3p. gedydon 71.6.

ge-**drēag**, n. *tumult, ?suffering*: as. 4.10 (ofer deop ~, *over the deep tumult? after severe suffering?*).

drēam, m. *joy, mirth, music*: ns. 26.7. *See* **seledrēam**.

drēfan, v.I. *stir up, disturb*: 1s. drēfe 5.2 (wado ~, *swim*); PRET. 3s. drēfde 20.16 (lagu ~, *swam*).

drēogan, v.2. 1. *do, work, perform*: inf. 37.17, 56.1; 3s. drēogeð 30.10; PRET. 3s. drēag 49.5, 54.7. —2. *endure, suffer*: 1s. drēoge 77.6.

drēorig, adj. *sad, bloody, afflicted*: dpn. drēorgum 1.75 [MS. dreontum].

drīfan, v.1. *drive*: 3s. drīfeþ 38.78. *See* **ā-, be-drīfan**.

drinca, m. *drink*: as. drincan (or inf?) 10.5, 70.8.

drincan, v.3. *drink*: 3p. drincað 12.12, 18.12, 61.3; PRET. 3p. druncon 53.1, 54.11, 65.14.

drohtað, m. *condition of life*: as. 4.10.

druncmennen, n. *drunken maid*: ns. 10.9.

drȳge, adj. *dry*: nsm. 38.77.

dryht, f. *multitude, (plural) men*: dp. dryhtum 10.15, 48.2; gp. dryhta 26.7, 39.4.

dryhten, m. *lord, master, God*: ns. 38.12, 81.2 [MS. dryht]; gs. dryhtnes 57.8,11 [MS. dryht]. *See* **in-, mon-dryhten**.

dryhtfolc, n. *nation, people*: gp.
dryhtfolca 24.17.

dryhtgestrēon, n. *noble treasure*: gp.
dryhtgestrēona 15.3.

dūfan, v.2. *dive*: PRET. 1s. dēaf 72.4;
3s. dēaf 49.5.

dugan, v.PP. *avail*: 3s. dēag 71.9;
PRET. 3s. dohte 59.7.

duguþ, f. 1. *troop*: as. duguþe 89.11.
—2. *benefit*: dp. dugþum 47.10.

dumb, adj. *dumb*: nsm. 51.6;
nsm.wk. dumba 47.10, 57.8; nsf.
dumb 29.16; asm.wk. dumban
47.2; dpm. dumbum 48.2.

dūn, f. *slope, hill, mountain*: ns. 1.51;
ap. dūna 36.6; dp. dūnum 25.3.

dūnþȳrel, n. *hill-hole, burrow*: as.
13.21 [MS. dum þyrel].

durran, v.PP. *dare*: 3s. dear 13.15.

duru, f. *door*: dp. durum 13.11, 26.7.

dūst, n. *dust*: ns. 27.12.

dwǣscan, v.I. *extinguish*: 3s.
dwǣsceð 80.39.

dwellan, v.I. *lead astray, deceive*: 1s.
dwelle 9.3.

ge-**dwolen,** adj. (pp. of unrecorded
gedwelan, v.4. *err, go astray*). *gone
astray, perverse, foolish*: npm. ge-
dwolene 9.7.

dȳfan, v.I. *dip*: PRET. 3s. dȳfde 24.3.

ge-**dȳgan,** v.I. *survive*: 3s. gedȳgeð
36.6; 3p. gedȳgað 1.87.

ge-**dyn,** m. *din, noise*: is. gedyne 1.75.

dynt, m. *blow*: dp. dyntum 25.17.

dȳp, n. *the deep, sea*: ds. dȳpe 1.51.

dȳre, adj. *dear, precious*: nsf. 80.23;
gsm.wk. dȳran 79.13; apm? dȳre
80.13; apn. dȳre 38.39; comp.
apn.wk. dȳrran 47.6. See **dēore.**

dysig, adj. *foolish*: apm. dysge 9.3.

E

ēac, adv. *also, likewise, moreover*:
34.12, 38.40. See **swylce ēac** *under*
swylce.

ēacen, adj. 1. *increased, endowed,
mighty*: nsm. 7.8; nsf. 80.21,27;
npn. 3.13. —2. *pregnant*: nsf.
31.11.

ēad, n. *prosperity, happiness*: as. 24.23.

ēadig, adj. *prosperous, happy*: dpm.
ēadgum 80.28.

ēadignes, f. *prosperity, happiness*: gs.
ēadignesse 28a.9, 28b.9.

eafora, m. *child, offspring*: ap. eaforan
13.12; ip. eaforan 18.21.

ēage, n. *eye*: ns. 23.11; as. 35.4, 82.3,
83.6; np. ēagan 38.11; ap. ēagan
34.7, 77.3; dp. ēagum 13.5; ip.
ēagum 80.32, 89.34; gp. ēagena
37.11 [MS. eage ne], ēagna 57.9.

eald, adj. *old, ancient, eminent*: nsm.
6.5; asm. ealdne 25.8; dsm. ealdum
38.63; comp. nsm. yldra 38.42,
70.10.

ealdor, n. *life*: ns. 7.3; ds? ealdre
65.11.

ealdorburg, f. *royal city*: as. 57.14.

ealdorgesceaft, f. *condition of life*: ns.
37.23.

ealfelo, adj. *entirely harmful, dire*:
asn. 21.9.

eall, A. adj. and subs. *every, the
whole of, all*: nsn. 90.6; asm. ealne
38.14, 64.9 [MS. ealdne]; asn. eal
38.33,40,84, eall 79.8; npm. ealle
53.10, 64.3; apm. ealle 80.9; apn.
ealle 89.23; dpm. eallum 27.8,
38.101, 49.7; gpm. ealra 38.4, 44.6;
gpn. ealra 11.1, 31.13; gpf. ealra
37.14, 38.88. —**B. adv.** *all, entirely*:
eal 3.6.

ealle, adv. *entirely*: 38.53 (or asf. of
eall?).

ealles, adv. *wholly, entirely*: 13.14.
eallgearo, adj. *entirely ready, eager*:
nsf. 21.4.
ēam, m. *uncle*: ns. 44.6.
ēar, m. *sea*: is. ēare 1.52.
earc, f. *chest, box*: ds. earce 59.2.
eard, m. *dwelling place, native land*: ns.
84.11; as. 58.5, 64.8, 77.6, 84.16; ds.
earde 31.4, 71.5, 79.8, 89.16.
eardfæst, adj. *fixed, ?earth-fast*: asm.
eardfæstne 47.1.
eardian, v.II. *dwell, abide*: inf. 84.24;
PRET. 3s. eardade 84.25.
ēare, n. *ear*: np. ēaran 13.5; ap. ēaran
77.3, 82.3.
earfoð, n. *hardship, labor*: gp. earfoða
70.15.
earm, m. *arm*: ap. earmas 30.6, 82.6.
earm, adj. *poor, wretched*: dpm. ear-
mum 80.28; supl. nsf. earmost
37.14.
earn, m. *eagle*: ns. 38.67; as. 22.4.
earp, *see* eorp.
ēaþe, adv. *easily*: 13.19, 21.11,
38.53,[84], 53.8.
ēawunga, adv. *openly*: 71.25.
eaxl, f. *shoulder*: np. eaxle 71.16; ap.
eaxle 67.3, 82.6, exle 30.6.
eaxlgestealla, m. *shoulder-companion,
comrade*: ns. 76.2.
ēce, A. adj. *eternal*: nsm. 38.1;
ipf.wk. ēcan 38.90. —B. adv. *eter-
nally*: 65.11.
ecg, f. *edge, blade, sword*: ns. 1.72, 24.6
[MS. ecge]; ds. ecge 1.72; np. ecge
31.4; ip. ecgum 3.3; gp. ecga 3.13.
See heard-, stīð-ecg.
ednīwe, adj. *renewed*: nsf. ednīwu
39.1.
efenlang, adj. *equally long, just as
long*: asn. (nsm?) 42.7 [MS. efe
lang].
efne, adv. *even, just*: 1. efne sēþēah,
conj. *nevertheless, even so*: 37.27,

63.1. —2. efne swā, conj. *just as,
even as*: 1.43.
efnetan, v.5. *eat as much as*: inf. 38.63.
eft, adv. 1. *again, afterwards*:
1.29,68,93, 4.9, 18.13, 24.3,10, 35.6,
37.6, 60.7, 63.2, 85.8, 89.10.
—2. *backwards*: 21.1.
egesful, adj. *fearsome, awful*: nsm.
31.4.
egle, adj. *hideous, painful*: npf. 70.18;
dpn. eglum 15.9.
egsa, m. *terror*: ns. 1.63,79.
eh, n. *horse*: ap. 20.11.
ehtuwe, num. *eight*: 34.4.
ellen, n. *zeal, strength, courage*: ns.
59.7, 71.9; as. 56.1 (*deed of strength*),
84.27.
ellenrōf, adj. *brave, powerful*: npm.
ellenrōfe 20.20.
ellorfūs, adj. *eager to depart*: npm.
ellorfūse 41.13.
ende, m. *end*: as. 80.10; ds. 76.9,
84.20,21.
endleofan, num. *eleven*: 20.3 [MS.
xi].
engel, m. *angel*: gp. engla 64.8.
engu, f. *confinement*: ds. enge 1.35,42.
eodor, m. *enclosure? protector?* ns.
15.2 (w. pun on both meanings?).
eofor, m. *boar*: ds. eofore 38.18.
ēoredmæcg, m. *horseman*: np.
ēoredmæcgas 20.3.
ēoredþrēat, m. *troop (of horsemen)*: ns.
1.79.
eorl, m. *man, nobleman, warrior*: gs.
eorles 58.13, 76.6; ap. eorlas 20.11;
dp. eorlum 6.5, 29.11, 53.8, 91.1;
gp. eorla 44.7.
eorp, adj. *dark, dusky*: nsm. 47.11,
?71.16; gsn. eorpes 89.27; npf.wk.
earpan 1.72.
eorðbūend, m. *earth-dweller, man*: dp.
eorðbūendum 27.8.
eorþe, f. *earth*: ns. 51.3; as. eorþan

1.17, 14.3, 27.12, 33.11, 38.1,21,
64.8, ?80.18, 80.42, 84.18, 91.10;
ds. eorþan 1.7,98, 4.3, 25.8,16,
38.40,50,82, 39.6, 48.1, 74.2, [80.1];
gs. eorþan 38.4,25, 65.13, 79.5,
84.24.

eorðgræf, n. *hole in the earth*: as. 56.9.

esne, m. **1.** *servant*: ns. 41.5,8,16, 52.8
(also meaning #2); gp. esna 20.13.
—**2.** *man*: ns. 42.4, 61.5; as. 25.8
[MS. efne]; ap. esnas 25.16.

ēst, m.f. *favor, grace, love*: dp. adv.
ēstum 24.24 (*gladly*).

etan, v.5. *eat*: 3s. iteþ 56.10, 74.8. *See*
efnetan.

ēþel, m. *home, native land*: ns. 14.3;
as. 64.7, 89.10; ds. ēðle 13.12.

ēþelfæsten, n. *fortress*: as. 71.25.

ēðelstōl, m. *ancestral seat, royal city*:
as. 1.37.

eðþa, *see* **oððe**.

exl, *see* **eaxl**.

F

fæcne, adj. *crafty, malicious*: dsm.
fæcnum 51.8.

fæder, m. *father*: ns. 7.2, 35.8, 38.34,
44.4, 80.9.

fæger, adj. *beautiful, pleasant*: nsn.
29.17; nsf. 80.5; comp. nsf. fægerre
38.46.

fægre, adv. *fairly, pleasantly, well*:
10.11, 18.2, 26.1, 48.8, 51.4, 61.2,
71.21.

fæhþ, f. *feud, vengeance*: ip. fæhþum
27.11 (adv.?).

ge-fǣlsian, v.II. *cleanse, purify*: pp.
gefælsad 79.4.

fǣmig, *see* **fāmig**.

fǣmne, f. *maiden, woman*: ns. 40.5,
72.1.

fǣr, m. *sudden danger*: as. 51.12. *See*
fērfæst.

fæst, adj. *firm, fixed*: nsm. 15.2, 58.3;
nsn. 19.13; npn. 32.6; apf. fæste
32.7; gpm. fæstra 50.7. *See* **bīd-,**
eard-, fēr-, hyge-, sige-, þrym-,
wīs-fæst.

fæste, adv. *fast, firmly*: 1.31, 10.3,
14.10, 24.26, 50.4, 54.6, 59.1, 69.4,
84.22.

fæsten, n. *prison, confinement*: as.
23.9. *See* **ēþelfæsten**.

fæt, *see* **lyft-, sīþ-, wǣg-fæt**.

fæt, adj. *fat*: comp. nsm. fættra
38.105.

fǣted, adj. *ornamented, plated*: asn.
49.7.

fæthengest, m. *riding-horse*: ns.
20.14.

fæðm, m. **1.** *embrace*: ds. fæðme 61.6;
dp. fæþmum 1.28, 8.6, 64.4; ip.
fæþmum 24.25. —**2.** *bosom*: ds.
fæðme 10.11. *See* **lagufæðm**.

fāg, *see* **blēo-, haso-, sinc-fāg, won-**
fāh.

fāh, adj. **1.** *hostile, inimical*: nsm.
79.4. —**2.** *outlawed*: nsm. 18.16.

fām, n. *foam*: ns. 1.19.

fāmig, adj. *foamy*: nsm. 1.49, fǣmig
1.62.

ge-fara, m. *companion*: ns. 76.3.

faran, v.6. *go, fare, depart*: inf. 30.4,8,
62.1; 3s. fareð 1.78, 15.11, 21.3,
80.3, fǣreð 19.4; 3p. farað 1.76;
PRET. 3s. fōr 34.9; prp. apf.
farende 1.87.

faru, *see* **wolcen-faru**.

fēa, adj. *few*: nsm. (or nsn?) 58.3
(~ ǣnig, *hardly any*); npm. 1.87.

ge-fēa, m. *joy*: ds. gefēan 39.5.

ge-feah, *see* **ge-fēon**.

fealdan, v.7. *fold*: PRET. 3p. fēoldan
24.7.

feallan, v.7. *fall*: inf. 1.76; 3s. fealleþ 19.13, 77.10, 89.26; PRET. 3s. fēol 27.12.

fealo, adj. *fallow, 'pale yellow shading into red or brown'* (W. Mead): nsm.wk. fealwa 53.10; nsn. fealo 13.1; npf. fealwe 71.18.

feax, n. *hair*: ds. feaxe 89.14 [MS. feax]. *See* **wonfeax.**

feaxhār, adj. *gray-haired*: nsf. 72.1.

fēdan, v.I. *feed, nourish, sustain*: 3s. fēdeð 32.2; 3p. fēdað 48.8; PRET. 3s. fēdde 7.9, 70.6, 74.1; 3p. fēddan 51.4, fēddon 71.1.

fēgan, v.I. *fix, join*: 3s. fēgeð 23.9; PRET. 3s. fēgde 59.6.

fēhð, *see* **fōn.**

fela, n. ind. *much, many*: 6.11, 19.8, 29.8, 30.8 [MS. fella], 32.2, 56.3, 79.10.

fēlan, v.I. *feel* (w. gen.): 3s. fēleþ 23.9, 80.50; 3p. fēlað 4.8.

felawlonc, adj. *proud, haughty, ?licentious*: nsf. 10.7.

feld, m. *field*: ap. feldas 30.8.

felde, *see* **fyllan.**

fell, n. *skin, hide*: as? .]ell 78.4; gs. felles 74.5; np. fell 11.3.

fen, n. *fen, swamp*: ns. 38.31.

fēng, *see* **fōn.**

fenȳce, f. *swamp-frog*: ns. 38.71.

feoh, n. **1.** *cattle, herd*: as. 32.2.
  —**2.** *money, property, wealth*: ds. fēo 52.12.

feohtan, v.3. *fight, contend*: inf. 4.5, 14.1; prp. npn. feohtende 1.76. *See* **bifeohtan.**

feohte, f. *battle*: as. feohtan 3.4.

fēol, f. *file*: is. fēole 87.2; gs. fēole 69.4.

fēolan, v.3CT. *pass*: inf. 20.5.

ge-fēon, v.5CT. *rejoice*: PRET. 3s. gefeah 62.5.

fēond, m. *enemy*: ns. 19.3, 48.4, 89.28; ds. fēonde 48.4; gp. fēonda 24.1.

fēondsceaþa, m. *enemy, robber*: ap. fēondsceaþan 12.19.

feor, adv. *far*: 21.5.

feorh, n. *life, soul*: ns. 7.2, 10.3; as. 8.6, 37.16; ds. fēore 1.62, 18.18, 24.1, 38.65, 89.22; is. fēore 21.14; ap. feorg 11.3, feorh 13.19. *See* **wīdeferh.**

feorhbealo, n. *life-bale, evil threat*: as. 21.5.

feorhberend, m. *life-bearer, man*: gp. feorhberendra 37.6.

feorhbora, m. *life-bearer, living creature*: ns. 88.2.

feormian, v.II. *cherish, care for, ?polish*: 3s. feormað 71.21.

feorran, adv. *from far, far off*: 4.8, 10.7, 26.6, 52.2.

fēower, num. *four*: 20.4 [MS. iiii], 36.3, 49.1,7, 53.2, 70.6; (infl.) apm. fēowere 34.3.

fēran, v.I. *go, travel*: inf. 27.11, 30.7, 34.1, 37.6, 38.69, 66.1, 73.1; 1s. fēre 1.5,101, 10.1, 19.1; 3s. fēreð 1.52, 56.2, 89.30, 91.3; 3p. fērað 1.74, 55.4; prp. nsm. fērende 5.9, nsf. fērende 80.5.

ge-fēran, v.I. *accomplish, ?suffer*: pp. gefēred 35.3.

fērfæst, adj. *danger-fast, perilous*: asn.wk. fērfæste 21.14 [MS. wer fæste].

fergan, v.I. *carry, bring*: inf. 13.13, 50.1 (w. passive sense); 3s. fereð 12.7, 30.10 [MS. fere], 56.4,11, 60.7 [MS. fareð]; PRET. 3s. ferede 17.6; 3p. feredon 25.4. *See* **oþfergan.**

fēring, f. *journeying*: gs. feringe 71.27.

ferþ, m.n. *mind, spirit, life*: as. 72.5

[MS. forð]; ds. ferþe 24.21; dp.
ferðþum 52.12, 57.3, ferþum 80.34.
ferðfriþende, adj. *life-sustaining*:
apm. 36.3.
ge-**feterian,** v.II. *fetter, bind*: pp.
npm. gefeterade 50.4.
fēþe, n. *walking, going*: ds. 13.2.
fēþegeorn, adj. *eager to go*: nsf. 29.9.
fēþelēas, adj. *without power to walk,
immobile*: asf. fēþelēase 74.3.
fēþemund, f. *walking-hand, fore-paw*:
ip. fēþemundum 13.17.
feþer, f. *feather*, (plural) *wings*: np.
feþre 25.4. *See* **halsrefeþer.**
fīf, num. *five*: (infl.) fīfe 44.6.
findan, v.3. *find*: inf. 3.11; 3s. findeð
32.6, 84.31; 3p. findað 41.7; pp.
funden 25.1. *See* **onfindan.**
finger, m. *finger*: np. fingras 24.7,
38.52.
firas, m.p. *men*: dp. firum 31.12; gp.
fīra 65.4.
firen, f. *crime, sin*: as. firene 80.39.
firenian, v.II. *chide, revile*: 3s. firenaþ
18.34.
firgenstrēam, m. *big or mountainous
stream, ocean-stream*: dp.
firgenstrēamum 8.2.
fisc, m. *fish*: dp. fiscum 72.4.
fiþere, n. *wing*: ap. fiþru 34.7.
flā, f. *arrow, dart*: ap. flān 1.87; gp.
flāna [MS. flan] 54.12 (or from *flān*,
m.f., *arrow*?).
flǣsc, n. *flesh, body*: as. 74.5, 78.4; ap.
1.13.
flēam, m. *flight*: is. flēame 13.13.
flēogan, v.2. *fly*: inf. 1.86, 29.8,
38.66, 56.3; 3s. flēogeð 21.12; 3p.
flēogað 15.6; PRET. 1s. flēah 72.3;
3s. flēag 20.16, 49.4 [flēag on: MS.
fleotgan], flēah 35.4, 62.5.
flēon, v.2CT. *flee*: PRET. 1s. flēah
13.29. *See* **flēogan.**

flet, n. *floor, hall*: as. 53.2, 54.12; ds.
flette 40.5.
flint, m. *flint*: ds. flinte 38.78.
flintgrǣg, adj. *flint-gray*: asm.
flintgrǣgne 1.49.
flōcan, v.I. *clap*: 3s. flōceð 18.34.
flōd, m. *flood, wave, stream*: ns. 20.6;
as. 1.49; ds. flōde 5.9, 8.2, 20.14,
38.77 [MS. flonde], 72.3, 74.3; np.
flōdas 64.4; ap. flōdas 12.7, 75.1.
See **lagoflōd.**
flōdweg, m. *flood-way, sea*: ap. flōd-
wegas 34.9.
flot, n. *sea*: ds? flote 75.7 [MS.
...flote].
flȳman, v.I. *put to flight*: inf. 12.19;
3p. flȳmað 14.6.
flȳs, n. *fleece, wool*: ip. flȳsum 33.3.
fōddurwela, m. *provision, store*: ap.
fōddurwelan 30.10.
folc, n. *people, race, nation*: ds. folce
31.12; gs. folces 62.6; ap. folc 5.6;
dp. folcum 1.73, 91.3. *See*
dryhtfolc.
folcsǣl, n. *hall, house*: ap. folcsalo
1.5.
folcscipe, m. *people, nation*: ds. 30.10.
folcstede, m. *people-place, dwelling-
place*: ds. 3.11.
folcwiga, m. *warrior*: np. folcwigan
12.13.
foldbūend, m. *earth-dweller, man*: gp.
foldbūendra 1.13.
folde, f. *earth, land, world*: as. foldan
1.5, 10.1, 37.10, 72.5; ds. foldan
5.9, 31.12; gs. foldan 26.1, 39.5,
64.4, 88.2.
folgian, v.II. *follow as a servant, at-
tend*: PRET. 3s. folgade 35.2, 83.2.
folm, f. *palm, hand*: ns. 38.52; as.
folme 37.10 [MS. folm]; ds. folme
71.8, ?folm[. 61.6; np. folme 29.7;
ap. folme 30.5; ip. folmum 18.34,
57.18, 59.3; gp. folma 25.15.

fōn, v.7CT. *take, seize, receive*: 3s. fēhð
25.9 (~ ongēan, *struggles against*);
PRET. 3s. fēng 54.3 (w. gen.). *See*
an-, bi-fōn.

for, prep. w. dat. 1. *before, in the*
presence of: 16.2, 18.12, 33.12, 46.1
[MS. fer],4, 53.8, 58.15. —2. *for, on*
account of: 69.6, 89.21.

fōr, f. *journey, course*: ns. 17.8; ds.
fōre 38.71, 41.10, 49.3; gs. fōre 9.5.

foran, adv. *in front, before*: 42.2, 51.8.

forht, adj. *afraid*: nsm. 41.10.

forhtmōd, adj. *timid, afraid*: nsm.
13.13.

forlǣtan, v.7. 1. *allow, let*: PRET. 3s.
forlēt 36.2. —2. *let go, release*: 3s.
forlǣteð 21.7. *See* ānforlǣtan.

forma, adj. *first*: nsm. 56.15 [MS.
furum].

forst, m. *frost*: ns. 38.54, 89.14,
?[.]orst 77.10.

forstelan, v.4. *rob, steal*: pp. forstolen
12.18 *(that which has been stolen)*.

forstondan, v.6. *hinder from, prevent*
(w. dat. of person): 1s. forstonde
14.8.

forstrang, adj. *very strong*: asm.
forstrangne 48.4 [MS. fer
strangne].

forswelgan, v.3. *swallow up, devour*:
3s. forswilgeð 47.11 [MS. fer
swilgeð]; PRET. 3s. forswealg 45.3.

forð, adv. 1. *forth, onward, away*:
19.6, 27.11,13, 61.2,8, 81.5, 87.6.
—2. *hence, henceforth*: 18.24.

forðcuman, v.4. *come forth*: pp. npn.
forðcymene 11.10.

forðgesceaft, f. *creation*: ns. 80.9.

forþon, adv. *therefore, consequently*:
13.12, 18.30, 24.13, 65.10.

forðsīþ, m. *going forth*: gs. forðsīþes
60.2.

forðweard, adj. *pointing forward, ad-*
vancing: nsm. 71.26; nsn. 19.13.

forðweg, m. *journey*: gs. forðweges
28a.3, 28b.3 *(death-road?)*.

forweorðan, v.3. *perish, die*: SUBJ.
pres. 1s. forwurðe 3.6 [MS. for
wurde].

fōt, m. *foot*: as. 29.20, 37.10, 89.27,
foot 77.3; ds. fōte 29.17, fēt 30.6;
np. fēt 29.7; ap. fēt 34.3, 65.7, 82.4;
ip. fōtum 10.1,7, 38.77, 78.4; gp.
fōta 25.15, 54.6.

fōðor, m. *fodder, food*: gs. fōþres
56.11.

ge-frǣge, adj. *known, famous*: nsm.
91.3.

frǣtwan, v.I. *ornament, adorn*: 3p.
frǣtwað 33.10; pp. frǣtwed 12.11,
26.6, 29.20, asm. frǣtwedne 59.8.

ge-frǣtw(i)an, v.I,II. *adorn*: pp.
gefrǣtwad 29.2, 30.2, gefrǣtwed
51.8.

frǣtwe, f.p. *ornaments, trappings*: np.
5.6; ap. 11.10; dp. frǣtwum 38.46;
ip. frǣtwum 12.7.

fram, *see* from.

frēa, m. *lord, master*: ns. 1.31, 4.5,
89.1, ?89.7, frēo 15.5; ds. frēan
18.2,24, 41.10, 53.10, 59.3, 60.2,
76.3; gs. frēan 1.96, 42.2, 71.8,
87.6.

frēcne, A. adj. *dangerous*: asf. 3.4.
—B. adv. *fiercely, dangerously*:
18.16.

frēfran, v.I. *comfort, aid*: 1s. frēfre 4.7.

fremde, adj. *foreign, strange*: nsm.
14.3, 91.4 [MS. fremdes].

fremman, v.I. 1. *do, accomplish, make*
(trans.): inf. [14.2], 71.11; 1s.
fremme 18.25; ger. fremmanne
84.26. —2. *get on, do (its task)*
(intr.): inf. 29.9.

fremu, f. *benefit*: ip. fremum 48.8.

frēo, adj. *noble, precious*: gpm. frēora
13.19.

frēo, *see* frēa.

frēogan, v.III. *love*: 3p. frēogað 52.12.

frēolīc, adj. *free, noble, beautiful*: nsm. 88.2; nsn. 12.13; nsf. 80.29, frēolicu 59.1; npn. frēolico 44.4.

frēond, m. *friend*: ds. frēonde 18.16; dp. frēondum 91.4; gp. frēonda 24.21.

frēorig, adj. *cold*: nsm. 33.1.

freoþian, v.II. *care for, protect*: 3s. freoþað 87.7; PRET. 3s. freoþode 7.5. See **friþian**.

fretan, v.5. *devour, eat*: inf. 74.5; PRET. 3s. fræt 45.1.

fricgan, v.5. *ask*: imp. 2s. frige 12.19, 14.10, 24.26, 25.15.

fridhengest, m. *horse*: ap. fridhengestas 20.4.

ge-frignan, v.3. *learn by asking, discover*: PRET. 1s. gefrægn 43.1, 45.2, 46.1, 65.1.

frið, n. *peace, security*: as. 71.26.

friþemǣg, f. *protectress, woman of peace*: ns. 7.9.

friþian, v.II. *protect*: inf. 14.7. See **freoþian**.

friþospēd, f. *peace, prosperity*: gs. friþospēde 57.3 [MS. friþo spe].

frōd, adj. **1.** *wise, prudent*: apm. frōde 57.3; comp. npm. frōdran 24.21. —**2.** *old*: nsm. 51.4, 89.8; nsn. 79.1; asm. frōdne 71.3; comp. nsm. frōdra 80.36.

frōfor, f. *comfort, aid, joy*: ds. frōfre 37.19; gs. frōfre 3.4.

from, prep. w. dat. *from, away from*: 18.23, 20.19, 31.2, 41.12.

from, adj. *active, bold, strong*: nsm. 60.2, 71.27; comp. nsm. framra 49.4; supl. nsf. fromast 80.29. See **orlegfrom**.

fromcynn, n. *the race from which one springs, ancestry, origin*: ns. 79.1 [MS. from cym]; as. 79.7.

fromlīce, adv. *boldly, strongly, swiftly*: 13.17, 38.69; comp. fromlīcor 38.66.

fruma, m. *beginning, commencement*: is. fruman 79.7 (adv. *at first*).

frumbearn, n. *first-born*: np. 44.4.

frumsceaft, f. *creation*: ds. frumsceafte 1.44.

frumstaþol, m. *original place or state*: ds. frumstaþole 58.3.

frymþ, f. *beginning*: ds. frymþe 38.6,34.

fugol, m. *bird*: ns. fugul 34.9; ds. fugele 29.7; gs. fugles 24.7, 34.11; dp. fuglum 49.4, 72.3. See **gūð-fugol**.

ful, adj. *full*: asm. fulne 1.60; comp. nsf? fulre 61.8. See **dēgol-, þrym-ful**.

ful, adv. *very*: 23.6, 28a.5, 28b.5, 38.104, 79.6, 84.12.

fūl, adj. *foul*: nsm.wk. fūla 38.48; comp. nsf. fūlre 38.31.

full, n. *cup, vessel*: as. 21.14; ap. 1.68.

fullēstan, v.I. *help, support*: 3s. fullēsteð 22.8.

fundian, v.II. **1.** *hasten*: 3s. fundað 80.5. —**2.** *strive, intend*: PRET. 3p. fundedon 20.6.

furðum, adv. *first*: 1.44.

fūs, adj. *striving forward, eager (for), ready (for)*: nsm. 28a.3, 28b.3, 71.27; dsm. fūsum 89.14; npn. fūs 1.73. See **ellorfūs**.

fyllan, v.I. *fell, cut down*: 1s. fylle 1.9.

fyllan, v.I. *fill*: inf. 59.8; PRET. 3s. felde 35.4.

ge-fyllan, v.I. *fill*: 1s. gefylle 64.8; 3s. gefylleð 12.8; PRET. 3s. gefylde 42.7; pp. gefylled (w. gen. of thing) 15.2.

fyllo, f. *fullness, satiety, impregnation*: as. 40.5; gs. fylle 15.5.

fȳr, n. *fire*: as. 38.78; ds. fȳre 1.73, 10.11; is. fȳre 28a.3, 28b.3, 79.4; gs. fȳres 69.4.

fyrd, f. *military expedition*: as. 71.21.

fyrdrinc, m. *warrior*: gs. fyrdrinces 76.3.

fyrdsceorp, n. *war-ornament*: ns. 12.13.

fyrn, adj. *ancient*: nsf. 80.9.

G

gæst, m. **1.** *guest, stranger*: ns. 5.9 (or *gǣst?*); as. giest 41.2 (w. pun on *gǣst?*). —**2.** *stranger, enemy*: ns. 13.10. See **brim-, hilde-, ryne-, stæl-giest.**

gǣst, m. **1.** *spirit, soul, life*: ns. 57.14; as. 10.2; ds. gǣste 57.4; is. gǣste 7.8; ap. gǣstas 1.13; gp. gǣsta 46.5, gēsta 38.41. —**2.** *man, human being*: dp. gēstum 20.15 (or *gestum,* from *gæst?*); gp. gǣsta 1.60.

gǣstberend, m. *soul-bearer, man*: as. 18.8.

gafol, n. *tribute, gift*: as. 36.2, gaful 30.12.

galan, v.6. *sing, chant*: 3s.gæleð 18.35.

galdorcwide, m. *incantation*: as. 46.7. See **wordgaldor.**

gān, v.AN. *go*: 3s. gǣð 38.77; PRET. 3s. ēode 2.6.

gangan, see **gongan.**

gārsecg, m. *ocean* (lit. *spear-man,* the ocean apparently conceived of as a personified warrior; see B-T., p. 362): gs. gārsecges 1.18, 38.93.

gāt, f. *goat*: ns. 22.2.

gēar, n. *year*: dp. gēarum 71.3; gp. gēara 30.12.

gēara, adv. *formerly, of old*: 18.29 [MS. gearo].

geard, n. *enclosure, dwelling*: ap. geardas 18.8; dp. geardum 41.2 (in ~, *in residence*), 88.4. See **middangeard.**

gearo, adj. *ready, willing*: comp. nsm. gearora 80.37 *(more attainable?)*. See **eallgearo.**

gearu, adv. *swiftly*: 38.17.

gearwe, adv. *readily, well*: 79.6.

geatwan, v.I. *prepare, equip, adorn*: pp. geatwed 26.6.

geatwe, f.p. *ornaments, decorations*: ip. geatwum 33.10.

gegnpæþ, m. *hostile or opposing road*: ds. gegnpaþe 13.26.

gēn, adv. **1.** *yet, still*: 7.2, 47.8, gēno 18.29, gēna 38.58. —**2.** *hitherto, continually*: gīen 18.25.

gēoc, f. *aid, help*: ns. 3.5.

geofu, see **gifu.**

geoguðcnōsl, n. *youthful family, progeny*: ds. geoguðcnōsle 13.10.

geoguðmyrþ, f. *pleasure of youth*: gs. geoguðmyrþe 36.2 [MS. geoguð myrwe].

geolo, adj. *yellow*: asn. 33.10.

geond, prep. w. acc. *through, throughout, (all) over*: 1.5, 10.13, 32.5 *(by, along)*, 37.17,19, 79.10, 80.41, 84.8.

geondsprengan, v.I. *sprinkle over*: PRET. 3s. geondsprengde 24.8 [MS. geond].

geong, adj. *young*: nsm. 12.2, ?84.6; nsf. 38.44, 72.1; comp. nsm. gingra 89.15 [MS. gingran], npm. gingran 84.17.

geonge, see **gongan.**

gēopan, v.2. *take to oneself, receive*: PRET. 1s. gēap 21.9.

georn, adj. *desirous, eager*: nsf. 29.16. See **clǣn-, fēþe-georn.**

georne, adv. *gladly, eagerly*: 2.2.

gest, *see* **gæst.**

gēst, *see* **gæst.**

gied, n. **1.** *word, speech, song*: as. 45.3; ds. giedde 76.11. —**2.** *saying, riddle*: gs. gieddes 53.14.

giefan, *see* **gifan.**

gieldan, v.3. *yield, pay*: 3s. gieldeð 30.11.

giellan, v.3. *yell, cry*: 1s. gielle 22.3; prp. asn. giellende 30.4.

gielpan, v.3. *boast, boast of* (w. dat.): 3s. gielpeð 56.12.

gīen, *see* **gēn.**

gierwan, *see* **gyrwan.**

giest, *see* **gæst.**

giestron, adv. *yesterday*: 38.44.

gif, conj. *if*: 1.59,84, 9.10, 10.3, 13.7,14,20,24, 14.4,5,8, 18.19,24, 19.14, 21.12, 24.18, 25.12, 27.6, 30.13, 34.12, 36.6,7, 37.28, 40.4, 41.4,8, 48.6, 51.12, 57.9, 59.7, 70.18, 71.9, 81.7, 91.5.

gifan, v.5. *give*: 3s. giefeð 38.19; PRET. 3s. geaf 18.4,23, ?70.3. *See* **ā-, of-gifan.**

gifen, n. *sea*: ns. 1.18.

gifre, adj. *useful*: nsm. 24.28; dpn. gifrum 47.3.

gīfre, adj. *greedy, voracious*: supl. nsf. gīfrost 80.30.

gifu, f. *gift, favor*: dp. gifum 56.13, geofum 80.37. *See* **wōð-giefu.**

gimm, m. *gem*: dp. gimmum 80.37. *See* **wælgim, wuldorgimm.**

gingra, *see* **geong.**

gītsian, v.II. *desire, crave for* (w. gen.): 3s. gītsað 56.11.

glæd, adj. *bright, shining, cheerful*: nsm. 61.3; nsf. glado 22.7; comp. nsf. glædre 90.3.

glēaw, adj. *clever, skilled, wise*: nsm. 30.14, 33.13, 80.34; npm. glēawe 46.7 (or adv?); apm. glēawe 57.2; comp. nsm. glēawra 45.6.

glēawstōl, m. *seat of wisdom*: as. 89.15.

glēd, f. *coal of fire, ember*: ns. 28a.4, 28b.4.

glida, m. *kite*: gs. glidan 22.5.

glisian, v.II. *shine, glitter*: PRET. 3p. glisedon 24.13 [MS. gliwedon].

God, m. *God*: ns. 38.21; as. 57.4; ds. Gode 46.8; gs. Godes 57.14.

gōd, n. *good thing, goods, wealth*: as. 91.6 (or ap?).

gōd, adj. *good*: nsf. good 76.11; asm. gōdne 42.3; npm. gōde 52.11; gpm. gōdra 24.22; comp. nsf. betre 38.28, apm. sēllan 10.4; supl. gsn.wk. sēlestan 39.3. *See* **ungōd.**

gōdlīc, adj. *good*: nsm. 83.4.

godwebb, n. *precious web, fine cloth*: as. 33.10.

gold, n. *gold*: ns. 88.4; as. 18.8, 49.7, 53.3, 69.6; ds. golde 24.13, 47.6, 61.3; is. golde 12.2, 65.14; gs. goldes 38.46, 46.6, 57.10.

goldhilted, adj. *gold-hilted*: asm. 53.14.

gōma, m. *palate*: as. gōman 47.6; ds. gōman 38.58.

gong, m. *movement, course*: ds. gonge 38.72. *See* **hingong.**

gongan, v.7. **1.** *go, walk, move*: inf. 29.8, 82.1, gangan 52.1; 1s. geonge 19.2; 3s. gongeð 32.3, ?gong[.. 78.4; prp. nsm. gongende 38.17, nsf? .]ongende 78.2, dsf. gongendre 19.9. —**2.** *happen, turn out*: 3s. gongeð 37.23; SUBJ. pres. 3s. gonge 34.14. *See* **ofer-, tō-gongan.**

gōp, m. *servant?* gs. gōpes 47.3.

gor, n. *dirt, dung*: gs. gores 38.72.

gōs, f. *goose*: ns. 22.3.

grǣdan, v.I. *cry*: 1s. grǣde 22.3.

grǣdig, adj. *greedy*: nsf. 36.2 (w. gen.); supl. nsf. grǣdgost 80.30.

græs, n. *grass*: as. 13.6.
grafan, v.6. *dig, dig up or into*: 1s.
græfe 19.2; PRET. 3s. grōf 31.6,
89.12.
grāpian, v.II. *grasp*: PRET. 3s.
grāpode 43.3.
grēne, adj. *green*: nsm.wk. grēna
38.51,83; nsn. grēne 19.9; asn.
grēne 13.6 [MS. grenne]; npm.
grēne 64.5; apm. grēne 10.2.
grēot, m. *sand, dirt*: ds. grēote 30.4,
grēate 78.2.
grētan, v.I. *greet, approach*: inf. 2.6,
42.6; PRET. 3s. grētte 85.6 (or *took
hold of*?).
grīma, m. *ghost*: ns. 38.17.
grimm, adj. *fierce, savage, severe*:
nsm.wk. grimma 41.2; asf.wk.
grimman 1.60; supl. isn.wk.
grymmestan 26.3. *See* heoru-
grimm, hete-, wæl-grim.
grimman, v.3. *rage, roar*: 3s. grim-
með 1.20.
grimme, adv. *grimly, fiercely*: 48.9,
80.3.
grindan, v. 3. *grind*: inf. 30.4. *See*
begrindan.
grīpan, v.1. *grab (onto)*: 3s. grīpeð
23.7; PRET. 3s. grāp 83.4.
gripe, m. *grip, grasp*: ds. 69.6.
grom, adj. *fierce, hostile*: npm. grome
71.3; gpm. gromra 18.19.
gromheort, adj. *angry-hearted*: dpm.
gromheortum 2.6.
grōwan, v.7. *grow*: inf. 32.9.
grund, m. 1. *ground, earth*: ds.
grunde 19.2, 20.15, 80.3. —2. *bot-
tom, depth (of sea)*: as. 1.18, 38.93;
dp. grundum 64.5 (or as meaning
#1?). *See* sǣgrund.
grundbedd, n. *ground*: as. 80.30.
grymetian, v.II. *rage, roar*: 3s.
grymetað 80.3.

gryrelīc, adj. *horrible, terrible*: nsm.
31.3.
guma, m. *man*: np. guman 30.12,
46.7, 61.3, 65.14; gp. gumena
21.10, 26.3, 79.6.
gumcynn, n. *mankind*: gs. gumcyn-
nes 84.17.
gumrinc, m. *man, warrior*: ns. 83.4.
gūþ, f. *war, battle*: as. gūþe 18.25; ds.
gūþe 18.19.
gūðfugol, m. *war-bird*: gs. gūðfugles
22.5.
gūþgemōt, n. *battle-meeting*: gs.
gūþgemōtes 13.26.
gūðgewinn, n. *battle*: gs. gūðgewin-
nes 3.5.
gūðwiga, m. *warrior*: gs. gūðwigan
88.4.
gyddian, v.II. *speak, sing*: inf. 46.1
[hring gyddian: MS. hringende
an].
gylden, adj. *golden*: asm. gyldenne
57.1 [MS. gylddenne].
gȳman, v.I. *care for, heed* (w. gen.): 1s.
gȳme 18.35.
gyrdan, v.I. *gird, encircle*: pp. gyrded
87.4.
ge-gyrdan, v.I. *gird*: pp. npf. gegyrde
71.16.
gyrdels, m. *girdle, belt*: as. 52.4; ds.
gyrdelse 52.11.
gyrn, m.n. *sorrow, misfortune*: ns.
13.6; ds. gyrne 79.6.
gyrwan, v.I. *adorn*: 3s. gyrweð 18.9;
PRET. 3s. gierede 24.13.
ge-gyrwan, v.I. *adorn, furnish, pre-
pare*: pp. gegyrwed 18.2,
gegierwed 26.1, 27.3, 34.2, 65.14,
66.2.

H

habban, v.III. *have*: inf. 1.95, 18.28, 91.5; 1s. hæbbe 1.12, 16.2, 19.8, 76.7, 77.2, 79.10, 89.27, hafu [9.2], 33.5, 38.98; 3s. hafað 29.21, 32.2, 37.3,10,[11],12,13,16,18,27, 42.3, 56.7, 63.3, 65.6, 67.3, 80.2; 3p. habbaþ 24.21, 29.15 [MS. habbad], 53.11; PRET. 1s. hæfde 8.6, 24.5, 70.13, 72.5; 3s. hæfde 7.11, 17.4, 29.5, 30.8, 34.3,7, 35.3 (aux.), 71.26, 82.3, 83.1, 85.2; 3p. hæfdon 11.3, 20.3. NEG. **nabban,** *have not*: PRET. 3s. næfde 30.5.

ge-habban, v.III. *hold*: inf. 14.10.

hād, m. *person*: ap. hādas 1.12.

hæft, n. *bond, bondage*: ds. hæfte 71.22.

hæftan, v.I. *bind*: pp. hæfted 2.2.

hæftnȳd, f. *captivity, bondage*: as. 79.9.

hægstealdmon, *see* **hagostealdmon.**

hægl, m. **1.** *hail*: ns. 77.9. —**2.** *name of runic* H: np. Hægelas 40.11.

ge-hǣlan, v.I. *heal, save*: PRET. 3s. gehǣlde 3.12; SUBJ. pres. 2s. gehǣle 46.5.

hǣlend, m. *Healer, Savior*: as. 57.6.

hæleð, m. *hero, man*: ns. 24.12, 60.6; np. 25.5, 53.1, 54.11; dp. hæleþum 6.10, 24.28, 33.12, 46.1, 57.17, 68.2, 80.23,36,54; gp. hæleþa 1.1,38, 5.3, 18.31, 38.96.

hǣlo, f. *safety*: as. 46.8.

hǣmed, n. *sexual intercourse, marriage*: as. 18.28.

hǣmedlāc, n. *sexual intercourse, marriage-game*: gs. hǣmedlāces 40.3 (plegan ~, *play at intercourse*).

hǣr, *see* **hēr.**

hǣst, *see* **hēst.**

hafoc, m. *hawk*: ns. 22.3, 38.67.

hagosteald, n. *celibacy, bachelorhood*: ds. hagostealde 18.31.

hagostealdmon, m. *bachelor, warrior*: ns. 12.2, hægstealdmon 52.3.

hālig, adj. *holy*: nsm. 24.28.

hals, m. *neck*: ns. 13.1; ds. halse 29.21, healse 70.13.

halsrefeþer, f. *pillow-feather, down*: ds. halsrefeþre 38.80.

halswriþa, m. *necklace, neck-ring*: as. halswriþan 2.4.

hām, m. *home*: ds. 27.4,9, 32.4, 41.6, 75.6.

hāmlēas, adj. *homeless*: nsf. 37.9.

hangelle, f. *hanging thing*: gs. hangellan 42.6.

hār, adj. *hoary, gray*: nsm. 19.3; nsm.wk. hāra 38.74, 89.13. *See* **feaxhār.**

haso, adj. *gray*: nsf.wk. heasewe 38.61; asm.wk. haswan 22.4; npm. haswe 1.7; apf. haswe 11.9.

hasofāg, adj. *gray*: nsn. 9.1.

hāt, adj. *hot, fiery*: nsm.wk. hāta 41.3; asm. hātne 60.7; comp. nsm. hātra 38.57.

hātan, v.7. **1.** *command, order*: 3s. hāteþ 4.5, 38.38; PRET. 3s. hēht 38.8, hēt 87.10; pp. hāten 59.4. —**2.** *call, name*: inf. 33.12; pp. hāten 22.9, npf. hātne 40.17. —**3.** *be called*: 1s. hātte 1.15,102, 6.8, 8.11, 10.13, 12.19, 14.10, 21.16, 24.26, 25.15, 60.9, 64.10, 71.29, 76.12, 79.14; 3s. hātte 17.9, 37.29, 41.15, 53.16, 82.7.

hē, hit, hēo, pron. *he, it, she*: nsm. hē 1.61, 13.14, 25.11,12, 35.5,8, 36.7, 38.5,6,7,19,55,94,108, 42.7, 45.6, 46.2, 48.5,8, 51.4,8, 52.1, 53.6, 57.17, 63.5, 71.27, 74.6, 81.3,4,5, 87.10; nsn. hit 17.9 [MS. ic], 27.6; nsf. hēo 7.11,12, 18.33, 23.7,

29.13,14, 32.6, 37.5,27 [MS. he],
38.26,28, 66.2, hīo 29.16,21, 31.5,
32.7, 34.8, 36.6, 37.7,8,10,16
(twice), 18,20,21,29, 52.9 [MS. hie
ó], 59.4, 65.3, 76.6, 80.28, 82.7
[MS. ic], 83.6,7; asm. hine 1.59,
13.15, 20.13, 21.12, 48.5,8,10, 51.3,
53.15; asn. hit 35.4, 37.4, 38.47,
58.16; asf. hīe 52.1, 56.4; dsmn.
him 1.83,84, 13.25, 17.4, 35.6,8,
36.2, 41.4, 47.6,9 (or dp?), 48.6,
57.7, 79.8, 81.6, 85.9, 89.15; dsf.
hyre 1.51, 27.5,10, 29.17,21, 32.3,
52.5,10; gsmn. his 13.15, 18.16,
25.14, 33.2, 35.4, 38.13,39, 41.9,
42.4,6, 44.1,2 (twice), 48.4, 51.9,
52.3,6, 53.13, 57.8, 61.7, 67.4, 71.9,
84.27; gsf. hyre 18.33,34, 29.6,13,
31.8, 37.23, 54.6, 56.6, 67.1 [MS.
hyra], hire 7.6; np. hī 4.8, 9.10,
14.5, 20.6, 28a.7, 28b.7, hȳ 1.53,
11.6, 18.12, 20.19, 24.19, 41.6,12,
51.10, 55.6, ?80.15, hēo 9.6; ap. hī
24.25, hȳ 24.24; dp. him 2.6, 4.4,
9.8, 13.11, 14.8, 29.15, 41.7,11, 47.9
(or ds?), 48.5,6,8, 49.6, ?75.5; gp.
hyra 4.9, 11.2,5, 20.9,18,21, 24.23,
44.3 [MS. hyre], 46.8, 50.6.
hēa, see **hēah**.
headre, see **heaþor**.
hēafod, n. *head*: ns. 13.1, 87.1; as.
23.8, 56.7, 59.5, 63.3, 77.2; ds.
hēafde 19.12, 38.98,102, 42.6; gs.
hēafdes 51.9; ap. hēafdu 34.8; gp.
hēafda 82.4. See **wulfhēafedtrēo**.
hēafodbeorht, adj. *shining-headed*:
asm. hēafodbeorhtne 17.2.
hēafodlēas, adj. *headless*: nsm. 12.10.
hēafodwōþ, f. *voice, headvoice*: ds.
hēafodwōþe 6.3.
hēah, A. adj. *high, exalted*: nsm.
68.2, 84.25, ?89.4; nsn. 1.57,93;
nsf.wk. hēa 5.4; asm. hēane 77.2;

asm.wk. hēan 38.22; dsn. hēaum
20.19; npm. hēa 20.7; apm. hēa
1.54; ipf. hēahum 1.10 [MS.
heanū]; comp. nsm. hȳrra 84.12,
nsf. hȳrre 38.38, 90.2; supl.
asn.wk? hȳhste 80.12. —**B. adv.**
high: 9.9. See **stēaphēah**.
hēahcræft, m. *excellent skill*: as. 33.4.
hēahcyning, m. *high-king, God*: ns.
38.38.
healdan, v.7. **1.** *hold*: 1s. healde
38.37; 3s. healdeð 18.13; PRET. 3s.
hēold 40.14. —**2.** *hold to, maintain*:
1s. healde 6.4. —**3.** *cherish, foster*:
PRET. 3s. hēold 7.5. —**4.** *rule, gov-*
ern: 3s. healdeð 38.2,5,22. See **be-,**
bi-healdan.
healdend, m. *holder, possessor*: ds.
healdende 18.23.
healf, f. *side*: ds. healfe 19.9, 84.25.
heall, f. *hall*: ds. healle 53.1 [MS.
heall],13, 57.1,17.
heals, see **hals**.
hēan, adj. **1.** *low, deep*: nsm. 1.99
[MS. heah]. —**2.** *lowly, despised,*
poor: npm. hēane 30.13; dpm.
hēanum 91.2; comp. nsf. hēanre
37.9.
hēan, hēane, see **hēah**.
hēanmōd, adj. *low-minded*: npf.
hēanmōde 40.17.
hēap, m. *crowd, band*: ip. hēapum
55.4.
heard, adj. *hard*: nsm. 12.10, 60.1;
nsm.wk. hearda 38.54, 53.9, 77.9;
nsn. heard 42.3, 89.19; nsf. heard
24.5, 76.9, heord 1.35; asn. heard
77.4; dsm. heardum 87.5; dsn.wk.
heardan 38.79; apm. hearde 50.2,
84.10; comp. nsm. heardra 38.54,
80.36, nsf. heardre 38.78; supl.
isn.wk. heardestan 26.2. See
hrīmigheard.

hearde, adv. *hard*: 87.5.

heardecg, adj. *hard-edged*: npn. 3.8.

heardhīþende, adj. *hard-plundering*: nsf. 31.7.

heasewe, *see* **haso.**

heaþoglemm, m. *battle-wound*: gp. heaþoglemma 54.3.

heaþor, n. *restraint, confinement*: ds. heaþore 18.13, headre 63.3.

heaþosigel, m. *sun of battle*: ns. 71.19.

hebban, v.6. *raise, lift*: inf. 43.2; 3s. hefeð 42.5; PRET. 3s. hōf 52.3; prp. gsm. hæbbendes 62.3. *See* **ā-, on-hebban.**

hefig, adj. *heavy*: asm. hefigne 56.7; comp. nsf. hefigere 38.74.

hēht, *see* **hātan.**

hell, f. *hell*: as. helle 64.6; ds. helle 37.20.

helm, m. **1.** *covering, protection*: ns. 84.13; as. 1.94. —**2.** *protector*: as. 24.17. *See* **sundhelm.**

helpend, m. *helper*: ns. 46.5.

helwaru, f.p. *people of hell*: gp. helwara 53.6.

hengest, *see* **fæt-, frið-, mere-hengest.**

heofon, m. *heaven*: ns? 90.2; as. 38.22; ds. heofone 38.38; gs. heofones 38.4,33, 83.5; ap. heofonas 64.6; dp. heofonum 27.12, 37.20.

heofonwolcn, n. *cloud of heaven*: ns. 71.2 [MS. heofon wlonc].

heolfor, n. *blood, gore*: ns. 89.19.

heord, f. *flock, herd*: gs. heorde 15.1.

heoroscearp, adj. *terribly sharp*: npn. 3.8.

heorte, f. *heart*: ds. heortan 40.14; dp. heortum 24.20. *See* **gromheort.**

heorugrimm, adj. *savage, fierce*: nsm.wk. heorugrimma 38.55.

hēr, adv. *here*: 38.32,49,61,77,81, 39.6, 41.16, 47.10, 84.20.

hēr, n. *hair*: np. 13.4; dp. hērum 24.5; ip. hǣrum 33.4.

here, m. *army, troop*: gs. herges 76.9.

heresīþ, m. *war-journey, raid*: ds. heresīþe 27.4.

hēreð, *see* **hȳran.**

hēst, f. *violence, hostility*: as. 13.28; is. (adv?) hǣste 1.35 [MS. hǣtst].

hetegrim, adj. *fierce, cruel*: nsf. 31.5.

heterūn, f. *hateful mystery, terrible curse*: as. heterūne 31.7.

hild, f. *battle*: ds. hilde 12.4, 31.5.

hildegiest, m. *battle-guest, enemy*: ds. hildegieste 51.9.

hildepīl, m. *war-dart*: np. hyldepīlas 15.6; ip. hildepīlum 13.28.

hildeþrȳþ, f. *battle-power*: as. hildeþrȳþe 17.4.

hildewǣpen, n. *battle-weapon*: ns. 88.5.

hindan, adv. **1.** *from behind, behind*: 87.5. —**2.** **on hindan,** *behind*: 35.1, ?85.5.

hindeweard, adj. *behind, hindward*: dsf. hindeweardre 19.15.

hingong, m. *departure*: gs. hingonges 60.1 [MS. Ingonges].

hīþan, v.I. *plunder, ravage*: 3s. hīþeð 32.4; prp. nsm. hīþende 89.28, gpm. hīþendra 91.5. *See* **heard-hīþende.**

hladan, v.6. *load, heap up*: 1s. hlade 1.95; PRET. 3p. hlōdan 20.10 (or inf?).

ge-**hladan,** v.6. *load*: pp. gehladen 80.22.

hlǣder, f. *ladder*: as. hlǣdre 53.6 (or is?).

hlǣst, n. *burden*: ap. 1.15.

hlāford, m. *lord, master*: ns. 2.4, 19.3,15, 87.9; ds. hlāforde 41.9, 54.11; gs. hlāfordes 56.13.

hlāfordlēas, adj. *lordless*: nsm. 18.22.

hleahtor, m. *laughter*: ns. 31.3 [MS. leahtor].

hlēo, m. *shelter, cover*: as. 25.5.

hlēobord, n. *protecting board*: ip. hlēobordum 24.12.

hlēor, n. *cheek*: dp. hlēorum 13.4 [MS. leorum].

hlēortorht, adj. *bright-cheeked*: nsm. 68.2.

hlēosceorp, n. *protecting garment*: ds. hlēosceorpe 7.5.

hleoþa, *see* **hliþ.**

hlēoþor, n. *voice, speech, song*: ns. 29.17; as. 22.5; ds. hlēoþre 6.4; is. hlēoþre 12.4.

ge-**hlēþa,** m. *companion*: as. gehlēþan 89.29. *See* **wilgehlēþa.**

hlīfian, v.II. *tower, stand out*: inf. 51.1; 3p. hlīfiað 13.4.

hlimman, v.3. *resound, roar*: 3s. hlimmeð 1.20, 33.6.

hlin, m. *maple*: ns. 53.9.

hlinc, m. *bank, ridge, ?cliff*: ap. hlincas 1.54.

hlinsian, v.II. *sound, resound, ?call*: PRET. 3s. hlinsade 31.3.

hliþ, n. *hill, cliff, mountain-slope*: ap. hleoþa 1.22, hliþo 89.9. *See* **beorg-, burg-, stān-hliþ.**

hlōðgecrod, n. *press of troops*: ns. 1.93.

hlūd, adj. *loud*: nsm. 1.54, 81.1; supl. nsn. hlūdast 1.70.

hlūde, adv. *loudly*: 1.20,92, 5.7, 6.3,10, 31.3, 46.2, 55.4.

hlutter, adj. *bright, clear*: asm. hlutterne 18.7.

hlyn, m. *noise, tumult*: ns. 1.7.

ge-**hnāst,** *see* **hōp-, wolcen-gehnāst.**

hnecca, m. *neck*: as. hneccan 77.4.

hnesc, adj. *soft*: comp. nsf. hnescre 38.80.

hnīgan, v.1. *bend, bow down, descend*: 1s. hnīge 1.93; prp. npm. nīgende 6.8. *See* **on-, under-hnīgan.**

hnītan, v.1. *push, thrust*: inf. 87.4.

hnossian, v.II. *beat, strike*: 3p. hnossiað 3.7.

hol, n. *hole*: as. 42.5; ds. hole 60.7.

hold, adj. *kind, gracious, faithful*: dsm. holdum 59.4. *See* **welhold.**

holdlīce, adv. *faithfully*: 32.4.

holen, m. *holly*: ns. 53.10.

holm, m. *wave, water, ocean*: as. 1.99; is. holme 1.10.

holmmægen, n. *force of waves*: is. holmmægne 1.24.

holt, n. **1.** *forest, wood*: ds. holte 88.1; gs. holtes 19.3; np. holt 84.12.
—**2.** *piece of wood, beam*: as. 54.3.

homer, m. *hammer*: is. homere 87.1; gp. homera 3.7.

hond, f. *hand*: ns. 10.12, 58.12; as. 47.3, 76.5; ap. honda 82.5; dp. hondum 28a.5, 28b.5 (æfter ~ , *from hand to hand*); ip. hondum 43.4, 52.4.

hondweorc, n. *handiwork*: as. 18.7; np. 3.8 [MS. 7weorc].

hondwyrm, m. *hand-worm*: ns. 38.96, 64.2.

hongian, v.II. *hang*: 1s. hongige 12.11; 3s. hongaþ 19.11, 42.1; PRET. 3p. hongedon 11.3.

hōpgehnāst, n. *crash of waves in the bay*: gs. hōpgehnāstes 1.57.

hord, n.m. *hoard, treasure*: as. 29.21, 51.11, 89.28; gs. hordes 87.9; ip. hordum 80.23; gp. horda 9.9. *See* **wombhord.**

hordgeat, n. *treasure-door*: gs. hordgates 40.11.

hordword, n. *treasure-word, valuable speech*: ap. 80.54.

horn, m. *horn*: dp. hornum 27.2 [MS. horna].

hornsæl, n. *gabled hall*: np. hornsalu 1.38.

hors, n. *horse*: ns. 34.5; gs. horses 34.11; ap. hors 20.10.

horsc, adj. *clever*: nsm. 1.1.

hræd/hreþ, adj. *quick, active*: nsm. 51.11; comp. nsm. hrædra 38.72, nsf. hreþre 38.71.

hrægl, n. *dress, garment, cloth*: ns. 5.1, 9.1, 11.9; as. 42.4, 52.4; ds. hrægle 8.7 [MS. hrægl], 60.6; is. hrægle 43.4.

hraþe, adv. *quickly*: ?hr[.]þe 74.7.

hreddan, v.I. *save, rescue*: inf. 12.18. *See* **āhreddan.**

ge-hrēfan, v.I. *roof, cover*: pp. gehrēfed 1.10.

ge-hrēodan, v.2. *adorn*: pp. gehroden 80.23. *See* **bēaghroden.**

hrēoh, adj. *fierce, wild*: nsf. 80.2.

hrēran, v.I. *move, stir, shake*: 1s. hrēre 1.8,38 [MS. hrera]; 3s. hrēreð 77.7; SUBJ. pres. 3p? hrēren 80.52.

hreþ, *see* **hræd/hreþ.**

hreþer, m. *breast, bosom*: ds. hreþre 59.5, 89.19.

hrif, n. *belly, womb*: as. 38.45, 80.52; ds. hrife 15.6, 21.12.

hrīm, m. *hoar-frost*: ns. 38.55, 77.9.

hrīmigheard, adj. *frozen hard*: apm. hrīmighearde 89.13.

hrīnan, v.1. *touch, reach, strike* (w. acc. or dat.): 1s. hrīne 4.4, 64.5, hrīno 13.28; 3s. hrīneð 21.12, 80.47; PRET. 3s. hrān 37.10,20.

hrindan, v.3. *push, thrust*: PRET. 3s. hrand 52.4 [MS. rand].

hring, m. *ring, chain, fetter, anything round*: ns. 46.8, 57.6; as. 46.1 [hring gyddian: MS. hringende an], 57.1; is? hringe 88.5; gs. hringes 57.17; ap. hringas 18.23; ip. hringum 69.8, 87.4, hringan 2.2.

hrīsil, f. *shuttle*: ns. 33.7.

hrōf, m. **1.** *roof*: as. 50.2; gs. hrōfes 25.5 (*roof? sky?*); dp. hrōfum 1.7. —**2.** *top, summit*: as. 13.27, 27.7.

hrōr, adj. *strong, vigorous, ?lusty*: nsm. 52.3.

hrung, f. *pole*: as. hrunge 20.10.

hrūse, f. *earth, ground*: ns. 1.36, 71.2; as. hrūsan 1.24, 5.1, 25.11; ds. hrūsan 38.55, 80.36,47.

hrūtan, v.2. *make a noise, whir, whiz*: prp. nsf. hrūtende 33.7.

hrycg, m. *back*: as. 1.95, 19.11, 77.4, 82.5 [MS. hryc]; ds. hrycge 1.12,36, 17.4, 34.6; is. hrycge 25.11; ip. hrycgum 1.63.

hū, adv. *how*: 1.15, 15.6, 29.19, 34.14, 37.23, 40.16, 41.15, 53.16, 57.16, 58.12, 80.8,56.

hund, num. *hundred*: 82.4.

hund, m. *dog*: ns. 22.2; gs. hundes 34.11.

hungor, m. *hunger*: ns. 41.3.

hunig, m. *honey*: ds. hunige 38.59.

hūþ, f. *booty, plunder*: as. hūþe 27.2,4,9.

hwā, pron. *who, what, what kind (of)*: nsm. 1.2,14,28,65,103,104, 79.7; nsn. hwæt 1.102, 6.8, 8.11, 10.13, 12.19, 14.10, 17.9, 21.16, 24.26, 25.15, 26.13, 29.24, 30.14, 33.14, 34.8, 37.29, 39.9, 60.9, 64.10, 65.16, 71.29, 76.12, 79.14, 82.7; asn. hwæt 59.9, 61.14. *See* **æghwā, nāthwæt.**

ge-hwā, pron. *each (one), every(one)*: dsm. gehwām 1.27, 9.8, 58.6; dsn. gehwām 30.12, 31.13, 78.6; dsf. gehwām 52.9.

hwæl, m. *whale*: ns. 38.92.

hwælmere, m. *sea*: ns. 1.20.

hwǣr, adv. *where*: 84.23. *See* **æg-, nāt-hwǣr, nōwēr.**

hwæt, adj. *active, bold*: comp. npm. hwætran 24.20. *See* **blēdhwæt.**

hwæþre, adv. 1. *yet, however,*
nevertheless: 1.84, 20.17, 29.8,9,17,
37.18, 52.8, 56.5. —2. **hwæþre**
sēþeah, conj. *nevertheless*: 33.11.

hwearft, m. *circuit, expanse*: ds.
hwearfte 38.33.

hweorfan, v.3. 1. *turn, depart*: inf.
18.22; 3p. hweorfað 41.12.
—2. *move, wander, roam*: inf. 30.3,
37.9; 3s. hweorfeð 38.5; prp. asn.
hweorfende 54.3. *See* **hwyrfan.**

hwettan, v.I. *encourage, incite*: 1s.
hwette 9.3.

hwīl, f. *a while, space of time*: as. hwīle
26.9; dp. adv. hwīlum, *sometimes,*
at times: 1.16,31,47,66,68,98
(twice),99,100, 2.8, 4.6,7, 5.3,
10.4,5,6,7,10, 12.3,4,5,6,8,9,11,13,
16,17, 15.7, 18.5,13, 22.2 (twice),
3 (twice),4,5,6, 23.5, 25.8, 47.4,
54.8, 55.5, 59.2, 60.6,7, 61.4, 69.5,
71.7,25, 76.4,8, 79.9, 81.5, 85.8,
87.8, 89.5,9 [MS. hwilu],10,13,
91.12, ? .]wīlum 89.6.

hwīt, adj. *bright, white, fair*: nsm.
13.1; npf. hwīte 8.8; apm. hwīte
38.98.

hwītloc, adj. *fair-haired*: nsf. 40.3.

hwītlocced, adj. *fair-haired*: nsf.
hwītloccedu 76.5.

hwonne, adv. *when, until*: 13.10,
29.13 (~ ǣr, conj. *when, until*).

hwylc, pron. 1. *who, which*: nsm. 1.1.
—2. *anyone, each one* (indef.): nsm.
18.19, 65.16; dsm. hwylcum 21.10.
See **ǣghwylc.**

ge-**hwylc,** pron. *each, all, every*: nsm.
70.7; dsm. gehwylcum 39.8, 79.12,
91.13; gsn. gehwylces 11.5, 38.36.

hwyrfan, v.I. *turn, move about*: 3s.
hwyrfeð 10.12. *See* **hweorfan,**
onhwyrfan.

hwyrftweg, m. *escape*: gs. hwyrft-
weges 1.36 (partitive).

hycgan, v.I. *think, consider, under-*
stand: ger. hycganne 26.12,
hycgenne 29.23.

hȳd, f. *skin, hide*: as. 74.7; is. hȳde
24.12 [MS. hyþe].

hygeblīþe, adj. *glad at heart*: comp.
npm. hygeblīþran 24.20.

hygecræftig, adj. *wise*: nsm. 1.1.

hygefæst, adj. *mind-fast, secure*: asf.
hygefæste 40.14.

hygegāl, adj. *lascivious, wanton*:
gsf.wk. hygegālan 10.12.

hygeþonc, m. *thought*: ip. hygeþon-
cum 33.4.

hygewlonc, adj. *proud, haughty*:
nsf. 43.4 (*licentious?*), asm. hyge-
wloncne 17.2.

hȳhste, *see* **hēah.**

hyht, m. *hope, joy*: ns. 62.3, 91.5; ds.
hyhte 23.1.

hyhtlīc, adj. *joyful, pleasant*: nsn.
88.5; asn. 33.12.

hyhtplega, m. *joyous play, sport*: gs.
hyhtplegan 18.28.

hyldepīl, *see* **hildepīl.**

hyll, m. *hill*: gs. hylles 13.27.

hȳran, v.I. *hearken to, obey* (w. dat.):
inf. 2.2, 21.15; 1s. hȳre 18.24; 3s.
hȳreð 41.9, 56.13, hēreð 48.5.

hyrde, m. *keeper, herdsman*: as. 87.9;
ds. 70.11.

hȳred, m. *company, congregation*: ds.
hȳrede 57.6.

hȳrra, *see* **hēah.**

hyrst, f. *ornament, trapping*: np.
hyrste 5.4, 8.8; ap. hyrste 9.1; ip.
hyrstum 12.11, 29.20, 51.7, 84.12.

hyrst, m. *copse, wood*: dp. hyrstum
38.61.

ge-**hyrstan,** v.I. *adorn*: pp. gehyrsted
69.8.

hyse, m. *boy, youth*: ns. 52.1.

I

ic, pron. *I*: ns. 1.3,8,15,16,23,36,37,
42,45,47, etc. (269 times); as. mec
1.2,14,26,28,30,31,43 (twice),103,
104, etc. (92 times); as. mē 10.13,
18.18,19, 38.34, 63.5, 71.2, 79.4,
81.5; ds. mē 1.12,35,46,66,95, 2.4,
10, 3.5 [MS. mec],13, 7.2, etc.
(70 times); gs. mīn 24.18, 33.4; for
possessive, *see* **mīn**; nd. wit 61.5,
81.7, 84.11,26,28; ad. unc 81.7,
84.12,14; dd. unc 58.15, 61.15,
70.4, 81.2, 84.15; gd. uncer 84.27;
np. wē 34.13, 38.73, 39.6,7; dp. ūs
40.16, 53.5 (or ap?).
ides, f. *woman*: ns. 59.2; as. idese
73.3; gp. idesa 44.7.
in, A. prep. 1. w. dat. *in, on, within,
among*: 3.9, 6.6, 10.10, 25.6, 32.1,
35.7, 38.98, 39.6, 41.2, 45.4,
51.6,13, 52.2, 53.1,13, 56.14,
57.1,17, 79.2, 81.6, 91.6. —**2.** w.
acc. *into, upon*: 13.6, 50.1, 57.7,9,
89.10,11. —**B. adv.** *within*: 30.11.
In innan, *see under* **innan.**
indryhten, adj. *noble*: nsm. 91.1; asm.
indryhtne 41.1.
ingeþonc, m. *thought, intention*: ns.
58.13.
innan, adv. **1.** *within, inside*: 15.2,
84.29. —**2. in innan,** *inside*: 7.3,
26.7.
innanweard, adj. *inward*: asm. in-
nanweardne 89.17 (semi-adv.).
innaþ, m. *inside of body, entrails,
stomach*: ns. 15.9, [84.18]; as. 35.6;
ds. innaþe 33.2.
inne, adv. *within, inside*: 44.4, 54.1.
insittende, adj. *sitting within*: gpm.
insittendra 44.7.
īsern, n. **1.** *iron*: gs. īsernes 56.9.
—**2.** *iron instrument or weapon*: ns.
70.15, 89.17; is. īserne 3.1.

īu, adv. *formerly, once*: 69.2.
īw, m. *yew*: ns. 53.9.

L

lāc, n.f. *gift*: dp. lācum 47.3 (or from
lacu, f. *stream, pool?*). *See* **hǣmed-
lāc.**
lācan, v.7. **1.** *move, jump, fly*: PRET.
3s. lēolc 54.8. —**2.** *play (an instru-
ment)*: inf. 29.19. —**3.** *sport, con-
tend, fight*: 1s. lāce 28a.1, 28b.1. *See*
belācan.
lǣcecynn, n. *leech-kin, race of physi-
cians*: as. 3.10.
lǣdan, v.I. *lead, bring, carry*: inf. 27.2;
pp. lǣded 26.6.
ge-lǣdan, v.I. *lead, conduct*: inf.
13.20.
lǣran, v.I. *teach, instruct*: PRET. 3s.
lǣrde 38.34.
lǣs, adv. (comp. of *lȳt*) and substan-
tive noun, n. *less*: as. 7.11 (þȳ ~,
the less).
lǣsse, *see* **lȳtel.**
lǣtan, v.7. *let, allow, let go*: 1s. lǣte
1.68; 3s. lǣteð 1.86, 18.13, 32.7,
48.10; 3p. lǣtað 1.76; PRET. 3p.
lēton 11.10; SUBJ. pres. 3s. lǣte
1.26. *See* **forlǣtan, ānforlǣtan.**
lāf, f. *what is left, remnant, legacy*: ns.
69.3; as. lāfe 87.10; np. lāfe 3.7; ap.
lāfe 54.10.
lagoflōd, m. *water*: as. 56.12.
lagu, m. *sea, water*: ns. 1.41; as. 20.16.
lagufæðm, m. *watery embrace*: is.
lagufæðme 58.7.
lagustrēam, m. *sea, stream, water*: gp.
lagustrēama 1.68.
land, *see* **lond.**
lang, *see* **long.**
lār, f. *teaching, doctrine*: ip. lārum
37.22.

lāreōw, m. *teacher*: ns. 65.10.
lāst, m. *track, step*: as. 1.51 (on ~, *behind*); ds. lāste 11.11 (on ~, *behind*), 37.8, 70.14 (on ~, *behind*); np. lāstas 49.2; ap. lāstas 91.11. *See* sweart-, wīd-last.
lāttēow, m. *leader*: ns. 1.26.
lāþ, adj. *grievous, hateful*: comp. gsn. lāþran 3.10.
lāðgewinna, m. *hated enemy*: ds. lāðgewinnan 13.29 [MS. laðgewinnum].
laðian, v.II. *invite, summon*: 1s. laðige 12.16.
lēad, n. *lead*: gs. lēades 38.75.
lēaf, f. *leaf*: ip. lēafum 54.10.
lēanian, v.II. *reward, repay* (w.dat.): 3s. lēanað 48.9.
lēas, *see* bān-, brōþor-, fēþe-, hām-, hēafod-, hlāford-, mūð-lēas.
lecgan, v.I. *lay, place*: 3s. legeð 76.5; PRET. 3s. legde 1.44, 18.30. *See* bilecgan.
lēg, *see* līg.
lēgbysig, *see* līgbysig.
lengan, v.I. *lengthen, delay, linger*: 3s. lengeð 26.8.
lēod, f. *folk, people*: gp. lēoda 65.10.
lēodan, *see* ā-, up-lēodan.
lēof, adj. *dear, beloved*: nsm. 38.34, 76.3; nsf. 18.2, 38.27, 80.28; comp. nsf. lēofre 90.6.
leofaþ, *see* libban/lifgan.
lēoht, adj. *light (in weight)*: comp. nsf. lēohtre 38.76, 90.6 (or = *brighter*?).
lēoht, adj. *bright, shining*: dsm.wk. lēohtan 38.57; comp. nsf. lēohtre 64.2.
lēoht, n. *light*: ns. 90.6; ds. lēohte 25.17, 61.11.
lēohtlīc, adj. *bright, shining*: asn. 27.3.
lēolc, *see* lācan.

lēoma, m. *light, glare*: ds. lēoman 38.57.
leoþo, *see* liþ.
leþer, n. *leather*: is? leþre 85.4 (or from lȳþre?).
libban/lifgan, v.III. *live*: inf. lifgan 37.22, 38.64, 39.6, 65.11; 1s. lifge 81.6; 3s. leofaþ 37.27; PRET. 3s. lifde 38.107; prp. lifgende nsm. 10.14, nsf. 26.9, asm. 8.9.
līc, n. *body*: as. 63.4; is. līce 8.5.
ge-līc, adj. *like* (w. dat.): np. gelīce 29.7. *See* ungelīc.
licgan, v.5. *lie (down), remain*: inf. 11.11, 12.10; 3s. ligeð 38.49.
ge-līcnes, f. *likeness, image*: ns. 34.10. *See* onlīcnes.
līf, n. *life*: ds. līfe 48.9, 56.12, 87.10. *See* worldlīf.
lifgan, *see* libban/lifgan.
lift, *see* lyft.
līg, m. *fire, flame*: ds. līge 1.74, lēge 38.57; is. līge 79.3 [MS. life].
līgbysig, adj. *busy with fire, troubled by fire*: nsm. 28b.1, lēgbysig 28a.1.
lilie, f. *lily*: ns. 38.27.
lim, n. *limb* (either *branch* or *human limb*): ns. 2.7; as. 37.27.
līne, f. *line, row*: ds. līnan 40.10.
liss, f. *kindness, grace, joy*: dp. lissum 48.9; ip. lissum 24.25, 31.13 (adv.?).
list, f. *art, skill*: ds. liste 25.4; ip. adv. listum 27.3, 85.7.
liþ, n. *limb*: ap. leoþo 21.7.
līþan, v.1. *go, move, sail*: inf. 31.1; prp. dsm. līþendum 8.5.
locc, m. *hair, lock*: np. loccas 38.104; ap. loccas 38.98. *See* hwītloc, wundenlocc.
ge-lōme, adv. *frequently, constantly*: 29.11.
lond, n. *land, ground, province*: as. 10.14, 11.11; ds. londe 1.41,94,

31.2, 54.8, lande 20.12; gp. londa
31.13. *See* **mearclond**.

londbūend, m. *land-dweller, inhabi-tant*: gp. londbūendra 91.11.

long, adj. **1.** *long* (space): asf. lange
56.8; comp. nsf. lengre 21.7.
—**2.** *long* (time): nsn. 37.22; asf.
longe 26.9. *See* **uplong, efenlang**.

longe, adv. *long, a long time*: 13.29,
38.8, 65.10.

losian, v.II. *escape, depart* (w. dat.):
inf. 1.26; 3s. losað 10.3.

lūcan, *see* **bi-, on-lūcan.**

lufe, f. *love*: gs. lufan 24.25.

lufian, v.II. *love*: 3p. lufiaþ 91.7.

lust, m. *pleasure*: as. 70.9.

lyft, f. *air, sky*: ns. 1.41, 5.4, 8.9, 55.1;
as. lyfte 54.8, 56.12; ds. lyfte 20.16,
38.81, 49.4, 80.31, lifte 25.4; gs.
lyfte 1.94.

lyftfæt, n. *air-vessel*: as. 27.3.

lȳt, adv. *little*: 58.7.

lȳtel, adj. *little, small*: nsm. 70.1;
nsm.wk. lȳtla 38.76; asn. lȳtel 56.7;
apf. lȳtle 55.1; comp. nsf. læsse
38.95, 64.2. *See* **unlȳtel**.

lȳþre, adj. *evil, wicked*: nsm? lēþre
85.4 (or from *leþer*?).

M

mā, n. ind. *more*: 16.4, 24.21, 58.16.

mæcg, m. *man*: np. mæcgas 48.7. *See*
ēoredmæcg.

ge-mǣdan, v.I. *madden, make foolish*:
pp. npm. gemǣdde 9.6.

mǣg, m. *kinsman, brother*: np. māgas
84.15.

mǣg, f. *woman, kinswoman*: ns. 29.23.
See **friþemǣg**.

mǣgburg, f. *family*: ns. 18.20; as.
mǣgburge 13.20.

mægen, n. **1.** *strength, power*: ns.
80.8,24,56; as. 51.9 [MS. mæg],
79.11, 80.33 [MS. mæge]; ds.
mægene 25.14, 38.95, mægne
29.23; is. mægene 80.21, mægne
21.13. —**2.** *host, troop*: ns. 20.13.
See **holmmægen**.

mægenrōf, adj. *very strong*: nsm.wk.
mægenrōfa 35.3.

mægenstrong, adj. *mighty*: nsm.
83.3.

mægenþise, f. *force, violence*: ds.
mægenþisan 25.10.

mægð, f. *maiden, woman*: np. mægeð
48.7; gp. mægða 12.8, 31.9 [MS.
mæg da].

mǣl, n. *time, occasion*: gp. mǣla 78.6.

mǣldan, *see* **meld(i)an.**

mǣnan, v.I. **1.** *mean, signify*: 1s.
mǣne 59.9. —**2.** *tell (of), relate*: 3s.
mǣneð 18.11; SUBJ. pret. 3p.
mǣnden 58.17.

ge-mǣnan, v.I. *utter*: 1s. gemǣne
22.6.

ge-mǣne, adj. *mutual*: npm? 70.4.

mǣran, v.I. *make known, celebrate*:
SUBJ. pres. 3p. mǣre 24.16.

mǣre, adj. *famous, great*: nsm. 24.27;
nsn. 80.11; nsf. 38.45; dpm.wk.
mǣran 84.15; gpf. mǣrra 80.4.

mǣrþu, f. *glorious deed*: ap? mǣ[.]þa
71.11.

mǣst, *see* **micel.**

mæðel, n. *assembly*: ds. mæðle 82.2.

mǣw, m. *sea gull*: gs. mǣwes 22.6.

magan, v.PP. *may, can, be able*: 1s.
mæg 1.25, 13.19, 16.1, 38.62,64,66,
40.5, 53.7, 61.10, 84.30; 3s. mæg
29.8, 38.16,20,52,69,90, 41.2, 56.3,
57.12, 80.6,17, ?m[.]g 65.10; 1p.
magon 39.6; 3p. magon 80.43;
PRET. 1s. meahte 3.11, 7.10, 89.21;
3s. meahte 27.6, 38.43,67; 3p.

meahton 20.5; SUBJ. pres. 1s.
mæge 2.12; 2s. mæge 37.28; 3s.
mæge 1.2, 29.19.

māge, f. *kinswoman*: ns. mēge 7.4; gs.
māgan 41.13.

ge-magnad, adj. (pp. of *mægnian*).
established, strengthened: nsn. 1.96
[MS. ge manad].

magorinc, m. *youth, warrior*: np.
magorincas 20.5.

man, *see* mon.

māndrinc, m. *evil drink, death-drink*:
as. 21.13.

māra, *see* micel.

maþelian, v.II. *speak*: PRET. 3s.
maþelade 36.5.

māðm, m. *treasure*: as. 53.13.

meaht, f. *might, power*: ns. 80.24; ip.
meahtum 1.10,96, 11.8, 38.90.

meahtelīce, adv. *mightily*: comp.
meahtelīcor 38.62.

meahtig, adj. *mighty*: nsm. 38.12.

mearc, f. *boundary, region*: ap. mearce
12.6.

mearclond, n. *border-land, sea-coast*:
ds. mearclonde 1.53.

mearcpæþ, m. *country path*: ap.
mearcpaþas 70.12.

mēdan, v.I. *encourage, instill courage
(in)*: SUBJ. pres. 3s. mēde 53.15.

medwīs, adj. *foolish, stupid*: dsm.
medwīsum 2.10.

mēge, *see* māge.

meld(i)an, v.I,II. 1. *announce, declare*:
inf. meldan 26.12, mældan 16.2.
—2. *inform against, accuse* (w. dat.):
PRET. 1s. meldade 70.17.

mengo, f. *multitude, crowd*: ds. 18.12;
?80.35.

meodu, m. *mead*: as. 18.12.

meodubenc, f. *mead-bench*: ds.
meodubence 58.9 [MS. meodu].

meotud, m. *Creator, Lord*: ns. 1.84,
84.14; gs. meotudes 80.11.

mēowle, f. *maid, woman*: ns. 2.5,
23.7, 59.1.

mere, m. *sea*: as. 20.5. *See* hwælmere.

merefaroþ, m. *shore, bank*: ds.
merefaroþe 58.2.

merehengest, m. *sea-horse, ship*: ns.
12.6.

merestrēam, m. *sea-stream*: ap.
merestrēamas 64.9.

mēsan, v.I. *eat*: inf. 38.62.

ge-met, n. *measure*: is. gemete 48.7.

micel, adj. *great, much, many*: nsm.
1.80, 83.3; nsm.wk. micla 38.92;
nsn. micel 26.12, 29.23; asn. micel
35.3; asf. micle 83.1; ism. micle
1.75,91; dpf. miclum 37.2; ?micle
80.43; comp. nsm. māra 38.92,105,
nsf. māre 15.4, 64.1, asm. māran
37.4 [MS. maram]; supl. nsm.
mǣst 1.69.

micle, adv. *much, more*: 37.4, [38.23],
38.42,74,76,80.

ge-miclian, v.II. *enlarge, increase*: pp.
gemiclad 80.24, nsf. gemicledu
18.20.

mid, A. prep. 1. w. dat. *with* (as-
sociation): 3.6 (or as meaning
#2?), 13.9,10, 28a.1, 28b.1, 29.23,
37.2, 38.59, 40.16, 44.1, 72.3,4.
—2. w. dat. or occasionally w. inst.
with, by means of (manner): 3.12,
4.4, 24.13, 25.4, 26.2 (twice),3,
28a.2,8, 38.13,14,30,35, 42.6, 48.7,
52.12, 60.6, 61.3, 64.10. —B. adv.
at the same time, likewise: 11.2,
20.18, 44.5.

middangeard, m. *earth, world*: ns.
29.1, 30.1, 38.43, 64.1 [MS. mindan
geard]; as. 37.19, 38.12, 64.9; gs.
middangeardes 79.11 (adv?).

midde, f. *middle*: ds. middan 30.9,
middum 77.5.

middelniht, f. *midnight*: dp. middel-
nihtum 87.7.

midwist, f. *presence, society*: as. 91.8.
milts, f. *humility, joy*: ds. miltse
  28a.8; ip. miltsum 28b.8.
mīn, poss. pron. *my*: nsm. 1.26,31,
  4.5, 13.1, 14.8, 15.9, 19.3,15, 21.1,
  23.4, 24.27, 81.1, 84.10 [MS. mine],
  18,20,23, 87.9, 89.1,16; nsn. 5.1,
  8.1, 9.1, 19.1,10, 79.1, 87.1; nsf.
  18.3, 31.9,10, 70.5, 76.9,11; asm.
  mīnne 12.8, 58.4, 79.14; asn. mīn
  2.3,11, 19.6, 23.8, 63.3, 74.5, 79.7,
  89.28; asf. mīne 6.4, 9.7, 13.20,
  18.12, 22.1, 63.4, 71.5,28, 77.12,
  89.22, 91.8,13; dsm. mīnum 2.1,9,
  18.2,26, 54.11, 58.2, 69.6, 76.3;
  dsn. mīnum 38.95, 71.6, 75.2; dsf.
  mīnre 25.10, 38.30; isn. mīne 8.5;
  isf. mīnre 6.11, 12.18; gsm. mīnes
  1.96, 71.8, 87.6; gsn. mīnes 16.4,
  23.10; gsf. mīnre 15.1,5, 38.45;
  npn. mīn 7.7, 38.11; npf. mīne
  5.4,6, 8.8; apm. mīne 13.12, 91.11;
  dpf. mīnum 13.11; ipm. mīnum
  18.21; ns? mīn 84.3.
mislīc, adj. *various, diverse*: nsn.
  80.8,56.
mislīce, adv. *variously*: 26.12.
missenlīc, adj. *various, diverse*: ipf.
  missenlīcum 29.1, 30.1.
missenlīce, adv. *variously*: 65.12.
ge-mittan, v.I. *meet*: 3p. gemittaδ
  1.53.
mīþan, v.1. **1.** *conceal*: inf. 61.10 (w.
  inst.), 79.12. —**2.** *avoid, refrain from*
  (w. dat.): 1s. mīþe 6.4. *See*
  bemiþan.
mōd, n. *heart, mind, spirit, temper*: ds.
  mōde 9.6, 80.35, 82.2; gs. mōdes
  25.14; ap. mōd 4.6; dp. mōdum
  57.2. *See* **forht-, hēan-mōd.**
mōdig, adj. *brave, high-spirited*: npm.
  mōdge 28b.8.
mōdor, f. *mother*: ns. 7.2, 31.9, 80.4,

mōddor 39.2, 80.21; gs. mōdor
  38.45, mōddor 41.14.
mōdþrēa, m. *torment of mind, anguish*:
  ns. 1.80.
mōdwlonc, adj. *proud, haughty,*
  ?licentious: nsf. 23.7.
mōdwynn, f. *heart's joy*: as.
  mōd · Þ · 87.7.
mon, m. *man*: ns. 1.27, 33.11 (indef.
  = *one*), 36.5, 38.47 (indef. = *one*),
  41.14, 80.35, monn 34.5, man 35.3;
  ds. men 2.10, menn 26.13; gs.
  monnes 34.11, 57.13; np. men
  1.16, 15.11, 37.4, 52.11, 91.7,
  menn 65.12; ap. men 10.4, 57.2;
  dp. monnum 16.2, 28a.8, 37.12,
  38.45; gp. monna 1.80, 20.1, 58.4,
  70.17, 74.4, 79.12, 91.13. *See*
  hagostealdmon, rȳnemonn.
mōna, m. *moon*: ns. 64.2.
moncynn, n. *mankind, men*: ds. mon-
  cynne 30.9, 37.2, 38.27.
mondryhten, m. *lord*: ds. mon-
  dryhtne 53.13, 56.6 [MS. dryht ne].
ge-mong, n. *company*: ds. gemonge
  (on ~ , *in the midst of,* w. dat.):
  29.4,11.
monig, adj. *many*: npm. monige
  28a.8, 63.6, 82.2; dpm. monigum
  91.8, mongum 28b.8; dpn. mon-
  gum 37.19; dpf. monegum 56.6;
  ipf. mongum 6.1; gpm. monigra
  4.6; gpn. monigra 39.2; gpf.
  monigra 80.4.
monna, m. *man*: as. monnan 63.5.
mōr, m. *moor*: ap. mōras 70.12.
mōs, n. *food*: ds? mōs[. 75.4.
ge-mōt, n. *meeting*: gs. gemōtes 3.10,
  23.10. *See* **gūδgemōt.**
mōtan, v.PP. *may, must*: 1s. mōt
  1.45,103, 13.20, 18.27, 79.8; 3s. mōt
  37.20; 3p. mōton 14.9, mōtan
  38.103; PRET. 1s. mōste 38.35,100;

3s. mōste 51.13; SUBJ. pres. 1s.
mōte 18.22; 3s. mōte 29.13.

mo**ð**ð**e, f. *moth*: ns. 45.1.

ge-**munan,** v.PP. *remember*: 1s.
gemon 79.6; 3p. gemunan 15.11.

mundbora, m. *protector*: ns. 15.1.

mundrōf, adj. *strong of hand*: nsm.
83.3.

mūþ, m. *mouth*: ns. 30.9; as. 6.1,
15.11, 16.2, 37.12, 65.6, 74.4; is.
mūþe 22.6, 61.4; ip. mūþum 11.8.

mūðlēas, adj. *mouthless*: nsm. 58.9.

ge-**myltan,** v.I. *burn, melt*: pp.
gemylted 28b.3.

ge-**mynd,** f. *memory, recollection*: as.
57.7.

N

nā, *see* **nō.**

naca, m. *boat, ship*: ns. 56.5.

næfde, *see* **nabban** *under* **habban.**

næfre, *see* **æfre.**

ge-**nægan,** v.I. *attack*: 3s. genǣgeð
18.19.

nægledbord, adj. *with nailed boards*:
nsm. 56.5.

næglian, v.I,II. *nail, rivet*: pp. asm.
nægledne 17.5.

nænig, *see* **ænig.**

nænne, *see* **ān.**

ge-**næstan,** v.I. *contend*: 3s. genǣsteð
25.10.

nætan, v.I. *oppress, afflict*: 1s. nǣte
4.4.

nāh, *see* **nāgan** *under* **āgan.**

nāles, adv. *not, not at all*: 24.17.

nama, m. *name*: ns. 24.27, noma 21.1;
as. naman 53.11, 57.8; ds. naman
56.14; ap. naman 40.8.

ge-**namna,** m. *companion*: ds.
genamnan 51.13.

nard, m. *spikenard, unguent*: gs.
nardes 38.29.

nāthwǣr, adv. *somewhere* (lit. *I know
not where*): 23.5, 60.8.

nāthwæt, pron. *something* (lit. *I know
not what*): ns. 59.9, 89.27; as. 43.1,
52.5.

ne/nē, negative particle. *not, nor*:
A. adv. *not*: 1.16,25,45,83,103, 3.4,
5.8, 6.4, 7.2, 9.10, etc. (66 times).
—**B. conj.** *nor, neither*: 11.6, 18.20,
20.13,14 (twice),15,16 (twice),17,
25.15, etc. (41 times).

nēah, adv. prep. w. dat. *near*: 1.53,
54.8, 58.1; comp. nēar 1.94.

nēahbūend, m. *neighbor*: dp.
nēahbūendum 23.2.

ge-**neahhe,** adv. *sufficiently, abun-
dantly, frequently*: 6.2, 10.12, 24.8,
29.10.

nearo, adj. *narrow*: asf. nearwe 13.24;
ip. nearwum 50.3.

nearo, f. *confinement, difficulty, danger*:
as. 59.6, 60.8; ds. nearwe 8.1,
nearowe 51.13.

nearogrāp, f. *tight grasp, clutch*: ns.
80.6.

nearwian, v.II. *confine, cramp, force in*:
3s. nearwað 23.10.

ge-**nearwian,** v.II. *confine*: 3s. ge-
nearwað 1.31; pp. genearwad 69.4.

neb, n. *beak, nose, face*: ns. 8.1, 19.1,
29.6, nebb 32.3; as. nebb 77.4; is.
nebbe 87.8. *See* **saloneb.**

nefa, m. *nephew*: ns. 44.6.

nelle, *see* **nellan** *under* **willan.**

nemnan, v.I. *name*: inf. 47.9; 1p.
nemnað 38.73; 3p. nemnað 22.7,
55.6; PRET. 3s. nemde 57.6.

nēol, adj. *prone, low, deep down*: nsf.
19.1, 80.6, nīol 83.8.

neoþan, adv. *beneath, below, from be-
neath*: 8.1, 23.5, 29.20, nioþan 59.6.

nergan, v.I. *save*: inf. 13.13; prp. asm.
(uninfl.) nergende 57.4.
ge-nergan, v.I. *save*: inf. 13.19.
nēþan, v.I. *venture, dare*: inf. 51.13;
3s. nēþeð 23.5.
nīgende, *see* hnīgan.
niht, f. *night*: ns. 27.13; as. 37.7; dp.
nihtum 3.14, 10.9, 84.13. *See* mid-
delniht.
ge-niman, v.4. *seize, hold*: pp. npm.
genumne 50.3 [MS. genamne]. *See*
biniman.
nīol, *see* nēol.
nioþan, *see* neoþan.
nīþ, m. *enmity, spite*: ds. nīþe 4.4.
niþerweard, adj. *downward*: nsn.
19.1, 29.6 [MS. niþer wearð]; nsf.
32.3.
nīðsceaþa, m. *malignant enemy*: ns.
13.24.
niþþas, m.p. *men*: dp. niþum 24.27;
gp. niþþa 55.6.
ge-nīwian, v.II. *renew*: pp. genīwad
11.9.
nō, adv. *not (at all), never*: 4.4, 26.10,
29.8, 37.9, 89.20, 91.9, nā 34.9.
noma, *see* nama.
nōwēr, adv. *nowhere*: 29.4 [nōwēr
werum: MS. onwerum].
nōwiht, n. *nothing*: as. 9.5.
nū, adv. *now*: 12.1, 22.9, 24.15, 25.6,
38.1,102, 40.15, 47.8, 51.8, 53.14,
65.10, 69.3, 71.8, 74.4, 79.4, 84.15,
29 [MS. hu], 88.4, 89.24,28, 91.7,10.
nȳd, f. *name of runic* N: ns. 40.8. *See*
hæftnȳd.
nȳdan, v.I. *urge, press*: 3s. nȳdeþ
60.8.
nȳde, adv. *necessarily*: 38.29.
nymþe, conj. *unless, except*: 18.22,
21.16, 23.3, 38.21, 39.7, nympþe
63.5.
nyt, adj. *useful*: nsm. 30.9, 52.7; nsf.

23.2, 56.5; gsf. nyttre 9.5; npn. nyt
53.11.
nytt, f. *use*: ds. nytte 24.27, 32.3, 47.9,
48.2, 68.2.

O

of, prep. w. dat. *of, out of, from*:
1.28,37,42,46,77,78,86, 8.6,10, 10.6,
12.15, 13.12, 15.6, 19.7, 20.16,21,
21.12, 25.2 (twice),3 (twice), 27.4,
33.2, 38.79, 48.2, 60.7, 71.4,5,28,
74.6, 79.8, 87.10, 89.14,16,19,30.
ofer, prep. **A.** w. dat. *over, above*:
1.7,40,41,51,70,73,75, 13.5, 58.9,
77.6. —**B.** w. acc. **1.** *over, above,
across, through*: 1.92, 4.10, 5.3,6,
8.11, 12.6,7, 17.3, 18.8, 20.5,12,18,
24.9, 27.7, 30.8, 42.5, 49.7, 51.7,
55.2, 62.1,5, 64.8. —**2.** *throughout*
(of distribution or extent): 33.11,
38.21, 39.5, 80.42, 84.18, 91.10.
—**3.** *against, contrary to*: 27.10.
ōfer, m. *bank, shore*: np. ōfras 20.7.
ofergongan, v.7. *overtake, come upon*:
3s. ofergongeþ 38.10.
oferstīgan, v.1. *rise above*: 1s.
oferstīge 64.6.
oferswīþan, v.I. *overpower, overcome*:
inf. 38.20; 1s. oferswīþe 38.29.
ofest, f. *haste*: ds. ofeste 60.4; ip.
ofestum 38.11 (adv.).
ofgifan, v.5. *give up, abandon*: PRET.
1s? .]fgeaf 84.8; 3p. ofgēafun 7.1
[MS. ofgeafum].
oft, adv. *often*: 2.5, 3.3, 4.2, 14.1,
15.3, 18.8,15,32, 28a.5, 28b.5,
29.11, 42.7, 47.2,7, 48.4, 51.10,
52.11, 53.12, 56.11, 59.1, 61.1,
65.8,13, 70.6,15, 74.3, 75.1, 76.10,
80.40,49, 84.8,12, 87.3, 89.30, 91.2.
ōhwonan, adv. *from anywhere*: 33.8.

on, prep. **A.** w. dat. or inst. **1.** *on,*
upon: 1.7,12,27,36,66, 9.2, 11.4,11,
12.[9],12,[14], 13.3,4,25,26, 17.[1],
4, 18.18, 19.5,8,9,10,12, 25.16,
29.14,21, 30.6, 31.12, 34.1,6, 38.25,
58,77,102,103, 40.5, 41.6,10, 48.1,
49.3, 56.2, 62.2, 66.3, 67.4, 70.13,
14,16, 71.1, 73.1 (or w. acc. as
meaning #1?), 76.8,9 (*at*), [80.1],
84.11 (adv?),19,20, 21, 89.14
[MS. of],22, an 40.10. —**2.** *in,*
within, among: 1.14,34,35,81, 3.11,
6.7, 8.1,3,7, 10.11, 13.16, 16.4,
18.10,13, 20.14, 21.3 [MS. of],
23.4, 24.3, 25.4, 27.5, 29.3,4,11,17,
30.9, 31.4,12,13, 32.8, 38.61,
81 (twice),87,106, 43.1, 47.4, 49.4
[flēag on: MS. fleotgan], 51.1,2,5,
57.6, 59.2,5, 61.4,?6,11, 63.3,
64.4, 65.1, 71.13, 72.3 (or as
meaning #1?), 76.7 (twice), 77.5,
84.23, 88.1,4. —**3.** *at, in* (manner):
2.9, 13.2, 17.7, 18.31, 25.13, 38.23,
28,95, 58.5,11, 60.4, 71.22, 82.2,
89.12. —**4.** *during*: 7.1. —**5.** *for, as*
(marking purpose): 23.1, 48.9.
—**B.** w. acc. **1.** *upon, on, onto*:
1.2,11,22,43,51,58,65,[95], 4.7,
13.21, 18.29, 19.13, 20.9,20, 23.7,8,
24.10, 27.12, 37.6, 43.3, 53.2,
54.12, 66.1, 72.5, 76.5, [77.11], 83.4
(obj. understood), ?84.5, 89.31.
—**2.** *in, into*: 1.33, 19.6, 23.9,
24.4, 53.15 (postpositional with
adverbial sense?), 54.8, 56.12, 59.6,
60.8, 63.3,4, 71.21, 83.6, 89.26.
—**3.** *on, in, at* (temporal): 1.60,
72.2. —**4.** *for, as, according to*:
36.2,4, 38.3, 48.3, 71.7. —**5.** in
other phrases where motion is
sometimes but not always clearly
implicit: 1.85 (~ geryhtu), 2.12
(~ spēd), 18.1 and 21.2 (~ gewin,

in battle(s)? for battle?), 18.14
(~ gerūm), 18.26 (~ þonc), 70.9
(~ lust); an 51.10 (~ yst). **On**
hindan, *see under* **hindan.**
on, adv. *on, forward*: 60.5.
onbūgan, v.2. **1.** *bend*: 1s. onbūge
21.3. —**2.** *turn aside, escape*: inf.
1.45.
oncweþan, v.5. *answer, respond* (w.
dat. of person): 1s. oncweþe 2.7.
ond, conj. *and*: 1.1,13,22,23,33,41,45,
48,70,74, etc. (205 times).
ondfenga, m. *receiver*: gs. ondfengan
59.7.
ondrǣdan, v.7. *fear, be afraid of* (w.
refl. dat.): 3s. ondrǣdeð 1.83.
ondswaru, f. *answer, reply*: as.
ondsware 53.15.
ōnettan, v.I. *hurry, hasten*: PRET. 3s.
ōnette 27.11 [MS. o netteð], ōn-
nette 52.7.
onfindan, v.3. *find out, discover*: 3s.
onfindeð 13.7, 25.9.
onga, m. *dart, arrow*: ns. 21.4.
ongēan, prep. *opposite to, against*:
1. w. dat. 74.3, 87.3. —**2.** w. acc.
25.9 (or adv., *opposite?*).
ongietan, v.5. *perceive, understand*:
inf. 57.10; SUBJ. pres. 3p. ongietan
46.6.
onginnan, v.3. *begin*: 1s. onginne
15.7; 3s. onginneð 26.11, 29.9;
PRET. 3s. ongon 7.3, 52.10; 3p.
ongunnon 20.8.
onhǣle, adj. *hidden*: asf. 13.7.
onhebban, v.6. *raise, exalt*: 1s.
onhæbbe 28a.7, 28b.7.
onhlīdan, v.1. *open, reveal*: imp. 2s.
onhlīd 80.54.
onhnīgan, v.1. *bow, bend down*: 3p.
onhnīgaþ 28a.7 [MS. on hin gaþ],
28b.7.
onhwyrfan, v.I. *turn, change*: PRET.

3p. onhwyrfdon 71.2; pp.
onhwyrfed 21.1 (eft ~ , *reversed,
turned around backwards*), [29.6].

onhyrgan, v.I. *imitate*: 1s. onhyrge
6.10, 22.4.

onlīcnes, f. *likeness*: as. onlīcnesse
38.37.

onlūcan, v.2. *unlock, open*: PRET. 1s.
onlēac 40.12.

ōnnette, *see* **ōnettan.**

onsittan, v.5. *fear, dread* (w. dat.
refl.): inf. 13.23.

onsundran, adv. *separately*: 70.7.

ontȳnan, v.I. *open*: PRET. 1s. ontȳnde
74.4.

onþēon, v.1,3CT. *to be of service,
succeed*: inf. 61.2; SUBJ. pret. 1p.
onþungan 84.28.

onþunian, v.II. *exceed one's bounds*:
inf. 31.91 [MS. onrinnan].

onwald, m. *power*: ds. onwalde
38.13.

onwendan, v.I. *turn, change*: PRET.
3p. onwendan 71.5.

onwrēon, v.1,2CT. *uncover, reveal*:
imp? 2s? ..]wrēoh 80.55.

ge-**openian**, v.II. *reveal, disclose*: imp.
2s. geopena 80.55.

ōr, n. *beginning, origin*: as. 1.89,
80.10.

ord, n. *point, dart*: ns. 58.12,13; is.
orde 74.6; dp. ordum 15.8; ip.
ordum 13.5 *(toes)*.

ordstapu, f. / **ordstæpe**, m. *prick of a
goad*: np. ordstæpe 70.18.

orlege, n. *strife, battle*: gs. orleges
1.89.

orlegfrom, adj. *valiant in battle*: asm.
orlegfromne 18.15.

orþonc, m.n. *understanding, skill*: as.
75.8; ip. orþoncum 67.3 (adv.).

orþoncbend, f. *cunning bond*: ip. or-
þoncbendum 40.15.

orþoncpīl, n. *cunning dart*: ns. 19.12.

oðberan, v.4. *bear off*: PRET. 3s.
oðbær 20.10.

ōþer, adj. and pron. *one (of two),
other, another*: nsm. 54.7 (twice);
nsn. 19.12, ?80.18; nsf. 1.52, 38.86,
40.9; asm. ōþerne 20.20; asf. ōþre
37.7 (*next?*); dsm. ōþrum 1.71,
18.15, 35.6, 41.11, 50.5, 51.5,10,
80.6, ?88.7; dsf. ōþre 19.10; gsn.
ōþres 4.9; apn. ōþre 47.5; dpm.
ōþrum 9.4.

oþfergan, v.I. *bear off*: inf. 14.7.

oþþæt, conj. *until*: 1.42, 7.7,10, 21.8,
51.4, 70.10, 71.2, 89.15.

oþþe, conj. *or*: 1.15,103,104, 2.5, 5.2
(twice), 38.24,43,49,67 (twice),75,
58.8, 71.10, 91.6, eðþa 41.16.

oðþringan, v.3. *snatch, seize*: inf.
84.16.

ōwiht, adv. *at all*: 39.6.

oxa, m. *ox*: ns. 20.13.

P

pæþ, *see* **gegn-, mearc-pæþ.**

pæððan, v.I. *traverse, travel over*: 3s.
pæþeð 56.9; PRET. 1s. pæðde
70.12.

pernex, m. *a supposed bird* (mistrans-
lation of Latin *pernix = swift*): ns.
38.66 [MS. p´nex].

pīl, *see* **hilde-, orþonc-, searo-pīl.**

plegan, v.I. *play, amuse oneself*: inf.
40.2 (w. gen.).

R

rād, f. **1.** *riding, course*: ds. rāde 17.7.
—**2.** *name of runic* R: ns. 56.15.

rādwērig, adj. *travel-weary, weary of
riding*: asm. rādwērigne 18.14.

rǣcan, v.I. *reach, extend*: 1s. rǣce 64.7.

ge-rǣcan, v.I. **1.** *reach, strike*: 3s. gerǣceð 1.88. —**2.** *reach, arrive*: 1s. gerǣce 13.27.

rǣced, n. *hall, house, building*: as. 50.1; ds. rǣcede 29.3; ap. rǣced 1.6.

rǣd, m. *good counsel, wisdom*: as. 13.16; gs. rǣdes 84.32. *See* **unrǣd**.

rǣdan, v.7,I. *read, explain, solve (a riddle)*: SUBJ. pres. 3s. rǣde 57.15; imp. 2s. rǣd 59.9.

rǣdelle, f. *riddle*: as. rǣdellan 40.13.

rǣping, m. *captive*: ap. rǣpingas 50.1.

rǣran, v.I. *raise*: PRET. 3s. rǣrde 53.6; SUBJ. pres. 3s. rǣre 1.103. *See* **ārǣran**.

rǣsan, v.I. *rush*: 3s. rǣseð 23.8. *See* **þurhrǣsan**.

rēad, adj. *red*: nsm.wk. rēada 24.15; asm. rēodne 23.8; gsn.wk. rēadan 46.6; apf. rēade 9.2.

rēade, adv. *redly, with a red color*: 69.1.

rēaf, n. *robe, garment*: ds. rēafe 9.2, 11.7.

rēafian, v.II. *rob, ravage, plunder*: 1s. rēafige 1.6, 10.14; 3s. rēafað 23.8, 63.2.

rēc, m. *smoke*: np. rēcas 1.6.

reccan, v.I. *be interested in, care for* (w. gen.): 3s. recceð 74.5.

reccan, v.I. **1.** *explain*: imp. 2s. rece 30.13. —**2.** *rule*: inf. 38.35; 1s. recce 38.33.

reccend, m. *ruler, God*: ns. 38.3.

recene, adv. *quickly, straightway*: 37.28.

regn, m. *rain*: as. 1.85.

regnwyrm, m. *rain-worm, earthworm*: ns. 38.70.

ge-rēne, n. *ornament*: np. gerēno 24.15.

rēod, *see* **rēad**.

reord, f. *voice, speech*: as. reorde 22.5; ip. reordum 6.1.

ge-reord, n. *speech, voice*: ip. gereordum 12.16.

rēsele, f. *answer, solution*: as. rēselan 37.28.

restan, v.I. *rest, remain*: inf. 1.103; 1s. reste 81.5 (refl.), 91.2.

rēþe, adj. *fierce, cruel*: nsm. 1.3; nsf. 80.2; gsm. rēþes 13.16.

ribb, n. *rib*: gp. ribba 30.8.

rīce, adj. *rich, powerful, great*: nsm. 38.3 [MS. ric]; gsm. rīces 69.1; npm. rīce 30.13; dpm. rīcum 91.2.

rīce, n. *power, authority*: ds. 1.61.

rīcels, n. *incense*: ns. 38.24.

rīdan, v.1. *ride, swing*: inf. 1.62, 20.2; 1s. rīde 76.8; 3s. rīdeð 1.66, 56.3; PRET. 1s. rād 89.14; 3s. rād 17.5.

riht, *see* **ryht**.

rīm, *see* **dæg-, un-rīm**.

rinc, m. *man*: ns. 60.4, 61.15, 72.2; ap. rincas 12.16; dp. rincum 40.6. *See* **fyrd-, gum-, mago-rinc**.

rinnan, v.3. *run, flow*: inf. 81.5 [MS. yrnan]. *See* **yrnan, upirnan**.

rod, f. *cross*: gs. rōde 53.5.

rodor, m. *sky, heavens*: dp. roderum 53.5; gp. rodera 57.15, rodra 11.7.

rōf, adj. *strong, bold, noble*: asm. rōfne 17.7. *See* **ellen-, mægen-, mund-rōf**.

rōp, adj. *liberal, bountiful*: npf. rōpe 55.3.

rōse, f. *rose*: ns. 38.24.

rūh, adj. *rough, hairy*: nsm. 23.5; gsn. rūwes 59.9.

ge-rūm, n. *space, room*: as. 18.14 (on ~ , *at large*).

ge-rūma, n. *space, room*: ds. gerūman 13.16.

rūnstæf, m. *runic letter*: np. rūnstafas 56.15; ap. rūnstafas 40.6.

ge-**rȳde,** adj. *agreeable, pleasing*: nsn?
61.15.

ryht, adj. **1.** *straight, direct*: asm.
ryhtne 60.4. —**2.** *right, true*: isn.
ryhte 48.7; npm. ryhte 56.15.

ryht, n. *that which is right, justice*: as.
38.3; ds. ryhte 38.35.

ge-**ryhte,** n. *straight direction*: ap.
geryhtu 1.85 (on ~ , *straight*).

rȳman, v.I. *make room, clear a way*: 3s.
rȳmeð 51.10.

ge-**rȳman,** v.I. *clear, open up*: 1s.
gerȳme 60.4.

ryne, m. *running, course*: as. 80.2.

rȳne, n. *mystery, mysterious saying*: as.
46.6.

rynegiest, m. *swift traveller* or *foe,
?swift spirit, ?rain-foe*: gs.
rynegiestes 1.88.

rȳnemonn, m. *mystery-solver, rune-
decoder*: ap. rȳnemenn 40.13.

rynestrong, adj. *strong-flowing,
swift-flowing*: nsm. 17.7.

S

sacan, v.6. *fight, contend*: 3p. sacað
65.8.

sacu, f. *strife, battle*: ds. sace 18.6. *See*
sæcc.

sǣ, m.f. *sea, ocean*: ns. 1.59, 74.1 [MS.
Se]; np. sǣs 64.3.

sæcc, f. *strife, contest*: as. sæcce 14.2,
84.26; gs. sæcce 1.59. *See* **sacu.**

sæd, adj. *sated, weary* (w. gen.): nsm.
3.2.

sǣgrund, m. *bottom of the sea*: ap.
sǣgrundas 1.25.

sæl, n. *hall*: gs. sales 50.2. *See* **burg-,
folc-, horn-sæl.**

sæl, m. *time, opportunity*: gs. sǣles
29.12.

ge-**sǣlig,** adj. *happy, blessed*: nsm.
38.64.

sǣlwong, m. *plain*: as. 17.3; gs. sāl-
wonges 1.32 [MS. sal wonge].

sǣne, adj. *slow, sluggish*: nsf. 31.5.

sǣweall, m. *sea-wall, cliff, shore*: ds.
sǣwealle 58.1.

sāgol, m. *pole, rod*: as. 77.5 [MS. sag].

sales, *see* **sæl.**

salo, adj. *dark, dusky*: nsm. 76.12.

saloneb, adj. *dark-faced*: nsm. 47.5.

salopād, adj. *dark-coated*: npf.
salopāde 55.3.

sālwong, *see* **sǣlwong.**

samed, *see* **somod.**

sang, *see* **song.**

sār, adj. *sore*: comp. nsf. sārre 11.6
[MS. sarra].

sāre, adv. *sorely*: 70.16.

sāwan, v.7. *sow*: 3s. sāweþ 19.6.

sāwol, f. *soul*: as. sāwle 37.16; ds?
sāwle 84.32.

sceacan, v.6. *move rapidly, shake*: inf.
18.14; PRET. 3s. scōc 89.13.

ge-**sceaft,** f.m.n. **1.** *creature, shape*:
np. gesceafte 1.72; gp. gesceafta
38.88. —**2.** *nature, condition*: as.
31.8. *See* **ealdor-, forð-gesceaft;
frum-, un-, won-sceaft.**

scēam, m. *shiner? bright creature?
white horse?* ap. scēamas 20.4.

ge-**sceap,** n. **1.** *fate, destiny*: np. ge-
sceapu 7.7, 37.24, gesceapo 67.4
(or ap? w. uncertain meaning
because of lacuna). —**2.** *nature,
mind, pleasure*: as. gesceap 36.4
(on ~ , *in pleasure*); ds. gesceape
71.6 (wiþ ~ minum, *against my
nature*).

scearp, adj. *sharp*: nsm. 1.71, 60.1;
npf. scearpe 31.4; ipn. scearpum
1.82; supl.isn.wk. scearpestan
26.2. *See* **heoroscearp.**

scearp, n. *ornament, apparel, fitting*:
as. 67.4 (or ap?). *See* fyrd-, hleo-
sceorp.

sceat, m. 1. *region, surface (of the
earth)*: as. 39.5; ap. sceatas 65.13;
gp. sceata 84.24. —2. *lap, bosom*:
ds. sceate 7.7. —3. *covering, gar-
ment*: ds. sceate 42.2.

sceaþa, *see* feond-, nið-sceaþa.

sceawendwise, f. *dramatic or narrative
song*: ap. sceawendwisan 6.9.

sceawian, v.II. *look at, behold*: inf.
57.2; 1s. sceawige 38.40.

sceo, m. *cloud*: ns. 1.71.

sceotan, v.2. *shoot, rush*: inf. 36.4.

sceran, v.4. *cut, shear*: 3s. scireþ 63.3.

sceþþan, v.6. *hurt, injure* (w. dat. or
acc.): inf. 41.3; 1s. sceþþe 23.2; 3s.
sceðeð 41.11; PRET. 1s. scod 18.15;
3s. scod 70.15.

scildan, v.I. *shield, protect*: PRET. 3p.
scildon 84.14.

scin, n. *specter, phantom*: np. 1.82.

scinan, v.1. *shine*: inf. 38.103. *See*
bescinan.

scip, n. *ship*: ns. 56.4.

scir, adj. *bright, shining, clear*: nsm.
71.20; asm. scirne 56.4; apm. scire
36.4; apf. scire 9.2.

scirenige, f. *minstrel? actress?* ns. 6.9.

scotian, v.II. *shoot*: 3p. scotiað 1.81.

scriþan, v.1. *go, glide, wander, stalk*:
3s. scriþeð 33.7; prp. npn.
scriþende 1.82.

sculan, v.AN. *be obliged, have to,
must*: 1s. sceal 1.47,64,95,98, 2.1,
3.9, 12.9,14,17, 13.12,17, 14.1,7,
18.26,30, 28a.8, 28b.8, 38.91, 61.1,
69.7, 79.12, 84.21, 87.4, 91.5,8; 3s.
sceal 25.11, 30.6, 31.12, 33.8, 35.5,
37.8,16,21, 40.8, 41.5, 78.6, 81.5,
84.24; 3p. sculon 84.16; PRET. 1s.
sceolde 58.8,14, 71.6; 3s. sceolde

59.8, 89.9; 3p. sceoldon 11.6;
SUBJ. pres. 3s. scyle 1.61.

scur, m. *shower, storm*: dp. scurum
84.14.

ge-scyldru, n.p. *shoulders*: dp. ge-
scyldrum 38.103, 67.4.

scyppan, v.6. *create, shape, order, des-
tine*: PRET. 3s. scop 81.2; pp.
sceapen 18.1, 21.2.

ge-scyppan, v.6. *create, form*: PRET.
3s. gescop 21.6, 84.14.

scyppend, m. *creator (God)*: ns.
38.1,101.

se (se), þæt, seo, dem. adj., def. art.,
pron. *the, this (one), that (one)*:
1. adj., def. art. *the, this, that*:
nsm. se, (or weakly stressed) se,
13.24 [MS. re], 14.3, 21.6, 24.15,
33.1, 38.1,3,21,54,68,74,92,96,
40.9, 41.2,3,8,15,16, 42.4, 45.3,
46.8, 47.4,10, 51.12 (twice), 53.9,
10,16, 54.5, 67.2, 77.9; nsn. þæt
23.11, 51.2, 80.33; nsf. seo 7.9,
26.13, 29.19, 36.6, 37.1, 39.9,
58.12, 65.16, sio 18.20, [29.24],
30.14, 58.6, 80.21; asm. þone 18.4,
21.13, 22.4, 89.15; asn. þæt 21.5,6,
32.2, 42.5, 43.3, 45.2, 47.8, ?80.12;
asf. þa 1.60, 27.9, 35.1, 36.1, 40.13,
66.1, 89.20; dsm. þam 13.26, 18.23,
27.4 (twice), 35.6, 41.6; dsn. þam
1.37, 84.31; dsf. þære 27.5, 54.5,
57.12, 71.4, 84.28; isn. þy 26.2
(twice),3; gsm. þæs 9.8, 18.28, 45.5
(or dem. pron.?), 53.7, 57.11,16,
59.7; gsn. þæs 1.89, 4.9, 14.4,
31.10, 38.72, 39.3 (twice),4, 40.4,11
[MS. wæs], 52.10, 57.9, 62.6, 87.9;
gsf. þære 27.14, 34.14; npm. þa
22.10; npn. þa 24.15,16, 39.7; npf.
þa 40.16; apn. þa 1.15,83, 5.2,
20.10; apf. þa 32.7, 40.12; dpn.
þam 45.6, 47.4, 71.28; gpm. þara

44.5; gpn. þāra 80.8,56; gpf. þāra
40.8, 54.12. —**2. dem. pron.** *that
(one), those, he, she, they,* etc.: nsm.
sē 1.69; nsn. þæt 31.11, 34.9,
37.24, 39.2,8, 41.11, 45.1, 53.12,
58.10, ?65.5; nsf. sēo 31.12, 37.14;
asn. þæt 1.2,65,87, 2.9 (þæt sylfe,
see **sylf**), 13.16, 14.8, 15.5, 25.9,
65.13, 70.10, ?77.11; isn. þȳ 61.10;
isn. þȳ (as adv. w. comp.) *by that,
the*: 7.11, 11.5,6, 15.4, 17.8, 24.19
(twice),20 (twice),21 (twice), 37.9,
45.6, 84.11,12; isn. þon 38.16
(to ~ , *to such an extent*); gsm.
þæs 1.46, 45.5 (or art?); gsn. þæs
4.8, 9.5, 14.5, 18.35, 21.10; ap. þā
32.6; dp. þām 14.2; gp. þāra 50.5,
63.6, ?80.16. —**3. rel. pron.** *who,
which,* etc.: nsm. sē 18.5, 21.6,
38.1,22,90, 47.2, 49.6, 60.5, 79.5,
84.25; nsn. þæt 38.32,69 (= ind.
rel. w. masc. *zefferus*?), 58.4 (= ind.
rel. w. m.n. *fea*?), 71.26, 89.24
(= ind. rel. w. neut. pl. *ealle*? or
MS. reading originally *þætte*?);
nsf. sēo 27.8, 32.2, 34.2, 38.81,
50.6, sīo 29.5; asm. þone 38.73,
48.3; asn. þæt 21.9, 42.7; dsm.
þām 41.2; np. þā 24.23, 50.3,
55.2; ap. þā 47.7; gp. þāra 56.15,
70.7. —**4. rel. pron. with ante-
cedent omitted,** either as a 'double
relative' (e.g., *þæt* = *þæt þæt,*
'that which') or as an indefi-
nite relative (e.g., *sē* = 'he who,'
'whoever'). [**Note:** Since the
cases of the relatives are most
often determined by the function
of the pronoun in the relative
clause, I have classified the 'double
relatives' under their relative
clause function. Occasionally the
cases of the relatives in this section

appear to be determined by an
originally demonstrative function
within the main clause (with
possible loss of relative *þe* by
attraction), and such occurrences
are indicated here by an asterisk.]
nsm. sē 1.43, 18.29, 53.15; nsn.
þæt 1.12,66, 15.11, 19.15 (= ind.
rel. w. masc. *hlaford*?), 21.12,
31.10, [35.4], 76.7, 87.3,6, 89.26;
asn. þæt 1.95, 14.7, 19.14, 21.11,
34.13, 47.10, 52.11; dsm. þām
54.9*; gsmn. þæs 39.7*, 53.5*; np.
þā 71.3; ap. þā 4.7. —**5. w. þe as
compound rel. pron.,** *he who,* etc.
[**Note:** The cases of the compound
relatives are normally determined
by their function within the rela-
tive clause (though the function is
sometimes the same in the main
and subordinate clauses); this is
the common or *se þe* relative
(Mitchell, *A Guide to Old English,*
162, pp. 73–74). Occasionally the
relative case is determined by the
case of the antecedent in the main
clause; this is the *se'þe* relative
(Mitchell, ibid., 163, pp. 75–76)
and is indicated in this section by
an asterisk. Sometimes the relative
case is determined by the sense
and function of the demonstrative
element as it operates in the main
clause without a direct antecedent
of equivalent case; this 'relative'
(which is really the demonstrative
plus indeclinable *þe,* each with its
own largely independent status) is
indicated here by a plus sign.]
nsm. sē þe 1.26, 25.9, 36.5, 38.93,
96*, 41.5,14, 57.5,15, 65.15, 69.6,
71.28, 77.7, 84.31, 89.29; nsf. sēo
þe 23.10 [MS. seþe]; dsm. þām þe

13.29*, 48.10⁺ [MS. þe], 58.11*
(or 58.11⁺?), 67.1⁺; gsn. þæs þe
29.15⁺, 30.12, 39.4*, 80.31⁺; np.
þā þe 32.6, 33.10; dp. þām þe
11.10⁺, 24.5*, 40.7*; gp. þāra þe
1.88⁺, 3.12⁺, 37.15*,26⁺, 38.89*,
87.10⁺.

sealt, n. *salt*: ns. 90.5.

searo, n. **1.** *art, skill*: dp. adv. sear-
wum: 27.6, 54.5, 80.49. —**2.** *work of
art, cunning device*: as. 30.3.

searobunden, adj. *skillfully bound*:
asn. 53.4.

searocēap, m. *skillfully made merchan-
dise*: ns. 30.7.

searocræftig, adj. *skillful, cunning*:
nsf. 31.8.

searolīc, adj. *ingenious, curious, mar-
velous*: nsn. 58.11.

searopīl, n. *skillfully made dart or
pointed tool*: gp. searopīla 87.2 (in-
strumental gen.).

searosæled, adj. *skillfully bound*: nsf.
21.16.

searoþonc, m. *ingenuity, sagacity, skill*:
ip. searoþoncum 33.13.

searoþoncol, adj. *sagacious, ingenious*:
npm. searoþoncle 38.97.

sēaw, n. *moisture, liquid*: ap. 1.77.

seax, n. *knife*: is. seaxe 38.97; gs.
seaxes 58.12 [MS. seaxeð], 74.6,
seaxses 24.6.

sēcan, v.I. **1.** *seek, look for*: inf. 25.11
(or as meaning #2?), 89.11; 3s.
sēceþ 13.25, 32.5; 3p. sēcað 91.12;
PRET. 3s? sōhte 89.6. —**2.** *visit, go
to*: inf. 1.17, 14.2.

ge-sēcan, v.I. *seek, visit*: inf. 37.5,
57.14.

secg, m. *man*: ns. 2.5, 60.9; np.
secgas 38.97; dp. secgum 46.4,
secgan 61.1. See **gārsecg.**

secgan, v.III. *say, tell, declare*: inf.

40.6, 53.8,16; 3p. secgað 37.1,13;
PRET. 3s. sægde 31.8; SUBJ. pres.
3s. secge 65.15; imp. 2s. saga
1.14,27,102, 6.8, 8.11, 10.13, 17.9,
21.16, 33.13, 34.8, 37.29, 60.9,
64.10, 76.12, 79.14, 82.7; ger.
secganne 37.22. See **āsecgan.**

ge-secgan, v.III. *say, tell, narrate*: inf.
2.12, 37.28; PRET. 3s. gesægde
36.5; ger. gesecganne 34.13, 37.25.

sefa, m. *mind, understanding*: ds.
sefan 58.11.

segnberend, m. *standard-bearer, war-
rior*: gp. segnberendra 38.20.

ge-selda, m. *companion*: ns. 76.4.

sele, m. *hall, house*: ns. 81.1; ds.
18.10; gs. seles 11.4.

seledrēam, m. *hall-joy*: ds. sele-
drēame 61.1.

sellan, see **syllan.**

sēllan, sēlestan, see **gōd.**

sellīc, adj. *strange, wonderful, excel-
lent*: nsf. 80.29, sellīcu 30.5; asn.
sellīc 29.3, 30.3.

semninga, adv. *suddenly*: 38.10.

sendan, v.I. *send*: 3s. sendeð 1.32,
47.5; 3p. sendað 28a.5, 28b.5; pp.
sended 1.11.

seolfor, n. *silver*: is. seolfre 18.10,
65.15, sylfre 12.2 [MS. sylfore]; gs.
seolfres 53.4.

seolhbæþ, n. *seal's bath, sea*: ap.
seolhbaþo 8.11.

seomian, v.II. *lie, rest*: 3s. seomað
18.3.

sēon, v.5CT. *see, behold*: 1s. sēo 3.3;
PRET. 1s. seah 11.1, 17.1, 29.3,
30.3, 40.1, 49.1, 50.1, 51.1, 53.1,
57.1, 62.1, 83.1; SUBJ. pres. 1s. sȳ
38.65; SUBJ. pret. 3p. sāwe 80.32.

ge-sēon, v.5CT. *see, behold*: PRET. 1s.
geseah 27.1, 32.1, 34.1, 35.1, 36.1,
54.1,10, 65.13, 66.1, 73.1,3.

settan, v.I. 1. *place, set*: PRET. 3s.
sette 24.4. —2. *create, establish*:
PRET. 3s. sette 38.7. *See* āsettan.
ge-settan, v.I. *create, establish*: PRET.
3s. gesette 4.1.
sēþēah, adv. or conj. 1. *yet, however,*
nevertheless: 2.9, 83.7. —2. hwæþre
sēþēah, conj. *however, nevertheless*:
33.11. —3. efne sēþēah, conj.
nevertheless, even so: 37.27, 63.1. *See*
swā þēah *under* swā.
sēþēana, conj. *yet, nevertheless*: 84.7.
See swā þēana *under* swā.
ge-sibb, adj. *reláted, familiar*: apm.
gesibbe 13.22; gpm. gesibbra 24.22.
See ungesibb.
sīd, adj. *wide, spacious*: apm. sīde
1.25.
sīde, adv. *amply, extensively*: 64.10.
sīde, f. *side*: ns. 11.6; as. sīdan 19.13;
ds. sīdan 70.16, 74.6; np. sīdan
13.2, 71.18; ap. sīdan 67.2, 77.5,
82.7.
siex, num. *six*: 22.10, 34.8, six 11.2
[MS. vi].
sigefæst, adj. *victorious*: comp. npm.
sigefæstran 24.19.
sigor, m. *victory*: gp. sigora 4.1.
ge-sihð, f. *sight*: as. 57.9.
sīn, poss. pron. *his, her, its*: dsm.
sīnum 56.14, 57.4; isn. 21.14; apm.
sīne 29.22; ipm. sīnum 87.11, 89.2;
ipf. sīnum 59.3.
sinc, n. *treasure, wealth*: ns. 46.4; as.
18.6, 53.4; is. since 18.10, 65.15.
sincfāg, adj. *richly adorned*: nsm.
12.15.
sinder, m. *impurity*: dp. sindrum
24.6.
singan, v.3. *sing*: inf. 29.3; 1s. singe
6.2; 3s. singeð 67.2; 3p. singað 5.8.
sittan, v.5. *sit*: inf. 73.3; 1s. sitte 22.7;
3s. siteð 1.35, 29.12; 3p. sittað 6.8

[MS. siteð]; PRET. 3s. sæt 44.1; 3p.
sǣton 82.1. *See* onsittan.
ge-sittan, v.5. *sit*: PRET. 1s. gesæt
75.6.
sittende, *see* burg-, in-sittende.
sīð, adv. *afterwards*: 58.8.
sīð, m. *journey, course, wandering, fate*:
as. 1.2, 27.14, 81.3; ds. sīþe [17.1],
50.7, sīþþe 62.2; ap. sīþas 7.11,
37.16; ip. sīþum 30.3; gp. sīþa 1.27.
See forð-, here-, unrǣd-sīþ.
ge-sīð, m. *companion*: np. gesīþas
28a.5, 28b.5.
sīþfæt, m. *journey, course*: ns. 17.9; as.
79.14; ds. sīðfate 41.6.
sīþian, v.II. *go, travel, wander*: inf.
49.2; PRET. 1s. sīþade 70.11; 3s.
sīþade 24.11.
sīþþan, A. adv. *after, afterwards, then*:
7.9, 8.10, 13.22, 24.2,5,11, 25.5,
27.13, 38.9, 59.5, 74.7, 89.17.
—B. conj. *when, after, since*: 9.9,
13.27, 21.6, 74.6, 79.2, ?85.10.
sīþþe, *see* sīð.
six, *see* siex.
sixtig, num. *sixty*: 20.1 [MS. lx].
slǣp, m. *sleep*: ns. 38.10.
slǣpan, v.7. *sleep*: SUBJ. pret. 1s.
slēpe 38.9.
slǣpwērig, adj. *weary from sleep?*
weary from a lack of sleep? asm.
slǣpwērigne 2.5.
slītan, v.1. *slit, tear*: inf. 11.8; 1s. slīte
10.1; 3p. slītað 84.29; prp. npm.
slītende 14.6. *See* tōslītan.
slīþe, adj. *dangerous, cruel*: gsf. slīþre
1.59.
slūpan, v.2. *slip, glide*: inf. 1.69.
smæl, adj. *slender*: nsm. 71.18.
smēah, adj. *subtle, penetrating*: comp.
nsf. smēare 90.5.
smēþe, adj. *smooth, soft*: comp?
smēþr[. 90.1.

smiþ, m. *smith*: gp. smiþa 3.8, 18.7,
24.14.

snægl, m. *snail*: ns. 38.70.

snāw, m. *snow*: ns. 77.10.

snel, adj. *quick, swift*: comp. nsm.
snelra 38.70 [MS. snel ro þōn].

snīðan, v.1. *cut*: PRET. 3s. snāð 24.6.

snottor, adj. *wise, clever, discerning*:
nsm. 80.35; npm. snottre 82.2,
91.7.

snyþian, v.II. *nose, go along sniffing
the ground*: 1s. snyþige 19.6.

ge-sōm, adj. *united*: npm. gesōme
84.26.

some, *see* swā some *under* swā.

ge-somnian, v.II. *unite, collect*: pp.
gesomnad 28a.2, 28b.2.

somod, adv. *together, at the same time*:
1.14, 14.2, 20.9, 58.13, samed 49.2.

sōna, adv. *soon, immediately*: 14.6,
23.9, 25.7,9, 61.13, 83.4.

sond, n. *sand, shore, bank*: ds. sonde
1.22, 58.1.

sond, f. *message*: ns. 88.3.

song, m. *song*: as. 22.6; gs. sanges
55.3.

sōð, adj. *true, just*: nsm. 1.84, 4.1;
nsn. 37.25; ipn. sōþum 37.29; gpm.
sōþra 24.22.

sōð, n. *truth*: as. 34.13.

sōðcwide, m. *true saying*: ip.
sōðcwidum 33.13.

spǣtan, v.I. *spit*: 1s. spǣte 15.4, 21.8.

spēd, f. *success, prosperity*: ns. 15.4;
as. 2.12 (on ~ , *successfully*), 84.31.
See friþospēd.

spēddropa, m. *useful drop*: ip. spēd-
dropum 24.8.

spel, n. *story, history*: as. 2.12.

spere, *see* āttor-, dēað-spere.

sperebrōga, m. *spear-terror*: as.
sperebrōgan 15.4.

spild, m. *destruction*: is. spilde 21.8.

spor, n. *track*: ds. spore 84.31.

spōwan, v.7. *succeed* (impers. w.
gen.): 3s. spēow 40.4 [MS. speop].

sprǣc, f. *speech*: ds. sprǣce 25.13. *See*
ǣrendsprǣc.

sprecan, v.5. *speak*: inf. 16.1, 58.9,
91.9 [MS. sprecað]; 1s. sprece 6.1,
sprice 21.11, 41.16; 3s. spreceð
18.33, spriceð 26.10; PRET. 3s.
sprǣc 37.12.

spyrian, v.II. *make a track, travel*:
PRET. 3s. spyrede 24.8.

stæf, m. *letter, character*: np. stafas
22.10. *See* ār-, rūn-stæf.

stælgiest, m. *thievish guest*: ns. 45.5.

stæpe, m. *step*: ds. 89.12. *See*
wrōhtstæpe.

stæþ, n. *bank, shore*: ds. staþe 1.48,
stæðe 20.19; ap. staþu 1.21. *See*
wǣgstæþ.

stæððan, v.I. *stay, contain*: SUBJ.
pres. 3s. stæðþe 1.104.

stān, m. *stone*: ns. 38.74; ds. stāne
1.22; np. stānas 14.9; ip. stānum
80.44.

standan, *see* stondan.

stānhliþ, n. *rocky cliff*: np. stānhleoþu
1.56.

stānwong, m. *stony plain*: ap. stān-
wongas 89.12.

staþol, m. *place, foundation*: ns. 23.4,
69.2; as. 45.5 (w. pun on meaning,
intellectual foundation or *content?*),
?84.5, 84.22. *See* frum-, wynn-
staþol.

staþolwong, m. *a place or field where
someone or something is established or
fixed*: ds. staþolwonge 32.8.

stealc, adj. *steep*: npn. 1.56; apn.
1.22, 89.9.

stēap, adj. *high, steep*: asm. stēapne
13.18, 77.4; npm. stēape 1.40.

stēaphēah, adj. *very high*: nsm. 23.4.

The Old English Riddles of the *Exeter Book*

stēapwong, adj. *steep-cheeked*: nsm. 69.2.
stede, m. 1. *site, position.* —2. *stability, firmness*: as. 42.3 (w. pun on both meanings?). See folc-, wīc-stede.
stefn, f. *voice*: as. stefne 22.1; is. stefne 6.7, 12.18, 46.3.
stelan, see be-, bi-, for-stelan.
stenc, m. *odor, fragrance*: as. 38.29; ds. stence 38.23.
steort, m. *tail*: ns. 14.8; as. 56.7, 77.2; ds. steorte 19.4.
stēpan, v.I. *exalt* (w. dat.): 3s. stēpeð 48.8.
steppan, v.6. *step, go*: 1s. steppe 13.5; 3s. steppeð 89.31; PRET. 1s. stōp 72.5; 3s. stōp 24.10, 52.2; 3p. stōpan 20.19.
stician, v.II. 1. *stick, thrust, pierce* (trans.): 3s. sticað 87.3; PRET. 3s. sticade 59.5. —2. *stick, be stuck* (intr.): 3s. sticaþ 10.11.
stīg, f. *way, path*: as. stīge 13.24.
stīgan, v.1. *rise, ascend, climb*: inf. 20.8, 89.9; 1s. stīge 1.100; 3p. stīgað 1.6. See ā-, ofer-stīgan.
ge-stillan, v.I. *quiet, calm*: 3s. gestilleð 1.65.
stille, A. adj. *still, quiet*: nsm. 1.104, 14.4; nsf. 1.40; npm. 1.29, 6.7.
—B. adv. *quietly*: 1.55, 32.8. See unstille.
stincan, v.3. 1. *stink*: 3s. stinceð 38.32. —2. *rise*: PRET. 3s. stonc 27.12.
stīð, adj. *stiff, hard, strong*: nsm. 69.2; nsn. 42.3; asm. stīþne 14.9; asn. stīð 89.31; gsn. stīþes 52.5.
stīðecg, adj. *strong-edged*: nsn. 89.20.
stīðweg, m. *hard way, fierce path*: as. 1.65.
stīwita, m. *steward? householder?* dp. stīwitum 1.40.

stōl, see ēþel-, glēaw-stōl.
stondan, v.6. *stand*: inf. 31.13, 32.8, 52.2, 84.22 [MS. stodan], standan 47.1; 1s. stonde 23.4, 68.1, 84.19, 89.26; 3s. stondeþ 38.61, 91.4 (me . . . stondeð, *stands on me? shines from me?*); 3p. standað 13.3; PRET. 1s. stōd 84.9; 3s. stōd 54.9; 1p. stōdan 84.11; prp. asm. (uninflected) stondende 77.8, dsf. stondendre 52.5. See forstondan.
storm, m. *storm*: ip. stormum 80.44.
strǣl, f. *arrow*: ap. strǣle 1.86.
strǣt, f. *street, road*: as. strǣte 13.18.
strang, see strong.
strēam, m. *stream, flood*: gs. strēames 24.10; np. strēamas 1.21,29, 20.8, 77.8; ap. strēamas 1.[48],100. See firgen-, lagu-, mere-strēam.
strēamgewinn, n. *strife of waters*: gs. strēamgewinnes 1.56.
strengu, f. *strength, power*: ns. 5.5; ds. strengo 25.13. See woruldstrengu.
ge-strēon, n. *wealth, possession*: gp. gestrēona 18.31, 26.3. See bearn-, dryht-gestrēon.
strong, adj. *strong, firm, powerful*: nsm. 1.3,65, 14.4, 25.13, 52.9, 60.1, 89.12; asm. strongne 80.2; asm.wk. strangan 45.5 (or gsm.wk.?); dsn.wk. strongan 38.79; npm. stronge 20.8; ipn. strongum 46.3; comp. nsm. strengra 38.92, 81.4, nsf. strengre 38.23. See for-strang, mægen-, ryne-strong.
strūdan, v.2. *plunder*: PRET. 3p. strudon 51.10.
ge-stun, n. *noise, whirlwind*: ds. gestune 1.86.
stund, f. *moment, time*: as. stunde 89.20; dp. adv. stundum (*eagerly, exceedingly*) 1.3,21; gp. stunda 52.9.
stȳle, n. *steel*: ns. 89.20, ?90.4; ds. 38.79.

stȳran, v.I. **1.** *guide, rule*: 3s. stȳreð 38.13. —**2.** *restrain, hinder* (w. dat. of person and gen. of thing): 1s. stȳre 9.4.

styrgan, v.II. *stir, agitate*: inf. 1.48; 1s. styrge 1.24,100.

styrman, v.I. *cry*: 1s. styrme 6.7.

suē, *see* **swā**.

sum, pron. and adj. *one, a certain (one), some*: nsm. 1.63, 24.1, 71.23, 74.4; nsf. 12.8; asm. sumne 1.34; asn. sum 76.10; gsm. sumes 12.15, 45.3; npf. sume 8.8.

sumor, m. *summer*: as? 84.2.

sumsende, adj. *humming, buzzing*: apn. sumsendu 1.77.

sund, m. *sea, water*: ds. sunde 1.14, 8.3.

ge-**sund**, adj. *safe, sound*: npm. gesunde 41.6; npn. gesund 20.21; comp. npm. gesundran 24.19.

sundhelm, m. *sea-guard, water-covering*: ns. 74.1; ds. sundhelme 1.25.

sundor, adv. *separately, individually*: 37.5.

sundorcræft, m. *special power or capacity*: as. 37.3.

sunne, f. *sun*: ns. 64.3, 89.33, 90.3; as. sunnan 24.4.

sunu, m. *son*: ns. 38.72, 80.10; as. 35.8; np. suno 44.2,3; gp. suna 7.12.

sūþerne, adj. *southern*: nsm. 60.9 (or asm?).

swā, **1.** adv. *so, in such a manner, in like manner, accordingly*: 1.97, 7.12, 9.6, 11.6, 25.16, 27.6, 31.11, 38.14, 69, 40.11 [swā ic: MS. hwylc], 47.9, 68.1, 80.33. —**2.** conj. *as, just as, in such a way that, when*: 1.16, 4.4, 6.9, 7.7, 18.25, 19.2, 20.6,13, 22.2 (twice),3 (twice),10, 28b.8, 38.5,34,

46.8, 57.11, 58.16, 59.4, 75.5, ?84.6, 84.28, swē 13.4. —**3.** **swā . . . swā**, adv. and conj. *as . . . as, just . . . as*: (swā ārlīce swā, *as kindly as*) 7.6 [MS. snearlice swa]. —**4.** **efne swā**, conj. *just as, even as*: 1.43. —**5.** **swā some**, adv. *likewise, as well*: 13.2, 40.11. —**6.** **swā þeah**, conj. *yet, nevertheless*: 56.11; *see* **sēþeah**. —**7.** **swā þeana**, conj. *yet, nevertheless*: 56.13; *see* **sēþeana**.

swǣs, adj. *own, favorite, dear*: npf. swāse 44.3; apm. swǣse 13.22, 70.7; gpm. swǣsra 7.11, 24.22.

swǣsende, n. *food*: dp. swǣsendum 85.11.

swǣtan, v.I. *sweat* (w. dat.): 3p. swǣtað 1.73.

swæð, n. *track, footprint*: ns. 19.10; as. 19.6; np. swaþu 49.3.

swaþu, f. **1.** *track*: as. swaþe 91.12; ds. swaþe 73.1 (or as?). —**2.** **on swaþe**, *behind*: 13.25.

swē, *see* **swā**.

sweart, adj. *dark, black*: nsm. 38.94, 47.5; nsn. 19.10; nsn.wk. swearte 38.31; asm. sweartne 10.13; dsm. sweartum 70.11; npm. swearte 49.2; npf. swearte 55.3; apm. swearte 10.4; apn. sweart 1.77; dpn. sweartum 15.7; supl. gsn.wk. sweartestan 39.3.

sweartlāst, adj. *dark-tracked, leaving a black track*: nsf. 24.11.

swēg, m. *noise, tumult*: gp. swēga 1.69.

swelgan, v.3. *swallow, imbibe* (w. dat. or inst.): inf. 12.15, 15.7; 1s. swelge 89.24; 3s. swelgeþ 56.10, swilgeð 47.2, 78.2; PRET. 3s. swealg 24.9, 45.6 (w. pun on meaning, *take into the mind, understand*?). *See* **for-swelgan**.

sweora, m. *neck*: ns. 67.2, swīora
71.18; as. sweoran 82.6. *See* **bel-
cedsweora**.

sweord, m. *sword*: as. 53.14.

sweorfan, v.3. *rub, file, scour, polish*:
pp. sworfen 26.4, 87.2.

sweostor, f. *sister*: ns. 70.5; gs. 41.14;
np. 11.2.

ge-**sweostor**, f.p. *sisters*: np. 44.3.

sweotol, adj. *manifest, evident, per-
ceivable*: nsn. 19.10; nsf. 37.3; npn.
11.4.

sweotule, adv. *clearly, plainly*: 22.10.

ge-**sweotulian**, v.II. *manifest*: pp.
gesweotlad 80.24.

swēte, adj. *sweet*: comp. nsm. swētra
38.58.

swētnes, f. *sweetness*: ds. swētnesse
38.30.

ge-**swīcan**, v.1. *desist (from), cease*
(w. gen.): 3s. geswīceð 25.12; 3p.
geswīcaþ 9.10.

swifan, v.1. *move, sweep, glide* (intr.):
inf. 30.7; 3s. swīfeð 10.13.

swift, adj. *swift, quick*: nsm. 1.102,
13.2, 49.3; nsm.wk. swifta 38.68;
asm. swiftne 17.3 [MS. swist ne],
73.1; comp. nsm. swiftra 38.70,
nsf. swiftre 64.3, 81.3 [MS. swis-
tre].

swīge, adj. *silent, still*: nsm. 1.41,
81.1.

swīgian, v.II. *be silent, become quiet*:
3s. swīgað 5.1; PRET. 1s. swīgade
70.16; prp. nsn. swīgende 46.4.

swimman, v.3. *swim, float*: PRET. 1s.
swom 72.3; 3s. swom 20.14.

swīn, n. *swine, pig*: ns. 38.105.

swingere, m. *beater, scourger*: ns.
25.7.

swinsian, v.II. *sing, sound melodi-
ously*: 3p. swinsiað 5.7.

swīora, *see* **sweora**.

swīþ, adj. **1.** *strong, powerful*: comp.
nsf. swīþre 38.94, npm. swīþran
14.5; supl. nsf. swīþost 80.29.
—**2.** comp. **swīþre**, *right (hand)*:
nsf. 58.12.

swīþe, adv. **1.** *very, especially, exceed-
ingly*: 8.3 (*deep*), 49.3, 55.2, 91.12;
supl. swīþast 91.7 (*especially,
chiefly*). —**2.** *vigorously, fiercely*: 4.8,
17.3 (or as meaning #3?), 60.8.
—**3.** *quickly*: 24.4, 30.7.

swīþfeorm, adj. *strong, violent, ?swol-
len*: nsm. 1.102.

swōgan, v.7. *make a noise, resound,
whistle*: 3p. swōgað 5.7.

swylc, adj. and pron. *such, such a
one, such a thing*: asn. 58.11; asf?
swylce 85.11; gpm. swylcra 17.9.

swylce, **1.** adv. *likewise, also, in such a
manner*: 18.3, 38.29,60,95, 62.4.
—**2.** conj. (*such*) *as, as well as, thus*:
4.9, 22.8, 80.10. —**3.** **swylce swē**,
conj. *as well as*: 13.4. —**4.** **swylce
ēac**, conj. *likewise, moreover*: ?61.13.

swyltan, v.3. *die, perish*: 3s. swylteð
1.84, 35.5.

sȳ, *see* **bēon/wesan** *or* **sēon**.

sylf, adj. and pron. *self, one's own*:
nsm. 24.28; nsm.wk. sylfa 35.8,
60.3, 76.12, 81.1; asn.wk. sylfe
(*þæt sylfe = likewise, in like manner*)
2.10; dsm. sylfum 18.6, 64.10; gsn.
sylfes 62.6 (*same*); gsf. sylfre 31.8;
apf. sylfe 55.6.

sylfor, *see* **seolfor**.

syllan, v.I. *give, grant*: inf. 35.5; 1s.
selle 10.5; PRET. 3s. sealde 2.4,
59.3, 70.8.

symbel, n. *feast*: ds. symble 29.12.

symle, adv. *always, ever*: 35.5, 38.30,
64, 65.3.

sȳn, f. *sight, eye*: ap. sȳne 30.5. *See*
ansȳn.

ge-sȳne, adj. *evident, manifest, perceivable*: nsf. 37.3; npn. 11.4.

T

tācn, n. *sign, token*: as. 53.5, tācen 57.10 *(significance)*.
ge-tācnian, v.II. *betoken, signify*: pp. getācnad 61.14.
tǣcnan, v.I. *mark out, designate*: 3s. tǣcneð 1.46, 49.6.
ge-tǣse, adj. *convenient, useful, beneficial*: nsf. 80.28.
tān, m. *twig, branch*: ip. tānum 51.2.
tēah, *see* tēon.
teala, adv. *well, rightly*: 19.14, tila 46.2.
teale, *see* tellan.
telg, m. *dye*: ns. 24.15. *See* beamtelg.
tellan, v.I. *consider*: 1s. teale 13.16.
tēn, num. *ten*: 11.1 [MS. x].
ge-tenge, adj. *near to, resting upon* (w. dat.): nsm. 5.8, 8.4, 80.26; nsn. 54.9; nsf. 50.5; asf. 74.2; apn. 4.3; ? .]etenge 80.48.
tēon, v.2CT. 1. *pull, draw, drag* (trans.): 3s. tȳhð 60.6; PRET. 1s. tēah 70.6; 3s. tēah 20.13. —2. *go, proceed* (intr.): 3s. tȳhð 32.4. *See* ātēon.
tēon, n. *injury, harm*: as. 48.3.
tēorian, v.II. *tire, grow weary*: PRET. 3s. tēorode 52.8.
teran, v.4. *tear*: 1s. tere 19.14.
tīd, f. *time, hour*: as. 1.60, 72.2; dp. tīdum 37.2, 56.6. *See* dægtīd.
til, adj. *good, useful, excellent*: nsm. 15.9; gpm. tilra 24.23.
tila, *see* teala.
tillfremmend, m. *one who does good, righteous man*: gp. tillfremmendra 57.7.

tillic, adj. *good, capable*: nsm. 52.8, 61.5.
timbran, v.I. *build*: pp? timbred 80.45. *See* ātimbran.
tō, prep. A. w. dat. 1. *to, unto, towards, into, upon*: 1.48, 12.4,17, 13.11, 18.6, 20.2,12, 25.8, 26.7, 27.4,9,12, 28a.7, 28b.7, 31.2, 32.4, 37.20, 38.55, 46.8, 53.5, 57.17, 66.3. —2. *as, for* (marking purpose, function, service, etc.): 4.2, 24.27, 31.5, 37.19, 38.16 (~ þon, *to such an extent*),65, 39.5, 47.9,10, 48.2, 68.2, 71.15, 75.4, 79.6. —3. *on, at, among* (marking sphere of action or juxtaposition): 10.11, 38.45. —B. w. gerund (which may be inflected or uninflected), *to, for*: 26.12, 29.23, 34.13, 37.22,25, 39.8, 84.26.
tō, adv. 1. *too, excessively*: 20.6. —2. *thither, to that place, there*: 52.2.
tōberstan, v.3. *burst apart, be rent*: 3s. tōbirsteð 36.7.
tōgædre, adv. *together*: 50.4. *See* ætgædre.
tōgongan, v.7. *pass away* (impers. w. gen.): 3s. tōgongeð 21.10.
torht, adj. *bright, splendid*: nsm. 48.3; nsm.wk. torhta 40.9; asm. torhtne 46.2, 51.2; ipf.wk. torhtan 54.9. *See* hlēor-, wlite-torht.
torhte, adv. *clearly, brightly*: 5.8, 57.7.
tōsǣlan, v.I. (impers. w. dat. of person and gen. of thing): 1. *fail, be unsuccessful*: 3s. tōsǣleð 14.5. —2. *lack, be wanting*: 3s. tōsǣleþ 13.25.
tōsomne, adv. *together*: 1.69. *See* ætsomne.
tōð, m. *tooth*: as. 56.8; is. tōþe 83.5; ip. tōþum 19.14; gp. tōþa 32.2.
tōþringan, v.3. *drive apart, scatter*: 1s. tōþringe 1.67.

tredan, v.5. *tread (upon), trample*: inf. 11.1,11; 1s. trede 5.1; 3s. trideþ 80.30, triedeð 10.6; 3p. tredað 55.5; PRET. 1s. træd 70.12.

trēow, n. *tree*: ns. 51.2, 54.9. *See* **wudutrēow, wulfhēafedtrēo.**

ge-**trēowe,** adj. *faithful*: gpm. ge-trēowa 24.23.

tunge, f. *tongue*: ns. 76.9 (= *mouthpiece*); as. tungan 56.8; ds. tungan 46.2.

turf, f. *turf, soil*: as. 11.1; ds. tyrf 38.25.

twēgen, num. *two*: nm. 40.10, 44.2,3; nn. tū 13.4, 61.5; nf. twā 40.17, 44.2; am. twēgen 50.2, 82.4 [MS. ii]; an. tū 34.7; af. twā 40.1, 77.5, 82.3,5,7, tuā 67.3; dm. twām 48.2, 58.15 [MS. twan], 84.15; dn. twām 44.1; gn. twēga 37.11; gf. twēga 40.9.

twelf, num. *twelve*: 34.7, 82.4 [MS. xii].

tȳdran, v.I. *increase, be prolific*: 3s. tȳdreð 80.38.

tȳhð, *see* **tēon.**

tȳnan, *see* **be-, on-tȳnan.**

tȳr, m. *honor, glory*: as. 24.23.

tyrf, *see* **turf.**

þ

þā, A. adv. *then*: 7.2,3, 8.9, 20.8, 10, 27.7,9, 38.35, 69.2. —**B. conj.** *when*: 8.6, 38.7, 45.2, 57.17, 61.15.

þæh, *see* **þēon.**

þǣr, A. adv. *there*: 1.54,58,63, 13.9, 21.11, 28a.8, 29.14, 34.10, 37.7, 40.8, 44.4, 53.9, 54.9, 58.4, 91.9. —**B. conj. 1.** *where*: 1.35, 12.12, 13.8, 18.12, 22.7, 24.4, 28b.6, 52.1, 53.1, 54.11, 61.3,5, 65.14, 71.1,

82.1, 84.1,9, 89.26. —**2.** *when*: 35.4, 77.7. —**3.** *if*: 2.11. —**C.** adv. and conj. þǣr þǣr, *there where*: 54.1, þār þār 1.64 [MS. þara þe], 26.9 [MS. þara þe].

þæs, adv. *so, to such an extent*: 1.1 (twice).

þæt, conj. **1.** *that* (in substantive clauses): 2.4, 3.5, 9.6, 18.18,26, 23.7, 25.11, 31.12, 37.1,14, 45.3, 58.8, 71.23, 80.43. —**2.** *that, so that* (in result and purpose clauses): 1.2,45,53,61, 20.19, 21.5,13, 28a.6, 38.9,16,35,91,103,108, 58.14, 71.6, 80.42.

þār, *see* **þǣr.**

þe, A. ind. particle serving as relative pronoun, *who, which, that,* etc.: 1.15,30,46, 6.9 [MS. þa], 10.14 (compound rel. þe ic = *I who*), 18.4,21,23, 25.16, 38.49,[61],77,78, [106], 40.13, 41.16, 47.9, 63.6, 68.1, 70.4, 71.4. —**B. conj.** (in þȳ . . . þe correlative w. comp. adj., *the more . . . in that*) *in that, because*: 45.6, 84.11. For forms of the **se þe** and **se' þe** relatives, see under **sē,** category 5.

þēah, 1. adv. *though, however*: 4.8. —**2.** conj. *though, although*: 11.6, 16.2, 38.47,65, 46.2, 76.6, 89.19, 91.10. —**3. þēah þe,** conj. *though, although*: 38.27, 80.34,51. *See* **sē-þēah; swā þēah** *under* **swā.**

þēana, *see* **sē þēana; swā þēana** *under* **swā.**

þearle, adv. *abundantly*: 70.9.

þēaw, m. *custom, habit, behavior*: gs. þēawes 9.8.

þeccan, v.I. *cover*: inf. 7.4 [MS. weccan]; 3s. þeceð 12.1, 77.9; PRET. 3s. þeahte 43.4, 74.1; SUBJ. pres. 3s. þecce 1.14; pp. þeaht 8.4, 14.3. *See* **biþeccan.**

þecen, f. *covering,* ?*garment*: as.
þecene 43.2; is. þecene 80.40.
þegn, m. *servant, attendant, man*: ns.
35.2, 47.4, 52.7, 83.2; ds. þegne
2.1,9.
þegnian, v.II. *serve* (w. dat.): 3s.
þēnaþ 19.14, 41.5; 3p. þegniað 48.6.
ge-þencan, v.I. *reflect, consider*: ger.
geþencanne 39.8. See beþencan.
þenden, conj. *while*: 10.2, 65.12, 81.6.
þēnian, see þegnian.
þēo, see þēoh.
þēod, f. *people, nation*: ds. þēode
71.13; gp. þēoda 39.8. See wer-
þēod.
þēodcyning, m. *people's king, God*: gs.
þēodcyninges 65.1.
þēoden, m. *chief, lord, master*: ds.
þēodne 18.26, 56.14, 59.4; gs.
þēodnes 43.5.
þēof, m. *thief*: ns. 45.4; gs. þēofes
71.23.
þēoh, n. *thigh*: ds. þēo 42.1.
þēon, v.1,3CT. *grow up, flourish,
prosper*: PRET. 1s. þǣh 70.9. See
onþēon.
ge-þēon, v.I. *see* ge-þȳwan.
þēotan, v.2. *murmur, resound*: inf.
36.4.
þēow, m. *servant*: ns. 1.97.
þēowian, v.II. *serve* (w. dat.): 1s.
þēowige 10.15; 3s. þēowað 48.6.
þēs (þes), þis, þēos, dem. adj. and
pron. *this*: nsm. þēs, (or weakly
stressed) þes, 29.1, 30.1, 38.42 [MS.
þæs],43,48,51,76,83, 64.1,4 [MS.
þas]; nsn. þis 33.14, 38.31,49, 90.6;
nsf. þēos 5.4, 55.1; asm. þisne 37.19,
38.7,12,15,22; asn. þis 38.78; asf. þās
37.17,26, 38.1,2; dsn. þissum 38.79;
gsn. þisses 53.14; apn. þās 38.5;
dpm. þissum 7.1.
þicce, adj. *thick*: apn. 38.36.

þicgan, v.5. *take, partake of, receive*:
inf. 87.10; 3s. þigeð 29.14; ?þygan
85.9.
þindan, v.3. *swell (up)*: inf. 43.2.
þing, n. 1. *thing*: ns. 37.24; as. 29.3,
43.5; ap. 38.39; ip. (adv?) þingum
58.14 *(for this purpose)*; gp. þinga
38.36. —2. *meeting, council*: ds.
þinge 65.1.
þolian, v.II. 1. *suffer, endure*: 1s.
þolige 89.23; 3s. þolað 14.8.
—2. *lack, do without* (w. gen.): inf.
18.26.
þon, see sē.
þonan, adv. *thence*: 24.3, 27.10, 71.27.
þonc, m. *thanks, gratitude*: as. 18.26
(on ~ , *in gratitude, willingly, gladly*);
ds. þonce 2.9 (on ~ , *according to the
pleasure, pleasing, acceptable*). See
hyge-, or-, searo-þonc, ingeþonc.
þoncian, v.II. *thank* (w. dat. of per-
son): PRET. 3s. þoncade 85.9.
þoncol, adj. *thoughtful, wise*: nsm.
1.27. See searoþoncol.
þonne, A. adv. *then*: 1.32,93, 5.5,
18.6, 26.11. —B. conj. 1. *when*:
1.3,8,23,29,57,71,81,90,103,104,
4.5,9, 5.1,8, 6.6, 12.14, 14.2, 21.3,
28a.7, 28b.7, 29.21, 35.5, 37.4 (or
as meaning #2?), 38.19,55, 41.12,
42.4, 61.2,?8, 69.7, 71.19, 87.4,9,
89.32. —2. *than* (w. comp.): 14.5,
21.7, 38.24,26,28,31,42,48,51,54,
59,60,66,74,76,83,92,94,96,105,
52.9 [MS. þon], 64.1,2 (twice),3,
80.19 [MS. þon], 81.3, 90.2,3,5,
6a,6b [MS. þon].
ge-þræc, n. *press, tumult, crash*: ns.
20.7; as. 1.17,91; ap. geþræcu 33.6.
þrǣd, m. *thread*: ns. 33.6.
þrǣgan, v.I. *run*: inf. 17.3.
þrafian, v.II. *restrain, constrain*: 3s.
þrafað 1.34.

þrāg, f. *time, space of time, period*: as. þrāge 85.11; dp. adv. þrāgum, *sometimes, at times*: 1.4,97, 52.7, 81.4.

þrāgbysig, adj. *periodically busy? continually busy?* nsm. 2.1.

þrēat, m. *crowd, multitude*: gp. þrēata 33.6. See **ēoredþrēat**.

þreohtig, adj. *enduring*: comp. nsm. þreohtigra 81.4.

þrimm, see **þrymm**.

þrindan, see **þrintan**.

ge-þring, n. *press, tumult*: ns. 1.57.

þringan, v.3. *press on, force a way*: inf. 1.91. See **ā-, oð-, tō-þringan**.

ge-þringan, v.3. *swell*: pp. asf. geþrungne 83.2.

þrintan, v.3. *swell*: prp. asn. þrindende 43.5. See **āþrintan**.

þrīst, adj. *bold, audacious*: gp. þrīstra 71.23 [MS. þrista].

þrīþ, see **þrȳþ**.

þrōwian, v.II. *suffer, endure*: PRET. 1s. þrōwade 70.14.

þrȳ, num. *three*: 38.52, 56.14.

þrymfæst, adj. *mighty, glorious*: asm. þrymfæstne 45.4.

þrymful, adj. *glorious, mighty*: nsm. 1.4,97.

þrymm, m. *might, power*: is. þrymme 38.91, þrimme 1.91; gp. þrymma 1.34.

þrȳþ, f. *might, power*: ip. adv. *greatly*: þrȳþum 83.2, þrīþum 35.2; gp. þrȳþa 62.4. See **hildeþrȳþ**.

þū, pron. *you*: ns. 30.13, 34.12 (twice), 37.28, 38.59; ds. þē 58.14.

þunian, v.II. 1. *stand out, stick up, be prominent*: inf. 43.2. —2. *resound, thunder*: 1s. þunie 1.4. See **onþunian**.

ge-þuren, see ge-þweran.

þurfan, v.PP. *need, have reason to*: 1s. þearf 13.22, 18.17.

þurh, prep. w. acc. 1. *through* (place): 1.85, 13.18,21,27, 15.11, 19.11, 29.20 (or as meaning #3?), 35.4, 67.2, 70.9. —2. *through, during* (time): 18.7, 56.4. —3. *through, by means of, because of* (condition, cause, agency): 1.91, 3.14, 6.1, 13.28, 33.4,6 (or as meaning #1?), 38.45 (or as meaning #1?), 40.6, 47.3, 51.9, 75.8, 80.11.

þurhræsan, v.I. *rush through*: 1s. þurhrǣse 1.66.

þurst, m. *thirst*: ns. 41.3.

ge-þwǣre, adj. *gentle, peaceable, obedient*: nsm. 48.6 (or adv?), npf. 1.30.

ge-þweran, v.4. *beat, ?forge*: pp. geþuren 87.1.

þȳ, conj. *as, because*: 7.12.

þygan, see **þicgan**.

þyncan, v.I. *seem, appear* (impers. w. dat.): 3s. þynceð 1.40, þinceð 29.18; PRET. 3s. þūhte 45.1, 83.3.

þynne, adj. *thin*: apn. 38.36.

þȳrel (þyrel), n. *hole, aperture*: ns. 42.2 (or adj. þȳrel, *pierced?*); as. 70.9, 87.5. See **dūnþȳrel**.

þyrelwomb, adj. *with pierced belly*: asm. þyrelwombne 77.11.

þyrran, v.I. *dry*: pp. þyrred 26.4.

þyrs, m. *giant*: ds. þyrse 38.63 [MS. þyrre].

þȳstru, f. *darkness*: ds. þȳstro 45.4 (*ignorance?*); dp. þȳstrum 1.34.

þȳwan, v.I. *urge, press*: inf. 1.48 [MS. þyran]; 3s. þȳð 10.8, 19.5, 60.5, 61.6.

ge-þȳwan/ge-þēon, v.I. 1. *press, afflict, impress*: PRET. 3p. geþȳdan 58.14. —2. *oppress, subdue*: inf. geþēon 38.91.

U

ufan, adv. **1.** *from above, down*: 1.47,85,99, 89.26. —**2.** *above*: 8.4, ufon 34.6.

ufemest, adj. (supl. of *uferra*). *highest*: nsf. 38.88 [MS. ufor].

ūhta, m. *early morning, (just before) dawn*: gp. ūhtna 58.6.

Ulcanus, m. *Vulcan*: gs. Ulcanus 38.56.

unbindan, v.3. *unbind, loosen*: pp. unbunden 21.15.

uncer, poss. pron. *our* (of two): npm. uncre 84.15; apm. uncre 58.17.

undearnunga, adv. *openly*: 40.2. *See* **undyrne.**

under, A. prep. *under, beneath*: **1.** w. dat. (at rest): 1.98, 7.7, 20.15, 34.3, 38.33,40,86, 40.4, 42.2, 52.11, 70.13, 80.31. —**2.** w.acc. (of motion): 1.17,32,94, 20.10,17 [MS. on der], 25.5, 47.6, 49.5, 50.2, 52.4, 60.3, ?71.24, 72.4, 87.8. —**B. adv.** *beneath, below*: 19.11.

underflōwan, v.7. *flow beneath, go under*: pp. underflōwen 8.2.

underhnīgan, v.1. *descend beneath*: inf. 1.99; 1s. underhnīge 64.6.

undyrne, adj. *not secret, revealed, known*: nsn. 40.15. *See* **undearnunga.**

unforcūð, adj. *not ignoble, honorable, reputable*: nsm. 60.2.

ungefullod, adj. *unfulfilled*: dsf. ungefullodre 57.13 [MS. ungaful lodre].

ungesibb, adj. *unrelated*: dsm. ungesibbum 7.8.

ungōd, n. *evil*: as. 18.35.

unlæt, adj. *unwearied, quick*: nsm. 51.11.

unlȳtel, adj. *not little, large, great*: nsm. 38.75; asn. 79.11.

unrǣd, m. *folly, mischief, crime*: gs. unrǣdes 9.10, 25.12.

unrǣdsīþ, m. *foolish enterprise*: gs. unrǣdsīþas 9.4.

unrīm, adj. *innumerable*: apn. unrīmu 4.3.

unrīm, n. *countless number*: as. 41.8.

unsceaft, f. *monster* (lit. *uncreation*): np. unsceafta 84.29.

unsoden, adj. *uncooked*: asf. unsodene 74.8.

unstille, adv. *not still, restlessly*: 49.5.

unwita, m. *ignorant person, fool*: ns. 47.11.

up, adv. *up, above*: 1.42,100, 20.19, 52.4, 53.5, 59.2, 89.10, upp 8.9.

upcyme, m. *up-springing, ?growth*: as. 28a.9, 28b.9.

upirnan, v.3. *rise up, soar*: prp. dsm.wk. upirnendan 38.56.

uplēodan, v.2. *grow up*: pp. uploden 31.11 [MS. upliden].

uplong, adj. *upright, erect*: nsm. 84.9.

upp, *see* **up.**

upweard, adj. *turned upwards*: asm. upweardne 59.6.

ūser, poss. pron. *our*: nsm. 38.89.

ūt, adv. *out, forth*: 60.6, 89.18.

ūtan, adv. *outside, from outside*: 38.5,15,47,53, 71.13, 80.40.

ūte, adv. *outside, abroad*: 40.2; comp. ūttor 38.84.

W

wā, interj. *woe!* (w. dat. of person and gen. of thing): 9.8.

wacan, v.6. *be born, spring*: PRET. 1s. wōc 18.21.

wadan, v.6. *go, proceed*: 1s. wade 60.3; PRET. 3s. wōd 20.15, ?89.7. *See* **bewadan.**

wǣcan, v.I. *weaken*: pp. wǣced 26.5.

wæccan, v.I. *watch, wake*: prp. asf. wæccende 38.8.

wæd, n. *water, sea*: ap. wado 5.2.

wǣd, f. *garment, dress*: dp. wǣdum 40.4, wēdum 7.4.

ge-wǣde, n. *garment*: ns. 33.14 [MS. ge wædu]; as. 33.12.

wæg, see **weg.**

wǣg, m. *wave*: ns. 1.50; ds. wǣge 1.23, 8.10, 14.1, 20.21, wēge 31.1, 66.3.

wǣg, see **wāg.**

wǣgan, v.I. *torment, afflict*: 3s. wēgeð 77.7.

wǣgfæt, n. *water-vessel, cloud*: ap. wǣgfatu 1.67.

wægn, m. *wagon, wain*: ns. 20.12; as. 20.9; ds. wægne 19.8.

wǣgstæþ, n. *shore, bank*: ds. wǣgstæþe 20.2.

wælcræft, m. *deadly power*: is. wælcræfte 87.11.

wælcwealm, m. *violent death, slaughter*: ns. 1.8.

wælgim, m. *slaughter-gem, death-gem*: as. 18.4.

wælgrim, adj. *slaughter-fierce, bloodthirsty*: nsm. 13.8.

wælhwelp, m. *slaughter-whelp, murderous dog*: gs. wælhwelpes 13.23.

wǣpen, n. *weapon*: ns. 1.88, 12.1; as. 53.12; dp. wǣpnum 18.17; ip. wǣpnum 1.82. See **beadu-, comp-, hilde-wǣpen.**

wǣpnedcynn, n. *male kind, male sex*: gs. wǣpnedcynnes 36.1.

wæstm, m.n. **1.** *growth, plant, fruit*: ns. 88.2; ip. wæstmum 80.38. —**2.** *shape, form*: as. wæstum 29.5.

wǣt, adj. *wet, moist*: nsm.wk. wǣta 33.1; nsn. wǣt 23.11.

wǣta, m. *moisture, liquid*: as. wǣtan 1.78; ds. 56.10.

wǣtan, v.I. *wet, moisten*: 3s. wǣteð 10.10; PRET. 3s. wǣtte 24.2.

wæter, n. *water*: ns. 51.3, 66.3; ds. wætre 8.1, 10.10, 24.3; is. wætre 89.25; gs. wætres 20.12.

wǣþan, v.I. *wander about, hunt*: 3s. wǣþeð 32.5.

wǣweð, see **wāwan.**

wāfian, v.II. *wonder, be amazed*: 3p. wāfiað 80.42.

wāg, m. *wall*: ds. wāge 12.12, wǣge 11.4.

wagian, v.II. *move, shake, totter*: 3p. wagiað 1.38; PRET. 3p. wagedan 52.6.

waldend, m. *master, possessor, ruler, Lord*: ns. 4.1, 18.4, 21.6, 38.89; gs. waldendes 38.14.

waldende, adj. *ruling, powerful*: comp. nsf. waldendre 38.87.

Wāle, f. *Welshwoman, female servant*: ns. 10.8, 50.6.

wamb, see **womb.**

wancian, v.II. *waver? stagger? reel?* PRET. 3s. wancode 83.7.

wanian, see **wonian.**

wār, n. *seaweed*: ds. wāre 1.23.

warian, v.II. *hold, possess, guard*: 3s. warað 29.21, 79.4, 89.28.

wāroð, n. *seaweed*: ns. 38.49.

wāþ, f. *wandering, journey*: as. wāþe 1.11.

wāwan, v.7. *blow, flutter (in wind)*: 3s. wǣweð 38.81.

wēa, m. *woe, misery*: ns. wēo 54.5; gs. wēan 70.14.

ge-wealcan, v.7. *roll*: pp. gewealcen 1.19.

ge-weald, n. *power, dominion*: as. 25.14; ds. gewealde 1.46. See **on-wald.**

wealdan, v.7. *have power over, control, rule* (w. gen. or acc.): 3s. wealdeð

38.[2],5,22; PRET. 3s. wēold 50.6.
See **waldende**.

Wealh, m. *Welshman, slave, servant*:
ap. Wēalas 10.4.

weall, m. **1.** *natural wall, hill, cliff*: ns?
80.45; ds. wealle 1.50; gs. wealles
27.7 (or as meaning #2?). —**2.** *wall
(of a building)*: np. weallas 1.39; ap.
weallas 32.5. *See* **bord-, sǣ-weall**.

weard, m. *guardian, protector, lord*: ns.
19.4, 79.2; gs. weardes 11.7.

-weard, *see* **æftan-, æfter-, forð-,
hinde-, innan-, niþer-, up-weard**.

weardian, v.II. *hold, occupy, guard*:
inf. 84.22.

wearm, adj. *warm*: nsn. 2.7.

wearp, m. *warp*: as. 33.5.

weaxan, v.7. *wax, grow, increase*: inf.
43.1 [MS. weax], 52.10; 3s. weaxeð
38.26; 3p. weaxað 38.102; PRET. 1s.
wēox 84.1; prp. nsm. weaxende
51.3. *See* **āweaxan**.

ge-**weaxan**, v.7. *grow (up)*: PRET. 3s.
gewēox 76.7.

wecgan, v.I. *lift, move, shake*: 3s.
wegeð 10.8, 19.5; PRET. 3p. wege-
don 71.5.

wēd, *see* **wǣd**.

weder, n. *wind, storm*: is. wedre
28a.2.

wefan, v.5. *weave*: 3s. wifeð 80.33.
See **āwefan**.

ge-**wefan**, v.5. *weave*: pp. gewefen
38.85.

wefl, f. *woof, weft*: np. wefle 33.5.

weg, m. *way, course, road*: as. 13.21,
37.6, 60.3, 66.1, wæg 51.8; ds.
wege 34.1, 68.1; ap. wegas 1.46,
wægas 49.6. *See* **flōd-, forð-,
hwyrft-, on-, stīð-weg**.

wēg, *see* **wǣg**.

wegan, v.5. *carry, bring, move*: 1s.
wege 18.6; 3s. wigeð 30.11, 48.3,

69.6, 71.21; 3p. wegað 12.14; PRET.
3p. wǣgun 25.3; pp. wegen 19.8.

wegeð, wegedon, *see* **wecgan**.

wēgeð, *see* **wǣgan**.

wel, adv. *well, fully, very (much)*: 48.5.

wela, m. *wealth*: ds? welan 65.8. *See*
fōddurwela.

welhold, adj. *very faithful*: nsf. 7.4.

wella, m. *fountain*: ap. wellan 36.3.

wēn, f. *hope, expectation*: ns. 1.58.

wēnan, v.I. *believe, suppose, expect* (w.
gen., acc., or obj. clause): inf.
18.17; 1s. wēne 3.4; 3p. wēnaþ
1.16; PRET. 1s. wēnde 58.7.

wendan, v.I. **1.** *move (something),
turn (it) round or over* (trans.): PRET.
3s. wende 57.5; pp. wended 57.18.
—**2.** *go, proceed* (intr.): 3s. wendeð
71.28. *See* **onwendan**.

ge-**wendan**, v.I. *turn, ?escape*: inf.
84.30.

wēo, *see* **wēa**.

weorc, n. *work, toil, handiwork, deed*:
as. 70.14; gs. weorces 40.4, 52.10;
np. weorc 24.14. *See* **beadu-,
hond-weorc**.

weorpan, v.3. *throw, cast* (w. acc. or
dat.): 1s. weorpe 25.7 [MS. weor-
pere]; 3p. weorpaþ 1.21. *See* **ā-,
be-weorpan**.

weorð, adj. *valuable, worthy*: nsm.
25.1; comp. nsm. weorðra 84.11.

weorþan, v.3. **1.** *be, become* (as inde-
pendent verb): inf. 48.10; 1s.
weorþe 14.4; 3s. weorþeð 13.14; 3p.
weorþað 1.29, 3.13; PRET. 3s.
wearð 7.8, 37.18, 65.9, 66.3 (twice),
79.5; 3p. wurdon 71.3. —**2.** *be* (as
aux. w. past participle forming
passive or perfective): inf. 1.61; 3s.
weorþeð 18.20; PRET. 3s. wearð
51.5; SUBJ. pret. 3s. wurde 80.31.
See **forweorðan**.

ge-**weorþan,** v.3. *become*: inf. 38.43.
weorþian, v.II. *honor*: 3s. weorþað 18.10.
ge-**weorþian,** v.II. *honor, adorn*: pp. geweorþad 69.5, 80.25.
wēpan, v.7. *weep*: 3s. wēpeð 69.5; PRET. 1s. wēop 89.21.
wer, m. *man*: ns. wær 44.1; gs. weres 42.1, [88.3]; np. weras 12.3,12, 20.9,21, 28a.6, 28b.6, 80.42, 82.1; dp. werum 25.1, 29.4,14, 30.11, 39.9, 40.16; gp. wera 1.8,39, 24.18, 27.14, 32.1, 45.3, 79.3, 84.23.
wērig, adj. *tired, weary*: nsm. 3.3, 52.10. See **rād-, slǣp-wērig.**
wermōd, m. *wormwood, absinthe*: ns. 38.60.
werþēod, f. *people, nation*: as. werþēode 80.41.
wesan, see **bēon/wesan.**
west, adv. *west, westward*: 27.10.
wīc, n. *house, dwelling-place* (frequently plural w. singular meaning): as. 13.8; ap. 5.2; dp. wīcum 6.7, 47.4, 71.28.
wicg, n. *horse*: ns. wycg 12.5; ds. wicge 12.14, 76.8; np. wicg 20.21; ap. wicg 20.9; ip. wicgum 20.2.
wīcstede, m. *dwelling-place*: np. 1.39.
wīd, adj. *wide, broad*: asf. wīde 16.3.
wīde, adv. *far, widely, far and wide*: 1.11,67,101, 5.5, 8.10, 18.16, 24.16, 25.1, 33.11, 37.17, 38.99, 56.2, 64.7, 71.22, 79.10, 89.29, 91.3; comp. wīddor 7.10, 58.17, 70.11.
wīdeferh, adv. *always, forever*: 37.8,21.
wīdgiel, adj. **1.** *wide-spread, extensive*: comp. nsm. wīdgielra 38.51, wīdgelra 38.83. —**2.** *wandering*: dsm. wīdgalum 18.5.
wīdlāst, m. *wide road*: ns. 17.6.
wido, see **wudu.**

wīf, n. *woman, wife*: ns. 23.11, 48.5, wiif 34.5; ds. wīfe 18.32; gs. wīfes 34.12, 88.3; np. wīf 28a.6, 28b.6; dp. wīfum 23.1, 44.1.
wifel, m. *weevil, beetle*: as. 38.73.
wīg, n. *fight, battle, war*: as. 3.3, 13.23.
wiga, m. *warrior*: ns. 13.8, 48.1, 49.6, 71.28; gs. wigan 12.1 [MS. wiga], 89.22. See **folc-, gūð-wiga.**
wiht, f.n. **1.** *creature, being, person*: ns. 16.1, 18.1, 21.2, 22.1, 23.1, 26.13, 27.7, 29.4,19,24, 30.5,14, 31.1, 36.6, 37.1, 38.87, 39.9, 65.16, 67.1, 78.1, 80.1, 82.1, 85.2; as. 27.1, 32.1, 34.1, 36.1, 37.26, 54.2, 56.2, 65.2, 66.1, 83.1, wihte 35.1; ds. wihte 54.5; gs. wihte 27.14, 34.14; np. wihte 40.16; ap. wihte 55.1, wyhte 40.1, wuhte 49.1; gp. wihta 26.8, 37.14, 40.8, 80.4. —**2.** *anything* (or w. neg. *nothing*): as. 2.11, 29.14, 56.10, 63.1. See **nō-, ō-wiht.**
wiht, adv. *at all*: 13.23, 26.10 [MS. wið].
wihte, adv. *at all*: 45.6.
wilcuma, m. *welcome, that which is welcome*: gp. wilcumena 6.11.
wilgehlēþa, m. *familiar companion, comrade*: ap. wilgehlēþan 12.5.
willa, m. *will, wish, desire, pleasure*: ns. 76.1; as. willan 18.33, 27.10, 52.6, 71.7, ?willa[. 61.7; ip. willum 83.7 (adv.), 87.11, 89.2; gp. wilna 26.10.
willan, v.AN. *wish, will, desire*: 1s. wille 47.9; 3s. wile 33.11, 37.5, 41.10, 42.5, 74.4, 87.9; 3p. willað 14.7, 24.18; PRET. 3s. wolde 83.7, walde 27.5; SUBJ. pres. 3s. wille 41.14, 57.15. NEG. **nellan,** *wish not, will not*: 1s. nelle 21.15.
wilnian, v.II. *desire*: 3p. wilniað 47.7.

ge-**win**, n. *battle, strife*: as. 18.1, 21.2;
gs. gewinnes 14.4. *See* **gūð-,
strēam-gewinn.**

wīn, n. *wine*: ds. wīne 12.17, 40.16,
44.1.

wincel, m. *corner*: ds. wincle 43.1,
52.2 [MS. winc sele].

wind, m. *wind*: ns. 8.10, 38.68; ds.
winde 12.14, 14.1, 28a.1, 28b.1,
38.81.

windan, v.3. *twist, roll, curl*: pp.
wunden 26.5, 53.3, npm. wundne
38.104, npf. wundene 33.5. *See*
be-, ymb-windan.

ge-**windan**, v.3. *wind, twist*: pp. apm.
gewundne 38.99.

winnan, v.3. *strive, struggle, labor*:
inf. 14.1; 1s. winne 1.97, 4.7 *(fight,
make war)*; 3s. winneð 1.49; prp.
nsm. winnende 1.23,78, 49.6, asf.
winnende 54.2.

winterceald, adj. *wintry-cold*: nsm.
2.7.

wīr, m. *wire, ornamental wire*, (plural)
ornaments: ns. 18.4; is. wīre 24.14,
69.5; ip. wīrum 15.2, 18.32, 38.47.

wīrboga, m. *twisted ornamental wire*:
ip. wīrbogum 12.3.

wīs, adj. *wise, learned*: nsm. 30.14;
dsm. wīsum 29.24. *See* **medwīs.**

wīsdōm, m. *wisdom*: as. 91.9; ds.
wīsdōme 65.5.

wīse, f. **1.** *manner, custom, nature*: ns.
34.14, 76.11 (w. pun on meaning
#2?); as. wīsan 9.8, 18.11, 67.1
(w. pun on meaning #2?), 71.5,29,
80.7; ip. wīsum 29.2, 30.2.
—**2.** *melody, song*: as. wīsan 6.4.
—**3.** *stalk*: as. wīsan 63.4. *See*
scēawendwīse.

wīsfæst, adj. *wise, learned*: nsm.
33.14; dsm. wīsfæstum 26.13;
dpm. wīsfæstum 39.9; gpm.
wīsfæstra 65.16.

wīsian, v.II. *guide, direct* (w. dat. or
acc.): 3s. wīsað 1.43, 18.5, 19.2.

wist, f. *sustenance, food*: as. 30.11,
wiste 41.7; ip. wistum 80.22. *See*
midwist.

ge-**wit**, n. *mind, understanding*: as.
37.13.

wita, *see* **stī-, un-wita.**

witan, v.PP. *know*: 1s. wāt 9.5, 33.3,
41.1, 47.1, 56.1, 84.23; 2s. wāst
34.12; 1p. witan 34.13; 3p. witan
40.7; PRET. 3s. wisse 52.1; SUBJ.
pres. 1s. wite 2.11; 3p. witen 37.4.
See **bewitan.**

ge-**witan**, v.PP. *know*: PRET. 3s.
gewiste 27.14.

witan, v.1. *find fault, blame*: SUBJ.
pres. 3s. wīte 24.17.

ge-**wītan**, v.1. *go, depart*: 1s. gewīte
1.16,90, 14.2; 3s. gewīteð 37.6;
PRET. 3s. gewāt 27.10 (w. refl.
hyre),13, 89.10; 3p. gewitan 11.11.

wīte, n. *punishment, pain, woe*: as.
21.6.

witod, adj. *decreed, appointed, or-
dained*: nsm. 13.6,11, 81.7; nsn.
18.24; apf. witode 41.7.

wið, prep. *against, with, beside*: **1.** w.
dat. 1.50,71,72, 14.1 (twice),2,
18.27, 25.10, 30.4, 37.12, 58.14,
71.6, 84.14, 87.5. —**2.** w. acc. 14.9,
40.13.

wlanc, *see* **wlonc.**

wlītan, v.1. *look, gaze*: 3s. wlīteð
89.34.

wlite, m. *aspect, appearance, counte-
nance*: ns. 34.12, 80.25; as. 80.7.

wlitetorht, adj. *bright, brilliant*: gpf.
wlitetorhtra 69.3.

wlitig, adj. *beautiful*: nsm. 12.12,
?80.20; nsn. 15.10; apf.wk. wliti-
gan 32.7.

wlitigian, v.II. *beautify, adorn*: 3s.
wlitigað 80.38.

ge-**wlitigian**, v.II. *beautify, adorn*: pp.
gewlitegad 29.2, 30.2, 80.41.

wlonc, adj. *magnificent, proud, exul-
tant, spirited*: nsm. 12.1; nsf. wlanc
40.4; asm. wloncne 48.10; dsn.
wloncum 76.8; npm. wlonce 28a.6,
28b.6; apm. wlonce 12.17; dpm.
wloncum 15.10, 80.26; gpm.
wloncra 57.18. *See* **fela-, hyge-,
mōd-wlonc**.

wōh, adj. **1**. *curved, bent, twisted*:
nsm. 19.4, 67.2; npn. 37.24 *(devi-
ous? obscure?)*; ipm. wōum 12.3.
—**2**. *perverse, wrong, evil*: asf. wōn
9.8.

wolcen, m.n. *cloud*: gp. wolcna 5.5.
See **heofonwolcn**.

wolcenfaru, f. *drifting of clouds*: as.
wolcnfare 1.101.

wolcengehnāst, f. *clash of clouds*: is.
wolcengehnāste 1.90.

wom, m.n. *insult, evil speech*: as.
18.33.

wom, adj. *evil, foul*: apn. 38.41.

womb, f. *womb, belly*: ns. 35.1; as.
wombe 16.3, 82.5, 83.1, 85.2,
wambe 60.3; ds. wombe 1.78, 34.3,
84.30, 89.30. *See* **þyrelwomb**.

wombhord, n. *womb-hoard, contents
of belly*: ns. 15.10.

won, adj. *dark, dusky, lurid*: nsm.
38.107, wonn 84.19; nsm.wk.
wonna 47.4; nsf. wonn 1.50; apn.
won 1.67; dpf. wonnum 84.13; ipf.
wonnum 51.7.

wōn, *see* **wōh**.

wonfāh, adj. *dark-colored*: nsf. 50.6.

wonfeax, adj. *dark-haired*: nsf. 10.8.

wong, m. *plain, field, place, world*: ns.
33.1, 38.51,83; as. 62.1; ds. wonge
19.5, 29.14, 56.2, 71.1; np. wongas
64.5; ap. wongas 10.2, 79.10. *See*
sǣl-, stān-, staþol-wong.

wonian, v.II. *diminish, lessen, curtail*:
1s. wonie 18.33.

wonsceaft, f. *misfortune, misery*: as.
77.12, wonnsceaft 89.22.

word, n. *word, speech*: as. 16.1, 91.9;
ds. worde 38.14 *(command?)*; ap.
word 45.1, 57.5; dp. wordum 45.6,
58.10; ip. wordum 2.11, 18.34,
29.19, 33.14, 37.26,29, 38.73, 46.3,
53.16, 80.7,55; gp. worda 30.14. *See*
cyne-, hord-word.

wordcwide, m. *speech, words*: ap.
wordcwidas 58.17.

wordgaldor, n. *incantation, charm*:
gp. wordgaldra 65.2. *See* **gal-
dorcwide**.

wordlēan, n. *reward for words*: gp.
wordlēana 76.10.

wordlof, n. *praise in words*: gs.
wordlofes 18.11.

world/woruld, f. *world*: as. world
38.2, worulde 80.38. *See* **wundor-
woruld**.

worldbearn, n. *child of the world, man*:
gp. worldbearna 80.33.

worldlīf, n. *worldly life, secular life*:
ds. worldlīfe 38.87.

woruldstrengu, f. *world-strength,
physical strength*: gp. woruld-
strenga 24.2.

wōþ, f. *sound, voice, song*: is. wōþe
6.11. *See* **hēafodwōþ**.

wōðbora, m. *singer, speaker, poet*: ds.
wōðboran 29.24, 76.10.

wōðgiefu, f. *gift of song*: ns. 29.18.

wōum, *see* **wōh**.

wrǣc, f. *vengeance*: is. wrǣce 1.4.

wrǣd, f. *band, bond*: ap. wrǣde 1.43.

wrǣsnan, v.I. *vary, change, modulate*:
1s. wrǣsne 22.1.

wrǣst, adj. *delicate*: comp. nsf.
wrǣstre 38.26.

wrǣste, adv. *delicately*: 38.99.

wrǣtlīc, adj. *wondrous, rare, magnificent, elegant, artistic*: nsn. 29.18, 37.24, 42.1; nsf. 21.2, 67.1, wrǣtlīcu 31.1, 45.2; asn. wrǣtlīc 53.3; asf. wrǣtlīce 65.2; gsm.wk. wrǣtlīcan 57.16; npn. wrǣtlīc 24.14; apf. wrǣtlīce 40.1, 49.1.

wrǣtlīce, adv. *wonderfully, strangely, magnificently, artistically*: 34.2, 38.6,85,102,104, 66.2, 68.1.

wrǣtt, f. *ornament, jewel*: dp. adv. wrǣttum, *splendidly*: 29.2, 30.2.

wrāh, *see* wrēon.

wrāþ, adj. **1.** *hostile, terrible, cruel*: dpm. wrāþum 12.17 [MS. wraþ-þum]; gpm. wrāþra 38.41; gpn. wrāþra 69.3. —**2.** *bitter*: comp. nsf. wrāþre 38.60.

wrāðscræf, n. *foul den, pit of misery, hell*: ap. wrāðscrafu 38.41.

wrēah, *see* wrēon.

wrecan, v.5. **1.** *drive, press on*: 3s. wriceð 1.33; SUBJ. pret. 3s. wrǣce 1.2 (or SUBJ. pres. *wrǣce*?); pp. wrecen 1.11 [MS. wrecan], 19.11. —**2.** *avenge*: inf. 89.21; SUBJ. pres. 3s. wrǣce 18.18. *See* āwrecan.

wrecca, m. *exile, wanderer*: as. wreccan 27.10; gs. wreccan 37.8.

wrēgan, v.I. *rouse, excite*: inf. 1.47; 1s. wrēge 1.101.

ge-wrēgan, v.I. *stir up, excite*: pp. gewrēged 1.18.

wrenc, m. *modulation of the voice*: ip. wrencum 6.2.

wrēon, v.1,2CT. *cover*: 3s. wrīð 48.5; PRET. 3s. wrāh 7.5, 24.11, wrēah 1.12; 3p. wrugon 1.30, 74.2, 84.12. *See* be-, on-wrēon.

wreðstuþu, f. *support*: ip. wreð-stuþum 38.2.

wrigian, v.II. *strive, press forward*: 3s. wrigaþ 19.5.

ge-writ, n. *writing, book*: np. gewritu 37.1,13.

wrīð, *see* wrēon.

wriþa, m. *band, ring*: as. wriþan 57.5. *See* halswriþa.

wrīðan, v.1. *bind, fetter*: pp. wriþen 51.7.

wrixlan, v.I. *change (voice), exchange (words), speak* (w. dat.): inf. 58.10; 1s. wrixle 6.2.

?wrōhtstæpe, m. *crime-going? injurious charge?* ds? wrōhtstæp[. 71.15.

wrōtan, v.7. *root, dig up the soil*: prp. nsm. wrōtende 38.107.

wrugon, *see* wrēon.

wudu, m. **1.** *wood (material), thing of wood*: ns. 38.48, 54.5; as. wido 54.2; ds. wuda 8.5 (w. pun on meaning #4?), 84.19; is. wuda 89.25. —**2.** *tree*: ns. 51.3, 53.16. —**3.** *wood, forest*: as. 1.8, 77.7. —**4.** *ship*: ns. 1.54. *See* bōcwudu.

wudubēam, m. *forest tree*: gp. wudubēama 84.13.

wudutrēow, n. *forest tree*: as. 53.3.

wuhte, *see* wiht.

wuldor, n. *glory*: ns. 80.33; is. wuldre 28a.2; gs. wuldres 64.7.

wuldorcyning, m. *king of glory, God*: gs. wuldorcyninges 37.21 [MS. wuldor cyninge].

wuldorgesteald, n.p. *glorious possessions, splendid treasures*: np. 24.16.

wuldorgimm, m. *glorious gem*: ns. 80.26.

wuldornyttung, f. *(things of) noble use, glorious service*: ip. wuldornyttingum 80.25.

wulf, m. *wolf*: gs. wulfes 89.29.

wulfhēafedtrēo, n. *wolfshead-tree, gallows, cross*: as. 53.12.

wull, f. *wool*: gs. wulle 33.3.

wund, f. *wound*: ds. wunde 89.21;

np. wunda 57.16; ap. wunda 51.7,
wunde 3.12; gp. wunda 79.10.
wund, adj. *wounded*: nsm. 3.1; nsn.
87.2.
wundenlocc, adj. *curly-haired*: nsn.
23.11.
wundian, v.II. *wound*: SUBJ. pres.
3p. wundigen 80.52.
wundor, n. *wonder, miracle*: ns. 65.5,
66.3; as. 45.2; gs. wundres 58.10;
dp./ip. adv. wundrum, *wonder-
fully*: 33.1, 34.2, 48.1, 66.2,
80.1,22,41; gp. wundra 19.8, 80.35.
wundorcræft, m. *wondrous skill*: is.
wundorcræfte 38.85.
wundorlīc, adj. *wonderful, remarkable,
strange*: nsm. 84.19; nsf. wunder-
līcu 16.1, 18.1, 22.1, 23.1, wundor-
līcu 27.7; asf. wundorlīce 27.1,
83.1; comp. asm. wundorlīcran
29.5.
wundorworuld, f. *wonderful world*:
as. 37.17.
wunian, v.II. *dwell, remain, continue*:
inf. 38.8; 1s. wunige 81.6; 3s.
wunað 29.16; PRET. 1s. wunode
71.1 [MS. wonode].
ge-**wunian,** v.II. *dwell, remain*: PRET.
1s. gewunade 58.2.
wyltan, v.I. *turn, roll*: pp. wylted
57.18.
wyn, f. *joy, delight*: ns. 24.7; ds.
wynne 51.2; ip. wynnum 38.107
(adv?). See **mōdwynn.**
wynlic, adj. *pleasant, beautiful*: nsf.
38.26, wynlīcu 29.18.
wynnstaþol, m. *place of joy*: ns. 88.3
[MS. wym staþol].
wynsum, adj. *pleasant, delightful*:
nsm. 80.26, ?80.20.
wyrcan, v.I. **1.** *work, perform, carry
out*: inf. 71.12; 3s. wyrceð 61.7;
PRET. 3s. worhte 52.6, 85.7.

—**2.** *make, construct, create*: inf.
13.18; 3s. wyrceð 35.8; PRET. 3s.
worhte 38.6,89. See **bewyrcan.**
ge-**wyrcan,** v.I. *make, create*: pp.
geworht 67.3.
wyrd, f. *fate, chance, happening*: ns.
45.2 (w. pun on *gewyrd*, n., *speech,
conversation, collection of words, sen-
tence?*); gp. wyrda 33.9, 37.24 (w.
pun on *gewyrd* as noted above?).
wyrdan, v.I. *injure, harm*: 3p. wyrdaþ
84.30.
wyrm, m. *worm, creeping insect*: ns.
38.76, 45.3; np. wyrmas 33.9. See
hond-, regn-wyrm.
wyrman, v.I. *warm*: 3s. wyrmeð
10.10.
wyrnan, v.I. *refuse* (w. dat. of person
and gen. of thing): 3s. wyrneð
18.11,29.
wyrs, adv. (comp. of *yfle*). *worse*:
11.5.
wyrslīc, adj. *mean, vile*: comp. nsf.
wyrslīcre 38.48.
wyrt, f. **1.** *vegetable, plant, herb*: ap.
wyrte 32.5; dp. wyrtum 3.12; gp.
wyrta 69.3. —**2.** *root*: ip. wyrtum
32.7.

Y

ȳcan, v.I. *increase*: inf. 28a.9, 28b.9;
3p. ȳcað 24.24.
yfle, adv. *evilly, badly, ill*: 38.32, 41.9,
79.8.
yldo, f. *old age*: ns. 41.4.
yldra, see **eald.**
ymb, prep. w. acc. **1.** *about, around,
near*: 18.4, 38.5, ?81.2. —**2.** *about,
concerning*: 21.11, 31.8, 37.26, 41.16
(w. ind. *þe*).
ymbclyppan, v.I. *embrace*: inf. 38.53;
1s. ymbclyppe 38.15.

ymbhwyrft, m. *earth, world*: ns.
38.42; as. 38.7,15.

ymbwindan, v.3. *entwine, embrace*:
1s. ymbwinde 38.84.

yrnan, v.3. *run, hasten, flow*: inf. 1.64
[MS. hyran]. *See* rinnan, upirnan.

ȳst, f. *storm, tempest*: as. 51.10 (on ~,
violently).

ȳð, f. *wave*: ns. 58.6; as. ȳðe 49.5,
72.4; np. ȳþa 1.30, 74.2; ap. ȳþa
1.47,98; ip. ȳþum 8.4, 14.3, 75.8;
gp. ȳþa 1.17,63, 20.7.

ȳþan, v.I. *destroy*: inf. 69.7.

ȳwan, v.I. *show, reveal*: SUBJ. pres.
3s. ȳwe 53.15.

ge-ȳwan, v.I. *show, reveal*: pp.
geȳwed 1.64.

Z

zefferus, m. *Zephyrus, west wind*: ns.
38.68.

Runes

Both textual and marginalic runes are listed here in order of their appearance in the *Riddle* portions of the manuscript. References to textual runes are in regular type; references to marginalic runes, in italics. For each rune, the Old English name is given; presumably for textual runes the name was read for the rune in the riddlic line. The Old English letter equivalent for each rune is also given (these are sometimes debated, however, and the reader should see the notes to the individual runes). Runes are used in different ways in different riddlic contexts, and the reader should consult the appropriate headnote and line notes in each case. For the marginalic rune references below, the following abbreviations are used: *l.m.* = *lower margin; u.m.* = *upper margin; r.m.* = *right margin.*

Rune	**O.E. Name**	**Letter Equivalent**	**Riddle and Line Number**
ᛋ	Sigel	S	*3.l.m., 4.l.m.*, 17.1, 62.6.
ᛇ	Ēoh (Īh)	E? I?	?*10.15.r.m.*
ᛚ	Lagu	L	*15.u.m.*, 73.2.
ᛒ	Beorc	B	*15.u.m., 62.r.m.*, 62.2.
ᚱ	Rād	R	17.1, 22.8, *62.r.m.*
ᚩ	Ōs	O	17.1,5,7,8, 22.8.
ᚻ	Hægl	H	17.2,8, 22.9, 62.3, 73.2.
ᚾ	Nȳd	N	17.5, *62.r.m.*, 73.2.
ᛗ	Mon	M	17.5.
ᚪ	Āc	A	17.6,8, 62.3.
ᚷ	Gifu	G	17.6, 22.7 [MS. x].
ᛖ	E(o)h	E	17.6, 62.2,4.
ᚹ	Wyn	W	17.6, 62.1, 87.7.
ᚳ	Cēn	C	17.7.
ᚠ	Feoh	F	17.8, 62.5.
ᚫ	Æsc	Æ	22.8, 62.5.
ᛁ	Īs	I	22.9, 62.1.
ᚢ	Ūr	U	*62.r.m.*
ᚦ	Þorn	Þ	*62.r.m.*, 62.4.
ᛠ	ĒAr	EA	62.5.
ᛈ	Peorð	P	62.6.
ᛞ	Dæg	D	73.2.

Bibliography

T he items in this bibliography are listed alphabetically by author or editor, and in rare cases where there is neither author nor editor, by title. When a modern author has a number of titles to his credit, these are listed chronologically under the author's name after the modern practice. When a classical or medieval writer has several titles to his credit, these are listed alphabetically by title under the author's name. In all cases an author's edited work(s) follows his own work. Some of the articles that appeared in 1975 or early 1976 received limited treatment in the Notes and Commentary because of the exigencies of publication.

Adams, John F. "'Wulf and Eadwacer': An Interpretation." *MLN* lxxiii (1958): 1–5.
_____. "The Anglo-Saxon Riddle as Lyric Mode." *Crit.* vii (1965): 335–48.
Aelfric. *Aelfric's Colloquy.* 2d ed. Edited by G. N. Garmonsway. London, 1947.
_____. *Aelfric's De Temporibus Anni.* Edited by Heinrich Henel. EETS, o.s. 213. London, 1942.
_____. *Aelfric's Lives of the Saints.* Edited by Rev. Walter W. Skeat. EETS, o.s. 76, 82. London, 1881–85.
_____. *Homilies of Aelfric.* Edited by John C. Pope. EETS, o.s. 259–60. London, 1967–68.
_____. *The Old English Version of the Heptateuch, Aelfric's Treatise on the Old and New Testament, and His Preface to Genesis.* Edited by S. J. Crawford. EETS, o.s. 160. London, 1922.
Aldhelm. *Aldhelmi Opera.* Edited by R. Ehwald. Berlin, 1919.
_____. *The Riddles of Aldhelm.* Edited by James Hall Pitman. New Haven, 1925. Reprint. Hamden, 1970.
_____. *Sancti Aldhelmi Opera.* Edited by J. A. Giles. Oxford, 1844.
Alfred. *King Alfred's Old English Version of Boethius' De Consolatione Philosophiae.* Edited by W. J. Sedgefield. Oxford, 1899.
_____. *King Alfred's West-Saxon Version of Gregory's Pastoral Care.* Edited by Henry Sweet. EETS, o.s. 45, 50. London, 1871–72.

Bibliography

Ambrose. *Hexaemeron. PL.* xiv, 133–288 [for the series, *see* Migne].
Anderson, George K. *The Literature of the Anglo-Saxons.* Princeton, 1949.
———. "Aldhelm and the *Leiden Riddle*." In *Old English Poetry: Fifteen Essays,* edited by Robert P. Creed, pp. 167–76. Providence, 1967.
André, Jacques. *Les Noms d'Oiseaux en Latin.* Paris, 1967.
Andrew, S. O. *Syntax and Style in Old English.* Cambridge, 1940.
Assmann, Bruno, ed. *Bibliothek der angelsächsischen Poesie.* Vol. 3. Leipzig, 1898 [for the series, *see* Wülker].
Barlow, Frank; Dexter, Kathleen M.; Erskine, Audrey M.; and Lloyd, L. J. *Leofric of Exeter.* Exeter, 1972.
Barnouw, A. J. *Textkritische Untersuchungen nach dem Gebrauch des bestimmten Artikels und des schwachen Adjectivs in der altenglischen Poesie.* Leiden, 1902.
———. Review of *Die altenglischen Rätsel (die Rätsel des Exeterbuchs)* by Moritz Trautmann. *Neoph.* iii (1917): 77–78.
Bately, J. M. "Interpretation of the Runes on the Gilton Pommel." *Archaeologia* ci (1967): 99–102.
Baum, Paull F., tr. *Anglo-Saxon Riddles of the Exeter Book.* Durham, N.C., 1963.
Bede. *Bede's Ecclesiastical History of the English People [Historia Ecclesiastica Gentis Anglorum].* Edited by Bertram Colgrave and R. A. B. Mynors. Oxford, 1969.
———. *De Natura Rerum. PL.* xc, 187–278 [for the series, *see* Migne].
Bern Riddles [Aenigmata 'Tullii' seu 'Bernensia']. Edited by Fr. Glorie. *CCL.* cxxxiii A, pp. 547–610. Turnhout, 1968.
Blackburn, F. A. "The Husband's Message and the Accompanying Riddles of the Exeter Book." *JEGP* iii (1900): 1–13.
Blair, Peter Hunter. *An Introduction to Anglo-Saxon England.* Cambridge, 1956.
Blakeley, L. "Riddles 22 and 58 of the Exeter Book." *RES,* n.s. ix (1958): 241–52.
Bliss, A. J. *The Metre of Beowulf.* Oxford, 1958.
———. "Single Half-lines in Old English Poetry." *NQ* ccxvi (1971): 442–49.
Bloomfield, Leonard. "Old English Plural Subjunctives in -E." *JEGP* xxix (1930): 100–113.
Bloomfield, Morton. "Understanding Old English Poetry." *Annuale Mediaevele* ix (1968): 5–25.
Bosworth, Joseph, and Toller, T. Northcote. *An Anglo-Saxon Dictionary.* London, 1898. *Supplement* by T. Northcote Toller, 1921. With *Revised and Enlarged Addenda* by Alistair Campbell, 1972.
Bouet, G. "De l'Ancienneté des Coqs sur les Tours d'Églises." *Bulletin Monumental* xv (1849): 532–33.
Bouterwek, K. W. *Cædmon's des Angelsachsen biblische Dichtungen.* Vol. 1. Gütersloh, 1854.
Bowen, H. C. *Ancient Fields.* London, 1963.

Bradley, Henry. Review of *English Writers*, vol. 2, by Henry Morley. *Academy* xxxiii (1888): 197–98.

———. "Two Riddles of the Exeter Book." *MLR* vi (1911): 433–40.

Brett, Cyril. "Notes on Old and Middle English." *MLR* xxii (1927): 257–64.

Bridge, T. W. "Cyclostomata." In *Fishes* (*Exclusive of the Systematic Account of Teleostei*), pp. 421–30. *Cambridge Natural History*, vol. 7. London, 1904.

British Museum. *Additional Manuscript 9067* [A transcript of the *Exeter Book*, made by Robert Chambers and collated with the MS. by Sir Frederick Madden]. 1831–32.

———. *A Guide to the Anglo-Saxon and Foreign Teutonic Antiquities in the Department of British and Mediaeval Antiquities*. London, 1923.

Brøgger, H. W., and Shetelig, Haakon. *The Viking Ships: Their Ancestry and Evolution*. Oslo, 1951.

Brooke, Stopford A. *The History of Early English Literature*. New York, 1892.

Brown, Carleton. "*Poculum Mortis* in Old English." *Spec.* xv (1940): 389–99.

Bruce-Mitford, R. L. S. "A New Wooden Ship's Figure-Head Found in the Scheldt, at Moerzeke-Mariekerke." *AA* xxxviii (1967): 199–209.

———. "Ships' Figure-heads in the Migration Period and Early Middle Ages." *Antiquity* xliv (1970): 146–48.

———. *The Sutton Hoo Ship-Burial: A Handbook*. 2d ed. London, 1972.

———. *Aspects of Anglo-Saxon Archaeology*. London, 1974 [containing a number of earlier articles, some of which are revised, along with previously unpublished materials].

———, and Bruce-Mitford, Myrtle. "The Sutton Hoo Lyre, *Beowulf*, and the Origins of the Frame Harp." *Antiquity* xliv (1970): 7–12.

Brunner, Karl. *Altenglische Grammatik nach der angelsächsischen Grammatik von Eduard Sievers*. 3d ed., rev. Tübingen, 1965.

Bülbring, Karl D. Review of *Die Räthsel des Exeterbuches und ihr Verfasser* by Georg Herzfeld. *Literaturblatt* xii (1891): 155–58.

Burke, Kenneth. "What Are the Signs of What?" *Anthropological Linguistics* iv, no. 6 (1962): 1–23.

Burrows, Roger. *Wild Fox*. Newton Abbot, 1968.

Caesar. *The Civil Wars* [*De Bello Civili*]. Edited by A. G. Peskett. Loeb Library Series. London and New York, 1914.

———. *The Gallic War* [*De Bello Gallico*]. Edited by H. J. Edwards. Loeb Library Series. London and New York, 1917.

Campbell, Alistair. *Old English Grammar*. Oxford, 1959.

———. *Revised and Enlarged Addenda* to Toller's *Supplement*. *See* Bosworth.

Campbell, Jackson J. "Learned Rhetoric in Old English Poetry." *MP* lxiii (1966): 189–201.

———. "A Certain Power." *Neoph.* lix (1975): 128–38.

Cassidy, Frederic G., and Ringler, Richard N., eds. *Bright's Old English Grammar and Reader*. 3d ed. New York, 1971.

Cassirer, Ernst. "Structuralism in Modern Linguistics." *Word* i (1945): 99–120.

Bibliography

Catholic Encyclopedia. See *New Catholic Encyclopedia.*

Chambers, Robert. *See* British Museum.

Cicero. *Tusculan Disputations [Tusculanae Disputationes].* Edited by J. E. King. Loeb Library Series. London and New York, 1927.

Clark Hall, John R. *A Concise Anglo-Saxon Dictionary.* 4th ed. With a supplement by Herbert D. Meritt. Cambridge, 1960.

Cleasby, Richard, and Vigfusson, Gudbrand. *An Icelandic-English Dictionary.* 2d ed. With Supplement by William A. Craigie. Oxford, 1957.

Cockayne, Rev. Oswald, ed. *Leechdoms, Wortcunning, and Starcraft of Early England.* 3 vols. London, 1864–66. Reprint. New York, 1965.

Colgrave, B. "Some Notes on Riddle 21." *MLR* xxxii (1937): 281–83.

————, and Griffiths, B. M. "A Suggested Solution of Riddle 61." *MLR* xxxi (1936): 545–47.

Collins, Douglas C. "Kenning in Anglo-Saxon Poetry." *Essays and Studies,* n.s. xii (1959): 1–17.

Conybeare, John J., ed. *Illustrations of Anglo-Saxon Poetry.* London, 1826.

Cook, Albert S., ed. *The Christ of Cynewulf.* Boston, 1900.

Corpus Christianorum, Series Latina, vols. 1–. Turnhout, 1953–.

Cosijn, P. J. "Anglosaxonica. IV." *Beiträge* xxiii (1898): 109–30.

Crawford, S. J., ed. *See* Aelfric.

Crossley-Holland, Kevin, tr. *Storm and Other Old English Riddles.* London, 1970.

Davidson, H. R. Ellis. *The Sword in Anglo-Saxon England, Its Archaeology and Literature.* Oxford, 1962.

De Baye, Baron J. *The Industrial Arts of the Anglo-Saxons.* Translated by T. B. Harbottle. London, 1893.

De Laet, Sigfried. "Wooden Animal Heads of Carolingian Times Found in the River Scheldt (Belgium)." *AA* xxvii (1956): 127–37.

Dietrich, F. *De Kynewulfi Poetae Aetate.* Marburg, 1859.

————. "Die Räthsel des Exeterbuchs: Würdigung, Lösung und Herstellung." *ZfdA.* xi (1859): 448–90.

————. "Die Räthsel des Exeterbuchs: Verfasser; Weitere Lösungen." *ZfdA.* xii (1865): 232–52.

Du Cange, Charles Du Fresne, ed. *Glossarium Mediae et Infimae Latinitatis.* New edition. 10 vols. Paris, 1937–38.

Dunning, T. P., and Bliss, A. J., eds. *The Wanderer.* London, 1969.

Ebert, Adolf. "Die Rätselpoesie der Angelsachsen." *BudV.* xxix (1877): 20–56.

Ekwall, Eilert. Review of *Three Northumbrian Poems: Cædmon's Hymn, Bede's Death Song, and the Leiden Riddle,* edited by Albert H. Smith. *MLR* xxix (1934): 78–82.

Eliason, Norman E. "Riddle 68 of the *Exeter Book.*" In *Philologica: The Malone Anniversary Studies,* edited by Thomas A. Kirby and Henry Bosley Woolf, pp. 18–19. Baltimore, 1949.

_____. "Four Old English Cryptographic Riddles." *SP* xlix (1952): 553–65.

Elliott, Ralph W. V. "The Runes in *The Husband's Message*." *JEGP* liv (1955): 1–8.

_____. "Runes, Yews, and Magic." *Spec.* xxxii (1957): 250–61.

_____. *Runes: An Introduction*. 2d corrected printing. Manchester, 1963.

Encyclopaedia Britannica. 24 vols. Chicago, 1969.

Erhardt-Siebold, Erika von. *Die lateinischen Rätsel der Angelsachsen*. Heidelberg, 1925.

_____. "History of the Bell in a Riddle's Nutshell." *ESn.* lxix (1934): 1–14.

_____. "Old English Riddle No. 4: Handmill." *PMLA* lxi (1946): 620–23.

_____. "Old English Riddle No. 39: Creature Death." *PMLA* lxi (1946): 910–15.

_____. "The Anglo-Saxon Riddle 74 and Empedokles' Fragment 117." *MÆ* xv (1946): 48–54.

_____. "Old English Riddle No. 57: OE *Cā 'Jackdaw.'" *PMLA* xlii (1947): 1–8.

_____. "Old English Riddle 95." *MLN* lxii (1947): 558–59.

_____. "The Old English Hunt Riddles." *PMLA* lxiii (1948): 3–6.

_____. "The Old English Loom Riddles." In *Philologica: The Malone Anniversary Studies*, edited by Thomas A. Kirby and Henry Bosley Woolf, pp. 9–17. Baltimore, 1949.

_____. "The Old English Storm Riddles." *PMLA* lxiv (1949): 884–88.

_____. "Old English Riddle 23: Bow, OE *Boga*." *MLN* lxv (1950): 93–96.

_____. "Old English Riddle 13." *MLN* lxv (1950): 97–100.

_____. "Note on Anglo-Saxon Riddle 74." *MÆ* xxi (1952): 36–37.

Erlemann, Edmund. "Zu den altenglischen Rätseln." *Archiv* cxi (1903): 49–63.

Erlemann, Fritz. "Zum 90. angelsächsischen Rätsel." *Archiv* cxv (1905): 391–92.

Ettmüller, Ludwig, ed. *Engla and Seaxna Scôpas and Bôceras*. London, 1850.

Eusebius. *Aenigmata Eusebii*. Edited by Fr. Glorie. *CCL.* cxxxiii, pp. 211–71. Turnhout, 1968.

Evans, A. H. *Birds. Cambridge Natural History*, vol. 9. London, 1900.

Evans, Angela Care, and Fenwick, Valerie H. "The Graveney Boat." *Antiquity* xlv (1971): 89–96.

Evison, Vera I. "The Dover Ring-sword and Other Sword-rings and Beads." *Archaeologia* ci (1967): 63–118.

The Exeter Book of Old English Poetry. Facsimile edition. With introductory chapters by R. W. Chambers, Max Förster, and Robin Flower. London, 1933.

Foote, Peter G., and Wilson, David M. *The Viking Achievement: A Survey of the Society and Culture of Early Medieval Scandinavia*. New York, 1970.

Forman, Maurice B., ed. *See* Keats.

Frankis, P. J. "*Deor* and *Wulf and Eadwacer*: Some Conjectures." *MÆ* xxxi (1962): 161–75.

Bibliography

Frye, Donald K. "*Wulf and Eadwacer*: A Wen Charm." *The Chaucer Review* v (1971–72): 247–63.

Garvin, Katharine. "*Nemnað hy sylfe*: A Note on Riddle 57, Exeter Book." *Classica et Mediaevalia* xxvii (1966): 294–95.

Gerlach, P. "Hahn." In *Lexicon der Christlichen Ikonographie*, edited by Engelbert Kirschbaum, vol. 2, pp. 206–10. Rome, 1970.

Gerritsen, Joh. "þurh þreata geþræcu." *ES* xxxv (1954): 259–62.

Giraldus Cambrensis. *Topographia Hibernica*. *Giraldi Cambrensis Opera*, edited by James F. Dimock, Rolls Series xxi.5, pp. 3–204. London, 1867.

Goldsmith, Margaret E. "The Enigma of *The Husband's Message*." In *Anglo-Saxon Poetry: Essays in Appreciation: For John C. McGalliard*, edited by Lewis Nicholson and Dolores Warwick Frese, pp. 242–63. Notre Dame, 1975.

Green, Charles. *Sutton Hoo: The Excavation of a Royal Ship-Burial*. London, 1963.

Greenfield, Stanley B. *The Interpretation of Old English Poems*. London and Boston, 1972.

Greenhill, Basil. "The Graveney Boat." *Antiquity* xlv (1971): 41–42.

Grein, Christian W. M. "Kleine Mittheilungen." *Germania* x (1865): 305–10.

———. "Zur Textkritik der angelsächsischen Dichter." *Germania* x (1865): 416–29.

———. *Sprachschatz der angelsächsischen Dichter*. In collaboration with F. Holthausen, revised by J. J. Köhler. Heidelberg, 1912.

———, ed. *Bibliothek der angelsächsischen Poesie*. 2 vols. Göttingen, 1857–58.

Grimm, Jacob, and Grimm, Wilhelm, eds. *Deutsches Wörterbuch*. 16 vols. Leipzig, 1854–1960.

Hacikyan, Agop. "The Exeter Manuscript: Riddle 19." *ELN* iii (1965): 86–88.

———. *A Linguistic and Literary Analysis of Old English Riddles*. Montreal, 1966.

Hall, John R. Clark. See Clark Hall, John R.

Hammett, Ian. "Ambiguity, Classification and Change: The Function of Riddles." *Man* ii (1967): 379–92.

Hardison, O. B. *Christian Rite and Christian Drama in the Middle Ages*. Baltimore, 1965.

Herzfeld, Georg. *Die Räthsel des Exeterbuches und ihr Verfasser*. Berlin, 1890.

Hickes, George. *Grammaticae Islandicae Rudimenta. Linguarum Veterum Septentrionalium Thesaurus*, pt. 3. Oxford, 1703.

Hicketier, F. "Fünf Rätsel des Exeterbuches." *Anglia* x (1888): 564–600.

Hill, Thomas. "Notes on the Eschatology of the Old English *Christ III*." *NM* lxx (1969): 672–79.

Hoffmann, Marta. *The Warp-weighted Loom: Studies in the History and Technology of an Ancient Implement*. Oslo, 1964.

Hollister, C. Warren. *Anglo-Saxon Military Institutions*. Oxford, 1962.

Holthausen, Ferdinand. Review of "Komposition und Quellen des Exeterbuches" by August Prehn. *Anglia* vii (1884): Anzeiger, 120–29.

_____. "Zu alt- und mittelenglischen Dichtungen." *Anglia* xiii (1891): 357–62.

_____. "Beiträge zur Erklärung und Textkritik altenglischer Dichter." *Indogermanische Forschungen* iv (1894): 379–88.

_____. Review of *Bibliothek der angelsächsischen Poesie*, vol. 3, pt. 1, edited by Bruno Assmann. *Anglia Beibl.* ix (1899): 353–58.

_____. "Zu alt- und mittelenglischen Dichtungen. XV." *Anglia* xxiv (1901): 264–67.

_____. "Zur altenglischen Literatur." *Anglia Beibl.* xvi (1905): 227–31.

_____. "Zur altenglischen Literatur. IV." *Anglia Beibl.* xviii (1907): 201–8.

_____. "Zur Textkritik altenglischer Dichtungen." *ESn.* xxxvii (1907): 198–211.

_____. "Zu den altenglischen Rätseln." *Anglia* xxxv (1911): 165–77.

_____. "Nochmals die altenglischen Rätsel." *Anglia* xxxviii (1914): 77–82.

_____. "Zu altenglischen Denkmälern." *ESn.* li (1917): 180–88.

_____. "Zu den altenglischen Rätseln." *Anglia Beibl.* xxx (1919): 50–55.

_____. Review of "Jubilee Jaunts and Jottings: 250 Contributions to the Interpretation and Prosody of Old West Teutonic Alliterative Poetry" by Ernst A. Kock. *Anglia Beibl.* xxx (1919): 1–5.

_____. "Zu altenglischen Dichtungen." *Anglia* xliv (1920): 346–56.

_____. "Zu altenglischen Gedichten." *Anglia Beibl.* xxxii (1921): 136–38.

_____. "Studien zur altenglischen Dichtungen." *Anglia* xlvi (1922): 52–62.

_____. "Anglosaxonica Minora." *Anglia Beibl.* xxxvi (1925): 219–20.

_____. Review of *The Exeter Book*, pt. 2, edited by W. S. Mackie. *Anglia Beibl.* xlvi (1935): 5–10.

_____. "Zu altenglischen Dichtungen." *ESn.* lxxiv (1940): 324–28.

_____. *Altenglisches etymologisches Wörterbuch*. 2d ed. Heidelberg, 1963.

Hoops, Johannes. *Waldbäume und Kulturpflanzen im germanischen Altertum*. Strassburg, 1905.

Hymes, Dell H. "The 'Wife' Who 'Goes Out' Like a Man: Reinterpretation of a Clackamas Chinook Myth." *Social Science Information* vii (1968): 173–99.

Isidore of Seville. *Etymologiarum sive Originum*. Edited by W. M. Lindsay. 2 vols. Oxford, 1911.

_____. *Traité de la Nature [De Natura Rerum]*. Edited by Jacques Fontaine. Bordeaux, 1960.

Jenkins, J. T. *A Textbook of Oceanography*. New York, 1921.

Jónsson, Finnur, ed. *Brennu-Njálssaga (Njála)*. Halle, 1908.

Jordan, Richard. *Die altenglischen Säugetiernamen*. Heidelberg, 1903.

Joyce, John H. "Natural Process in *Exeter Book* Riddle 29: 'Sun and Moon.'" *Annuale Mediaevale* xiv (1974): 5–8.

Jungmann, Rev. Joseph A. *The Mass of the Roman Rite: Its Origins and Development*. Translated by Rev. Francis A. Brunner, revised by Rev. Charles K. Riepe. New York, 1959.

Bibliography

Kaske, R. E. "A Poem of the Cross in the Exeter Book: 'Riddle 60' and 'The Husband's Message.'" *Traditio* xxiii (1967): 41–70.

Kay, Donald. "Riddle 20: A Revaluation." *TSL* xiii (1968): 133–39.

Keats, John. *The Letters of John Keats*. Edited by Maurice B. Forman. Oxford, 1935.

Keller, May Lansfield, *The Anglo-Saxon Weapon Names*. Heidelberg, 1906.

Kendrick, T. D. *Anglo-Saxon Art to A.D. 900*. London, 1938.

Kennedy, Charles W. *The Earliest English Poetry*. Oxford, 1943.

Kennedy, Christopher B. "Old English Riddle No. 39." *ELN* xiii (1975): 81–85.

Ker, N. R. *Catalogue of Manuscripts Containing Anglo-Saxon*. Oxford, 1957.

Ker, W. P. *The Dark Ages*. New York, 1904.

King, Cuchlaine A. M. *An Introduction to Oceanography*. New York, 1963.

Klaeber, Friedrich. "Emendations in Old English Poems." *MP* ii (1904): 144–46.

_____. "Wanderer 44; Rätsel XII 3 f." *Anglia Beibl.* xvii (1906): 300–301.

_____. Review of *Die altenglischen Rätsel (die Rätsel des Exeterbuchs)* by Moritz Trautmann. *MLN* xxxi (1916): 426–30.

_____. "Das 9. altenglische Rätsel." *Archiv* clxxxii (1943): 107–8.

_____, ed. *Beowulf and The Fight at Finnsburg*. 3d ed. with supplements. Boston, 1950.

Kluge, Friedrich. "Zur Geschichte des Reimes im Altgermanischen." *Beiträge* ix (1884): 422–50.

_____. *Etymologisches Wörterbuch der Deutschen Sprache*. 19th ed. Revised by Walther Mitzka. Berlin, 1963.

Klump, Wilhelm. *Die altenglischen Handwerkernamen*. Heidelberg, 1908.

Kock, Ernst A. "Jubilee Jaunts and Jottings: 250 Contributions to the Interpretation and Prosody of Old West Teutonic Alliterative Poetry." *Lunds Universitets Årsskrift*, NF. Avd. 1, Bd. 14, Nr. 26 (1918).

_____. "Interpretations and Emendations of Early English Texts. V." *Anglia* xliii (1919): 298–312.

_____. "Interpretations and Emendations of Early English Texts. VI." *Anglia* xliv (1920): 97–114.

_____. "Interpretations and Emendations of Early English Texts. VII." *Anglia* xliv (1920): 245–60.

_____. "Interpretations and Emendations of Early English Texts. VIII." *Anglia* xlv (1921): 105–31.

Konick, Marcus. "Exeter Book Riddle 41 as a Continuation of Riddle 40." *MLN* liv (1939): 259–62.

Krapp, George Philip, and Dobbie, Elliott Van Kirk, eds. *The Anglo-Saxon Poetic Records*. 6 vols. New York, 1931–53. Vol. 1, *The Junius Manuscript*, edited by George Philip Krapp, 1931; Vol. 2, *The Vercelli Book*, edited by George Philip Krapp, 1932; Vol. 3, *The Exeter Book*, edited by George Philip Krapp and Elliott Van Kirk Dobbie, 1936; Vol. 4, *Beowulf and*

Judith, edited by Elliott Van Kirk Dobbie, 1953; Vol. 5, *The Paris Psalter and the Meters of Boethius*, edited by George Philip Krapp, 1932; Vol. 6, *The Anglo-Saxon Minor Poems*, edited by Elliott Van Kirk Dobbie, 1942.

Lactantius. *De Ave Phoenice*. Edited and translated by Mary Cletus Fitzpatrick. Philadelphia, 1933.

Lancaster, Lorraine. "Kinship in Anglo-Saxon Society." *BJS* ix (1958): 230–50, 359–77.

Latham, R. E., ed. *Revised Medieval Latin Word List from British and Irish Sources*. London, 1965.

Lawrence, W. W. "The First Riddle of Cynewulf." *PMLA* xvii (1902): 247–61.

Leclercq, H. "Coq." In *Dictionnaire d'Archéologie Chrétienne et de Liturgie*, vol. 3, pt. 2, pp. 2886–2906. Paris, 1948.

Leechdoms. See Cockayne, ed.

Leeds, E. T. *Early Anglo-Saxon Art and Archaeology*. Oxford, 1936.

Lehmann, Ruth P. M. "The Metrics and Structure of 'Wulf and Eadwacer.'" *PQ* xlviii (1969): 151–65.

Leo, Heinrich. *Quae de se ipso Cynevulfus (sive Cenevulfus sive Coenevulfus) poeta Anglosaxonicus tradiderit*. Halle, 1857.

Leslie, Roy F. "The Integrity of Riddle 60." *JEGP* lxvii (1968): 451–57.

_____, ed. *Three Old English Elegies*. 1961. Reprint with corrections. Manchester, 1968.

Lewis, Charlton T., and Short, Charles. *A Latin Dictionary*. Oxford, 1879.

Liebermann, F. "Das angelsächsische Rätsel 56: 'Galgen' als Waffenständer." *Archiv* cxiv (1905): 163–64.

_____, ed. "Gerefa." *Anglia* ix (1886): 251–66.

_____. *Die Gesetze der Angelsachsen*. 3 vols. Halle, 1903–16. Reprint. Aalen, 1960.

Lindheim, Bogislav von. "Traces of Colloquial Speech in OE." *Anglia* lxx (1951): 22–42.

Lindsay, W. M. "Bird-Names in Latin Glossaries." *CP* xiii (1918): 1–22.

Logeman, H. "Anglo-Saxon Minora." *Anglia* xii (1889): 497–518.

Lorsch Riddles [*Aenigmata 'Laureshamensia'*]. Edited by Fr. Glorie. *CCL.* cxxxiii, pp. 347–58. Turnhout, 1968.

Lucan. *Civil War* [*De Bello Civili*]. Edited by J. P. Duff. Loeb Library Series. London and New York, 1928.

Lucretius. *De Rerum Natura*. Edited by W. H. D. Rouse. 2d ed. Loeb Library Series. London and New York, 1928.

Mackie, W. S. "Notes on Old English Poetry." *MLR* xxi (1926): 300–301.

_____. "Notes on the Text of the 'Exeter Book.'" *MLR* xxviii (1933): 75–78.

_____, ed. *The Exeter Book*. Part 2. EETS, o.s. 194. London, 1934.

MacLean, G. E., ed. *An Old and Middle English Reader*. New York, 1893.

Madan, Falconer. *Books in Manuscript*. London, 1920.

Madert, August. *Die Sprache der altenglischen Rätsel des Exeterbuches und die Cynewulffrage*. Marburg, 1900.

Malone, Kemp. "Two English Frauenlieder." In *Studies in Old English Literature in Honor of Arthur G. Brodeur*, edited by Stanley B. Greenfield, pp. 106–17. Eugene, 1963.

Maranda, Elli Köngäs. "The Logic of Riddles." In *Structural Analysis of Oral Tradition*, edited by Pierre and Elli Köngäs Maranda, pp. 189–232. Philadelphia, 1971.

Marckwardt, Albert H., and Rosier, James L. *Old English Language and Literature*. New York, 1972.

Mead, William E. "Color in Old English Poetry." *PMLA* xiv (1898): 169–206.

Meritt, Herbert Dean. "Old English Glosses, Mostly Dry Point." *JEGP* lx (1961): 441–50.

Meyvaert, Paul. "The Solution to Old English Riddle 39." *Speculum* li (1976): 195–201.

Middle English Dictionary. Edited by Hans Kurath, Sherman M. Kuhn, and John Reidy. Vols. 1–. Ann Arbor and London, 1952–.

Migne, J. P., ed. *Patrologiae Cursus Completus. Series Graeca.* 161 vols. plus index. Paris, 1857–76.

———, *Patrologiae Cursus Completus. Series Latina.* 217 vols. plus indexes (4 vols.). Paris, 1841–64.

Mitchell, Bruce. *A Guide to Old English.* 2d ed. Oxford, 1968.

Morley, Henry. *English Writers.* Vol. 2. London, 1888.

Müller, Eduard. *Die Rätsel des Exeterbuches.* Cöthen, 1861.

———. "Zwei angelsächsische Gedichte." *Archiv* xxix (1861): 205–20.

Müller, Ludv. Chr., ed. *Collectanea Anglo-Saxonica, maximam partem nunc primum edita et vocabulario illustrata.* Copenhagen, 1835.

Müller, Max. *Lectures on the Science of Language.* 2d ser. London, 1864.

Muratori, Ludovico Antonio. *Antiquitates Italicae.* Vol. 4. Arezzo, 1774.

Napier, Arthur S. *Old English Glosses.* Oxford, 1900.

Needham, A. *English Weathervanes: Their Stories and Legends from Medieval to Modern Times.* London, 1953.

Nelson, Marie. "The Rhetoric of the Exeter Book Riddles." *Spec.* xlix (1974): 421–40.

New Catholic Encyclopedia. 15 vols. New York, 1967.

Newton, Alfred, and Gadow, Hans, et al. *A Dictionary of Birds.* London, 1899.

Norman, F., ed. *Waldere.* London, 1933.

Nuck, R. "Zu Trautmanns Deutung des ersten und neunundachtzigsten Rätsels." *Anglia* x (1888): 390–94.

Ogilvy, J. D. A. *Books Known to the English, 597–1066.* Cambridge, 1967.

Ohl, Raymond Theodore, ed. *See* Symphosius.

Ohlert, K. *Rätsel und Rätselspiele der alten Griechen.* Berlin, 1912.

Okasha, Elisabeth. *Hand-list of Anglo-Saxon Non-runic Inscriptions.* Cambridge, 1971.

Olcott, William Tyler. *Olcott's Field Book of the Skies.* 4th ed. Revised by R. N. and M. W. Mayall. New York, 1954.

Olsen, Olaf, and Crumlin-Pedersen, Ole. "The Skuldelev Ships (II): A Report of the Final Underwater Excavation in 1959 and the Salvaging Operation in 1962." *AA* xxxviii (1967): 73–174.

Ovid. *Metamorphoses.* Edited by Frank J. Miller. 2 vols. Loeb Library Series. London and New York, 1916.

The Oxford English Dictionary. 13 vols. Oxford, 1933. Originally published as *A New English Dictionary on Historical Principles,* 1884–1928.

Padelford, Frederick Morgan. "Old English Musical Terms." *BBzA.* iv (1899): v–xii, 1–112.

Page, R. I. "Language and Dating in Old English Inscriptions." *Anglia* lxxvii (1959): 385–406.

————. "The Old English Rune *ear.*" *MÆ* xxx (1961): 65–79.

————. "A Note on the Transliteration of Old English Runic Inscriptions." *ES* xliii (1962): 484–90.

————. "The Old English Rune EOH, ÍH, 'YEW-TREE.'" *MÆ* xxxvii (1968): 125–36.

————. *Life in Anglo-Saxon England.* London and New York, 1970.

————. *An Introduction to English Runes.* London, 1973.

Patch, Howard R. "Anglo-Saxon Riddle 56." *MLN* xxxv (1920): 181–82.

Patzig, H. "Zum ersten Rätsel des Exeterbuchs." *Archiv* cxlv (1923): 204–7.

Perret de la Menue, Émile. "Recherches Historiques et Philologiques sur les Girouettes chez les Anciens et les Modernes." *Société Littéraire, Historique et Archaéologique de Lyon: Memoires* i, no. 1 (1885): 69–88.

Pinsker, Hans. "Neue Deutungen für zwei altenglische Rätsel (Krapp-Dobbie 17 und 30)." *Anglia* xci (1973): 11–17.

Pitman, James Hall, ed. *See* Aldhelm.

Platt, J. "Angelsächsisches." *Anglia* vi (1883): 171–78.

Pliny. *Natural History* [*Historia Naturalis*]. Edited by H. Rackham and W. S. Jones. 10 vols. Loeb Library Series. Cambridge and London, 1938–62.

Pompeius. *Commentum Artis Donati.* Edited by Heinrich Keil. *Artium Scriptores Minores Grammatici Latini,* vol. 5. Leipzig, 1868. Reprint. Hildesheim, 1961.

Pontán, Runar. "Three O.E. Textual Notes." *MLR* xii (1917): 69–72.

Pope, John C. *The Rhythm of Beowulf.* Rev. ed. New Haven, 1966.

————. "An Unsuspected Lacuna in the Exeter Book: Divorce Proceedings for an Ill-matched Couple in the Old English Riddles." *Spec.* xlix (1974): 615–22.

————, ed. *Seven Old English Poems.* Indianapolis, 1966.

Prehn, August. "Komposition und Quellen der Rätsel des Exeterbuches." *NS* iii (1883): 143–285.

Quinn, John J. "Some Puzzling Lemmata and Glosses in MS. Cotton Cleopatra A III." *PQ* xlv (1966): 434–37.

Quirk, Randolph, and Wrenn, C. L. *An Old English Grammar.* 2d ed. London, 1957.

Renoir, Alain. *"Wulf and Eadwacer*: A Noninterpretation." In *Franciplegius: Medieval and Linguistic Studies in Honor of Francis Peabody Magoun, Jr.*, edited by Jess B. Bessinger, Jr., and Robert P. Creed, pp. 147–63. New York, 1965.

Rissanen, Matti. *The Uses of 'One' in Old and Early Middle English*. Mémoires de la Société Néophilologique de Helsinki, vol. 31. Helsinki, 1967.

Robinson, Fred C. "The Significance of Names in Old English Literature." *Anglia* lxxxvi (1968): 14–58.

―――――. *Old English Literature: A Select Bibliography*. Toronto, 1970.

―――――. "Artful Ambiguities in the Old English 'Book-Moth' Riddle." In *Anglo-Saxon Poetry: Essays in Appreciation: For John C. McGalliard*, edited by Lewis E. Nicholson and Dolores Warwick Frese, pp. 355–62. Notre Dame, 1975.

Rudeaux, Lucien, and de Vaucouleurs, Gérard. *Larousse Encyclopedia of Astronomy* [*Larousse Astronomie*]. Rev. ed. Translated by Michael Guest and John B. Sidgwick. With an introduction by F. L. Whipple. London, 1966.

Schlauch, Margaret. "The 'Dream of the Rood' as Prosopopoeia." In *Essays and Studies in Honor of Carleton Brown*, pp. 23–34. New York, 1940.

Schlutter, Otto B. "Anglo-Saxonica." *Anglia* xxx (1907): 239–60.

―――――. "Das Leidener Rätsel." *Anglia* xxxii (1909): 384–88.

―――――. "*Afog* 'Perversus' im 24ten Rätsel, Die Balliste bezeichnend." *ESn.* xli (1910): 453–54.

―――――. "Zum Leidener Rätsel." *Anglia* xxxiii (1910): 457–66.

Scott, Charles T. "Some Approaches to the Study of the Riddle." In *Studies in Language, Literature, and Culture of the Middle Ages and Later*, edited by E. Bagby Atwood and Archibald Hill, pp. 111–27. Austin, 1969.

Sedgefield, W. J. "Suggested Emendations in Old English Poetical Texts." *MLR* xvi (1921): 59–61.

―――――, ed. *An Anglo-Saxon Verse Book*. Manchester, 1922.

Seneca. *Naturalium Quaestionum Libros VIII*. Edited by Alfred Gercke. *Opera Quae Supersunt*, vol. 2. Leipzig, 1907.

Senghor, Léopold Sédar. *Liberté I: Négritude et Humanism*. Paris, 1964.

Shook, Laurence K. "Old English Riddle I: 'Fire.'" *MS* viii (1946): 316–18.

―――――. "Old English Riddle 28—Testudo (Tortoise-Lyre)." *MS* xx (1958): 93–97.

―――――. "Old English Riddle No. 20: *Heoruswealwe*." In *Franciplegius: Medieval and Linguistic Studies in Honor of Francis Peabody Magoun, Jr.*, edited by Jess B. Bessinger, Jr., and Robert P. Creed, pp. 194–204. New York, 1965.

―――――. "Riddles Relating to the Anglo-Saxon Scriptorium." In *Essays in Honour of Anton Charles Pegis*, edited by J. Reginald O'Donnell, pp. 215–36. Toronto, 1974.

Siebold, Erika von Erhardt. *See* Erhardt-Siebold.

Sievers, Eduard. "Erklarung (gegen J. Platt)." *Anglia* vii (1884): 222.
_____. "Zur Rhythmik des germanischen Alliterationsverses II." *Beiträge* x (1885): 451–545.
_____. "Der angelsächsische Schwellvers." *Beiträge* xii (1887): 454–82.
_____. "Zu Cynewulf." *Anglia* xiii (1891): 1–25.
_____. *Altenglische Grammatik. See* Brunner.
Sisam, Kenneth. Review of *The Poetical Dialogues of Solomon and Saturn,* edited by R. J. Menner. *MÆ* xiii (1944): 28–36.
_____. *Studies in the History of Old English Literature.* Oxford, 1953.
Smith, Albert H., ed. *Three Northumbrian Poems: Cædmon's Hymn, Bede's Death Song, and The Leiden Riddle.* London, 1933.
Smith, Edward H. *The Marine Expedition to Davis Strait and Baffin Bay Under Direction of the United States Coast Guard, 1928, Part 3, Arctic Ice, with Especial Reference to Its Distribution to the North Atlantic Ocean.* Washington, 1931.
Sonke, Emma. "Zu dem 25 Rätsel des Exeterbuches." *ESn.* xxxvii (1907): 313–18.
Stanley, E. G. "The Chronology of *R*-Metathesis in Old English." *EGS* v (1952): 103–15.
_____. "The Search for Anglo-Saxon Paganism: VIII–IX: C—*Wyrd.*" *NQ* ccx (1965): 285–93, 322–27.
Stenton, Sir Frank, et al., eds. *The Bayeux Tapestry.* 2d ed. London, 1965.
Stevens, W. O. *The Cross in the Life and Literature of the Anglo-Saxons.* New Haven, 1904.
Storms, G. *Anglo-Saxon Magic.* The Hague, 1948.
Strobl, Joseph. "Zur Spruchdichtung bei den Angelsachsen." *ZfdA.* xxxi (1887): 54–64.
Swaen, A. E. H. "Contributions to Anglo-Saxon Lexicography VI." *ESn.* xl (1909): 321–31.
_____. "Het 18e Oudengelsche Raadsel." *Neoph.* iv (1919): 258–62.
_____. "Riddle XIII (XVI)." *Neoph.* xxvi (1941): 228–31.
_____. "The Anglo-Saxon Horn Riddles." *Neoph.* xxvi (1941): 298–302.
_____. "Riddle 9 (6, 8)." *SN* xiv (1941–42): 67–70.
_____. "Riddle 63 (60, 62)." *Neoph.* xxvii (1942): 220.
_____. "Riddle 9 (12)." *Neoph.* xxx (1945): 126.
_____. "Riddle 8 (10, 11)." *Neoph.* xxx (1945): 126–27.
_____. "Notes on Anglo-Saxon Riddles." *Neoph.* xxxi (1947): 145–48.
Swanton, Michael, ed. *The Dream of the Rood.* Manchester, 1970.
Symphosius. *The Enigmas of Symphosius.* Edited by Raymond Theodore Ohl. Philadelphia, 1928.
Tacitus. *Germania.* Edited by Maurice Hutton. In *Dialogus, Agricola, Germania,* pp. 255–354. Loeb Library Series. London and New York, 1914.
Tatwine. *Aenigmata Tatvini.* Edited by Fr. Glorie. *CCL.* cxxxiii, pp. 167–208. Turnhout, 1968.

Bibliography

Taylor, Archer. *The Literary Riddle Before 1600*. Berkeley, 1948.
————. "The Varieties of Riddles." In *Philologica: The Malone Anniversary Studies*, edited by Thomas A. Kirby and Henry Bosley Woolf, pp. 1–8. Baltimore, 1949.
————, ed. *English Riddles from Oral Tradition*. Berkeley, 1951.
Thomson, Sir A. Landsborough, ed. *A New Dictionary of Birds*. New York, 1964.
Thorpe, Benjamin, ed. *Ancient Laws and Institutes of England*. 2 vols. London, 1840.
————, *Codex Exoniensis: A Collection of Anglo-Saxon Poetry*. London, 1842.
Toller, T. Northcote. *See* Bosworth.
Traugott, Elizabeth Closs. *A History of English Syntax: A Transformational Approach to the History of English Sentence Structure*. New York, 1972.
Trautmann, Moritz. "Cynewulf und die Rätsel." *Anglia* vi (1883): Anzeiger, 158–69.
————. "Zum 89. Rätsel." *Anglia* vii (1884): Anzeiger, 210–11.
————. "Die Auflösungen der altenglischen Rätsel." *Anglia Beibl.* v (1894): 46–51.
————. "Zu den altenglischen Rätseln." *Anglia* xvii (1895): 396–400.
————. "Auflösung des 11ten (9ten) Rätsels." *BBzA.* xvii (1905): 142.
————. "Alte und neue Antworten auf altenglische Rätsel." *BBzA.* xix (1905): 167–215.
————. "Zum Streit um die altenglischen Rätsel." *Anglia* xxxvi (1912): 127–33.
————. "Das sogenannte erste Rätsel." *Anglia* xxxvi (1912): 133–38.
————. Review of *Sprachschatz der angelsächsischen Dichter* by Christian W. M. Grein in collaboration with F. Holthausen, revised by J. J. Köhler. *Anglia Beibl.* xxiv (1913): 36–43.
————. "Die Zahl der alteng. Rätsel." *Anglia Beibl.* xxv (1914): 272–73.
————. "Zu den Lösungen der Rätsel des Exeterbuchs." *Anglia Beibl.* xxv (1914): 273–79.
————. "Die Quellen der altenglischen Rätsel." *Anglia* xxxviii (1914): 349–54.
————. "Sprache und Versbau der altenglischen Rätsel." *Anglia* xxxviii (1914): 355–64.
————. "Zeit, Heimat und Verfasser der altengl. Rätsel." *Anglia* xxxviii (1914): 365–73.
————. "Das Geschlecht in den altenglischen Rätseln." *Anglia Beibl.* xxv (1914): 324–27.
————. "Zu meiner Ausgabe der altenglischen Rätsel." *Anglia* xlii (1918): 125–41.
————. "Weiteres zu den altenglischen Rätseln und Metrisches." *Anglia* xliii (1919): 245–60.
————, ed. *Die altenglischen Rätsel (die Rätsel des Exeterbuchs)*. Heidelberg, 1915.

Tucker, Susie I. "Sixty As an Indefinite Number in Middle English." *RES* xxv (1949): 152–53.

Tupper, Frederick, Jr. "Originals and Analogues of the Exeter Book Riddles." *MLN* xviii (1903): 97–106.

_____. "Solutions of the Exeter Book Riddles." *MLN* xxi (1906): 97–105.

_____. "The Cynewulfian Runes of the First Riddle." *MLN* xxv (1910): 235–41.

_____, ed. "The Holme Riddles (MS. Harl. 1960)." *PMLA* xviii (1903): 211–72.

_____. *The Riddles of the Exeter Book*. Boston, 1910. Reprint. Darmstadt, 1968.

Turner, Sharon. *The History of the Anglo-Saxons*. 7th ed. Vol. 3. London, 1852.

Vierck, H. E. F. "The Origin and Date of the Ship's Figure-Head from Moerzeke-Mariekerke, Antwerp." *Helinium* x (1970): 139–49.

Virgil. *Aeneid*. Edited by H. Rushton Fairclough. Rev. ed. 2 vols. Loeb Library Series. London and Cambridge, 1934.

Vitruvius. *On Architecture [De Architectura]*. Edited by Frank Granger. 2 vols. Loeb Library Series. London and New York, 1931–34.

Walker, Ernest P., et al., eds. *Mammals of the World*. 2d ed. Baltimore, 1964.

Walz, John A. "Notes on the Anglo-Saxon Riddles." *Harvard Studies and Notes* v (1896): 261–68.

Waterman, D. M. "An Early Medieval Horn from the River Erne." *Ulster Journal of Archaeology*, ser. 3, vol. xxxii (1969): 101–4, and plate IV.

Wattenbach, Wilhelm. *Das Schriftwesen im Mittelalter*. 3d ed. Leipzig, 1896.

Webster, Graham. *The Roman Imperial Army*. London, 1969.

Webster, James Carson. *The Labors of the Months in Antique and Medieval Art to the End of the Twelfth Century*. Evanston, 1938.

Webster's Third New International Dictionary. Edited by Philip Babcock Gove et al. Springfield, 1967.

Wender, Leo. *Animal Encyclopaedia: Mammals*. New York, 1949.

Wheeler, R. E. M. "The Roman Lighthouses at Dover." *Archaeological Journal* lxxxvi (1930): 29–46.

Whitelock, Dorothy. *The Audience of Beowulf*. Oxford, 1951.

_____. *The Beginnings of English Society*. Baltimore, 1952.

Whiting, Bartlett Jere, and Whiting, Helen Wescott. *Proverbs, Sentences, and Proverbial Phrases from English Writings Mainly before 1500*. Cambridge, 1968.

Whitman, Charles H. "The Birds of Old English Literature." *JEGP* ii (1898): 149–98.

_____. "The Old English Animal Names: Mollusks; Toads, Frogs; Worms; Reptiles." *Anglia* xxx (1907): 380–93.

Whitman, Frank H. "OE Riddle 74." *ELN* vi (1968): 1–5.

_____. *The Influence of the Latin and the Popular Riddle Traditions on the Old English Riddles of the Exeter Book*. Ph.D. dissertation, University of Wisconsin, 1968.

_____. "The Origin of Old English 'Riddle LXV.'" *NQ* ccxiii (1968). 203–4.

_____. "The Christian Background to Two Riddle Motifs." *SN* xli (1969): 93–98.

_____. "Medieval Riddling." *NM* lxxi (1970): 177–85.

_____. "Riddle 60 and Its Source." *PQ* l (1971): 108–15.

Wilde, W. R. *Catalogue of the Museum of Antiquities of the Royal Irish Academy.* Dublin, 1857.

Wilson, David M. "The Fejø Cup." *AA* xxxi (1960): 147–73.

_____. *Anglo-Saxon Ornamental Metalwork 700–1100 in the British Museum.* With appendixes by R. L. S. Bruce-Mitford and R. I. Page. *Catalogue of Antiquities of the Later Saxon Period*, vol. 1. London, 1964.

_____. "Anglo-Saxon Carpenters' Tools." In *Studien zur europäischen Vor- und Frühgeschichte* [dedicated to Herbert Jankuhn], edited by Martin Claus, Werner Haarnagel, and Klaus Raddatz, pp. 143–50. Neumünster, 1968.

_____. *The Anglo-Saxons.* Rev. ed. Middlesex, 1971.

_____. "The Bowls and Miscellaneous Silver: Form and Function." In *St. Ninian's Isle and Its Treasure*, edited by Alan Small, Charles Thomas, and David M. Wilson; with contributions by Kenneth Jackson, Hugh McKerrell, and T. B. Smith, 2 vols.; vol. 1, pp. 106–24. Oxford, 1973.

Wright, Thomas. *Biographia Britannica Literaria.* Vol. 1. London, 1842.

_____, ed. *A Volume of Vocabularies.* Liverpool, 1857.

_____, and Wülker, Richard P., eds. *Anglo-Saxon and Old English Vocabularies.* 2d ed. London, 1884. Reprint. Darmstadt, 1968.

Wülker, Richard P., ed. *Bibliothek der angelsächsischen Poesie.* 3 vols. Kassel and Leipzig, 1881–98. Vol. 3 [including the *Riddles*], edited by Bruno Assmann, q.v.

Wyatt, A. J., ed. *Old English Riddles.* Boston, 1912. Reprint. Folcroft, 1970.

Young, Jean I. "Riddle 8 of the *Exeter Book*." *RES* xviii (1942): 308–12.

_____. "Riddle 15 of the *Exeter Book*." *RES* xx (1944): 304–6.

Zandvoort, R. W. "The Leiden Riddle." *EGS* iii (1949–50): 42–56.

Index of Solutions

Index of Solutions